DOWNLOADS FOR STUDENTS AND FACULT

*D*etailed PowerPoint presentations and end-of-chapter/end-of-module review questions are available for students to download. New to the second edition website is a secure faculty section where instructors can download the Instructor's Manual, Model Syllabi, Teaching Suggestions, and more.

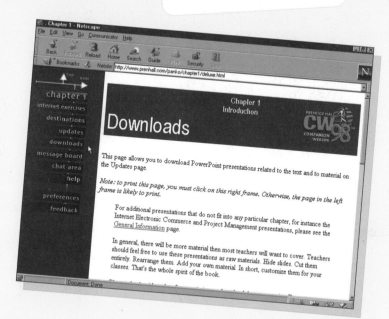

CHAPTER UPDATES

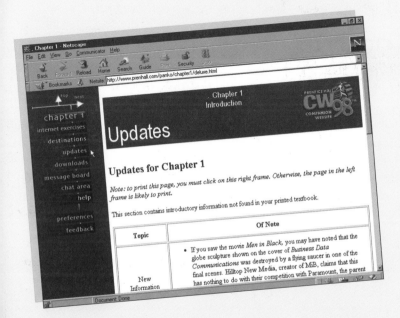

*C*hapter and module updates, including new information and supplemental readings, are provided by the author on the website. Updates are posted every month to help students and instructors stay abreast of the latest developments in data communications and networking.

Business Data Communications and Networking

Second Edition

Business Data Communications and Networking

RAYMOND R. PANKO

University of Hawaii

PRENTICE HALL

Upper Saddle River, New Jersey 07458

Acquisitions Editor:	David Alexander
Assistant Editor:	Lori Cardillo
Editorial Assistant:	Keith Kryszczun
Editor-in-Chief:	P. J. Boardman
Marketing Manager:	Nancy Evans
Production Editor:	Carol Samet
Permissions Coordinator:	Monica Stipanov
Managing Editor:	Dee Josephson
Manufacturing Buyer:	Lisa DiMaulo
Senior Manufacturing Supervisor:	Paul Smolenski
Manufacturing Manager:	Vincent Scelta
Design Manager:	Patricia Smythe
Interior Design:	Digitext
Cover Design:	Robin Hoffman
Cover Illustration/Photo:	Wendy Grossman
Composition:	UG

Copyright © 1999, 1997 by Prentice Hall, Inc.
A Simon & Schuster Company
Upper Saddle River, New Jersey 07458

Library of Congress Cataloging-in-Publication Data

Panko, R. R.
  Business data communications and networking / Raymond R. Panko.—
2nd ed.
    p. cm.
  Rev. ed. of: Business data communications. © 1997.
  Includes index.
  ISBN 0-13-082182-9
  1. Business enterprises—Computer networks—Study guides.
2. Computer networks—Management—Study guides. 3. Data
transmission systems—Study guides. I. Panko, R. R. Business data
communications. II. Title.
HD30.37.P36 1999
005.7′1—dc21
                                                             98-19428
                                                               CIP

Prentice-Hall International (UK) Limited, London
Prentice-Hall of Australia Pty. Limited, Sydney
Prentice-Hall Canada, Inc., Toronto
Prentice-Hall Hispanoamericana, S.A., Mexico
Prentice-Hall of India Private Limited, New Delhi
Prentice-Hall of Japan, Inc., Tokyo
Simon & Schuster Asia Pte. Ltd., Singapore
Editora Prentice-Hall do Brasil, Ltda., Rio de Janeiro

Printed in the United States of America

10 9 8 7 6 5 4 3 2 1

*To the great teachers who
inspired me to try to follow them:
Leonard Kauffer, Don Knuth,
Bruce Lusignan, Ed Parker,
Gerald Steckler, and John Toutonghi.*

Brief Contents

Contents

Preface

Features of the Book
- *Unique Modular Design*
- *Detailed PowerPoint Presentations*
- *Interactive Website*
- *Market-Driven Content*
- *TCP/IP and the Internet*
- *Begins with What Students Already Know*

What's New in the Second Edition
- *Even More on TCP/IP, the Internet, Intranets, and Extranets*
- *More on Security, More on Propagation, Quality of Service*
- *More on Switching, Focus on Servers*

Model Syllabi
- *A One-Quarter Course (or More Time for Hands-On Work)*
- *A Typical Course*
- *A TCP/IP-Focused Course*
- *A More Heavily Transmission-Oriented Course*
- *A Telecommunications Course*
- *An MBA Course*
- *A Two-Semester Course*

Contacting the Author

FEATURES OF THE BOOK

Unique Modular Design

We in a field as complex as networking, will never have agreement on what to teach in introductory networking courses. Based on individual judgment, each teacher must decide what to include and what to omit in order to meet time limits and to cover the most important material.

To respect the professional judgment of teachers, this book has a unique modular design. There are eight core chapters that cover the central concepts of networking. Most teachers will cover these eight, although the last two, which are application chapters, may be covered in other courses.

The eight advanced modules that follow the core chapters give more information on selected topics. Teachers can use these modules to tailor the book to their specific objectives without having to assemble other resources.

In addition to the core chapters and the advanced modules, the book's website has updates to cover new developments. There are pieces written by the author, and there also are selected links to online articles from major trade magazines.

Detailed PowerPoint Presentations

To help teachers present material, there is a detailed PowerPoint presentation for each core chapter that includes full coverage of the core chapter, and multislide builds for complex figures. The PowerPoint presentations for core chapters even include relevant materials from the advanced modules, and new information from the book's website updates.

We encourage adopters to "own" these presentations by modifying them for their needs. Given the inclusion of advanced module material and website material, the presentations are quite long. Cut out slides, rearrange them, add your own slides, or make them available at your local server for students. The only restrictions are the usual ones: only book adopters may use them, do not remove the copyright notice, and do not reuse the clip art, which the author and Prentice Hall do not own but use only under license that specifically prohibits reuse.

Interactive Website

The author personally maintains the book's website and updates it monthly. The website has a wealth of information for students, including interactive Internet exercises, in which the students search online catalogs for recent NIC, hub, and switch prices, and then send their results by e-mail to you, the instructor. For each chapter, there are objectives, updates, and downloads pages. Downloads pages allow you or your students to download the PowerPoint presentations. They also allow students to download the end-of-chapter and end-of-module review questions to reduce their typing time when answering them.

Market-Driven Content

Some textbooks try to cover every technology, even technologies that never made it in the marketplace, or that have insignificant market share. As a result, the textbooks have less space for the things that are truly important in the market today, such as Ethernet and TCP/IP. Many students who finish these courses don't even know how to build a simple Ethernet LAN.

This book focuses on the things that corporations are really looking for in our graduates today. The book covers such topics as TCP/IP, Ethernet switching, VLANs, Layer 3 switching, security (SSL, SET, digital certificates, IPsec, etc.), directory servers, intranets, extranets, high-speed Internet access, network management, groupware, videoconferencing, desktop conferencing, third-generation cellular telephony, IP telephony, and Internet electronic commerce.

TCP/IP and the Internet

The Internet and its TCP/IP standards already dominate corporate networking. The book introduces these standards in Chapter 1. By the end of Chapter 2, students get more TCP/IP than most texts cover in total. TCP/IP is woven through all other chapters. There is another really big gulp available in Module A.

Starting Early

Some other textbooks place TCP/IP and the Internet late in the books, to ease the work of writing new editions. Keeping TCP/IP early and expanding it required an 85% rewrite for this second edition.

OSI's Détente with TCP/IP

What about OSI? In the real world, TCP/IP and OSI have reached a comfortable working relationship. Networks use OSI standards at the physical and data link layers. They then use TCP/IP at the Internet, transport, and application layers. This dominant hybrid TCP/IP-OSI framework is used throughout the book.

Other Standards Issues

This book does not spend a great deal of time on higher levels of OSI beyond defining what they do because, quite simply, they are not used significantly in corporations and probably never will be.

IPX/SPX is also fading, and even SNA data is beginning to move more than TCP/IP. Although we cover IPX/SPX (Chapter 4) and SNA (Module H) somewhat, we focus more on TCP/IP-OSI.

Unique Pedagogy: Begin with What the Student Already Knows

Almost all students walk into introductory networking classes with a good deal of networking experience. Almost all have surfed the Net, and almost all have worked on a PC network in the school's lab. Some have even used PC networks in business.

The first three chapters tell students what is going on when they use the World Wide Web. The fourth chapter tells students about simple LANs and PC networks. The usual reaction is "Wow, so that's how it works!"

By the time students get to the abstract stuff involving large networks, they have already internalized the key concepts of networking, especially layered standards.

Best of all, students see the difficult concept of layering in a series of contexts. They see all layers in the context of web access. Students then see them again in the context of PC networking on a LAN. They also see them again in the context of large networks. I find that it takes these three passes for students to fully grasp layered communication.

Many other books work up through the layers one at a time. Although this has many virtues, it makes it difficult for students to deal with real multilayer contexts. Only at the end of such books do students get the full context. There is no time afterward to reinforce it.

WHAT'S NEW IN THE SECOND EDITION

There is a lot new in the second edition. In fact, as an 85% rewrite, most things are different in the second edition. Here are the biggest changes.

Even More on TCP/IP, the Internet, Intranets, and Extranets

As noted above, TCP/IP coverage begins in Chapter 1, and by the end of Chapter 2, the book has more TCP/IP than most of its competitors. TCP/IP coverage continues throughout the book, including the two application chapters. Chapter 7 looks at intranet communication services and Internet standards for e-mail and similar services. Chapter 8 covers extranets for Internet electronic commerce. Module A covers TCP/IP in more depth, and Module G looks at common Internet applications.

Security

In many polls, security has risen to first place on the list of chief information officer concerns. Chapter 5 introduces secure virtual private networks using the Internet. Chapter 6 discusses the core of Internet-related security concerns, including public key encryption, single key (symmetric) encryption, message digest authentication, and digital certificate authentication. It also discusses firewalls. Chapter 8 returns to security in the context of Internet electronic commerce, discussing the SSL and SET security approaches. Module F offers much more detail on the specifics of security approaches, including the details of SSL and SET, comprehensive new Internet IPsec standards, Kerberos, and other security issues. Throughout the discussions, the book focuses on the need for comprehensive policy-based security.

Propagation

The second edition brings more physical-level propagation material to the core chapters, especially in Chapter 3. This is a direct response to requests made by adopters of the first edition. Chapter 3 also examines various alternatives for faster home and small office (SOHO) access, including V.90 modems, cable modems, and ADSL. Module B covers more propagation topics, including detailed information on modulation, multiplexing, and carrier trunk lines, including satellite trunking.

Quality of Service

Ethernet and IP have always been "best effort" services whose throughput is highly variable. But in recent years, both the IEEE 802 Committee and the IETF have been working to bring prioritization to all 802 LANs and to IP. Their efforts, furthermore, are beginning to merge. This will allow us to handle time-dependent services. Of course prioritization is only one aspect of quality of service. In general, as Chapter 6 discusses, the tagging approaches that are being used for quality of service improvements have much broader application in quality of service, security, and other management concerns.

More on Switching

Once we had only two basic choices: routers, which were expensive and slow but highly functional; and bridges, which were fast and cheap but frankly rather stupid. Today, however, switches have replaced bridges, have brought greater functionality, and have actually increased speed. Some routers, in turn—thanks to ASIC technology—are approaching switch speeds. Switches, finally, are beginning to handle routing. The switch explosion and the router cost-revolution are central concerns in organizations today, and students must understand the issues that new devices are raising, including virtual LAN management.

Servers

Network administrators do not only manage wiring, carrier lines, switches, and routers. They are also responsible for servers. The book strengthens the first edition's focus on server technology. The first chapter introduces basic types of servers. Chapter 4 presents more on the servers found in PC networks. Chapter 6 looks at the superserver technology used on larger enterprise networks, and Module C presents more information on these enterprise servers. Chapter 8 discusses the steps needed to create a website using company-owned servers.

MODEL SYLLABI

A One-Quarter Course
(or More Time for Hands-On Work)

For a one-quarter course, or to leave more time for hands-on work, it is possible to cover only the eight core chapters and still give students a good grounding in networking. In fact, if applications are covered in other courses, the first six chapters alone give a full treatment of non-application concerns. Even if you supplement your course with some material from the modules, there should be sufficient time.

A Typical Course

A typical course will cover the first six or eight core chapters and will draw from two to five modules' worth of information from the advanced modules. Module D, which deals with telephone service, is a good addition to balance data communications with traditional telecommunications concerns. Module H is attractive if your graduates might work in mainframe environments.

A TCP/IP-Focused Course

In this increasingly TCP/IP-focused world, students benefit from more in-depth knowledge of TCP/IP standards. The core chapters cover many TCP/IP concerns, especially in Chapter 2 (HTTP, TCP, and IP operation), Chapter 5 (virtual private networks using the Internet), Chapter 7 (Internet e-mail and other standards), and Chapter 8 (extranets for Internet electronic commerce).

Beyond the core chapters, Module A focuses on TCP/IP, covering TCP and IP in more depth, and covering a number of supervisory protocols. Module F covers the IPsec security standards that will make TCP/IP systems far more secure. Module G covers Internet applications.

A More Heavily Transmission-Oriented Course

If you wish to give students a stronger technical focus at the physical, data link, and network/Internet layers, you can cover the first six chapters and material in Modules A through C, and E, F, and H. This will give a very strong foundation in technology and standards below the application layer.

A Telecommunications Course

Most schools do not have the luxury of a separate telecommunications course. Module D covers traditional telephone concepts, including carriers, regulation, services, and pricing. The chapter also looks at customer premises wiring and PBXs.

Module D also presents new developments in cellular telephony, hand-held satellite telephones, and IP telephony (which is outgrowing its Internet roots as a poorly functioning toy).

Module B covers the technology used for trunking in the public switched telephone network, including wire-based systems from T1 to SONET/SDH and radio systems using microwave, GEOSATS, LEOs, and VSATs. You can have a telecommunications course while still focusing heavily on data communications, which is growing ever larger in importance in corporate communications functions.

An MBA Course

For MBAs, you can be more selective in your coverage, reducing what you cover in Chapter 2 (TCP/IP functioning), Chapter 3 (propagation) and Chapter 4 (propagation and small PC networks).

You can focus more on the application chapters dealing with human communication (Chapter 7) and networked database and electronic commerce (Chapter 8). You may also wish to cover telephony (Module D), pricing for Frame Relay and ATM (Module E), and Internet applications (Module G). Module F (security) is more difficult material, and it seems to resonate well with many MBA students.

A Two-Semester Course

Until recently, few undergraduate MIS programs had even a single data communications course. Today, the battle of getting datacoms or telecoms into the curriculum has been won, and we are beginning to see that one course is not enough given the growing importance of the networking career track for graduates. This book is perfect for a full-year sequence.

One possibility is to cover each core chapter and relevant advanced module material before going on to the next chapter. My preference is to cover all core chapters first and then cover material in the advanced modules. This second approach covers less material, because students have to relearn information they previously learned and forgot, yet the repetition seems to be very helpful for long-term retention.

CONTACTING THE AUTHOR

One of the nicest things about writing a book in the Internet era is that I get so much great feedback from faculty members and students. If you have comments, questions, corrections, or simply want to get acquainted, please drop me a note. I'd love to hear from you. I'm panko@hawaii.edu. My home page is www.cba.hawaii.edu/panko.

About the Author

Ray Panko is a professor of business administration at the University of Hawaii. Before coming to the UH, he worked as a physicist at the Boeing Company and as a project manager at SRI International (formerly Stanford Research Institute). He received his BS and MBA from Seattle University and his PhD from Stanford University.

By a stroke of incredible good fortune, he arrived at Stanford during the "telecommunications mafia" era of the early 1970s. His combination of physics and business administration experience got him into a number of great projects, including early technical and business research on VSATs (Module B), early LAN technology, document retrieval, and early forays into electronic commerce. His dissertation was funded by the executive office of the president of the United States. (That sounds good, but Nixon's political problems delayed its release.) He even worked in Washington, DC on satellite communications.

An even greater stroke of luck brought him to SRI International, where he did some of the pioneering research on e-mail, videoconferencing, and the interactions between communication and travel. More than that, he spent a year working for Doug Engelbart, who gave us the mouse, hypertext, and much more.

When he came to the University of Hawaii, he spent four years teaching marketing, on the tenuous grounds that he had been doing marketing research at SRI International. Although he eventually moved back into information technology full time, electronic commerce is increasingly dragging his interest back to marketing.

His current research interests include the vulnerabilities that companies face now that they have become dependent on information technology. They also include the broad question of what the Internet (or what succeeds the Internet) will look like in the year 2020. Finally, they include reinventing the university. As an old guy, he will probably retire while universities look a lot like they do today. However, in your career, the way you engage in lifelong learning will resemble nothing like today's classroom instruction.

CHAPTER 1

Introduction

THE NETWORKING REVOLUTION

Toward a New Tomorrow

Until the 1980s, there was only one major career path for **Information Systems (IS)** graduates. This was the programmer/analyst track. You began your career as a programmer and eventually moved into systems analysis. Later, you would enter IS management. You might even become your company's *Chief Information Officer (CIO)*.

THE PC REVOLUTION

In the 1980s, the personal computer explosion created a new career path. Many graduates became user support specialists. They helped PC users with problems and upgraded user hardware and software. User support specialists needed to know both PC hardware and software to succeed.

SMALL PC NETWORKS

In the 1990s, networking began to explode. Earlier, high costs had kept networking simple. In the last decade of the twentieth century, however, transmission and switching costs fell dramatically, fueling massive growth in networking. At first, the major focus was small local area networks (LANs) for personal computers. These small *PC networks* allowed users to move beyond their desktops and work with nearby colleagues.

THE INTERNET

By the middle of the decade, the Internet had begun to dominate the networking picture. The Internet allowed a person at home to reach out to a vast amount of information around the world. As Steve Wosniak of Apple Computer once asked, "Why should I have one computer on my desk when I can have a million computers on my desk?" Soon, large numbers of corporate computers connected to the Internet as well. Internet electronic mail (e-mail) addresses and personal home page URLs became as widespread on business cards as facsimile numbers.

TRANSFORMING THE CORPORATION

During the first part of the twenty-first century, many businesses will be transformed by networking technology. Externally, the Internet allows businesses to work with their customers and suppliers in ways never before possible. Companies are beginning to make major investments in **extranets,** which are secure systems that use the Internet to communicate with business partners. Some businesses have already leveraged Internet connectivity into critical strategic advantages over their competition. In the coming years, we may see a business revolution as profound as the Industrial Revolution, with new companies rising to the top of what will be increasingly global markets.

Internally, companies are also being transformed by networking technology. PC networks, for instance, are no longer limited to single LANs. Many companies now have internal *enterprise networks* that span multiple corporate sites and that allow any authorized user to work with any authorized resource in the company. Given the importance of the Internet, companies are increasingly basing the enterprise networks on **intranet** technology, which applies Internet standards and applications to internal corporate communication.

Careers

Networking is having a profound impact on the career paths of information systems (IS) graduates.

NETWORKING

Networking itself has become one of the hottest career ladders for new graduates. However, although networking is a high-demand area, it is broadening far beyond what networking professionals had to know just a few years ago.

Today, it is not enough to know low-level wiring and propagation effects as signals travel down wires. In fact, standards have made the installation of simple networks very routine at the physical level.

Now demand is greatest for people who can work with higher-level standards, especially those of the popular TCP/IP standards architecture. At higher layers, it is critical to understand how software on different machines communicates through the exchange of highly structured messages, in order to achieve performance and reliability.

DISTRIBUTED PROGRAMMING

Networking is also transforming other career paths of IS graduates. Programmers once wrote single programs that ran on single machines. Now programmers must write increasingly distributed programs consisting of modules that run on two or more different machines and that work by communicating with one another over a network.

NETWORKS AND USER SUPPORT

When a user support specialist encounters an end user with a problem today, the problem is as likely to be a network matter as a PC hardware or software matter. Indeed, network support and PC support are increasingly becoming integrated into a single department. In addition, networking allows user support specialists to diagnose a growing number of problems remotely, without having to make a costly visit to the user's office.

Information Systems, Computer Science, and Electrical Engineering

Information systems professionals in business schools are not the only networking professionals. Computer science (CS) and electrical engineering (EE) graduates are also likely to deal with networking in their careers. Some IS students in business schools are confused about what they will do compared to what CS and EE graduates will do in their careers.

MAKE VERSUS BUY

The basic difference is that CS and EE graduates are being trained to work for companies that will produce new networking technologies. These vendor companies will produce the next generations of switches and transmission line technologies.

In contrast, IS graduates are being trained to work in **end user organizations,** such as banks and automobile producers. End user organizations use **Information Technology (IT)** to help their companies work more efficiently and effectively. This is why you graduate with a full business degree instead of a narrow technical degree.

SYSTEMS INTEGRATION

One result of this difference is that IS graduates seldom build network systems from scratch. Rather, their job is to build integrated corporate systems using hardware and software components available on the market. At a technical level, they are systems integrators, rather than box builders. Although they do program, their programs usually exist to link purchased components together. Being able to work with purchased components allows IS professionals to build complex systems very rapidly. Integration is a key skill for IS networking graduates.

CHOOSING AMONG COMPETING PRODUCTS AND TECHNOLOGIES

Of course, the final system will depend heavily on the quality and appropriateness of the components that are purchased. As a result, IS graduates need to understand how to compare alternative technologies, products, and vendors. To do this, they must consider many factors. Most of these factors, however, fall into three major categories.

1. **Performance** can be measured in many different ways, depending on the technology. For instance, if we are comparing local area network (LAN) technologies, we would be concerned with such factors as speed, reliability, and security. If we are concerned with wide area networking (WAN), we might focus on efficiency and management functions.
2. **Feasibility** asks whether the organization can implement the technology. For example, one concern with new technologies is that standards may be immature. It usually takes two or three revisions of a standard before products from different vendors can work together easily. Similarly, new technologies often are difficult to install and may lack critical features. Of course, what is feasible for one company may not be feasible for another company.

3. **Cost** is the third major selection factor. Although user demands for network services are growing exponentially, many networking budgets are constant or even shrinking. Even those that are growing are growing very slowly. So it is important not to buy technology whose costs are excessive compared to user requirements.

Cost is perhaps the most difficult factor to measure.

▶ **Total Purchase Cost for Hardware and Software.** It is important to identify all initial purchase costs for hardware and software. Often, you must buy many components to make a system work. An organization inexperienced with a new technology might not realize the need to buy one or two expensive components.

▶ **Labor Costs.** It is important to measure not only the cost of hardware and software purchases but also the cost of the labor needed to plan the project, install the system, and maintain the system. Labor costs often far exceed hardware and software costs.

▶ **Life Cycle Costs.** It is important to measure costs over a system's total life cycle, not just its purchase and installation costs. The costs of ongoing use and maintenance can be much higher than initial costs. In addition, some systems have moderate initial costs but high ongoing costs. Their total life cycle costs might make them unattractive. So it is important to compare the costs of all alternatives over your planning horizon.

Cost is always a very major consideration in technology selection. As noted above, companies need to buy the least expensive technology that will do the job. Although the trade press typically focuses on the newest and most expensive technologies, less expensive technologies typically win in the marketplace. In local area networks, for instance, Ethernet became the dominant technology despite the early availability of better technologies, such as the Token-Ring Networks championed by IBM. Ethernet did the job that users needed at a reasonable cost.

USER NEEDS

Of course, technology evaluation must always be done on the basis of a clear and detailed understanding of *user needs*. User needs are extremely complex, and there is no way to anticipate these needs without extensive and constant communication between end users and the networking staff. In addition, user needs change over time. The networking staff must both anticipate these changes and accommodate changes that take place unexpectedly.

The president of a tool company once told his board of directors, "Last year, we sold ten million drills that nobody wanted." What customers wanted, he went on to explain, were holes. Drills are expensive and difficult to use. Customers merely tolerated them, and they tolerated them only because they needed holes. A network is just another drill. It is a means to a corporate end.

Standards

In this first chapter, we will begin by discussing **standards.** *Standards are rules of operation that are followed by most or all vendors.* Standards bring many benefits.

- If there are good standards in an area, you do not have to buy all your products from a single company.
- Being able to buy from multiple vendors brings the benefits of competition, including lower prices and feature-rich products.
- You do not have to worry if one of your key vendors fails or falls behind the pace of development.

Standardization is a complex topic. Rather than dealing with the full complexities of standards initially, we will look at a single example of standards in this chapter. Specifically, we will look at dialing into the Internet from home, in order to use the World Wide Web. We will first look at the technology involved. We will then look at the specific standards that make Web access work. Note that we said "standards," not "standard." All practical networking situations involve multiple standards. As we will see, these standards work together to produce overall communication between a browser on your home PC and the webserver program on an Internet webserver.

Network Environments

The first part of this chapter focuses on Internet standards. In the remainder of this chapter, we will look at other important networking environments, including PC networks, client/server database processing, and terminal–host systems.

ACCESSING THE WORLD WIDE WEB FROM HOME

One of the most familiar network environments for many students is accessing the World Wide Web (WWW) from home, using a PC, a telephone line, and a modem. Because this network environment is so familiar to users, we will begin our discussion of networking and standards by examining this apparently simple situation. We will see that it is anything but simple, however.

The Internet: Networks, Packets, Routers, Host Computers, and Addresses

Figure 1.1 shows the essential elements of the Internet: networks, packets, routers, host computers, and addresses.

MULTIPLE NETWORKS

A **network** *is a collection of computers that are interconnected so that any computer can send messages to any other computer simply by giving the receiver's network address at the start of the message.*

You work with one network every day, the telephone network. Of course, this is a network designed for voice communication, not data communication. However, connection is essentially the same. You dial the address (telephone number) of the person you wish to call, and the network does all the rest.

The Internet, however, is not a single network. Rather, as Figure 1.1 indicates, the Internet consists of thousands of networks scattered around the globe. This is why we call it "the Internet." Universities, corporations, and other organizations often own individual networks. Your own university's network is probably a network on the Internet.

FIGURE **1.1**

The Internet

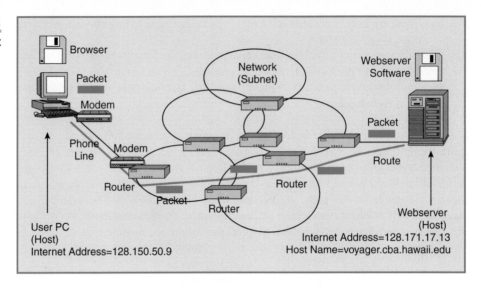

Figure 1.1 The Internet

PACKETS, ROUTERS, AND ROUTES

Messages on the Internet are called **packets.** How do packets get from one computer on one network to another computer on another network? Figure 1.1 shows that devices called **routers** make this possible. When you send a message, your computer sends the message to a router. Figure 1.1 shows that this first router passes your packet to another router on another network. Your packet hops from one router to another, across multiple networks, until it eventually reaches the destination computer. We call the path it travels its **route.**

HOSTS

Any computer attached to the Internet is called a **host.** Note the word *any.* Most students do not find it surprising that large computers that provide services to desktop client machines are called hosts. However, they often have a difficult time thinking of their own underpowered home PC as being a host as well. Yet that is the way it is.

In fact, the Internet makes no distinctions among different types of host computers. So while you are connected to the Internet with a home PC, you can become a temporary World Wide Web host. Of course, for most people, the distinction between *client hosts* (desktop machines) and *server hosts* (large machines that provide services to clients) is a very useful distinction, and we will make it in this book.

INTERNET ADDRESSES AND HOST NAMES

To reach someone by telephone, you need to know his or her phone number. You simply enter this number via your telephone keypad, and the telephone network does the rest.

On the Internet, the equivalent of the telephone number is the **internet address.** Currently, the internet address is a string of 32 bits (1s and 0s). A new version of the Internet Protocol (IP) will raise this to 128 bits to allow for the enormous growth expected in the number of IP hosts in the future.

To make internet addresses easier to remember, it is customary to divide the 32 bits of the internet address into four 8-bit *segments* and then to convert each string of 8

FIGURE **1.2**

**Internet
Addresses
and Host Names**

Internet Address	Host Names
32-bit IP number	cnn.com
10000000101010110001000100001101	www.microsoft.com
	voyager.cba.hawaii.edu
Divided into Bytes	
10000000 10101011 00010001 00001101	
Bytes Converted to Decimal Numbers	
128 171 17 13	
Segments Separated by Dots	
128.171.17.13	

zeros to a decimal number. Figure 1.2 illustrates this process. These four decimal segments are separated by decimal points, called dots. So the internet address

10000000101010110001000100001101

would be written as

128.171.17.13

Even dot numbers are difficult to remember. So the Internet also defines for **host names**,[1] which consist of several *labels* of *text* separated by dots. Examples are cnn.com, www.microsoft.com, and voyager.cba.hawaii.edu. Although all internet addresses have four decimal segments, host names can have as few as two text segments.

Carriers

A **carrier** is an organization that transmits your data for a price. Figure 1.3 shows that when you use the Internet in the United States, two very different types of carriers are involved: Internet service providers and network service providers. The situation is different in other countries, but many other countries are now considering this model, so you should be familiar with it.

INTERNET SERVICE PROVIDERS (ISPs)

When you connect to the Internet in the United States, you first connect to an organization called an **Internet service provider (ISP).** Figure 1.3 shows that when you dial into an Internet service provider, you dial into a router owned by the ISP. The ISP also has a router connected to the Internet backbone. This second router is your gateway to the whole Internet. For this connection to the Internet and for other services such as an e-mail mailbox, the ISP typically charges $15 to $30 per month.

---

[1] In the next chapter, we will see that host names are a subset of the concept of "domain names."

FIGURE **1.3**

Internet Carriers in the United States

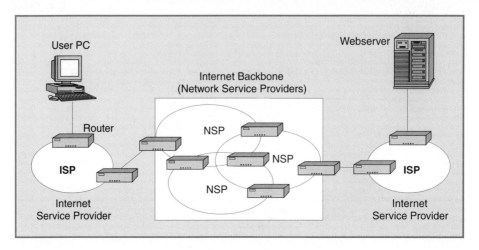

NETWORK SERVICE PROVIDERS (NSPS)

The backbone of the Internet in the United States consists of a number of competing companies called **network service providers (NSPs).** These NSPs are interconnected. So if a PC attached to one ISP is connected to a different NSP than the webserver's ISP, then the one NSP will transfer the packet to the other NSP for delivery. Although they compete for ISP business, network service providers nevertheless work together to provide total interconnection.

Network service providers do not work for free. Most are for-profit organizations. All have costs to cover. To connect to an NSP, the ISP must pay the NSP a certain amount of money per month. Where does it get this money? From the fees that you and other subscribers pay to the ISP. Part of these fees pays for the ISP's internal operation and profit, and part of these fees goes to the ISP's network service provider.

In the early years, the Internet was largely free. The government provided access and backbone services, and the only costs were those associated with reaching the nearest Internet access point. As the Internet became commercialized in the mid-1990s, however, government subsidies for commercial enterprises came under intensive scrutiny. This led to the complete commercialization of Internet transmission services in the United States. Other countries, also faced with the uncomfortable prospect of government payments to support commercial services, are considering commercializing the Internet within their countries.

Of course, to the routers involved in packet delivery, none of this is relevant. Routers work together regardless of who owns them and how their costs are paid.

Internet Standards

Earlier, we saw the importance of standards. Figure 1.4 shows that Web access from home requires five types of standards. For reasons we will see below, they are organized as five layers. These five layers work together to provide the functionality you need to connect an application program on your machine to an application program on another machine.

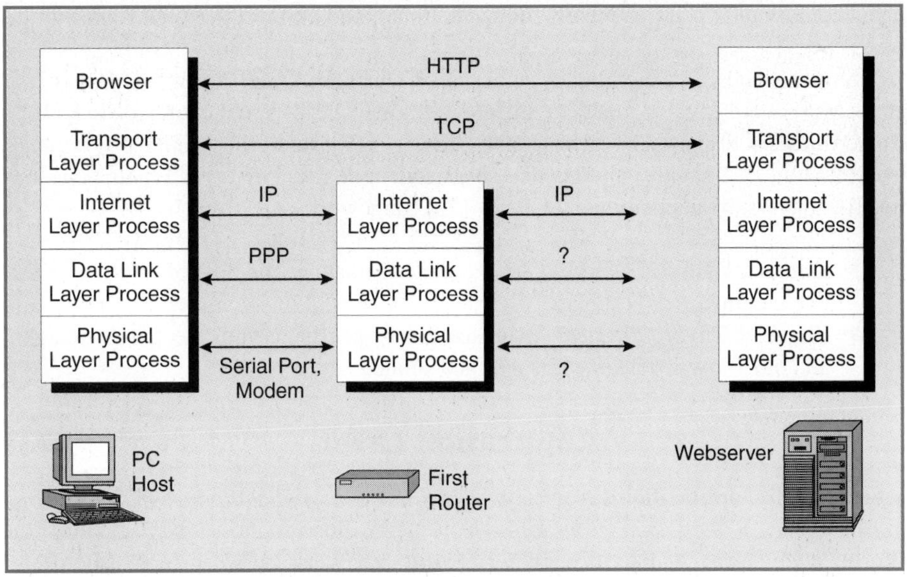

FIGURE **1.4**

**TCP/IP–OSI
Standards
Framework**

Browser	HTTP →			Browser	

Figure diagram:

- Browser — HTTP — Browser
- Transport Layer Process — TCP — Transport Layer Process
- Internet Layer Process — IP — Internet Layer Process — IP — Internet Layer Process
- Data Link Layer Process — PPP — Data Link Layer Process — ? — Data Link Layer Process
- Physical Layer Process — Serial Port, Modem — Physical Layer Process — ? — Physical Layer Process

PC Host   First Router   Webserver

TCP/IP and OSI

The Internet was created in the early 1980s by the U.S. *Defense Research Projects Agency (DARPA)*. DARPA commissioned the Information Sciences Institute (ISI) at the University of Southern California to create standards for this network.

ISI first created a framework (called an architecture) for setting standards. Such a framework defines a limited number of things required for two application programs on different machines to be able to communicate effectively. Once this general framework was in place, ISI could then create individual standards, confident that the individual standards would mesh together to achieve complete interoperability.

The framework that ISI created is known as **TCP/IP.** As shown in Figure 1.4, ISI realized that standards were needed in several basic "layers" ranging from high-level concerns like application program standards to low-level concerns, such as the thickness of wires in the network. We will define each of these layers briefly now. Then we will look at each layer in more depth.

▶ **Application Layer.** *Application layer* standards allow the two application programs to communicate effectively. In webservice, these two programs are the browser and the webserver application programs.
▶ **Transport Layer.** *Transport layer* standards allow the two computers to exchange messages effectively. These two computers are the user PC and the webserver.
▶ **Internet Layer.** *Internet layer* standards coordinate the routers that lie between the two computers, so that messages will be routed effectively between the two machines.

Finally, TCP/IP needed standards for delivering messages within single networks (called **subnets**). Subnet transmissions connect your PC to your ISP's access router, connect individual pairs of routers along the route, and connect the final router to the webserver.

Subnet standards were already widespread when the TCP/IP framework was created. Most were created under a different framework or architecture called OSI.[2] Rather than try to create competing standards, TCP/IP uses OSI standards for subnet transmission. OSI usually divides its subnet standards into two layers. This gives the final two layers in the combined **TCP/IP–OSI** framework.

▶ **Data Link Layer.** *Data link layer* standards manage the flow of traffic between two computers on a subnet.

▶ **Physical Layer.** *Physical layer* standards specify wiring, electrical voltages, and other low-level concerns within a subnet.

Application Layer

More formally, **application layer** *standards allow two application programs to work together, even if they come from different vendors.* For instance, when you surf the World Wide Web, it does not matter if you buy your browser from Microsoft, Netscape, or some other company. (The exceptions to this general rule are the features that browser vendors add beyond current standards.)

As Figure 1.4 shows, your browser and the webserver application program communicate via the **HTTP (HyperText Transfer Protocol)** standard. In HTTP, the browser sends an **HTTP request message** to the webserver application program asking for a particular file. The webserver finds the desired file and downloads it to the browser in an **HTTP response message.** Nor does it matter what company made the webserver software.

Note the word *protocol* in *HyperText Transfer Protocol. A* **protocol** *is a standard to govern communication between two peer processes at the same layer on different systems.* In the case of HTTP, the two processes are application layer programs. We will deal with protocols extensively in later chapters and modules. For now, think of them as a set of rules for what messages each process can send to its peer and when it may send these messages.

Transport Layer

More formally, **transport layer** *standards allow two computers to exchange messages even if they come from different vendors and even if they are of different platform types.* Figure 1.4 shows that the transport layer protocol in Web access is the **Transmission Control Protocol (TCP).** Thanks to TCP, we do not care what type of machine the other computer is. For instance, Figure 1.5 shows that the client host may be a PC and the server can be a workstation server (discussed later). As long as both communicate via TCP, neither knows what type of computer platform (type of computer) the other machine is.[3] Overall, TCP gives **platform independence.**

---

[2] The full name is Reference Model of Open Systems Interconnection. Given a name like this, almost everyone uses the contraction *OSI*. OSI actually has three layers for subnets, but modern network technologies do not use the third (network) layer for single networks. They only use the physical and data link layers.

[3] An analogy in the human world is anonymous e-mail. If you receive an anonymous e-mail message, you cannot tell if the other person is male or female.

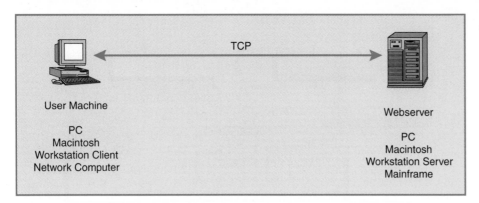

FIGURE **1.5**

Platform Independence through TCP

The Transmission Control Protocol is the TCP in TCP/IP. Unfortunately, the fact that TCP/IP is named after two of its specific standards, TCP and IP, causes confusion. Please remember that TCP/IP is the overall framework, not a specific standard. TCP and IP, which we discuss next, are specific standards, not multilayer standards frameworks.

Internet Layer

More formally, **internet layer** *standards allow packets to be routed across multiple routers from a source host to a destination host, even if the routers come from different vendors.* Figure 1.1 showed that messages may travel over multiple routers to reach their destination. Internet layer standards make this possible. The chief TCP/IP standard at the internet layer is the **Internet Protocol (IP)** standard.

Note in Figure 1.4 that the application and transport layer protocols govern interactions between software processes on the two host computers. However, the internet layer and lower layers are concerned only with interactions between the user PC host and the first router on the Internet. There also are internet layer and lower-layer connections between each pair of routers along the route and between the final router and the webserver.

Data Link Layer

More formally, **data link layer (DLL)** *standards organize transmissions into collections of bits called frames and manage the transmissions of these frames within a single network.* Note that, at the data link layer, these messages are called **frames.** (They are called **packets** at the internet layer.)

Specifically, Figure 1.6 shows that the data link layer standardizes how bits are organized into frames and transfers these frames from one machine to another on a single network. The data link layer also standardizes the management of data transmission on a single network, including how to deal with errors and how to be sure that two stations do not transmit at the same time if they would interfere with each other by transmitting simultaneously.

Figure 1.4 shows that when you use your home PC and a modem to reach the Internet, the data link layer standard you are using is probably the **Point-to-Point Protocol (PPP).** Some older routers require you to communicate with them via the Com-

FIGURE **1.6**

**Data Link and
Physical Layers
for Subnets (Single
Networks)**

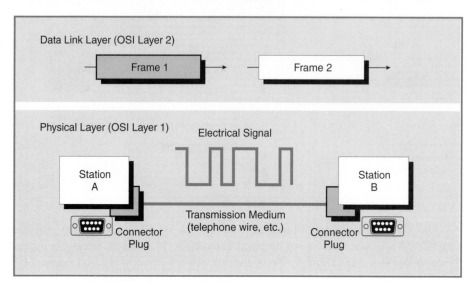

pressed Serial Line Protocol (CSLIP), but this is uncommon today. PPP is newer, and it is also the default standard in Windows 95, Windows 98, and Windows NT. If you wish to use CSLIP with one of these operating systems, in fact, you have to add additional software.

Physical Layer

More formally, Figure 1.6 shows that the **physical layer** *standardizes connector plugs, transmission media, electrical signaling, and other physical matters you can see and touch, even if the components come from different vendors.*

When you connect your PC at home to the Internet via a modem, two physical layer standards are involved. First, if you have an external modem, you need to connect it to one of your PC's *serial ports* on the back of the PC. Figure 1.6 shows a 9-pin serial port. There are physical layer serial port standards for plug size and shape, for the meaning of voltages on each pin, for voltage levels representing ones and zeros on each pin, and for transmission speed; that is, how often the voltage can change between two or more levels. Serial ports generally follow the EIA/TIA-232-F standard, although most depart from the standard in several ways, as discussed in Chapter 3.

Second, you also need physical layer standards for *modems*, which allow two computers to communicate over the telephone network. Both computers have modems, and these modems must be compatible. Fortunately, nearly all modems sold today are compatible. The most popular modems today follow the V.34 standard, which allows them to transmit and receive at 33.6 kbps. We will see other modem standards in Chapter 3.

Subnet and Internet Standards

Many people have a hard time distinguishing between subnet and internet layer standards because both deal with transmission. Figure 1.7 shows how they are different.

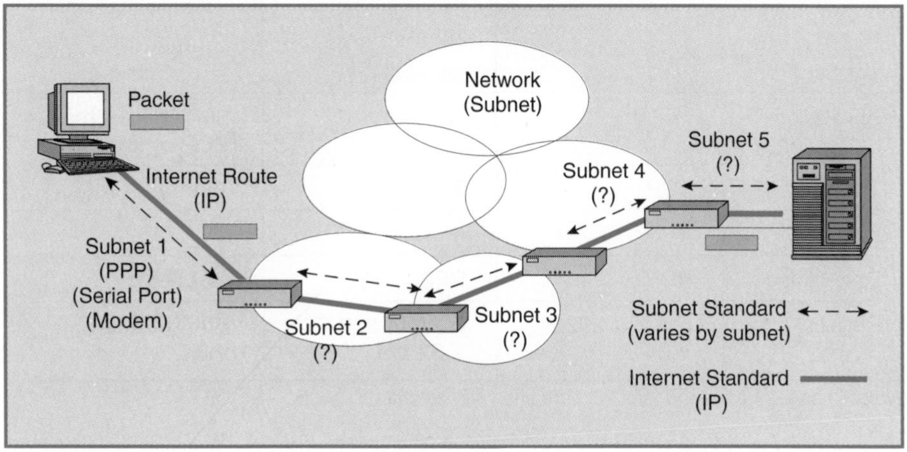

FIGURE **1.7**

Subnet and Internet Standards

Note that internet layer standards are concerned with end-to-end routing of messages (packets) *across multiple subnets*. They exist to create a single route between the two host computers.

Furthermore, there is only one internet layer standard for transmitting the packets. This is IP. All routers communicate with hosts and with other routers via the Internet Protocol.

In contrast, subnet standards are concerned with routing messages (frames) *within single networks (subnets)*. Subnet processes are not even aware that they are part of a larger internet.

Furthermore, each subnet may have different data link and physical layer standards. So if there are six subnets between the source and destination hosts, there may be six different data link and physical layer standards. Just because you use a modem and PPP to communicate with the first router does not mean that other subnets along the route use modems and PPP.

In this book, we will look mostly at subnet standards. This is because subnet standards have to serve many different needs, ranging from simple communication within a single office to the linking of corporate sites using expensive and comparatively unreliable long-distance transmission lines. The great diversity that exists in data link and physical layer standards gives us the flexibility we need to select the best subnet technology for each need.

The Flexibility of Standards Layering

Dividing standards into layers gives great flexibility. To move between different network environments, you may have to change standards only at a single layer or at a few layers. For instance, consider Figure 1.8.

The base case, accessing a webserver from home, is shown in the second column. Here, the standards in the five layers are HTTP, TCP, IP, PPP, the EIA/TIA-232-F serial port standard, and the V.34 modem standard.

Suppose instead that you have an older and slower V.32 *bis* modem. The third column shows that the only thing that is different is the physical layer, and even there, the serial port standard does not change.

FIGURE **1.8**

Flexibility in Standards Layering

LAYER	BASE CASE	SWITCH TO V.32 *BIS* MODEM	SWITCH FROM WEB ACCESS TO E-MAIL
Application	HTTP	HTTP	**SMTP and either POP or IMAP**
Transport	TCP	TCP	TCP
Internet	IP	IP	IP
Data Link	PPP	PPP	**CSLIP**
Physical	EIA/TIA-232-F, V.34	EIA/TIA-232-F, **V.32 *bis***	EIA/TIA-232-F, V.34

Note: Changes from the Base Case are shown in boldface.

At the opposite extreme, consider switching from Web access to e-mail. Figure 1.8 shows that at the application layer you will use the SMTP protocol (for sending e-mail) and either the POP or IMAP protocol (for receiving e-mail). Suppose also, in this case, that you use CSLIP rather than PPP as your data link layer standard. In this case, the application and data link layer standards both change, but the transport, internet, and physical layer standards do not.

Overall, layering means that you normally can reuse many standards from one situation to another. Throughout this book, we will do exercises requiring you to create figures like Figure 1.8. This will help you see how the standards in that situation fit into the overall five-layer TCP/IP–OSI framework.

OTHER NETWORK ENVIRONMENTS

Although most people are familiar with the Internet, corporations have other network environments that are equally or even more important. In the remainder of this chapter, we will discuss these other network environments.

PC Networks with File Servers

In corporations today, the *personal computer (PC)* is the dominant desktop machine. Most PCs in organizations are on PC networks, such as the PC network shown in Figure 1.9.

CLIENT PCS

Networked PCs that sit on the desks of ordinary managers and professionals are called **client PCs.** Client PCs usually begin their lives as simple stand-alone PCs. However, by adding a little hardware and software, as discussed in Chapter 4, they become client PCs able to reach out to the resources on many servers on their PC networks.

FILE SERVERS

There are several different types of **servers** on PC networks. These machines provide services to client PCs. A typical PC network will have hundreds or even thousands of client PCs and dozens or hundreds of servers.

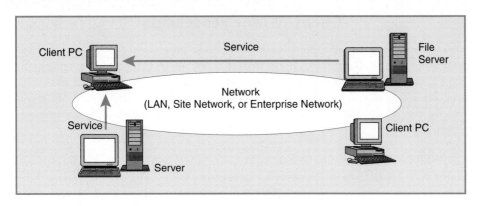

FIGURE 1.9

PC Network

The most common server in PC networks is the **file server.** As the name implies, a file server stores files, both data files and program files. In effect, it gives the user additional hard disk storage. It also allows groups of users to share common files, such as progress reports for project teams.

FILE SERVER PROGRAM ACCESS

For program execution, note that the file server merely *stores* programs. It does not *execute* them. Figure 1.10 shows that when you run a program, the file server downloads the program to your client PC. *The program actually executes on your client PC*, just like a program stored on your local hard disk drive. (File servers are merely remote hard disk drives.) *This process of downloading programs for execution on the client PC is* **file server program access.**

LIMITATIONS OF FILE SERVER PROGRAM ACCESS

Although executing programs on a client PC is simple, many corporate PCs are old and slow and have little RAM. They can run only small programs. As a result, software has to be limited in complexity and therefore functionality, so that programs can run on older PCs. Even for personal productivity applications, such as word processing programs, this limitation on functionality can be problematic. For database programs, however, the constraint to run on old client PCs is severe. Quite simply, the low processing power of many corporate PCs limits the size and therefore the functionality of software.

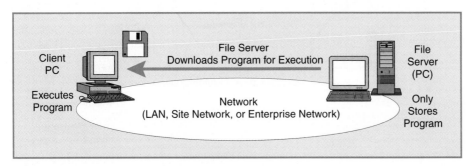

FIGURE 1.10

File Server
Program Access

Client/Server Processing

Many people have a hard time accepting file server program access. Why do all the processing on a small client PC, rather than on a fast file server, which is often a high-end PC far more capable of doing the processing work? The answer is that file server program access is simple and easy to implement. However, for more complex applications, corporations are turning to a newer form of program execution, client/server processing.

COOPERATIVE PROCESSING

Figure 1.11 illustrates how **client/server processing** works. The most important thing to note is that processing is handled by *two* programs working cooperatively, rather than by a single program. The **client program** runs on the client PC. The **server program** runs on the server. In client/server processing, the server is called an **application server.**

In order to get their work done, the two programs communicate. First, the client program sends a **request message** to the server program on the application server. This request message specifies what the client program needs the server program to do. In webservice, the request specifies the webpage to be retrieved.

The server program does the required work, such as retrieving certain data from its database. The server program then packages this information in a **response message,** which it sends to the client program on the client PC. In webservice, the response message includes the requested webpage or a code to explain why the request could not be fulfilled.

In human teamwork, the goal is to have individuals do whatever they do best. The same is true in client/server processing. The client program focuses on helping the user formulate requests. It also helps the user process information after the server program has delivered it. The client software responds immediately to the user's input, because it does all of its processing on the PC's microprocessor.

The server program, in turn, does the heavy processing work that cannot be done on limited client PCs. In database applications, for instance, it can store a massive

FIGURE 1.11
Client/Server Processing

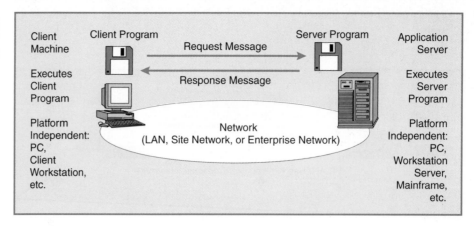

database and do processing-intensive data searching. *In other words, client/server processing eliminates the processing limitations of file server program access.*

PLATFORM INDEPENDENCE

In file server program access, the client machine is a personal computer. The file server is almost always a personal computer also. In other words, with rare exceptions, file server program access is for PC networks. There is no platform independence.

In contrast, client/server processing is inherently platform independent, because it uses transport layer standards that hide the identities of the client and server machines.

In Figure 1.11, for instance, the server machine is not a personal computer. It is a workstation server. These machines, discussed below, have far more processing power than personal computers, so they can support larger applications.

In Figure 1.11, the client machine is a personal computer. Given the importance of desktop PCs, most clients in client/server processing are PCs. However, the client machine can be an Intel PC, a Macintosh, or one of the newer platforms we discuss below.

SCALABILITY

When you build a client/server application, you can first install it on a high-end PC server, which is large enough to serve quite a few users. Later, if you run out of speed, you can shift the application from a PC server to a workstation server. You will be able to get higher processing power without changing application programs or data files. *The ability to grow to much larger sizes without changing an application or its data files is called* **scalability.** Given the insane growth rates for many applications, server scalability is critical to corporations, and the platform independent nature of client/server processing creates a high degree of scalability by allowing a broad range of server technologies to be used.

CLIENT/SERVER PROCESSING ON THE INTERNET

In most corporations, client/server processing first appeared in database applications on internal corporate networks. However, the Internet also uses client/server processing for most of its applications, including World Wide Web service, electronic mail, and file transfer protocol. Client/server operation is why the Internet can bring such rich and powerful services to low-power desktop PCs in corporations and to small home PCs.

File Server Program Access versus Client/Server Processing

Many students have a difficult time distinguishing between file server program access and client/server processing. Figure 1.12 compares these two platforms. It also shows terminal–host systems, which we will see below.

Networks

In both file server program access and client/server processing, the client machine needs a network to reach its server. Figure 1.13 shows that most corporations have a hierarchy of networks.

	FILE SERVER PROGRAM ACCESS	CLIENT/SERVER PROCESSING	TERMINAL-HOST SYSTEMS
Server name	File server	Application server	Host computer
Location of processing	Client PC (*not* on the file server)	Client computer and application server (2 programs)	Host computer (terminals are dumb)
Application program size and therefore functionality	Limited	Relatively unlimited	Relatively unlimited
Scalability	Low	High	Very high
Rich user interface and short response times because of local processing on client machine	Very good	Very good	Poor
Platform independent?	No. For PCs only	Yes. Client and server machines may be of any platform type. The two machines may be of different platform types	No. For terminals and hosts only

FIGURE 1.12

Processing in Different Computer Platforms

LANS

The first networks were very small, consisting of only a few machines in a single office or small company. These small networks are called **local area networks (LANs).** They usually are limited to 200 to 300 devices.

FIGURE 1.13

Networks in Corporations

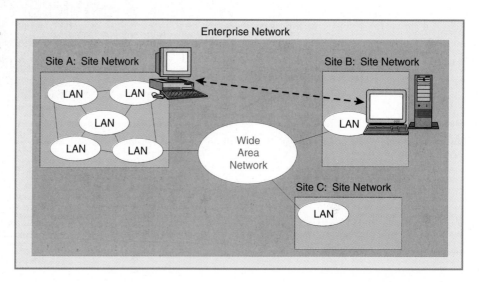

SITE NETWORKS

Figure 1.13 shows that the next level of networking is the **site network.** A site network links the various LANs that exist within a single site. For university campuses and industrial parks, site networks can be very large. In other cases, they connect a few LANs within a single building.

ENTERPRISE NETWORKS

Organizations with multiple sites normally use **enterprise networks.** These enterprise networks use the services of transmission carriers. The most popular of these services is the **wide area network (WAN),** which carries data between sites. It is easy to confuse enterprise networks with WANs. Note that WANs carry traffic only *between sites*, whereas enterprise networks also *include the site networks* at the connected sites.

LARGE PC NETWORKS

When PC networking first began, only LANs commonly existed. So early PC networks were very small. Many people still think of PC networks as small and confined to single LANs. In fact, many textbooks equate "PC network" and "LAN."

However, Figure 1.13 shows that site networks and enterprise networks have led to the creation of enormous site and enterprise PC networks with thousands of client PCs and hundreds of servers. As shown in Figure 1.13, a client PC on a LAN in Site A can reach a server on a Site B LAN without difficulty. Just as people in different offices cannot be constrained to internal communication, the PCs in every organization need to communicate. Today, it is possible technically to build such networks, but the human effort required to manage such huge networks is very great.

Terminal–Host Systems

Although the Internet and PC networks dominate networking today, this was not always true. Until the personal computer explosion of the 1980s, most corporations relied primarily on an older computer platform, the **terminal–host system.** Figure 1.14 illustrates this platform.

TERMINALS

The figure shows that users worked through desktop machines called **terminals**. Outwardly, terminals look a great deal like PCs. However, they are far less powerful. A

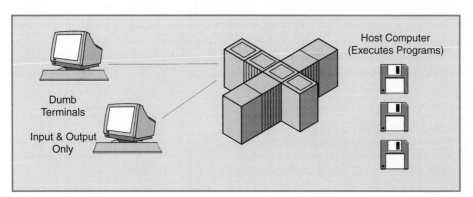

FIGURE **1.14**

Terminal–Host System

Host Computer
(Executes Programs)

Dumb
Terminals

Input & Output
Only

terminal is basically just a keyboard and a display, plus enough electronics to communicate with a distant host computer. For this reason, terminals are often called **dumb terminals.**[4]

HOST COMPUTER PROCESSING

The central **host computer**, in turn, is the brain of the system. All processing is done on the host computer, and all data are stored at the host site. When a terminal user types a command at the keyboard, the command first goes to the host computer, which executes the command. The host then sends information back to the terminal's screen. The terminal merely portrays what the host computer sends it.

A host computer can serve many terminals simultaneously. It does this by doing a little work for the first terminal, then doing a little work for the second, and so on, until it gets back to the first terminal. This is called **time sharing.** It resembles a chess master playing simultaneous games with many opponents, moving from one to another to make a single move in each game. However, host computers work so quickly that each terminal user has the illusion that he or she has the entire host computer. Of course, this illusion breaks down when the host is overloaded.

The largest host computers used in most businesses are **mainframes.** The largest mainframes can execute around a billion instructions per second, giving them the processing power to serve hundreds of terminal users simultaneously. Mainframes are designed for database use, because most business processes involve databases. As a consequence, mainframes not only have extensive processing power. They also have massive disk capacity and ultrahigh-speed disk access. In contrast, **supercomputers** are designed to do complex numerical calculations at very high speeds. However, complex calculations are rare in database processing, and supercomputer disk performance usually lags far behind that of mainframes. IBM dominates the mainframe industry, and most other mainframe vendors build host computers that are compatible with IBM mainframes.

Smaller hosts are called **minicomputers.** Minicomputers that are configured for database processing are called **small business computers.** The IBM AS/400 is the most popular small business computer.

"HOST" IN TERMINAL–HOST SYSTEMS AND ON THE INTERNET

Note, by the way, that *host computer* has two different meanings in networking. *In terminal–host systems*, the host is the machine that provides processing power to dumb terminals. *On the Internet*, any computer is a host.

This Internet use of the term *host* occurred because when the Internet started, only hosts in terminal–host systems connected to the Internet. Later, when other computers, such as PCs, began to connect to the Internet, they were simply added to the Internet definition of *host*. Although it is unfortunate that you have to master two different meanings for the term **host computer,** this is simply a fact of life in networking.

---

[4] It may seem strange to put so little computer intelligence on the desktop. However, terminal–host systems were created in the 1960s, long before microprocessors. There was no way to bring processing to the desktop economically. By the time microprocessors appeared, host computer operation was set.

THE FALL AND RISE OF TERMINAL–HOST SYSTEMS

Although terminal–host systems can serve hundreds of users simultaneously, this ability comes at the cost of great complexity. As a result, terminal–host systems are very expensive.

Because of these high expenses, most corporations have been **downsizing**[5] many of their applications—that is, moving them from terminal–host systems to PC networks. In database systems, for instance, client/server processing on application servers is less expensive.

In addition, as shown in Figure 1.1, because PCs have local processing power, they provide a rich user interface, and there usually is no delay when a user hits a key. In contrast, in terminal–host systems, where the processing is done on a distant host, response time can be very long when a user hits a key. In addition, graphics usually are limited or nonexistent, due to the cost of the high-speed long-distance lines needed to transmit rich graphics images.

As a result of this gradual abandonment of terminal–host systems, applications on such systems are often called **legacy** applications. In human terms, a legacy is what your parents leave to you when they die. In networking, a legacy application is one "bequeathed" to you by your predecessors in your job.

Most corporations are working to downsize their legacy applications to PC networks. However, budgets are always limited, so the conversion of legacy systems cannot take place overnight. Every organization has a mixture of new systems and legacy systems.

Less Common Platforms

We have now looked at the major computer platforms today, including file server program access, client/server processing, and terminal–host systems. However, there are a few other platforms we should note briefly.

WORKSTATIONS

Before personal computers even existed, the Xerox Palo Alto Research Center built machines that looked like PCs but were far more powerful. Xerox called these machines **workstations.** Other vendors began to produce workstations as well, including Hewlett-Packard, IBM, and SUN. Soon, UNIX became the main operating system for these workstations.

When low-cost PCs emerged in the early 1980s, workstations found themselves limited to specialized areas needing higher computer power than PCs could provide. Engineering design is a good example of such an area.

Figure 1.15 shows that a workstation network has both client machines and server machines. In fact, the creation of client and server machines first appeared in the workstation community.

---

[5] This is an unfortunate term because *downsizing* often means to lay people off in an organization. As a result, other terms are sometimes used to refer to the transfer of host application to PC networks.

FIGURE 1.15
Workstation
Network

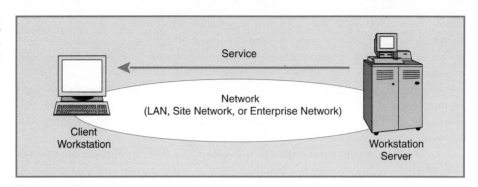

NETWORK COMPUTERS (NCs)

In recent years, there has been increasing concern about the cost of networked personal computers. These machines are expensive to buy. They are also expensive to maintain. Analysts have begun to focus on the **total cost of ownership (TCO)** of a networked personal computer over its entire life cycle, including purchasing, upgrading, software installation, and user learning. The TCO can be several times the initial purchase price.

One potential way to lower the TCO is to replace expensive personal computers on user desktops with less expensive **network computers (NCs).** As Figure 1.16 illustrates, NCs are simple boxes with a processor and RAM but no hard disk drive. They typically are sealed boxes that cannot be upgraded.

Another characteristic of NCs is that they do not run the Windows operating system. Instead, they have an operating system that only runs programs written in the Java language. As Figure 1.16 shows, when a user needs a program, a special server downloads the software to the network computer.

Oracle and SUN Microsystems have been pushing network computers heavily. Because NCs do not need Windows to operate, Oracle and SUN see the NCs as a way to break Microsoft's dominance on the desktop. However, the inability of these machines to run most Windows applications and concerns about the costs of servers and transmission lines to support NCs has limited them so far to niche applications, generally involving the replacement of dumb terminals.

FIGURE 1.16
Network
Computer (NC)

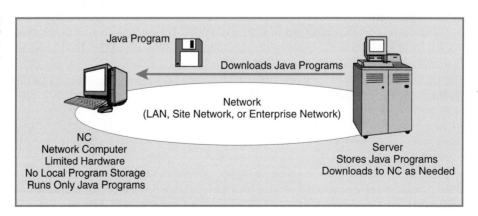

FIGURE 1.17

Distributed Processing

DISTRIBUTED PROCESSING

In client/server processing, *two* programs communicate. Both are complete programs. Many analysts feel that client/server processing is only a first step toward a radically new approach to program execution in network environments. This is **distributed processing,** which is illustrated in Figure 1.17.

Here, there is no complete program. Instead, there are a number of small *objects*. Each object contains a piece of software plus associated data. Each object does a single, well-defined task.

To accomplish their work, objects often call (send messages to) other objects. In effect, they send one another well-defined messages similar to structured e-mail. When objects receive messages, they take well-defined actions.

Dividing a process into objects is the essence of **object oriented programming.** In the past, all objects were on the same machine. This made calls to other objects fairly simple. In distributed computing, however, the objects are spread across multiple machines, perhaps to take advantage of available computer capacity on these various machines. In distributed processing, messages between objects must travel across the network.

Programmers know that object oriented programming has a number of advantages over traditional programs. Distributed computing has the potential to extend these advantages to networked environments. Today, distributed computing is still in the experimental stage. During your future career, however, it is likely to become very important both to networking professionals and to programmers in general.

INFORMATION APPLIANCES

Most computers in organizations today are *general-purpose computers* designed to run many different programs, such as word processing, spreadsheeting, electronic mail, and other applications. However, the falling cost of microprocessors and RAM means that we may soon see specialized machines called **information appliances**, which are created to do a single specific task.

Figure 1.18 illustrates information appliances in an office. One example is the intelligent copier, which can have embedded PC-like intelligence for internal diagnostics, memorizing user preferences, and communicating with client PCs in the office.

FIGURE **1.18**

Information Appliances

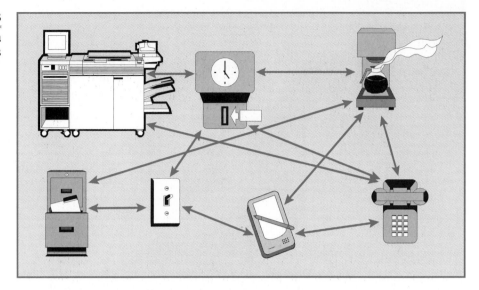

Another information appliance is an even more specialized device, the intelligent coffee maker. Although this seems like a trivial information appliance, it illustrates the fact that intelligence will soon be so cheap that it will become almost universal.

One feature of information appliances is that they will communicate constantly with one another. When an intelligent copier is out of paper or is having other problems, it can notify the secretary responsible for it. The coffee maker can call for help when the pot is empty or when the coffee is too old. It can even receive commands from a desktop PC to turn itself on at a certain time.

The key thing to keep in mind is that today's costs are far higher than they will be ten or even five years from now. During most of your career, there may be dozens of intelligent devices even in small offices, communicating in a dense web that will make today's corporate network look simple.

STANDARDS ARCHITECTURES

Now that we have looked at the broad spectrum of networking environments that exist in organizations, we will again return to standards, to see how they differ among networking environments.

As discussed earlier, TCP/IP is a **standards architecture** or framework. When you build a house, you first create an overall architecture for the house. This specifies what rooms you will have and how they will work together to produce an overall goal—providing a good place to live. To achieve this, you create a number of subgoals, such as designing the bedrooms, designing the kitchen, and so forth.

In standards architectures, the goal is to allow two application programs to work together despite being on different machines and on different subnets. A standards architecture also divides this large goal into a number of smaller subgoals. In the TCP/IP architecture, for instance, the subgoals are to standardize 1) application program communication, 2) computer-computer communication, 3) end-to-end routing across multiple subnets, and 4) transmission within subnets. Each of these subgoals has its own layer in the architecture.

Standards Architectures versus Individual Standards

Most standards architectures were developed in the 1970s and early 1980s. Since then, the focus has been on developing standards at individual layers. You might think that a four-layer architecture would need only four standards, one at each layer. However, this is not the case for several reasons:

1. Different user conditions might require different standards. For example, different subnet technologies are needed for local area networks, in which speed is inexpensive, than for wide area networks, in which transmission speed is very expensive.
2. New standards are developed to take advantage of technological advances. For instance, in the Ethernet standards we will see in Chapter 4, speeds were originally 10 Mbps. Today, we can run Ethernet at 100 Mbps or even 1,000 Mbps.
3. Although it is sad to say, battles in standards committees often result in two or more standards that do almost the same thing.

Standards Architectures and Standards Agencies

There are four major standards architectures, and, as you might guess, they use different layering principles and have different standards even when their layers match up. This causes deep incompatibilities. We will briefly characterize these four major standards architectures and the agencies that manage them.

OSI

The full name for the **OSI** architecture is the Reference Model of Open Systems Interconnection. *Reference model* is another name for architecture. The OSI architecture is overseen by two standards agencies.

1. The **International Organization for Standardization (ISO)**[6] is the premier international standards agency for industrial products, including motor oil, nuts and bolts, and computers.
2. The **International Telecommunications Union–Telecommunications Standards Sector (ITU-T),** in turn, is the premier standards organization for telecommunications, including telephony, facsimile, radio, and television.

Networking involves the convergence of computers and telecommunications, so having these two superstar standards agencies work together seemed like a winning combination.

OSI standards are very **open,** meaning that they are not under the control of one organization. In fact, OSI development leans over backward to ensure proper procedure and broad representation.

Unfortunately, OSI standards development practices have created so much overhead that it takes a very long time to develop an OSI standard. The standards that OSI

---

[6] Why not International Standards Organization? Because "International Organization for Standardization" is ISO's official name in English. *ISO* does not mean anything in any other language, either. *ISO* is simply from the Greek for "true." Similarly, all ITU sectors (divisions) have single-character extensions, so it is ITU-T, not ITU-TSS.

develops, furthermore, are extremely complex. Because standards are late, product development begins late. Because of the complexity of OSI standards, furthermore, it takes a long time to develop products. Also thanks to the complexity of OSI standards, products are complex and therefore expensive.

"Late to market and expensive" is not a winning combination in the real world. As a result, OSI standards have not fared well in the marketplace with two exceptions. First, as noted earlier, they dominate standards for subnets (single networks). In addition, several OSI application layer standards have succeeded in the marketplace or have at least been used as a starting point for application standards in other architectures.

As you might suspect, OSI uses a complex layering system, as shown in the box "TCP/IP versus OSI." Once, this layering was widely taught in networking classes, because it was assumed that OSI would eventually become dominant. This has not happened, but you will need to know it for job interviews. In your actual future work, you will rarely see OSI standards between the data link layer and the application layer. Instead, as in the case of our five-layer hybrid TCP–OSI framework, you will see *protocol stacks* with OSI at the bottom two layers and another architecture's layers above that.

TCP/IP

The Internet Engineering Task Force (IETF) manages TCP/IP. Although the IETF is an open body and sets open standards, it has a strong culture of moving quickly and developing simple standards. This is the opposite of OSI, and the market effects have also been opposite. TCP/IP standards tend to be inexpensive and quick to market. This makes them very attractive and in fact has made them dominant in the marketplace above the subnet layers.

Many people believe that TCP/IP succeeded because of the Internet's popularity. In fact, industry and government adopted TCP/IP for internal systems in the 1980s. TCP/IP was already the most widely used architecture before the Internet captured the eye of corporations in the 1990s. The emergence of the Internet as a corporate tool, of course, has solidified the dominance of TCP/IP in the marketplace.

Although the layers of the TCP/IP architecture are likely to remain the same in the future, most analysts expect that major changes will be needed in key standards in the future. Current standards, especially IP and TCP, were designed when the Internet was far smaller than it is today and when high performance was less critical than it is today. Current standards are simply not good enough for many current and future applications. The IETF has already developed a new version of IP, called IPng (IP, the next generation[7]) or, more officially, IP Version 6. However, this is just the beginning.

TCP/IP VERSUS OSI

As discussed in the text, whereas TCP/IP architecture uses a four-layer standards architecture, OSI uses a more complex seven-layer standards architecture. Figure 1.19 shows how the layers match up.

---

[7] Many IETF members are Star Trek fans.

TCP/IP	OSI
Application	Application (layer 7)
	Presentation (layer 6)
	Session (layer 5)
Transport	Transport (layer 4)
Internet	Network (layer 3)
Subnet	
	Data Link (layer 2)
	Physical (layer 1)

Application Layers

TCP/IP has a single application layer. OSI has two and a half.

- OSI's *application layer (OSI layer 7)* is for standards allowing two applications to talk together.
- OSI's *presentation layer (OSI layer 6)* is a catch-all layer for standards that are used in multiple applications, such as standards for representing text and graphics. The OSI presentation layer also offers a computer-neutral language for transferring files between computers with different storage and display screen formats.
- OSI's *session layer (OSI layer 5)* manages the connection between two applications, including how to handle disrupted message exchanges. In TCP/IP, managing connections is done at the computer–computer transport layer. This is a major philosophical difference between OSI and TCP/IP.

Computer–Computer Layers

For computer–computer standards, TCP has only a single layer, the transport layer. OSI has one and a half.

- As just noted, the OSI session layer handles many of the connection management functions handled by TCP/IP's transport layer.
- The OSI *transport layer (OSI layer 4)* handles the rest of the functions needed for two computers to communicate effectively. Note that both TCP/IP and OSI have transport layers, but they have different functions.

Lower Layers

For transmission across single networks, OSI created three layers. We have already discussed the physical and data link layers in this chapter. The *physical layer (OSI layer 1)* moves individual bits encoded as electrical signals across a single physical data link. The *data link layer (OSI layer 2)* manages frame transmission across a single physical data link.

OSI originally assumed that subnets would also need *network layer (OSI layer 3)* standards, which guide packets across a number of data links within a single subnet. However, as discussed in Chapters 4 and 5, this proved to be unnecessary for both LANs and wide area networks. Except for X.25 wide area networks, Chapter 4 notes that all OSI subnet standards stop at layer 2. Even X.25 would be classified as a layer 2 network if it were developed today by the same principles used to create Frame Relay and ATM network standards.

This "freeing" of the network layer from subnet use was fortunate, because in creating the OSI architecture, ISO and ITU-T had ignored internetting. When the need for internetting became apparent to OSI developers, it was added into the network layer (layer 3).

Together, the addition of internetworking standards to layer 3 and the lack of subnet standards in layer 3 means that OSI's networking layer is effectively used only for internetworking. So although Figure 1.19 shows the OSI network layer spanning the TCP/IP subnet and internet layers, OSI's layer 3 is really an internet layer in practice.

SNA

IBM developed large mainframe networks long before OSI and TCP/IP appeared. To manage these large networks, IBM created its own standards architecture. This was **Systems Network Architecture (SNA),** which is discussed in Module H. SNA is still very common because IBM mainframes are still widely used. In addition, other mainframe vendors either have adopted SNA or have developed derivative architectures. Especially for long-distance networking, SNA transmission needs to be considered carefully in corporate network planning.

SNA is a **proprietary** architecture, meaning that it is controlled by one company. To IBM's credit, however, when OSI was formed, IBM submitted SNA standards to be the basis of OSI. However, SNA was then strongly a **master–slave** architecture, with the mainframe in control of "lesser units." ISO and ITU-T correctly decided to develop a **peer–peer** architecture with no central device in charge. Especially at the data link layer, however, OSI initially borrowed from SNA.

IPX/SPX

Until very recently, the dominant vendor in PC networking was Novell. In the early 1990s, Novell's NetWare operating system for servers had more than a 60% market share. NetWare developed a proprietary architecture called **IPX/SPX.** Recently, it has begun to offer versions of NetWare in which TCP/IP is the native standards architecture. However, many organizations still have large installed bases of IPX/SPX equipment.

SUMMARY

In this chapter, we focused on two key issues: standards and computer platforms. These are the two key issues for this book overall.

Standards allow you to buy products from competing vendors, resulting in lower prices and more features. In Chapter 1, we looked at standards in a specific, familiar context—accessing a webserver from home using a telephone line and a modem. This allowed us to look at how the Internet works. It also let us see the widely used hybrid TCP/IP–OSI standards framework, with its application, transport, internet, data link, and physical layers. One important concept is platform independence, which brings scalability, among other benefits.

We also looked at other standards architectures besides TCP/IP, including OSI, SNA, and IPX/SPX. Almost every organization of significant size supports multiple architectures. So multiprotocol support is always a key issue in network planning and product selection.

In Chapter 1, we also looked at a number of computer platforms, including file server program access on PC networks, client/server processing, terminal–host systems, workstations, network computers, distributed processing, and information appliances. It is very important to understand the difference between file server program access and client/server processing because they are easily confused.

The beginning of the chapter discussed the fact that IS networking professionals typically buy and integrate products instead of building them from scratch. It noted that technology selection normally depends on three main criteria: performance, feasibility, and cost.

REVIEW QUESTIONS

CORE REVIEW QUESTIONS

1. What are the three main factors you must consider when selecting a product or technology? What are the three major considerations within the cost factor? Which usually wins—the best technology or the least expensive technology that does what users need?
2. Give the exact definition of *standard*. (See Page 4.) What benefits do standards bring?
3. Give the exact definition of *network*. (See Page 5.) Why does the fact that you only need to know the receiving computer's address make life simpler?
4. Does *network* mean the same thing as *the Internet*? Explain. Why do we have *inter* in the name *Internet*?
5. What is the function of a router? What is a route?
6. What are the two types of addresses on the Internet?
7. Is a webserver on the Internet a host computer? Is a home PC on the Internet a host computer?

8. Name the five layers in the hybrid TCP/IP–OSI architecture. Give the exact definition of each. (See Pages 10–12.) What standard or standards are used at each layer when you access the World Wide Web from home? What is a frame? What is a packet?

9. Give the exact definition of *protocol*. (See Page 10.) Are all standards protocols?

10. Distinguish between subnet and internet transmission.

11. What is platform independence? Standards at which layer bring platform independence?

12. Distinguish between file server program access and client/server processing in terms of where processing is done, the implications for program functionality, scalability, user interface richness, and platform independence. For file server program access, explain why you cannot simply say "processing is done on the PC." What program runs on an application server?

13. What is scalability? Why is it needed? What is the link between platform independence and scalability?

14. Distinguish between LANs, site networks, and enterprise networks. Distinguish between WANs and enterprise networks.

15. Where is the processing done in terminal–host systems? What are the implications of your answer for response time and rich graphics?

16. What is downsizing? What is a legacy application? Why is it impossible to downsize all host legacy applications in two or three years?

17. Distinguish between PCs and workstations in terms of processing power. Do PC networks and workstation networks both use client machines and server machines?

18. Distinguish between standards architectures and individual standards. What are the four major standards architectures? Why has TCP/IP emerged as the predominant standards architecture? In what situations are OSI, SNA, and IPX/SPX important?

DETAILED REVIEW QUESTIONS

1. How are the programmer/analyst and user support career tracks changing as a result of networking? Distinguish between what IS professionals and computer science or electrical engineering professionals do in networking.

2. Is the Internet free in the United States? Distinguish between ISPs and NSPs. Why is it possible for two hosts using different ISPs linked to different NSPs to communicate? Do all countries use ISPs and NSPs?

3. When you link to a webserver from home, which two standards layers deal with communication between processes on your PC and on the webserver? (These are called end-to-end layers, by the way.) Which three standards layers deal with communication between processes on your PC and on the first router—the one that you dial into at your Internet service provider?

4. Why is there only one main internet layer standard, IP, whereas there are many different sublayer standards?

5. Do the terms *LAN* and *PC network* mean the same thing? Explain.

6. What is an information appliance? Why are they likely to be common?

7. Distinguish between PCs, workstations, and network computers (NCs) in terms of processing power and the ability to run Windows applications.

8. Distinguish between client/server processing and distributed processing.
9. Distinguish between mainframes and minicomputers. Distinguish between mainframes and supercomputers. Distinguish between minicomputers and small business computers.
10. (From the Box: TCP/IP versus OSI). Briefly explain how TCP/IP and OSI layers match up. At what layer in each are connections managed? Explain why the OSI network layer (layer 3) is effectively the same as the TCP/IP internet layer.
11. (From the Box: TCP/IP versus OSI). Characterize the seven layers of the OSI architecture. For each, give the layer's name and number, followed by a brief description of what it standardizes.

THOUGHT QUESTIONS

1. Do you think that it is good that less expensive technologies that meet user requirements usually win in the marketplace over better technologies?
2. Distinguish between the Internet and the World Wide Web. Distinguish between the Internet and electronic mail.
3. Distinguish between the data link layer and the physical layer. Do not just repeat the two definitions. Why do you think standards developers created two layers for subnets instead of just one?
4. In Figure 1.8, what changes relative to the base case if you use the Compressed Serial Line Interface Protocol to dial in from home to a File Transfer Protocol host on the Internet? File transfer protocol uses the FTP application layer protocol.
5. What operating system do you think information appliances will run?
6. How do you think TCP/IP standards will have to change in the future to meet the needs of the Internet?

PROJECTS

1. Go to the book's website, http://www.prenhall.com/panko, and read the Updates Page for this chapter to see any reported errors and for new and expanded information on the material in this chapter.

2. Go to the book's website, http://www.prenhall.com/panko, and do the Internet Exercises for this chapter.
3. On the Internet, go to http://www.yahoo.com and look up an estimate for the number of hosts on the Internet.
4. From cnet.com, download the shareware program "neotrace.exe." Try several known host names, such as www.prenhall.com, to see how many routers sit between you and each host.

CHAPTER 2

Using the Internet from Home: Standards at Higher Layers

INTRODUCTION

In the last chapter, we began to look at the Internet, which is arguably the most important networking environment today. In this chapter, we will look at the Internet in more detail, again using World Wide Web access from home as our example.

We will examine how structured messages called *protocol data units (PDUs)* are exchanged at the application, transport, internet, and data link layers. The physical layer is very different because it does not involve the exchange of structured messages. We will look at the physical layer in detail in the next chapter.

After looking at PDU transmission in general, we will look in more detail at HTTP, TCP, and IP. If you use a different application, such as e-mail, the application layer standard changes, of course. Yet you probably continue to use TCP at the transport layer, and you certainly continue to use IP at the internet layer. We will also look at two "helper" standards you probably use unknowingly every time you use the Internet. These are DNS and autoconfiguration standards. By the end of this chapter, you should have a good understanding of key TCP/IP standards and concepts.

At the very start, you should be warned that this chapter is probably the most difficult in the book. Interactions at individual layers are highly complex, and the processes at different layers work together in complex ways. You will need to read this chapter carefully and read it several times if you are to master this material.

Protocol Data Units (PDUs)

We saw in the last chapter that peer processes at the same layer on different hosts or routers need to communicate with one another. At the application layer, for instance, the browser must send HTTP request messages to the webserver application program on the webserver.

PROTOCOLS

For two processes to communicate, they must interact according to some standard. A **protocol** *is a standard that governs interactions between peer processes at the same layer but on different machines*. For instance, the standard governing interactions between a browser and server (HTTP) is a protocol. The two processes (programs) are at the same layer (application) but are on different machines.

PDUs AT VARIOUS LAYERS

Figure 2.1 shows that peer processes at the application, transport, internet, and data link layers communicate via messages called **protocol data units (PDUs).** The protocol at each layer defines the organization of the PDU.

The physical layer, which is concerned only with the transmission of individual bits in isolation, does not send messages, which are organized collections of bits.

PDU ORGANIZATION

Figure 2.2 shows that most PDUs have two parts. The **data field** contains the information to be delivered. The **header,** in turn, contains supervisory information to tell the receiving process what to do with the data field.

The figure also shows that some PDUs, typically those at the data link layer, may contain a third part, namely a **trailer.** This also contains supervisory information to tell the receiving process what to do with the PDU.

The header and trailer themselves have internal organization. As we will see below, a header or trailer may consist of several **fields.** For instance, headers usually have source and destination address fields, which give the addresses for the two processes that are communicating through the PDU.

END-TO-END LAYERS

Figure 2.1 shows that the application and transport layers are **end-to-end layers**, meaning that their PDUs are aimed at peer processes on the *other host computer* in the interaction.

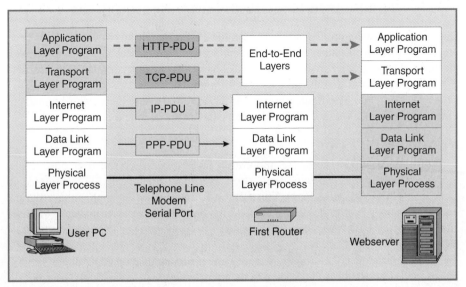

FIGURE 2.1

Protocol Data Units (PDUs)

FIGURE **2.2**

**Protocol Data
Unit (PDU)
Organization**

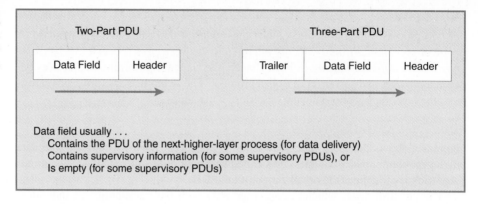

Yet the internet and data link layers are not end-to-end layers. The internet and data link processes on your PC communicate with their peer processes *on the first router*, not with their peer processes on the destination host. The physical layer process, which does not create a PDU, also communicates only with the physical layer process on the first router.

As you would suspect, and as we will see below, the first router has internet, data link, and physical layer processes that communicate with their peers on the second router. All routers along the route from the source host to the destination host communicate at the internet, data link, and physical layers.

At the other end, the final router has internet, data link, and physical layer processes that communicate with their peer processes on the destination host.

FRAMES AND PACKETS

We saw in Chapter 1 that messages (protocol data units) at the data link layer are called **frames.** PDUs at the internet layer, in turn, are called **packets**. We will use these terms in this chapter.

The Source Host Transmits: Nested PDUs

One question that Figure 2.1 raises is *how* the PDU at each layer can reach its peer process on another machine. After all, the application layer processes (the browser and the webserver programs) are on different machines. They cannot communicate directly.

Figure 2.3 shows that the processes at different layers on the source host work together to send data. The figure shows that the PDUs are nested, one inside another. Later, we will look at *nested PDUs* on routers and on the destination host.

AT THE APPLICATION LAYER

In World Wide Web access, the application layer process on the user host is the browser. The browser creates the application layer PDU. Specifically, in webservice, it creates an **HTTP-Request-PDU.** This PDU asks the webserver application program on the webserver host to download a file to the browser. If we were using a different application, say FTP, then the application program on the user PC would create an FTP-PDU.

The application layer program cannot deliver the application PDU directly. So it passes the HTTP-Request-PDU down to the transport layer program on the user PC.

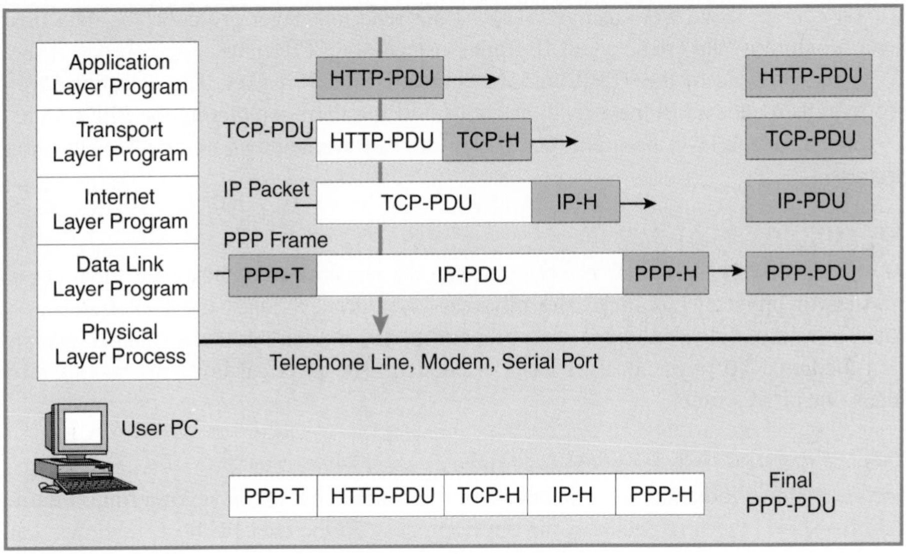

FIGURE 2.3

Nested PDUs on
the Source Host

AT THE TRANSPORT LAYER

The transport layer program receives the HTTP-PDU. It then creates a transport layer PDU.

Because TCP is the required transport layer protocol in HTTP interactions, this transport layer PDU is a TCP-PDU. The TCP-PDU has a data field and a header field.

The data field of the TCP-PDU is just the HTTP-PDU passed down by the application layer program. Figure 2.3 shows that the transport layer program then adds a TCP header, to create a full **TCP-PDU.**

Finally, the transport layer program passes the TCP-PDU down to the next-lower-layer program, the internet layer program.

In effect, the transport layer receives the PDU from the next-higher-layer process and adds a header. It then passes the new PDU down to the next-lower-layer process. This cycle of receiving a PDU, adding a header (and perhaps a trailer), and passing the new PDU down is repeated at the internet and data link layers.

AT THE INTERNET LAYER

The internet layer program accepts the TCP-PDU from the transport layer program. The internet layer program uses the TCP-PDU as the data field of a new internet layer PDU. The Internet Protocol is the standard used at the internet layer for HTTP, so the internet layer program adds an IP header, to create a full IP-PDU. Because this is the internet layer, we call this IP-PDU the **IP packet.**

Finally, the internet layer program passes the IP packet down to the data link layer program.

AT THE DATA LINK LAYER

The data link layer program accepts the IP packet from the internet layer program and creates a new data link PDU. Because we are using the PPP standard in our example, the data link layer specifically creates a PPP-PDU. This is happening at the data link layer, so we call the PPP-PDU the **PPP frame.**

Of course, if we were using CSLIP as our data link layer protocol, the data link layer program would create a CSLIP frame instead of a PPP frame.

The data field of the PPP frame, of course, is the IP packet. The data link layer program then adds a PPP header. It also adds a PPP trailer, completing the PPP frame.

The data link layer program then passes the PPP frame down to the physical layer process.

AT THE PHYSICAL LAYER

At most layers, the "process" is a program. At the physical layer, however, the process consists of physical circuitry. The physical layer process takes the PPP frame and changes it into a physical signal that propagates down a wire or some other transmission medium. No physical layer PDU is created. The physical layer process merely sends one bit at a time.

THE PPP-PDU: AN OVERALL LOOK

So far, we have looked at what happens on the source host one layer at a time. Figure 2.3 also shows the final result of the entire process on the user PC host. It shows that the data link layer frame consists of a PPP header, an IP header, a TCP header, an HTTP protocol data unit, and the PPP trailer. The HTTP-PDU also has a header and a data field, as we will see later.

Communication at Each Router

Recall from Figure 2.1 that the PPP frame goes from the source host to the *first router*, not to the destination host directly. When the first router receives the PPP frame from the source host, it takes a series of actions on the nested PPP frame. Figure 2.4 illustrates these actions.

The first router (and every other router) has two or more ports or connections. When a data link layer frame (PDU) arrives in one port over the physical connection, the router must decide which port to use to send the frame back out, so that the frame and its contents will go to the destination host or at least to a router nearer the destination host.

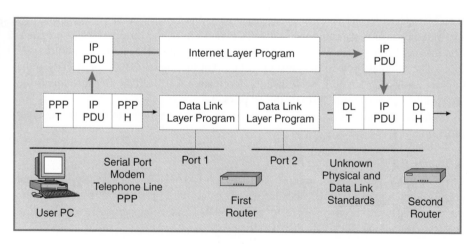

FIGURE **2.4**

Nested PDUs on the First Router

Recall from Chapter 1 that routers and hosts use many different data link layer protocols and physical layer protocols to connect to one another. In our example, you use PPP, a serial port, a modem, and a telephone line to connect to the first router. This does not mean that the first router will use such low-performance technology to connect to other routers. If a router has four ports, it may use a different physical and data link layer standard on each port.

AT THE RECEIVING PORT'S DATA LINK LAYER PROGRAM

The data link layer process on the first router's receiving port receives the incoming PPP frame. It reads the PPP header and the PPP trailer.

When the data link layer program on the receiving port finishes taking any required actions, it removes the IP packet from the PPP frame's data field. It passes the IP packet to the next-higher-layer process, the router's internet layer program.

AT THE INTERNET LAYER PROGRAM ON THE ROUTER

When the internet layer program receives the IP packet, it studies the IP header and takes appropriate actions.

Most importantly, it reads the internet address of the ultimate destination host, the webserver. The internet layer program then considers what it knows about network conditions. Considering these network conditions, the internet layer program decides which of its several ports to use to send the IP packet back out, so that the IP packet and its contents will move closer to the final destination.

The internet layer program then modifies the IP header[1] and passes the reconstituted IP packet down to the data link layer program on the selected port. (Remember that each port has its own data link layer and physical layer process.)

AT THE SENDING PORT'S DATA LINK LAYER PROGRAM

The data link layer program on the selected output port receives the IP packet and uses it as the data field of a new data link frame. The data link layer program then adds the header and perhaps a trailer, as required by the data link layer protocol on that port.

What is the data link layer protocol for the outgoing link on the first router? We simply do not know. The Internet hides the details of all data link layer protocols (and physical layer protocols) beyond the link connecting your user PC to the first router.

The data link layer program on the outgoing port passes the data link layer frame to the physical layer process, which is hardware. The physical layer process on the selected outgoing port delivers the data link layer frame to the next router.

Repeating the Process at Each Router

The process we have just seen at the first router is repeated at each router.

▶ The physical layer process delivers the data link layer frame to the data link layer program on the receiving port.
▶ That data link layer program passes the IP packet to the router's single internet layer program.

---

[1] Normally, the internet layer program on a router changes only one field, which counts the number of "hops" the packet has made among routers.

- ▶ The internet layer program selects an outgoing port and passes a newly consti-
tuted IP packet down to the data link layer on that outgoing port.
- ▶ The data link layer program creates a new data link layer frame.
- ▶ The data link layer program passes the data link layer frame to the physical
layer process (usually hardware) on the outgoing port.
- ▶ The physical layer process delivers the data link layer frame to the next device—either the next router or, eventually, the ultimate destination host.

At the Destination Host

At some point, if everything goes well, a data link layer PDU reaches the destination
host, as shown in Figure 2.5.

- ▶ The data link layer program on the destination host inspects the header of the
incoming data link layer frame. If everything goes correctly, the data link layer
program removes the IP packet from the data link layer frame and passes this
IP packet to the internet layer program on the destination host.
- ▶ The internet layer program on the destination host inspects the header of the incoming IP packet. If everything goes correctly, the internet layer program removes the TCP-PDU from the IP packet and passes the TCP-PDU to the transport layer program on the destination host.
- ▶ The transport program on the destination host inspects the header of the incoming TCP-PDU. If everything goes correctly, the transport layer program
removes the HTTP-Request-PDU from the TCP-PDU and passes the HTTP-
Request-PDU to the application layer program on the destination host.
- ▶ The application layer program—the webserver application program—examines
the HTTP-Request-Header. If everything goes correctly, it acts upon the contents of the HTTP-Request-PDU's data field by retrieving the desired file.

FIGURE 2.5

**Nested PDUs on
the Destination
Host**

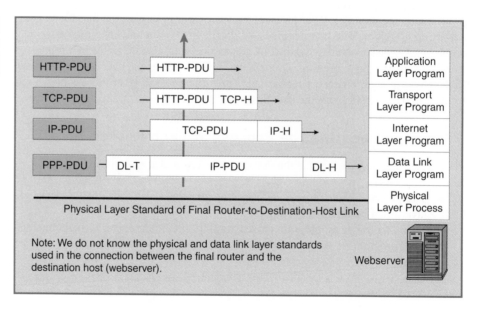

▶ The webserver application program then creates an HTTP-Response-PDU containing the requested file. This generates a new cycle of nested communication, mirroring the cycle that began with the HTTP-Request-PDU.

When Other Layer Processes Initiate Communication

In the example we have been following in detail, the browser application program on your client PC initiated the communication. This is a common occurrence, as is the initiation of the response communication by the application layer program on the webserver.

However, it is not always the application layer program that initiates a communication sequence. In fact, *every layer process on every router and host may initiate a communication sequence*. (Of course, at the physical layer, this is limited to two adjacent physical layer processes and does not involve PDUs.) We will look briefly at one example to see how this works.

ERROR CORRECTION AT THE DATA LINK LAYER

In our preceding discussion, we frequently said, "if everything goes correctly." Sometimes it does not. For instance, a receiving process may detect an error during transmission. Figure 2.6 shows what happens if the data link layer program on the first router finds a transmission error in the frame that your client PC's data link layer program has transmitted across the physical link connecting your client PC and the first router.

Note that we did not say "PPP frame." PPP uses a more complex error correction process that tends to obscure underlying principles. So we assume a simpler data link layer process. It does data correction by sending **negative acknowledgments (NAKs)** when there are errors. If it does not detect an error, it simply passes the IP packet up to the next-higher layer.

In this case, there is an error in transmission. So the data link layer program on the first router cannot continue to send your data toward the destination host. There is no

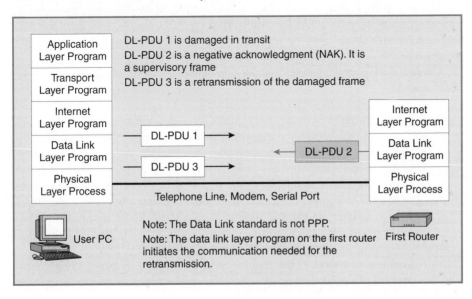

FIGURE 2.6
Error Correction at the Data Link Layer

point sending on bad data. So it discards your damaged frame instead of continuing to process it.

However, the data link layer protocol in this case is a **reliable** protocol, which means that it does error correction. It creates a new frame to be sent back to the data link layer program on your user PC. This new frame has a header field that asks for the retransmission of the damaged frame. This frame is the negative acknowledgment.

The router's data link layer program on the original receiving port sends this new NAK frame back to your user PC over the physical link that connects them.

The data link layer program on your user PC then retrieves the original (undamaged) frame from memory and retransmits the lost or damaged frame to the data link layer program on the router, via the physical layer connection.

LESSONS: THE DATA FIELD OF A PDU

There are several lessons in this example. One is to reinforce the fact that *any layer process* may initiate communication sequences. In this case, the data link layer program on the first router initiated the communication. However, internet layer programs on routers also can initiate communication, as can the application, transport, internet, and data link programs on each of the hosts.

Another lesson is what is in the data field of the NAK frame that the router's data link layer program sends back to your client PC. Many students assume that the first router's data link layer program will send back the damaged frame that it received. Yet why should it do that? Your user PC's data link layer program has no use for a damaged frame!

Figure 2.2 shows there are two possibilities for the content of the data field in a **supervisory PDU**; that is, in any PDU that contains a supervisory message instead of data. The NAK frame is a supervisory PDU.

Some protocols place the retransmission request information in some field in the header. In this case, there is *nothing* in the data field. The data link layer process initiated the communication process, and the internet layer had nothing to do with it. So there cannot be an internet layer PDU.

Figure 2.2 shows that in other cases, a header field merely indicates that supervisory information is contained in the data field of the PDU. In this case, then, the data field is not empty. It contains the supervisory information addressed to the receiving process.

Overall, then, Figure 2.2 notes that the data field of a PDU normally has three possible contents.

> ▶ First, when a layer process is *not initiating* a communication, its data field usually contains the *PDU of the next-higher-layer process*. Only when there is need for supervisory communication does this change.
> ▶ However, when a layer process *initiates* a communication, its data field either is *empty* or contains *supervisory information*. It does not put the PDU of the next-higher-layer process in the data field because the next-higher-layer process is not involved in the communication at all. There simply is no PDU from the next-higher-layer process.

The one exception, of course, is the application layer. When it initiates a communication, the data field of the application PDU contains application data.

AT THE APPLICATION LAYER (HTTP)

Hypertext

Nearly everyone is familiar with the World Wide Web. The Web is based on the concept of **hypertext,** in which documents may contain associative links to other documents. Although hypertext has been around for many years, the real breakthrough came when Tim Berners-Lee created hypertext standards for the Internet. The Internet already offered standards at the transport layer and at lower layers. So Berners-Lee only had to create application layer standards.

HTTP

In fact, he had to create *two* standards, as shown in Figure 2.7. First, he had to create a standard that would allow the client host to send a request to the webserver application program and for the webserver application program to send back a response. In Chapter 1, we saw that this was the **HyperText Transfer Protocol (HTTP).** To keep things simple, Berners-Lee based HTTP on the simple Internet standard for exchanging messages between e-mail systems. By adapting an existing simple standard, Berners-Lee made transfers easy to implement.

HTML

Second, Berners-Lee had to create a standard to represent the structure of webpages themselves. As an editorial note, at the application layer, it usually is necessary to create two standards—one for application exchanges and another for document structure. Figure 2.7 shows that the document structure standard that Berners-Lee created was the **HyperText Markup Language (HTML).** Most students are familiar with HTML documents, which consist of text and also of tags to indicate formatting, the need to

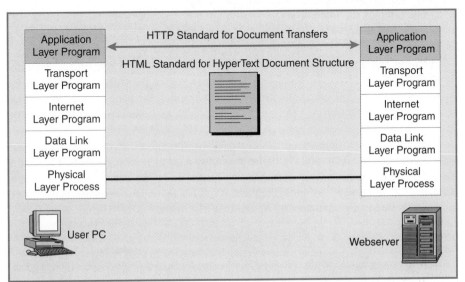

FIGURE 2.7

World Wide Web Standards

HTTP PDU	PHASE STARTING	BROWSER → ← WEBSERVER	MEANING
1	Initial Request	HTTP Request →	Browser asks server for the main (HTML) document
2		← HTTP Response	Webserver application program finds the HTML document file and sends it to the browser
3	Request for Image File	HTTP Request →	Browser reads the HTML file. Sees reference to an image file, Big.jpg. Sends request for the image file
4		← HTTP Response	Webserver sends the Big.jpg file
5	Request for Java File	HTTP Request →	Browser reads the HTML file. Sees reference to a Java applet (small program). Sends request for Java applet
6		← HTTP Response	Webserver sends the Java applet

FIGURE **2.8**

HTTP Request-Response Cycle: Downloading a Webpage with an Image and Java Applet

insert an image file in a certain place, links to other documents, and other explanatory information.

Multiple HTTP Request-Response Cycles

When we download an HTML document, we tend to assume that there is a single HTTP-Request-PDU from the browser to the webserver application program and a single HTTP-Response-PDU in the opposite direction.

In fact, things are more complex, as shown in Figure 2.8. Here, we are downloading a very simple webpage with one image and one Java applet. A Java applet is a small program that makes some aspect of the webpage active.

Figure 2.8 shows that the initial **HTTP request-response cycle** downloads only the HTML page, which consists of only text characters for information and tags. After downloading the HTML page, the browser looks through the page for tags that represent image files, sound files, video files, Java applets, and other nontext objects to be added to the page.

The browser then initiates an HTTP request-response cycle for each of the additional objects. In our example, it initiates two more request-response cycles. The first is for the image file containing the image to be displayed on the page. This image file is Big.jpg. Note in Figure 2.8 that this requires a full HTTP request-response cycle. Next, the browser needs the Java applet. Again, this requires a full HTTP request-response cycle.[2]

---

[2] Actually, a Java applet may consist of multiple files. So downloading a Java applet typically requires multiple HTTP request-response cycles.

So downloading even this simple webpage with only one image and one Java applet requires *three request-response cycles*. Complex webpages with many elements need a dozen or more HTTP request-response cycles.

This process of multiple cycles is why webpages appear the way they do on your screen. First, text appears. Then, individual images and other elements appear, one at a time.

The HTTP-Request-PDU

Most protocol data units are complex. The **HTTP-Request-PDU,** however, is extremely simple. It consists of a single line of text:

GET voyager.cba.hawaii.edu/panko/home.htm HTTP/1.0

This command asks the webserver application program to retrieve the *home.htm* file and send it to the browser.

SYNTAX

The syntax of the HTTP-Request-PDU has only three elements: a keyword, a URL, and the version of HTTP being used. The "GET" keyword tells the webserver application program that the browser wishes to retrieve the specific webpage designated in the URL.

In essence, this is a header with three fields (keyword, URL, and version). It has no data field because it is not delivering data.

DOWNLOADING NONTEXT FILES

When we download image files or other files, the syntax is exactly the same. The only difference is that the extension of the file is not *htm* or *html*. For example, the HTTP-Request-PDU to download Big.jpg would have the following form:

*GET voyager.cba.hawaii.edu/panko/**Big.jpg** HTTP/1.0*

Note that the file named in the URL is Big.jpg, our image file. URLs are not limited to HTML files.

The HTTP-Response-PDU

The header of the **HTTP-Response-PDU** also consists of simple text. However, it typically consists of many lines of text. The first is a response status line, telling the browser what follows. Next come additional header lines resembling the header fields of an electronic mail message. (As noted earlier, HTTP was modeled after e-mail standards.) Then there is a blank line, followed by the file being retrieved.

HTTP/1.0 200 OK
Date: Tuesday, 20-JAN-1999 18:32:15 GMT
Server: *name of server software*
MIME-version: 1.0
Content-type: text/plain

HTML document

Everything before the HTML document constitutes the HTTP-Response-PDU header. The data field consists of the HTML document.

Note that the HTTP-Response-PDU tells the browser several things.

▶ First, it notes that the target file was found. The "200" is the code for a successful retrieval. If there had been a problem, a different code would have been used, such as the famous "404" code when the webserver program cannot locate the requested file.
▶ Next, it tells the date and time of the retrieval.
▶ Next, it names the webserver application software that the webserver is using. This allows the browser to adjust to the characteristics of that particular webserver program.
▶ Next, recall that the file to be retrieved does not have to be an HTML file. If you download a webpage with an image and a Java applet, you will need three downloads, and two of these will not be HTML files. The MIME (Multipurpose Internet Mail Extensions) standard, developed for e-mail but borrowed by HTTP, allows the webserver application program to tell the browser the specific format of the file being downloaded. In this case, the content type is plain text. This is appropriate because an HTML document is indeed plain text.

AT THE TRANSPORT LAYER (TCP)

Recall from Chapter 1 that the transport layer allows two machines to communicate even if they are of different platforms. The most widely used protocol at the transport layer is **TCP**, the **Transmission Control Protocol**. In fact, HTTP mandates the use of TCP at the transport layer.

THE TCP-PDU

Figure 2.9 shows the TCP protocol data unit. Note that the header consists of several different parts called **fields**. The header, like the data field, is merely a long string of ones and zeros. However, the TCP standard allows us to make sense of this bit string by dividing it into fields based on the position of the bits in the string. Figure 2.9, for instance, shows that the first 16 bits (0 through 15) constitute the source port number field. The next 16 bits (16 through 31) form the destination port number field.

BITS, BEGINNING WITH ZERO

For convenience, 32 bits are shown on each line. Note that the first bit in the TCP-PDU is designated as "0" rather than "1." This is the normal way to count in binary. It will seem strange at first, but you have to get used to it because it is almost universal.

OCTETS

Most fields are multiples of eight bits. In computing, a string of eight bits is a *byte*. In data communications, it is called an **octet**. So *byte* and *octet* mean the same thing. We will use the term *octet* in most cases, to help you get used to this common piece of network terminology.

Transmission Control Protocol (TCP) PDU

source port number (16 bits)	destination port number (16 bits)
sequence number (32 bits)	
acknowledgment number (32 bits)	

header length (4 bits)	reserved (6 bits)	flag fields (6 bits)	windows size (16 bits)

TCP checksum (16 bits)	urgent pointer (16 bits)

options (if any)
data field

Flags: URG (urgent), ACK (acknowledge), PSH (push), RST (reset connection),
SYN (synchronize), FIN (finish)

Downloading a Single File

At the application layer, the browser and webserver application program communicate through simple HTTP request-response cycles. Although downloading multiple files complicates the picture, each request-response cycle generates only two HTTP-PDUs. The first is the request, and the second the response.

At the transport layer, things are much more complex when the TCP protocol is used. We will see that each HTTP request-response cycle at the application layer generates a flurry of TCP-PDU exchanges at the transport layer. It is critical for you to distinguish between what happens at the application layer and what happens at the transport layer. We have finished the application layer and are now at the transport layer.

APPLICATION AND TRANSPORT LAYERS

In Figure 2.8, we see the application layer program (the browser) sending its first HTTP-Request-PDU. This PDU asks for the basic HTML document file.

When the browser has created the HTTP-Request-PDU, it does not deliver it directly to the webserver application program. Rather, as we saw earlier in the chapter, in Figure 2.3, it passes this application layer PDU down to the transport layer program. The figure shows the transport layer program placing the application PDU into the data field of a transport layer PDU and passing the resultant TCP-PDU down to the internet layer. We will now show that the situation actually is really more complicated.

Time	TCP (Connection-Oriented)	HTTP (Connectionless)	IP (Connectionless)
1	Open the connection (requires several TCP-PDUs)	Send an HTTP-Request-PDU. No need to wait for a connection	Send a data IP-PDU (IP packet). No need to wait for a connection
2	Send data TCP-PDU #1. Contains a sequence number		
3			Send a data IP-PDU (IP packet). No relationship to the previous IP-PDU
4	Send data TCP-PDU #2. Contains a sequence number		
5		Send an HTTP-Request-PDU. No relationship to the previous HTTP-Request-PDU	Send a data IP-PDU (IP packet). No relationship to the previous IP-PDU
6	Send data TCP-PDU #3. Contains a sequence number		
7	Close the connection (requires several TCP-PDUs)	No need to close a connection because no connection exists	No need to close a connection because no connection exists

FIGURE **2.10**

Connection-Oriented TCP Service versus Connectionless HTTP and IP Service

CONNECTIONLESS AND CONNECTION-ORIENTED SERVICE

In a sense, HTTP at the application layer is rude. The browser does not even say hello to the webserver application program before sending its demand for a file. Nor does the webserver say hello when it returns the requested file. At the end, neither says "good-bye." No enduring relationship exists between the browser and webserver.

We say that HTTP is **connectionless** (see Figure 2.10). Each HTTP request and response is a separate interaction. Although Figure 2.8 showed multiple request-response cycles, different cycles were not related in any way through the HTTP protocol.[3]

In contrast, at the transport layer, TCP is a **connection-oriented** protocol. Figure 2.11 shows that TCP first opens a connection between the transport layer program on your PC and the transport layer program on the webserver. Then, the transport layer programs implement the file transfer. Finally, the two transport layer programs close

---

[3] This actually causes problems in electronic commerce, where single transactions may require several HTTP request-response cycles. To create an enduring relationship across multiple HTTP request-response cycles, the webserver may place a text file called a cookie on your PC. This text file contains information about previous exchanges.

TCP PDU	PHASE STARTING	PC →	← SERVER	MEANING
1	Open Connection	SYN →		PC transport program asks server transport program to open a connection
2			← ACK SYN; SYN	Server acknowledges PC request, sends own open request
3		ACK SYN →		PC acknowledges
4	Send HTTP-Request-PDU	HTTP-Request-PDU →		PC sends TCP-PDU containing HTTP-Request-PDU.
5			← ACK	Server acknowledges
6	Send HTTP-Response-PDU		← HTTP-Response-PDU	Server sends HTTP-Response-PDU
7		ACK →		PC acknowledges
8	Close Connection		← FIN	Server sends notice that it is closing its side of the connection
9		ACK →		PC acknowledges
10		FIN →		PC sends notice that it is closing its side of the connection
11			← ACK	Server acknowledges

FIGURE **2.11**

TCP Interactions to Implement One HTTP Request-Response Cycle: The Simplest Case

the connection. Although this seems like a great deal of unnecessary work, we will see later why connection-oriented service is good for error detection and fragmentation. For now, we will focus on the basic process.

OPENING A CONNECTION

When you call someone on the telephone, the person first answers, "Hello," and you reply.[4] Figure 2.11 shows that the two transport layer programs do something similar.

1. The PC's transport layer program sends an "Open" request to the webserver's transport layer program (TCP-PDU (1)). This is called a **SYN** message because the SYN flag in the header is set to one.

---

[4] The ritual varies by country, but in general, both sides speak to indicate to the other that they are ready to talk.

2. The webserver transport program sends back a TCP-PDU (2) that serves two purposes. First, it sends the PC transport layer program the webserver's own open (SYN) request. Second, it acknowledges the PC's original open request.

3. The PC transport layer program sends back a TCP-PDU (3) acknowledging the webserver transport layer program's SYN request.

TRANSFERRING THE HTTP-PDUs

To put things in perspective, we have already exchanged three TCP-PDUs, and we have not yet begun to pass the HTTP-Request-PDU to the webserver. Now that we have opened a connection, however, we are ready for the HTTP-PDU transmissions.

4. The PC's transport layer program finally does what was shown in Figure 2.3. While opening the connection, it held the HTTP-Request-PDU temporarily. It now takes the HTTP-Request-PDU and places it in the data field of a TCP-PDU (4). It adds the required header and passes the TCP-PDU containing the HTTP-Request-PDU to the PC's internet layer program.

5. The webserver's transport layer program creates a TCP-PDU (5) acknowledging receipt of the TCP-PDU containing the HTTP-Request-PDU.

6. On the webserver, the transport layer program delivers the PC's HTTP-Request-PDU to the webserver application layer program, as shown in Figure 2.5. The webserver application program retrieves the requested file and passes it down to the webserver transport layer program as the HTTP-Response-PDU. The webserver transport layer program places the HTTP-Response-PDU in the data field of a TCP-PDU (6) and sends this TCP-PDU to the PC transport layer program.

7. The PC transport layer program sends back a TCP-PDU (7) acknowledging the TCP-PDU containing the HTTP-Response-PDU.

CLOSING THE CONNECTION

In a telephone conversation, you do not just hang up on the other party. Both sides indicate that they are finished speaking. Connection-oriented services must do the same thing, as Figure 2.11 indicates.

8. When the webserver transport layer program receives its acknowledgment of the TCP-PDU containing the HTTP-Response-PDU, it knows that its job is finished. So it sends a **FIN** (finish) TCP-PDU (8) to the PC's transport layer program. This TCP-PDU has a one in its FIN field, to indicate that it wishes to close the connection.

9. The PC's transport layer program acknowledges the close request (TCP-PDU (9)).

10. The PC transport layer program then sends its own FIN TCP-PDU (10), indicating that it will no longer send messages either.

11. Finally, the webserver's transport layer program acknowledges the close TCP-PDU from the PC's transport layer program (TCP-PDU (11)).

In a human telephone call, one party can initiate the call, but both parties agree to terminate it. It is the same with TCP connections. This is why it takes only three TCP-PDUs to open a connection, whereas it takes four to close it. Both sides must initiate close messages.

In this example, the PC and webserver transport programs produced 11 TCP-PDUs.

Note that this was for *a single HTTP request-response cycle.* We saw in Figure 2.8 that downloading a single webpage usually requires several HTTP request-response cycles (three, in that simple example).

Let's put these two examples together. There were 3 HTTP request-response cycles. Each would generate 11 TCP-PDUs. So it would take 33 TCP-PDUs to download this simple webpage! TCP is a "chatty" protocol.

Reliable versus Unreliable Service

Although TCP's chattiness gobbles up transmission capacity, its connection-oriented operation is necessary for several features that we need in transport connections.

The first of these features is reliability. TCP is a **reliable protocol,** *meaning that it does error detection and correction.* Figure 2.12 illustrates how TCP implements error correction. The portion of the TCP connection that illustrates error correction is shaded.

In TCP-PDU 4, the PC's transport layer program transmits the HTTP-Request-PDU from the application layer. The webserver sends back an acknowledgment in TCP-PDU 5. This tells the PC transport layer protocol that TCP-PDU 4 has been received correctly.

In TCP-PDU 6, the webserver's transport layer program transmits the HTTP-Response-PDU to the PC transport layer program. It expects to receive an acknowledgment from the PC's transport layer program.

However, the acknowledgment for TCP-PDU 6 never comes from the PC transport process. Somehow, TCP-PDU 6 was damaged or lost in transit.

After a while, the webserver's transport layer program automatically retransmits the HTTP-Response-PDU as TCP-PDU 7. This time, the PC transport layer program acknowledges receipt of the TCP-PDU in TCP-PDU 8. The webserver transport layer program then knows that TCP-PDU 7 has arrived safely.

How does a transport layer protocol know which of its TCP-PDUs have arrived safely? As shown in Figure 2.9, the TCP header has a *sequence number* field. Each outgoing TCP-PDU has a different value in the sequence number field. In acknowledgment TCP-PDUs, the *acknowledgment number* field specifies the TCP-PDU being acknowledged.

Every TCP-PDU is acknowledged if it is received correctly, so if a transport layer program does not receive an acknowledgment, it knows that it must resend the TCP-PDU.

Sequence numbers require connection-oriented service. In connectionless service, a PDU has no memory of prior messages. There would be no way to tell which PDU needed to be retransmitted.

ACK AND NAK

In this chapter, we have seen that there are two general ways to do error correction. TCP uses *positive acknowledgment*, sending an ACK message for each TCP-PDU it receives correctly. If there is no acknowledgment, then the sending process knows that the TCP-PDU was either lost or damaged during transmission.

TCP PDU	PHASE STARTING	PC → ← SERVER		MEANING
1	Open Connection	SYN →		PC transport layer program asks server transport layer program to open a connection
2			← ACK SYN; SYN	Server acknowledges PC request, sends own open request
3		ACK SYN →		PC acknowledges
4	Send HTTP-Request-PDU	HTTP-Request-PDU →		PC sends TCP-PDU containing HTTP-Request-PDU
5			← ACK	Server acknowledges
6	Send HTTP-Response-PDU		← HTTP-Response-PDU	Server sends HTTP-Response-PDU
				Error in transmission. PC does not send ACK
7	Resend HTTP-Response-PDU		← HTTP-Response-PDU	Server resends unacknowledged TCP-PDU containing the HTTP-Response-PDU
8		ACK →		TCP-PDU containing the HTTP-Response-PDU arrives correctly. PC acknowledges
9	Close Connection		← FIN	Server sends notice that it is closing its side of the connection
10		ACK →		PC acknowledges
11		FIN →		PC sends notice that it is closing its side of the connection
12			← ACK	Server acknowledges

Note: the blue shaded area illustrates an error correction episode.

FIGURE **2.12**

TCP Interactions to Implement One HTTP Request-Response Cycle: Error Correction

We saw a *negative acknowledgment* protocol earlier, in the case of the hypothetical data link layer protocol. That protocol sent only NAK messages, indicating that a PDU was damaged or, in the case of connection-oriented service with sequence numbers, lost. Negative acknowledgment is less chatty than positive acknowledgment because only errors generate error messages. However, there is a danger that the NAK

TCP PDU	PHASE STARTING	PC → ← SERVER	MEANING
1	Open Connection	SYN →	PC transport layer program asks server transport layer program to open a connection
2		← ACK SYN; SYN	Server acknowledges PC request, sends own open request
3		ACK SYN →	PC acknowledges
4	Send HTTP-Request-PDU	HTTP-Request-PDU →	PC sends TCP-PDU containing HTTP-Request-PDU
5		← ACK	Server acknowledges
6	Send HTTP-Response-PDU in 2 Fragments	← HTTP-Response-PDU, Part 1	Server sends first part of HTTP-Response-PDU. (The HTTP-Response-PDU is too large to fit into one TCP-PDU.)
7		ACK →	PC acknowledges
8		← HTTP-Response-PDU, Part 2	Server sends second part of HTTP-Response-PDU
9		ACK →	PC acknowledges
10	Close Connection	← FIN	Server sends notice that it is closing its side of the connection
11		ACK →	PC acknowledges
12		FIN →	PC sends notice that it is closing its side of the connection
13		← ACK	Server acknowledges

Note: Blue shaded area describes fragmentation with two fragments.

FIGURE **2.13**

TCP Interactions to Implement One HTTP Request-Response Cycle: Fragmentation

message will be lost. With positive acknowledgment, if the ACK message is lost, the sending process may retransmit the frame, but it is fairly trivial for a receiving process to deal with duplicate frames.

Flow Control

Sequence numbers also allow **flow control**—the ability to ask the other side to pause or slow down.

The TCP-PDU header has a **window size** field. This field tells the other transport layer program how many bytes may transmit *beyond the last message acknowledged.* If the window size is 100 for instance, the transport layer program may send only 100 more bytes beyond the last TCP-PDU acknowledged.

The nice thing about this approach to flow control is that it is automatic. If a receiving transport layer program is being overloaded, it will not be able to send acknowledgments. After a few more transmissions, the other transport layer program has to stop transmitting. This gives the receiving transport layer program time to handle unprocessed PDUs.

The end of flow control is also automatic. When the overloaded transport layer program is no longer overloaded, it automatically begins to send new acknowledgments.

Fragmentation

There is a maximum size for TCP-PDUs. By default, the TCP-PDU data field is set to a maximum of 536 bytes. Using an optional field in the TCP header, the two transport layer programs can negotiate a higher maximum size for the data field (called a **maximum segment size, MSS**).

Suppose that the default of 536 bytes is in effect. Suppose also that the HTTP-Response-PDU is 750 bytes long. Obviously, the entire HTTP-Response-PDU will not fit in a single TCP-PDU.

As Figure 2.13 shows, the answer to this problem is *fragmentation*. The HTTP-Response-PDU is fragmented into two pieces, and the pieces are sent in successive TCP-PDUs. TCP-PDUs 6 through 9 (shaded) illustrate this process.

Perspective

We noted that TCP is a chatty protocol. Even in the simplest case, there are 11 transport layer TCP-PDUs for each application layer HTTP request-response cycle. If there is extensive fragmentation, or if there are several errors, the number of TCP-PDUs will rise far above this number.

We also noted, in the title of each figure on TCP exchanges, that what we are showing is a time diagram for a *single HTTP request-response cycle*. In many webpages, there are one dozen to three dozen files to be downloaded. So to download a single page may require hundreds of TCP-PDUs.[5]

---

[5] Given this heavy load, it is often desirable to fine-tune connections. At the transport layer, the window size and maximum segment size parameters for TCP must be set astutely. Making them either too large or too small can harm performance.

In addition, PCs sometimes open multiple transport layer connections with the webserver. They may use different transport connections to download different files. This can increase throughput because sometimes there is delay on the webserver while downloading the file in one connection. (For instance, there may be a wait for information to be brought into RAM from the disk drive.) If this happens, the download in another connection might be able to proceed instead of nothing happening.

Future versions of HTTP may open a connection at the beginning of all file downloads and may close it only after the completion of all file downloads. Recall that our base example with 3 HTTP cycles and 11 TCP-PDUs per HTTP cycle required 33 TCP-PDUs. If the connection could be left open, this would decrease to 19.

AT THE INTERNET LAYER (IP)

Just as the application layer uses the transport layer to deliver application PDUs, the transport layer uses the internet layer to deliver transport layer PDUs.

In many ways, the internet layer is the heart and soul of the TCP/IP architecture. The **Internet Protocol (IP)** allows two hosts to exchange messages across complex internets consisting of multiple networks linked by routers from many different vendors.

The Internet Protocol (IP) Header

Figure 2.14 shows the IP-PDU. The typical IP header is 20 octets long. Options can extend this, but IP options are not commonly used.

VERSION FIELD

The first four bits of the IP header constitute the **version field.** Once the receiving internet program reads the version number, it knows what fields will follow according to that version standard. The current version of the Internet Protocol is Version 4.[6] A new version of the IP protocol, Version 6,[7] promises to offer new delivery capabilities.

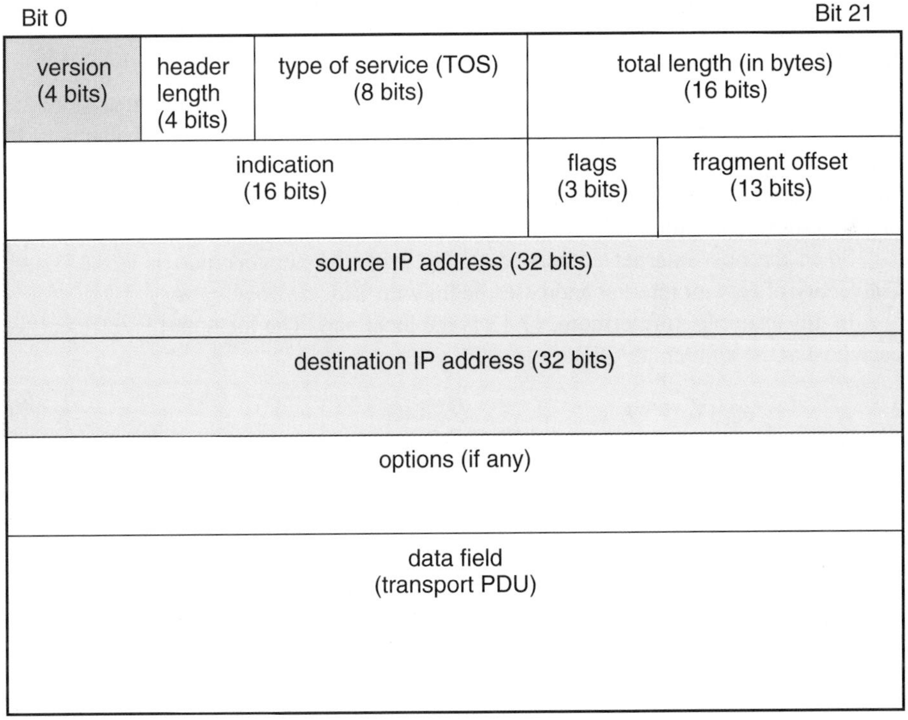

Bit 0   Bit 21

version (4 bits)	header length (4 bits)	type of service (TOS) (8 bits)	total length (in bytes) (16 bits)	
indication (16 bits)			flags (3 bits)	fragment offset (13 bits)
source IP address (32 bits)				
destination IP address (32 bits)				
options (if any)				
data field (transport PDU)				

FIGURE 2.14

The Internet Protocol (IP) PDU

---

[6] There were no Versions 1 through 3.

[7] There was a Version 5, but it was not implemented.

HEADER CHECKSUM FIELD

For error checking, there is a 16-bit **checksum field.** This allows the receiving internet program to check the header for transmission errors. Note that the IP checksum field *is not for the entire IP packet.* It is only for errors in the IP header. A bad header can cause problems such as sending the packet to the wrong destination host. So IP packets with bad headers must be detected and discarded. As discussed earlier, the Internet Protocol is not reliable. It does not ask for the retransmission of damaged IP packets. It merely discards IP packets with bad headers. Because the IP header usually contains only 20 octets, and because costly retransmission processes are not implemented, header error checking in IP does not place a significant load on routers.

SOURCE AND DESTINATION INTERNET ADDRESSES

Both the **source** and **destination addresses** are 32-bit fields. This is why internet addresses are always 32-bit numbers. Nothing else will fit into the source or destination field.

Two-Part Internet Addresses

DOTTED DECIMAL NOTATION

We saw in Chapter 1 that internet addresses normally consist of four segments that contain decimal numbers between 0 and 255 and that are separated by dots. So a typical internet address would be 128.171.17.13 in **dotted decimal notation.**

NETWORK AND LOCAL PARTS

Actually, as Figure 2.15 shows, the IP standard specifies that 32-bit internet addresses have two parts, a **network part** and a **local part.** For instance, at the University of Hawaii, the 32 bits are divided into a 16-bit network part that is unique to the University of Hawaii and a 16-bit local part that the UH can assign to individual hosts.[8] Figure 2.15 shows this situation.

So in the host internet address 128.171.17.13, the network part is 128.171. All University of Hawaii internet addresses begin with 128.171.

In this example, furthermore, 17.13 is the local part. The local part is different for each host at the University of Hawaii.

FIGURE 2.15

Hierarchical Internet Address Organization

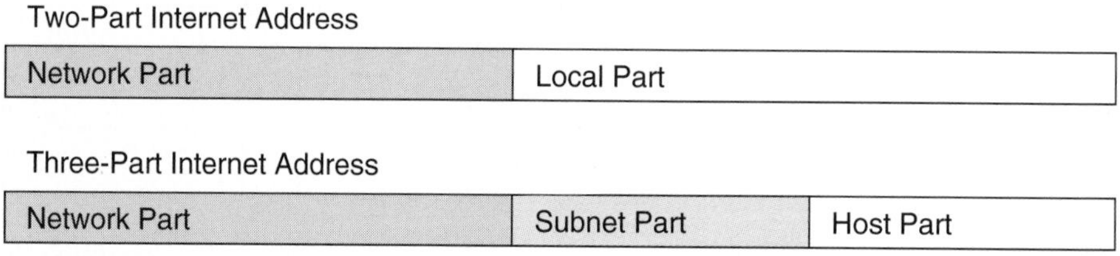

Two-Part Internet Address

Network Part	Local Part

Three-Part Internet Address

Network Part	Subnet Part	Host Part

Note: Shaded part is used by a router to determine if the router can deliver an IP packet directly to the destination host computer. See Figure 2.16 to see how this is done in two-part addresses.

---

[8] There are three basic classes of networks. Class A networks have 8-bit network parts and so have 24-bit local parts. Class B networks, like the one at the University of Hawaii, have 16-bit network and local parts. Class C networks have 24-bit network parts and only 8-bit local parts.

Looked at another way, the address 128.171.17.13 tells a router, "This host is on network 128.171, and it is host 17.13 on that network." We will see later how this is useful information in routing.

ASSIGNING THE NETWORK PART

This two-part internet address has two advantages. The first advantage is that it simplifies the assignment of internet addresses.

Suppose you wish your organization to be a network on the Internet. You contact an *internet address registrar* and ask for a network part. The registrar will then assign you a unique network part, such as 128.171 for the University of Hawaii.

In essence, the internet address registrar has assigned you a block of addresses. If your local part is 16 bits, as it is in this example, you can have 2^{16} hosts on your network—65,536. This is good for universities and other large organizations.

ROUTER OPERATION IN NETWORKS WITH TWO-PART INTERNET ADDRESSES

We have said that two-part network addressing has two advantages. We have just seen that one of them is the assignment of blocks of internet addresses to organizations for internal assignment to individual hosts.

The other is router operation. Figure 2.16 shows that a router is always attached to two or more networks. In this figure, Router A is attached to two networks, whose network parts are 128.171 and 133.287. (Of course, segments cannot be greater than 255. So the latter network part is fictitious. Fictitious network parts were selected for this example to avoid legal problems.)

Direct Delivery to the Destination Host Suppose, as shown in Figure 2.16, that Host 1 is located on the network with the network part 128.171. This host (128.171.15.12) sends Router A an IP packet addressed to host 133.287.180.6.

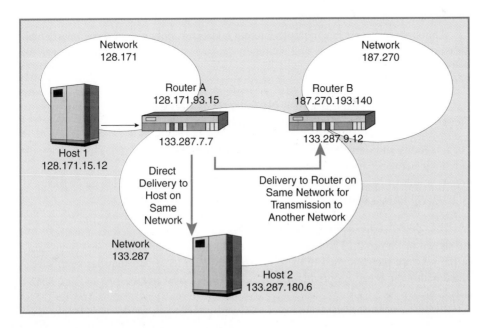

FIGURE **2.16**

Internet Addresses and Router Operation

To determine what to do with the IP packet, *the router first looks at only the network part of the destination internet address*. In this case, the network part of the destination host is 133.287. This is on one of Router A's attached networks. So the router can deliver the IP packet to the destination host directly.

To deliver the IP packet, the router places the IP packet in a frame addressed to Host 2's data link layer address.[9] It sends this frame out the port connected to network 133.287.

Passing a Packet on to Another Router Suppose, instead, that the destination host's internet address is 144.260.27.201. As shown in Figure 2.16, Router A again *first looks at only the network part of the internet address*, in this case 144.260. (This is another fictitious network part.) Router A notes that neither of its two attached networks (128.171 and 133.287) has this network part. So the router cannot deliver the IP packet directly to a host.

Instead, the router would pass the IP packet to a router on one of its two attached networks, for further routing. In this case, it sends it to Router B (133.287.9.12) on network 133.287.

ROUTERS AND INTERNET ADDRESSES

A router must be able to receive IP packets from hosts and from other routers. For this to be possible, the router must have an internet address just like a host computer.

In fact, a router must have *multiple* internet addresses—one for every network to which it is attached. For example, Router A has two networks, so it has two internet addresses. These are 128.171.93.15 and 133.287.7.7.

Why must a router have a separate internet address for each network? Recall that internet addresses always begin with a network part that is unique to that network.

For Host 1 (128.171.15.12) on network 128.171 to be able to recognize Router A as being on the host's own network, the router must have the same network part in its internet address, 128.171. So on network 128.171, Router A is 128.171.93.15.

For the same reason, hosts on network 133.287 need to be able to address Router A with an internet address beginning with 133.287. So on this network, Router A is 133.287.7.7.

Although the router has multiple internet addresses, only one of these internet addresses is visible to the hosts and routers on each network—the one appropriate for that network.

Three-Part Network Addresses through Subnetting

Organizations with large networks often create a second level of delegation. They divide their networks into a number of *subnets* controlled by suborganizations. For example, at the University of Hawaii, the local area network in the College of Business Administration is a subnet.

THREE-PART INTERNET ADDRESSES

As shown in Figure 2.15, subnetting requires three-part internet addresses, consisting of the network part assigned to the organization and a local part that has been subdivided within the organization into a **subnet part** and a **host part.**

---

[9] Transmission within a subnet is done at layer 2, so the layer 2 address is used to deliver the frame.

Most commonly, a 16-bit local part is subdivided into an 8-bit subnet part and an 8-bit host part. This creates 256 (2^8) subnets, each with 256[10] possible host computers.

Other combinations are possible. For instance, if you have a 16-bit local part, you might assign only 4 bits for the subnet part, leaving you with 12-bit host parts. This would give you 16 (2^4) large subnets with 4,096 (2^{12}) hosts apiece. Or, by having more than 8 subnet bits, you can have more than 256 subnets, each with fewer than 256 hosts.

ROUTERS AND SUBNETS

We saw in Figure 2.16 that when two-part addressing is used, a router *has to look first at only the network part* of an internet address. This is enough information for the router to decide whether it can deliver the IP packet to a host on one of the router's attached networks or must pass the packet onto another router.

When subnetting is used, in turn, routers connect subnets instead of networks. By extension, then, *a router now has to look first at only the combined network part and the subnet part of the internet address*. These bits will tell the router whether it can deliver the IP packet directly to a host on one of its attached subnets or just pass it to another router for delivery on another subnet.

TWO OTHER COMMON PROTOCOLS

We have focused on the protocols involved in HTTP request and response messages. However, there are two other common protocols that you use most times you type a URL or connect to the Internet.

The Domain Name System (DNS)

Suppose that you give your browser a URL containing the host name of a webserver. This host name is not enough for delivery. As we have just seen, the browser needs to know the *internet address* of the destination host because only a 32-bit internet address can be placed in the destination address field of an IP packet.

DNS HOST LOOKUPS

Figure 2.17 shows that your browser must contact a **domain name system (DNS)** host. This DNS host contains a table listing host names and the internet address associated with each host name. It is like a telephone book that contains human names (similar to host names) and telephone numbers (similar to internet addresses).

The internet layer on the user PC, without the user's knowledge, sends a DNS-Request-PDU to the DNS host. This PDU contains the host name you typed in the URL. In this case, it is voyager.cba.hawaii.edu.

The DNS host looks up the host name in its file. It notes the internet address associated with that host name. In this case, the internet address is 128.171.17.13.

The DNS host then sends the internet address of the webserver back to your internet layer process, through a DNS-Response-PDU.

---

[10] Well, almost 256. Some addresses are reserved. For hosts, a host part of all ones is a broadcast address. IP packets sent to this address should be read by all hosts on the subnet. The host address with all zeros, in turn, means "this computer." It is used when a host sends an IP packet to itself during "loop-back" testing.

FIGURE **2.17**

Domain Name System (DNS)

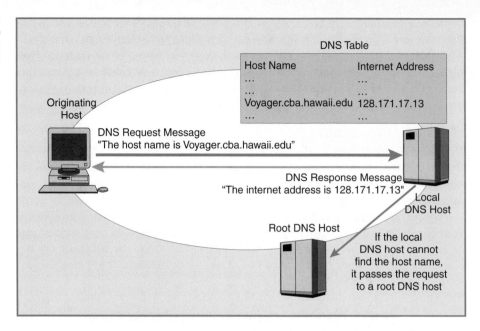

DISTRIBUTED OPERATION

The figure also shows that the domain name system is distributed. Your organization's DNS host normally knows only the host names and internet addresses of hosts on your network. If you wish to know the internet address of a webserver on a different network, your local DNS host will pass your request on to another DNS host.

AUTOMATIC OPERATION

Normally, all of this takes place without the knowledge of the person typing the URL. However, if you mistype a host name, or if the DNS hosts that your PC contacts do not recognize the host name, you will get an error message telling you that there was a "DNS error." In addition, if your local DNS host goes down, your PC will tell you that a certain host name does not exist, even if you reached it successfully a few minutes earlier. This can be very confusing to users.

DOMAINS

We have said that the domain name system looks up information on host names. Actually, its role is broader. *A host name really is a special case of a broader concept called a domain name*. Broadly speaking, a **domain** is a set of resources under the control of an organization. A host name is the lowest level of domain.

Domain names are hierarchical. At the very top is the root, which contains all domains. Beneath the root are top-level domains. There are **generic top-level domains**, such as *com* and *edu*, which tell the type of organization owning the domain name, and there are **national top-level domains**, such as *UK* and *AU*, which tell the country in which the host resides. Traditionally, generic top-level domains have been used within the United States and national top-level domains have been used in other countries. However, nothing in domain naming requires this.

Beneath the top-level domains are **second-level domains**, such as *hawaii.edu* and *microsoft.com*. Second-level domains define individual organizations. **Domain name registrars** assign second-level domain names to individual organizations. These are not necessarily the same as the internet address registrars we saw earlier.

Organizations can create subdomains internally. For instance, the University of Hawaii, hawaii.edu, created cba.hawaii.edu for the College of Business Administration subdomain.

Finally, domain names can be assigned to individual host computers and routers. For instance, one webserver in the College of Business Administration is voyager.cba.hawaii.edu. Another is www.cba.hawaii.edu. A mail host in the college is busadm.cba.hawaii.edu. We call domain names applied to individual host computers "host names."

Although domain names are important in helping people remember host names, they are not essential. Only internet addresses are official addresses on the Internet. Although every host must have an internet address, it does not have to have a host name.

ROOT HOSTS

In Figure 2.17, we saw that if a local DNS host cannot recognize a host name, it passes the request to another DNS host. Now that we have learned about domain names, we can be more specific. The DNS host for your organization, such as the University of Hawaii, must know the full domain names of all of its own host computers (and routers). It should be able to give you the internet address of all local hosts. There are also a small number of **root hosts** (currently 13) that have comprehensive knowledge of the Internet. At a minimum, they must be able to recognize second-level domain names and pass your request on to the local DNS host for that second-level domain name.

Autoconfiguration

Every host on the Internet needs a 32-bit internet address. This includes every user PC in homes, on organizational desktops, and in school computer labs.

One way to ensure that every PC has an internet address is to assign it a *permanent* internet address. However, few organizations and Internet service providers have enough internet addresses to assign permanently to all of the individual computers they serve. In most organizations today, permanent internet addresses are assigned only to servers and routers.

For client PCs, organizations normally use **autoconfiguration hosts** to assign *temporary* internet addresses to user PCs on an as-needed basis. As Figure 2.18 shows, when a user PC wishes to connect to the Internet, its internet layer sends an Autoconfiguration-Request-PDU to the autoconfiguration host.

The autoconfiguration host has a pool of internet addresses to assign. It selects an unused internet address from the pool and sends this internet address back to the user PC in an Autoconfiguration-Response-PDU. The user PC uses this temporary internet address during its session on the Internet. When the user PC stops using the Internet, the autoconfiguration host puts the internet address back into its pool of available addresses.

There are several **autoconfiguration protocols.** The most common today is *DHCP*, the Dynamic Host Configuration Protocol. Its popularity is due in part to the fact that Windows 95 made DHCP its standard autoconfiguration protocol. Other popular autoconfiguration protocols are *bootp* and *RARP*.

FIGURE **2.18**

**Autoconfiguration
Host**

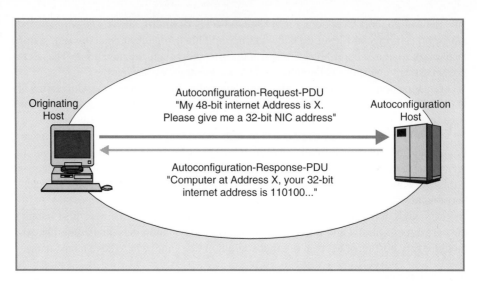

Originating
Host

Autoconfiguration-Request-PDU
"My 48-bit internet Address is X.
Please give me a 32-bit NIC address"

Autoconfiguration
Host

Autoconfiguration-Response-PDU
"Computer at Address X, your 32-bit
internet address is 110100..."

SUMMARY

This chapter begins our discussion of Internet technology. It focuses on the application, transport, internet, and data link layers of the hybrid TCP/IP–OSI framework. Specifically, it focuses on the way these layers communicate through nested protocol data units (PDUs). This chapter is perhaps the most difficult material in this textbook. You will have to go through it several times, each time gaining more insight on the broad rhythms and specifics of nested PDU transmission.

PROTOCOL DATA UNITS (PDUs)

A PDU consists of a header, a data field, and sometimes a trailer field. The header and trailer field tell the receiving program what to do with the PDU. The data field normally is the PDU of the next-higher-layer process. However, this is not true for layers that initiate a communication. If a layer initiates a communication, there is no next-higher layer. Then, the data field either is nonexistent or contains supervisory information. The exception is the application layer, which contains data for the application program.

NESTED PDUs

Except at the physical layer, two hosts cannot communicate with each other directly. When other layer processes, such as the browser at the application layer, send messages to their peers on the other host, they must pass their PDU down to the next-lower-layer process. That layer embeds the PDU into the data field of its own PDU. This process continues until the data link layer process, which passes its PDU to the physical layer process for direct delivery.

When the receiving host (or router) receives a data link layer PDU from its physical layer process, it removes the IP packet from the data link layer PDU's data field and passes it to the internet layer. This process continues until the final layer process is reached.

PROCESSES AT THE APPLICATION, TRANSPORT, AND INTERNET LAYERS

We next looked in more detail at what happens at the application, transport, and internet layers. We saw that downloading a webpage typically requires multiple HTTP request-response cycles, one for the text-only HTML webpage and one for every image or other element to be portrayed on the browser's screen.

Furthermore, every HTTP request-response cycle generates a stream of TCP-PDUs. For each HTTP request-response cycle, the transport layer processes on the two machines open a connection, transfer HTTP request and response PDUs, manage problems during the exchanges, and finally close the connection. If there are 10 HTTP request-response cycles, and if each HTTP cycle generates 20 TCP-PDUs on average, then it will take 200 TCP-PDUs to complete the exchange.

At the internet layer, we focused on internet addresses. We saw that a basic internet address has two parts—a network part shared by every host and router on the network and a local part under the organization's control. With subnetting, there are three parts to the address: a network part, a subnet part, and a host part.

We saw that, in two-part addressing, routers use the network part to decide whether they can deliver an IP packet directly to the destination host or must pass it on to another router on another network. In three-part addressing, routers use both the network and subnet parts to decide whether they can deliver an IP packet directly to the destination host or must pass it on to another router on a different subnet.

DNS AND AUTOCONFIGURATION

We finished the chapter with two supervisory protocols that you probably use every time you connect to the Internet and surf the World Wide Web. A DNS host translates between the unofficial host name you have for a webserver in the URL and its official internet address, which must be used in all IP packets sent to the webserver. An autoconfiguration host, in turn, gives you a temporary internet address to use when you first connect to the Internet.

GENERAL THEMES

The chapter also presented a number of general concepts that we will see throughout this book. One key theme was *reliability*. Not all layers are reliable, because checking for errors at all layers is not necessary and would add too much to costs.

Another theme was *connection-oriented service*. Establishing a connection, maintaining it, and breaking it down afterward add overhead, slowing transmission. However, connection-oriented service makes many things possible, including error correction and flow control.

In *flow control*, if one side is transmitting too much information too quickly, the receiver must be able to tell the sender to slow down or pause.

Fragmentation divides information to be sent into several PDUs. At the receiving end, the information from several PDUs must be defragmented before being passed to the next-higher-layer process.

CORE REVIEW QUESTIONS

1. Define *protocol*. Define *protocol data unit (PDU)*. Which layers have PDUs? Which layers have end-to-end communication?
2. Why do we need nested PDU transmission (why can't the two application layer programs merely exchange PDUs without nesting)?
3. In nested PDU transmission, what three things normally can be in a PDU's data field? What is the exception to this rule?
4. Why are there multiple HTTP request-response cycles to download a single webpage?
5. What is an octet?
6. What is reliability? Why is it good? Why is it not used at all layers?
7. What is connection-oriented service? Explain the benefits of sequence numbers.
8. What is flow control?
9. What is fragmentation? Why is it necessary? What program does reassembly?
10. What are the two parts in two-part internet addresses? What are the three parts in three-part internet addresses?
11. With two-part internet addressing, a router connects two or more networks. To what do routers connect in three-part network addressing?
12. What does a router look at in two-part addressing to decide whether it can deliver the IP packet to its destination host or must pass it on to another router? What does a router look at in three-part addresses?
13. Why do we need the Domain Name System (DNS)? What information does the client PC send in a DNS-Request-PDU? What new information does the DNS host send back in its DNS-Response-PDU?
14. Distinguish between top-level domains, second-level domains, and host names.
15. You wish to get internet addresses and host names for the computers in your firm. Describe what you would do to accomplish this.
16. Why do we use autoconfiguration instead of assigning permanent internet addresses to each client PC? What new information is returned in an Autoconfiguration-Response-PDU?

DETAILED REVIEW QUESTIONS

1. Trace the steps that begin when your webserver issues an HTTP-Response-PDU and end when the browser receives the requested file.
2. Why are there usually two standards at the application layer?
3. Create the HTTP-Request-PDU for the following URL:
   http://voyager.cba.hawaii.edu/panko/home.htm
4. Does the transport layer program on the destination host ask for the retransmission of a specific PDU? If not, what transport layer program decides which TCP-PDUs to retransmit, and how does it know which ones to retransmit?
5. Compare ACK and NAK error correction.
6. How does TCP implement flow control?

7. How do reliable and unreliable layers work together to ensure unreliability? Is there any error checking in IP? What does the internet layer program do if it finds an error?

8. You are downloading a webpage with four images. How many HTTP-PDUs will be generated? How many TCP-PDUs will be generated if there are no errors and no fragmentation? Show your calculations. How many TCP-PDUs will be generated if the maximum segment size if 536 bytes, if the webpage is 1,000 bytes in size, and if each image is 20,000 bytes in size? Show your calculations.

9. Express the following 32-bit internet address in dotted decimal notation. Show your work. (Hint: You can use Excel's Dec2Bin function for each octet, or you can use the Windows Calculator accessory set to scientific mode.)

10000000101010111000100011010000

10. Why does a router need multiple internet addresses?
11. What are root hosts? How do they work with your local DNS host?
12. What is the most common autoconfiguration protocol for users of Windows 95?

THOUGHT QUESTIONS

1. Why do we not use connection-oriented service at each layer?
2. Why does a single TCP-PDU often both send new information and acknowledge correctly received PDUs? (Hint: The correct answer is not "to confuse students.")
3. A router has internet addresses 128.171.17.13, 128.171.15.4, and 128.171.9.34. The network part is 16 bits, and the host part is 8 bits. There is a host, 128.171.9.7. It wishes to send an IP packet to 128.171.9.88. What will happen? There is a host, 128.171.9.7. It wishes to send an IP packet to 128.171.15.12. What will happen? There is a host, 128.171.9.7. It wishes to send an IP packet to 128.171.6.88. What will happen? (Hint: Draw a picture of the subnets and hosts involved.)
4. If you type a URL and your browser tells you that the host could not be found, what might have happened? (Hint: There are several possibilities.)

PROJECTS

1. At the book's website, http://www.prenhall.com/panko, read the Updates Page for new information since the book went to press.
2. At the book's website, http://www.prenhall.com/panko, do the Internet Exercises for this chapter.

CHAPTER 3

Using the Internet from Home: The Physical Layer

INTRODUCTION

Chapter 1 introduced the Internet and TCP/IP. Chapter 2 looked at Internet standards above the physical layer. This chapter completes the basic picture by looking at the physical layer.

The telephone line to your home is called "the final mile." This is because it is roughly a mile between the last switching office of a carrier and the subscriber's household or business. This terminology is a little loose, because the distance sometimes is two or even three miles, but the imagery is roughly accurate.

TRANSMISSION THEORY

There are several technologies for the physical layer connection used in the final mile. The simplest, of course, is the ordinary telephone line that reaches your home. However, we will soon see faster access available through wires, optical fiber, and radio propagation. In this section, we will look at the theories that underlie propagation in general.

Transmission Speeds

The first question that people ask about their home connection is how fast it will run.

BITS PER SECOND

A bit is either a one or a zero. So we can measure transmission speed as the *bit rate*, in terms of *bits per second*. Note that transmission speed does not measure how fast bits travel in kilometers per second or some other measure of speed. Rather, it determines the *duration* of each bit. If I transmit at 10 bits per second, then each bit period will be one tenth of a second. If I transmit at a million bits per second, then each bit period will be only one millionth of a second long. As speed constantly increases, receiving equipment must become ever more sensitive to high-speed signal changes.

Of course, if we transmitted at only a few bits per second, it would take forever to download even simple files. So in increasing factors of 1,000, we measure speed in *kilobits per second (kbps), megabits per second (Mbps), gigabits per second (Gbps),* and *terabits per second (Tbps)*. Data communications professionals write kilobits per second with a small *k* (kbps), as dictated by the metric system.

If you are familiar with computer memory measurement, you will have to alter a few expectations. First, transmission speeds are measured in factors of 1,000, not in factors of 1,024, as in computer memory. Also, transmission speeds are almost always given in bits per second, rather than bytes per second. Finally, computer people sometimes write kilobits per second as Kbps.

BAUD RATE

Bit rate measures the rate at which we send actual information, which usually is encoded as ones and zeros. In contrast, the **baud rate** is the number of times per second the **state** (typically, the voltage level) of the transmission line changes.

Figure 3.1 shows a situation in which a line has only two states for each bit period, either a high voltage or a low voltage. A high voltage represents a one, while a low voltage represents a zero. In this case, each line change sends a single bit of content. The bit rate is equal to the baud rate.

In contrast, Figure 3.1 also shows a situation in which each line change can put the line in any of four states—high, medium high, medium low, and low. We can associate two bits with each state. For instance, high can be 11, medium high can be 10, medium low can be 01, and low can be 00. In this example, each line change transmits two bits. So if the baud rate is 1,000 baud—in other words, if the line state changes 1,000 times per second—then the bit rate will be 2,000 bps. So in this example the bit rate will be twice the baud rate. Although the bit rate is faster than the baud rate in this case, it is slower under certain conditions (see Chapter 4).

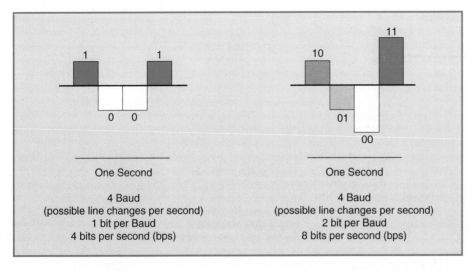

FIGURE 3.1

Bits per Second (bps) and Baud Rate

Unfortunately, salespeople often find it easier to say that a device such as a modem can transmit at 33.6 kilobaud. However, such modems really transmit at 33.6 kbps, and their baud rates are far lower. This drives some networking teachers crazy, and they insist on accuracy in the use of the term *baud rate*. Others accept the degradation of the term *baud* with resignation.

Digital and Analog Transmission

DIGITAL TRANSMISSION

The type of transmission shown in Figure 3.1 is called digital transmission. In **digital transmission,** *time is divided into periods of fixed length; the line is kept in one of only a few possible states (conditions) during each time period; at the end of each time period, it may change abruptly to another of these states.* The duration of each time period determines the baud rate. In the figure, there are two and four states (voltage levels). Note that states do not change within each time period. They may then change abruptly, to another of these two or four states.

To give another example, you may have a digital wristwatch. A digital watch shows individual numbers, not a hand that moves smoothly around the dial. At each second or hundredth of a second, depending on the watch, the individual digits (0 to 9) may change abruptly. In fact, having 10 states from 0 through 9 was the original meaning of the term *digital*, because our 10 fingers are called our *digits*. Today, however, any time we have abrupt changes among 2, 4, 10, or any other limited number of states, this is digital transmission.

BINARY TRANSMISSION

There is a special case of digital transmission in which there are only two states. We call this **binary transmission.** Each bit period can be only a zero or a one, as shown in Figure 3.2. Note that binary transmission is a special case of digital transmission. *Binary transmission is always digital, but not all digital transmission is binary.*

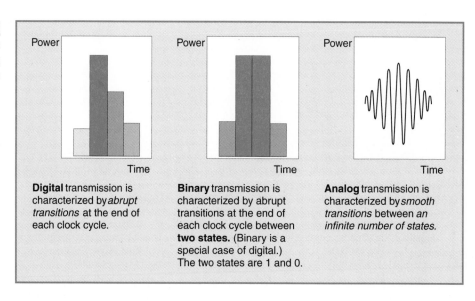

FIGURE 3.2

Digital versus Analog Transmission

Digital transmission is characterized by *abrupt transitions* at the end of each clock cycle.

Binary transmission is characterized by abrupt transitions at the end of each clock cycle between **two states.** (Binary is a special case of digital.) The two states are 1 and 0.

Analog transmission is characterized by *smooth transitions* between *an infinite number of states.*

ANALOG TRANSMISSION

Figure 3.2 also compares digital and analog transmission. We have seen that digital transmission uses abrupt transitions between a limited number of states. In contrast, as the figure illustrates, in **analog transmission,** *the state of line can vary continuously and smoothly among an infinite number of states.*

The human voice, for instance, does not move abruptly between a few sound levels. Rather, our loudness increases and decreases smoothly. Even when we give a sudden shout, the rise and fall in our sound volume are relatively slow compared to the detection speeds of transmission equipment. The human voice, unlike computer signals, is inherently analog. Analog clocks, in turn, have hands that move smoothly around the clock face, instead of jumping from one tick to another.

THE BENEFITS OF DIGITAL TRANSMISSION

All early transmission systems such as the telephone system, were analog. Analog systems were easy to build with nineteenth-century technology. In contrast, digital transmission requires complex integrated circuits to recognize the state of the line at any moment. Even more sophisticated circuitry is needed for the kinds of complex digital signal processing we will see next.

As a result, even first-generation cellular telephony, which was created in the 1980s, was analog. However, new types of cellular telephony are digital. In fact, almost all new transmission systems are digital because falling chip prices have made digital transmission not only better but cheaper as well.

DIGITAL SIGNAL PROCESSING

Reliability One advantage of digital transmission is reliability. We will see in the next section that when we transmit signals down a wire, they tend to be changed slightly by propagation effects. With digital signal processing, however, the receiving station can analyze the changed signal and, in most cases, recognize the voltage changes that correspond to ones and zeros or to the multiple states of the transmission (see Figure 3.3). This is called **regeneration.** It dramatically lowers signaling errors, which is one reason why digital sound and video usually sound and look much better than traditional radio and television signals, which are analog.

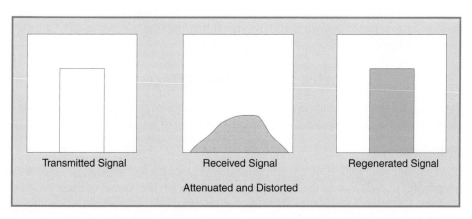

Transmitted Signal   Received Signal   Regenerated Signal

Attenuated and Distorted

FIGURE 3.3

Regeneration in Digital Signal Processing to Remove Propagation Effects

FIGURE 3.4

Multiplexing

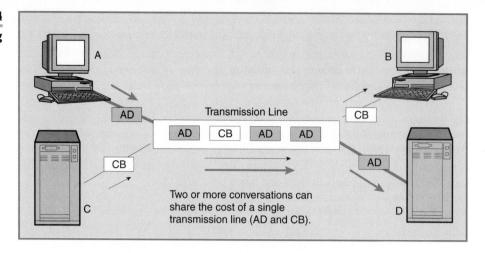

Transmission Line

AD | CB | AD | AD

Two or more conversations can
share the cost of a single
transmission line (AD and CB).

Error Detection and Correction In addition, because digital signals essentially represent streams of ones and zeros, digital signals can be treated as binary numbers, and digital signal processing chips can perform computations on these numbers. For instance, we saw in Chapter 2 that error detection and correction are used in data transmission to give even cleaner transmission than regeneration can provide. This is possible because of computations performed on the PDUs as if they were large binary numbers.

Compression In addition, it is often possible to use digital signal processing to *compress* a bit stream before transmission. For instance, a facsimile machine can transmit a page in less than a minute, thanks to compression. Without compression, most pages would take six minutes to transmit or even longer. Compression removes redundancy in data. In facsimile, for instance, there may be a whole line of white. So compression signals that "the next N dots are white."

Multiplexing Finally, as Figure 3.4 shows, we can *multiplex* (mix) digital signal transmissions from multiple conversations onto single transmission lines. With multiplexing, each conversation pays for only the fraction of transmission line capacity it actually uses. This can dramatically lower transmission costs.

In general, regeneration, error detection and correction, compression, multiplexing, and other digital signal processing benefits are very strong. Almost all data transmission today is digital, so we will show digital transmission systems in all of the discussions in this chapter.

Wire Propagation Effects

Typically, we send computer signals through a closed propagation media, such as telephone wires. Because this situation is so common, we will look at it first.

PROPAGATION

If we change the voltage of the medium, that disturbance in the voltage level will **propagate** (travel) down the transmission medium at the speed of light in that medium. The effect is similar to throwing a pebble in a quiet lake. Propagation allows a distant receiver to detect the disturbance and so hear your transmission.

Unfortunately, propagation is never perfect. There are always *propagation effects* that change the signal as it travels down the medium. Figure 3.3 shows such propagation effects. Propagation effects can make it difficult or impossible for the receiver to identify the line state represented by the disturbance. All propagation effects have the same impact. They make the received signal (disturbance) different from the transmitted signal.

ATTENUATION

The most obvious effect is **attenuation,** meaning that the signal gets weaker as it propagates. Figure 3.3 illustrates this effect. If the signal gets too weak, the receiver will not be able to detect it. For instance, in the EIA/TIA-232-F serial ports used in personal computers, a zero is 3 to 15 volts. If the signal begins at 12 volts and weakens to 2 volts, the receiving serial port will reject it as a zero. The farther a signal travels, the more it will attenuate.

DISTORTION

Figure 3.3 also illustrates another common propagation effect, **distortion.** As signals travel, they tend to spread out in time. So a nice sharp square wave will tend to become rounded. Worse yet, it will begin to overlap the signals before and after it, making them impossible to distinguish by the receiver as separate ones or zeros.

NOISE

A signal is electrical energy. However, unless the propagation medium is at absolute zero temperature, its electrons will move around, creating random energy called **noise.** As shown in Figure 3.5, the average noise intensity is called the noise floor. However, because noise is random, there can be momentary *noise spikes* that will make individual ones and zeros unreadable or that will flip ones to zeros and zeros to ones.

The ratio of signal power to noise power is called the **signal-to-noise ratio (SNR).** If the SNR is very high, then few noise spikes will cause propagation errors. However, if the SNR is low, then quite a few noise spikes will cause errors. (Try listening to a conversation in a noisy restaurant.)

Attenuation reduces the signal strength, thus reducing the signal-to-noise ratio. So noise errors increase as distance increases.

In addition, noise errors increase as transmission speed increases. If a bit period is very long, say a tenth of a second, then there will be few random noise spikes large

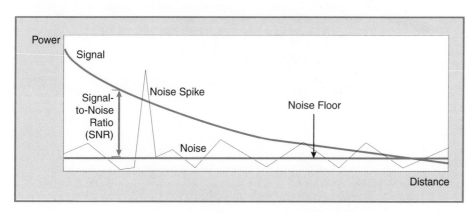

FIGURE 3.5

Noise and Attenuation

enough to cause errors. Most noise spikes will average their energies with normal noise levels during that long period. Noise spikes are very brief, and noise power over a comparatively long period of time will tend to be very close to its average level, the noise floor. However, as the duration of a bit decreases, there will be a greater probability of a damaging noise spike that has not averaged out.

INTERFERENCE

Noise is inherent in any transmission medium. In contrast, interference is an external signal. The transmission medium, acting like an antenna, will pick up the external signal and convert it into electrical energy, where it will have the same effect as noise. However, whereas noise is relatively constant, apart from brief noise spikes, interference comes and goes, making it difficult to diagnose.

Figure 3.6 shows that if two transmission wires are placed side by side, they will each radiate some of their signal, and the other wire will pick up leaked signal as interference. This is called **cross-talk.**

One way to reduce interference problems is to twist adjacent pairs of wires several times per foot or even several times per inch. (You need two wires for an electrical circuit, as in electrical wires and telephone wires.) Interference on adjacent halves of the twists will tend to be opposite in direction, adding to the signal in one half of the twist and subtracting from it during the second half of the twist. So interference tends to cancel out.

However, when the wire is terminated in a connector, each pair must be untwisted to allow the individual wires to be placed in the connector. This untwisting must be limited to about a half inch, or there will be *near end cross-talk* where the wires are untwisted. It is very difficult to do connections when you are allowed to untwist wires only a half inch. As a result, some installers "cheat" and untwist the wires a bit farther. This often creates unacceptable cross-talk.

TERMINATION PROBLEMS

The near end cross-talk problem raises an important point. Although propagation effects may cause problems as a signal travels down the line, errors often occur at the very beginning and the very end of propagation, where the medium is connected to a

FIGURE 3.6

Cross-Talk Interference: A Termination Problem

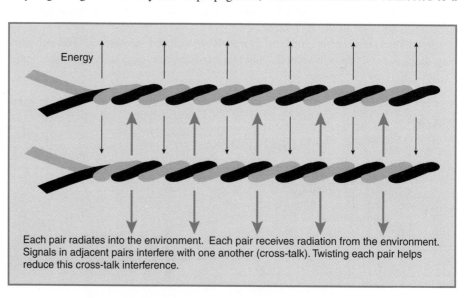

Each pair radiates into the environment. Each pair receives radiation from the environment. Signals in adjacent pairs interfere with one another (cross-talk). Twisting each pair helps reduce this cross-talk interference.

device. Such *termination problems*, in fact, may be far more common than propagation effects we have been discussing during the propagation between the termination points.

Wire Media

We have been speaking about wire media in the abstract. Now we will look at the three specific wire media in common use. The first two are widely used in new networks, but the third is seen almost exclusively in legacy networks.

UNSHIELDED TWISTED PAIR (UTP)

The cheapest transmission medium is copper wire, such as ordinary telephone wire. As noted above, you need a pair of wires for data transmission, and these are usually twisted around each other. Although twisting reduces interference problems, data transmission wiring usually does not have any other shielding against electrical interference. So it is called **unshielded twisted pair (UTP).**[1]

In home telephone wiring, you have only a single pair of wires. However, as Figure 3.7 illustrates, business telephone wiring usually comes in a multipair bundle. A common configuration is four pairs (eight wires). This requires a wider telephone jack, the RJ-45 jack, than the normal RJ-11 telephone jack used in the home.

What about the final mile in telephony? Telephone companies bring only a single twisted pair to each household. Nor do telephone companies use amplifiers along the way if the signal weakens. Because the distance from a residence to the switching office varies from a few meters to several kilometers, attenuation varies considerably from one residence to another.

OPTICAL FIBER

UTP wiring uses voltage levels to indicate ones and zeros. In contrast, *optical fiber* uses light. It turns light on or off in each bit period to signal a one or zero.

As Figure 3.8 illustrates, when light rays reach the outside of the central glass core, they hit a layer of glass cladding with a different index of refraction. The indices

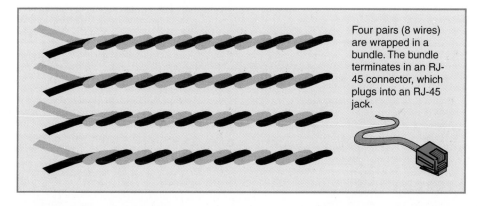

Four pairs (8 wires) are wrapped in a bundle. The bundle terminates in an RJ-45 connector, which plugs into an RJ-45 jack.

FIGURE 3.7

Unshielded Twisted Pair (UTP) Bundle

---

[1] Some local area networks use shielded twisted pair (STP) wiring, in which a metal mesh is wrapped around each twisted pair and another mesh is wrapped around a multipair bundle. This reduces interference but increases media cost and makes the wiring thick and difficult to lay.

FIGURE 3.8
Optical Fiber

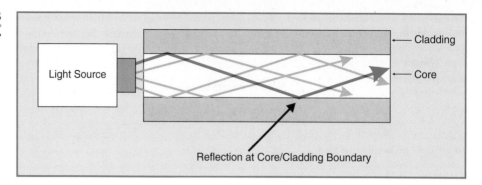

of refraction are set so that there is total internal reflection at the boundary—none of the light escapes. Because none of the light energy escapes, there is very little attenuation. Nor is there interference, because few interference sources operate at light frequencies, and the outer cladding is wrapped in a nontransparent covering.

A major propagation problem with optical fiber is distortion. Note, in Figure 3.8, that light rays enter the core at slightly different angles. Over a long enough distance, different rays will travel different distances because they will be internally reflected a different number of times. So adjacent ones and zeros will begin to overlap.

UTP AND OPTICAL FIBER

In corporations today, there is a strong division of labor between UTP and optical fiber. UTP is normally used for the final run to the desktop, as Figure 3.9 illustrates. UTP is less expensive than optical fiber and is easier to connect. Even more importantly, UTP is more durable. (Hey, optical fiber is glass!) Because desktop runs often have to lie on the floor, optical fiber links would break constantly.

The figure also shows that for other connections within a building or site, it is normal to use optical fiber. Optical fiber has the capacity needed to multiplex many desk-

FIGURE 3.9
UTP and
Optical Fiber

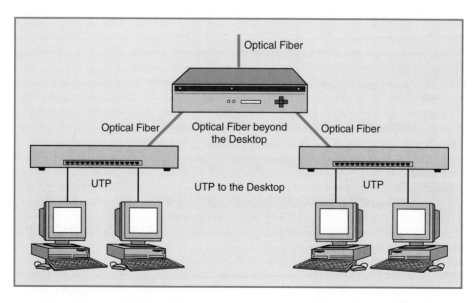

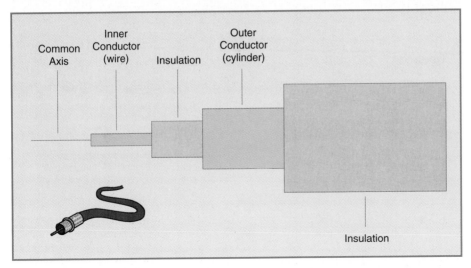

FIGURE **3.10**

Coaxial Cable

top connections and is much less expensive than a many-wire UTP bundle of comparable capacity. In addition, the optical fiber can be laid within false ceilings, conduits, and other places where it will be protected.

COAXIAL CABLE

Although UTP and optical fiber now dominate new network development at individual sites, many legacy local area networks still use an older technology, coaxial cable, as shown in Figure 3.10.

Electrical transmission requires two conductors. In coaxial cable, they are a wire and a cylinder on a common axis. The cylinder, which normally is wire mesh, both shields the cable from interference and traps the signal within the cylinder, preventing the energy loss that causes attenuation.

However, UTP is less expensive than coaxial cable and now offers comparable speeds or even higher speeds. For really high speeds, in turn, optical fiber offers far more throughput. There is no realm of speed in which coaxial cable is still a good choice today, although it continues to be rather common in business.

Radio Propagation

In the past, radio propagation was confined to the microwave towers and satellites of telephone networks. Now, however, some companies have their own satellite networks for data, and we are beginning to see radio local area networks, which allow you to roam with your computer within a building.

CHANNEL BANDWIDTH AND TRANSMISSION SPEED

Radio frequencies are measured in **Hertz**. One Hertz is one cycle per second. For higher frequencies, we have kilohertz (kHz), megahertz (MHz), gigahertz (GHz), and even terahertz (THz).

The range of frequencies from zero Hertz to infinity is called the **frequency spectrum.** In practice, the entire spectrum is divided into *service bands* for particular uses, such as the cellular telephony band. As Figure 3.11 shows, these service bands are sub-

FIGURE 3.11

Radio Frequency Bands and Channels

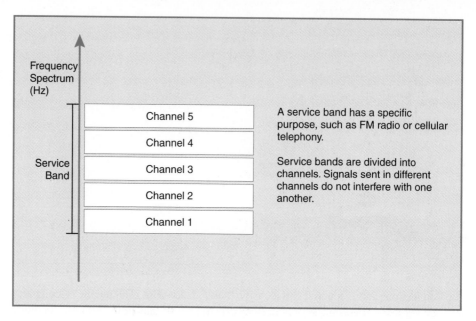

divided into *individual channels*. Individual transmissions are sent in channels. Signals in different channels generally do not interfere with one another.

Shannon[2] discovered that there is a relationship between channel bandwidth, noise, and the maximum possible transmission speed within a channel. Equation 3.1 shows this relationship.

$$W = B \, \text{Log}_2 \, (1 + S/N) \qquad \qquad \textbf{3.1}$$

Here, W is the maximum throughput in bits per second. B is the bandwidth in Hertz. S/N is the ratio of signal strength to noise energy strength.

Equation 3.1 shows that as the signal-to-noise ratio increases, the maximum possible speed, W, increases, because there will be fewer errors that require retransmission.

The second factor limiting the maximum transmission speed is the bandwidth, B. The more bandwidth the channel has, the faster you can send information. To use an imperfect analogy, a thick hose can carry more water than a thin hose.

In the telephone network, there is a filter where your signal reaches the first switching office, as Figure 3.12 illustrates. The human voice has a broad range of frequencies, and a young and healthy human ear can hear up to about 20 kHz.

Frequencies below about 300 Hz are filtered out, in order not to pick up the hum caused by 50 to 60 Hz electrical currents in the telephone network.

Frequencies above about 3,400 Hz are also filtered out. By reducing the telephone bandwidth, the telephone system can stack more telephone calls into adjacent channels when it uses radio transmission.

[2] C. Shannon, "A Mathematical Theory of Communication," *Bell System Technical Journal*, July 1948, pp. 379–423; October 1948, pp. 623–656.

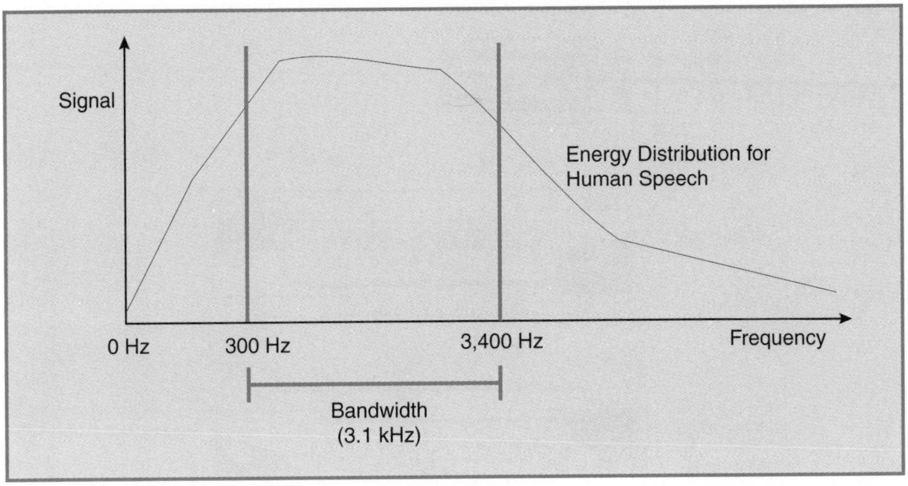

FIGURE **3.12**

**Telephone
Bandwidth**

The **bandwidth** is the difference between the maximum frequency and the minimum frequency of a channel. For the telephone network, the bandwidth is about 3.1 kHz, although this varies from location to location.

Given typical signal-to-noise ratios and a 3.1 kHz bandwidth, Equation 3.1 indicates that you can transmit at only about 35 kbps over the telephone network. Current modems can transmit at 33.6 kbps, very close to the ultimate limit of telephone networks. (We will see later how so-called 56 kbps modems seem to avoid this limit.)

In radio LANs, speeds of one to two Mbps are common. This is a good balance between speed in each channel and the number of channels. (If your channels are narrower, you can have more of them in a service band.)

BASEBAND AND BROADBAND TRANSMISSION

With UTP and optical fiber, we inject the signal directly into the medium. In effect, this means that we have a single channel. This situation is called **baseband transmission.** When channels are used, this is called **broadband transmission.**

As we have just seen, high bandwidth in a channel means high potential speed, so in radio, "broadband" is synonymous with high speeds. Although it is not correct technically, there is a growing tendency to refer to all high-speed systems as "broadband" signals, even when baseband transmission is being used.

PC Serial Ports

Physical layer standards also govern connector plugs and their operation. On a personal computer, a **port** is a physical connector plug, plus the electronic circuit needed to send and receive data using this plug. Most PCs come with at least one *serial port* and usually two. As Figure 3.13 shows, there are two possible plugs for serial ports: a 9-pin plug and a 25-pin plug. The types of modems commonly used can work with either because most modems use only 9 pins, and the 9-pin plug's pins match that subset of pins from the original 25-pin standard.

FIGURE **3.13**

PC Serial and Parallel Ports

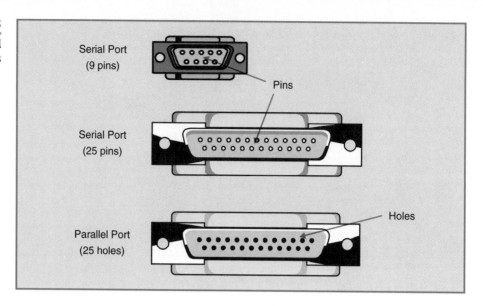

Serial Port
(9 pins)

Pins

Serial Port
(25 pins)

Holes

Parallel Port
(25 holes)

STANDARDS

The first PC serial ports followed the RS-232-C standard, which was later upgraded to EIA/TIA-232-F. However, serial ports today usually depart from the basic standard.

First, as just noted, many PC serial plugs have 9 pins, although the standard calls for 25 pins. This departure occurred when IBM began producing 9-pin serial plugs. Most other PC vendors soon followed suit.

Second, the standard specifies a maximum speed of 20 kbps. However, most new serial ports can operate at speeds up to 115.2 kbps. There were two reasons for adding speed. First, modems are now faster than 20 kbps. Most transmit at 28.8 kbps to 33.6 kbps.

Third, most modems can do *data compression*, so although they can send data out to the telephone system at only 33.6 kbps, they can accept a much faster incoming data stream from the serial port. For instance, with 4:1 compression, a modem can accept an incoming data stream at 115.2 kbps and send it out at 28.8 kbps.

The compression ratio of 4:1 is a maximum and is not frequently achieved. So if a modem is receiving data from the serial port at 115.2 kbps, it will often have to tell the serial port to pause. We will see below how it does this.

DATA TRANSMISSION

Figure 3.14 shows how the serial plug and the modem exchange data. Note that the serial plug is called **DTE (data terminal equipment)** whereas the modem is called **DCE (data circuit terminating equipment).** This is common terminology when a computer attaches to a device at the end of a data communications line.

To transmit data, you always need two pins to complete an electrical circuit. (This is why your home electrical and telephone lines have two wires.) When the serial port transmits to the modem with a 9-pin plug, it transmits on Pin 3. Pin 5 is an electrical ground, providing the second pin for DTE-to-DCE transmission.

Going in the other direction, the modem transmits on Pin 2. It also uses Pin 5 as an electrical ground. So serial plugs transmit on Pin 3 and receive on Pin 2.

FIGURE 3.14

Pin	Pin Name	Initiator	Use in Modem Communication
1	*Received line signal detector*	*DCE*	*Modem detects carrier of modem at other end of line*
2	*Received data*	*DCE*	*Modem sends data to PC*
3	Transmitted data	DTE	PC sends data to modem
4	DTE ready	DTE	PC indicates it is ready to receive
5	Signal common	Both	Common zero voltage for all other pins
6	*DCE ready*	*DCE*	*Modem indicates that it is ready to receive*
7	Request to send/ Ready for receiving	DTE	PC indicates that it wishes to send and is ready to receive
8	*Clear to send*	*DCE*	*Modem gives PC permission to transmit*
9	*Ring indicator*	*DCE*	*Modem detects ringing on the line*

FIGURE 3.14

Data Transmission between 9-Pin Serial Port and Modem

Notes:

DTE is the data terminal equipment (the PC's serial port)
DCE is the data circuit terminating equipment (the modem)
Information for pins for which the modem is the initiator is shown in italics

ELECTRICAL SIGNALS

When the serial port sends data on Pin 3, how does it represent a one or a zero? Figure 3.15 shows that the standard specifies a voltage of -3 volts to -15 volts for a one and $+3$ to $+15$ volts for a zero. The figure shows these voltages as -12 and $+12$ volts, which are typical of practice. It may seem odd that a one is the lower voltage and zero is the higher voltage, but the decisions of standards committees are often perplexing.

Figure 3.15 shows how signals are sent. Here, the serial port sends 1, 0, 1, 1. During the first bit's time period, the voltage is kept at -12 volts, signifying the first one. During the next time period, the signal switches to $+12$ volts, to signal a zero. During the third time period, the signal switches to -12 volts to represent another one. Then, during the final time period, the voltage stays at -12 volts to represent the final one.

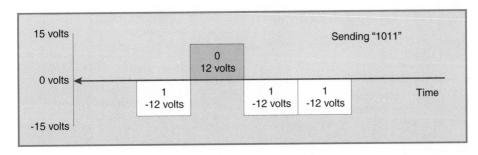

FIGURE 3.15

Electrical Signaling in Serial Ports

OTHER PINS

The other six pins facilitate the transmission of data on Pins 2, 3, and 5. On these supervisory pins, an "on" is indicated by +3 to +15 volts, and "off" is indicated by −3 to −15 volts. The committee chose this reversal of voltage meanings in order to confuse networking students.

What are the purposes of these other six pins? Two pins allow the modem to tell the PC about signals on the line. Pin 9 is the Ring Indicator pin. The modem turns this pin "on" when it detects ringing on the telephone line. Pin 1, in turn, is turned "on" when it detects a modem signal at the other end of the line.

The other four pins control when the DTE and DCE plugs may transmit. The PC turns "on" Pin 7 to request permission to send. The modem replies with a Clear to Send by turning "on" Pin 8. In addition, the DCE indicates in general that it is ready by turning "on" Pin 6. So the DTE plug does not send unless it has turned "on" Pin 7 and sees "on" signals on Pins 6 and 8.

The modem, in turn, does not send unless the DTE has turned On Pin 4 (DTE Ready) and has also turned "on" Pin 7 (Request to Send/Ready for Receiving).

FULL-DUPLEX AND HALF-DUPLEX TRANSMISSION

If you use a walkie-talkie, only one person can transmit at a time. The other person must wait until the first person has finished talking. Then, the other person can reply. This is called **half-duplex** transmission. As Figure 3.16 shows, in half-duplex transmission, both sides share a single channel. Only one side can transmit at a time.

In a telephone conversation, in contrast, both parties can talk at the same time. Although they do not both talk constantly, one side can interrupt the other to ask the other party to slow down, correct an error the other party has made, and so forth. This is **full-duplex** transmission. As Figure 3.16 shows, full-duplex transmission requires two channels, one in each direction.

Note that full-duplex transmission does not mean that both sides *always are* transmitting at the same time, only that they *can* transmit at the same time. In data commu-

FIGURE **3.16**

Full-Duplex and Half-Duplex Transmission

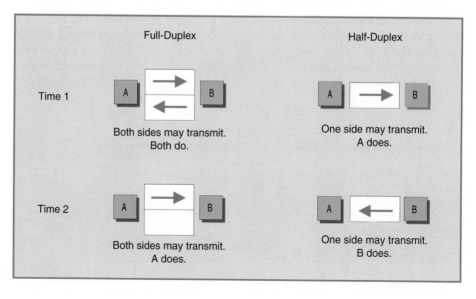

nications, full-duplex transmission allows one side to do most of the transmission, while the other side interrupts only as needed. This allows *flow control*; that is, asking the other side to slow down or pause because it is sending too quickly for the receiver to process the information. It also allows *error correction*, in which the receiver asks the sender to retransmit incorrect information.

When channel capacity is given in full-duplex transmission, it usually is given only for a single channel, even when two channels are used. For instance, we will see below that ISDN supports two 64 kbps *B channels*. These are full-duplex channels, so each B "channel" is really two 64 kbps channels, one in each direction. However, we still say that each B channel is 64 kbps.

SERIAL AND PARALLEL TRANSMISSION

The PC serial port is called a **serial** port because it sends information in each direction one bit at a time, along a single wire. The bits follow one another in series. In each clock cycle, one bit is sent along the wire in each direction.[3] Figure 3.17 illustrates this process.

In contrast, Figure 3.17 shows that parallel transmission uses *several* wires to send information in one direction. If there are eight wires, a parallel system can send eight bits per clock cycle. This obviously moves information faster than one bit per clock cycle—eight times faster. Parallel transmission is always faster than serial transmission, given comparable clock cycles.

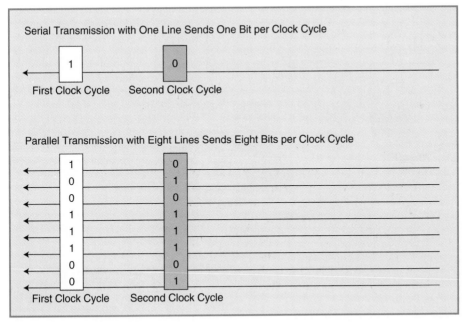

FIGURE 3.17

Serial and Parallel Transmission

---

[3] Of course, this is true only for binary transmission, in which there is one bit per baud (line change). More correctly, there is one baud per clock cycle in serial transmission and several baud per clock cycle in parallel transmission.

There is nothing magic about having eight wires. We selected eight wires for our example because PC parallel ports use eight wires. However, many parallel transmission systems use a different number of wires—from as few as two to over a hundred.[4]

MODEMS AND BEYOND

So far in this chapter, we have looked at transmission in terms of abstract principles. Now, we will look at how these principles apply to the transmission and reception of data from home, using a transmission line offered by a telephone company or data carrier. We will begin with modems and then move to faster alternatives to modem transmission.

Modems

Ordinary telephone lines are very useful for low-speed data transmission. Most homes already have a telephone line, so there is no incremental transmission cost in using this line to carry data.

Unfortunately, telephone transmission has a problem. Ordinary telephone technology, created long before digital transmission was economical, uses analog transmission line to and from the home. In contrast, computer signals are digital. So there must be a way to translate between them, so that digital signals will travel over analog telephone lines. As Figure 3.18 illustrates, a **modem**'s *job is to transform digital computer*

FIGURE 3.18

Modem

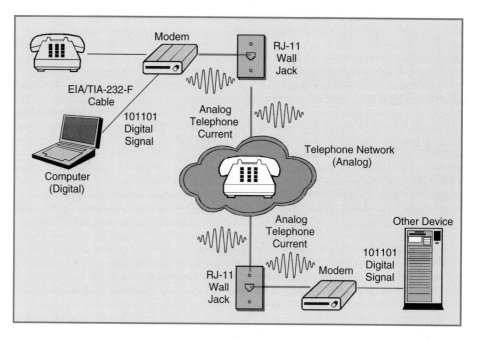

---

[4] Unfortunately, parallel transmission is good only for short distances. Think about a marching band with several rows of musicians. Now blindfold the band members, so that they cannot see one another. Unless the musicians in each row walk at exactly the same speed, a musician in the second row might end up in the third row or the first row after a short distance.

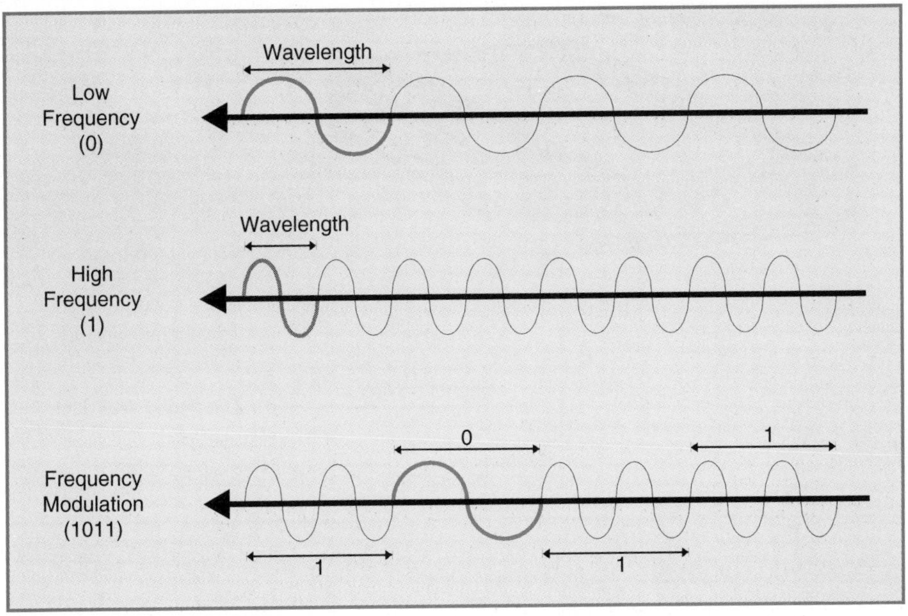

FIGURE **3.19**

**Frequency
Modulation**

FIGURE **3.19**

**Frequency
Modulation**

*signals into an analog form that will travel over an analog telephone line. At the other
end, the analog telephone signal is translated back into a digital computer signal.*

Modulation

If you try to transmit a digital signal over the telephone system, the digital signal will
be cut out at the first switching office. So to transmit digital computer data over a telephone line, you must convert it into electrical vibrations. For instance, Figure 3.19
shows frequency modulation, in which a 1 is represented by a high-frequency vibration
and a 0 is represented by a low-frequency vibration. The modem jumps between the
two frequencies to transmit 1s and 0s. To send 1011, you would send high-low-high-
high.

Converting a digital source signal into an analog transmitted signal is **modulation.** At the other end, the receiving modem *demodulates* the transmitted signal
back to a digital source signal. The term "modem," then, is a merciful contraction
for *modulator/demodulator.*

Modem Forms

Modems come in three basic forms: external modems, internal modems, and PC Card
modems.

EXTERNAL MODEMS

First, as shown in Figure 3.20, an *external modem* sits outside the system unit. You
connect it to the PC's serial port with a serial cable. External modems are easy to install because you do not have to open your PC to install it. You merely connect it to a
serial port.

FIGURE 3.20

External Modem

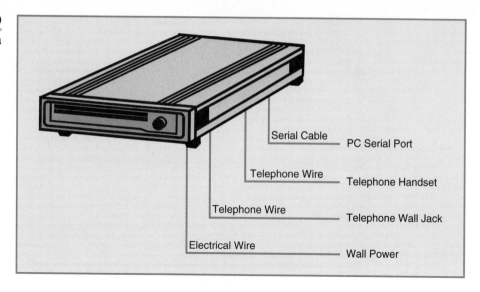

INTERNAL MODEMS

Second, there are **internal modems.** As shown in Figure 3.21, internal modems are printed circuit boards that sit inside the system unit. They do not need a serial port; they have one built in. Internal modems are attractive because they do not take up valuable desktop real estate.

PC CARD MODEMS

Figure 3.22 shows yet another type of modem. This is a *PC Card modem*. It is inserted into a PC card slot found in most notebook computers. Installation usually is easy, yet the modem does not sit outside the computer, adding to desktop clutter. Unfortunately,

FIGURE 3.21

Internal Modem

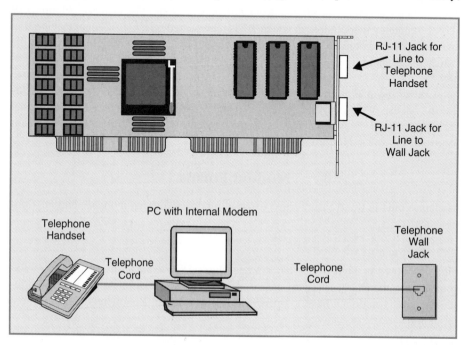

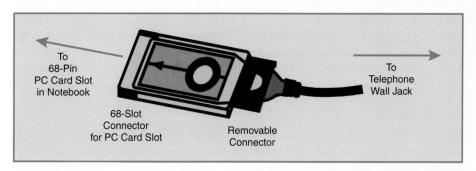

FIGURE **3.22**

PC Card Modem

few desktops have such slots. In addition, PC card modems are more expensive than internal or external modems.

Modem Standards

The International Telecommunications Union–Telecommunications Standards Sector (ITU-T), sets most new modem standards. This is the same standards organization that, along with ISO, manages OSI. As Table 3.1 illustrates, ITU-T has created a number of modem standards.

TABLE **3.1**

Modem Standards

SPEED STANDARDS

Name	Speed	Origin
V.90*	56 kbps receiving 33.6 kbps sending	ITU-T
V.34	33.6 kbps	ITU-T
V.32 *bis*	14.4 kbps	ITU-T
V.32	9,600 bps	ITU-T
V.22 *bis*	2,400 bps	ITU-T
V.22	1,200 bps	ITU-T
212A	1,200 bps	AT&T

ERROR CORRECTION AND DATA COMPRESSION STANDARDS

Name	Type	Origin
V.42	Error correction	ITU-T
V.42 *bis*	Data compression	ITU-T
MNP (Microcom Network Protocol)	Error correction and data compression	Microcom

FACSIMILE MODEM STANDARDS

Name	Speed	Origin
V.14	14.4 kbps	ITU-T
V.29	9,600 bps	ITU-T
V.17 *ter*	4,800 bps	ITU-T

*Called V.pcm during development, V.90 resolved the competition between two competing 56 kbps modem standards, X2 and K56Flex.

SPEED STANDARDS

The most important standards govern modem *transmission speed*. Most new modems today follow the *V.34* standard, which allows a 33.6 kbps transmission speed. (When V.34 was first released, its speed was 28.8 kbps.) However, in the field you may still encounter older *V.32 bis* modems (*bis* means second edition), which operate at only 14.4 kbps.

TRAINING

What if there is a V.34 modem at one end of a telephone line and a V.32 *bis* modem at the other end? Before two modems begin to transmit data, they go through a *training period*, during which they exchange messages to learn what the other modem can do. The faster modem automatically slows down to match the speed of the slower modem. In this case, then, transmission would take place at V.32 *bis* speed, which is only 14.4 kbps.

ERROR CORRECTION AND COMPRESSION

Most modems today can do error correction during transmission. This involves retransmitting information that was garbled during transmission. Error correction is governed by the *V.42* standard.

In addition, most modems today can do data compression, using the *V.42 bis* standard. Under ideal circumstances, you can get up to 4:1 compression. So if your modem is transmitting at 28.8 kbps, you can feed it data at a speed of 115.2 kbps through the serial port. Your modem will compress the data down to 28.8 kbps for transmission over the telephone network.

What if a modem that does not do compression is at one end of the line and a modem that does compression is at the other end? During the training period, the modem that can do compression automatically agrees not to compress its data before transmission.

FACSIMILE MODEM OPERATION

We have been focusing on data transmission. However, most modems today can also act as *facsimile modems*, transmitting and receiving facsimile images at 14.4 kbps (V.14) or at 9,600 bps (V.29).

Alternatives to Ordinary Modems

Even with a 33.6 kbps modem and compression, downloading webpages can take an excruciatingly long amount of time. For this reason, you would like to have faster transmission speeds.

THE SPEED PROBLEM

Unfortunately, we cannot expect to get much higher speeds with traditional modems. As discussed earlier, Equation 3.1 indicates that an analog telephone line has a theoretical maximum speed of about 35 kbps when we transmit. Modems today are very close to this theoretical transmission limit.

For this reason, some home users of the Internet are turning to higher-speed connection devices. Unfortunately, this also increases costs. First, the devices are more expensive than modems. Second, the telephone company will charge more for monthly transmission service to connect you to the ISP. Third, Internet service providers will charge more because you are placing a heavier load on the ISP's network.

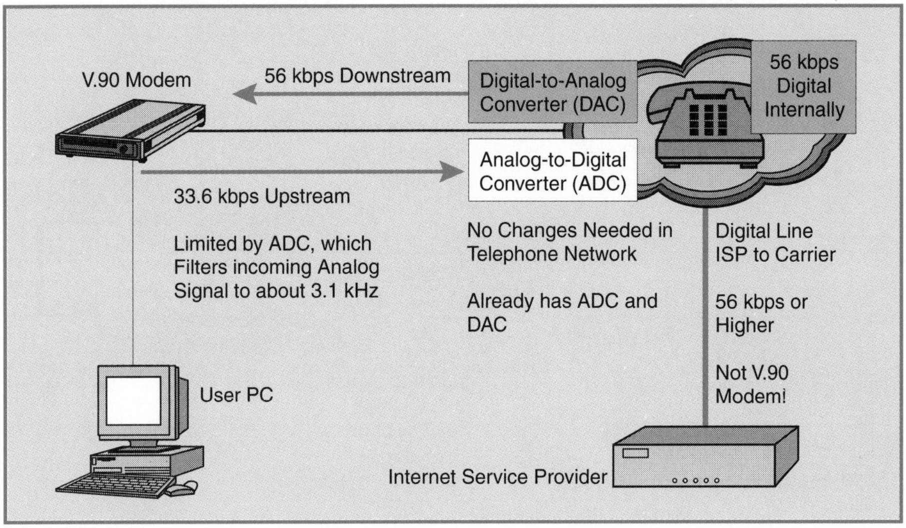

FIGURE **3.23**

V.90 Modem

FIGURE **3.23**
V.90 Modem

V.90 MODEMS

Although there is a rather firm limit on *transmitting* data at more than about 35 kbps into the telephone system, the telephone system is actually designed to carry digital signals at about 56 kbps. As a result, Figure 3.23 shows that companies have begun selling *56 kbps modems* that allow you to *receive* data at 56 kbps, over ordinary telephone lines. These modems follow the *V.90* modem standard.

Figure 3.23 shows that when you transmit, your signal goes through an *analog-to-digital converter (ADC)* at the telephone switching office. This ADC is what creates the 35 kbps limit on telephone transmission. So although you can *receive* at 56 kbps, you can still *send* at only 33.6 kbps with a 56 kbps modem.

When your ISP transmits, however, it does not use an analog telephone line to the telephone system. Rather, it uses a digital line. Note that there is no ADC when the ISP uses a digital leased line. So there is no 35 kbps limit.

However, there is a limit of 64 kbps because the telephone system internally is all-digital and uses channels of 64 kbps. In the United States, the telephone company "steals" 8 kbps for supervisory signal, giving a net speed of 56 kbps. By not going through an ADC, the ISP can send at 56 kbps.

Unfortunately, there are some problems with V.90 modems at the time of this writing, including the fact that not all telephone lines will support these modems. In fact, even very good lines will typically limit you to between 40 and 50 kbps.

Not all ISPs, furthermore, support V.90 modems, and those that do usually charge more for 56 kbps service, because it places a greater load on their switches and on their transmission link to the Internet backbone.

ISDN

For guaranteed faster speeds, you need to move beyond your current dial-up voice telephone service. Many transmission carriers now offer a competing service, the *Integrated Services Digital Network*, or *ISDN*. Figure 3.24 shows an ISDN connection.

FIGURE **3.24**

**Integrated
Services Digital
Network (ISDN)**

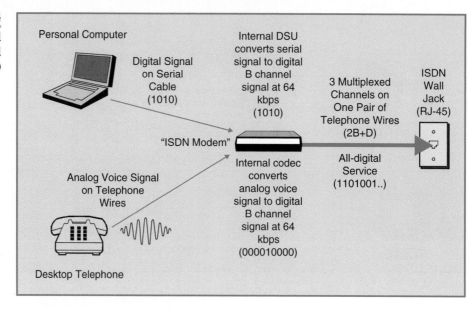

What is not obvious in this picture is that ISDN is a purely digital system. Also not obvious from the figure is that ISDN is a dial-up service. You can dial up any other ISDN subscriber.

The figure does show that the ISDN line into your home terminates in a device that is usually called an **ISDN modem.** (The proper name is *terminal adapter*.) It costs substantially more than an ordinary telephone modem.

The ISDN line coming into your home multiplexes (mixes) three distinct data channels onto the single pair of UTP wire running from your home to the first switching office. Two of these are 64 kbps "B" channels, and one is a 16 kbps "D" channel. For this reason, the service that ISDN brings to the desktop is called *2B+D*.

Many ISDN modems have one RJ-11 input port for a telephone connection plus one serial port for a computer connection. This allows you to talk on the telephone while simultaneously transmitting and receiving computer data at 64 kbps. Some ISDN modems allow you to transmit and receive data at 128 kbps without a telephone connection. (In the latter case, your ISP must support 128 kbps service.)

Unfortunately, ISDN service costs about twice as much per month as ordinary telephone service, and most households would find this cost prohibitive.

In addition, as in the case of 56 kbps V.90 modems, ISPs usually charge more if you use ISDN connections, because you place a heavier load on their router and transmission link to the Internet.

DATA SERVICE UNITS (DSUs)

Although the device that connects your computer to the ISDN system is called an ISDN modem, it really is not a modem at all. Figure 3.25 shows that different data translation devices are needed depending on the type of *device* that is sending and the type of the *transmission line* being used. If you have a digital computer device and an analog transmission line, you truly do need a modem.

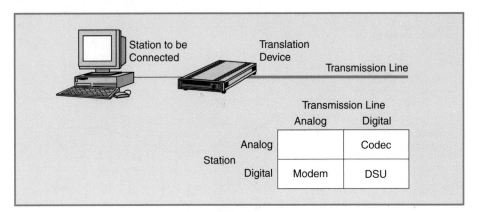

FIGURE **3.25**

Signal Translation Devices

However, the figure shows that if you have a *digital device* and a *digital transmission line*, as you do in ISDN, then you do not need a modem. Rather, as Figure 3.26 shows, you need a device called a **data service unit (DSU).** Although both the source signal and the digital transmission line are digital, there are different digital formats, involving different signaling rates, different numbers of bits per baud, different voltage levels, and so forth. In your ISDN "modem," there is a DSU to translate between your serial port signal from the PC into the digital transmission format used by the ISDN system.

CODECS

If you tie your telephone into the ISDN "modem," you have another problem. Your *device* (telephone) is *analog*, but the ISDN *transmission line* is *digital*. As Figure 3.25 illustrates, you need a translation device called a **codec.**

Codecs work through a technique called sampling. Figure 3.27 illustrates this process. It shows that a sound signal is nothing more than a loudness level that varies smoothly with time. In sampling, each second is divided into many time periods. For voice, there usually are 8,000 sampling periods per second.

For each sample, only the loudness level is recorded. Historically, it was recorded as an 8-bit binary number, giving 256 possible loudness levels. This is enough that the human ear cannot pick up differences between loudness levels, effectively giving a smooth loudness range. If we have 8 bits per sample and 8,000 samples per second, then digital voice sampling gives a data stream of 64 kbps. This is why most digital transmission lines operate at multiples of 64 kbps.

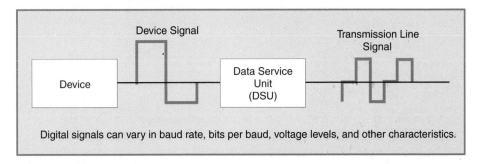

Digital signals can vary in baud rate, bits per baud, voltage levels, and other characteristics.

FIGURE **3.26**

DSU Translates between Digital Formats

FIGURE **3.27**

Codec Sampling

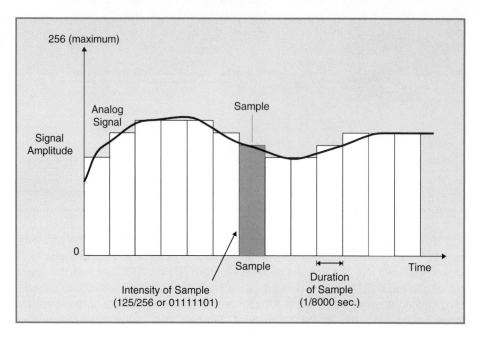

DIGITAL SUBSCRIBER LINE (DSL) MODEMS

The telephone companies are beginning to offer an even faster service, the *digital sub-scriber line (DSL)*. As in the case of ISDN, these digital subscriber lines are all-digital and are faster than ordinary voice modems. In fact, they are much faster than even ISDN, offering transmission speeds of 384 kbps to several megabits per second.

Unfortunately, there are several types of DSL lines. You must get the proper DSL modem for the particular DSL service your telephone company offers. As Figure 3.28 shows, *ADSL (A* is for asymmetrical) offers very high-speed downstream service (up

FIGURE **3.28**

Asynchronous Digital Subscriber Line (ADSL)

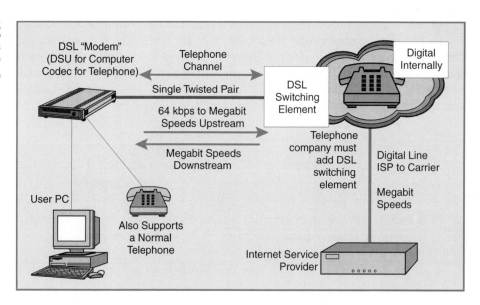

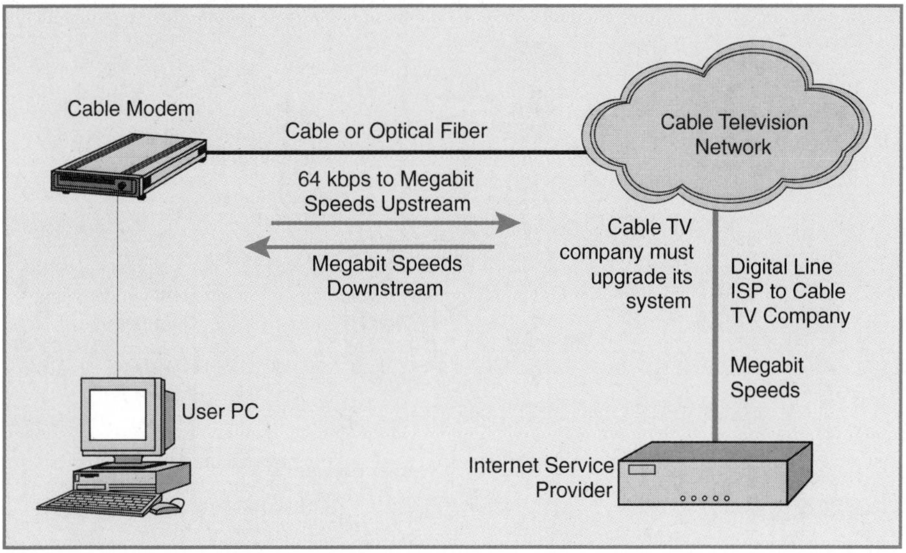

FIGURE **3.29**

Cable Modem

to several megabits per second) but only ISDN-speed upstream service. This is particularly good for Web surfing. In addition, the speed you actually receive may vary, depending on how far you are from the nearest telephone company switch.

Most importantly, transmission carriers will charge much more for DSL service than for ISDN service, and, as usual, expect your ISP to charge more if you connect with a faster line.

Figure 3.28 shows that a digital subscriber line delivers more than data traffic. It also multiplexes an ordinary full-duplex telephone channel on the pair of wires coming into the home. This allows you to talk on the telephone at the same time you are surfing the World Wide Web.

CABLE MODEMS

Not to be outdone, cable television companies are beginning to offer data transmission services at DSL speeds or at even higher speeds, as shown in Figure 3.29. To use this service, you need a *cable modem*. The cable television company usually operates as both a transmission carrier and an ISP. Many cable companies price their services aggressively, at under $50 per month for both transmission and Internet access. This is competitive with 56 kbps access for subscribers who install a second telephone line for Internet access. Cable modems offer speeds of up to 10 Mbps, but many customers share this capacity, so the real throughput for individual customers is much lower.

WIRELESS ACCESS

As Internet access grows increasingly important in organizations, mobile computer users will want to link their laptops to the Internet. Today, they need to find a telephone to do this. Figure 3.30 shows an alternative: *wireless Internet access*. Wireless Internet access systems use a radio **transceiver** (transmitter/receiver) in the computer to link it to the wireless Internet access supplier's central site. As you might expect, this is a very expensive option today.

FIGURE **3.30**

Wireless Internet Access

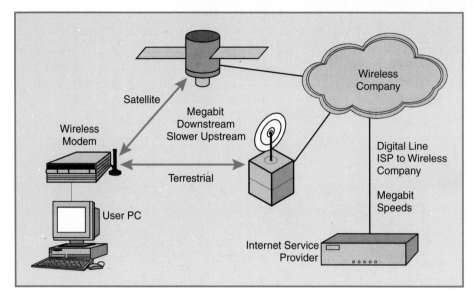

ETHERNET NICs VERSUS THE UNIVERSAL SERIAL BUS (USB)

Serial ports are good for speeds of up to 115.2 kbps. This is adequate for high-speed modems and is only a little constraining for ISDN. However, for faster services, we need to move bits into the PC and out of it at much higher speeds.

One alternative is to install an Ethernet network interface card (NIC). As discussed in Chapter 4, this is a printed circuit board resembling an internal modem (see Figure 3.21). However, an Ethernet NIC is designed to work with 10 Mbps Ethernet LANs, so it can send and receive at 10 Mbps. Ethernet NICs are attractive because they are very inexpensive. They begin at $25 to $35. Unfortunately, like internal modems, they require you to open your computer and go through a potentially complex installation procedure.

Many new PCs will avoid the need to install anything. They come with a new type of port built to send and receive at much higher speeds than serial ports. This is the *universal serial bus (USB)*. A USB port operates at 12 Mbps, although several devices attached to a USB port may share that speed.

Another new port is the *IEEE-1394* port, which is often called **firewire.** IEEE-1394 ports operate at 400 kbps, which is a little low for some high-speed Internet lines.

When you order an ISDN, DSL, or cable "modem," you will soon have to specify whether you wish an EIA-TIA-232-F connection, an RJ-45 port for your Ethernet NIC, a USB connector, or a firewire connector. You will also need an RJ-11 port for your telephone line.

OVERALL

Businesses can now connect to Internet service providers via ISDN lines or other high-speed lines. For most homes, however, such lines are likely to be prohibitively expensive. Most home users are still likely to be limited to 56 kbps downstream modems or, at best, cable modems. In other words, surfing the Web will continue to be a slow process for the foreseeable future for most people.

SUMMARY

Chapter 2 introduced the standards needed to use the Internet from home, via a telephone line and a modem. However, Chapter 2 limited itself to standards above the physical layer. This chapter completes the picture by looking at the physical layer in Internet access from home. The next chapter discusses how things differ at the physical and data link layers if you access the Internet through a corporate network.

The chapter began with a number of basic transmission concepts that networking professionals have to master when dealing with physical layer standards and processes. This included such things as:

▶ Transmission speed measured in both bits per second and baud
▶ The difference between digital and analog transmission and why digital transmission now dominates new communication technologies
▶ Propagation effects in closed transmission media, including attenuation, distortion, noise, and interference
▶ Wire media, including unshielded twisted pair (UTP) wire, optical fiber, coaxial cable, and the trend toward using UTP to the desktop and optical fiber for longer runs
▶ Radio transmission, including the relationship between channel bandwidth and maximum possible transmission speed and baseband versus broadband transmission
▶ PC serial ports, in order to give the reader an understanding of how connector plugs in general tend to work, in terms of pin organization, pin meaning, and electrical signaling

The remainder of the chapter looked at modem transmission over telephone lines and at newer alternatives that will provide higher speeds, albeit at a higher price.

We focused on modem transmission over ordinary telephone lines because this is the most common form of home access today and, given the costs of other alternatives, is likely to dominate in the near future. The chapter discussed modulation, followed by modem forms and modem standards.

The discussion of modem standards emphasized that there are several standards for modems.

▶ In terms of speed, V.34 modems transmit and receive at 33.6 kbps. V.90 modems transmit at 33.6 kbps but can receive at speeds up to 56 kbps. However, V.90 modems require the Internet service provider (ISP) to have a digital connection to the telephone company.
▶ In addition to speed standards, there are separate standards for error correction, data compression, and facsimile.
▶ When two modems connect, they go through a training period that can last for several seconds. During this period they negotiate the highest common denominator for these various standards.

Modems are inexpensive and can use your ordinary telephone line. However, modem speeds cannot rise much above V.90 levels, given the nature of telephone transmission.

Higher speeds will require new technologies. Fortunately, several of these new technologies are now available or are becoming available.

- ▶ ISDN multiplexes three channels to the user's desktop. Two of these are 64 kbps B channels that can sometimes be combined to provide 128 kbps transmission and reception speeds. The ISDN "modem" really contains DSU and codec circuitry rather than modem circuitry.
- ▶ Cable modems can download data at several megabits per second, although this speed is shared.
- ▶ Telephone carriers are introducing digital subscriber lines (DSLs) that offer high kilobit to megabit downstream speeds and, in asymmetric digital subscriber lines (ADSL), slower upstream speeds.
- ▶ Wireless access will allow portable computers to use the Internet at any time.

Although these new transmission options are attractive in terms of speed, they are also very costly.

- ▶ First, you must have a translation device between your PC (and possibly your telephone line) and the transmission line. This can be a modem, codec, or DSU.
- ▶ Second, you must pay the carrier for the transmission line. You cannot use your ordinary telephone line, so this is an incremental cost.
- ▶ Third, your ISP probably will charge you more because your higher download speeds (and perhaps upload speeds) will require more ISP resources.
- ▶ Fourth, you will need a port faster than a serial port.

REVIEW QUESTIONS

CORE REVIEW QUESTIONS

1. What is the difference between the bit rate and the baud rate?
2. Define *digital transmission*. Define *analog transmission*. What is the difference between *digital* and *binary*?
3. Explain the main propagation effects.
4. What are the three main wire transmission media? Which is used most frequently to the desktop? Why? Which is used most frequently over longer distances? Why?
5. As bandwidth increases in a channel, how does maximum transmission speed through that channel change? What does *broadband* mean literally? How is the term *broadband* commonly used?
6. In PC serial ports, how many pins are used for data transmission? In general, what are other pins for?
7. Define *modulation*. Define *demodulation*. Do not just say translation between digital and analog or analog and digital. For both modulation and demodulation, characterize whether the transmission line is analog or digital and whether the device attached to the transmission line is analog or digital.

8. Which modem form is easier to install—internal or external? What is the advantage of internal modems over external modems? What is the most expensive modem form?

9. What is the speed of a V.34 modem? What are the speeds of a V.90 modem? Be specific.

10. What is "training" in initial modem communication? If a V.42 modem tries to communicate with a 14.4 kbps V.32 *bis* modem, what will happen?

11. What is the maximum reception speed for V.90 modems? What is the maximum transmission speed? To use a V.90 modem, can you use your ordinary home telephone line, or do you need an additional line?

12. Distinguish between full-duplex and half-duplex transmission in terms of who can communicate simultaneously. What is flow control, and why does full-duplex transmission allow it? What is error correction, and why does full-duplex transmission allow it?

13. Distinguish between serial and parallel transmission in terms of bit rate for a given clock cycle (and baud rate).

14. In ISDN, what is 2B+D? What is the maximum reception speed for ISDN? What is the maximum transmission speed? To use ISDN, can you use your ordinary home telephone line, or do you need an additional line?

15. What is multiplexing? How does it apply to ISDN?

16. What type of organization offers cable modems? What type of organization offers digital subscriber lines (DSLs)? How do cable modems and DSLs compare to 56 kbps V.90 modems in terms of speed and cost?

17. When you use an alternative to ordinary modem transmission, what four additional costs do you incur?

18. If you have a *digital device* communicating over an *analog transmission line*, what type of translation device do you need, if any? If you have an *analog device* communicating over a *digital transmission line*, what type of translation device do you need, if any? If you have a *digital device* communicating over a *digital transmission line*, what type of translation device do you need, if any?

DETAILED REVIEW QUESTIONS

1. Why is digital transmission dominant in new communication systems?

2. What is the relationship between distance traveled and noise errors? What is the relationship between bit rate and noise errors?

3. Why is UTP twisted?

4. What is the difference between baseband and broadband transmission?

5. In general, as noise increases, what happens to the maximum transmission speed in a channel?

6. What does V.42 standardize? What does V.42 *bis* standardize?

7. What are the two standards for facsimile modem speeds?

8. What device limits your speed when you transmit over the telephone system? Where is this device located?

9. In using a V.90 modem, what does the PC user need, compared to using a V.34 modem? What does the ISP need? What does the telephone company need?

10. Full-duplex transmission at 100 kbps requires two 100 kbps channels, one in each direction. However, do we say that this is a 100 kbps system or a 200 kbps system?

11. If you attach a telephone and a computer to an "ISDN modem," are you dealing with a modem at all? What type of translation device(s) are you really using?

12. A cable modem can often give you download speeds of 10 Mbps. Why will you usually not achieve anything like this speed?

13. In codec encoding, what do you measure in each sampling period?

14. A DSU translates between digital formats. What things could be different between two digital formats?

15. Distinguish between DSL and ADSL. What does the *A* in *ASDL* mean?

16. When you buy an ISDN, DSL, or cable "modem," what types of ports might you specify? What are the advantages of each port type?

THOUGHT QUESTIONS

1. Why is serial port transmission binary?

2. What happens if a modem that follows the V.42 standard tries to communicate with a modem that does not follow the V.42 standard?

3. When a teacher is lecturing in class, is this half-duplex transmission or full-duplex transmission? Explain.

4. Which is better for downloading, a 10 Mbps cable modem or a 10 Mbps DSL line? Explain.

5. Several forms of transmission are asymmetric, with downstream speeds being higher than upstream speeds. For what application is this good? For what applications are asymmetric transmission speeds not good?

6. Besides the speed of your line to the ISP, what determines download speed in World Wide Web access?

7. In encoding, the general rule is that you need to sample at twice the bandwidth. In addition, for each sample, if you store N bits, you can have 2^N loudness levels. How many bits per second would you generate if you wanted to encode music? Assume a bandwidth of 20 kHz and 65,536 loudness levels. Assume stereo music, in which you have two channels. Second, convert this into bytes per second. How much storage would you require on a disk holding 60 minutes of stereo music? How does this compare to the storage capacity of a CD-ROM disk of about 550 MB? What do you conclude about CD-ROM disks? Can you think of why the calculation did not equal exactly 550 MB?

PROJECTS

1. Go to the book's website, http://www.prenhall.com/panko, and read the Updates Page for this chapter to see any reported errors and new and expanded information on the material in this chapter.

2. Go to the book's website, http://www.prenhall.com/panko, and do the Internet Exercises for this chapter.

3. Create a one-meter length of UTP wiring, ending at both ends with an RJ-45 terminator. For this, you will need a spool of Category 5 UTP wire, a bag of RJ-45 terminators, and a crimping tool for RJ-45. When you look at the back of

the RJ-45 connector, the pins are numbered 1 through 8 left to right. The table below lists the wire you will place in each slot. To do the work, place the connector on a table. Use a crimping tool's cutter to strip off no more than a half inch of the covering over the bundle and around each wire pair. Be sure to place the wires in the appropriate holes. When you hold the connector plug away from you, as if you are plugging it into a jack, and when you look down at the plug, hole 1 is on your left and hole 8 is on your right. Make sure that some of the wiring bundle jacket is inside the connector; then crimp the connector to tighten it. Try pulling the wiring bundle out of the connector to make sure that the crimping worked. If you have a wiring tester, test the connection.

HOLE	PAIR	WIRE COLOR
1	2	white/orange
2	2	orange
3	3	white/green
4	1	blue
5	1	white/blue
6	3	green
7	4	white/brown
8	4	brown

CHAPTER 4

A Simple PC Network

INTRODUCTION

Chapter 1 introduced the Internet as arguably today's most important networking environment. Chapters 2 and 3 fleshed out the standards and technology involved in using the Internet from home via a telephone line and modem.

This chapter takes us into another very important networking environment: a simple PC network built on a single local area network (LAN). The next two chapters look at larger networks that span large sites or multiple sites within a firm. If the Internet is today's glamour environment, the PC network is the workhorse networking environment for day-to-day business. It handles most of the typical office worker's daily processing tasks.

Of course, the PC network is also the way that most office workers reach the Internet. Instead of using PPP or CSLIP at the data link layer and serial ports and modems at the physical layer, the office worker uses the LAN's physical and data link layer standards. Standards at the internet, transport, and application layers are exactly the same.

The discussion of PC networking will extend our understanding of layered standards. We will see that in PC networking, the IEEE (Institute of Electrical and Electronics Engineers), which sets most LAN standards, divides the data link layer into two layers, the logical link control (LLC) layer and the media access control (MAC) layer. So for PC networking, we must learn to work with a *six-layer* hybrid TCP/IP–IEEE framework consisting of the application, transport, internet, logical link control, media access control, and physical layers.

We will also extend our understanding of layered standards because Novell NetWare, one of the most popular server operating systems for PC networking, adopted the TCP/IP architecture only recently. Many NetWare servers still use Novell's proprietary IPX/SPX architecture. At the lower layers, IPX/SPX and TCP/IP follow the same logical link control, media access control, and physical layer standards. At the application, transport, and internet layers, however, IPX/SPX has its own standards.

The IEEE has produced many LAN standards at the LLC, MAC, and physical layers. We will focus on the most widely used LAN standards, namely the Ethernet standards from the 802.3 Working Group. Furthermore, we will concentrate on the 802.3 MAC layer standard and the 802.3 10Base-T and 100Base-TX physical layer standards because these are the most widely used Ethernet standards.

Elements

Figure 4.1 shows that simple PC networks consist of client PCs, servers, server software, network interface cards, hubs, and wiring.

CLIENT PCs

The PCs that sit on the desks of ordinary managers, professionals, and clerical workers are **client PCs.** As the name suggests, these client PCs are the clients or customers of the network, receiving various services from the servers. Only one client PC is shown in the figure, but even a small PC network will have a half dozen or more client PCs.

PCs with newer operating systems, beginning with Windows 95, are inherently capable of working with servers over a network. PCs with older operating systems, such as Windows 3.1, must add "client shell" software to be client PCs on a PC network.

SERVERS

Servers provide services to the client PCs. Again, only one server appears in the figure. However, it is common to have about one server for every ten or so PCs. Typically, different servers offer different services.

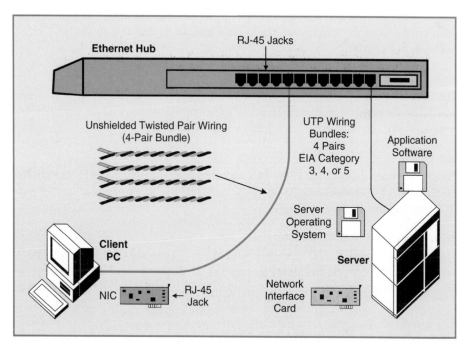

FIGURE **4.1**

Simple PC Network

Server Hardware Although some servers use high-power computer platforms, such as workstation servers (see Chapter 1), *most servers on a PC network are themselves personal computers.* This is especially true on smaller PC networks. In fact, as we will see later, some PC servers are not even high-end PCs.

Server Operating Systems (SOSs) You are probably most familiar with operating systems designed for stand-alone PCs and client PCs, such as Windows 3X, Windows 9X, and Windows NT workstation.[1] Servers, however, have special needs, such as the ability to provide services to many client PCs simultaneously. So instead of running operating systems designed for client machines, a server runs an operating system designed to run servers. The most popular **server operating systems (SOSs)** today are Novell NetWare, Microsoft Windows NT Server, and UNIX. In the small networks discussed in this chapter, Windows NT Server and Novell NetWare are the most popular SOSs. UNIX is found mostly in large PC networks and is used even there primarily for client/server applications.

Server Application Software Although server technology and the server operating system are expensive, the real cost of PC networks comes from the *application software* installed on the server. It is the application software—such as electronic mail and webservice—not the SOS itself, which provides services to the client PCs. To be fair, however, most SOSs come bundled with some application software.

Network Interface Cards (NICs)

To communicate over a telephone line, your PC needs a modem. To communicate over a PC network, your PC needs an expansion board called a **network interface card (NIC).** As Figure 4.2 shows, the NIC normally fits into an expansion slot on the PC's mother board, which contains the microprocessor, RAM, and other electronics. This connection allows the microprocessor to send commands and data to the NIC and to read data from the NIC.

HUBS

The **hub,** shown in Figure 4.1, links all of the client PCs and servers together. It allows any PC on the network to send messages to any other PC. As we will see later, hub operation is very simple in Ethernet 10Base-T and 100Base-TX.

WIRING

Finally, we must connect the client PCs and servers to the hub. We will see that the Ethernet 802.3 10Base-T and 100Base-TX standards use the *unshielded twisted pair (UTP)* wiring that we saw in Chapter 3.

PC NETWORKS VERSUS LANs

Many textbooks equate "PC network" with "LAN." However, this is inaccurate. A LAN is a single network, so it involves only the physical and data link layers. In contrast, PC networks require all layers to operate successfully, because they involve

---

[1] Confusingly, Windows NT workstation is used primarily on PCs, rather than on RISC client workstations. However, it does run on some RISC client workstations. Microsoft chose to use the name *workstation* for all client computers it supports with the client version of Windows NT.

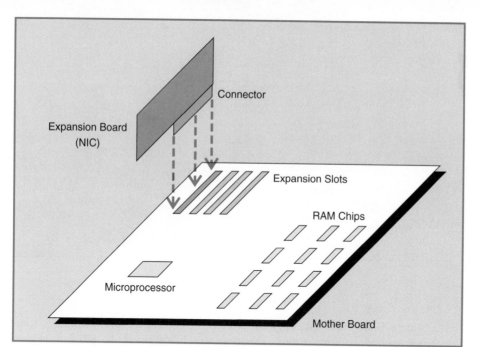

FIGURE **4.2**

Network Interface Card (NIC)

Connector

Expansion Board
(NIC)

Expansion Slots

RAM Chips

Microprocessor

Mother Board

application–application interactions. In a sense, the LAN is the transmission service for a small PC network.

In addition, as we will see in the next two chapters, PC networks are not limited to single LANs. Enterprise PC networks can span the entire corporation. They can contain thousands of client PCs and dozens of servers spread across multiple sites. Any client PC at any site can reach any server at any other site, as long as it has administrative permission.

IEEE 802 LAN MAN Standards Committee

Now that we have seen the elements of a fairly simple PC network operating on a single local area network, we will look at the way that LAN standards are set.

THE IEEE

LANs are *subnets*—single networks. We saw in Chapter 1 that subnet standards predominantly follow the OSI architecture. However, the two organizations that manage OSI, namely the International Organization for Standardization (ISO) and the International Telecommunications Union–Telecommunications Standards Sector (ITU-T), do not always create standards themselves. Often, they ratify standards submitted by other organizations. In the case of LAN standards, Figure 4.3 shows that the usual pattern is to ratify LAN standards created by the **Institute of Electrical and Electronics Engineers,** the **IEEE.**

THE IEEE 802 LAN MAN STANDARDS COMMITTEE

The IEEE has many standards committees. It created the **802 LAN MAN Standards Committee** to develop standards for LANs and also for citywide metropolitan area networks. Since the 1970s, this committee has created a large number of LAN standards.

FIGURE **4.3**

**Accepting OSI
LAN Standards**

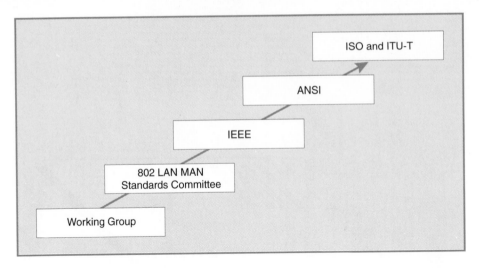

WORKING GROUPS

Actual standards are created in **working groups.** The 802 LAN MAN standards committee has several working groups. The most widely known is the **802.3 Working Group,** whose *Ethernet*[2] standards have dominated LAN technology. Another is the **802.5 Working Group,** which creates the competing *Token-Ring Network* standards used in many organizations. The **802.11 Working Group,** to give a third example, creates standards for radio and infrared wireless local area networks.

ACCEPTING 802 STANDARDS

Figure 4.3 shows that once a working group creates a standard, the standard goes through several steps in order to be ratified as an OSI standard.

▶ The working group sends the standard to the 802 Committee for review.
▶ The 802 Committee sends the standard to the IEEE as a whole.
▶ The IEEE does not have official standing to submit standards to ISO or the ITU-T. So it submits the standard to the *American National Standards Institute (ANSI)*, which is authorized to submit standards to ISO.
▶ ANSI submits the standard to ISO.
▶ Finally, ISO ratifies the standard, and the ITU-T ratifies the standard as well. It is now an official OSI standard.

This process sounds cumbersome and slow, but it has become almost completely automatic. Each group above the working group almost always accepts the standard without substantive change. So once working groups complete their work, manufacturers begin to create products based on the working group version.

---

[2] Technically, Ethernet predated the 802.3 committee, and the 802.3 Working Group ratified only a modified form of the Ethernet II specification. However, few LANs still use Ethernet II technology, and it is common practice to call 802.3 standards "Ethernet" standards.

FIGURE **4.4**

Hybrid TCP/IP–IEEE Framework for LANs

TCP/IP	TCP/IP–OSI	TCP/IP–IEEE
Application	Application	6 Application
Transport	Transport	5 Transport
Internet	Internet	4 Internet
Subnet	Data Link	3 Logical Link Control
		2 Media Access Control
	Physical	1 Physical

The TCP/IP–IEEE Standards Framework

In Chapter 1, we noted that TCP/IP standards use OSI layers for individual networks. This leads to the five-layer hybrid *TCP/IP–OSI framework*, with application, transport, internet, data link, and physical layers.

Figure 4.4 shows that the situation is slightly different for LANs. The IEEE further subdivides the data link layer into two layers—the logical link control layer and the media access control layer. The data link layer is fairly complex in LANs because hundreds of devices must be coordinated. Breaking it into two layers allows for greater division of labor in standards development.

Overall, then, LANs use a hybrid **TCP/IP–IEEE** framework that has six layers: application, transport, internet, logical link control, media access control, and physical.

PHYSICAL LAYER STANDARDS

Physical layer standards deal with things you can see and feel, including media, connector plugs, and electrical signaling.

The Ethernet (802.3) 10Base-T and 100Base-TX Physical Layer Standards

In this chapter, we focus on the *Ethernet 802.3 10Base-T* and *100Base-TX* physical layer standards.

▶ "802.3" tells us that this standard comes from the 802.3 Working Group—the working group that develops all Ethernet standards.

▶ The "10" says that the 10Base-T standard operates at 10 Mbps. The "100" says that the 100Base-TX standard operates at 100 Mbps.

▶ "Base" means baseband transmission. As we saw in Chapter 3, this means that signals are injected directly into the wire, instead of being placed in multiple channels at different frequencies (broadband transmission). Baseband transmission is simpler than broadband transmission and, therefore, less expensive.

▶ Finally, the "-T" tells us that these standards use ordinary UTP telephone wire, which we saw in the last chapter.

The 10Base-T versus
100Base-TX Physical Layer Standards

TECHNOLOGY AND 10BASE-T

Initially, the 802.3 Working Group created 10 Mbps physical layer standards. The technology of the early 1980s could not support higher speeds. The working group created several 10 Mbps physical layer standards (see Module C), but **10Base-T** soon dominated corporate use. As Figure 4.1 shows, 10Base-T uses a hub to link stations together.

THE EMERGENCE OF 100BASE-TX

Since the creation of 10Base-T, technology has improved to the point where 100 Mbps networks make sense economically in many situations. So the 802.3 Working Group created the Ethernet 802.3 100Base-TX standard.

OTHER 100BASE-X STANDARDS

Actually, it created *three* 100 Mbps standards. The **100Base-TX** standard is the most popular. It uses the Category 5 UTP wiring discussed in the next section. The 100Base-T4 standard, in turn, can use older Category 3 and Category 4 wiring, also discussed in the next section. However, this option has not become popular because most current installations and almost all new installations use Category 5 wiring. Finally, 100Base-FX uses optical fiber. The 100Base-FX standard is used mostly to connect hubs to other devices. Optical fiber, being glass, is not as rugged as wire and cannot take the beating that desktop wiring receives.

EASY UPGRADING

Given the high installed base of 10Base-T networks, the 802.3 Working Group worked hard to make upgrading existing 10Base-T networks to 100Base-TX easy and inexpensive. To upgrade to 100Base-TX, you first remove your 10Base-T hub and replace it with a 100Base-TX hub.

The wiring between stations and the hub remains the same. This is far more crucial than it may seem at first. Wiring is very inexpensive to buy but very expensive to install. In nice installations that hide wires in false ceilings and under carpets, it may cost $100 to $200 to wire each desk. By leaving the desktop-to-hub wiring in place, 100Base-TX removes the massive cost of new wire installation.

Of course, you also have to change the NICs in client PCs and in servers if you want them to be able to send and receive at 100 Mbps.

MIXING AND MATCHING

Although a station cannot send and receive at 100 Mbps unless it has a 100Base-TX NIC, 100Base-TX gives you choices in upgrading. You may wish to upgrade only some of your NICs immediately, for instance, those in servers, whose transmission needs are high. Many hubs offer a mix of 10Base-T and 100Base-TX ports. Many even have *autosensing* ports that supply either 10Base-T or 100Base-TX service, depending on the NIC in the computer at the other end of the wire.

WHICH TO CHOOSE?

In terms of pricing, we are at a transition point today. A new 10Base-T LAN is still somewhat less expensive to install than a new 100Base-TX LAN. However, as you will see if you do the Internet Exercises for this chapter, the price differences between the two technologies for NICs and hubs are small enough for many firms to install 100Base-TX in new LANs. The most common situation in firms today is a mixture of 10Base-T and 100Base-TX LANs.

The UTP Transmission Medium

We have just seen that the "-T" in 10Base-T and 100Base-TX stands for telephone wire, specifically, the unshielded twisted pair (UTP) wiring we saw in the last chapter. UTP is inexpensive and rugged enough to be run under carpets.

As Figure 4.1 shows, both 10Base-T and 100Base-TX specify a bundle of four UTP pairs, for eight wires total. This bundle is fairly standard in building telephone wiring. Having eight wires in the bundle makes UTP somewhat stiff, but it is still pliable enough to be run easily to desktops.

As discussed in Chapter 3, eight-wire bundles require the use of an RJ-45 telephone jack, which is slightly larger than the RJ-11 telephone jack normally used in homes.

Plugging in UTP wire bundles is just as easy as plugging in home telephone wiring. You simply snap the RJ-45 connectors on your wire into the RJ-45 jacks in the wall and in your NIC.

CATEGORIES OF UTP WIRING

There are three basic quality grades of UTP wiring under the **EIA/TIA-568** standard. In terms of increasing quality, these are **Category 3, Category 4,** and **Category 5.** Price differences between the three categories are small, so all new installations and most existing installations use **"Cat 5"** wiring. Cat 5 wiring has several twists per inch. This allows very high speeds without having much cross-talk interference between adjacent pairs of wires (as discussed in Chapter 3). However, as discussed in Chapter 3, installation must be done very carefully. Problems occur if the installer untwists more than a half inch of the wires to place them in an RJ-45 connector.

Hub Operation

Figure 4.5 shows how *hubs* operate under both the Ethernet 802.3 10Base-T and 100Base-TX physical layer standards. In basic hub operation, only speed differs in these two standards.

NIC TRANSMISSION

When a station transmits, it sends the signal to the hub on Pins 1 and 2.[3] In the figure, Station A, which is connected to hub Port 2, is transmitting.

BROADCASTING TO ALL STATIONS (BUS TRANSMISSION)

When the hub receives each bit, it repeats (broadcasts) this bit out all of its ports, so that every station receives the bit. This **broadcasting** is called **bus transmission,** so we say that the Ethernet 802.3 10Base-T and 100Base-TX standards use bus transmission. In fact, *all* Ethernet 802.3 physical layer standards use bus transmission. Bus transmission (broadcasting) is a hallmark of Ethernet physical layer transmission.

---

[3] Two wires are always needed to form a complete circuit. Pins 1 and 2 contain the orange and white/orange wires for Pair 2. Pins 3 and 6 contain the green and white/green wires for Pair 3.

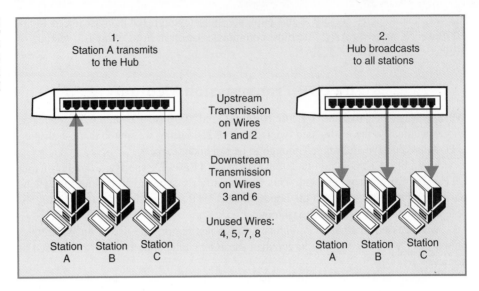

FIGURE **4.5**

Hub Operation in Ethernet 802.3 10Base-T and 100Base-TX

1.
Station A transmits
to the Hub

2.
Hub broadcasts
to all stations

Upstream
Transmission
on Wires
1 and 2

Downstream
Transmission
on Wires
3 and 6

Unused Wires:
4, 5, 7, 8

Station
A

Station
B

Station
C

Station
A

Station
B

Station
C

In networks, we use the term **topology** to describe how devices are connected when they communicate. Topology is a physical layer concept. In Ethernet, stations use broadcasting to connect at the physical layer. So we say that Ethernet uses a **bus topology.**

Note that the hub received the signal on Pins 1 and 2. When it broadcasts the bit back out, however, it uses Pins 3 and 6. This way there is no interference between transmissions and receptions.

Note also that each bit is broadcast to all stations attached to all ports. This includes the station doing the transmission. Sending the bit back to the transmitting station allows the station to confirm that its signal is being retransmitted correctly.

Note, finally, that transmission works a bit at a time. Recall from Chapter 2 that the organization of PDUs is limited to upper layers. The physical layer does not worry about message organization. It merely handles one bit at a time.

ELECTRICAL SIGNALING

Physical layer standards determine how ones and zeros will be represented as electrical signals. In Chapter 3 we saw that serial ports represent a one as -3 to -15 volts and a zero as $+3$ to $+15$ volts.

The Problem of a Long Series of Ones and Zeros

Such simple representations of ones and zeros as constant voltages over the bit period are attractive, but they create a potential problem. Suppose that you transmit a long series of ones or zeros. In this case, the voltage will remain constant for a long period of time. If the receiver's clock is slightly different from the sender's clock, the receiver may lose track of when each bit period starts.

	Bit							
Sender	1	2	3	4	5	6	7	8
Receiver	1	2	3	4	5	6	7	8	9	10

FIGURE **4.6**

Improper Synchronization of the Sender's and Receiver's Clocks

Figure 4.6 shows how loss of synchronization can cause problems. Here, the sender's clock is 20% slower than the receiver's clock. Suppose that the receiver measures the voltage in the *middle* of each bit period. When the receiver thinks it is sampling bit four, it is really sampling the third bit transmitted by the sender. Although clocks would never be 20% off, a frame may contain several thousand bits. Even if clocks are different by only a tiny fraction of a percent, this will create errors if there is a long series of ones or zeros.

Synchronization in Manchester Encoding

Ethernet 10Base-T faces the clock synchronization problem by placing a transition in the middle of each bit period, as Figure 4.7 illustrates. This transition effectively resynchronizes the receiver's clock every bit period. Even if the receiver's clock is substantially off, it will be resynchronized with every bit so that errors do not accumulate.

This is called **Manchester encoding**. Figure 4.7 shows that a one is a low voltage (-2.05 volts) for half of the bit period and a high voltage (0 volts) for the second half. A zero is the opposite. It is high for the first half and low for the second half. One way to remember this is that the ending tells whether the bit is a one or a zero. A high ending is a one, whereas a low ending is a zero.

10 Mbps but 20 Mbaud

Recall from Chapter 3 that the bit rate tells the number of information bits transmitted per second. In Ethernet 10Base-T, this is 10 Mbps. The baud rate, in turn, is the

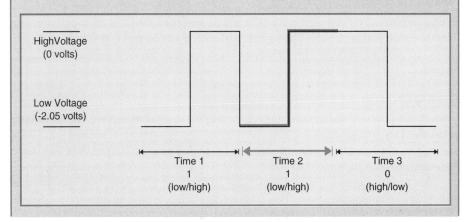

FIGURE **4.7**

Manchester Signal Encoding in Ethernet 802.3 10Base-T

number of times per second the line can change state per second. In Manchester encoding, the line can change twice for each bit transmitted—once at the beginning of the period and once in the middle. So the baud rate is 20 Mbaud. In other words, the baud rate is twice the bit rate in Ethernet 10Base-T.

4B/5B Encoding

The baud rate is limited by technology. If you need 20 Mbaud to get 10 Mbps in bit rate, this is not very efficient. Indeed, faster versions of Ethernet use more efficient but also more complex encoding schemes. For instance, the 100Base-TX standard uses 4B/5B encoding.

In 4B/5B, a high or a low voltage represents a bit for its *entire bit period*. To prevent loss of synchronization because of a long series of ones and zeros, each five bits transmitted carry four data bits. The 5-bit combinations are chosen to contain at least two line changes in the five bits. This is almost as good as synchronization for every bit.

This 4B/5B synchronization has a bit rate of 100 Mbps and a baud rate of 125 Mbaud. Manchester encoding would require a baud rate of 200 Mbaud for the same speed. So 4B/5B encoding gives both good synchronization and efficiency.

DATA LINK LAYER STANDARDS

As noted above, the IEEE 802 LAN MAN Standards Committee subdivided the data link layer into two layers—the media access control layer and the logical link control layer. We will now look at those standards.

Media Access Control: CSMA/CD

We have seen that hub operation is very simple at the physical layer. The hub merely repeats (broadcasts) everything it hears—much like a snoopy neighbor. This is fine if only one station is transmitting. But what if two stations transmit at the same time? We call this a **collision.** The voltages of the two stations will add together, and the resulting combined voltage generally will not make sense to NICs looking for either 0.00 or −2.05 voltage levels. The signals will effectively be scrambled beyond recognition. To give an analogy, two broadcast radio stations cannot transmit on the same channel.

SHARED MEDIA NETWORKS

If scrambling occurs when two stations transmit, we call the network a **shared media network.** The multiple stations effectively share the transmission medium, and only one may transmit at a time. Even if there are a hundred or more stations attached to the hub, only one may transmit at a time.

As a result, although stations transmit at 10 Mbps or 100 Mbps, they may have to wait before sending each frame. This reduces their *effective* transmission rate. To send

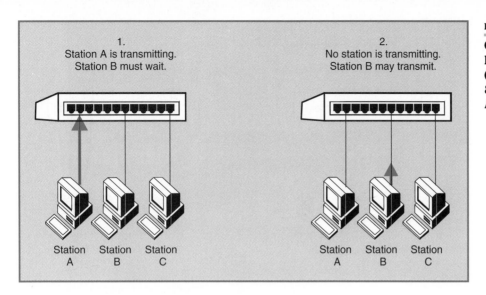

a message containing many frames, a station will be lucky to get even 1 Mbps to 3 Mbps of throughput.

MEDIA ACCESS CONTROL

This limitation to one transmission at a time at the physical layer means that shared media networks must have **media access control (MAC).** The devices must be controlled in terms of when they transmit (access the medium).

Ethernet uses a media access control method called **carrier sense multiple access with collision detection (CSMA/CD).** Although this sounds very complex, it really is very simple.

CARRIER SENSE MULTIPLE ACCESS

"Carrier sensing" simply means listening to the signal (carrier) that is coming to the station on Pins 3 and 6. The NIC always listens to these two pins.

"Carrier sense multiple access" is used to create a very simple rule for access control. Figure 4.8 shows that if you hear another NIC transmitting, you may not transmit. You must wait your turn. However, if you do not hear another NIC transmitting, then you are free to transmit. In other words, NICs obeying CSMA behave as people do in polite conversation.

COLLISION DETECTION

Sometimes, however, there will still be a collision because two NICs begin transmitting at the same time (see Figure 4.9). Perhaps several NICs have been waiting to transmit while another is sending. As soon as the NIC that is currently transmitting finishes, the waiting NICs all begin to transmit at the same time. Or, suppose that one station transmits. It takes time for the signal to travel up the wire to the hub and back down again to the attached stations. During that delay, another station, hearing nothing yet, may start transmitting.

If a collision happens, the transmitting NICs will note that what they are hearing

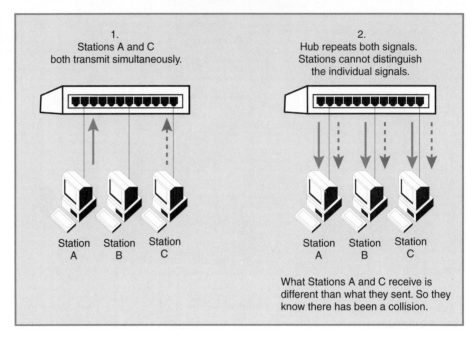

on Pins 3 and 6 is not what they are sending on Pins 1 and 2. This tells them that there is a collision. This is **collision detection.**

Again, if a collision does occur, there is a very simple rule. All transmitting NICs stop transmitting immediately. Each waits a random amount of time and transmits if the line is free. If there is another collision, each waits a longer random amount of time before trying again. After a few collisions and waits of increasing duration, one of the colliding NICs will be able to send its frame.

Media Access Control: The 802.3 MAC Layer Frame

We have just seen that the **802.3 Media Access Control (MAC) Layer Standard** governs the operation of CSMA/CD. In other words, physical layer transmission is controlled by MAC layer protocols. The 802.3 MAC layer standard also governs the structure of the **802.3 MAC layer frame,** shown in Figure 4.10. Both 10Base-T and 100Base-TX use this frame.

THE PREAMBLE AND START OF FRAME DELIMITER FIELDS

The frame begins with the preamble and start of frame delimiter fields. The **preamble** field consists of seven octets (bytes) of "10101010." The **start of frame delimiter** field, in turn, has the form 10101011. Together, the preamble and start of frame delimiter fields consist of eight octets with a very strongly repeating "10" rhythm terminating in "11" to signal the end of the rhythm.

In American football, the quarterback may yell "Hut, hut, hut" to synchronize the team for the play. The "10" rhythm of the preamble and start of frame delimiter synchronizes the receiver's clock.

FIGURE **4.10**

**Ethernet 802.3
MAC Layer Frame**

Preamble	7 Octets of 10101010 for synchronization
Start of Frame Delimiter	1 Octet of 10101011 to show start of frame
Destination Address	6 Octets for address of receiving station
Source Address	6 Octets for address of transmitting station
Length	2 Octets for length of data field in octets
Data (LLC Frame)	Data to be delivered (PDU of next higher layer, LLC)
PAD	Padding if needed to make frame 64 octets long
Frame Check Sequence	4 Octets of error checking information

DESTINATION AND SOURCE ADDRESSES

The Internet Protocol (IP) uses a 32-bit address field, the internet address. The 802.3 MAC layer frame, in contrast, uses 48-bit **source addresses** and **destination addresses.** The choice of 48-bit addresses means that there are 2^{48} possible source and destination addresses. This is a huge number, ensuring that there will be ample Ethernet addresses for many years to come.

In practice, each NIC vendor is given a large block of addresses by assigning it a unique 24-bit initial sequence. The NIC vendor then assigns a unique 24-bit final sequence to each NIC it produces. This ensures that, across NIC vendors, the default address preset at the factory will be unique for every NIC produced.

LENGTH FIELD

The 802.3 MAC standard does not specify a fixed length for frames. Ethernet frames can be anywhere from 64 octets to 1,518 octets.[4] The 802.3 MAC frame has a two-octet **length field,** which tells the number of octets in the *data field* (not in the entire frame).

---

[4] Without a frame length limit, one station could "hog" the shared media network by sending very long frames. For statistical reasons, this would harm maximum throughput. It might even be noticeable to users.

The minimum length is set for collision detection. Signals travel only at the speed of light in the transmission medium. If two stations at opposite ends of a network with multiple hubs (see the next chapter) transmitted simultaneously, their signals would collide in the middle of the network. If frames were very short, the sending stations would be finished transmitting before the frame arrived from the other station. They would not perceive a collision and so would not realize that they need to retransmit the frame for the benefit of stations in the middle of the LAN.

DATA FIELD

The **data field** holds the information being sent. Although we discuss the other fields in much greater depth, the data field normally is far larger than all of the other fields combined. Recall from Chapter 2 that it usually contains the PDU of the next-higher layer, namely the logical link control layer.

PAD FIELD

If the data field were very small, the frame would fall below the 64-octet minimum. If this happens, the NIC adds a **PAD** field to bring the total length of the frame up to the minimum size (64 octets).

FRAME CHECK SEQUENCE FIELD

To keep the error rate very low, the MAC frame specifies a four-octet error-handling field, the **frame check sequence** field. To compute this field, the transmitting station ignores the preamble, start of frame delimiter, and frame check sequence fields. It then performs a calculation on the remaining bits and places the results in the frame check sequence field.

The receiving MAC layer process redoes the calculation and determines if its result is consistent with the value in the frame check sequence field. If the results are consistent, the receiving MAC layer process accepts the MAC frame.

If the results are inconsistent, the MAC layer process **discards** the MAC layer frame. There is no request to retransmit the damaged packet at the MAC layer. A higher-layer process must detect a problem and retransmit the lost information. The Ethernet 802.3 MAC layer standard offers error detection but not error correction.

A four-octet frame check sequence field will miss only about one error in 4 billion. Yet although this field is 32 bits long, it adds little overhead. In a frame size of 1,000 octets, the 4-octet frame check sequence represents less than 0.5 percent of all bits sent.

The Logical Link Control Layer

As noted earlier, the data field of the MAC layer frame contains the PDU of the next higher layer, the **logical link control (LLC)** layer. All IEEE LANs, regardless of their physical and MAC layer standards, use the same LLC standard, **802.2.**

ERROR HANDLING

In the terminology we saw in Chapter 2, the MAC layer offers connectionless unreliable service. This minimizes overhead, but it fails to offer error correction. The 802.2 LLC layer standard gives the network administrator more options.

Given the low rate of errors on well-built LANs, and given the fact that the transport layer normally uses a reliable standard to correct errors at lower layers, most LANs use the *802.2 Type 1 option* (unacknowledged connectionless service). This option does not add error correction at the logical link control layer. It has very low overhead.

However, some administrators select the *802.2 Type 2 option*, which provides connection-oriented service with full error correction. As we saw in Chapter 2, connections and error correction require substantial overhead and reduce throughput on a network.

The LLC layer sits at the top of the data link layer, OSI layer 2. The LLC standard must create a link to the next higher layer, layer 3. In networks that use TCP/IP, the most common standard at layer 3 is the Internet Protocol (IP). Yet as Module A discusses, TCP/IP also has other protocols at layer 3 to handle supervisory work. In addition, we will see later that Novell NetWare networks typically use IPX at layer 3.

Note that the IEEE created only a single standard for the logical link control layer, 802.2. This means that designers of layer 3 standards have to create an interface to deal with only a single LLC layer standard, not several. All IEEE LANs look exactly the same to the layer 3 program, regardless of the physical and MAC technology used by the LAN.

THE 802.2 LLC FRAME

Figure 4.11 shows the organization of the 802.2 LLC frame.

The DSAP and SSAP Fields

As noted in the text, one role of the LLC layer is to connect to whatever layer 3 program wishes to use the LAN. To do this, the LLC layer frame must have a way to designate what standard is used at the next-higher layer, so that the LLC process on the NIC can pass the LLC frame up to the correct layer 3 program on the receiving computer. This could be a TCP/IP program, an IPX/SPX process on the receiving computer, or some other layer 3 program. Yes, a computer may run several layer 3 programs simultaneously, as discussed later (see Figure 4.16).

802.2 Logical Control Link (LLC) Frame

DSAP	SSAP	Control	Information (PDU of next higher layer)

Subnet Access Protocol (SNAP) Alternative

DSAP	SSAP	Control	SNAP PDU		
DSAP	SSAP	Control Code	Organization Type	Ethernet	Information
AA	AA	03	00-00-00	0800 (IP)	...
AA	AA	03	00-00-00	8137 (IPX)	...
AA	AA	03	00-00-00	8145 (SNMP)	...
AA	AA	03	00-00-00	0806 (ARP)	...

FIGURE 4.11

802.2 LLC Frame and SNAP Frame

To accomplish this, the DSAP and SSAP[5] fields of the 802.2 LLC layer frame shown in Figure 4.11 designate the standard used at layer 3. When the receiving LLC layer process examines an incoming LLC layer frame, it reads the DSAP field and, therefore, knows what layer 3 program should receive the PDU within the LLC layer frame's data field.

Subnet Access Protocol (SNAP)

The DSAP and SSAP are merely strings of ones and zeros. There must be some way to tie each one-octet binary number to a layer 3 protocol.

The IEEE has its own list of layer 3 protocols and the DSAP and SSAP bit sequence associated with each. If the IEEE list is used, then the second bit in the DSAP octet is set to one.[6]

DECIMAL	BINARY*	HEXADECIMAL
0	0000	0
1	0001	1
2	0010	2
3	0011	3
4	0100	4
5	0101	5
6	0110	6
7	0111	7
8	1000	8
9	1001	9
10	1010	A
11	1011	B
12	1100	C
13	1101	D
14	1110	E
15	1111	F
16**	00010000	10

*Usually, leading zeros are dropped. They are included in this field to show the 4-bit boundaries used in hexadecimal counting.
**Requires two octets of storage.

Figure 4.11 shows that the IEEE also created a way for other lists of layer 3 protocols to be used to link DSAP and SSAP addresses to specific layer 3 protocols. If the second bit in the DSAP address is set to zero, this means that another organization's list is to be used.

---

[5] Destination Service Access Point and Source Service Access Point. The terminology is not very enlightening. Basically, the LLC layer provides "access points" at which the LLC layer connects to the internet layer.

[6] The first bit also has a supervisory meaning. A computer may have several protocol stacks at layer 3 and above, as shown later in Figure 4.16. So there really are only six bits used to designate a layer 3 protocol. If the first bit in DSAP is one, all service access point programs will read the LLC frame to see if it is for their protocol. A zero in the first bit of the DSAP means that only the service access point program whose SAP number is listed in the following six bits should read the frame.

If the second DSAP bit is set to zero, then the logical control link control layer process on the receiver's NIC must look at the **Subnet Access Protocol (SNAP)** PDU within the frame. Figure 4.11 shows that the SNAP PDU first lists the organization that created the list. It then gives the specific value of the layer 3 protocol corresponding with DSAP addresses in the organization's list.

Figure 4.11 gives some specific examples of how the SNAP PDU can be used. Here, values are given in hexadecimal notation, in which symbols run from 1 through 9 and then A through F. Table 4.1 shows that each "hex" symbol represents a four-bit sequence from 0000 (0) to 1111 (F).

The examples show that 802.2 LLC layer frames with SNAP PDUs place AA hex (10101010) in both the DSAP and SSAP fields. They use a single-octet control field with the value 03 hex.

In the examples listed in Figure 4.11, the three-octet **organization code** of the SNAP PDU is all zeros, indicating that Xerox is the responsible organization. Xerox created Ethernet and created a list of standards to be used at layer 3.

Different values in the **Ethernet type** field specify different layer 3 standards. For instance, 0800 hex tells the receiving LLC layer process that the 802.2 frame contains an Internet Protocol packet.

Control Field

The **control field** allows the sending LLC process to send commands to the receiving LLC process. This field can be either one or two octets long, depending on the options being used.

Other Ethernet Standards

So far, we have looked at the elements of layered standards in isolation. Figure 4.12 brings these elements together. It shows the layers that are involved when you have TCP/IP standards at higher layers and use Ethernet (802.3) standards for subnet transmission.

Figure 4.12 shows that there are several Ethernet (802.3) physical layer standards. In fact, there are even more than the figure indicates. The network administrator then selects the physical layer standard best for his or her network, based on cost and performance.

However, regardless of the 802.3 physical layer standard, Ethernet (802.3) networks all use the same 802.3 MAC layer standard, which governs CSMA/CD transmission and defines the 802.3 MAC layer frame shown as Figure 4.10. (Actually, the 1000Base-X standard modifies synchronization in the frame slightly, but this does not change the basic picture.)

Nor do other layers change with different 802.3 physical layer standards. The logical link control (802.2), internet (IP), and transport (TCP) layers all remain the same.

FIGURE **4.12**

Layering in Ethernet PC Networks

LAYER	STANDARD(S)
Application	HTTP, FTP, NCP, etc.
Transport	TCP, SPX, NCP, etc.
Internet	IP, IPX, etc.
LLC	802.2 (may include the SNAP PDU)
MAC	802.3 MAC Layer Protocol
Physical	10Base-T, 100Base-TX, 100Base-FX, 1000Base-X, 10Base2, 10Base5, etc.

The application layer standard, of course, depends on the specific application. However, changing the physical layer will not require any change in the application layer standard.

TOKEN-RING NETWORKS

Although Ethernet dominates LANs today, there are other LAN technologies in use. Several of these are token-ring networks, which are very different from Ethernet CSMA/CD networks. Module C discusses these other LAN technologies in more detail, including 802.5 Token-Ring Networks and FDDI. In this chapter, we will focus on the key differences between token-ring technology and CSMA/CD bus technology.

Physical Layer Ring Topology

We saw earlier that a network technology's *topology* describes ways that stations are interconnected. Ethernet uses a *bus topology*, which is characterized by *broadcasting*. One station transmits, and this transmission is broadcast to all other stations. In Ethernet 10Base-T and 100Base-TX, the hub does the actual broadcasting.

In contrast, Figure 4.13 shows that token-ring network stations connect to **access units,** which are themselves connected in a **ring** (loop). Signals travel around the ring in one direction, so there is only a single possible path between any two access units on the ring.

Token Passing at the Media Access Control Layer

At the MAC layer, Figure 4.14 shows that whereas Ethernet uses CSMA/CD for media access control, token-ring networks use **token passing** to determine when each station may transmit.

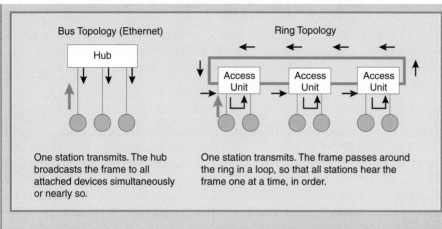

FIGURE 4.13

Bus versus Ring Topology at the Physical Layer

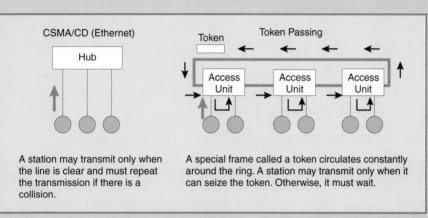

In token passing, a special frame called a **token** circulates constantly around the ring when no station is transmitting. This gives rise to a very simple rule for media access control: A station may transmit only when it has the token. Otherwise, it must wait. This ensures that only one station may transmit at a time.

802.2 at the Logical Link Control Layer

Like all other LANs, token-ring networks are designed to use 802.2 as the logical link control layer standard.

Perspectives on Token-Ring Networks

In many ways, token-ring network technology is superior to 802.3 Ethernet technology. However, most firms find Ethernet sufficient for their needs. Token passing, although offering some advantages over CSMA/CD, is also more complex, and this has led to high-priced products. On LANs, neither the 802.5 Token-Ring Networks nor the FDDI token-ring networks discussed in Module C have enjoyed large market shares.

Figure 4.12 shows layering if TCP/IP is used for higher-layer standards. In UNIX, this is always the case. For Microsoft Windows NT Server, this is usually the case. In the newest version of the Novell NetWare server operating system, this is also the case.

IPX/SPX

However, older versions of Novell NetWare used a different architecture for higher layers. This was **IPX/SPX,** Novell's own proprietary architecture. Many firms continue to use IPX/SPX on their NetWare systems to avoid the cost of converting their networks.

Figure 4.15 shows that IPX/SPX and TCP/IP have similar layering. This is not surprising because they have a common ancestor, the Xerox Network Systems (XNS) architecture. However, they use different standards.

▶ At the internet layer, TCP/IP specifies IP, whereas IPX/SPX specifies IPX.

▶ At the transport layer, IPX/SPX offers the SPX standard as an alternative to TCP.

▶ However, for most file service and print service operations, IPX/SPX uses the Network Core Protocol (NCP), which encompasses both the application and transport layers, as shown in Figure 4.15.

CONNECTING TO MULTIPLE SERVERS SIMULTANEOUSLY

As described in the box "Connecting a Client PC to Multiple Servers Simultaneously," client PCs are extremely versatile. A single client PC can connect simultaneously to a Novell NetWare file server running IPX/SPX and to a Microsoft Windows NT server or UNIX application server running TCP/IP. So although having multiple internet and transport layer protocols operating at the same layer makes life more complex for network administrators, it should not do so for users.

For LAN transmission, there is even less problem running multiple transport and internet protocols. An 802.2 LLC frame does not care whether it is carrying an IP packet, an IPX packet, or a packet following some other network layer protocol.

FIGURE 4.15 **IPX/SPX and TCP/IP**	Layer	TCP/IP	IPX/SPX	
	Application	various	various	NCP
	Transport	TCP	SPX	
	Internet	IP	IPX	
	Subnet	Use OSI Standards	Use OSI Standards	

CONNECTING A CLIENT PC TO MULTIPLE SERVERS SIMULTANEOUSLY

In a single PC network, there can be a Novell NetWare file server running IPX/SPX and a Windows NT Server file server running TCP/IP, as shown in Figure 4.16. A user at a client PC might like to connect to both at the same time. Figure 4.16 shows how this is possible.

The client PC must have two sets of higher-layer software, called **protocol stacks.** One will be the TCP/IP stack. The other will be the IPX/SPX stack.

The Adaption Layer Handles Sending Conflicts

Having two stacks can cause a problem. Suppose, for instance, that one application program submits a file retrieval job to the TCP/IP stack while another application program simultaneously submits a print service job to the IPX/SPX stack, as shown in Figure 4.16.

Both stacks will want to send their packets (IP or IPX packets) out through the NIC. Of course, NICs were not designed to process two different jobs at the same time.

The solution is to place a layer of software between the NIC and the upper-level stacks. This **adaption layer** software acts like a traffic officer at a crowded intersection. It controls which stack goes first in passing its packets to the NIC. The adaption layer removes the problems that occur when both stacks submit transmission requests at the same time.

The Adaption Layer Handles Reception Problems

Having multiple stacks also causes problems in reception. When a frame comes into the NIC, the NIC has no way of knowing which stack should receive the frame.

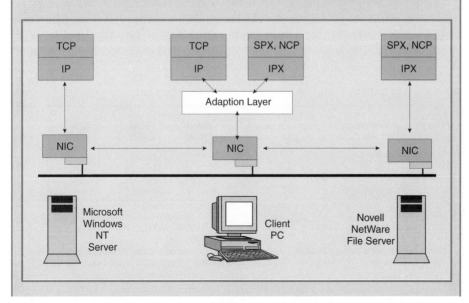

FIGURE 4.16

Simultaneous Connection to TCP/IP and IPX/SPX Servers

Again, the adaption layer comes into play. The NIC merely passes the frame up to the adaption layer software. The adaption layer software then examines the frame to see whether the data field inside the LLC frame is an IP packet or an IPX packet. Based on the answer, it passes the IP packet to the TCP/IP stack or the IPX packet to the IPX/SPX stack.

The bottom line is that there is no practical difficulty in mixing TCP/IP and IPX/SPX servers on the same PC network. In fact, client PC users can connect to both simultaneously. For instance, it is possible for a client PC to open a folder on a Novell NetWare server running IPX/SPX, to open another folder on a Microsoft Windows NT server running TCP/IP, and to copy files between the two folders as if they were two local disk drives.

APPLICATION LAYER: TYPES OF SERVERS

Although all layers are important, it is only at the application layer that we get the services that users really want to do their work. Everything at every other layer exists merely to support application services.

Servers and Services

In this section, we will use such terms as *file server* and *application server* as if they were separate machines as well as distinct services. However, one of the strengths of PC networking is that an organization can decide on the basis of performance, reliability, and economics whether to have one server or many.

For example, Figure 4.17 shows multiple services on a single server. To the server operating system, services are merely application programs. All server operating systems are multitasking operating systems that can run several application programs at a time.

The figure also shows the other extreme—several servers, each running a single application. This case allows the organization to optimize each server for that single application. For example, file servers need a great deal of very rapid disk storage. Client/server application servers, in turn, need a very fast processor. Communication servers often need very little processing power or disk storage.

FIGURE **4.17**

Single Server versus Multiple Servers

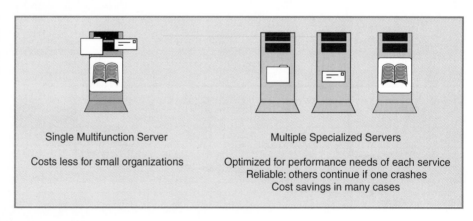

Single Multifunction Server

Costs less for small organizations

Multiple Specialized Servers

Optimized for performance needs of each service
Reliable: others continue if one crashes
Cost savings in many cases

PERFORMANCE

For performance, it typically is best to distribute the processing across multiple servers.

- ▶ First, the hardware and software can be optimized for high throughput.
- ▶ Second, the server operating system does not waste processing cycles constantly shifting among many tasks.
- ▶ Third, you do not have to worry about restricting a heavy application's processing time versus giving smaller applications too little processing time.

RELIABILITY

For reliability, applications that tend to crash frequently can be given their own servers. This way, when they fail, they are not likely to cause the entire server to crash. Although multitasking server operating systems should not crash when a single application crashes, this can still happen. Communication servers often have reliability problems because they cannot control the environment outside themselves.

ECONOMICS

Economics is a difficult matter to assess. Certainly, a firm with only a handful of people is unlikely to benefit from a dozen separate servers. However, in larger groups, the benefits of optimizing usually outweigh the costs of having a few multiple-service machines.

File Servers

The first type of server on PC networks was the file server. In **file service,** the server acts like a very large hard disk that is shared by many client PCs. Figure 4.18 shows this situation.

VIRTUAL DRIVES

The figure shows that individual users see directories on the file server's hard disk as merely additional disk drives. In this case, the client PC has real (local) disk drives A:,

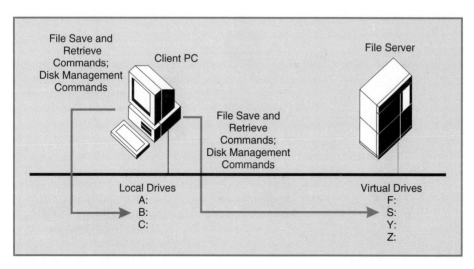

FIGURE 4.18
File Server

B:, and C:. However, it also has **virtual drives** F:, S:, Y:, and Z:. Each additional virtual drive points to a different folder on the file server's hard disk drive.

Different users can use the same virtual drive letter. For instance, two users can have virtual drives F: and Z:. In some cases, the drives will point to the same directory. For instance, Z: might point to the e-mail program for both users. In other cases, the same letter might point to different directories. For instance, for different users, the F: drive might point to their (different) private home directories.

To the user, virtual drives act almost exactly like regular disk drives. When users save a file to the file server, they do it the same way that they save a file to a local disk drive. They merely specify the drive, directory, file name, and extension. They can even add subdirectories, copy files between virtual drives, copy files between virtual drives and real drives, and do many other disk maintenance operations. They can even copy files between virtual drives on two different file servers if they are connected to both at once! So if users already know how to use regular drives, using a file server requires no relearning.

SHARING AND ACCESS RIGHTS

One of the big advantages of file service is file sharing. Figure 4.19 shows that members of a project team might have a directory for the team's work products. In addition, all employees on a PC network might get access to an application program.

One of the most time-consuming jobs of PC network administrators is to assign **access rights** to individual people and groups in each directory. For instance, in the case of the project team, should anyone be allowed to delete files, or should only the team leader have those rights? What about creating new files?

Also, if someone on the team is editing a document, should others be allowed to read the old version on disk until it is changed? This is called read-only access. Files in use often are **locked** by making them read-only, to prevent conflicting edits and other problems.

FIGURE 4.19

Sharing Data and Application Files

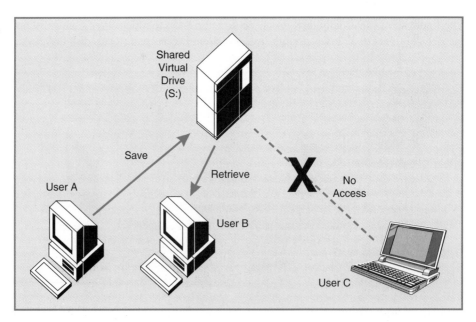

FILE SERVER PROGRAM ACCESS

For network administrators, perhaps the biggest advantage of sharing is the ability to install new programs and updates only once, on the file server. Previously, new programs and updates had to be installed on each individual PC separately. This was very time consuming and costly.

Program files shared this way, however, can be run only via file server program access. We saw in Chapter 1 that file server program access limits the size of programs because these programs must be able to fit on most corporate PCs, even older underpowered PCs. File server program access has very limited scalability.

Print Servers

File servers appeared in the early days of PC networking because many client PCs had no hard disk drives or only very small disk drives. Another limit of early PCs was printing. Laser printers and other good printers were prohibitively expensive for individual client PCs. So **print service** was created to allow all of a PC network's users to share a few very good printers.

Print service works the same way as printing to a local printer. When a user prints in a Windows program, for example, he or she merely selects the printer from the list on a pop down menu. There is no distinction between local printers and remote printers.

The one difference that does occur is beneficial. When you print, your print job goes to a print queue, where it waits until its printer is free. There is a print queue management program to which most users have access. (In Windows 9X, you right click on the printer icon in the lower right-hand corner of the screen to bring up the print queue manager.) You can delete your print job from the queue and take other actions, depending on your access rights.

IMPLEMENTING PRINT SERVICE

Figure 4.20 shows that print service actually is fairly complex. It also shows that the file server is involved in print service. In fact, the **print server** attached to the remote printer plays only a small role in print service.

The Print Server and Printer

To see why the role of the print server is limited, note that there is a print server for each remote printer. Obviously, print servers must cost much less than the server if you are to get economic benefits from print service. In practice, the print server is a very simple device. It has a built-in NIC to work with the network. It has a parallel port to feed the print job to the attached printer. It has a small amount of buffer RAM to hold print jobs. And it has just enough electronics to receive commands from the file server and to tell the file server when the print buffer is empty enough to accept another print job.

FIGURE **4.20**

Print Service

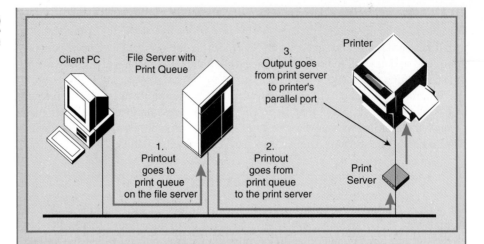

The printer, by the way, does not even know that a print server is feeding it. The output comes into the printer through the parallel port, just as it would if the PC were directly attached to the printer.

At the same time, some newer printers have built-in print servers. This allows them to receive data at 10 Mbps or at even higher speeds, instead of having to receive data through low-speed parallel ports. It also allows richer interactions with the file server, so problems can be assessed quickly.

Print Queues on the File Server

When the user at the client PC prints, Figure 4.20 shows that the print job first goes to the file server, where it is placed in a print queue. A **print queue** is nothing more than a directory on the file server. As new print jobs come in for that printer, they are added to the printer's print queue directory.

Typically, there is one print queue for each printer. When a person at a client PC prints, he or she selects a printer for the output. What the person is really selecting, however, is a print queue.

The file server has a printer **queue manager program** that oversees all of the print queues and the printers they serve. When a print server attached to a printer sends back a message indicating that it can accept another print job, the print queue manager reaches into the printer's print queue and sends a waiting print job to the print server.

Issuing the Print Command

To the user working at the client PC, the mechanics of network printing are largely hidden. The user uses his or her normal application program. When the user prints, he or she selects a printer from a list, which includes both printers directly attached to the client PC and remote printers.

Nor does the application program know that it is printing to a network printer. It simply prints to a normal parallel printer port. The PC operating system or client shell redirects the print job to the file server, where it is placed in the appropriate print queue.

Perspective

Overall, print service is a fairly complex process. However, the details normally are hidden from users. They merely select a printer by name and print to it as they normally do in their application programs.

Client/Server Application Servers

In Chapter 1, we saw that the limits of file server program access can be overcome through client/server processing. In client/server processing, the heavy work of information retrieval and other tasks is off-loaded from the client PC to the server application program on the application server. This frees the client PC's client program to focus on user interface matters. Freed from the confines of running only on the small client PC, application software can have unlimited scalability.

Recall from Chapter 1 that client/server processing is platform independent. Because we are talking about PC networking, the client machine will be a PC. However, the server can be a high-end PC, a workstation server, or some other high-end computer. This means that even on PC networks, where the client machines are PCs, there can be high scalability in applications.

Remote Access Servers

If you are at home or traveling, you sometimes need to get access to files on your PC network servers. As Figure 4.21 shows, many PC networks have **remote access servers**, which allow users to dial into the PC network via modems.

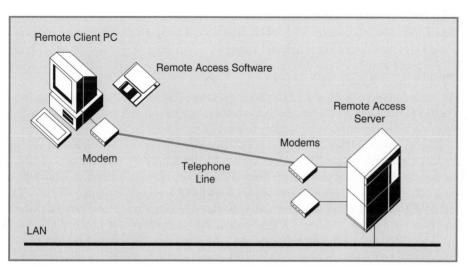

FIGURE 4.21

Remote Access Server

AUTHENTICATION

When the remote user first connects to the remote access server, the server asks the user to type his or her login name and password. The remote access server then compares the login name and password to an approved list. If the password **authenticates** the user (proves that the user is who the user says that he or she is), the user is given access to the same resources he or she could use through a desktop PC connected directly to the network. Once the user authenticates himself or herself, the remote access server basically becomes invisible to the user. Module F discusses more sophisticated forms of authentication.

REMOTE CONTROL CLIENT SOFTWARE

Figure 4.21 shows that the client PC dialing into the network needs **remote access client software** so that it can work with network resources after dialing in. This remote access client software must be matched to the remote access server software.

A remote user has access to exactly the same resources available to local users. However, remote access users typically use low-speed lines to reach the network. As a result, remote users do not enjoy the same response time that local users enjoy.

SUMMARY

In this chapter, we have looked at a simple PC network consisting of a few client PCs and servers on a single local area network (LAN). Although we will see in the next two chapters that many PC networks now have thousands of PCs and span multiple corporate sites, it is less confusing to start on a smaller scale. Even on a small scale, we have seen, PC networking on a LAN is fairly complex.

ELEMENTS

Figure 4.1 shows the elements of a small PC network on a single LAN. First, there are client PCs and servers. Client PCs receive services from servers. Usually, a stand-alone PC needs only a network interface card (NIC) to become a client PC. Servers require NICs as well. They also require a server operating system (SOS) designed for server operation, plus server application programs. The figure also shows the elements of the LAN itself, including a hub and wiring.

ETHERNET LAN TECHNOLOGY

We looked in some depth at LAN technology, at the OSI physical and data link layers. The IEEE 802 LAN MAN Standards Committee sets most LAN standards. The 802.3 Working Group of this committee sets Ethernet standards.

At the physical layer, we looked at Ethernet 802.3 10Base-T, which carries data at 10 Mbps, and at 100Base-TX, which operates at 100 Mbps. We saw that in both cases the hub merely repeats everything it hears. When a bit arrives at the hub, it is broadcast back out on all ports. This broadcasting is called a bus topology. Initially, 100Base-TX technology was far more expensive than 10Base-T technology. Now, however, their cost is so similar that 100Base-TX has become the standard for new installations.

The IEEE 802 Committee divided the data link layer into two sublayers: logical link control and media access control. This gives a six-layer TCP/IP–IEEE architecture: application, transport, internet, logical link control, media access control, and physical layers.

The media access control (MAC) layer specifies when stations may transmit. On shared media LANs, only one station may transmit at a time. Ethernet 802.3 uses CSMA/CD media access control, in which a station transmits only when it hears no other station transmitting, stops transmitting if another station transmits while it is transmitting, and tries again later when the line is free.

The logical link control layer (LLC) optionally does error detection and correction. It also links the logical link control layer program to the programs handling internet layer protocols.

OTHER LAN TECHNOLOGIES

The box "Token-Ring Networks" looked briefly at token-ring transmission. At the physical layer, token-ring networks use a ring topology, rather than the bus (broadcasting) topology of Ethernet networks. At the MAC layer, token-ring networks use token passing for media access control, rather than the CSMA/CD access control method used on Ethernet networks.

THE INTERNET AND TRANSPORT LAYERS

Above the logical link control layers, we have the internet and transport layers. Many server operating systems, including UNIX and Microsoft Windows NT, use TCP/IP standards at these layers. Novell NetWare can also use TCP/IP in its newer versions, but many organizations still implement its older IPX/SPX standards. Fortunately, a client PC can use both sets of internet and transport layer protocols. A client PC can even work with a TCP/IP server and an IPX/SPX server simultaneously.

APPLICATION LAYER SERVICES

At the application layer, we looked at a number of widely used services. The most common is file service, in which individuals and groups have access to both data and application program files on a file server. File servers essentially give the user additional and shareable disk storage capacity.

In print service, when the user prints, the output goes to a printer attached to the network. While the job is waiting to be printed, the user can delete the job or take other actions.

In file server program access, the application program and related data files are downloaded to the client PC for execution there. This limits the size of the program because many client PCs have very limited processing capacity. Client/server processing ends this size limit by doing heavy tasks on the application server.

Finally, in remote access service, users can connect to the network from home or while traveling. Remote users have access to the same resources as local users.

REVIEW QUESTIONS

CORE REVIEW QUESTIONS

1. Distinguish between client PCs and servers. What do you have to add to a Windows 95 or 98 PC to make it a client PC? What do you have to add to a PC to

make it a server? What are the elements of a LAN to connect the PCs of a PC network?

2. List the six layers of the hybrid TCP/IP–IEEE framework used for LAN standards. How does it differ from the five-layer TCP/IP–OSI framework introduced in Chapter 1? Which layers are subnet layers? Which layers are implemented by the NIC?

3. Explain each of the elements of "Ethernet 802.3 10Base-T" and "Ethernet 802.3 100Base-TX." At what layer are these standards defined? Why are many organizations upgrading from 10Base-T to 100Base-TX? Why is this upgrade easy and inexpensive?

4. When the first bit of a frame reaches the hub, what does the hub do? What is the characteristic of the bus topology at the physical layer?

5. (From the box "Electrical Signaling") How does Ethernet 802.3 10Base-T represent a one? Why does it do this instead of representing a one as a simple high or low voltage?

6. What is media access control? At what layer is it implemented? Explain how Ethernet 802.3 handles access control.

7. All the LAN standards discussed in this chapter are shared media standards. In a shared media network of any type, if you have 200 stations on the network, how many may transmit at a time?

8. Name each of the fields in the Ethernet 802.3 MAC layer frame, including the length (in octets) and the purpose of each. What does the receiving NIC do if it detects an error?

9. What is the single logical link control layer standard for all IEEE LANs? What error control options does it offer network administrators? What is its function other than error control?

10. (From the box "Token-Ring Networks") Compare Ethernet and token-ring networks in terms of physical layer topology. Compare them in terms of MAC layer media access control. Compare them in terms of LLC layer standards.

11. One file server uses TCP/IP standards. Another uses IPX/SPX standards. Both operate on an Ethernet LAN. At what layers do they have the same standards? At what layers do they have different standards? Can a client PC communicate with both an IPX/SPX server and a TCP/IP server at the same time?

12. What are the three factors to take into account in deciding how many servers to use to implement a PC network's services?

13. Does file service allow file sharing by several people? What happens if two users try to change the same file at the same time? What are access rights?

14. In print service, why is printing to a remote printer the same for a user as printing to a printer directly attached to the user's PC? In what good way is it different?

15. Distinguish between file server program access and client/server processing in terms of the size of applications that may be executed.

DETAILED REVIEW QUESTIONS

1. After the 802.3 Working Group creates a new candidate standard, what steps must the candidate standard go through to become a full OSI standard? When do vendors begin building products?

2. How many wires are there in an 802.3 10Base-T/100Base-TX wiring bundle? How many are actually used in transmission? How would you answer if someone asked you what "Cat 5" means?

3. (From the box "Electrical Signaling") What is the baud rate of Ethernet 10Base-T networks? How does Manchester encoding encode ones? How does it encode zeros? Why does it place a transition in the middle of each bit period? Why is the 4B/5B encoding used in 100Base-TX better?

4. What is the size of address fields in 802.3 MAC layer frames? Why does every NIC have a unique 802.3 MAC layer address when it comes from the factory? What is the minimum size of 802.3 MAC layer frames? What is the maximum size of these frames? What is in the data field of a typical MAC layer frame?

5. (From the box "802.2 Logical Link Control Layer Frame") In 802.2, what is the purpose of the DSAP and SSAP fields? What field is used to implement error control if error control is selected? What additional information is added by a SNAP PDU if there is one?

6. What problems can arise when a client PC **transmits** to a Novell NetWare file server, a UNIX application server, and a Windows NT webserver simultaneously? How does the adaption layer standard solve this problem? What problem occurs when a client PC **receives** from these three servers? How does the adaption layer software solve this problem?

7. (From the box "Implementing Print Service") Where does a print job go after it leaves your PC—to the file server or to the print server? Why is this done?

THOUGHT QUESTIONS

1. Your organization has 10 employees, each with his or her own stand-alone PC running Windows 98. List **all** the additional hardware and software you would have to buy to install a simple PC network. Be very sure that you list all the things the organization will have to buy. The organization wishes to use electronic mail, word processing, file sharing, and print sharing with one existing printer.

2. Explain the steps a receiving station takes when it receives an Ethernet 802.3 frame **not** intended for it. (Begin with "The receiving station's MAC layer process reads the preamble and start of frame delimiter fields to synchronize its clock with the sender's clock.")

3. Explain the steps a receiving station takes when it receives an Ethernet 802.3 frame intended for it, including what it does when it finishes processing the entire frame.

4. (From the box "802.2 Logical Link Control Layer Frame") Your NIC is receiving an 802.3 MAC layer frame containing an 802.2 LLC frame with no data field. The 802.2 control field is two octets. List all the fields your NIC will encounter through the end of the MAC layer frame. Give the size of each. Give the total size of the frame.

5. (From the box "802.2 Logical Link Control Layer Frame") Your NIC is receiving an 802.3 MAC layer frame containing an IP packet whose data field has 400 bytes of data. List all the fields your NIC will encounter through the end of the MAC layer frame. Give the size of each. Give the total size of the frame. The 802.2 control field is one octet long.

6. (From the box "802.2 Logical Link Control Layer Frame") Write the binary numbers for 0 through 17. Convert the following hexadecimal values to binary: 00-00-00 hex, 03 hex, and AA hex. What types of games use Base 13? How do they handle the values 11, 12, and 13?

7. You are a project leader with two project members. What rights might you want for yourself and for them in a shared project directory?

PROJECTS

1. At the book's website, http://www.prenhall.com/panko, read the Updates Page for errors found in the text and for new information since the book went to press.

2. At the book's website, http://www.prenhall.com/panko, do the Internet Exercises for this chapter.

3. The chapter's Internet Exercises page has you cost out the elements of an Ethernet 802.3 10Base-T LAN, including NICs, hubs, and wiring. Cost out the LAN needed in Thought Question 1. Cost it out again using 100Base-TX.

4. Using the same sources as in the last question, compare the prices of Microsoft Windows NT Server and Novell NetWare for 10 users. Also compare how much you would have to pay if you had 75 users.

5. Use the settings option to set up a Windows 95 computer or a Windows 98 computer to work with a Windows NT or Novell NetWare file server.

6. Install a NIC in a computer.

CHAPTER 5

Larger Networks I: Transmission

INTRODUCTION

In the last chapter, we looked at a small PC network using Ethernet 802.3 10Base-T or 100Base-TX technology. That small local area network (LAN) had only a single hub and a handful of personal computers.

In larger organizations, things are very different, as Figure 5.1 illustrates.

▶ **Site networks** connect multiple LANs at a corporate site (location). Site networks consist of individual LANs plus devices and transmission lines that link the LANs together.

▶ On a larger scale, **enterprise networks** connect computers across multiple sites in the firm. Enterprise networks consist of several site networks plus devices and wide area networks (WANs) to link the site networks together.

Creating site and enterprise networks is a challenging task. In this chapter, we will look at issues at the bottom layers of the TCP/IP–OSI architecture, namely the physical, data link, and internet layers, as shown in Figure 5.2. In the next chapter, we will look at upper-layer concerns in site and enterprise networks, as we deal with servers and network management.

Note that Figure 5.2 shows that hubs work only at layer 1, the physical layer. Their operation is purely physical and electrical. When a bit comes into a port, it is reflected out all other ports. This simplicity makes hubs extremely inexpensive.

To build larger networks, however, we will need to work with more sophisticated devices to connect stations, LANs, and site networks. Specifically, we will look at *switches* and *routers*. Figure 5.2 shows that switches operate at the data link layer (layer 2), whereas routers work at the internet layer (layer 3). Do not worry if you do

FIGURE **5.1**

**LANs, Site
Networks, WANs,
and Enterprise
Networks**

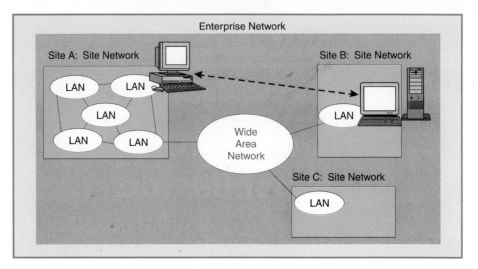

not understand the distinction now, but be sure you understand it by the end of the chapter, because it is fundamental.

EXTENDING SMALL NETWORKS

Before dealing with the full complexity of site networks, we will consider a simpler case, namely a single local area network somewhat larger than the single-hub network we saw in the previous chapter.

Both Ethernet 10Base-T and Ethernet 100Base-TX specify a maximum distance of 100 meters between each station and the hub that serves it. So there is a maximum distance of only 200 meters between the farthest two stations in such a network. (Think "station—100 meters—hub—100 meters—station.")

Multiple Hubs in Ethernet 10Base-T

A simple way to get around the limitation of 200 meters is to add another hub. Figure 5.3 shows that in 10Base-T you merely connect the two hubs. (We will look at 100Base-TX later.)

FIGURE **5.2**

**Layering in
Large Networks**

LAYER	DEVICE	DESCRIPTION
1	Hub	Single path between devices Transmission of one bit at a time without framing
2	Switch	Single path between devices Management of frame transmissions between devices Flat addressing
3	Router	Alternative routing Hierarchical addressing

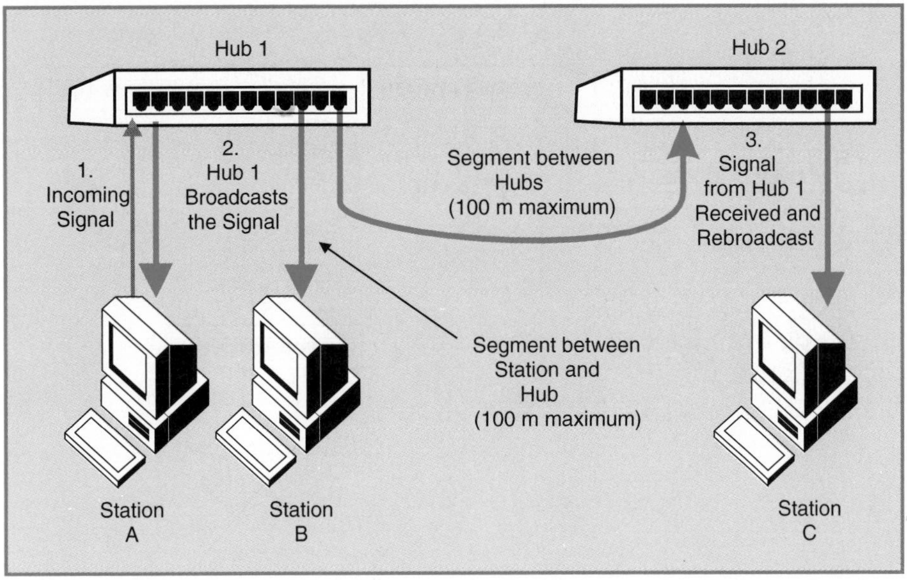

FIGURE **5.3**

**Two-Hub Ethernet
10Base-T LAN**

- In Figure 5.3, Station A is transmitting to Hub 1.
- Hub 1 broadcasts the signal back to Station A and to all other stations attached to Hub 1, including Station B. This is exactly what we saw in the previous chapter.
- In addition, Hub 1 broadcasts the signal out the line to Hub 2.
- When the signal reaches the second hub, Hub 2 treats the signal as if it were coming from a station. Hub 2 broadcasts the signal out to all stations attached to it, including Station C.

Overall, when any station attached to a hub transmits, its signal is broadcast to all other stations attached to both hubs. In effect, it is almost as if there were a single large hub rather than two connected hubs.[1]

MULTIPLE HUBS

Do you need to stop at two hubs? The answer is no. As Figure 5.4 shows, you can connect multiple 10Base-T hubs.

MAXIMUM DISTANCE SPAN

However, there are some rules for connecting hubs. First, you cannot have more than four hubs between the two farthest stations. If you connect hubs with 10Base-T wiring, this means a maximum distance of 500 meters between the farthest stations. (Think S—H—H—H—H—S, and think of the dashes as 100 meter links.)

NO LOOPS

The second rule is that you cannot connect the hubs in a loop. If you look at Figure 5.4, you will see that there are no loops among the hubs. If you want to see why there is a "no loops" rule, consider the case of three hubs connected in a loop. The first hub

---

[1] You cannot connect any port on one hub to any other port on another hub. Hubs that can be connected have special ports for connecting to other hubs. Module C discusses these special ports.

FIGURE **5.4**

**Multiple Ethernet
10Base-T Hubs**

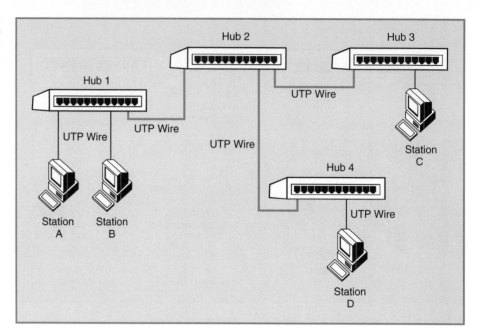

would broadcast to the second, which would broadcast to the third, which would broadcast back to the first. The first would then send the signal back out, beginning the second of an infinite number of cycles.

Multiple Hubs in Ethernet 100Base-TX

We have been focusing on Ethernet 10Base-T. We saw that an Ethernet 10Base-T LAN can have up to four hubs between the farthest two stations. What is the situation in Ethernet 100Base-TX?

The answer is that although Ethernet 100Base-TX is very fast, it pays for its high speed with distance limitations. First, there can be only two hubs between the farthest two stations, as shown in Figure 5.5. Second, the two hubs must be separated by at

FIGURE **5.5**

**Hubs in Ethernet
100Base-TX**

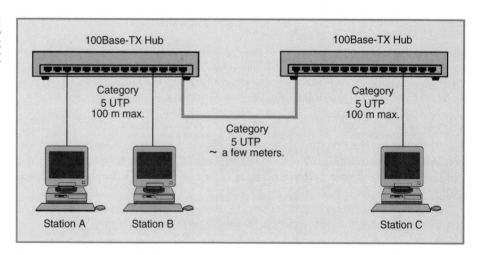

most a few meters. Typically, they are right next to each other or stacked one on top of the other. So the maximum distance between the farthest stations in a 100Base-TX LAN is only about 200 meters.

SITE NETWORKS

Distance limitations of 200 to 500 meters between the farthest stations are too restrictive for large sites. We need a way to connect multiple LANs into larger site networks.

Congestion in Shared Media LANs

An even bigger problem with individual LANs is traffic jams. Ethernet is a **shared media** technology. This means that all the devices attached to the network must share the limited transmission capacity of the network. Figure 5.6 shows that, when one station transmits, all other stations must wait. Even if you have a thousand-station LAN, only one station can transmit at a time, and all others must wait.

If you have only a few stations, the average waiting time will be negligible. However, as you add more stations, the delay (called **latency**) increases. As you add stations, latency first becomes annoying and eventually becomes crippling.

In essence, the LAN becomes **congested.** Although 10 Mbps sounds very fast, when it is shared with many stations, latency becomes unacceptable. Just as multilane freeways become congested at rush hour, shared media LANs become congested if you have too many stations. In Ethernet 10Base-T, congestion becomes crippling at 200 to 300 stations.

Of course, congestion is much less on 100Base-TX LANs than on 10Base-T LANs. When each station transmits on a 100Base-TX LAN, its transmission takes only a tenth as long as it would on a 10Base-T LAN. So waits to transmit fall to a tenth of what they would be on a 10Base-T LAN (approximately). So you can have about ten times as many stations on a 100Base-TX LAN as you would on a 10Base-T LAN.

Of course, the ability of 100Base-TX LANs to serve more stations is not very helpful in practice because of the 200-meter limit. Few organizations have hundreds of stations within such a small area. In addition, as multimedia applications grow, even 100Base-TX LANs with 200 to 300 stations will soon become congested or, as it is commonly said, LAN-locked.

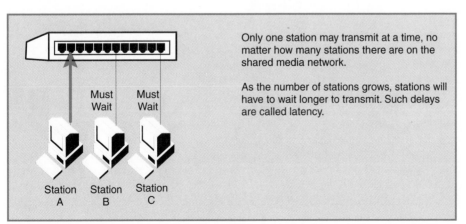

Only one station may transmit at a time, no matter how many stations there are on the shared media network.

As the number of stations grows, stations will have to wait longer to transmit. Such delays are called latency.

Must Wait   Must Wait

Station A   Station B   Station C

FIGURE 5.6

Shared Media LAN

FIGURE 5.7

**Hubs Permit Only
One Conversation
at a Time**

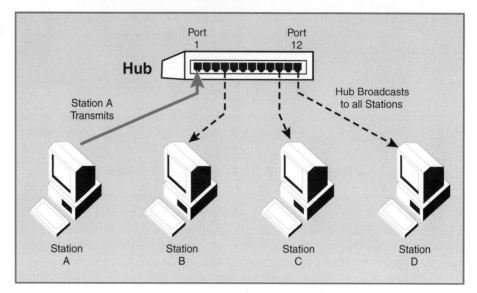

Hubs versus Switches

Congestion occurs because hubs broadcast incoming signals out to all attached stations, as Figure 5.7 illustrates. If Station A is transmitting to Station C, all other stations receive the message. If Station B wants to send to Station D, it must wait.

Figure 5.8 shows that devices called **switches** work differently. Again, Station A is transmitting to Station C. This time, however, there is a switch instead of a hub. Instead of blindly reflecting each bit back out, the switch looks at the Ethernet frame and examines the destination address. The switch has a table that shows it that the addressed station, Station C, is on Port 5. So the switch sends the signal only out Port 5. Stations B and D on Ports 2 and 6 do not hear the frame transmission.

FIGURE 5.8

**Switches Allow
Multiple
Simultaneous
Conversations**

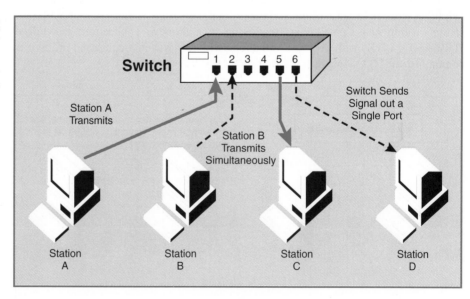

Now there is no problem with Station B transmitting to Station D. It sends its frame to the switch on Port 2. Reading the destination address in the 802.3 MAC layer frame, the switch recognizes that Station D is on Port 6. It sends the frame out Port 6.

Is there a problem with these two transmissions taking place at the same time? The answer is no. As long as the switch has sufficient switching capacity, Stations A and B can transmit frames at the same time. Because their signals travel in and out different switch ports, they do not interfere. There is no need to wait. So there is no latency.

Think of the telephone system, which uses switches. You and your neighbors can all use your telephones at the same time because telephone switches have many ports and each of you is attached to a different port. Only if someone tries to call someone who is already engaged in another conversation will there be a busy signal. Data switches work the same way.

Ethernet: 10Base-T, 100Base-TX, and 10Base-T Switching

Today, corporations have a difficult decision to make when they wire new offices. The cheapest solution is a 10Base-T LAN, but it costs only a little more to install a 100Base-TX LAN.

A 100Base-TX LAN, furthermore, costs only about as much as an all-switched LAN in which stations attach directly to 10Base-T switches. Pure 100Base-TX and switched 10Base-T LANs, furthermore, give comparable performance.

It is even possible to mix 10 Mbps and 100 Mbps devices on a single hub or switch. Figure 5.9 shows a switch that has 10Base-T connections for client PCs and a 100Base-TX connection for a server, which has heavier communication requirements.

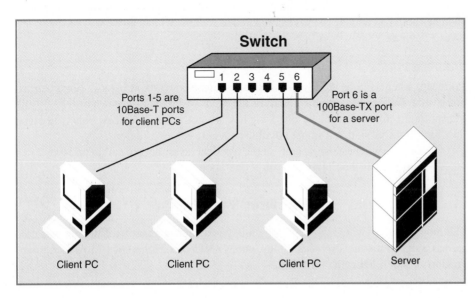

FIGURE **5.9**

Mixed 10Base-T and 100Base-TX Switch

Layer 2 Switch Operation

Recall that hubs operate only at layer 1, the physical layer. When the electrical signal for a bit arrives, the hub broadcasts the bit signal out over all ports. This is very simple and so very inexpensive. Note that the physical layer works one bit at a time. It does not examine the contents of frames.

LAYER 2: FRAME ANALYSIS

Switches are more sophisticated. They must examine every frame coming into them. They first determine the destination address of each frame. They then look at a table to see what port is associated with that frame. They then send the frame out that port. Because switches deal with the content of frame fields (specifically addresses fields), rather than just reflecting individual bits, they are data link layer devices. They work at layer 2.

LAYER 2: SINGLE PATH

Another characteristic of layer 2 operation is that there is only a single possible path between any two stations connected to the network.

In an Ethernet 10Base-T network with a single hub, for instance, there is only one possible path from the sending NIC to the receiving NIC. This is up to the hub and back down again.

With multiple hubs, Figure 5.4 shows that there is still only a single path between any two stations. Because the hubs must be arranged in a strict hierarchy, with no loops, there is one and only one possible path between any two stations.

We will see below that the two most popular switching technologies for site networks—Ethernet switches and ATM switches—use different approaches to reduce transmissions to a single possible path between sender and receiver. Both technologies, however, do restrict transmissions to a single possible path.

Layer 2 operation is attractive because if there is only a single possible path between devices, switches do not have to spend large amounts of processing capacity to compute alternative routes. They merely take in each frame, look at a table to see which port serves the destination address, and send the frame out that port. This makes switches both fast and inexpensive compared to routers, which, as we will see later, are layer 3 devices.

PERSPECTIVE

To recap, whereas hubs are layer 1 devices, switches operate at layer 2. Switches are not layer 1 devices because they analyze the fields of incoming frames instead of just transmitting information bit by bit. Switches are not layer 3 devices, either, because they limit transmission to a single possible path between two stations.

Of course, switches also operate at the physical layer, but we call them layer 2 devices because that is their highest layer of operation.

Ethernet Switches

The most popular switching technology today is switched Ethernet. Ethernet was created as a shared media LAN technology, not as a switched technology. However, many vendors now sell **Ethernet switches.**

WORKING WITH EXISTING TECHNOLOGY

Ethernet switching is attractive because it works with existing Ethernet components already in your LAN.

► If you attach a station directly to an Ethernet switch, your existing Ethernet NIC will work with the switch without change.

► If, instead, you connect an Ethernet hub to an Ethernet switch, you do not have to modify the hub or buy a new one.

The ability to work with existing NICs and hubs makes Ethernet switching very attractive. You get the benefits of switching with a minimum of equipment replacement and staff retraining.

FULL-DUPLEX ETHERNET SWITCHING

Although switched Ethernet can use existing NICs, you may wish to upgrade at least some of them to achieve *full-duplex* service. Figure 5.10 shows that normal Ethernet gives *half-duplex* service. This means that a device cannot simultaneously send to another station and receive from another station. In normal Ethernet, if two stations transmit at the same time, you have a collision. So if Station B is receiving, as it is in the figure, it cannot also be transmitting.

Switching eliminates that problem. Switches do not have collisions if two stations transmit simultaneously, as we saw in Figure 5.8. So nothing prevents a station from simultaneously sending and receiving. Nothing, that is to say, except the NIC. Standard Ethernet NICs are inherently half-duplex. Special full-duplex Ethernet NICs, however, are available. For some stations, especially servers, the ability to send and receive at the same time can boost throughput significantly.

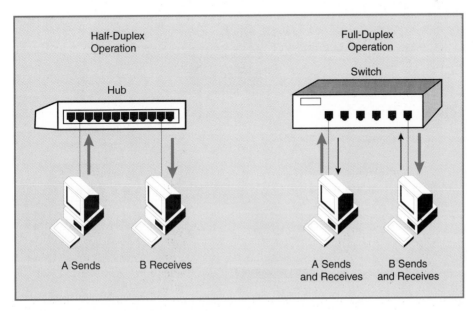

FIGURE 5.10

Half-Duplex and Full-Duplex Ethernet

LOW COST

Another reason Ethernet switches are attractive is cost. Ethernet switches are the least expensive switches available. Many vendors make Ethernet switches, creating intense competition that drives down prices and spurs vendors to introduce new features constantly.

SCALABILITY

Ethernet switches come in various speeds. By far the most popular are Ethernet 10Base-T switches, which offer speeds of 10 Mbps and work with 10Base-T NICs and hubs. Next come 100Base-TX and 100Base-FX switches, designed to work with NICs and hubs following that standard. Finally, there are 1000Base-TX Ethernet switches that work with gigabit Ethernet equipment.

DEVICE HIERARCHIES

Often, firms have a hierarchy of 10Base-T switches, 100Base-TX switches, and gigabit Ethernet switches, as shown in Figure 5.11. At each layer in the hierarchy, the firm can choose a switch in the required speed range.

When a technology can span a wide range of speeds without changing protocol, we say that it is highly **scalable.** Scalability is important because whenever the network staff must change technologies, there are large costs in retraining. The scalability of Ethernet switching makes it very attractive because it can serve demand from a few megabits per second to a gigabit per second.

LAYER 2 OPERATION

Figure 5.11 shows why Ethernet switches are layer 2 devices. Ethernet switches *must* be arranged in a hierarchy, as the figure illustrates. This means that there is only one possible path between any two stations. Hierarchical organization in switching forces single-path operation, just as it does for hubs.

FIGURE 5.11

Hierarchy of Ethernet Switches

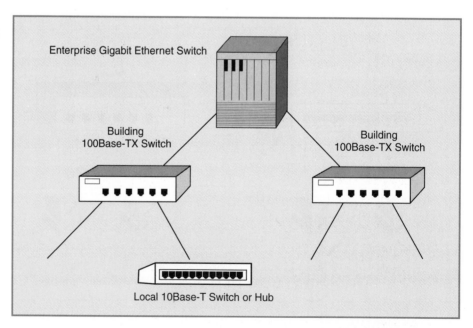

Enterprise Gigabit Ethernet Switch

Building 100Base-TX Switch

Building 100Base-TX Switch

Local 10Base-T Switch or Hub

Single-path operation also explains why Ethernet switches are inexpensive. They do not have to worry about alternative routes between any pair of NICs.

Ethernet switches also have the other characteristic of layer 2 devices: They analyze frames (unlike hubs). An Ethernet switch must analyze each frame to know which out port to use to retransmit the frame.

Virtual LANs

One especially important Ethernet switching feature is the **virtual LAN** or **VLAN.** Figure 5.12 shows that switches can cluster devices into groups called virtual LANs. A client PC on a virtual LAN can reach only file servers on the same VLAN. It is as if the switched network really consisted of multiple unconnected individual LANs.

SECURITY

One reason for VLANs is security. A client PC on the marketing VLAN cannot connect to a server on the accounting VLAN, even if the user has the correct password for the server. The switch's VLAN software blocks the transmission. Otherwise, anyone working at any client PC could get access to any server simply by knowing the password, which is easily compromised.

BROADCAST STORMS

A second reason for VLANs is to reduce the effect of broadcast messages. Recall that the 802.3 MAC layer frame has a destination field. Each NIC listens for its own unique address in the destination field. However, each NIC also looks in the destination field for a group of "broadcast addresses" that are designed to work like public address systems. Every NIC processes frames sent to these broadcast addresses. For example, file

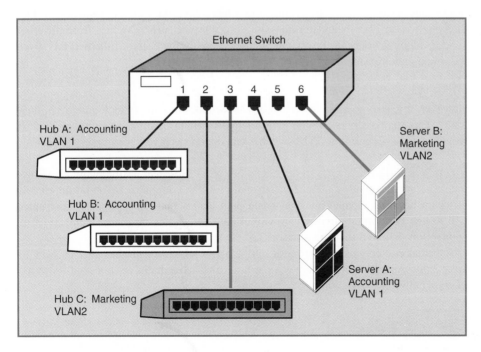

FIGURE 5.12
Virtual LAN (VLAN)

servers typically send broadcast frames advertising their availability every minute or so. All NICs should listen to these frames.

As networks get larger, broadcasting by servers and other stations begins to eat up a great deal of transmission capacity. Each broadcast message creates a *broadcast storm* that sends messages out every port on every switch. With a VLAN, however, a server's broadcast messages are allowed to go only to stations on the server's VLAN. This greatly reduces the traffic generated by broadcast frames.

CUTTING ACROSS VLANS

VLANs are very good for breaking a large site network into multiple smaller pieces. However, VLANs are less adept at linking client PCs and servers on different VLANs if cross-VLAN communication is necessary. For instance, it might be necessary to give a client PC on the marketing VLAN temporary or permanent access to the accounting server on the accounting VLAN. This requires extra functionality in the switching software because it must provide exceptions to the very nature of the way that VLANs operate.

Different vendors often implement VLANs and cross-VLAN communication in different ways. This prevents you from mixing switches from different vendors if you wish to use VLAN features. The IEEE is currently working on a VLAN standard.

ATM Switches

Another important switching technology is ATM switching. **ATM** does not stand for "automated teller machine." It means **"asynchronous transfer mode."** This name is not very enlightening, so everyone just calls the technology ATM.

ATM HIERARCHICAL SWITCHING

Sometimes ATM switches are arranged in a hierarchy, like Ethernet switches. In fact the widely used PNNI standard that is used to connect ATM switches from different vendors requires you to use a switch hierarchy.[2] As in the case of Ethernet, this gives the single-path transmission characteristic of layer 2 operation.

MESH ATM NETWORKS

However, it is also possible to arrange ATM switches in a mesh, as Figure 5.13 illustrates. This implies loops, which give alternative routes. So the presence of a mesh would seem to suggest that ATM switches can operate as layer 3 devices.

Virtual Circuits (Connection-Oriented Service) However, as the figure also illustrates, before two stations attached to the network can communicate, a **virtual circuit** is set up between them. This is a single path across multiple switches. All frames will follow this virtual circuit. This virtual path creates a connection. The service is **connection-oriented** transmission service.

Virtual circuits change the mesh into a single possible path, bringing us back to layer 2 operation. Although there is a mesh, its alternative paths are not used for transmission between two stations.

---

[2] Stephen Saunders and Jay Ranade, The *McGraw-Hill High Speed LANs Handbook* (New York: McGraw-Hill, 1991), p. 114. Within a hierarchical level, however, several switches can be connected in a simple daisy chain. Only one of these daisy-chained switches has an uplink to the next-higher-level switch.

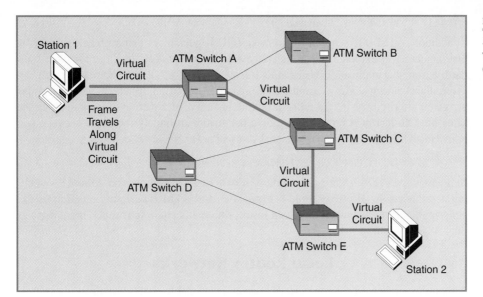

FIGURE **5.13**

**ATM Switch Mesh
with Virtual
Circuits**

Permanent Virtual Circuits Virtual circuits come in two types. First, a **permanent virtual circuit (PVC)** can be set up between a pair of stations. It will be used every time the two stations communicate.

Switched Virtual Circuits In contrast, a **switched virtual circuit (SVC)** is set up only when one station wishes to connect to another. If the first station wished to connect to the same partner the next day, it might receive an entirely different SVC. This requires more switching processing power and more complex switch software.

ATM Addresses The importance of virtual circuits in ATM is perhaps most obvious in ATM frame addresses. In the PDUs we saw in earlier chapters, each PDU had a destination address of some sort. In IP, for instance, the destination address was a 32-bit internet address. Every host on a TCP/IP network must have an internet address.

In contrast, ATM frames do not use the destination addresses of stations. Instead, each outgoing frame contains the **virtual circuit number** for the virtual circuit that connects the two stations. To give a rough analogy, if you are flying on a commercial airline, you give the flight number rather than the destination city.

ITU-T

The International Telecommunications Union–Telecommunications Standards Sector (ITU-T) sets ATM standards. This is the standards agency for telephony in general, and ATM grew out of efforts to produce a new high-speed, all-digital telephone network.

SCALABILITY

ATM switches, like Ethernet switches, are highly scalable. In fact, whereas Ethernet switching currently stops at one gigabit per second, ATM can operate at several gigabits per second. The most popular ATM speeds are 155 Mbps and 622 Mbps.

QUALITY OF SERVICE GUARANTEES

In addition, ATM offers **quality of service (QOS)** guarantees that switched Ethernet is just beginning to explore. If there is congestion in the network, quality of service standards ensure that applications that cannot tolerate delays, such as telephony and video, are given higher priority. This is similar to railroad transportation, in which passenger trains are given priority over freight trains if both trains arrive at a section of track at about the same time. In fact, it is possible to reserve bandwidth absolutely for traffic between two points in a virtual circuit. This means that you will never be cut off or suffer congestion.

HIGH SPEED, HIGH FUNCTIONALITY, HIGH COST

In many ways, ATM is the gold standard in switching. In comparison, Ethernet switching is rather crude. However, gold is expensive, and ATM is currently much more expensive than Ethernet switching. As a result, Ethernet switching is much more popular than ATM switching.

Local Router Networks

Although switches offer good performance at a reasonable cost, some firms use routers instead of switches for their local site networks, or at least for parts of these networks. Developed originally for the Internet, which has thousands of routers, routers can handle the most complicated local networking situations.

ALTERNATIVE ROUTES

As discussed above, switches operate at layer 2, in which there is only a single possible path between any two stations. Ethernet switches are layer 2 devices because they are arranged in a hierarchy, which has only one possible physical path between any two stations. Some ATM networks are also hierarchical. Others use a mesh but constrain transmissions to a single path through virtual circuits.

Having only one possible path between stations makes switching very simple and, therefore, fast and inexpensive. A switch does not have to waste CPU cycles deciding what to do with each incoming frame. It merely looks at a table relating the data link layer address of the destination station to a port number. It then sends the incoming frame out the appropriate port.

In contrast, when routers are connected in a mesh, as shown in Figure 5.14, they make use of the fact that there are many possible **alternative routes** between any two stations. The figure shows just one alternative route between two stations across the mesh of routers. You can trace a number of other alternative routes between the two stations. To give an analogy, if you drive from one place to another in a city, there are many possible ways to get between these two places.

LAYER 3 OPERATION

Alternative Routing In layer 2 operation, there is only a single possible path between two stations. Alternative routing requires layer 3 operation. Higher-level standards are needed for routing across complex meshes and for router–router coordination to ensure the best possible routing of messages.

Hierarchical Addressing Another characteristic of layer 3 operation is hierarchical addressing. In Ethernet, which operates at layer 2, there is **flat addressing.** You cannot tell from a station's MAC layer address what Ethernet switch serves that station. Nor

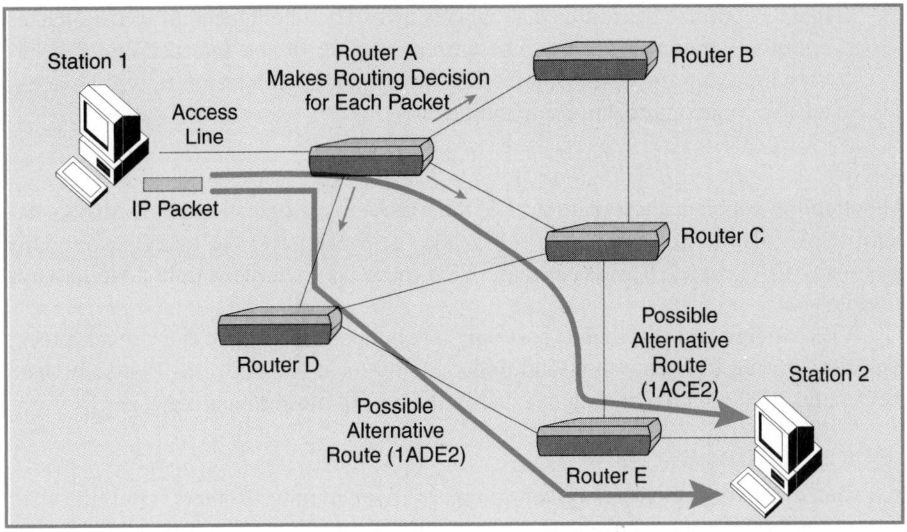

FIGURE 5.14

Mesh Router
Network

Figure content labels: Station 1, Access Line, IP Packet, Router A Makes Routing Decision for Each Packet, Router B, Router C, Router D, Possible Alternative Route (1ADE2), Router E, Possible Alternative Route (1ACE2), Station 2

can you tell from an ATM virtual circuit number what switch serves a particular station. Switching tables must be established within all the switches.

In contrast, routers use **hierarchical addressing.** As we saw in Chapter 2, IP uses either two-level or three-level hierarchical addressing. In three-level addressing, a router first looks at the network and subnet parts of the IP packet's internet address and compares it with the router's own network and subnet parts. If the network and subnet parts are different, the router knows that the destination host is on a different network. So the router sends the IP packet to a boundary router for packets going out of the organization. However, if the internet and subnet parts of the router and the destination host are the same, the router delivers the packet directly to the destination host.

BENEFITS OF ALTERNATIVE ROUTING

Alternative routing has three main benefits. Together, these make routers very attractive in complex local networks.

- ▶ **Routing around Failures.** Most dramatically, if a router or a line between two routers fails, routers automatically send packets through another route.
- ▶ **Routing around Congestion.** The outright failure of a router (or switch) does not happen too often. It is much more common for a router or a line between routers to become *congested* due to transient traffic conditions. In such cases, advanced routers will do **load balancing,** in which they reroute some traffic to other routes that transfer part of the load to more lightly used routers and transmission lines.
- ▶ **Optimized Routing.** In general, advanced routers in the mesh work together to ensure that each packet travels over the best possible route. This often means the *least expensive* route. Some packets, however, might require a different goal for the routers. For instance, a voice packet in a two-way conversation cannot tolerate delay, so you might want to send packets in this stream over the *lowest-latency* route. If the packet is part of a financial transaction, furthermore, you might want to send it over the *most secure* route. In general, you would

like to optimize the routes that packets take. The intelligence of routers makes *optimized routing* possible. The current version of the Internet Protocol has very limited route optimization. The next version, IP Version 6, will have extensive route optimization capabilities.

COSTS

Although the sophistication of routers is very attractive, sophistication is always expensive. A complex routing decision is made for every packet at every router. This uses many CPU cycles. This is far more CPU-intensive than the simple table lookups of switches.

Whereas entry-level switches cost only a few thousand dollars, entry-level routers typically cost ten to twenty thousand dollars. Only local site networks that truly need the benefits of alternative routing can justify the cost of mesh router networks.

ROUTER COORDINATION

In a routed network, there is no central control over routing. Routers, after all, were created for the Internet, whose tens of thousands of routers could not possibly be centrally controlled.

Yet somehow, each router must make a routing decision for every packet that arrives. A router will have multiple ports. If a packet arrives at Port 2, then a router with four ports must decide whether to send it out Port 1, 3, or 4.

How does the router know which port will lead to the best router for sending the packet toward its destination? The answer is that routers constantly talk to one another. As Figure 5.15 shows, routers frequently send *coordination packets* to nearby routers that tell other routers what the sender knows about nearby conditions. As a result, each router has a reasonably good understanding of which routers are nearby and whether failure or congestion conditions are occurring. This constant information exchange allows intelligent routing using only peer-peer communication.

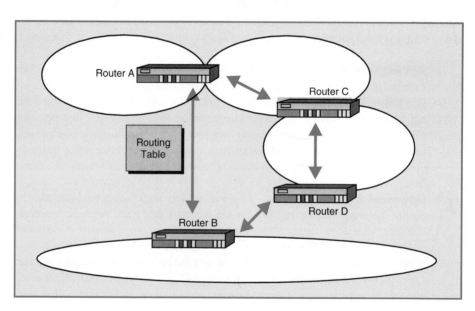

FIGURE 5.15

Exchange of Routing Information among Routers

Closing the Gap between Switches and Routers

Until recently, routers and switches represented extremes in speed and cost. In terms of speed, switches could process many more frames per second than routers could process packets per second. This speed difference stemmed primarily from the fact that routers had to do much more processing on each incoming packet than switches had to do on incoming frames, because routing a packet across an internet is much more complex than selecting an outgoing port in a switch.

In recent years, however, both switch and router vendors have been closing the gap between their products. Marketers have confused the picture considerably by offering up a wide variety of names for often similar technologies as well as by using the same name for different technologies.

SWITCHES WITH ADDED ROUTING

In general, switching vendors have attempted to add simple routing to their switching software. Often, there are many switches in a network. **Edge switches** connect these switching networks to the outside world. These edge switches analyze incoming IP packets, place the IP packets in frames, and create virtual circuits to send the frames across the switched network to the destination computer. Adding routing to edge switches can route IP packets to the proper destination while maintaining the cost effectiveness of switches. In ATM, the *Multiprotocol Over ATM (MPOA)* standard provides a standardized way to add routing to switching networks.

FLOW ROUTERS

Router vendors, in turn, have begun to add the equivalent of virtual circuits to the internet layer. These devices, called **layer 3 switches,** create flows that specify that a series of packets will all travel through the same series of switches without packet-by-packet decision making.

Figure 5.16 illustrates one approach to layer 3 switching. Here, an edge router observes that a series of incoming IP packets are going to the same destination host. The edge router then specifies that subsequent packets in the series will all be sent out the same port. No longer does the router have to do complex routing. Although the router is called a layer 3 switch, it is really a router with added software for **flow recognition.**

Another approach to layer 3 switching is **flow specification.** Here, special fields called tags are added to each IP packet. Tags specify that a particular IP packet is part of a flow. The routers in the network look up the flow designation in a table and send the tagged packet back out without going through all of the complexities of routing decisions.

ASIC ROUTERS

The reason that traditional routers were so slow was that they were really general purpose computers. The complex routing decisions that had to be made when a packet arrived had to be handled in a program that required many machine cycles.

Some new routers can do almost all routing work in hardware. They use **application-specific integrated circuits (ASICs).** These are integrated circuit chips that do almost all routing logic in hardware. ASIC routers have packet-per-second processing rates that are almost as fast as frame-per-second processing rates in switches. They are also relatively inexpensive. In essence, ASIC routers do all routing tasks at the internet layer yet still rival switches in cost and speed.

FIGURE 5.16

Layer 3 Switching

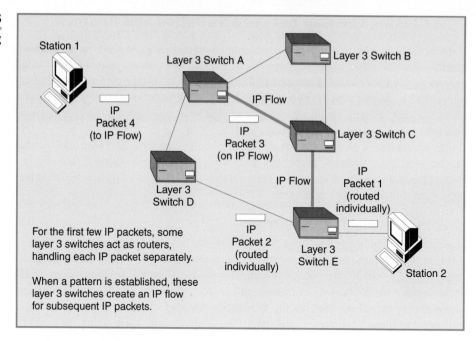

For the first few IP packets, some layer 3 switches act as routers, handling each IP packet separately.

When a pattern is established, these layer 3 switches create an IP flow for subsequent IP packets.

Unfortunately, ASIC routers create two concerns. First, because they do so much in hardware, buyers question what will happen if new internet layer standards are created. How will new functions be added? Most ASIC routers also have a general-purpose computer component and can add functions in software. However, this will slow processing speed.

A more immediate concern is that many ASIC routers handle only IP. Yet organizations also need to handle IPX/SPX and SNA traffic. Until most ASIC routers are multiprotocol routers, their usefulness in many organizations will be questionable.

ENTERPRISE INTERNETS

So far we have only been looking at networking at a single site. However, many organizations have multiple sites. These sites must be linked together into a coherent enterprise-wide network, so that any station at one site can send messages to any other station at any other site, using the destination station's address (usually its internet address).

Our discussion of enterprise networks will be shorter than our discussion of site networks, because many of the concepts we saw in site networks carry over to enterprise networks.

Carriers

The biggest difference between site and enterprise networks is ownership. On your own site, you can decide what technology you wish to use, and you can install it the way you see fit.

Once you cross your site's boundary, however, you do not own the land between that site and other sites. You cannot just run wires across the land between your two sites, because this would cut across property owned by other organizations.

Transmission between sites must be handled by a common carrier, usually called simply a **carrier**. Carriers are regulated organizations. The government gives them the right to lay wire where they need to do so. In turn, carriers must obey many rules designed to foster competition and to forbid unjustified bias in serving customers.

Leased Lines

One way to build a site network is to use a mesh of leased lines between pairs of sites. As shown in Figure 5.17, **leased lines** are point-to-point transmission lines that link only a single pair of sites. If you have more than two sites, you need to have multiple leased lines.

LEASED LINE MESHES

Point-to-point operation is awkward, because if you have many sites, you have to manage the mesh network yourself. In compensation, leased lines are fairly inexpensive.

LEASED LINE SPEEDS

Leased lines come in a wide variety of speeds. Table 5.1 shows the most widely used leased lines. They range from 64 kbps to several gigabits per second.

Although you can get very fast leased lines, speed is more expensive over longer

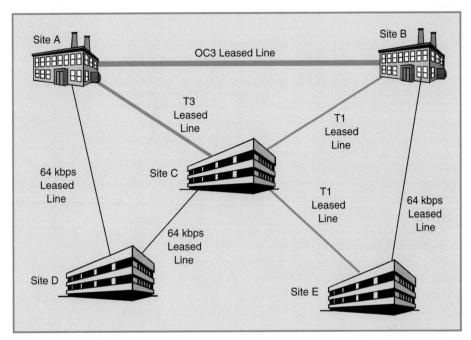

FIGURE 5.17

Leased Line Enterprise Network

TABLE **5.1**

Common Leased Line Speeds

LINE	SIGNALING	SPEED
Analog Voice-Grade Lines		
Analog		up to 30 kbps
North American Digital Hierarchy		
64 kbps	DS0	64 kbps
T1	DS1	1.544 Mbps
T3	DS3	44.7 Mbps
Fractional T1 (most carriers only offer one or two of these speeds)		
		128 kbps
		256 kbps
		384 kbps
		768 kbps
CEPT PCM Multiplexing Hierarchy		
E1		2.048 Mbps
E3		34.4 Mbps
Synchronous Optical Network (SONET)		
OC1	STS1	51.84 Mbps
OC3	STS3	156 Mbps
OC12	STS12	622 Mbps
OC24	STS24	1224 Mbps
OC48	STS48	2488 Mbps
Synchronous Digital Hierarchy (SDH)		
STM1		156 Mbps
STM4		622 Mbps
STM8		1224 Mbps
STM16		2488 Mbps

The slowest carrier transmission circuits are analog voice-grade lines designed to carry a single voice conversation. Faster circuits are digital, reducing error rates. Digital circuits run from as low as 64 kbps (sometimes 56 kbps) to more than 1 gigabit per second. Higher-speed circuits can multiplex many telephone calls to the carrier's switching center. Or they can be high-speed video and data pipes.

distances. As a result, most organizations today primarily use leased lines in the 64 kbps to 2 Mbps range. Even larger organizations use very fast leased lines only for some of their connections.

At each site, you have an **access device,** usually a router. As Figure 5.18 illustrates, routers have several ports. One port must connect to the local site network. For instance, this port might contain a NIC that connects to one of the site network's LANs. The other ports connect to leased lines going to other sites or to one of the public switched data networks we will see below. In Figure 5.18, two ports connect to 56 kbps leased lines. The last connects to a 45 Mbps T3 leased line.

FIGURE **5.18**
**Router with
Four Ports**

Enterprise Network

Site A: Site Network

LAN
LAN
LAN
LAN
LAN

Site B: Site Network

LAN

Site C: Site Network

LAN

LAN

Public Switched Data Networks (PSDNs)

For many years, organizations had to use leased lines to reduce costs. Much of this saving in transmission line cost, however, was eaten up by the cost of managing these networks. If a leased line fails or becomes congested, your network staff must solve the problem itself.

Because of the difficulty of managing multisite networks, organizations are increasingly turning to an alternative. This is the **public switched data network (PSDN)** shown in Figure 5.19.

FIGURE **5.19**
**Public Switched
Data Network
(PSDN)**

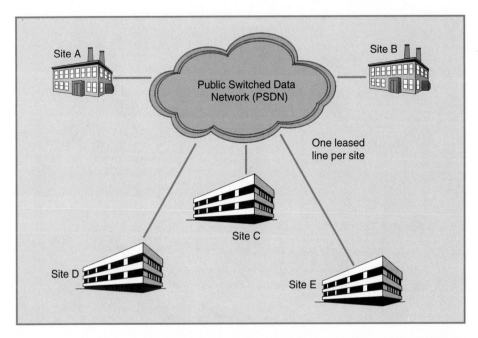

Site A

Public Switched Data
Network (PSDN)

Site B

One leased
line per site

Site C

Site D

Site E

PROBLEMS WITH MULTISITE NETWORKS

Meshes of leased lines are good only if you have only a few sites. In a fully connected mesh, there is a leased line between every pair of sites. If you have N sites, then a fully connected mesh of leased lines will require N*(N − 1)/2 leased lines. With 4 sites, the mesh needs only 6 leased lines for a full mesh. With 10 sites, however, the number of leased lines jumps to 45 leased lines! Even if you do not have a fully connected mesh, networks built from leased lines become very cumbersome as the number of sites increases.

THE CLOUD

The public switched data network itself is shown as a *cloud*. This emphasizes that you do not have to be concerned about what is inside the PSDN. The switched data network carrier manages all internal connections. This greatly simplifies the network manager's life.

ONE LEASED LINE PER SITE

Note that you only need one leased line for each site, no matter how many sites you have. If you have N sites, you need only *N* leased lines, not *N*(N − 1)/2 leased lines. For instance, if the router in Figure 5.18 were connected to a switched data network, it would need only two ports. One would connect it to the internal site network. The other would be the access line to the public switched data network "cloud."

Circuit Switching

Public switched data networks use two basic technologies. One is **circuit switched** service. As Figure 5.20 shows, a **circuit** is an end-to-end connection between two stations. This circuit may pass through multiple switches and transmission media (wire, satellite,

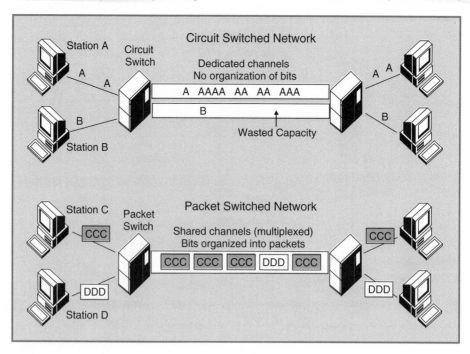

FIGURE 5.20

Circuit Switching and Packet Switching

TABLE **5.2**

Public Switched Data Network Technologies*

Service	Typical Speeds	Circuit or Packet?	Dial-Up or Dedicated?	Relative Maturity	Relative Cost
ISDN	2 64 kbps B Channels; 1 16 kbps D Channel	Circuit	Dial-up	Moderate	Low
X.25	9,600 bps–64 kbps	Packet	Dedicated	High	Low
Frame Relay	64 kbps–6 Mbps	Packet	Dedicated	High	Moderate
ATM	25 Mbps–2 Gbps*	Packet	Dedicated	Moderate	High

*Officially, ATM speeds start at 156 Mbps, but many vendors offer lower speeds.

and so forth). To the user, however, all of this is irrelevant. The user appears to have a simple transmission pipe to the other user, much like a string stretched between two cans.

GUARANTEED, DEDICATED CAPACITY

In circuit switching, the transmission capacity of the circuit is reserved for your use throughout the duration of a call. This way, you are always sure of being able to send messages. On the other hand, if you do not use the circuit constantly, you still have to pay for the capacity.

BURSTINESS AND THE WASTEFULNESS OF DEDICATED CAPACITY

Dedicated capacity is poorly suited to data transmission because data traffic tends to be *bursty*, with brief transmissions punctuating long silences. Under these conditions, you will be paying for dedicated circuit capacity constantly, but you will be using the line only a small fraction of the time you are connected. As Table 5.2 shows, only one popular switched data network service is circuit switched, ISDN.

Packet Switching

Packet switching is very different from circuit switching. For reasons we will soon see, packet switching is also much less expensive. As a consequence, three of the four PSDN services shown in Table 5.2 are packet switched data networks.

PACKETS

First, as Figure 5.20 shows, your computer divides each message into a number of short **packets** before transmission. For technical reasons, it is much easier for a network to handle short packets than to route messages of large size. Roughly speaking, it is like running sand versus pebbles through an hourglass.

LOWERING COST THROUGH MULTIPLEXING

Note that the transmission lines between packet switches are not dedicated to a single user. Instead, the packets of multiple conversations are multiplexed over the **trunk lines** that connect packet switches. This allows the multiple conversations to share the cost of the trunk line (and of switches), resulting in considerable cost savings. This is why packet switching is the dominant public switched data network technology.

FIGURE 5.21
**Virtual Circuits
and Access Lines**

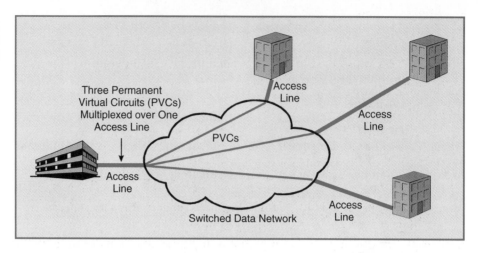

Three Permanent
Virtual Circuits (PVCs)
Multiplexed over One
Access Line

Access
Line

Access
Line

PVCs

Access
Line

Access
Line

Access
Line

Switched Data Network

VIRTUAL CIRCUITS

Earlier, we saw virtual circuits in the context of ATM networks (see Figure 5.13). Virtual circuits first appeared in public switched data networks that connect sites, specifically networks using the X.25 standard. Later, other popular public switched data network technologies—Frame Relay and ATM—also used virtual circuits. This is hardly surprising, because, like packetization, virtual circuits greatly reduce costs.

Until recently, all virtual circuits in PSDNs were permanent virtual circuits (PVCs). Wherever a company formerly had a leased line between two sites, it would establish a permanent virtual circuit. These PVCs allowed PSDN carriers to compete directly against the profitable leased line networks offered by telephone companies. As Figure 5.21 emphasizes, a company needs only one PSDN access line per site, rather than a complex mesh of leased lines. Multiple PVCs are multiplexed over that one leased access line. The site on the right side of the figure, for instance, has three PVCs multiplexed over its leased access line. So a company can replace its mesh of leased lines with a mesh of PVCs but with only one access line per site.

Permanent virtual circuits must be established long before a transmission between any pair of sites. However, the inflexibility of PVCs is not a problem if the goal is to replace mesh networks of leased lines among corporate sites.

Now, however, because of the growing importance of interconnecting different companies, public packet switched data network vendors are beginning to offer switched virtual circuits (SVCs). As noted earlier in the chapter, these are established at the time of the call, not beforehand. Carriers were initially reluctant to offer SVCs because accounting and billing are much more complex for SVCs, which come and go constantly, than for PVCs, which are established initially and are rarely changed.

Dedicated versus Dial-Up Connections

Some public switched data networks offer **dedicated connections.** They are always "live" and ready to receive and deliver packets. You normally pay a monthly fee for such connections. X.25, Frame Relay and ATM public switched data networks use dedicated connections.

Other public switched data networks offer **dial-up service,** which is similar to normal telephony. If you wish to reach someone, you must dial that party's number. This takes your connection live, and it remains live until the end of the call. ISDN works this way.

Sometimes a site has only occasional transmission needs, as in the case of a store that connects to the head office each night to download a half hour of sales data. In such situations, dial-up service is much less expensive than maintaining a dedicated connection.

Dedicated connections, in turn, are good for situations in which data flows will be significant throughout the day, as in connections between two large corporate sites. The line always has to be available to send and receive data. Under such constant-use conditions, dedicated services are also less expensive than dial-up services.

POPULAR PUBLIC SWITCHED DATA NETWORK TECHNOLOGIES

Table 5.2 illustrates the characteristics of the most popular public switched data network technologies today. These are ISDN, X.25, Frame Relay, and ATM.

ISDN

In Chapter 3, we saw that the Integrated Services Digital Network (ISDN) multiplexes three channels to the desktop. These are two 64 kbps "B" channels to carry user data and one 16 kbps "D" channel for supervisory communication. This is called the **Basic Rate Interface (BRI).**

PRIMARY RATE INTERFACE

Figure 5.22 shows that the ISDN carrier often provides a different service to the corporation. This is the **Primary Rate Interface (PRI).** In some countries, the PRI is based on the T1 leased line and provides 23B+D service, with twenty-three 64 kbps B channels and one 64 kbps D channel. In other countries, it is based on the E.1 leased line and provides 30B+D service. The figure shows that the company must have internal equipment to bring the Basic Rate Interface to user desktops.

DIAL-UP SERVICE

As noted earlier, ISDN is a dial-up service designed for occasional connections. For constant use, services that use dedicated connections, such as Frame Relay, are much more economical.

As a dial-up service, ISDN is **fully switched.** This means that every ISDN station has a telephone number. Any ISDN station can call any other, just as any telephone can call any other. There is nothing like virtual circuits to set up beforehand.

ISDN is even integrated with the telephone network, so that an ISDN subscriber can call a regular telephone number. Of course, when this happens, you move down to the lowest common denominator, telephone speed.

CIRCUIT SWITCHED SERVICE

Most carriers offer ISDN as a *circuit switched* service. This makes it relatively expensive compared to the other two PSDN technologies we will see, Frame Relay and ATM. You pay for the line's capacity even when you are not using it during a dial-up connection.

FIGURE 5.22

ISDN Service

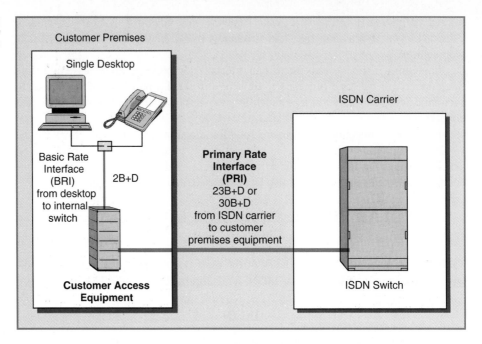

Frame Relay

The most popular public packet switched data network technology today is **Frame Relay.** Table 5.2 compares Frame Relay with ISDN and another public packet switching service, ATM.

PACKET SWITCHED WITH VIRTUAL CIRCUITS

First, note that Frame Relay is packet switched. As discussed above, this makes it inherently relatively inexpensive. In addition, carriers have priced Frame Relay fairly low in response to strong competition.

All Frame Relay vendors offer permanent virtual circuits, which, as we saw earlier, are limiting. Some are beginning to offer switched virtual circuits.

DEDICATED CONNECTIONS

In contrast to ISDN, which offers similar speeds, Frame Relay uses dedicated connections. Sites can send and receive at all times.

REASONS FOR POPULARITY

Note the speed range of Frame Relay. Typically, Frame Relay service begins at 64 kbps and extends to about 1 or 2 Mbps. Some Frame Relay services are slightly faster, but none at the time of this writing extends to 10 Mbps.

This is a narrow speed range, but it satisfies the bulk of today's corporate demand. Corporations sometimes use faster lines, but most of their long-distance demand falls into the speed range offered by Frame Relay.

Although higher speeds might be desirable, the additional cost would not be worth the added speed. You do not need a Ferrari to drive to the store.

In addition, Frame Relay is priced aggressively. When low prices are added to Frame Relay's fit with corporate speed requirements, it is not at all surprising that Frame Relay dominates the packet switching marketplace today.

Note, in the final analysis, that although low cost is an attractor, it is only one of two reasons for Frame Relay's popularity. If Frame Relay did not offer speeds in the range of greatest corporate demand, low price would not be enough to make it so popular.

ATM

We have already seen ATM in this chapter, as a switching technology for site networks. Yet ATM is not limited to site networking. In fact, it was created first as a wide area network (WAN) packet switching technology for public switched data networks. Like Frame Relay, ATM is packet switched, uses PVCs and sometimes SVCs, and uses dedicated connections.

COMPETITION WITH FRAME RELAY

In the past, it was expected that ATM would dominate both internal and external networking needs for corporations. We would even bring ATM to the desktop. However, the high cost of ATM service compared to Ethernet switching within sites and compared to Frame Relay switching between sites has slowed its acceptance.

HIGH SCALABILITY

In Table 5.2, note that ATM speeds typically span the range between 25 Mbps and a few gigabits per second. So Frame Relay and ATM services typically are not direct competitors.

PRICING FOR ATM AND FRAME RELAY

In fact, many carriers offer both Frame Relay and ATM service. Furthermore, they usually set prices so that if Frame Relay and ATM offer the same speeds, they have the same prices. In other words, by offering both Frame Relay and ATM, and by creating a smooth price curve, carriers provide a smooth growth path between 64 kbps and several gigabits per second.

Virtual Private Networks Using the Internet

The services we have just looked at—ISDN, Frame Relay, and ATM—require carriers to build dedicated networks and require corporations to pay for carrier services.

However, most organizations are already connected to another transmission network, namely the Internet. Why not use the Internet to send and receive corporate data, instead of a PSDN carrier?

CONCERNS

Although the idea of using the Internet for corporate data has attractions, it also raises concerns.

▶ **Reliability.** Corporations need 100% service availability. This is called **24 × 7** operation—24 hours a day, 7 days a week. The Internet does not offer this level of reliability.

- ▶ **Congestion.** Individual PSDN vendors offer **service-level agreements.** These guarantee such things as maximum delay. The Internet cannot do this. Technically, it is a "best-effort" delivery system, meaning that it cannot offer any guarantees. In addition, its components are owned and managed by several different organizations, so agreements would have to be made with all of them.

- ▶ **Throughput.** Although the Internet has many high-speed internal connections, actual end-to-end throughput between two hosts can be extremely low, sometimes little more than modem speed. Corporations need higher speeds for their internal traffic.

- ▶ **Security.** The Internet was not designed for security. For critical corporate data, this lack of security is unacceptable.

Creating Virtual Private Networks Using the Internet

Security problems, at least, can be solved. An organization creates a **virtual private network (VPN),** as Figure 5.23 illustrates. Here, when a PC connects to a corporate site or when two corporate sites connect, they add security to the Internet. They are said to create a secure **tunnel** through the insecure Internet.

We will look at security in Chapter 6. For now, we will simply mention several areas of security that are implemented in VPNs.

- ▶ **Authentication.** Before users can connect to a site, they must first authenticate themselves, that is, must prove that they are who they say they are. Passwords offer only weak forms of authentication. VPNs use stronger forms.

- ▶ **Encryption.** Before IP packets are sent, they are first encrypted so that if someone intercepts an IP packet, that person will not be able to read its contents.

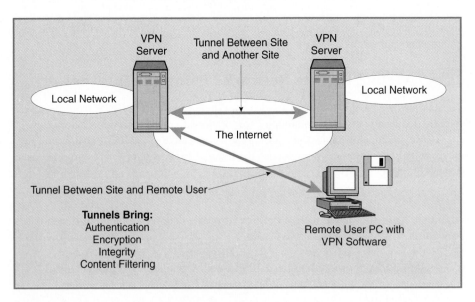

FIGURE 5.23
Virtual Private Network (VPN)

▶ **Integrity.** There is a danger that someone will change IP packets in transit. Integrity checks ensure that packets have not been destroyed, changed, or re-ordered in their passage from the sender to the receiver.

▶ **Content Filtering.** Some companies check transmissions for improper content, such as viruses.

Figure 5.23 shows that user PCs must be equipped with special software to participate in VPN transmissions. At each site, furthermore, there must be a **VPN server.**

THE FUTURE OF THE INTERNET

VPN security solves only one problem with VPNs. Reliability, congestion, and throughput are also serious problems for corporate use. They are also serious problems for Internet electronic commerce (see Chapter 8).

A number of efforts are now under way to make the Internet a solid transmission environment sufficient for corporate needs internally and in external electronic commerce. As Modules A and F discuss, however, these efforts are just getting under way.

SUMMARY

In the last chapter, we looked at a simple situation—a single Ethernet LAN using either a 10Base-T or a 100Base-TX hub. In a small firm, this is all you need. In large firms, however, you must have multiple site networks linked together by carrier transmission facilities into a single enterprise network.

Multihub 10Base-T Networks and 100Base-TX

This chapter looks at progressively larger networks. First, it looked at adding more hubs to increase the physical span of an Ethernet network. It noted that the maximum distance between two stations in a pure 10Base-T network is 500 meters. For 100Base-TX, however, there is a maximum span of only about 200 meters.

Congestion and Latency

Although distance is important, an even bigger limitation of hub-based networks is congestion, which leads to latency (delay). Ethernet 10Base-T and 100Base-TX are shared media networks, in which all stations share the available transmission capacity. Only one station can transmit at a time, so as stations are added, latency inevitably increases. Beyond 200 to 300 stations, latency becomes intolerable in Ethernet 10Base-T.

Reducing Congestion through Switches and Routers

For this reason, large site networks (networks at a single site) combine hubs with switches and routers. Stations connect directly to hubs, and hubs are linked by switches and routers. Switches and routers do not broadcast messages. This allows them to support multiple simultaneous conversations. Even with thousands of stations, there is no congestion. This is critical in large site networks.

Switches Operate at Layer 2

Switches operate at OSI layer 2, in which there is only a single possible path between any two stations and in which addressing is flat (nonhierarchical addressing).

Switches arranged in a physical hierarchy automatically have a single possible path between stations. Switches arranged in a mesh use virtual circuits to create a single path. Virtual circuits can be either permanent or switched.

Virtual LANs (VLANs)

Ethernet switching can create virtual LANs (VLANs). This provides security and the taming of broadcast storms. However, allowing stations on different VLANs to communicate can be very difficult.

Routers Operate at Layer 3

In contrast, routers can be arranged in a mesh to offer multiple alternative routes between any two stations. This allows routing around failed switches and lines, routing around congestion, and optimal route selection. Routers must operate at layer 3 (the internet layer) in order to do alternative routing. Alternative routing requires a complex decision for each packet. As a result, routers are expensive. Routers are also expensive because of complex peer management among the routers in a network.

Routers also operate at layer 3 because they use hierarchical addressing, which we saw in Chapter 2. Their two hierarchical layers are the network and the subnet.

Closing the Gap between Routers and Switches

Traditionally, switches have been fast and inexpensive. Routers have been very expensive and slow and were tolerated only because of their ability to route packets across multiple subnets. We saw that some switches are beginning to add some routing functions, whereas some routers can now process flows of packets instead of processing each packet individually, and ASIC routers offer switch-like speed and cost while doing full IP routing but sometimes not multiprotocol routing.

Carriers and Leased Lines

When you leave the individual site, you must deal with carriers, who transport your messages from site to site. Some carriers offer point-to-point leased lines.

Public Switched Data Networks: Circuit and Packet Switching

Other carriers offer public switched data networks. For PSDNs, all you need is a leased line from each site to the switched data network. The PSDN manages all internal switching and transmission. Circuit switched data networks maintain dedicated transmission capacity for the duration of a data call. Packet switched data networks divide messages into small packets and multiplex these packets onto transmission lines between packet switches. Multiplexing makes packet switching relatively inexpensive.

Dedicated versus Dial-Up Service

Some public switched data networks offer access lines that are always live. These dedicated lines are useful when you will be sending and receiving data fairly constantly. In contrast, other switched data networks offer dial-up lines. As in dial-up telephone service, services that offer dial-up connections make lines live only during a specific call.

ISDN, Frame Relay, and ATM

Among the popular public switched data network technologies, ISDN offers speeds of 64 kbps or 128 kbps. It gives moderate increases in speed and cost compared to telephone transmissions using a modem. ISDN is circuit switched and provides dial-up service. It is best for occasional use during the day.

Frame Relay and ATM are packet switched services that use dedicated connections. They are best when you will be sending and receiving frequently during the day.

Frame Relay usually offers speeds of 64 kbps to 1 or 2 megabits per second. This is the range of largest corporate need, and Frame Relay is also priced aggressively. These two factors make Frame Relay the most popular PSDN technology.

ATM offers much higher speeds but also much higher costs. Many carriers offer both Frame Relay and ATM, to give users access to a broad range of speed options.

Virtual Private Networks (VPNs)
Using the Internet

In ISDN, Frame Relay, and ATM, the carriers build their own transmission networks. Yet corporations are already connected to the Internet. Virtual private networks (VPNs) use the Internet but provide additional security. The company appears to have its own secure private network within the broader insecure Internet. Although VPNs solve security problems involving the Internet, they do not solve other Internet problems—reliability, congestion, and throughput.

REVIEW QUESTIONS

CORE REVIEW QUESTIONS

1. How far apart can the farthest stations be in an Ethernet **10Base-T** network with a single hub? With multiple hubs? Can you have loops in an Ethernet 10Base-T network with multiple hubs?
2. How far apart can the farthest stations be in an Ethernet **100Base-TX** network with a single hub? With multiple hubs?
3. What is a shared media network? Why do you inevitably have congestion in a shared media network as the number of stations grows? Is Ethernet 10Base-T a shared media network? Ethernet 100Base-TX?

4. Are switched networks shared media networks? What does this imply for congestion as a switched network grows?

5. Why do we say that switches operate at layer 2? How do Ethernet switches restrict traffic to a single path between stations? How do ATM networks do this? Distinguish between permanent and switched virtual circuits. Is virtual circuit operation connection-oriented or connectionless?

6. What are the advantages of Ethernet switches compared to ATM switches? What are the advantages of ATM switches compared to Ethernet switches? Consider cost, scalability, and quality of service.

7. What is a virtual LAN (VLAN)? What are the two reasons why organizations use virtual LANs? What is the disadvantage of virtual LANs?

8. What is alternative routing? What is the other characteristic of layer 3 operation? What are the advantages of alternative routing? What type of device gives alternative routing? Given the advantages of alternative routing, why are routers not used everywhere?

9. Distinguish between layer 1 and layer 2 operation. Distinguish between layer 2 and layer 3 operation. What type of connector box operates at layer 1? At layer 2? At layer 3? How do layer 3 switches, flow routers, and ASIC routers give some of the advantages of both layer 2 and layer 3 operation?

10. What are layer 3 switches?

11. What is a carrier?

12. What is a leased line? Why do organizations use leased lines? What are the disadvantages of networks made from leased lines?

13. Why is a public switched data network (PSDN) represented as a cloud? How many leased lines does a **site** have using a public switched data network? How many leased lines does a **site** have using a network of leased lines?

14. Distinguish between circuit switching and packet switching in terms of guarantee of transmission capacity and cost. Why is packet switching less expensive than circuit switching?

15. Distinguish between dedicated and dial-up switched data networks. When would you use each?

16. All commercial public packet switching services offer permanent virtual circuits. How does this make their services competitive with meshes of leased lines?

17. Which public switched data networks are circuit switched? Packet switched? Which public switched data networks use dedicated lines? Which use dial-up lines?

18. What is the most popular public switched data network service? Why is it the most popular?

19. Compare ISDN, Frame Relay, and ATM in terms of scalability.

DETAILED REVIEW QUESTIONS

1. Why is Ethernet normally half-duplex? Why can Ethernet switches be full-duplex? For full-duplex switching, do you have to change the NIC?

2. Distinguish between permanent virtual circuits and switched virtual circuits.

3. In ISDN, distinguish between the Basic Rate Interface (BRI) and the Primary Rate Interface (PRI).

4. How do the speeds and prices of Frame Relay and ATM compare?

THOUGHT QUESTIONS

1. How do virtual circuits reduce costs?

2. The College of Business Administration building at the University of Hawaii was built in a circle. One of the towers had to be demolished shortly after construction (Don't ask), leaving a C-shaped building. The farthest points in the building are about 300 meters apart. The building has 250 personal computers. Ten of these are file or application servers. Briefly evaluate the following options: Ethernet 10Base-T, Ethernet 100Base-TX, switched 10Base-T Ethernet, switched 100Base-TX Ethernet, ATM, and routers. Evaluate each option in terms of performance, cost, and technical feasibility. Select a good working solution for the college.

PROJECTS

1. Go to the book's website, http://www.prenhall.com/panko, and read the Updates Page for this chapter to see any reported errors and for new and expanded information on the material in this chapter.

2. Go to the book's website, http://www.prenhall.com/panko, and do the Internet Exercises for this chapter.

3. Create a high-level design for a site network for a real site. First, draw a rough diagram of the site. Second, draw the locations of various connector boxes, including hubs, switches, and routers (as applicable). Mark each box, indicating its type and number of ports. (Be sure to leave room for growth in the number of ports.) Indicate how the connector boxes will be linked (UTP, optical fiber, etc.). Write a few paragraphs about the design choices you faced and how you resolved them.

4. Create a high-level design for linking sites in an enterprise network in a real organization. Do this as in the previous question but this time adding leased lines, switched data networks of various types, and so forth. Note that you are concerned here only with linking sites. You are not concerned with the design of the site networks within the sites, except for the type of device that links each site to the outside world (router, etc.).

CHAPTER 6

Larger Networks II: Servers, Management, and Security

INTRODUCTION

The last chapter looked at site networks and enterprise networks. These large networks may serve thousands of users working at client PCs and other desktop devices. They may also have hundreds of servers. The last chapter focused on transmission concerns. This chapter looks at servers, management, and security for site and enterprise networks.

The servers we have seen so far, including file servers, client/server application servers, and webservers, exist to serve *users* working at desktop machines. However, to manage large networks, we also need servers that focus on the needs of network administrators. Large site and enterprise networks are so complex that they are extremely difficult to manage. Administrative servers are critical for getting and keeping control of networks in large organizations.

Large servers holding sensitive information must be highly secure. Otherwise, company employees, outside hackers, or both will attack resources on the network. We will look at some of the security precautions that organizations must take on large networks.

SERVER TECHNOLOGY

Servers for very large networks are very different from servers for small networks. We will look at important goals in selecting server technology for large systems and at basic ways to achieve those goals.

Scalability and Reliability

SCALABILITY

Servers that need to support large numbers of users are complex and expensive. Our goal is to find *scalable* server technology that will allow us to keep pace with user growth, including the enormous growth often seen in webserver usage. If you run out of power on a server using a scalable technology, you can simply replace your existing server hardware with a larger computer of the same type. After transferring your program and data files, you can immediately serve more users.

RELIABILITY

Another goal is **reliability**. This means that the server should almost never be unavailable because it has crashed. For electronic commerce and other important applications, servers must support **24 × 7** operation. This means that they must be available 24 hours a day, 7 days a week, month after month. Even maintenance and hardware upgrades should be done without disrupting service. Such an extreme level of reliability is very difficult to achieve.

Server Categories

There are four main types of servers in common use today.

HIGH-END INTEL-BASED PERSONAL COMPUTERS

First, there are **high-end Intel-based**[1] **personal computers.** These are top-of-the-line ordinary PCs with very fast Intel microprocessors, ample RAM, large and fast disk drives, and other advanced hardware technologies.

In contrast to other large servers we will see, high-end PC servers can be purchased at a computer store. Faster servers must be purchased from the vendor or from a company that specially configures high-end servers.

However, you would not run Windows 3.1, Windows 95, or Windows 98 on these machines. Such desktop operating systems are not sufficiently reliable for server operation. Instead, you must install a **server operating system (SOS)** designed for server use. Such server operating systems, sometimes called network operating systems, include Windows NT Server, Novell NetWare, IntranetWare, and versions of UNIX that operate on Intel microprocessors. SOSs have strong management tools for assigning rights to multiple users and for doing other tasks needed in highly reliable environments that support many users.

INTEL-BASED SUPERSERVERS

Beyond high-end PCs that you can buy at a store, there are **Intel-based superservers** with much higher processing power. These superservers have Intel processors but add technology not sold in computer stores.

RISC SUPERSERVERS

Other superservers are **RISC superservers.** These are workstation servers that use RISC microprocessors that give higher performance than even the highest Intel processor.

---

[1] Yes, this includes Intel-cloned and Intel-similar microprocessors from competitors.

FIGURE 6.1

Symmetric
Multiprocessing
(SMP)

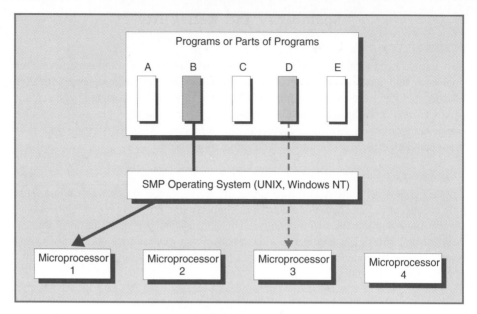

MAINFRAME SERVERS

For really high speeds, you can use a **mainframe** computer. IBM is now beginning to call some of its biggest mainframes "enterprise servers." This is more than a name change. IBM is equipping its mainframes with the software needed to turn mainframes into super superservers.

Symmetric Multiprocessing

Both Intel and workstation superservers have multiple microprocessors, as shown in Figure 6.1. This is called **symmetric multiprocessing (SMP).**

Several microprocessors obviously can do more work than one. However, it is difficult to keep multiple microprocessors constantly busy, so an eight-microprocessor SMP machine will not be eight times faster than a machine with a single microprocessor.

Server Clustering

SMP allows servers to scale by placing several microprocessors in a single machine. Another way to scale servers is through **server clustering,** in which several servers are linked together to act as a single machine. Figure 6.2 illustrates server clustering.

There are two reasons to do server clustering. First, in line with our overall discussion, server clustering gives *scalability*. Server clusters have far more processing power than do single servers.

The second reason to cluster is *reliability*. If one server in the cluster fails, there is no interruption of service.

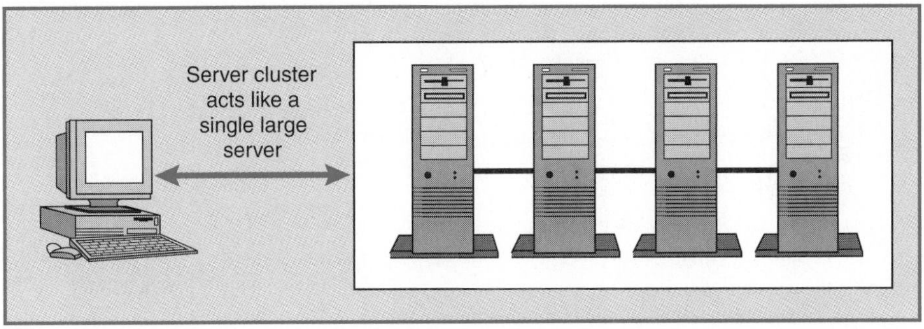
Server cluster
acts like a
single large
server

FIGURE 6.2
Server Cluster

Load Balancing

One way to have many of the benefits of server clustering is to buy multiple single servers (or clusters) and to connect them with a load balancing router, as shown in Figure 6.3. When HTTP request messages arrive at the router, the router considers the load on each server and passes the request message on to the least heavily loaded server. If a server fails, it is simply not sent additional requests.

Load balancing routers can even support a server farm of single servers that support different services, such as HTTP, FTP, and newsgroups. This requires the load balancing router to examine each incoming packet to determine the standard used by the application layer request message it contains.

Geographical Decentralization

Another way to increase performance in servers is **geographical decentralization.** Figure 6.4 illustrates this concept. Here, a central server either is **replicated** at multiple servers around the world or has its most widely used webpages **cached** at multiple servers. In replication, the main server's *entire contents* are available at each remote server. In caching, *only some* webpages are made available at remote servers.

Server replication and data caching allow client PCs to use the server nearest them. This reduces the number of router hops between the user and the server, lowering access time. It also reduces the load on the Internet backbone. Unfortunately, geo-

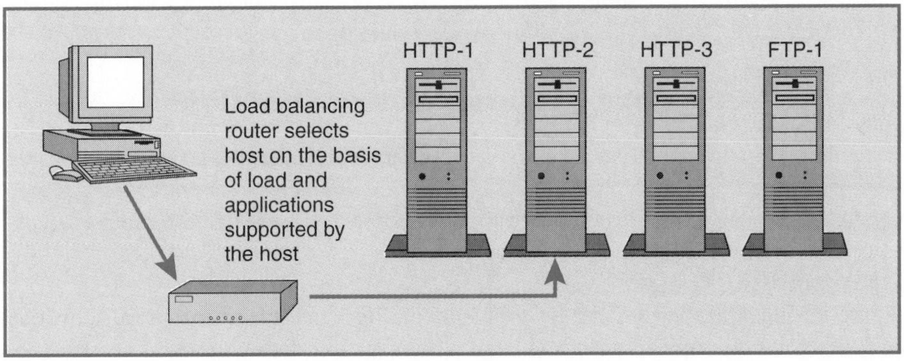
HTTP-1
HTTP-2
HTTP-3
FTP-1
Load balancing
router selects
host on the basis
of load and
applications
supported by
the host

FIGURE 6.3
Load Balancing Router

FIGURE **6.4**

**Server Replication
and Caching**

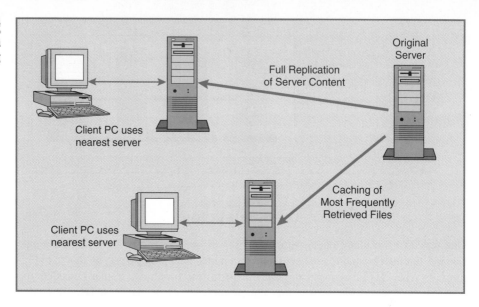

graphical distribution is not standardized in TCP/IP at this time, so existing solutions are proprietary and are limited to intranets.

DIRECTORY SERVERS

Administrative Servers

To this point in the book, we have focused on servers that provide services to **end users.** These are employees in functional departments who use information technology to do their functional work in marketing, finance, production, purchasing, or some other corporate function. File servers, client/server application servers, and the other servers that we have discussed so far in this book were created to help end users be more effective and efficient.

In larger networks, however, we see a number of servers that support the needs of **network administrators.** We call them **administrative servers.** As networks grow ever more complex, network administrators will have to turn increasingly to administrative servers. In effect, administrative servers use network technology to help administrators cope with the complexity of network technology.

Directory Servers: Lookup Functions

At the heart of administrative services is the **directory server,** *which maintains information about all resources on the network, allowing it to help users find resources they need and allowing it to help administrators control end user access to these resources.*

E-MAIL LOOKUP NEEDS

Figure 6.5 illustrates two common problems that end users have on large networks. First, it shows a user who wishes to send a message to a fellow worker, Wendy Lee. Unfortunately, the company has several mail servers. E-mail addresses usually have

FIGURE **6.5**

Finding Resources

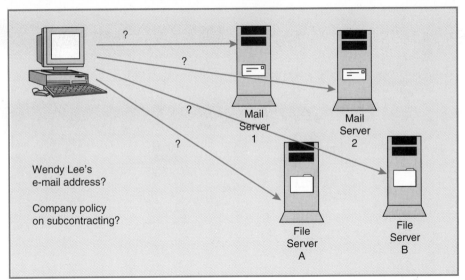

the form *userid@host.* So to send mail to Wendy Lee, the user first has to know which mail host she uses. The user also has to know her user ID on that mail host. This is difficult in a company with dozens or hundreds of mail hosts.

FILE LOOKUP NEEDS

Another problem is finding data files. Suppose, for instance, you wish to download the company's policy statement on subcontracting. You have to know which of the company's many file servers holds that information. Then, you have to locate the file on the server's disk drives.

DIRECTORY SERVER E-MAIL LOOKUP

Figure 6.6 shows how a directory server helps a user locate information. When a user gets onto the network, he or she first logs into a directory server. This server has an organized list of all information on all servers on the entire enterprise network.

When you go to a large office building, you first need to find the room number of the company or person you are seeking. You go to the building's *directory,* which is a simple list giving the name of the company or person and the pertinent floor and room number. Directory servers provide similar information for resources on multiple servers on the network.

For instance, to send e-mail to Wendy Lee, you indicate that you wish to send e-mail and indicate that you wish to send it to "Wendy Lee." The directory server tells you that there are three Wendy Lees. It gives you more information on each, allowing you to select the right Wendy Lee.

FILE LOOKUP

Similarly, for locating the company policy on subcontracting, the directory server provides search tools. At the simplest level, all data files in the firm are shown as a single hierarchical tree that cuts across servers. At more advanced levels, the directory server provides search tools.

FIGURE **6.6**
Directory Server Lookup

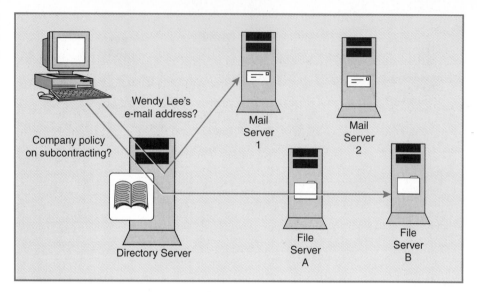

Access Control Functions

ACCESS CONTROL PROBLEMS

Another problem users face is that they may have to log into multiple servers. Figure 6.7 illustrates this process. For each server, a user must remember his or her user ID and password.

The need for end users to log into multiple servers is also a problem for network administrators. Suppose you have only 100 end users and 10 servers. If each end user needs to log into each server, the network administrator will have to set up access rights for 1,000 accounts. **Access rights** determine which directories and other resources end users should be able to use on each host and what specific rights they have in those directories and other resources.

FIGURE **6.7**
Access to Multiple Servers

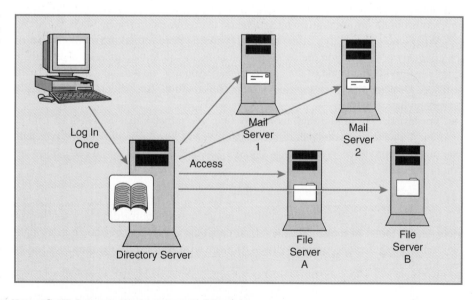

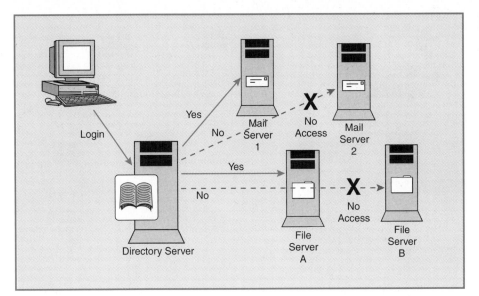

FIGURE **6.8**

Access Control with a Directory Server

IMPLEMENTING USER ACCESS

Figure 6.8 shows that a directory server allows a user to log in just once, to a directory server itself. The directory server then looks up the profile created for that end user. Without additional logins (except for very sensitive information), the directory server will then give the user access to all resources specified in the user's profile.

Directory servers also make the network administrator's life easier. The network still has many resources, but these may be groupable in ways that focus on content instead of servers. The network administrator may give a user access to a certain type of content and thereby assign rights on multiple servers with a single action.

Directory Access Protocols

We have spoken of users querying the directory server for information. However, dealing with directory servers is normally done by application programs rather than by the users themselves. For instance, Figure 6.9 shows that when a user wants to send an e-mail message to Wendy Lee, the e-mail program gets the needed information from the directory server. The e-mail program then presents this information to the end user.

Figure 6.9 shows that standards for user applications to request information from a directory server are called **directory access protocols.**

X.500

The first international standards for directory access protocols were the **X.500** series of standards from OSI. Like most standards from the OSI architecture, the X.500 standards were full-featured and extensible. This, unfortunately, also made them difficult and expensive to implement.

LDAP

In response to the perceived need for a less elaborate directory access protocol, a simpler protocol was developed, based on X.500 standards. This was the **Lightweight Directory Access Protocol (LDAP).** In addition to being simpler than X.500, LDAP

FIGURE 6.9

Directory Access Protocol

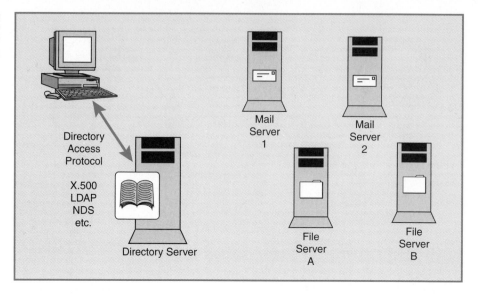

runs over TCP/IP, whereas X.500 was designed to run over an OSI protocol stack. Today, LDAP is becoming very popular. Its standardization is managed by the IETF.

PROPRIETARY DIRECTORY ACCESS PROTOCOLS

Individual server operating system vendors also have created their own **proprietary** directory access protocols. For instance, Novell has a proprietary directory access protocol in NetWare Directory Service (NDS), and Microsoft has one in Active Directory. Most vendors are now moving to become compatible with LDAP.

NETWORK MANAGEMENT SYSTEMS

When you are sitting at home watching television, you probably use a remote control to send commands to your television and VCR. Network administrators would like something similar to manage devices on their networks. Today, we have the beginnings of such "push-button" tools. We call them **network management systems**.

Network Management System Elements

As shown in Figure 6.10, network administrators would like to be able to manage their entire network from a single **network control center** at a single site.

NETWORK MANAGEMENT CONSOLE

The heart of a perfect network control center would be a single **network management console,** either a personal computer or client workstation. This console would give the network administrator an overview of what is happening throughout the network. It would also allow the network administrator to reconfigure devices hundreds or thousands of miles away. Although single network management consoles today cannot control entire networks, most network control centers have several network manage-

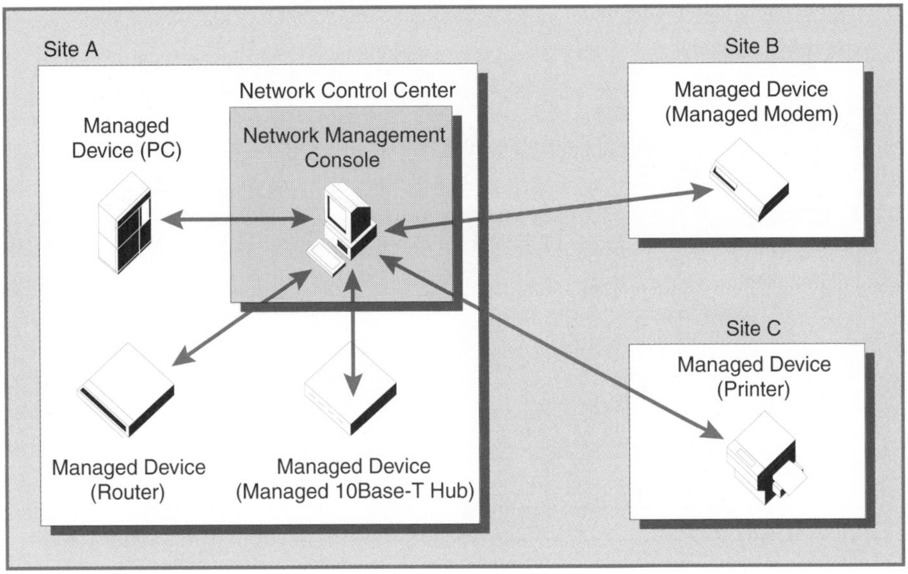

FIGURE **6.10**

Network Management System

FIGURE **6.10**
Network Management System

Figure contents:

Site A

Network Control Center

Managed Device (PC)

Network Management Console

Site B

Managed Device (Managed Modem)

Site C

Managed Device (Printer)

Managed Device (Router)

Managed Device (Managed 10Base-T Hub)

ment consoles that give such control over parts of the network. One might control routers, whereas another might control carrier transmission lines, and so forth.

The software on the network management console is the **network management program.** The network management program collects data on the network constantly. It then digests the data and presents summarized information to the network administrator in the form of statistical profiles and fault (problem) diagnoses.

To do its work, whenever the network management program obtains information from devices on the network, it stores this information in an organized database called the **management information base (MIB).** This structured database allows the network management program to analyze patterns in the data.

MANAGED DEVICES AND AGENTS

The devices controlled by the network management system are called **managed devices.** These can be client PCs, servers, hubs, switches, routers, carrier services, or any other piece of hardware on the network.

In contrast to unmanaged devices, managed devices contain **network management agents.** In the arts, agents act on behalf of artists in negotiations. In networks, a network management agent communicates with the network management program on behalf of a managed device, as Figure 6.11 illustrates.

For an intelligent device, such as a personal computer or a router, the network management agent may be purely software—a program added to the machine. For a dumb device, such as a hub or a printer, the network management agent may be a printed circuit board with enough intelligence to handle interactions with the network management program.

Note also that the network management agent maintains a management information base (MIB) for the device. This **local MIB** contains information about that single device.

FIGURE 6.11

Network Management Protocols

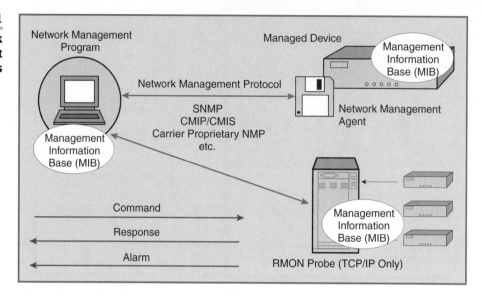

RMON PROBES

If the network management program has to get information constantly from individual network management agents, it is likely to be overloaded with work.

TCP/IP network management standards provide another tool, called the **RMON** (Remote Monitoring) probe. Figure 6.11 shows that an RMON probe actively collects data about its section of the network, including many traffic statistics. From time to time, the network management program collects this data from the RMON probe. The RMON probe can also send the network console alarm messages, called **traps**, if dangerous conditions appear to exist.

Network Management Protocols

Network management protocols allow the network management program and the network management agent to communicate. Figure 6.11 illustrates the request-response nature of most of these communications, with the network management program initiating the request. In addition, if a network management agent detects a problem, it is able to send **alarm** messages to the network management program.

SNMP

The most popular network management protocol is the **Simple Network Management Protocol (SNMP).** The *simple* in its name tells you that SNMP was created by the IETF as part of the overall TCP/IP standards. Simplicity has brought SNMP to the market quickly. Unfortunately, simplicity has also left SNMP fairly limited in what it can do. However, like most TCP/IP standards, SNMP will grow in functionality over time. The newest version, SNMP v3, adds a number of security enhancements.

CMIP/CMIS

OSI has its own network management protocol, **Common Management Information Protocol/Common Management Information Services (CMIP/CMIS).** Even the abbreviation is complex, reflecting the complexity of CMIP/CMIS. However, these

OSI protocols also possess a high degree of sophistication (for instance, object oriented design). This could make them widely adopted in the future if SNMP does not deliver the functionality that network administrators need in a timely manner.

COMPREHENSIVE NETWORK MANAGEMENT PROGRAMS

Although it would be nice if all vendors supported a single standard, that is not the case. Nor are SNMP and CMIS/CMIP the only alternatives. Many carriers have their own internal network management systems, and network administrators are gaining greater access to carrier management information bases.

There is a growing trend toward the purchase of **comprehensive network management programs** that can collect data using multiple network protocols and integrate this information, as illustrated in Figure 6.12.[2]

Layers of Concerns in Network Management

Figure 6.13 shows that there are three basic layers in network management. These are the transmission, systems, and application layers.

▶ **Transmission management** deals with the things we have seen in Chapters 3 through 5, including hubs, switches, routers, modems, and carrier transmission lines.

▶ **Systems management** moves us up to the management of individual servers and client PCs. This includes such things as establishing access rights and backing up files.

▶ **Application management,** finally, is concerned with the management of distributed applications, such as database applications. This includes such things as application access control and the collection of application use statistics across servers.

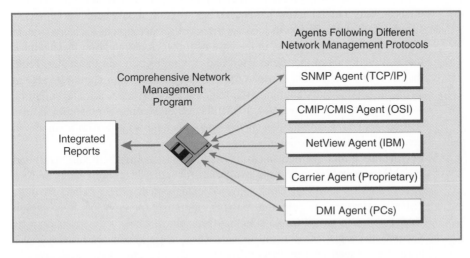

FIGURE 6.12

Comprehensive Network Management Program

---

[2] One popular comprehensive network management program is Computer Associates' TNG Unicenter. To give another example, Tivoli Systems developed TME. Tivoli Systems was purchased by IBM and now also manages IBM's older NetView comprehensive network management program. Tivoli will eventually merge TME and NetView.

FIGURE 6.13

**Network
Management
Layers**

LAYER	CHARACTERISTICS
Application Management	Software distribution Software metering (amount of use) Application access control Virus detection and removal
Systems Management	Organizing resources on servers Adding users on servers Access rights on servers Backup for servers Systems management for client PCs
Transmission Management	Fault management Configuration management Performance management Security management Accounting management

TRANSMISSION MANAGEMENT

The most obvious layer in Figure 6.13 is **transmission management.** This is the management of transmission assets in the network, including wiring, hubs, switches, routers, and carrier transmission facilities. The goal of transmission management is to move bits efficiently and effectively between computers on the network. This requires several types of capabilities in the network management program.

▶ **Fault management** tools help the network administrator identify the cause of a network failure and then take action to remove the problem or to route packets around it. Diagnosis can be very difficult because a failure in one place will cause failures in other places as well. The network administrator must identify the root fault, and the network management program should help him or her.

▶ **Configuration management** looks at the specific operation of each component of the network. For instance, in the case of routers, configuration management looks at the status of the router itself and of various ports on the router. From the network management console, the network administrator should be able to change a component's configuration remotely. For instance, a router might be told at night to shut down a port, so that the use of expensive transmission lines will be stopped. Configuration management also allows a firm to maintain an inventory of its network components.

▶ **Performance management** measures such things as **speed (throughput)** and **reliability (percentage of time available)** for individual components and for the network as a whole. Good network management programs should offer "what-if" analysis to help the network administrator envision how certain changes in the network would affect performance.

▶ **Security management** prevents unauthorized access to network resources. We have already seen security matters above. The next section looks at security in more depth.

▶ **Accounting management** will be needed if firms stop viewing network use as an overhead cost and begin assigning costs to individual departments, employees, or other units.

SECURITY

A firm with a few PCs has simple security needs. As networks grow in size, however, security problems also increase.

SECURITY PRINCIPLES

Figure 6.14 shows that security is needed against a number of *threats*. All major threats need to be countered if a firm is to be safe. Determined attackers search for any weakness in corporate defenses. In security, if you do not take required steps everywhere, being excellent in most areas will do little good.

AUTHENTICATION

Figure 6.14 shows someone who wishes to use a resource server. **Access control** limits use of the server to authorized people. The person claims to be an authorized user. However, the person may not be who he or she claims to be. To address this threat, we require **authentication,** *which means requiring the person to prove his or her identity.*

The simplest form of authentication is the use of a **password.** Unfortunately, passwords are easily compromised. Larger firms need stronger forms of authentication.

CONTENT FILTERING

Another danger is that once the person is authenticated, he or she may send unauthorized requests to the resource. For instance, someone may enter the system with authorization to use e-mail. However, after admission, he or she may then begin to use another service, send a message containing a virus, or take some other harmful action.

To prevent inappropriate behavior after authentication, it is necessary to pass each subsequent message from the user through a **content filter.** The filter examines the contents of each message before passing it on. One reason for content filtering is **viruses.** Good virus filtering is critical in large networks.

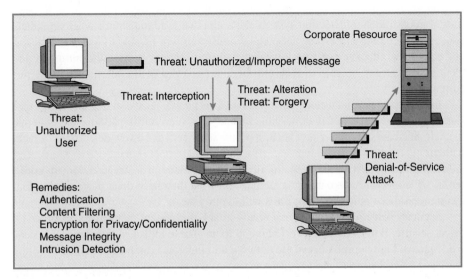

FIGURE 6.14

Security Threats and Remedies

Corporate Resource

Threat: Unauthorized/Improper Message

Threat: Interception

Threat: Alteration
Threat: Forgery

Threat: Unauthorized User

Threat: Denial-of-Service Attack

Remedies:
Authentication
Content Filtering
Encryption for Privacy/Confidentiality
Message Integrity
Intrusion Detection

ENCRYPTION FOR PRIVACY AND CONFIDENTIALITY

Suppose the user in Figure 6.14 is legitimate and takes only legitimate actions. There is still the danger of **third-party threats.** Someone between the user and the resource may **intercept** one or all messages.

The figure shows an interception taking place during transmission. However, interception can also take place afterward, when the message contents are stored on the resource server. Someone can hack into the computer to read messages. Or, the computer's supervisor, who normally has very broad power to access files on the computer, may read files without authorization.

If someone does intercept messages, you would like to prevent that person from benefiting from this action. This requires that you **encrypt** your messages, that is, transform your messages into a form that will be unreadable by anyone intercepting the message. That person will see only an unreadable sequence of ones and zeros. Encryption gives **privacy,** which is also called **confidentiality.**

MESSAGE INTEGRITY

Another danger is that someone can intercept your message, change it, and place it back into the transmission network. **Message integrity** controls ensure that if a message is altered, the receiving party will be able to detect the alteration. In a postal letter, for example, we may be able to tell if the flap has been opened after being glued shut.

DENIAL-OF-SERVICE ATTACKS

Denial-of-service attacks are aimed at making systems useless to their normal users. Figure 6.14 shows one common denial-of-service attack—to deluge a server with hundreds of thousands of computer-generated messages. The system will be so overloaded that it will not be able to serve its normal users. Other attacks use fewer messages, each of which requires the system to take a long period of time to handle.

ACTIVELY DETECTING AND ANTICIPATING ATTACKS

Perhaps the greatest weakness of most corporate networks is their lack of **intrusion detection** capabilities. If a network lacks the ability to detect intruders, attackers will be able to take their time, trying many different things until something works. In contrast, a good intrusion detection system alerts a network administrator when an attack appears to be taking place. The network administrator will be able to lock the attacker out before the attacker can find a weakness in the system. In fact, the intrusion detection system may be able to lock out the attacker even before alerting the systems administrator.

Intrusion detection systems have databases of known attack strategies. They constantly monitor traffic to detect possible matches between traffic patterns and patterns in their databases. Some, like the best virus scanners, can even detect new attack patterns.

One of the most basic elements of intrusion detection is the creation of **audit trails,** which record where users have gone and what they have done. If you know that a system has been attacked, audit trails will identify suspects.

Security self-analysis tools essentially attack the system themselves, in order to detect security holes before hackers can find them. These tools test the company's network against known problems so the network administrator can take action.

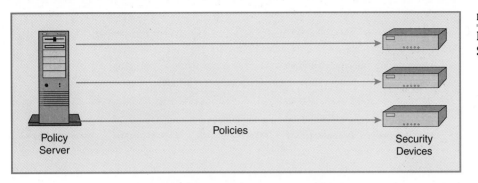

FIGURE **6.15**

Policy-Based Security

Policy Server

Policies

Security Devices

Developing a Security Policy

In large systems, security is extremely complex. Firms must develop comprehensive **security policies** that establish broad guidelines against which to judge individual security measures.

UNDERSTANDING THE BUSINESS

Developing security policies requires you to understand your organization's business. For instance, in banking it is not difficult to see that access control will be very important, given the dangers of monetary theft from databases. In other businesses, industrial espionage may be a major concern. In some firms, security threats will be fairly modest. In security policies, one size does not fit all.

POLICY-BASED SECURITY

Once major threats have been identified, the next step is to develop broad security policies. One example is to require strong authentication for access to any server classified as being subject to strong threats. Another is to check every message from the Internet for viruses. Figure 6.15 shows that some firms have a **policy server** that contains specific policies.

Other security devices check with the policy server to implement their security protocols. For instance, to prevent a hacker from finding a weak server to attack, every server might check with the policy server when it implements its access protocols.

A policy server allows the firm to change policies quickly. For instance, if a firm begins to experience a new type of denial-of-service attack, the policy server can be set to add a new type of filtering. All access servers would update their filtering protocols automatically.

Encryption

Encryption's goal is to make messages unreadable to anyone who intercepts them. Encryption provides **confidentiality,** also called **privacy.** We will see later that it is also essential in authentication.

THE ENCRYPTION PROCESS

As Figure 6.16 shows, the original message is called **plaintext.** Encryption converts this plaintext into **ciphertext,** which an interceptor will not be able to read. The receiver converts the ciphertext back to the original plaintext.

FIGURE **6.16**

Single Key Encryption

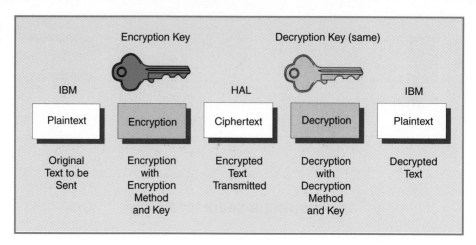

Encryption/decryption requires two things. One is an **encryption method.** To give an example that is too easy to break to be used in practice, suppose that the encryption method is to subtract *N* positions in the alphabet for each letter. So if we subtract two positions, we would encrypt the letter *C* by changing it to *A*.

Encryption also requires a **key.** In Figure 6.16, the key is "1" (position). So "IBM" becomes "HAL".[3] If the key had been "2", "IBM" would have been "GZK." It is impossible to keep the encryption method secret, so security *requires keeping the key secret.*

Even if the key is kept secret, an interceptor can still defeat the system if the **key length** (measured in bits) is small. For instance, suppose that the key length is only 2 bits. In this case, there are only four possible keys, 00, 01, 10, and 11. The interceptor will only have to try four keys before getting the correct one. To prevent **exhaustive search** from defeating encryption, the key length is made quite long. A key of 56 bits provides minimal commercial security, whereas a key of 128 bits provides good security.

Incidentally, there is tension between commercial organizations, which want large keys, and many governments, which want to keep keys short enough to allow legal wiretaps to listen in on criminals and terrorists.

SINGLE KEY ENCRYPTION

The encryption method used in Figure 6.16 is a **single key encryption** method. There is a single key that both sides must use. In our trivial example, the key is "1".

Single key encryption methods have two major problems. The first is that the key must be delivered securely to the two parties. This can be quite difficult. If your security system has already been breached, then you cannot send the key over the network. Hand delivery or complex network-based schemes make **key distribution** an awkward process.

The second problem is that if you have 10 business partners, you need 10 different single keys. (You would not want Supplier A to be able to read messages you send to Supplier B.) If you have many customers or suppliers, key distribution for multiple keys becomes a nightmare.

---

[3] Stanley Kubrick denies that this is how the HAL 9000 computer in *2001: A Space Odyssey* got its name.

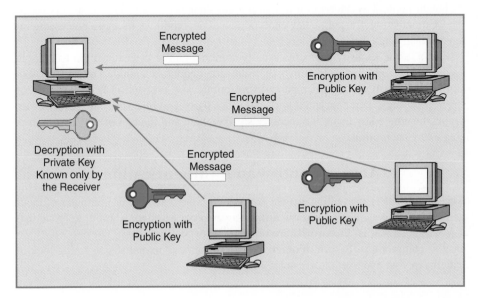

FIGURE 6.17
**Public Key
Distribution**

The advantage of single key systems is their speed. Single key encryption is much faster than the public key encryption we will see next.

PUBLIC KEY ENCRYPTION

To overcome the problems of single key encryption, systems today often use **public key encryption,** which Figure 6.17 illustrates. In public key encryption, each person has a **public key.** Instead of keeping it secret, everyone makes his or her public key available to everyone, as the figure indicates.

If a sender wants to send a receiver a message, the sender encrypts the message with the *receiver's public key*, as Figure 6.18 illustrates. Anyone can encrypt a message to a receiver with the receiver's public key.

FIGURE 6.18

**Encrypting
Messages
with Public
Key Encryption**

FIGURE **6.19**

Two-Way Public Key Encryption

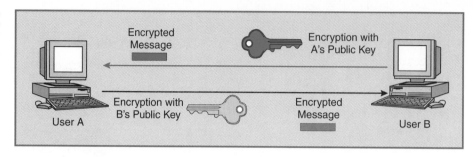

Although anyone can encrypt a message with a receiver's public key, the public key cannot **decrypt** the message afterward. Even the sender cannot decrypt the message after encrypting it. Only a second key, the receiver's **private key,** can decrypt the message. As the name suggests, although the receiver publishes his or her public key, the receiver keeps his or her private key secret. Anyone learning the receiver's private key could read encrypted messages sent to the receiver.

Note that the receiver does not need to give each business partner a different key. Everybody uses the receiver's public key. This reduces the problem of key distribution. Although private keys must still be distributed securely, there is only one secure key delivery per user, rather than two for each of a user's business partners.

TWO-WAY PUBLIC KEY ENCRYPTION

So far, we have discussed people sending messages to a receiver. Figure 6.19 illustrates two-way transmission. It shows two parties, A and B. When A sends to B, A encrypts the message with *B's public key*. When B sends a message to A, in turn, B encrypts it with *A's public key*. *In other words, a sender always encrypts messages with the receiver's public key.*

COMBINING PUBLIC AND SINGLE KEY ENCRYPTION

Although public key encryption has strong advantages, it also has a major disadvantage. Computationally, public key encryption and decryption is far more processing intensive than single key encryption.

As a result, security protocols usually combine public key encryption and single key encryption. Figure 6.20 shows that one side generates a single key for that session and sends it to the other party using public key encryption. The key creator sends this single key encrypted with the other party's public key. The receiver decrypts the single key using the receiver's private key and the rest of the session uses single key encryption.

Access Control and Authentication

Access control is preventing people from using your network or computer without permission. This requires **authentication**—a person or a system's ability to prove that it is who it says it is. **Passwords** are often used for authentication, but passwords are easy to compromise. In turn, **biometric** devices, such as retinal scanners that look at patterns in your eye's retina, are not widely available.

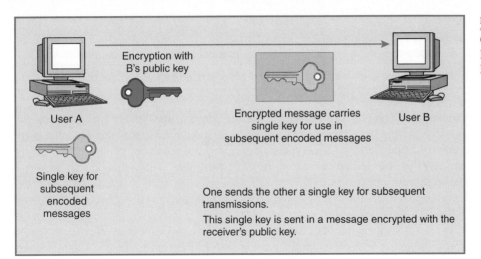

FIGURE **6.20**

Combining Single Key and Public Key Encryption

Encryption with B's public key

User A

Single key for subsequent encoded messages

Encrypted message carries single key for use in subsequent encoded messages

User B

One sends the other a single key for subsequent transmissions.

This single key is sent in a message encrypted with the receiver's public key.

PUBLIC KEY AUTHENTICATION

Authentication often uses **public key authentication.** More specifically, *the goal is for a sender to demonstrate that the sender holds his or her own private key*. Because private keys are supposed to be secret, if you can demonstrate that you hold your private key, the receiver is reasonably sure that you are who you say you are. Of course, if your private key is stolen, then the entire system is compromised.

Public key authentication relies on the fact that private keys can encrypt as well as decrypt. As Figure 6.21 shows, a sender encrypts a plaintext message with *the sender's private key* (not the receiver's public key). The receiver then decrypts the message with *the sender's public key*, which the receiver already knows. If the decryption works, then the sender definitely holds the sender's private key.

Note that public key authentication is the reverse of public key encryption. Figure 6.22 illustrates this. In public key *encryption*, the sender encrypts with the *receiver's*

FIGURE **6.21**

Public Key Authentication

Sender's Private Key, Which Only the Sender Knows

Sender's Public Key, Which the Receiver Knows

Challenge Text

101110101100

Challenge Text

| Plaintext | Encryption | Ciphertext | Decryption | Plaintext |

Original Text to be Sent

Encryption With *Sender's Private Key*

Encrypted Text Transmitted

Decryption with *Sender's Public Key*

Decrypted Text is Correct, so Sender Holds the Private Key and is Authenticated

FIGURE **6.22**

Public Key Encryption and Authentication

PUBLIC KEY METHOD	SENDER	ENCRYPTION	DECRYPTION
Encryption	Other party	Your public key	Your private key
Authentication	You	Your private key	Your public key

public key. In public key *authentication*, in contrast, the sender encrypts with the *sender's private key.* One way to keep this straight is to remember that the other party knows your public key. In encryption, the other party uses your public key to encrypt messages to you. In authentication, the other party uses your public key to decrypt a message sent from you.

DIGITAL SIGNATURES

One way to implement public key authentication on a per message basis is to send a *digital signature* with each message, as Figure 6.23 illustrates. When you sign a letter, you authenticate it by adding something (your signature) at the end. A digital signature, in turn, is added to the end of each message.

Figure 6.23 shows that a sender begins with the plaintext message to be sent. The next step is for the sender to generate a **message digest,** which is a sample of the message's content. For instance, the sender might create the digest by taking every tenth word. This would give the sender a message digest one-tenth the size of the original message.[4]

Figure 6.23 shows that the next step is to *encrypt the message digest with the sender's private key.* This creates the **digital signature.** Only the sender should be able to do this, so the digital signature authenticates the message.

FIGURE **6.23**

Digital Signature

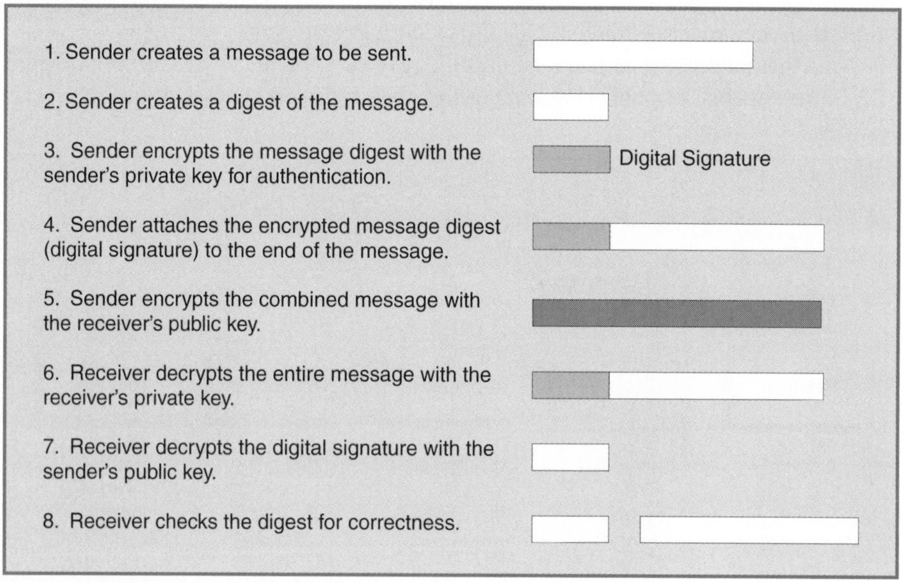

1. Sender creates a message to be sent.

2. Sender creates a digest of the message.

3. Sender encrypts the message digest with the sender's private key for authentication.   Digital Signature

4. Sender attaches the encrypted message digest (digital signature) to the end of the message.

5. Sender encrypts the combined message with the receiver's public key.

6. Receiver decrypts the entire message with the receiver's private key.

7. Receiver decrypts the digital signature with the sender's public key.

8. Receiver checks the digest for correctness.

---

[4] Such a simple digesting procedure would introduce enough redundancy to make the encryption easy to break.

Next, the sender attaches the digital signature to the end of the plaintext message, just as you put your signature at the end of a letter.

Finally, the sender takes the combined plaintext and digital signature and encrypts the entire combined message using the receiver's public key. This way, if the message is intercepted, the interceptor will not be able to read the message.

The receiver reverses the steps taken by the sender. The receiver first decrypts the entire message, using the receiver's private key. This decrypts the plaintext but leaves the digital signature encrypted in the sender's private key.

Next, the receiver decrypts the digital signature, using the *sender's public key*. The receiver then checks to make sure that the resulting message digest is every tenth word in the message.

DIGITAL CERTIFICATES

Another way to authenticate individual messages is to add a digital certificate. A certificate is something given to you by a third party to ensure people that you have certain desirable characteristics. For instance, your driver's license is given to you by your government to prove that you have permission to drive. Another form of third-party authentication is the medical diploma presented by a university. By seeing the diploma, patients can verify that their doctor is adequately trained.

In the digital world, a company can apply to a **certificate authority (CA)** for a **digital certificate.** This certificate contains information about the company, including its name and public key.

Figure 6.24 shows that a company attaches the digital certificate to every message it sends. The receiver, seeing the digital certificate, knows that a third-party certificate authority has checked the company's identity and has assigned it a digital certificate. If the receiver is suspicious, it can verify the company's identity and other characteristics by checking with the certificate authority.

Digital certificates can also be used within corporations. Each employee may be given a digital certificate for authentication when he or she deals with internal resources.

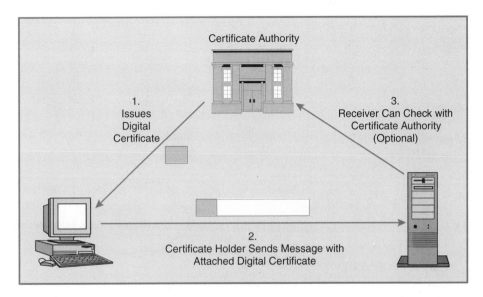

FIGURE **6.24**

**Digital Certificate
Authentication**

Certificate Authority

1.
Issues
Digital
Certificate

3.
Receiver Can Check with
Certificate Authority
(Optional)

2.
Certificate Holder Sends Message with
Attached Digital Certificate

Firewalls

Now that many firms are connected to the Internet, there is a danger that they will be attacked by Internet hackers who break into corporate computers for fun and profit.

Figure 6.25 shows that many firms now place firewalls at the border between their internal network and the Internet. **Firewalls** are designed to filter out messages from intruders.

IP FIREWALLS

As the name suggests, **IP firewalls** work at the internet layer by examining the source and destination address of each incoming IP packet. If the packet's source address or even source network part is from a person or organization that is not trusted, the IP firewall will discard the incoming message. In turn, if the packet's destination address is a system that should not be accessible through the Internet, the IP firewall will again discard the packet.

Although IP firewalls provide some protection, a skilled hacker can easily defeat them. For instance, the source address of each packet from the hacker can be changed to a trusted source address. This is called **IP spoofing.**

APPLICATION FIREWALLS

Application firewalls are more useful. As shown in Figure 6.26, these firewalls take into account the behavior of applications. For instance, if an application firewall receives an HTTP-reply-PDU addressed to a computer that has not just sent an HTTP-request-PDU, this would be highly suspicious. The application firewall would discard the HTTP-response-PDU.

Application firewalls are also called **proxy firewalls.** To be a proxy means to act in place of someone else. Figure 6.26 illustrates a browser sending an HTTP-request-PDU to a webserver. The browser actually sends the PDU to an HTTP proxy program on the application server. The proxy program then sends the HTTP-request-PDU to the webserver. The proxy server also receives the HTTP-response-PDU and passes it to

FIGURE 6.25

IP Firewall

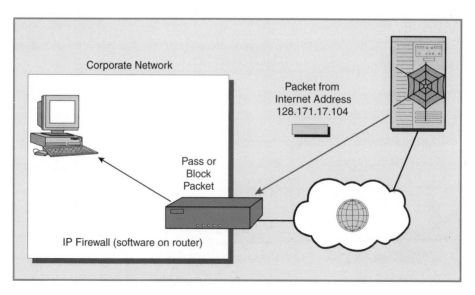

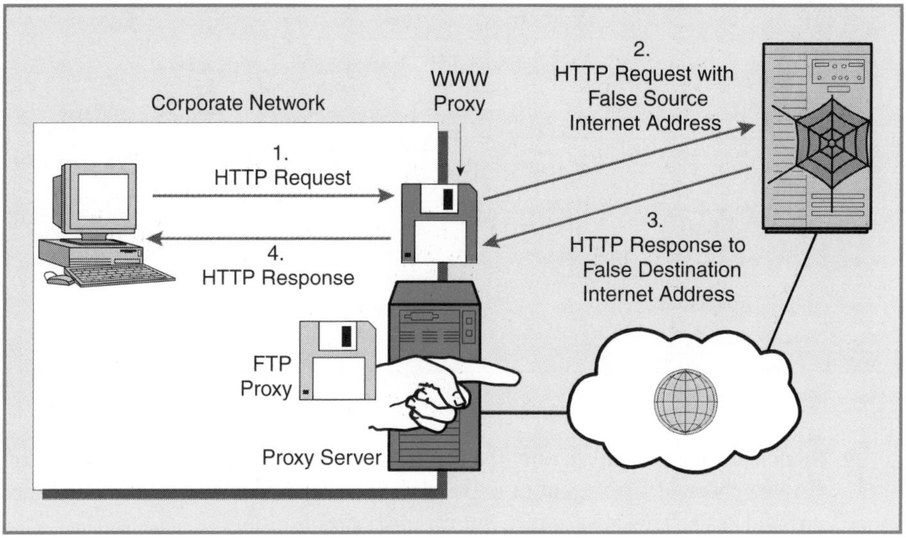

FIGURE **6.26**

**Application
Layer Firewall
(Proxy Server)**

the browser that originated the communication. This proxy operation allows strong filtering for both incoming and outgoing messages.

STATEFUL INSPECTION FIREWALLS

One problem with proxy servers is that formal proxy rules can be established for only some applications. In general, these applications are characterized by a series of interactions in a sequence, as in the case of HTTP request and response messages. At any moment, the proxy server can look at the history of the interactions and base decisions on the current state of the series.

Other applications do not have a series of well-defined states, including database applications, which are especially critical. **Stateful inspection firewalls** observe a series of transactions and keep track of states even if the application does not. Stateful inspection firewalls do not even need distinct proxies to be created for each application. Unfortunately, stateful inspection methods are proprietary and have not been analyzed independently for effectiveness at the time of this writing.

FILTERING

A persistent theme of this chapter and the previous chapter has been **filtering,** in which incoming messages are examined.

Depth of Filtering

In Chapter 2, we saw that an incoming frame will have a frame header (and perhaps trailer), a packet header, a transport layer header, and an application layer header and data field. Figure 6.27 illustrates this situation.

One key issue in any system is the **depth of filtering,** in other words, how deeply inspection examines headers and trailers.

FIGURE **6.27**

Depth of Filtering

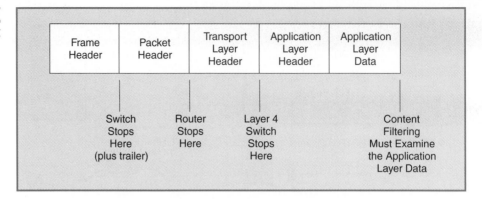

▶ Switches have to analyze only the frame header to deliver frames to stations on LANs or virtual LANs and to prevent stations from reaching stations on other virtual LANs. This is very fast, but it is also very limiting.

▶ Routers stop at the IP packet header. This gives them hierarchical addressing. It also gives them access to the internet layer's rich administrative protocols that are discussed in Module A.

▶ Newer "layer 4" routers examine the transport layer PDU. Among other things, this tells them the "port" number of the application (in TCP/IP). This usually specifies the particular application, such as HTTP.

▶ Finally, application layer devices, such as proxy firewalls, examine the details of the application layer PDU, including the data field. Virus filtering software, for instance, needs to look at the application layer PDU.

Purposes of Filtering

There are four general purposes in filtering.

1. **Effective, Efficient, and Reliable Delivery.** Most obviously, examining headers and trailers is required for efficient and reliable message delivery. Frame addresses are used to deliver messages within a subnet. IP packet addresses are used to deliver messages from subnet to subnet. Transport layer headers have port numbers to determine which application program should receive the application layer PDU. Error checking fields at several layers allow headers or entire PDUs to be checked for errors, so that messages with bad headers can be discarded and so that retransmission can be accomplished in some layers.

2. **Access Control.** A second purpose in filtering is to collect information needed for security. IP layer firewalls examine the IP packet header to decide whether to pass the packet or discard it. Application layer firewalls must examine the application layer PDU header to decide whether to pass or prevent the message.

3. **Quality of Service (QoS).** A third major reason to filter is to provide quality of service. For instance, header fields may request high priority for a frame or packet that cannot tolerate delays, such as a packet in a voice conversation. Filtering allows explicit QoS header fields to be read, so that a switch or router can assign appropriate priority to the frame or packet. In other cases, QoS can

be determined implicitly, by examining the type of application in the transport layer PDU's port field and giving priority based on application type.

4. **Translation.** The fourth reason to filter is translation. At the data link layer, for instance, switches may translate between the MAC layer frame formats for Ethernet and token-ring networks. At the highest level, devices called **gateways** translate between all layers—for instance, when a TCP/IP station on an Ethernet LAN needs to communicate with an SNA mainframe.

Integrated Transmission Networks

Today, we have many products that filter for many specific reasons. We have firewalls, routers, remote access devices, and many others. However, the inherent unity of filtering and its purposes suggests that we will eventually have fewer devices that do more things. Figure 6.28 illustrates such an **integrated transmission network.**

Instead of having many different devices, we may have only two types: **comprehensive relay devices** and **comprehensive policy servers.** The comprehensive relay devices will combine the functionality of switches, routers, firewalls, route optimization equipment, and translation equipment. These comprehensive relay devices will filter all incoming frames at all layers, in order to know how best to deliver them, prevent bad frames, provide the optimum quality of service for each frame, and provide any translations that are needed.

Today, vendors are too specialized to provide such comprehensive systems. In addition, the cost of such comprehensive relay devices would be prohibitive. However, vendor firms are already beginning to produce multilayer, multipurpose devices. Regarding costs, the same ASIC technology that is driving down router costs (as discussed in the last chapter) can make such simpler integrated transmission networks economically feasible. Although companies want to have the "best of breed" in each type of device, such as firewalls and routers, an integrated transmission network would be far easier to manage.

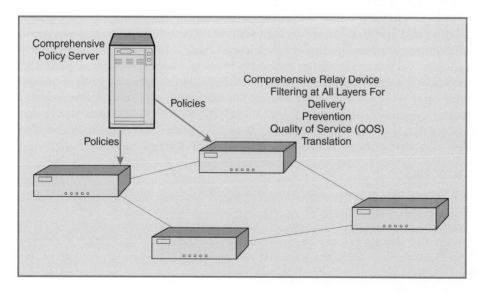

FIGURE 6.28

Integrated Transmission Network

Previous chapters have focused on technology and services from the end user's point of view. This chapter focuses on the tools that network administrators need to keep large networks operational and safe.

SERVER TECHNOLOGY

One issue is server technology. User demand for service is almost insatiable, and unless server technology is highly scalable, companies may suddenly find themselves unable to meet user demand. In addition, server technology must be highly reliable. Users have little patience when they need a critical service and it is unavailable. In terms of increasing scalability, we looked at high-end PC servers, Intel-based superservers, RISC workstation–based superservers, and mainframes. We also looked at ways to increase scalability and sometimes reliability through multiple processors on single machines and by combining multiple machines through server clustering, load balancing, and geographical decentralization.

NETWORK MANAGEMENT SYSTEMS

Large networks are very difficult to manage. Breakdowns and bottlenecks to performance can occur anywhere throughout the network and can be very difficult to diagnose and fix. The ideal network management system would allow a network administrator to handle all network management chores from a single network management console. Although we are far from that goal, we do have network management programs that can talk to many types of network management agents on managed devices. In addition, tools are moving beyond transmission management into systems management and application management. They are also moving beyond fault management into performance management and other types of higher-level concerns.

SECURITY

We also looked at security. Companies today are vulnerable to many types of internal and external security threats. We looked at these threats and the steps that companies take to guard against them. We focused particularly on authentication and encryption because they are used in many threat defenses. Public key encryption is particularly important, but it is also confusing because there are four keys: the sender's private key, the sender's public key, the receiver's private key, and the receiver's public key. You must know how each of these keys is used in encryption and authentication. We also looked at firewalls, which are designed to protect your firm from outside attack. One key concept in security is that you must have a comprehensive program. People who threaten your security are always looking for a weak link in your defenses.

FILTERING

We finished the chapter by noting that networks have many different devices that perform filtering at several different layers for several different purposes. We are already beginning to see devices that filter at multiple layers for multiple purposes, such as routers that also act as firewalls. If this trend continues, we will eventually see integrated transmission networks with just two major types of devices: comprehensive relay devices and comprehensive policy servers.

CORE REVIEW QUESTIONS

1. What are the two main performance characteristics one looks for in server technology? What are the main types of servers, and how do they differ from one another?

2. Distinguish between symmetric multiprocessing, server clustering, load balancing, and geographical decentralization. Which of these improves scalability? Which of these improves reliability?

3. Distinguish between servers aimed primarily at end users and servers aimed at network administrators.

4. How do directory servers help users? How do directory servers help administrators? What do X.500 and LDAP standardize? How are X.500 and LDAP different?

5. In network management, what should the network administrator be able to do from the network management console? Distinguish between network management programs, managed devices, network management agents, and MIBs. How do RMON probes differ from other managed devices?

6. What are the two major standards for network management? What are comprehensive network management programs, and why do we need them?

7. What are the three layers of functionality for network management? Briefly characterize each layer.

8. Characterize the following: authentication, encryption, privacy, confidentiality, message integrity, denial-of-service attack, intrusion detection, and security self-analysis. Why is intrusion detection, which is often ignored, critical for security?

9. Why is understanding the business the first step in developing a security policy? What are policy servers, and why are they important?

10. Characterize the following: plaintext, ciphertext, encryption methodology, and encryption key. Why is it important for keys to be as large as possible?

11. Distinguish between single key and public key encryption. Which reduces problems of key distribution?

12. In public key encryption, when A sends to B, what key does A use? When A authenticates himself or herself to B, what key does A use? If A and B send messages to each other, what keys do A and B use? If A encrypts a message to B, can A read it afterward?

13. How are public key encryption and single key encryption usually combined? Why are they combined?

14. In public key authentication, how do you prove you are who you say you are? What are the steps in creating a message containing a digital signature? How does a digital signature differ from a digital certificate?

15. What is the function of a firewall? Distinguish between IP firewalls and application firewalls. What happens between the time that you send an HTTP request message and the time that you get the HTTP response message when you have an IP firewall? When you have an application layer firewall?

16. What are the levels of depth in filtering? What are the purposes of filtering? Explain what an integrated transmission network of the future is likely to look like.

DETAILED REVIEW QUESTIONS

1. What is 24 × 7 operation? Why is it more important for some applications than for others?
2. What are the two types of superservers? How do they differ? How do server operating systems differ from operating systems for desktop PCs? What are the main server operating systems?
3. In symmetric multiprocessing, will a four-processor system be twice as fast as a two-processor system? Why or why not?
4. In geographical decentralization, distinguish between replication and caching.
5. Why is it normally difficult for an end user to find someone's e-mail address or the location of a file if the user does not have a directory server?
6. How is a user's having to log in only once—at the directory server—useful for end users? How is it useful for network administrators in terms of access rights and access control?
7. Between what two machines does a directory access protocol standardize interactions? Distinguish between X.500 and LDAP on the one hand and NDS and Active Directory on the other hand.
8. Will the network management agent in a managed device consist of software alone? When will it consist of a combination of hardware and software? Distinguish between the network management agent, the MIB, and the managed device.
9. What three types of messages are exchanged between the network management program and network management agents? What does RMON call an alarm message?
10. Characterize each of the following: fault management, configuration management, performance management, security management, and accounting management.
11. What are the major threats to security?
12. How many times does encryption take place when you send a message with a digital signature? List each, and explain whose private or public key is used and what this encryption accomplishes.
13. Do you need a different proxy program for each application? Can you get a proxy for every application?
14. Why will performance suffer if you have comprehensive relay devices for integrated transmission networks? How will ASIC technology help?

THOUGHT QUESTIONS

1. Why is intrusion detection central to security?
2. If you and I wish to communicate via public key encryption, what do you have to know? What do I have to know?
3. How many tries would it take to find the key through exhaustive search if the key length is 8 bits? 16 bits? 32 bits? 40 bits? 128 bits?
4. If I send you a message, I normally encrypt it with your public key. However, I could also encrypt it with my private key. You could decrypt it with my public key. This would work, but it would cause a serious problem. What is that problem?

5. Explain why it is important to begin with a comprehensive security policy.
6. Why do you think network management has taken so long to develop?
7. Many governmens would like to restrict the length of keys. Why do you think this is? Do you think it is a good policy?

PROJECTS

1. Go to the book's website, http://www.prenhall.com/panko, and read the Updates Page for this chapter to see any reported errors and for new and expanded information on the material in this chapter.
2. Go to the book's website, http://www.prenhall.com/panko, and do the Internet Exercises for this chapter.

CHAPTER 7

Human Communication Applications on Intranets and Other Networks

INTRODUCTION

In a real sense, everything we have studied so far has had one purpose—to show how to link application programs on different machines. The real key to networking—and to computing in general—is application software. Application software is what users need to do their daily work.

In this chapter, we will focus on human communication applications, including *e-mail* and a complex set of applications called *groupware,* which encompasses video-conferencing, workflow, and electronic document management, among other applications. These are tools for human communication involving words and images and conveying conceptual information.

In the next chapter, we will focus on applications that use more highly structured data in which information is organized in databases and similar repositories. The chapter examines client/server database systems, data warehouses, intranet-based information systems, electronic commerce, and other highly structured applications.

THE SHIFT TO INTRANETS

In recent years, there has been surging interest in **intranets**—the use of Internet technology and applications within businesses. Intranets use the TCP/IP standards architecture for internal corporate transmissions. They use routers to deliver messages within the company. They use Internet standards for e-mail, the World Wide Web, and other applications.

There are several reasons why organizations are turning to intranets. One is the lure of TCP/IP transmission technology, which is standardized, proven, and relatively inexpensive. It is also highly scalable. Technology that works for the worldwide Internet will work in even the largest corporations.

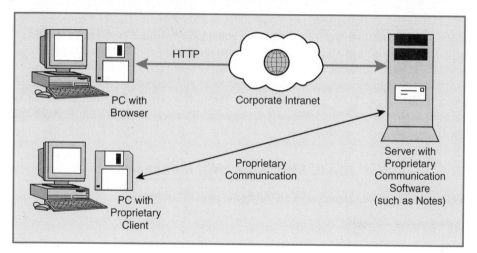

FIGURE 7.1

Web-Enabled
Proprietary
Communication
Application

More importantly, the Internet allows companies to move from proprietary applications, which lock them into a single vendor, to open Internet applications, such as Internet e-mail. With open application standards, companies can buy products from multiple vendors with reasonable assurance that they will work together.

For older Internet applications, such as e-mail, applications are sufficiently mature that one loses fairly little in moving from proprietary applications to open applications. However, for newer applications, such as groupware tools, proprietary applications offer a good deal more functionality than standard Internet applications even where such applications exist.

Companies are now attempting to mix the benefits of proprietary applications and intranet technology. Figure 7.1 shows that many vendors are **web-enabling** their proprietary applications. Here, we see a proprietary groupware application that traditionally required a proprietary client program on each PC. Now, however, if a user has a browser, he or she can also access the proprietary communication server, via a World Wide Web interface.

Do browser-based users have all the functionality of proprietary client users? Generally, they do not. Web-enabled users are still second-class citizens. However, they have at least basic services. This allows an organization to extend service to lighter users while still giving heavier users the full proprietary client program. Over time, however, the service gap between browser users and proprietary client users will diminish.

One problem in the conversion is pricing. Many companies with proprietary products charge relatively little for the server software and charge several hundred dollars for each client. In a web-enabled environment, however, they cannot charge for browsers and so will have to charge more for the server software.

ELECTRONIC MAIL

E-mail is the most widely used computer application of any type. It is not hard to imagine why. First, it is extremely *inexpensive*. It is much less expensive than facsimile and may even be cheaper than postal or interoffice mail delivery. It also helps users prepare their outgoing messages efficiently and to dispose of incoming messages (read, print, file, retrieve, delete, and so on), thus reducing labor time.

In addition, e-mail fills an important communication niche. The telephone provides instant communication, but only if the other person is available. Only about a quarter of all telephone calls reach the intended party. Managers often play telephone tag for days, leaving messages for someone and then not being in when that person returns the call.

Facsimile provides instant delivery, but facsimile images are difficult to use in other applications, except as raw images. In contrast, e-mail text can be copied into a document and edited after delivery if appropriate. Physical mail, in turn, is slow. On the Internet, it is called "snail mail."

Basic Elements of a Message

Figure 7.2 shows the elements of an electronic mail message.

HEADER

First, an e-mail message has a **header** with fixed-format fields such as To: and From:. These fixed-format fields can be processed automatically, like fields in business forms. For instance, a user can search for a message from "Pat Lee" received in the last two weeks.

BODY

Following the header is a free-prose **body.** Traditionally, the body has consisted of plain text. As we will see later, however, new standards will allow much greater flexibility in body content.

SIGNATURES

Many users end their messages with **signatures,** which give their full name, the name of their organization, their mailing address, their telephone numbers, their home page URL, and other information. This is like the information contained in corporate letterheads. The IETF is working on a standard for online business card exchanges, iCARD.

FIGURE 7.2

Elements of an Electronic Mail Message

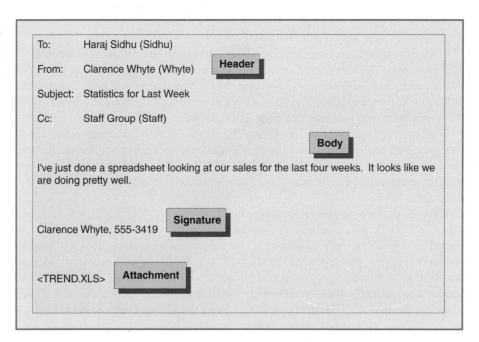

In the future, signatures may use iCARD format. The signature actually is a file that is appended to your messages automatically.

ATTACHMENTS

Finally, some messages contain **attachments.** Although the body may be limited to plain text, attachments can be word processing documents, spreadsheet files, graphics images, or files of any other type. Attachments turn e-mail into a general file delivery system. However, attachments are not easy to send because of multiple standards and sometimes poor interoperability among products that claim to follow the same standard.

Message Disposition

Research has shown that most e-mail commands are issued in the **disposition phase** after a message is received. People can scan through their mail quickly, read specific messages, dash off replies, file messages for later retrieval, or simply delete unneeded messages. People often get 10 to 100 messages a day, so automating the disposition phase is extremely important for productivity.

Distribution Lists

One reason why people often get many messages is that it is easy to create a **distribution list,** say of members of your department. To create a distribution list, you enter the e-mail addresses of your group's members in a file. You then give your file a name, perhaps *Department*. If you put *Department* in the *To* field, your mail program will send the message to everyone on the distribution list. In a typical mail system, one-to-one or one-to-few messages will dominate the number of messages *transmitted*, whereas distribution list messages will dominate the number of messages *received*.

Rules, Filters, and Agents

Although distribution lists bring many benefits, they tend to deluge users with more mail traffic than they can read. Fortunately, many systems now allow the user to automate how mail should be handled upon arrival. This capability is known by several different names, including **rules, filters,** and **agents.**

Whenever a new message arrives, the mail system looks up the **filtering rules** that the user has specified. For instance, one rule might be that if the From: field has the boss's name, then the message should be flagged with high priority.

Another rule might be that all mail from a certain distribution list should be automatically removed from the in-box and placed in a topical folder for reading when the receiver has time. Such a filtering rule might be used for distribution lists of low interest, such as those dealing with company social outings.

Most filtering rules follow the classic If-Then format. The "If" portion of the rule describes the fields to be considered and the content to seek. The "Then" portion describes what should be done with the message if it is flagged by the "If" portion.

Computer Conferencing

Electronic mail was created for private, one-to-one, and one-to-few messages. But *groups* also need to communicate. For example, suppose you are a member of a project team. In many cases, you have to send a message to everyone on the project team.

One way to do this is for each team member to create his or her own *distribution list* containing the addresses of all team members. Then, whenever someone sends a message, everybody gets it. This approach works well if group membership is static.

If group membership changes constantly, however, as it does in many groups, the mailing list approach breaks down. Even if everybody starts with the correct list, many lists will soon contain the addresses of people who are no longer in the group and no longer wish to get group mail. Worse yet, it will take some time before new members get on to most distribution lists. In the meantime, new members would get only some group messages.

Figure 7.3 shows how **computer conferencing** solves this problem. In conferencing, messages are sent to a conferencing system, which posts it to a common area. This area is often called a bulletin board, giving conferencing systems the synonym **bulletin board** systems. They are also called **forums** because members can broadcast their ideas to everybody, as in a physical political forum.

What happens next varies. Traditionally, when users wanted to see new postings, they had to log into the conferencing system and specify a conference name. Then they could look at the messages at their leisure. On the Internet, **USENET newsgroups** work like this. So do traditional computer conferencing programs. For more on USENET newsgroups, see Module G.

More recently, many conferencing systems have been based on the **LISTSERV** program or programs that act like LISTSERV. LISTSERV essentially keeps a centralized distribution list that is maintained by a conference moderator. When a message arrives, the LISTSERV program broadcasts it out to everybody on the distribution list. Members of the group receive the message in their regular electronic mail in-box, along with other e-mail. For more on LISTSERVs, see Module G.

Whatever the conferencing system, there are almost always special **moderator tools** to help the moderator run the conference. Most basically, there are functions for adding and dropping members who can access the conferencing messages.

FIGURE **7.3**

Computer Conferencing

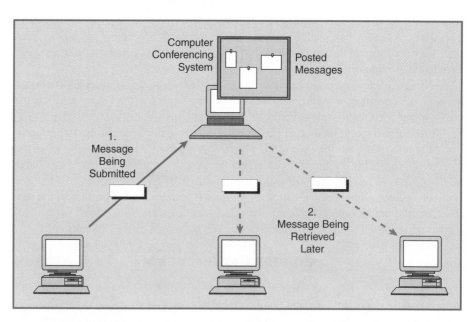

Mature conferencing systems have many other features. For instance, there usually is an area for storing group documents, such as working drafts, finished reports, and common data files. In addition, there are storage systems for many aspects of **group memory.** Hiltz and Turoff[1] present an extensive discussion of computer conferencing system features.

Electronic Mail Standards

Electronic mail began to grow rapidly in the late 1980s and early 1990s. Unfortunately, most companies soon found themselves with multiple mail systems, none of which would talk to any other. Some systems ran on PC networks. Others ran on workstation networks. Still others ran on mainframes or minicomputers.

Fortunately, there are now relatively good standards for electronic mail delivery. Although they are not everything we want, they typically provide basic connectivity among mail systems.

INTERNET MAIL STANDARDS

The most widely used e-mail standards are those produced by the Internet Engineering Task Force and used on the Internet. Even companies that are not on the Internet often use these standards. As shown in Figure 7.4, these TCP/IP standards assume the existence of **e-mail hosts.** These hosts accept incoming mail and hold the mail until the subscriber is ready to read it. This allows the receiver to work on a client PC, which will often be turned off. E-mail hosts also transmit outgoing messages to other mail hosts. Together, mail hosts function as a network of electronic post offices.

Internet electronic mail hosts exchange messages through the **Simple Mail Transfer Protocol (SMTP),** which is in the TCP/IP Internet architecture. As discussed in the box "Internet Electronic Mail Standards," several other standards work with SMTP to

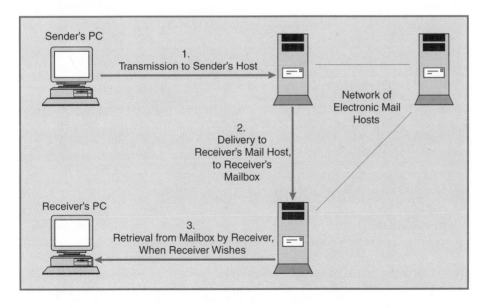

FIGURE 7.4

Internet Mail Hosts and Delivery

---

[1] S. R. Hiltz and M. Turoff, *The Networked Nation*, rev. ed. (Cambridge, MA: MIT Press, 1993).

standardize both delivery and message structure. For more on Internet electronic mail standards, see the box "Internet Electronic Mail Standards."

X.400

In the OSI architecture, mail delivery and structure are defined by the **X.400** family of standards. X.400 and Internet standards have similar functionality. As usual with OSI standards, X.400 standards are more sophisticated and slower to market.

Although X.400 standards have not had as extensive use as Internet mail standards, transmission carriers in many countries, particularly in Europe, favor them.

MESSAGE HANDLING SYSTEM (MHS)

In PC networking, the earliest widely used standard was the **Message Handling System (MHS)** standard promoted by Novell. It is still widely supported, although it has tended to give way to SMTP.

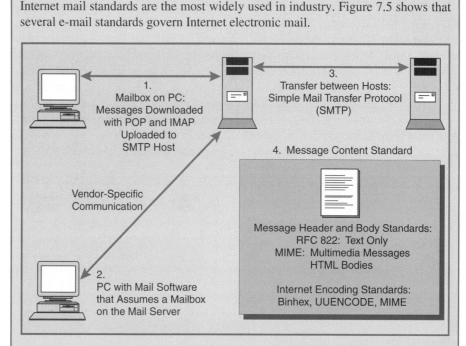

FIGURE 7.5

Internet Electronic Mail Standards

INTERNET ELECTRONIC MAIL STANDARDS

Internet mail standards are the most widely used in industry. Figure 7.5 shows that several e-mail standards govern Internet electronic mail.

Communication among Mail Hosts

In the body of the chapter, we saw that the core TCP/IP mail standard is the **Simple Mail Transfer Protocol (SMTP)**, which governs communication *among mail hosts*.

Communication with Subscribers

There are two basic ways for the mail host to interact with subscribers. As Figure 7.4 shows, the traditional way was to place the mail application program on the server. Then the user could log into the host from anywhere to read and maintain his or her messages.

POP

To handle mail the traditional way, the subscriber must remain logged onto the mail host. Another approach is to use client/server processing in which the user has a mail client on his or her PC. The PC mail client works with a server program on the mail server. Through request–response exchanges, the user can download mail, upload outgoing mail, and perform various supervisory tasks.

For such needs, the IETF initially defined the **Post Office Protocol (POP),** shown in Figure 7.5. POP downloads all new mail to the user's client program, where the user can read the mail at his or her leisure. In addition, these clients can upload mail to an SMTP mail host for delivery via an intranet or the Internet.

IMAP

Although POP has been very popular, having to download all new messages at once can cause problems. For instance, if someone has attached a 2-megabyte file to a message and you are using a 33.6 kbps modem, the bulk mail download could take a very long time.

A newer standard, the **Internet Message Access Protocol (IMAP),** offers more options. When you connect to your mail host, you can see a one-line summary of each message. You can then download only the messages you wish to receive. IMAP also allows you to do housekeeping chores on your mailbox, such as deleting messages selectively.

FRAGMENTED MAILBOXES

One problem with client programs that use standards like POP and IMAP is that a user may have several e-mail client programs, say one at work, one on a home desktop, and one on a laptop. Each may contain only some of a person's messages, especially if messages are deleted from the host PC after downloading.

Message Structure

SMTP, POP, and IMAP are concerned with message *delivery*. But the *structure* of a message also needs to be standardized. Recall that the structure consists of a header and a body.

RFC 822 TEXT MESSAGES

The standard for text messages on the Internet is **RFC 822.** This standard specifies that a message must have two parts: a header and a body. The header must contain specific fields, such as *date sent*, *to*, *from*, and *subject*. Other header fields are optional. Each field has a keyword, a colon (:), and the content of the field. The rigid header structure allows a mail program to search for messages from a specific e-mail address, sort messages by author or date, and do many other things to make message retrieval easier. The body contains free-form text.

RFC 822 was limited to 7-bit ASCII text, in which each byte represents one keyboard character and in which only the first seven bits of the byte can be used. Module H discusses 7-bit ASCII in more detail. According to David Crocker, an author of RFC 822, this limit was needed because RFC 822 was created for the original ARPANET, which could only guarantee 7-bit ASCII transmission. Packets whose data fields contained information in the eighth bit often failed to reach the destination host or were scrambled during transmission. Later, the Internet continued this restriction.

MIME

The IETF, however, has defined ways to put information other than text into both the message body and the message header. Collectively, these standards are referred to as **Multipurpose Internet Mail Extensions (MIME).** The IETF has added many MIME extensions since creating the MIME framework in 1993.

HTML

The popularity of the World Wide Web has led several mail vendors to offer **HTML** formatting in the body of the message. Unfortunately, this is nonstandard. To make matters worse, different mail program vendors use different nonstandard HTML tags. When messages with HTML in the body are sent to users of text-only or text-plus-MIME mail systems, receivers will see the tags used in HTML instead of the formatting these tags were designed to convey.

Internet Encoding for Attachments

As just noted, a peculiarity of the Internet is that it will transmit only 7-bit ASCII. PC ASCII, however, has 8 bits. So if you transmit a binary attachment, such as a word processing document, it will not travel through the Internet without being altered.

The solution is to **Internet encode** your attachment before transmission. Encoding takes your document and converts it into a legitimate 7-bit form that can travel through the network.

To give an example of Internet encoding, blocks of 3 data bytes (24 bits) are sent in blocks of 4 attachment bytes (32 bits). Each attachment byte then contains only 6 data bits.

Next, because the first 32 ASCII codes are supervisory control characters that are also forbidden on the Internet, the binary value for 32 is added to each attachment byte. After this is done, there are no forbidden control characters, and the seventh bit is still free.

Unfortunately, several Internet encoding schemes are in common use. Macintosh users have traditionally used **Binhex.** UNIX users have traditionally used **UUENCODE.** IBM PC compatible users find themselves using both. **MIME** (discussed previously) is also becoming common. Each Internet encoding scheme encodes the attachment differently, so both sides must use the same encoding scheme.

Before you send someone an attachment, then, you must know which Internet encoding schemes your mail program and the receiver's mail program support. This will allow you to identify a common Internet encoding standard.

You must agree upon a **file format** for the attachment. For instance, suppose that I am using the latest version of Word for Windows and the other party is using WordPerfect. Then if I send the other party an attachment, I will have to save my file either to an older version of Word for Windows (which the receiver can probably read) or to a version of WordPerfect that is the receiver's version or an earlier version.

Mail Etiquette and Legality

Although e-mail is widely used, it is still a very young medium of communication. Informal standards of behavior called **etiquette** and legal standards of behavior are still being worked out or are not understood by many users. For more on electronic mail behavior, see the box "Electronic Mail Etiquette and Laws."

ELECTRONIC MAIL ETIQUETTE AND LAWS

Unfamiliarity sometimes leads to rather unpleasant surprises. As a result, many organizations have published rules governing the behavior of e-mail users. Often these rules are informal and are classified as **etiquette.** In some cases, however, these rules represent corporate policy and can result in sanctions against those who break them. In yet other cases, the rules are set by outside legal institutions.

Flaming

The most frequently discussed behavioral problem is **flaming.** In flaming, a user sends a harsh emotional message to another user. Often this message is fired off in the heat of the moment after receiving a message from another person. For better or worse, e-mail allows us to dash off replies before we have had a chance to cool down.

There is disagreement over how serious flaming is in real corporations. It may well be that flaming in e-mail is correlated with flaming in other types of media and in meetings in an organization.[2] Some corporations have styles that are blunt or even rude. Even in these firms, however, flaming in permanent e-mail form may be frowned upon.

Some e-mail systems allow you to "take back" a message before the other party has read it, but most do not have this function, and there is no provision for it in standards for mail delivery from one system to another.

Spamming

In the television series *Monty Python*, there was a skit in which a group of Vikings yells "SPAM, SPAM, SPAM."[3] This drowns out other people who are trying to talk.

---

[2] E. Davidson, University of Hawaii, personal communication with the author, 1995.

[3] SPAM is a registered trademark of Hormel. It is *not* an acronym for "spongy pink animal matter."

On the Internet, **spamming** is the practice of developing mailing lists with millions of e-mail addresses and using these lists to broadcast commercial announcements, often of a sleazy nature.

In many cases, the spammer uses a false return address, and an innocent user at that address may be bombarded with mail from irate receivers of the spam. Spammers also tend to "hijack" an e-mail host in someone else's corporation to send out their mail. This can seriously degrade host performance. In addition, some hijacked mail servers are later attacked by angry spam receivers.

Several states in the United States have made spamming illegal, but this is difficult to enforce, especially when the spammer is in another state or country without anti-spam laws. Many Internet users already receive one or two spam messages a day, and given the Internet's potential growth, e-mail users could soon be drowning in spam.

Rules for Forwarding

If you receive a message, you can **forward** it to someone else. For instance, if you receive a request for a copy of something, you might forward it to your secretary.

Unfortunately, if you send someone a private message, that person can forward it to others—perhaps even to a distribution list. This unexpected forwarding can be done either maliciously or simply with lack of forethought to consequences. Two simple rules are never send anything that others should not see and never forward something without permission.

Care in Replying

When you get a message, you can send back an immediate **reply.** This is dangerous if the original message went to multiple people. Some reply functions automatically reply to everyone who received the original mail. If you do not realize this, you are likely to use reply to send a message to the author of the message. Yet everyone who got the original message will also get the reply. This can be acutely embarrassing.

Spoofing

It is not very hard in most mail systems to send a message that seems to be from someone other than yourself. This is **spoofing.** In one company, a message supposedly from the president announced that there would be layoffs the next week. The message really was from a prankster. It took weeks to make this clear to the employees, however, and even then, doubts remained.

Viruses

Many application programs have macro languages that do certain things when a program is loaded. Unfortunately, some hackers have learned ways to turn macros into malicious **viruses.** If you get an attachment and open it, there is a danger that the virus will affect data files of the same type. Although some mail programs and application programs filter out these macro viruses, you must be careful when opening attachments.

Urban Legends

Modern life has given us many **urban legends,** such as rumors about the presence of alligators in the sewer system. Unfortunately, there are also urban legends about e-mail systems. The most widespread of these is the "Good Times Virus Hoax." It is an e-mail message warning that if you open a message with "Good Times" in the title, your system may get a horrendous virus that will crash your hard disk. Although *opening* an attachment can cause macro virus infections, merely reading a message cannot. The Good Times message was a pure hoax. Nevertheless, it has circulated for several years and has hit some organizations several times. Well-meaning receivers, in order to warn their friends, immediately broadcast the message out to everyone they know. Several of their friends do the same, propagating the hoax message farther.

Corporate Privacy

Many employees believe that their electronic mail is **private** and that only they can read it. In fact, it appears that companies in most legal jurisdictions have extensive rights to read electronic mail sent or received by their employees. This has resulted in terminations and other sanctions. Unless companies have clear policies stating that e-mail is private, it is best to follow the simple rule that you should not state anything that you would not want your boss or another employee to read.

Even when companies have policies declaring e-mail to be private, they usually include exceptions for messages detrimental to the firm, such as criticism of other employees and especially superiors, messages that indicate that the employee is breaking nonmail corporate policies, and so forth.

Legal Discovery

Even if a company decides to make all e-mail private, this has no bearing on how courts view e-mail. When there is a lawsuit against a firm, there is a **legal discovery** process in which the plaintiff can require the defendant firm to produce all relevant documents, including e-mail messages, that bear on a case. Informal messages meant for internal consumption are often very influential with juries. A good rule is never send anything that you would not want a jury to read.

GROUPWARE

Perhaps no term in information systems today has been more abused by marketers than *groupware*. Almost any product that does not run on a stand-alone PC has been labeled "groupware" by corporate advertising staffs. Although definitions vary, for our purposes in this book we will define **groupware** as information technology aimed at supporting work processes in managerial or professional groups, where **group** means a workgroup of limited size (say 2 to 20 members) whose members are fairly interdependent.

Note the stress on managerial and professional work. In general, these products are not designed for *production systems*, that is, high-volume systems used by clerical workers or other production workers. We will look at production systems in the next section.

Note also the limitation on group size. Most groupware tools are well suited to the support of workgroups that are relatively flat, that is, do not have two or more levels of hierarchical structure with sharp divisions of labor among subgroups. This may (and should) change in the future, of course.

Another reason for limiting group size is that intensely interacting workgroups in corporations tend to be rather small. In a sample of 165 project teams, only 12% were larger than 16 people.[4] Subjects were allowed to select any project they had worked on in the last 6 months, so the data may not be representative, but the trend is impressive. In addition, in a study that examined data on 45 conference room meetings from 14 managers,[5] the average conference room meeting size was 7 people, and extremely large meetings were rare.

Categories of Group Processes

Figure 7.6 shows a taxonomy for group processes created by Johansen, Martin, and Sibbet at the Institute for the Future.[6]

FIGURE **7.6**

Taxonomy of Groupware Products

	Same Time (Synchronous)	Different Time (Asynchronous)
Same Place	Electronic Meeting Room	Departmental Electronic Document Management (EDM)
Different Place	Videoconferencing Desktop Conferencing	E-Mail Computer Conferencing Electronic Document Management Project Management

[4] S. T. Kinney and R. R. Panko, "Project Teams: Profiles and Member Perceptions: Implications for Group Support System Research and Products," *Proceedings of the Twenty-Ninth Hawaii International Conference on System Sciences*, Kihei, Maui (Los Alamitos, CA: IEEE Computer Society Press, January 1996).

[5] R. R. Panko and S. T. Kinney, "Meeting Profile: Size, Duration, and Location," *Proceedings of the Twenty-Eighth Hawaii International Conference on System Sciences*, Vol. 4, Kihei, Maui (Los Alamitos, CA: IEEE Computer Society Press, January 1995), pp. 1001–1012.

[6] R. Johansen, A. Martin, and D. Sibbet, *Leading Business Teams: How Teams Can Use Technology and Group Process Tools to Enhance Performance* (Addison-Wesley, 1991).

SAME TIME/DIFFERENT TIME

One key distinction is whether the people are working together at the **same time** or at **different times.** Same-time communication, which is called **synchronous communication,** includes face-to-face meetings, telephone calls, desktop videoconferencing, and a number of other types of human communication. Managers spend about 60% of their days in same-time communication.[7] In general, same-time communication is highly interactive, with extensive give and take. Ideas fly freely, and the result is a "group thinking" process in which it is very difficult to establish who produced what ideas and why particular decisions were made.

In contrast, different-time processes tend to use text and other permanent artifacts to a greater degree. Because people have more time to compose messages, there tends to be more rational organization to the communication. At the same time, work takes longer to perform.

SAME PLACE/DIFFERENT PLACE

The second dimension is whether the participants are in the **same place** or in **different places.** Same-place interactions can involve meetings at deskside or in conference rooms. Research has shown that managers spend 55% of their working days (not just communication time) in same-place face-to-face communication.[8] Obviously, supporting same-place communication is necessary if we wish to have a large impact on managerial work.

At the same time, it is often inconvenient to bring participants together for a meeting. In a sample of 105 project teams,[9] 31% of the project team members worked at a different site than the respondent. Over half of the project teams had at least one member from another site. A quarter had half or more of their members working at a different site than the respondent.

Different-place systems are also important because managers and professionals spend a quarter of their days dealing with written communication.[10]

KEYBOARD-BASED GROUPWARE

To many people, the term *groupware* is almost synonymous with Lotus Notes. However, Lotus Notes is only one example of a family of applications called **keyboard-based groupware.** In keyboard-based groupware, the user works at a client PC or some other desktop machine. He or she has one or more keyboard-based applications to help the user participate in group efforts.

Normally, desktop groupware is a different-time/different-place tool. Other members of the team work at different computers, often at different sites. When they work, furthermore, they work at different times, having access to what others have done previously.

---

[7] R. R. Panko, "Patterns of Managerial Communication," *Journal of Organizational Computing* 2, no. 1 (1992): 95–122.

[8] Panko, "Patterns of Managerial Communication," 95–122.

[9] Kinney and Panko, "Project Teams: Profiles and Member Perceptions."

[10] Panko, "Patterns of Managerial Communication," 95–122.

Services

Generally, desktop groupware has a number of related tools, as shown in Figure 7.7. This figure shows a customer tracking tool.

VERBAL COMMUNICATION

The most basic element in any keyboard-based groupware system is **verbal communication,** that is, communication using *words*. Keyboard-based groupware systems tend to use e-mail as their communication tool. In fact, one early study of groupware indicated that most systems were used primarily for e-mail.[11]

GROUP COMPOSITION

In stand-alone computing, word processing is the most widely used type of application software. Groups also need to compose word processing documents, as well as spreadsheet models and other group artifacts. **Group composition** tools extend word processing to groups.

Often one member creates a draft. Others add to it, approve it, or make modifications after the initial author has finished. There may be many iterations in this *different-time* process. In addition, one person may draft the whole document, or different people might draft different parts.

FIGURE 7.7

Desktop Groupware Tools

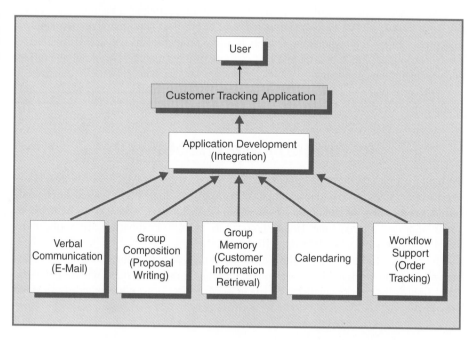

---

[11] V. V. Bullen and J. L. Bennett, "Learning from User Experience with Groupware," *CSCW'90: Proceedings of the Conference on Computer-supported Cooperative Work* (Los Angeles: October 1990), pp. 291–302.

GROUP MEMORY

Groups need to maintain records of what they have done and why they have done them. They need to maintain a common set of notes, documents, analyses, and other outputs.

Prose documents present special problems, which are addressed by **electronic document management (EDM)** tools. These systems store prose documents in electronic form. This allows rapid retrieval through **full-text searching** or through the searching of fixed-format **index entries** for each document. EDM is now being extended to include multimedia documents, including the ability to search for specific graphic elements.

Electronic document management also brings needed control to group memory. EDM can track **versions** of a document that is created over a long period of time. This will allow searchers to find the most recent version of a document. It will also allow the team to go back and look at the changes made over time. EDM also allows a team to create a **retention strategy** to dictate how long different group outputs will be maintained. Not only is storage expensive, but as you increase the number of items stored, you also increase the time and difficulty of locating any individual document.

In some cases, it is critical to retain knowledge of why certain decisions were made. This is especially true in design. **Design rationale** systems not only retain information about what design decision was made, but also retain information on the alternatives considered and the pros and cons of each. This allows the team to revisit its decision later. It also allows the team working on the next-generation design to understand why its predecessor made certain decisions that may at first seem counter-intuitive.

CALENDARING

Group members must coordinate their individual efforts over time. In many cases, such as in approving a document, processes must be handled in a certain sequence, often by multiple team members.

One important class of coordination applications is **calendaring.** If the members of a group maintain online calendars, software can check their availability for upcoming meetings. For instance, to set up a meeting among six people, you might give the calendaring program information about who should be there and a range of dates within which you wish to have the meeting. The calendaring program will then show you a list of possible days and times for the meeting. The calendaring program may even schedule the meeting by blocking out times in the calendars of the group members or at least sending them an e-mail asking them to attend the meeting.

Calendaring requires a very disciplined organization. Unless everyone keeps his or her online calendar completely up to date, "free" times may in fact be taken. Loosely structured firms are unlikely to use calendaring, except perhaps as a way to schedule facilities such as meeting rooms or as a way of posting a schedule of events. In many organizations that are highly time-driven, however, such as consulting firms, the organization may have the will to mandate calendar maintenance.

WORKFLOW SUPPORT

In a **workflow** system, a job has to pass from person to person in a preset sequence. These workflow systems can be as simple as the process for handling a travel expense reimbursement claim or as complex as the process needed to handle a customer order

FIGURE 7.8

Workflow for Clerical Applications

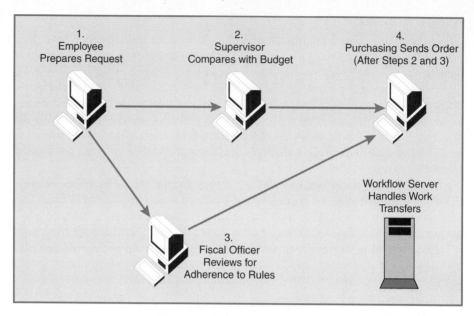

from the time of its reception until billing and shipping. There may be only a few people who must work on the order, or there may be dozens.

In the next chapter, we will look at large-scale clerical workflow. However, managerial and professional systems usually have limited workflow tools to handle simple situations in which a task must flow among several people in a sequence.

As shown in Figure 7.8, workflow systems define who should do what, in what order, for clerical tasks. The workflow system may even provide specific tools to each person, to help him or her do the assigned work. For instance, if the person is to fill out a form, the system may enter standard values or calculated values to save the person time.

When one person finishes a task, the workflow system passes the job to the next person. There is no interoffice delivery delay.

Finally, the workflow system tracks individual tasks. If a claim seems to be taking an unusually long time, you can see where it is in the process so that you can expedite it.

PROJECT MANAGEMENT SYSTEMS FOR MANAGERIAL AND PROFESSIONAL PROJECTS

Finally, groups need to plan their work. Figure 7.9 represents a **project management system.** In such systems, various tasks can be planned ahead of time. As each task is finished, it is checked off. If a task is taking longer than expected, the project manager can see the impact this will have on other tasks.

WORKFLOW VERSUS PROJECT MANAGEMENT SYSTEMS

Workflow and project management systems are similar, but there is a critical difference between them. Workflow systems are designed for *clerical* tasks (including clerical tasks performed by managers and professionals). They tend to be used in high-volume applications.

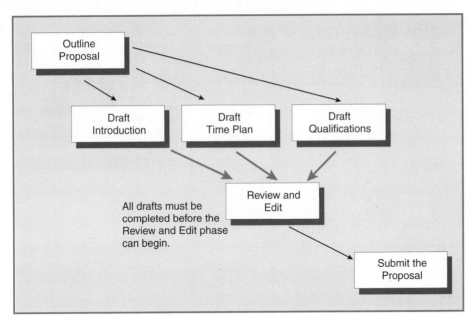

In contrast, project management systems are designed for high-level *managerial and professional* coordination. They describe sequences among project steps, but each step is complex and open-ended. Whereas workflow tasks should take only a few hours or days from start to finish, projects usually take weeks, months, or even years.

APPLICATION DEVELOPMENT

We have discussed a number of key components found in various groupware systems. Any particular project may require several. Figure 7.7 shows that **application development** tools allow the group leader to select a number of modules and link them into a single application with a single interface. For instance, an application might allow sales force users to track their customers. To group members, it is as if they had a custom-designed group support system.

Lotus/IBM Notes

If any product symbolizes keyboard-based groupware in corporations today, it is **Lotus/IBM Notes.** Notes is primarily a keyboard-based system originally designed for different-time, different-place work. Most Notes users work at their desks.

APPLICATIONS

When a person enters Notes, he or she sees a number of applications. These have been put together with Notes's application development tool. This ability to develop custom applications for sales staffs, project teams, and other groups is one of the most important features of Notes. Some would even argue that Notes is primarily an application development environment.

Notes offers a broad array of modules that may be incorporated into an application. Notes has e-mail, document composition, document retrieval, electronic forms processing, workflow, and other tools. It is adding capabilities constantly, so our de-

FIGURE **7.10**

**Replication in
Lotus Notes**

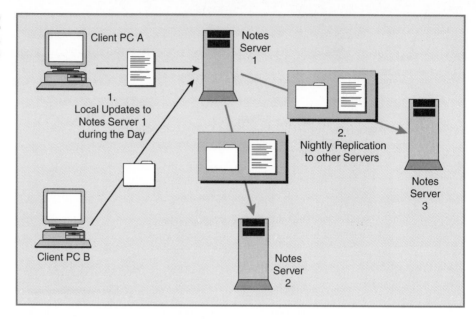

scription here is certainly out of date. In addition, many third-party companies are selling add-in modules that may be incorporated in applications. This is greatly strengthening the importance of Notes.

REPLICATION

What if a company has many Lotus Notes users? This will require supporting a number of Notes servers, as shown in Figure 7.10. Traditionally, Notes servers were limited to about a hundred users, but moving to larger servers can now increase this. Even so, most firms have multiple Notes servers.[12]

If you have multiple servers, the information on each server must be **replicated** (copied) to other servers. This allows any user to get to any document by logging into any Notes server in the firm. In database applications, such as airline reservation systems, replication across multiple databases must be almost instantaneous. The replication of groupware information, in contrast, usually can be done more slowly. Typically, replication is done overnight among Lotus Notes servers. Along with application development, replication is one of the two key strengths of Lotus Notes.

Internet Groupware

The growth of the Internet, including the World Wide Web, has created new possibilities for groupware that are just beginning to be explored. Using standard browsers, these systems bring many of the benefits of traditional systems while adding the features of the World Wide Web, including CGI processing on the webserver and downloading applications to the user's PC via the Java language. One pioneering effort was the *TCBworks* system at the University of Georgia. It provides group discussions and voting—tools often found in computer conferencing systems.

---

[12] Notes servers now come with World Wide Web support. Lotus (now owned by IBM) calls its proprietary client programs Notes and calls its servers Domino servers.

VIDEOCONFERENCING

When groups have geographically distant members, meetings can be difficult and costly to arrange. Particularly among groups that meet very often and find travel burdensome, it may make sense to hold at least some meetings via videoconferencing.[13]

Room-to-Room Videoconferencing

Figure 7.11 illustrates room-to-room videoconferencing in which the equipment is in a conference room. The users in the two rooms can see and hear one another, almost as if they were in the same room.

COSTS

Videoconferencing has been used since the 1960s, but two things have held it back in the past. One, of course, was cost. However, costs have fallen steeply and will continue to do so. A minimal videoconferencing system costs under $50,000 per site. This is still expensive, of course, but it is acceptable for many purposes, and the cost of an equipped room will continue to fall over time.

In addition to the cost of a room, there is transmission cost. Although room-to-room videoconferencing can be done at 64 kbps, the results are jerky pictures and poor image quality. Fractional T1 leased lines, 128 kbps ISDN, T1 leased lines, or Frame Relay service are needed for good service.

STANDARDS

Another problem in the past has been a lack of standards. Videoconferencing systems from different vendors would not work together. Recently, however, the ITU-T has developed a fairly comprehensive set of standards for videoconferencing. These are the **H.320 standards.** This family of standards already covers most key aspects of video-

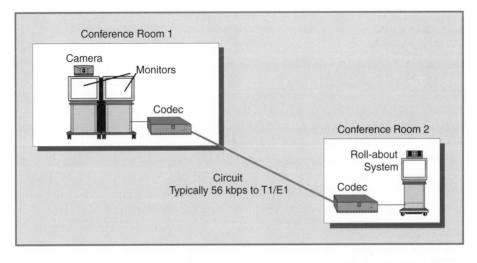

FIGURE 7.11

Room-to-Room Videoconferencing System

---

[13] A. M. Noll, "Teleconferencing Communications Activities," *IEEE Communications Society*, November 1976, 8–14.

conferencing, and ITU-T is constantly adding new standards and enhancing older members of the family. Today, interoperability among the systems of different vendors is quite good.

Actually, H.320 is a *family* of standards. **H.320** itself is the standard for videoconferencing over leased lines or circuit-switched networks, such as ISDN. On these circuits, there is little delay, and bits come out at the same rate they go into the network. This is a relatively easy situation to support.

Later, the ITU-T created the **H.323** standard for LANs and IP networks. For these networks, there may be brief delays, and frames and packets may not arrive at an even rate. H.323 is more sophisticated than H.320 because of the need to handle uneven frame and packet delivery.

Most recently, the ITU-T developed the **H.324** standard for videoconferencing over ordinary modems connected to telephone lines. The problem with modem videoconferencing is the low speed of modems. Low speed severely limits quality.

CODECS: CONVERSION AND COMPRESSION

Video signals are analog. High-speed transmission lines are digital. As discussed in Chapter 3, we need a **codec** to translate analog video source signals into digital transmitted signals.[14]

In videoconferencing, codec standards also cover compression. Digitizing a video signal generates a 96 Mbps data stream. By reducing quality and by compressing redundancy out of the signal, videoconferencing can use speeds as low as 64 kbps, at the cost of poorer audio and video quality.

CAMERAS AND MONITORS

The growth of consumer video has slashed the costs of both cameras and displays. Figure 7.11 shows a *roll-about* conferencing system that can be moved from room to room. More expensive units are built into the room's walls and furniture.

Typically, there are two monitors. One might be used to see the remote site, while another might show what the camera is transmitting from this room.

In addition, there usually are two cameras. One might show all of the people in the room, while another might point at the person speaking. This allows rapid switching between views.

At the desk facing the cameras and monitors, there are microphones. These tend to be mounted almost flush with the surface of the desk.

GRAPHICS

Showing graphics has always been a need in conferences. Many early systems had cameras pointing down from the ceiling, so that a participant could draw on a small pad. This worked, but television has very low resolution.

Today many videoconferencing monitors are computer monitors with at least VGA screen resolution (640 dots horizontally and 480 lines vertically). With such monitors, it is possible to link the display in one room with a computer in the other room. This will allow both sides to see documents and computerized "slide shows" in

---

[14] Note that a codec does not "translate between analog and digits." Modems also do that. Codecs translate between *analog devices* and *digital transmission lines*. Modems translate between *digital devices* and *analog transmission lines*.

high resolution. With ordinary television monitors, resolution is too low to show ordinary computer graphics.

CONTROL CONSOLES

The moderator at each end has a **control console.** This allows him or her to set up the conference and to control such things as sound volume, camera selection, and where cameras are pointing. In some cases, the moderator can even remotely control the camera in the other room, just as in a real meeting you can decide where to look.

MULTIPOINT CONFERENCES

Traditionally, videoconferences linked only two sites. Yet there are other possibilities. This requires a **multipoint control unit** at one of the sites. The multipoint control unit connects multiple sites so that all can see and hear the same input. It also controls which site transmits at any given moment.

BENEFITS OF VIDEOCONFERENCING

Videoconferences are less expensive than travel, although not by as much as one might think. When people travel, they usually attend several meetings.

In general, travel benefits are more subtle than straight one-for-one trade-offs between face-to-face meetings and videoconferences might indicate. Many groups meet periodically face-to-face, then meet by video in-between. Having video may allow them to meet more than they would if they had to travel. This adds to cost but improves communication.

Video has many other benefits. If travel is necessary, then most firms limit the number of participants. However, with video meetings, it is common to have additional people present at each end. This brings more people into the communication. If additional experts are needed, furthermore, they might be just down the hall.

Video meetings tend to be shorter than face-to-face meetings. Perhaps because of the cost involved or perhaps because video is less emotionally warm, video meetings tend to be more formal and businesslike. As long as there are adequate opportunities for getting to know other members of the team, this briefness can be very beneficial, given the number of people involved in many meetings, and given their salaries.

Desktop Conferencing

Standards for videoconferencing were first created for room-to-room conferencing. However, **desktop videoconferencing** is now becoming attractive, especially on LANs, where there is high transmission capacity. The growth of ISDN also allows fairly rapid transmission between desktop machines at different sites.

EQUIPMENT

Although in principle the H.324 standard allows videoconferencing over ordinary modem connections, adequate quality normally requires at least a 128 kbps ISDN connection. LANs allow higher-speed communication via the H.323 standard. IP connections also allow higher speeds if they travel over internal corporate systems, to avoid congestion on the Internet backbone.

Most personal computers sold today are multimedia systems that have the speakers needed to hear the other party. Faster PCs can also show video without additional hardware. Not all PCs come with video cameras to show the person at the keyboard, but adding a video camera is a small investment.

DOCUMENT CONFERENCING

You would like to be able to do more than see and hear the other party. **Document conferencing** allows the communicating partners to see the same document, as shown in Figure 7.12. Both parties can also mark up the document. This is a valuable feature because many telephone calls are made to discuss a document, spreadsheet, schedule, or some other form of visual information.

In general, document conferencing uses VGA resolution, rather than the lower television resolution of television-only conferencing systems. It can do this because it does not have to transmit many video images per second. It has to transmit only a single VGA screen image.

Whiteboard Document Conferencing The simplest document conferencing systems offer only **whiteboard** service, in which the two computers share only a screen image. Both parties, however, have tools for marking up the image. For instance, one might circle a problem or write a note on the image. The ITU-T **T.120** standard offers a whiteboard standard.

Application Sharing Document Conferencing More sophisticated document conferencing systems offer **application sharing.** One computer runs the application, but both computers show the same image. Both keyboards are "live," so it is possible for either side to take control of the program; for instance, to do a what-if analysis using a spreadsheet on the screen.

Combining Desktop Videoconferencing and Document Conferencing It is possible to combine document conferencing with videoconferencing. Both the other side's video image and the document appear in separate resizable windows.

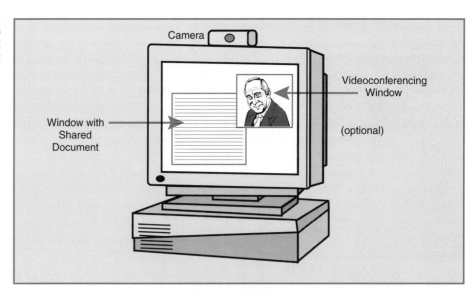

FIGURE 7.12

Document Conferencing

In one experiment,[15] M.B.A. students in different universities developed a spreadsheet using such a system. When they were concentrating on the spreadsheet, they tended to keep the video window very small. However, when they were in disagreement and wanted to argue a point, they tended to blow up the video window so that they could see the other person better.

Telephony

In the past, groupware was seen as standing in opposition to telephony. However, managers spend 5% of their days on the telephone,[16] and this is too much time to ignore. In the future, there may be no distinction between e-mail messages and voice mail messages. Both may arrive via a common in-box. The receiver may even be able to copy voice messages into document, as annotations. In the market, competing telephony application program interface (API) standards are now trying to link groupware with telephony. This is known as **computer-telephony integration (CTI).**

ELECTRONIC MEETING ROOMS

Videoconferencing links people at different sites, but traditional conference room meetings, in which everyone is present physically, also need support. Managers spend a quarter of their days in conference room meetings.[17] When they leave their desks, which are loaded with computer hardware and network connections, they often enter a world where the highest technology is an overhead projector. They need better support for the same-time/same-place conference room meetings that consume so much of their lives.

HARDWARE

Figure 7.13 shows the technology of an **electronic meeting room (EMR).** Each participant has a PC. In addition, there is a **moderator** who has a special PC that controls the functioning of the EMR. There is also an EMR server to hold EMR application programs and data. These machines are linked together by a LAN.

In addition, there is a **public screen** (sometimes several) large enough for everyone to see. A video projector paints shared images on this screen. This video projector can cost $5,000 or more and tends to be one of the two main costs in the EMR. The other is application software.

APPLICATION SOFTWARE

As in any system, application software is the real key to productivity and performance. Typically, EMR application software is organized around an **agenda system,** which specifies how the meeting will flow.

For each agenda item, the moderator either will have a traditional live discussion or will select an application software tool. For instance, suppose that an agenda item is

---

[15] M. Alavi, B. C. Wheeler, and J. S. Valacich, "Using IT to Reengineer Business Education: An Exploratory Investigation of Collaborative Telelearning," *MIS Quarterly* 19, no. 3 (1995): 293–312.

[16] Panko, "Patterns of Managerial Communication," 95–122.

[17] Panko and Kinney, "Meeting Profile: Size, Duration, and Location," 1001–1012.

FIGURE **7.13**

Electronic Meeting Room (EMR)

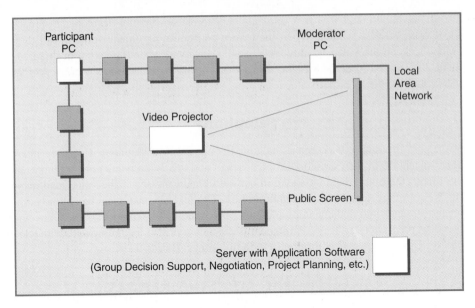

Figure: Electronic Meeting Room (EMR) — Participant PC, Moderator PC, Local Area Network, Video Projector, Public Screen, Server with Application Software (Group Decision Support, Negotiation, Project Planning, etc.)

a report. The moderator might call up PowerPoint or some other presentation tool. The presenter would then take over the presentation.

The next item might be an exploration of possible uses for a new product. A **brainstorming** tool would allow everyone to type in ideas. Because participants can type in parallel, electronic brainstorming groups almost always produce many more ideas than face-to-face groups.[18] In addition, contributions can be **anonymous,** so others will react to the quality of the suggestion rather than to the status (high or low) of the suggester.

When it is time for a decision, the moderator might call up a **voting tool.** The tool will not only handle voting but will also show any patterns in voting. For instance, if a ranking method is used, items that receive very different rankings from various people may be understood differently by the participants. An initial vote may turn up problems in understanding.

In a project meeting, the moderator might bring up the *project management system* and review the status of various tasks.

Another application with apparent potential is *group composition*. Groups can meet in an electronic meeting room to do joint writing or to review and edit a document produced before the meeting.

PRODUCTION SYSTEMS

So far, we have looked at groupware tools for managers and professionals. Organizations also have large **production systems,** which deal with high-volume operational work, usually involving large numbers of people who are often in multiple departments. A typical example is an order entry system, which drives internal processes until the product is delivered and paid for. Several network technologies (in addition to basic data processing) are promising for production systems.

---

[18] R. B. Gallupe, A. R. Dennis, W. H. Cooper, J. S. Valacich, L. M. Bastianutti, and J. F. Nunamaker, Jr., "Electronic Brainstorming and Group Size," *Academy of Management Journal* 35, no. 2 (1992): 350–369.

PRODUCTION IMAGING SYSTEMS

Many organizations have production systems that are drowning in paper. For example, even a moderate-size bank will process more than a million checks each night. Mailing these back to customers at the end of the month is extremely expensive. So is storing them physically. Many other firms, such as insurance firms, also have enormous paper storage problems.

One solution is **imaging;** that is, taking a digital picture of the paper and storing only the digital image. Production imaging systems are capable of enormously high volumes. The images they produce, although large in terms of bits, can be stored in a fraction of the room needed for paper documents.

When a document is stored, a *header* containing searchable fields that describe aspects of the document is stored with the electronic document image. This allows rapid retrieval whenever needed.

PRODUCTION ELECTRONIC DOCUMENT MANAGEMENT (EDM) SYSTEMS

As in the case of workflow, **electronic document management (EDM)** takes on a different meaning in production systems than in groupware systems. Groupware **docubases** may hold only several hundred documents for a particular team. In contrast, production EDM systems may contain several hundred thousand documents. These documents might be quite similar (for instance, insurance contracts), so finding a specific document can be quite difficult. This requires extremely sophisticated retrieval software.

ADOPTING GROUPWARE

E-mail is an "easy sell" in organizations. First, it offers good benefits yet is easy to use. Second, if some people do not use e-mail, they will increasingly find themselves "out of the loop" and see the need to use e-mail.

Perhaps most importantly, the adoption of e-mail is largely an individual decision. Although a mail system will work best if everybody uses it, you can have some nonuse and it will only be an annoyance.

However, with team-oriented groupware, such as Lotus Notes, videoconferencing, and electronic meeting rooms, the entire team must adopt the tool or it is likely to have little or no benefit. This can be a very "hard sell," and if the team leader leaves, the use of the tool may be discontinued.

WEB-BASED DOCUMENT SYSTEMS

One attraction of intranets is that they store a company's documents in a standard format, usually HTML. Any user with a browser can load these documents from a webserver and read them online.

Many companies with intranets now put a great deal of document-based information on their internal intranet webservers. Policy manuals on the webserver are accessible to anyone, can be kept completely up to date, and do not require expensive printing and storage. Companies post many other types of information of interest to internal users, such as job openings and the availability of surplus computers.

This chapter looked at human communication applications. These applications involve written prose or the spoken word. As a result, they are more open-ended than the structured database systems we will see in the next chapter.

We noted that companies are increasingly turning to intranets to provide communication tools. Intranets use Internet transmission technology and communication applications, such as Internet e-mail. We noted that even proprietary applications are beginning to be web-enabled by allowing at least limited browser access. We also noted the importance of document-based websites (and the tools needed to build them).

The chapter focused heavily on electronic mail because this is by far the most widely used electronic human communication tool. We discussed the elements of an e-mail message. We looked at message disposition, filtering, computer conferencing, and etiquette and laws. Boxes looked more specifically at Internet e-mail standards and at e-mail etiquette and laws.

We looked at the classic same-time/different-time–same-place/different-place taxonomy for groupware. We then looked at multiple keyboard groupware tools, such as group composition, group memory, electronic document management, calendaring, workflow, project management systems, and the ability of firms to combine them into single integrated applications.

We looked at room-to-room and desktop videoconferencing. We also looked at document conferencing, which often supplements videoconferencing but can also stand alone.

We finished with discussions of implementation problems for groupware beyond e-mail and the work needed to create a document-based intranet website.

REVIEW QUESTIONS

CORE REVIEW QUESTIONS

1. What are intranets, and why are they attractive to companies?
2. What are the main elements in an e-mail message?
3. Distinguish between e-mail and computer conferencing. List some tools that moderators have in conducting a computer conference.
4. In e-mail, what are the three main standards families?
5. (From the box "Internet Electronic Mail Standards") What is SMTP (in your answer, specify the entities between which SMTP governs communications)? What are POP and IMAP (in your answer, specify the entities between which POP and IMAP govern communications)? What does RFC 822 standardize? What are the limitations of RFC 822? What alternatives are there for the message body? Why do you need Internet encoding? What are the main Internet encoding standards?

6. (From the box "Electronic Mail Etiquette and Laws") Explain each of the following: flaming, spamming, rules for forwarding, care in replying, spoofing, viruses, and urban legends.

7. (From the box "Electronic Mail Etiquette and Laws") In the absence of a corporate policy, should you regard your e-mail messages as private? If corporations have a policy making e-mail private, what exceptions do they usually include? If a corporation has a policy making e-mail private, what can override this policy?

8. What is groupware? What are the two major dimensions of groupware? Give one example in each of the four quadrants.

9. What are the main services in keyboard groupware? How does application development tie them together?

10. What is web-enabled groupware? Why is it attractive? How is it usually limited?

11. What is the ITU-T standard for videoconferencing over circuit switched networks? LANs? IP networks? The ordinary telephone network?

12. What is desktop videoconferencing? What is document conferencing? What are the two types of document conferencing? What does the T.120 standard regulate?

13. What technology do you find in electronic meeting rooms? What software applications do you find in EMRs?

14. Why are companies increasingly turning to web-based document systems?

15. Explain the difference between groupware and production systems.

16. Explain differences in implementation issues between e-mail and more complex team-based groupware products.

17. For document-based websites, explain the difference between HTML editors, website development tools, and development utilities. What is the advantage of installing a search engine at a corporate website? Why do you need usage analysis tools?

DETAILED REVIEW QUESTIONS

1. What is the disposition phase in e-mail? Why is it important?

2. What are distribution lists? Why do they simplify group communication? How do they affect the ratio of messages received to messages sent?

3. What are the advantages of filtering rules?

4. What is electronic document management? Distinguish between full-text searches and index searches. Why do you need a retention strategy? In group memory, why is design rationale important?

5. What is group calendaring? Why is it needed? Why is it difficult to implement?

6. Distinguish between workflow and project management.

7. In Lotus/IBM Notes, explain replication and scalability.

8. In videoconferencing, what is a multipoint conferencing unit? What does it allow you to do?

9. What are the advantages of combining groupware with telephony?

THOUGHT QUESTIONS

1. At what layer in the TCP/IP–OSI hybrid architecture would you find e-mail standards?
2. Why do you think e-mail has grown so explosively while more sophisticated groupware products have lagged? Do not limit yourself to what was said in the text.
3. You want to send someone an attachment. What things should you negotiate beforehand?
4. What groupware services would you like to have for a team designing a new software product? Explain.

PROJECTS

1. Go to the book's website, http://www.prenhall.com/panko, and read the Updates Page for this chapter to see any reported errors and for new and expanded information on the material in this chapter.
2. Go to the book's website, http://www.prenhall.com/panko, and do the Internet Exercises for this chapter.

CHAPTER 8

Internal Database Applications and Internet Electronic Commerce

INTRODUCTION

Chapter 7 dealt with human communication applications. These applications support spoken and written communication. Although communication is very important, it is difficult to structure document repositories. Indexing, full-text searching, and hypertext all help, but identifying relevant information is very difficult.

This chapter looks at database applications. Databases are highly structured repositories consisting of files, records, and fields. In many ways, such tight structure is constraining. Who enjoys filling out forms? On the other hand, there is a basic rule in information retrieval called **SISO** (structure in, speed out). The more structured the information is, the faster and more precisely you can extract information you need. You can quickly find an employee's e-mail address, the average salary in the marketing department, and other facts and summarized information.

We will first look inside the corporation, at internal database applications that involve networking. We will look at client/server processing, web-enabled database applications, standards and middleware, network object oriented programming, data warehouses, and enterprise resource planning (ERP).

The internal reengineering section will look at changing business rules, centralizing work when possible, and supporting workflow applications where centralization will not work.

Afterward, we will look outside the corporation. The Internet has dramatically changed the way we can deal with our suppliers and customers. Under the broad category of electronic commerce, we will look at information services, consumer selling, advertising, and industrial buying and selling.

We will close with a discussion of how to build an electronic commerce website, examining the major elements of such websites and choices that organizations must face when building such websites.

INTERNAL DATABASE APPLICATIONS

A great deal of the information in a firm consists of highly structured information. In the 1970s, there were about as many pages of business forms sent in organizations as pages of prose memos, letters, and reports.[1] Data processing has now automated many form-handling processes. Data processing stores this highly structured information in *databases*.

Client/Server Databases

As discussed in Chapter 1, database systems often use **client/server processing.** As Figure 8.1 shows, the database processing is done on a powerful server. The **client program,** typically running on a PC on the user's desk, sends a **request message** to the **server program** on the **database server.** The database server in turn handles the request and sends back the desired information in a **response message.**

APPROPRIATE LOAD ON THE CLIENT MACHINE

Client/server database processing allows the two machines to be specialized for their respective roles. The database server can be optimized for database queries. This requires a powerful server computer. The client machine, in turn, can focus on two things. First, it can provide a graphical user interface to the user—a task at which desktop PCs excel. Second, it can analyze the data received from the server and present it in a format that aids understanding, such as a table or graph.

Compared to file server program access (see Chapter 1), client/server program access reduces the processing load on the client PC. This means that a firm may be able to use 80% to 90% of its existing PCs as clients for many database applications.

Of course, another alternative is to place all of the processing on a minicomputer or mainframe and to give the user a simple terminal. This might be inexpensive, but

FIGURE 8.1
Client/Server Database Processing

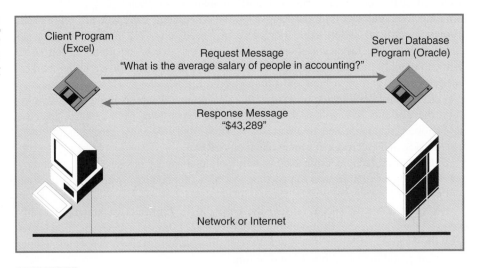

Client Program (Excel)

Request Message
"What is the average salary of people in accounting?"

Server Database Program (Oracle)

Response Message
"$43,289"

Network or Internet

---

[1] R. R. Panko and R. U. Panko, "An Introduction to Computers for Human Communication," Paper 21:1, *NTC '77 Conference Record* (Los Angeles, CA: National Telecommunications Conference, December 5–7, 1977).

terminals tend to have limited user interfaces. Graphical user interfaces require very fast communication between the microprocessor and the display. They cannot be handled adequately by a remote processor, even at LAN speeds.

REDUCED NETWORK LOAD

In file server program access, both the database program and a substantial part of the database must be downloaded from the file server to the client PC. For heavy database tasks, this could overwhelm even a fairly fast LAN.

In contrast, in client/server database processing, the response message only contains the information requested. Typically, this information is very small compared to the size of the database. The database program on the server does not have to be downloaded at all. So the load on the network in client/server processing is much lower than in file server program access.

DATA SAFETY

Database programs that use file server program access, such as Microsoft Access, have to be small to execute on client PCs. As a result, they lack many of the features possible in client/server database processing. If there is a network breakdown or the client program fails, there may be lost information, duplicated information, or simply confusion about what information has been entered into the database. Client/server database programs are much more robust, offering many of the **data safety** features of traditional mainframe database systems.

COMPILING DATA FROM MULTIPLE SOURCES

Figure 8.2 shows an even more important reason to use client/server processing. The information that a manager or clerical worker needs may be scattered across multiple databases on several database servers.

Almost all client/server database servers today are **relational database** systems. They deliver their responses as tables called **relations.** It is (relatively) easy for the client to join relations from different databases.

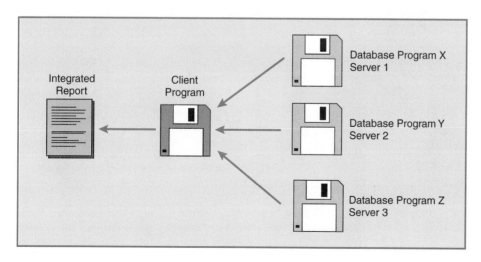

FIGURE 8.2

Access to Multiple Databases from a Single Client

Being able to join data from multiple sources means that managers and other workers can find whatever information they need fairly rapidly. There is no need to write complex programs to extract data from multiple incompatible databases, as there was in the days of mainframe database processing.

RAPID INCREMENTAL APPLICATION DEVELOPMENT

Perhaps the most important advantage of client/server computing is **rapid application development.** Traditionally, if you wanted to write a program for a business process, such as order entry, you would have to write an extremely large and complex program to handle all major functions. This might take two or three years. During that time, you would receive no benefits at all.

Figure 8.3 shows incremental application development in client/server computing. Once the database structure is built, the first increment is a program for entering data. In many cases, this can be built in two or three days. Once this is done, you can add increments as needed. You can add a clerical function to check for the purchaser's credit rating. You can add another to give management statistics. This process continues indefinitely.

With each increment, you get immediate benefits. The quick payoff allows you to recoup initial investments in server hardware and database server software fairly rapidly.

Initial increments might be built with simple programming languages, such as Visual Basic, which allow rapid development but are not highly efficient. Later, increments that are used extensively can be reprogrammed for efficiency in a more sophisticated language, such as COBOL or C++. This allows you to enjoy rapid development and ultimate efficiency. In addition, by the time the optimized version is needed, there will be considerable user experience, which may result in the development of a better application.

FIGURE 8.3
Rapid Application Development

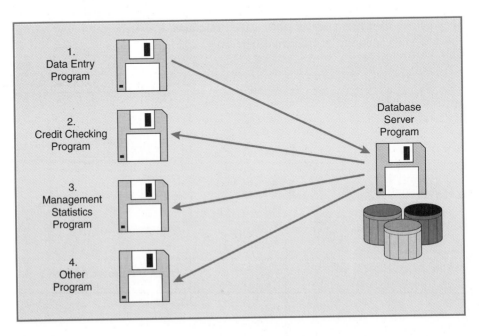

Server Software

Of course, the most critical piece of software in any client/server database system is the server database program. This might be Oracle, Informix, SQL Server, Sybase, or some other database server program.

Database is a sophisticated application that requires a sophisticated server operating system. Although Microsoft Windows NT server is seeing increasing use in the database server market, UNIX is still dominant for database servers. UNIX achieved this dominance because it is an extremely mature and sophisticated operating system.

As discussed in Chapter 6, both UNIX and Windows NT Server support high-powered PC servers. Both support symmetric multiprocessing and server clustering. Both can be used on workstation servers, although UNIX is available for far more types of workstation servers than is Windows NT Server.

Both UNIX and Microsoft Windows NT server are highly **scalable,** which means that you do not have to change your database as its size grows. You can begin by installing the database on a high-end PC server. You can then add symmetric multiprocessing and clustering. Later you can move the database to a RISC workstation server. Nowhere along the line will you have to redesign your database or applications.

Software to Web-Enable Database Applications

One important trend in client/server database processing is allowing the client program to be a browser. Figure 8.4 shows how this web-enabled database processing works.

BROWSER-BASED OPERATION

In the past, client/server processing required installing a **proprietary client program** on the client PC. However, nearly every PC in corporations has a **browser,** and installing a browser is quick and painless compared to installing a proprietary client program.

IMPLEMENTING WEB-ENABLED DATABASE APPLICATIONS

Figure 8.4 shows that the webserver creates pages and sends them to the browser as forms. Users fill out these forms and send them back to the webserver. So far, this sounds like an ordinary World Wide Web application.

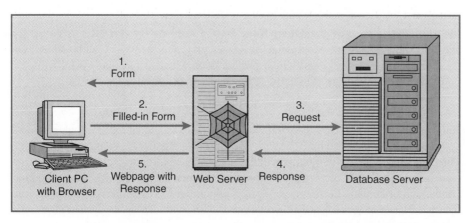

FIGURE 8.4

Web-Enabled Database Application

Normally, a webserver merely looks up a requested webpage and returns it to the browser in a response message. In web-enabled database processing, the webserver must do more. It first passes the data from the form to the database application program. This program often runs on a separate database server, as shown in Figure 8.4.

To the database server, the information coming from the webserver looks like a standard request message. The database searches through its files, retrieves the desired information, and, if necessary, performs computations to produce summarized information. The database application then sends this information to the webserver.

Next, the webserver creates a new webpage containing the retrieved information. It creates this webpage on the fly, instead of using a premade page. It sends this webpage back to the browser on the client computer.

ACTIVE WEBPAGES

In the preceding example, the processing was done on the webserver and on the database server. The browser was merely a data input device.

However, it is possible to build **active webpages** that contain Java applications or other active components. Users can do a good deal of work with the downloaded application before sending a request for data to the webserver.

In addition, the active webpage can process the data after retrieval. For instance, if the active webpage is designed to retrieve and show trends in a database, the active webpage may be able to show the data as a graph.

Standards and Middleware

The biggest problem today with client/server database processing is limited standards for client/server requests and responses. Without standards, a company tends to become locked into a single database vendor's proprietary protocols.

SQL

All client/server database programs send request messages in **Structured Query Language (SQL)** format. However, SQL merely specifies the query. It does not specify the full format of the request and response messages. For example, request protocols must add the details needed to manage request–response exchanges. They do it, furthermore, in different proprietary ways.

OPEN DATA BASE CONNECTIVITY (ODBC)

Microsoft has promoted the **Open Data Base Connectivity (ODBC)** standard for client/server interactions. Most database server programs will work with ODBC. On the client side, however, many client programs on Macintoshes and UNIX workstations cannot communicate via ODBC. ODBC is an application layer standard.

DATABASE MIDDLEWARE

Another limitation of ODBC is that it works only with relational database management systems. Many older database systems use other database organizational structures. There are also many old programs written in COBOL that create individual files rather than full databases. Older **legacy** applications cannot be ignored because they hold critical corporate data. Furthermore, even if you are going to replace a legacy system, your new database server program will have to work with the legacy system during the transition period for data transfer.

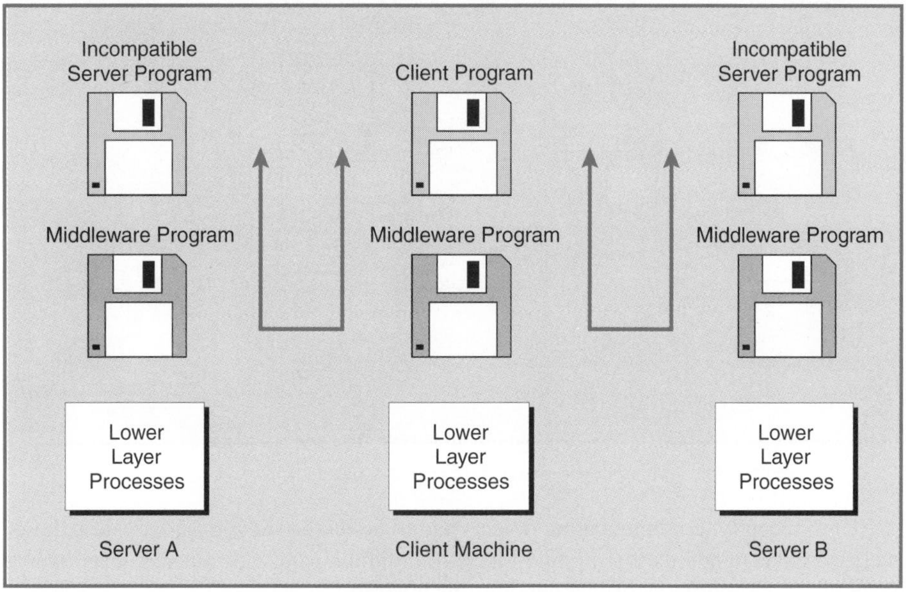

FIGURE **8.5**

Database Middleware

Figure 8.5 shows how the **middleware** concept applies to database processing. Note that the **database middleware** software, like all middleware software, sits between the application and transport layers. The client program merely sends a request message in some supported format. It passes this request to the middleware program via an interface call. The database middleware program grabs the request message, then passes it to the middleware program on the server or mainframe. The database middleware program on the server or mainframe translates the request into whatever format is needed to get the desired data. In other words, database middleware translates formats.

Middleware also handles interactions with the transport and network layers for the software developer. This limits the amount of computer platform and networking expertise the developer will need. By handling such details, it also increases programmer productivity.

Finally, database middleware links modern relational database servers with older legacy systems. This supports data transfers during the transition from a legacy system to a new system. It also allows data transfer with enduring legacy systems.

Still, middleware is not perfect. Database middleware products are very expensive. There are also several forms of middleware, so selecting middleware software is difficult. Also, at the present time, there are no standards for database middleware APIs.

Network Object Oriented Programming (OOP)

Object oriented programming (OOP) promises to be one of the most important developments in programming in the next few years. In object oriented programming, individual modules called **objects** contain both data and the logic to process the data. As Figure 8.6 illustrates, objects send **messages** to one another, asking their partners to do certain tasks.

FIGURE 8.6

Network Object Oriented Programming

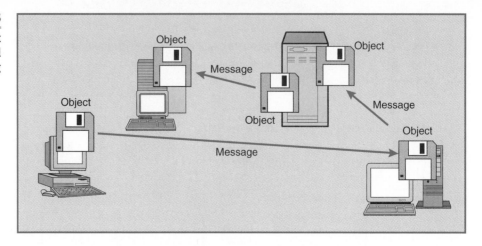

Until recently, communicating objects had to be on the same machine. Now, however, we have standards that allow objects to communicate with other objects over a network. This is **network object oriented programming.**

Unfortunately, we have *too many* standards for network object oriented programming. This excess of standards exists because Microsoft and other vendors (including SUN, Netscape, IBM, and Oracle) have been feuding over standards in this area. Microsoft has the Distributed Component Object Model (*DCOM*). The competitors' Object Management Group has a standard called the Common Object Request Broker Architecture (*CORBA*). Although there is movement toward interoperability, the future is still murky.

Whatever standards situation emerges in the future, network object oriented programming promises to increase dramatically in importance in the future. This will further erode the distinction between networking and programming.

Data Warehouses for Decision Support

We noted earlier that one promise of client/server processing was that it would allow ordinary managers and professionals to query databases directly. Unfortunately, this promise has failed to be fulfilled.

PROBLEMS IN CLIENT/SERVER ACCESS

The main problem is that client/server queries have been too complex for most managers and professionals. However, this is not the only problem. Another is that if managers and professionals are allowed to access production databases, complex queries may slow operational transaction processing. Yet another problem is that giving many people access to operational databases raises security issues.

DATA WAREHOUSE CONCEPTS

As Figure 8.7 illustrates, some companies avoid these problems by creating **data warehouses.** These systems draw data from multiple operational databases and combine them in accessible data formats. The data warehouse administrator also handles problems such as the same variable being defined differently in different sources. The

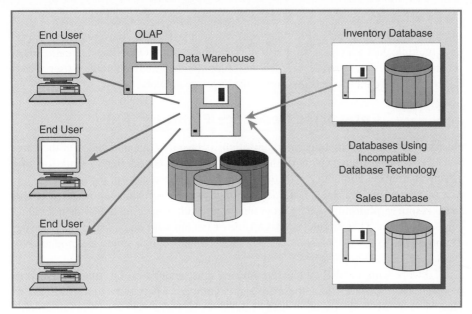

FIGURE **8.7**

Data Warehouse

End User

OLAP

Data Warehouse

Inventory Database

Databases Using
Incompatible
Database Technology

Sales Database

End User

End User

accessible data formats make data queries relatively easy, and storing the data in the data warehouse removes the problems of managers and professionals using operational databases.

ONLINE ANALYTICAL PROCESSING (OLAP)

The data warehouse usually offers more than data. Most importantly, it offers tools for analyzing the data. In general, these interactive tools are referred to as **online analytical processing (OLAP).** OLAP tools can do statistical analysis, trend projections, and other types of analysis that managers and professionals need to make sense of the data.

MULTIDIMENSIONAL DATABASES AND MOLAP

Most databases on client/server systems have been relational. However, it is difficult to browse through relational databases. As a consequence, many data warehouses offer **multidimensional databases.** For instance, in purchase transactions, dimensions might be sales amount, date, salesperson, item sold, and customer. **MOLAP** (multidimensional OLAP) tools allow managers to search through these multidimensional databases easily. For instance, if a manager wishes to see how sales of a product have been to date, the OLAP tool can produce a sales graph showing sales for that product over time. Many other two-dimensional "cuts" through the database are possible.

To add to the surplus of acronyms in the field, relational OLAP tools are referred to as **ROLAP** tools.

DATA MINING

Special **data mining** tools do even more. They can search a large database for associations, sequences of events, and other patterns that are difficult to see by looking at masses of data. They are not automatic. They need a manager or professional who is knowledgeable about the data. However, they can often find patterns that the user had not seen before.

DATA MARTS

Initially, many firms had only a single data warehouse. Now, however, many firms have multiple data warehouses for specific functional areas. Often they are called **data marts** because of their small sizes. Having multiple data marts simplifies user access but complicates data transmissions over the corporate network.

Enterprise Resource Planning (ERP)

Nearly every function in modern organizations is heavily computerized. Yet the computer systems in different parts of the organization may not be able to work together effectively to meet corporate needs for data to flow between parts of the firm.

A number of companies have developed integrated software suites called **enterprise resource planning (ERP)** programs. These suites have modules for individual parts of the firm. These modules are capable of talking with one another fairly easily. The most widely used ERP suite is SAP's R/3. Other popular suites are produced by Baan, Oracle, and PeopleSoft.

To work with an ERP system, a company must understand the suite's data communications processes. Often, these are highly complex. Many firms find that ERP implementation drives decisions in many related areas, including data communications. An ERP decision is also a network decision.

REENGINEERING THE BUSINESS WITH INTERNAL DATABASE SYSTEMS

In the early 1990s, Hammer and Champy's *Reengineering the Corporation* became a best-seller.[2] The ideas in the book were not really new. Hammer, for instance, had been promoting the basic ideas in the book for over a decade. Yet in the 1990s, faced with growing competition and shrinking profit margins, managers read the book in huge numbers.

Quite simply, the book argued that if you continue to work the same way you always have, you will get few benefits if you add networking and other information technology. In the Industrial Revolution, after all, the steam engine produced few gains until it was coupled with a revolution in work called the factory.

In the same way, the benefits can be great if you try to apply information technology to **reengineer** (redesign) current work practices. For instance, Hammer and Champy discussed the Ford Motor Company's accounts payable system (pp. 39ff.). They noted that the company expected to get only a 20% productivity gain by automating its current processes. By rethinking and reengineering the process, however, Ford was able to slash the number of jobs from 500 to 125.

Obliterate

One theme of reengineering is to completely **eliminate** as much work as possible. Look at the **business rules**—the written (and unwritten) assumptions that guide how people work.

---

[2] M. Hammer and J. Champy, *Reengineering the Corporation: A Manifesto for Business Revolution* (New York: Harper Business, 1993).

Next consider how things would improve if some rules were changed to eliminate whole processes. For instance, Ford decided to pay suppliers when a part was actually used rather than when it was delivered. This caused the parts companies to become expert in delivering parts on time, freeing Ford of the job and placing the job where the real expertise existed in the first place. Individual invoices and a tedious reconciliation step were completely eliminated in the new process, allowing a considerable reduction in staffing needs.

Many business rules that once made sense (or seemed to) no longer make sense today. They often impose high costs to address small risks. In many cases, they were present only because crude paper-based technology limited communication and forced the work to be spread over several departments. Many business rules, in other words, were created to cope with an inefficient manual system.

Unfortunately, many obsolete business rules are so integrated into business thinking that their potential inappropriateness is difficult to recognize, much less challenge. In addition, changing business rules always creates some real risks.

Consolidate

Another principle is **consolidation.** When you call a mail-order firm today, a single person can take your name, check your credit rating, determine if what you want is in stock, take your order, and sometimes even begin the automatic stock-picking process. In the past, multiple people in multiple departments would have to do all of this in sequence, and it would take days rather than seconds. This is an example of *consolidating* functions into the hands of a single person. Hammer and Champy call this person a **case worker.** Database technology and networking technologies have made case worker systems both possible and profitable.

Obviously, the first step in reengineering is to study the current system. Reorganization to allow the process to be handled by case workers or by small **case teams** may radically reduce the complexity of workflow processes.

Workflow Automation

We saw **workflow** processes in the previous chapter. In workflow processes, jobs pass from one person to another, often in different departments. As discussed in the last chapter, workflow processes tend to be very slow because of long delays at each transfer of the job. They also tend to be quite expensive because each person in the workflow for a job has to do a small amount of work processing the content of the job but a relatively large amount of time starting, stopping, and sending the job on.

Consolidation can eliminate workflow almost completely, but only in some cases. Even after consolidation, there still may be quite a few steps in the workflow process. Companies need to automate those steps as much as possible.

Workflow software often is designed for specific applications that will be used by people across the organization. For example, a typical workflow application is a *requisition system* for ordering supplies. To make a purchase requires a number of actions by a number of different people. Some of these actions, furthermore, must be taken in a particular order. This is exactly the thing workflow systems were designed to support.

One problem with workflow applications in the past has been the need to install client software on each user PC. Now, however, many workflow applications are web-enabled. This allows anyone with a browser to participate.

Best Practices

As noted earlier in this chapter, many organizations are installing comprehensive enterprise resource planning (ERP) systems. Many firms have a stated objective of installing "wall-to-wall ERP." Even this term is a misnomer because ERP is also beginning to look outside the walls of the firm to sales force automation and the management of the supply chain.

One advantage of ERP is that many ERP systems embody **best practices** in each area. In inventory control, for instance, they try to use what research has shown are the best algorithms and practices for inventory management.

Virtual Corporations and Interorganizational Systems

Up to this point, we have been looking at changing specific aspects of a company's work. Networked database technology, in combination with the human communication technology we saw in the last chapter, may support even more radical corporate-wide changes.

ADHOCRACIES

Long ago, Bennis and Slater[3] foresaw an age in which companies would become **adhocracies,** consisting entirely of teams that would be pulled together as needed and then quickly disbanded so that members could work on other teams.

VIRTUAL CORPORATIONS

More recently, authors such as Davidow and Malone[4] have used the term **virtual corporations.** The "adhocracy" concept looked primarily inside organizations. The virtual corporation concept acknowledges that participants in projects may not even be employees of the firm but members of other firms or consultants brought in for specific expertise.

Although adhocracies and virtual corporations might sound futuristic, as noted in Chapter 7, managers and professionals already spend a great deal of their time working on teams. As the pace of teamwork increases, electronic support will be ever more necessary.

INTERORGANIZATIONAL SYSTEMS

Virtual corporations loosen the boundaries between inside and outside *workers*. In turn, **interorganizational systems** involve building closely functioning systems out of buyer and seller *companies* and other combinations of companies that usually are thought of as competitors.

Outsourcing

Traditional interorganizational systems are *vertical*, involving interactions among separate firms in the marketing channel from manufacturer to customer. In turn, **outsourcing** is creating *horizontal* interorganizational systems. A firm retains only its *core busi-*

---

[3] W. G. Bennis and P. E. Slater, *The Temporary Society* (New York: Harper & Row, 1992), originally published 1968.

[4] W. H. Davidow and M. S. Malone, *The Virtual Corporation* (New York: Harper & Row, 1992).

ness functions in-house. These are functions in which the firm has specialized expertise that allows it to add value. It outsources all other business functions to specialists, as in the case of payroll processing. Many firms are also outsourcing much of their information systems function.

Although the work may be outsourced, computer systems still have to work together. It is important for computer systems in internal and outsourced units to be able to work together. It is equally important to implement networks to link in-house and outsourced systems.

EXTERNAL SYSTEMS: ELECTRONIC COMMERCE

Basic Concepts

Although the benefits from reengineering internal systems can be great, many businesses are focusing on changing the way they do business with the outside world by using networks, especially the Internet. We will use the term **electronic commerce**[5] to describe doing business in a networked environment of any type. We will use the term **Internet electronic commerce** if the network is the Internet.

MARKET CHANNELS

Marketers have long discussed the importance of **market channels** consisting of a manufacturer, a series of wholesalers, a retailer, and finally the customer. Unless each link in the chain is strong, it will be impossible to reach the customer.

New network technologies are beginning to reinvent market channels in many industries. For instance, the Internet allows residential customers to buy books, computers, and even automobiles online, bypassing traditional wholesalers and retailers.

RESIDENTIAL VERSUS INDUSTRIAL CUSTOMERS

Customers normally are divided into two types. First, there are residential customers, often called **consumers.** Second, there are **industrial customers.** Market channels to reach these two types of customers tend to be very different. The same is true of general business practices.

The popular press has tended to focus on consumer-oriented network innovations. However, corporations have been using computers to communicate with one another for years, and vendors and buyers are leveraging this long experience to implement sophisticated network systems while consumer selling is still in its infancy.

According to EMarketer,[6] consumer spending on the Internet was $4.5 million in 1998 and is projected to grow to $26 billion in 2002. Although this is large, it is small compared to industrial buying on the Internet. Again according to EMarketer, industrial purchasing over the Internet was already $16 billion in 1998 and is forecast to grow to $268 billion in 2002.

For industrial products, it is common to see very tight linkages between buyers and sellers. When such close links occur, the buyer–seller dyad begins to look like

---

[5] Many authors restrict the term *electronic commerce* to buying and selling activities.

[6] S. Deck, "Study Sees Growth in Online Shopping," *Computerworld* website, May 25, 1998, http://cnn.com/TECH/computing/9805/25/shopping.idg/index.html.

a single company. As noted earlier, we call such tight linkages interorganizational systems.

Internet Electronic Commerce

As noted above, Internet electronic commerce allows firms to do business over the Internet. Although the Internet appeared in the early 1980s, it did not become popular until the mid-1990s. Before then, costs were too high, a reliable and easy way to link customers to the Internet was not in place, and the World Wide Web had not yet been implemented widely.

Since then, the Internet has grown explosively. It should continue to grow rapidly in the foreseeable future. The Internet can already link companies to tens of millions of affluent and innovative customers around the world. It will soon be able to link companies to hundreds of millions of consumers anywhere in the world.

In such a rapidly expanding environment, there is the possibility of radically changing existing market channels. For instance, manufacturers can now bypass wholesalers and retailers to deal directly with customers. For example, Dell Computer sells millions of dollars' worth of equipment to Internet customers each year.

Retailers, in turn, are freed from the two traditional limitations of having to use expensive retail space and of being confined to a few locations. For instance, Amazon.com has grown to enormous size as a bookseller. Yet it stocks only a few best-selling books. When customers place orders, Amazon.com normally passes each order to a book distribution company. This company ships the book to the buyer, using an Amazon.com label.

To give another example, one small company sold Kona coffee in Hawaii, in a retail store. It began to offer its coffee on the World Wide Web. Soon, it was making half of its revenues and most of its profit from web purchases. When its landlord raised its rent, the company went completely to Internet selling. Later, the company's president left Hawaii to move to Seattle. There, in Starbucks country, the company continued to maintain its website selling Kona coffee from Hawaii. Although the coffee was still roasted in Hawaii to the company's specifications, this Hawaiian company was only in "virtual Hawaii."

Being able to reach customers worldwide is opening new possibilities. For example, Japan has a complex wholesaling and retailing system that makes it difficult for companies in other countries to reach Japanese customers. Many Japanese customers, frustrated with this system, are now making purchases directly over the Internet.

Although the Internet is promising, it still has many problems. As Chapter 3 discussed, modem access is very slow. This limits the use of graphics and other rich information. Congestion in the core Internet backbone often adds to the speed problem. At least for the near future, companies will have to reach most residential consumers over low-speed lines that limit the complexity of information.

In addition, because the Internet is so new, we do not yet have a body of law to govern it. Legislation is sketchy, and even where laws exist, we have had very little case law developed in courts to guide the interpretation of statutes. Most of the legislation that does exist, furthermore, applies only within single countries or even in single states within countries. Without predictable law and without legal recourses when problems arise in a business relationship, the growth of Internet electronic commerce will be somewhat retarded.

Information and Advertising Applications

INFORMATION WEBSITES

The first corporate websites were information repositories. They are still popular today. Their offerings have been called **brochureware,** and that is a good name. They hold the type of information one normally finds in corporate brochures and catalogs.

Information websites have to focus on the needs of multiple external constituencies. Obviously, we are focusing on customers in this section. However, these websites are also of interest to investors, potential employees, news organizations, and other interest groups that may have a particular reason for visiting a website. Within the "customer" category, furthermore, there may be residential consumers, small businesses, educational institutions, and large corporations. A major purpose of the home page is to route each constituency to a set of pages targeted to its needs.

Information websites try to build a **relationship** with the visitor, in order to get them to look deeply at the website and return frequently. This frequently involves related activities. For instance, food companies often have ample recipe sections. Automobile companies often have the latest standings in various types of racing series. At Nike's website at the time of this writing, there is so much information about sports and training that product information is difficult to find!

Once a relationship is built, the company tries to benefit from the visit. If the person is a potential customer, the site will give him or her a good deal of in-depth information about products, in order to move the prospect from general interest toward specific purchase intentions. If the company sells through dealers, the website might ask you to type the name of your city to find the nearest dealer.

Information websites also save money by reducing after-sales **service.** If customers have problems or questions, the website offers **24 × 7** service (24 hours, 7 days a week). Customers can see lists of frequent problems, solutions, and various other tips. This can reduce the need for live customer service agents on the telephone.

Selling to Residential Consumers

Although information websites are valuable in building relationships and providing services, the goal of any business is to sell products. If the person is already at your website, why not sell him or her something?

ATTRACTIONS OF ONLINE PURCHASING

Many people enjoy the online shopping experience, because they can shop without having to deal with salespeople. In addition, they do not have to get dressed and travel to the store. They can also shop without being observed by their friends and neighbors.

In addition, although physical stores have limited selection, online stores do not. Amazon.com offers millions of books, and you can often read the first chapter, see reviews from readers, and get other detailed information online.

Customers can even personalize their products online. For instance, if you go to Dell's website, www.dell.com, you can custom-configure your own computer. You can select a base model that fits your needs approximately. You can then substitute displays, hard disks of various sizes, and other parameters until you "build" the computer that best fits your needs and budget. In the future, many other products will be customizable this way, including automobiles coming off assembly lines.

Another reason that people like to shop online is rapid delivery. Often, if you order by late afternoon, your products will be delivered to you the next morning. Some Internet sellers even have warehouses near the hubs of major overnight shipping services.

Finally, there is price. Freed of the need to support expensive retail floor space and sales staff commissions, online selling can often give customers deep discounts.

MAKING THE PURCHASE

The application software to sell online is widely available. It is easy to let a visitor shop through an online catalog, adding products to an electronic "shopping cart" as he or she goes along. When the customer is ready to place the order, he or she enters personal information and a credit card number. If the customer feels uncomfortable typing his or her credit card number online, the customer can save what he or she has put in the basket, disconnect from the Internet, call a number, and give the credit card number by phone.

PROBLEMS WITH ONLINE SELLING: CREDIT CARD THEFT

In general, consumer purchasing on the Internet has been growing fairly rapidly yet more slowly than many analysts initially expected. Consumers have serious concerns with online purchasing. One concern is **credit card fraud.** Someone could steal your credit card number and use it to make purchases in your name.

One specific concern in credit card fraud is **interception.** Customers fear that someone may intercept their purchase order, stealing their credit card number and using it for illicit purposes.

Technically, interception is not likely. In fact, *none* have been reported to the time of this writing. Almost all financial transactions are highly secure. Purchase orders are encrypted during transmission, so there is no way for an interceptor to read them. Most consumer transactions today use the **Secure Sockets Layer (SSL)** encryption standard created by Netscape but also used by Microsoft. Module F discusses SSL in more detail.

Another concern is that the selling company itself may abuse the credit card number, either because it is a scam organization or because one of its employees is dishonest. The SSL standard does nothing to protect consumers relative to this concern, because the merchant sees the credit card number. The newer **Secure Electronic Transactions (SET)** standard created by VISA, MasterCard, and others encrypts the credit card number so that the merchant cannot read it. Instead, the merchant sends the encrypted credit card number to a third party for verification. Module F discusses the SET approach. However, although SET seems to protect the consumer, the current version of SET has a major loophole. If the merchant asks for the credit card number afterward, the third party will provide it!

What SET does do is protect you from bogus companies that offer great products at impossible prices, take your credit card number, and then disappear. Unless the company has a relationship with a "gateway" organization that can check with banks for authorization, it cannot get your credit card number. Companies cannot get such a relationship, furthermore, without some proof of legitimacy. Even if they can get a relationship with a gateway organization, fraud would be detected quickly, and they would lose the relationship.

Another protection against bogus companies is the use of digital certificates. As Chapter 6 noted, digital certificates are provided to the merchant by third parties called certificate authorities. The certificate gives the organization's name and its public key. Most browsers can now check the certificates of major certificate authorities. With a digital certificate, if a company claims that it is IBM, your browser will verify its claim. Note that a digital certificate only verifies names. It is not a guarantee that the company is trustworthy. Module F discusses digital certificates in more detail.

To reduce their risks, some consumers use **electronic cash.** They authorize merchants to debit a preestablished electronic cash account at an organization that acts like a bank. Electronic cash may even give the buyer anonymity, although this is not always the case.

Actually, credit card purchases are very safe. Even if your credit card number is abused, many countries and states have liability limits of about $50 if the fraud is reported promptly. In fact, whereas electronic cash cannot be stolen beyond the amount authorized, a credit card's liability limit may be safer financially.

Incidentally, credit card companies are not very alarmed over the problem of limited liability. They simply raise their rates to cover the cost of fraud.[7] If you present your credit card when you shop in a store, the merchant pays a fee of 1.2%. In purchases where the credit card itself is not presented, as in telephone orders and Internet purchases, this fee rises to 2.5%.

CONCERNS ABOUT NONDELIVERY

Another concern is **nondelivery.** The merchant may simply take your money and never deliver your goods. You may have no legal recourse, especially if you are in a different country than the supplier.

However, credit card purchasing actually helps you. You can put a stop payment on a purchase if your goods are not delivered or are defective. In fact, a more legitimate concern is the concern of merchants that they will deliver goods and not be paid.

CONCERNS ABOUT PRIVACY

A deeper concern is **privacy.** Electronic purchases are recorded online. Patterns of online purchases, even at a single company, can say a great deal about you and your interests. Furthermore, a growing number of sites ask you to register so they can satisfy the needs of advertising audit bureaus. This also helps them direct you to certain webpages. Privacy is a complex and subtle issue. What one customer sees as customization of service looks to another like an invasion of privacy.

THE CORE ISSUE OF TRUST

Although a great deal of effort has gone into technical security systems, the basic issue really is that of **trust.**[8] One reason that large companies have often done well in Internet selling is that customers recognize the name and trust the organization. If you are buying a program from Microsoft, you have good reason to trust that it will be delivered.

Consumer Advertising

Companies must advertise if they are to stay in business. They must reach customers and generate awareness, interest, and, if possible, purchase intentions. Although a company's information website is in effect an advertising vehicle, it works only when customers visit your site. You would like to be able to advertise at other sites.

---

[7] Ellen Messmer, "Visa and CompuServe get SET for Net Sales," *Network World*, September 29, 1997, 10.

[8] S. Singh, "Trust and Electronic Money across Cultures," *Proceedings of the 1997 Pacific Telecommunications Conference* (Honolulu, January 1997), pp. 760–767.

BANNER ADS

The dominant advertising vehicle for Internet advertising today is the **banner ad** on a World Wide Web page. If you visit a major search engine site, you will always see a banner ad at the top of the page. This ad is about 640 pixels wide, so that it will fit across a VGA display screen horizontally. It is about 60 pixels high so that it can attract attention yet not take up the entire screen.

CLICK-THROUGHS

Banner ads merely get attention or build awareness. Your goal is for the customer to click on the banner. If they do, they will go to your website, where you can entice them with much more information and may even be able to close a sale. When a reader clicks on the banner to go to your site, this is called a **click-through.**

COSTS OF ADVERTISING

In almost all media, advertising space is purchased on the basis of **cost per thousand impressions,** better knows as **CPM.** Website CPMs are around $20. This is $0.02 per individual impression. This number is similar to CPMs in radio and magazines. CPMs in television are higher.

For websites that cater to particular groups, the CPM may rise to $100 or more. For instance, if you sell mountain climbing gear, you would pay more to show your banner ads on a mountaineering website. Or, if you are advertising on a search engine, you would be willing to pay more if someone used the keyword *mountaineering* to get to a page or if a page itself dealt with mountaineering.

Advertisers normally require a magazine's circulation to be **audited.** This means that the magazine must prove that it really has as many subscribers as it claims. Auditing also requires the magazine to provide demographic data because advertising often has demographic targets. This, unfortunately, requires websites to ask visitors for demographic information.

Although consumer purchasing on the Internet is lagging, advertising is growing very rapidly. Within about 10 years, given current growth rates and expected developments, Internet advertising should be about as large as magazine advertising and perhaps radio. Check the book's website for recent projections.

In fact, advertising is becoming the key to financing content providers. Although some websites are corporate home page sites and others are labors of love, many websites need financial support. Advertising is already supporting the major search engines. In time, it may support a much broader range of content. Although some sites may be able to charge people for visits, there is tremendous resistance to this. Advertising may be annoying to some visitors, but it may be the price we have to pay for "free" websites.

Industrial Electronic Commerce

While consumer buying and selling has been growing fairly slowly, **industrial electronic commerce**—businesses selling to other businesses—has been booming.

Industrial electronic commerce has had a long history. Even in the days of terminal–host systems, some vendors allowed their customers to log into a vendor host, check stock for availability and price, and create a purchase order online. Pharmacists, for instance, can place orders with local drug supply warehouses at the end of a business day. The order will be delivered to them the next morning.

Some industrial buyers have tightly integrated their suppliers to them. For instance, when an automobile company needs front windows, the glass factory may be located just outside the auto plant's walls. In fact, the glass company may deliver windows without being asked because it constantly checks the plant's production schedule and inventory supplies. Although such close associations are legendary, most business takes place on a transaction-by-transaction basis at arm's length.

EDI

For many years, buyers and sellers have communicated through **electronic data interchange (EDI).** EDI standards specify standard formats for a number of **business documents,** such as invoices and purchase orders. EDI is also called electronic document interchange.

When a buying company wishes to purchase something, it enters information into its local EDI computer. The local EDI computer then connects to the EDI computer of the seller. There is no need to retype information, and the order is delivered immediately or overnight. Errors are also reduced.

Unfortunately, EDI has had its problems. One is that each industry has different purchase orders and other business documents. As a result, direct communciation between buyer and seller EDI computers is difficult. As a consequence, many firms deal with **EDI gateways.** These services accept business documents from one party and convert them into the format used by the other party.

Another problem is that participation in EDI traditionally required you to be on the same packet switched data network as the buyer or at least the same network as the EDI gateway.

INDUSTRIAL INTERNET ELECTRONIC COMMERCE

With the Internet, the need to find a common network is no longer a problem. Nearly every firm is connected to the Internet. Standards, however, are still a problem. There are no standard business documents as there are in EDI. Fortunately, the web browsers that are the standard client programs for industrial Internet electronic commerce have the security of SSL, as discussed above. Industrial buyers and sellers have evaluated SSL and have found it an acceptable way to deal with interception threats and authentication.

A lack of standards means that most systems are vendor-centric or buyer-centric. For instance, Dell has set up purchasing accounts with many corporations. This allows companies to place orders quickly and at low cost.

In the future, SET may provide a better basis for standardized transmission. In the automobile industry,[9] there are about 18,000 suppliers. They have been testing SET as the transmission and authentication basis for their Automotive Network Exchange (ANX) network. However, SET is used here only for transmission. ANX also has standardized business documents.

One promising direction for the future is an **Open Buying on the Internet (OBI)** standard now under development. It will combine EDI standards for some business documents with Internet transmission and security from SSL and possibly SET. Unfortunately, this standard is still in early stages of development, so its long-term impact is uncertain.

A more ambitious standard for Internet electronic commerce is the **Internet Open Transaction Protocol (IOTP)** standard now under development in the Internet Engi-

---

[9] B. Davis and G. Dalton, "VPNs SET to Take Off," *Informationweek*, January 5, 1998, 85–86.

neering Task Force. While the Open Buying on the Internet standard is primarily designed for the creation of catalog purchasing, the Internet Open Transaction Protocol promises to be a more comprehensive standard for industrial buying and selling. However, this standard is in an early state of development.

One goal for the future is to have purchasing and buying systems that not only make purchases and accept invoices but that also go more deeply into the buyer and seller firms. For instance, buyer firms would like to integrate electronic purchasing with their requisition and inventory systems. For small office supply purchases, for instance, they would like individual office managers to enter their requisitions through browser interfaces. A day's requisitions would be integrated and then passed as a group to an office supplies vendor. Sellers, on the other hand, wish order entry to be the beginning of a full cycle including order fulfillment, shipping, and after-sale accounting.

WEBSITE TECHNOLOGY

To present information or sell products online, you need to develop a website. This raises many business, artistic, and technical issues. We will focus on technical issues.

Hosting versus Owning

The first issue is whether to build a website at your own organization. This obviously gives you control. It also creates many maintenance issues that may not make sense, especially for smaller firms.

Many ISPs provide website **hosting.** They will begin by arranging a second-level domain name for your firm. They will then put your website on their own host computer. Visitors will not know that your site is hosted. They will see only your domain name in the URL. Of course, ISPs also offer other services, such as website design.

Of special note, ISPs have the special application software you will need if you wish to sell over the Internet. Setting up a sales site is relatively complex, and hosting ISPs provide assistance in setting up such sites.

A final reason to choose ISP hosting is that if hackers break into the website, they cannot get through to your internal corporate computers, because there is no permanent connection. The only connections come if you develop webpages on your own computer and then occasionally load them up to the ISP host.

Webserver Hardware Options

Chapter 6 discussed server options. Module E discusses some additional details of server technology. The important thing is to settle upon a scalable set of computers that all run the application software you select. This way, you will be able to upgrade simply by changing your hardware.

Protecting the Webserver

If you own your own webserver, there is always the danger that hackers will break in and damage it. They can even search its files for credit card information and other sensitive data.

As Figure 8.8 shows, protecting your webserver may require setting up a **security zone.**

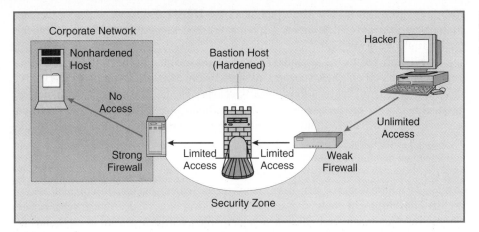

FIGURE **8.8**

Security Zone with a Bastion Host

INTERNAL AND EXTERNAL FIREWALLS

A security zone has a firewall between itself and the Internet. This **external firewall** must be comparatively weak, because you will have to deal in electronic commerce with many outside users.

There is a second firewall between the security zone and the company's internal network. This **internal firewall** should be very strong. Very few stations inside the organization should need access to a webserver or vice versa. Anyone really needing access to the server must put up with the strong security, like a traveler passing through an airport during wartime.

BASTION HOST

The heart of the security zone is the electronic commerce server itself. It is set up as a **bastion host.** In a castle, the bastion is a part of the castle that is likely to be attacked first. It is specially fortified. A bastion host, in turn, is one that is likely to be attacked by **hackers.** So it is "hardened" against attack. All programs not absolutely required to run the application program are removed. In addition, all known security bugs in the operating system are fixed.

It is impractical to take such steps for all servers in an organization. By isolating the bastion servers from the main corporate network through strong firewalls, it is hoped that access to internal servers will be so limited that they can be fairly soft from a security viewpoint.

Even with firewalls and hardening, bastion hosts will be defeated from time to time. So it is important not to put any information on the bastion hosts whose loss would be devastating. It is also important to identify a security breach, identify how it was done, and to plug the unexpected gap quickly.

Webserver Software

APPLICATION DEVELOPMENT TOOLS

To create a website requires a considerable investment in server hardware and software to provide service to users. It also requires a considerable investment in application development tools.

Webpage Creation Tools The simplest tools—**HTML Editors**—focus on the creation of individual HTML webpages. Even word processors often have good tools for creating individual webpages.

HTML was created as a standard for prose documents. In the future, many webpages will be based on a new standard, the **Extensible Markup Language (XML).** As Module G discusses, XML allows page developers to develop custom tags, such as ⟨product-number⟩, ⟨product-name⟩, and ⟨product-unit-price⟩. This will allow very rich searches. It also will allow many transaction processing tasks to be implemented by the browser and the webserver.

Website Development Tools The best tools go beyond the individual page, to the creation of entire websites that have many pages linked together in complex ways. **Website development tools** give users a visual overview of the entire website (see Figure 8.9). This is very helpful in keeping complex websites straight in the minds of developers.

Website development tools do more than show the organization of the website. They also help the developer make changes. If a user moves a page from one directory to another, for instance, the website development tool will examine all other webpages and update their links pointing to the moved document.

Development Utilities In general, HTML editors and website development tools focus on HTML documents. They typically have only very limited tools for creating graphics and other nontext elements in webpages.

Dedicated **graphics editors** create complex graphics. They can also optimize file size to limit download time. They typically do this by reducing the number of colors and other controllable elements in ways that minimize the loss of visual impact while greatly reducing download time.

Java editors, in turn, allow website creators to place sophisticated interactive elements in webpages.

SEARCH ENGINES

The best of these systems have **internal search engines.** Almost all users are acquainted with search engines because of Internet browsing. They can use the skills they have learned to search through internal collections of corporate web documents.

FIGURE 8.9

Website View in a Website Development Tool

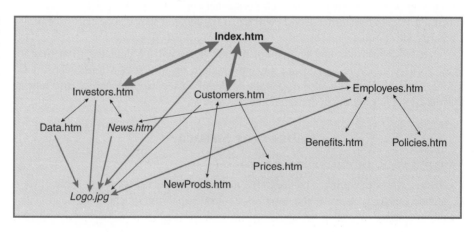

USAGE ANALYSIS

Another advantage of web-based document systems is that many webserver development tools allow document creators to collect data on which documents are the most highly used and which links within each document are the most followed. This allows companies to build "Top 25" lists that allow users to get to common information very quickly. It also helps companies plan information updating. If a section of an online procedure manual is accessed frequently, it will make sense to update that section frequently.

It is also important to monitor the performance of a webserver. If many connections are refused, or if download time is slow, users will stop going to the website.

TRANSACTION PROCESSING SOFTWARE

To sell over the Internet requires special **transaction processing software.** As shown in Figure 8.4, there must be special software on the webserver to communicate with the database program. This software must create forms for users, pass data from incoming forms on to the database program, and generate webpages on the fly based on responses from the database program. Of course, there must also be the database program itself, typically on a separate server.

TRANSMISSION LINES

You must connect your website to the Internet. Expect your ISP to charge quite a bit of money because you will be placing a heavy load on its system if you use a high-speed **access line.**

You will need a permanent connection to the Internet so that customers can always reach you. This suggests the use of Frame Relay or a T1 line. (A 64 kbps connection is too slow for a larger website.)

If you have your website hosted by an ISP, it is a good idea to have at least an ISDN connection from your company to the Internet. This will allow you to build the website on your own computer and then periodically upload it to the hosting computer at the ISP site. Most new development software, such as Microsoft FrontPage, can load entire websites with a single command if the hosting computer has supporting software.

SUMMARY

As the introduction noted, this chapter has four parts:

► First, there was a discussion of networked database technology, with special emphasis on client/server processing, web-enabled database applications, network object oriented programs, and data warehouses.

► Second, there was a discussion of corporate reengineering techniques made possible by networked database technology and the human communication technology we saw in the last chapter. A central concept was the importance of changing business rules. Unless business rules are changed, few benefits will follow. This section focused on work obliteration, work consolidation, workflow support, best practices, virtual corporations, interorganizational systems, and outsourcing.

▶ Third, there was a discussion of electronic commerce, especially Internet electronic commerce. This section focused on information websites, consumer selling, advertising, and industrial selling. There was a special focus on the concerns of consumers about fraud and privacy violations and the need for consumers to develop trust.

▶ Finally, there was a discussion of the hardware, software, and networking needed to implement an electronic commerce website.

REVIEW QUESTIONS

CORE REVIEW QUESTIONS

1. What does *SISO* stand for? Why does it make database applications attractive?
2. Why is client/server database processing attractive?
3. Why are web-enabled database applications attractive? Explain the steps that take place when a user at a client PC wishes to get information from a web-enabled database application.
4. How has client/server database processing proven to be inappropriate for managers' and professionals' information retrieval needs? How do data warehouses make information retrieval easier for nonprogrammers? Why do managers need OLAP tools to use a data warehouse effectively?
5. What is reengineering? What are business rules? Why are business rules central to reengineering?
6. Distinguish between reengineering through obliteration, consolidation, and workflow systems. Are these three approaches mutually exclusive?
7. Distinguish between adhocracies, virtual corporations, and interorganizational systems.
8. What is electronic commerce? What is Internet electronic commerce? What are marketing channels? Distinguish between consumers and industrial customers.
9. Why is Internet electronic commerce attractive? What limitations does it have today?
10. Distinguish between information websites and selling websites. Can they be combined?
11. What services do information websites provide to customers? How is the concept of "relationship" central to all of these services?
12. For customers, what are the attractions of online purchasing? What are the concerns? Distinguish between network security and trust.
13. Distinguish between banner ads and click-throughs. What is CPM? How do banner CPMs at websites compare to CPMs in radio, newspapers, and television?
14. Which is more developed—electronic commerce with consumers or industrial customers? Why is this the case?
15. Why is EDI attractive? What are its limits? Why is the Internet more attractive to companies than EDI? What is OBI? What is IOTP?
16. What is website hosting? Why is it attractive to businesses?
17. List what you will need to create an electronic commerce website.

DETAILED REVIEW QUESTIONS

1. Explain how client/server database processing allows rapid application development. When do the benefits of rapid application development appear compared to when benefits appear in traditional development?
2. How do active webpages make web-enabled database applications more attractive?
3. What do SQL and ODBC both do? How do they compare? What is middleware? Why does it simplify application development?
4. What is networked object oriented programming? Why is it attractive? What is the standards situation in networked OOP?
5. What is a multidimensional database? Distinguish among OLAP, MOLAP, and ROLAP.
6. What is a case worker? How does using case workers decrease costs and speed operations?
7. Explain the concept of "best practices." How do ERP systems help companies implement best practices?
8. What is outsourcing? What networking problems does it create?
9. What are two ways in which a customer's credit card can be stolen for fraudulent use? What can be done about the first threat? What can be done about the second? Is fraudulent credit card use likely to result in the customer losing a great deal of money or paying for a product that is not delivered? Why or why not?
10. Distinguish between SSL and SET. In what way is SET supposed to be better for customers? Is it really better in that way?
11. What are security zones? What business need do they address? What is a bastion host? Why must it be assumed that bastion hosts will fail?
12. Name and briefly characterize the main types of software you will need at an electronic commerce website.

THOUGHT QUESTIONS

1. Comparing adhocracies, virtual corporations, and interorganizational systems, in what order do you think they will appear? Justify your reasoning.
2. Why are marketing channels central to electronic commerce strategies?
3. Give your own assessment of the validity of customer concerns about credit card fraud in Internet electronic commerce.
4. Give your own assessment of the validity of customer concerns about privacy in Internet electronic commerce.

PROJECTS

1. Go to the book's website, http://www.prenhall.com, and read the updates page for this chapter.
2. Go to the book's website, http://www.prenhall.com/panko, and do the Internet Exercises for this chapter.

MODULE A

More on TCP/IP

INTRODUCTION

This module presents more information on TCP/IP protocols. It is designed to be read after Chapter 2. However, references to the Simple Network Management Protocol in the discussion of UDP use information in Chapter 6. This module is not designed to be read front-to-back like a chapter. However, different parts of the module sometimes refer to one another.

MORE ON THE TRANSPORT LAYER

TCP Sequence and Acknowledgment Numbers

Chapter 2 discussed basic TCP transmission. It noted that when a source host's transport layer process sends out TCP-PDUs, it places a 32-bit **sequence number** in each outgoing TCP-PDU. This allows the receiving transport layer process to determine if any TCP-PDUs have arrived out of order or are missing.

Chapter 2 noted that the transport layer process on the receiving host sends an acknowledgment for every TCP-PDU correctly received. It designates the TCP-PDU being acknowledged through the **acknowledgment number** field of a TCP-PDU going back to the source host.

To understand this process in more detail, you should realize that when the transport layer program on one machine establishes a TCP connection with the transport layer program on another machine, it views the data it sends as a very long sequence of bytes divided up into many TCP-PDUs. Every byte sent has a sequence value.

Figure A.1 shows that when a transport layer program initiates a TCP connection, it generates a random 32-bit **initial sequence number.** It places this number in the sequence number field of the first outgoing TCP-PDU. In the example, the random initial sequence number is 79.

TCP-PDU	BYTE	REMARK
Initial SYN for Open	79	Randomly chose Initial Sequence Number (ISN)
Data PDU 1	80	First byte in TCP-PDU 1 Placed in TCP-PDU 1's sequence number field
	81	
	82	
	83	
	84	
	85	
	86	Last byte in TCP-PDU 1 This number *plus 1* (87) is placed in the other host's ACK message's acknowledgment number field. This designates that the expected next sequence number will be 87
Date PDU 2	87	First byte in TCP-PDU 2. "87" placed in the sequence number field
	88	
	89	
	90	
	91	
	92	
	93	
	94	
	95	Last byte in TCP-PDU 2
Other TCP-PDUs . . .		

Figure A.1 shows that the next TCP-PDU carries bytes 80 through 86. This first data PDU will have "80" in its sequence number field, because 80 is the sequence number of its first byte. The next data PDU will carry bytes 87 through 95. It will have the value 87 in the sequence number field, because 87 is the sequence number of its first byte.

Figure A.1 also illustrates acknowledgment handling. When the destination host receives the initial open request, it treats the request as a single byte, 79. In its acknowledgment, it places the value 80 in the acknowledgment number field. In other words, the acknowledgment number field contains the sequence number of the next *byte* (not TCP-PDU) the destination host expects to receive.

For Data PDU 1, the last byte is 86. So the destination host sends back an acknowledgment with 87 in the acknowledgment field. For Data PDU 2, the last byte has sequence number 95. So the acknowledgment would have 96 in the acknowledgment number field.

UDP

In Chapter 2, we used the expression **transport layer program** instead of *TCP program*. The reason for this is that TCP is only one of the protocols handled by a TCP/IP transport layer program.

Another important transport layer protocol is the **user datagram protocol (UDP).** We saw in Chapter 2 that TCP is a ponderous protocol that spends a good deal of overhead establishing a connection, doing error checking on each TCP-PDU sent out, and then closing down the connection. It is a very safe protocol, to make up for the unreliability of IP at the next lower layer. However, it is also a very slow protocol.

UDP, in contrast, sacrifices safety for speed. Like IP, UDP does no error detection or correction. Also like IP, UDP does not establish a connection ahead of time. It merely sends its UDP-PDU. Reflecting this lack of connection establishment, the UDP-PDU is even called a **UDP datagram.**

Emphasizing the stripped-down nature of this protocol, UDP's header only has four fields. Two are 16-bit source and destination port numbers. **Port numbers** identify the program at the next-higher layer (the application layer) that should get the UDP datagram. For instance, HTTP almost always uses Port 80.

The remaining two fields are a 16-bit **UDP length** field, which is needed because UDP is a variable-length protocol, and a 16-bit **UDP checksum** that is only useful for discarding the UDP datagram in case of a header error.

What kinds of applications specify UDP for their application PDU (APDU) delivery? One example is voice. As Module D discusses, voice is extremely intolerant of delay. Doing only minimal error checking (on the header only) reduces the amount of time the APDU is delayed at the destination host's transport layer. In addition, minimizing delay precludes stopping to redeliver an incorrect APDU.

UDP is also used in many supervisory applications where it is not critical if some messages are lost. For instance, when the Simple Network Management Protocol discussed in Chapter 6 asks a network management agent to send data, there usually is little damage if the request or response APDU is lost. The SNMP program's database will be updated in the next information-gathering cycle, which usually is only seconds or minutes away.

Because SNMP uses UDP, there is only a single UDP datagram going in each direction for each information collection request. With TCP, in contrast, three TCP-PDUs are needed to open a connection, and four are required to close the connection. TCP would place a very heavy load on the SNMP server and also on network management agents.

MORE ON THE INTERNET PROTOCOL

Chapter 2 introduced the basic mechanisms for the Internet Protocol (IP). This section will look in more depth at internet addresses and at how the Internet Protocol will fragment an IP packet into several smaller IP packets if a subnet has a maximum packet size that is too small for the original IP datagram to get through.

Internet Addresses

As discussed in Chapter 2, the IP header contains a destination address and a source address. Each is 32 bits long. For instance, one host's internet address is the following 32-bit number:

10000000101010110001000100001101

Obviously, this is not very easy to memorize. To make life easier, we normally represent internet addresses in an equivalent but easier-to-remember way. First, we divide the 32-bit number into four bytes, in this case:

10000000   10101011   00010001   00001101

Second, we convert each byte into its decimal equivalent. For instance, the binary number 10000000 is 128 in decimal. The binary number 10101011, in turn, is 171 in decimal. The last two bytes are equivalent to 17 and 13.

Most spreadsheet programs have a binary-to-decimal converter that can perform the conversion of up to 8-bit binary numbers to their decimal equivalents. If you use these functions, you will see that 00000000 is 0, 00000001 is 1, 00000010 is 2, 00000011 is 3, and so on.

Each part of the address can range from 00000000 to 11111111 in binary. In decimal, this is 0 to 255.

We then represent the number as these four decimal numbers separated by periods. This gives us the following number internet address. We pronounce it as "128 dot 171 dot 17 dot 13." This is called **dotted decimal notation.**

128.171.17.13

Although the process of deriving this dotted decimal notation may seem complex, it actually is very straightforward. The first important thing to remember is that internet addresses really are strings of 32 ones and zeros. The only purpose of dotted decimal notation is to create a notation that is easier to memorize.

The second important thing to remember is that the process itself is straightforward.

▶ First, we divide the address logically into four octets.
▶ Second, we treat each octet as a binary number and then convert it to the equivalent decimal number.
▶ Finally, we then write the four decimal numbers and separate them with dots.

ASSIGNING INTERNET ADDRESSES

Every internet address must be unique. To see why, suppose that two hosts had the same internet address. If you sent an IP packet to their common address, both hosts would receive it.

One way to ensure uniqueness would be to create a central internet address registrar for the entire Internet. This central registrar would assign unique internet addresses

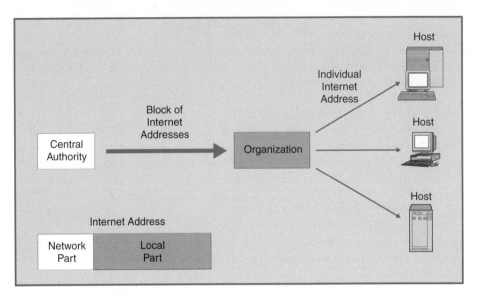

to all hosts directly. That actually was done for the ARPANET, which was the predecessor to the Internet. However, when the Internet standards were created in the early 1980s, it was clear that having one agency assign all addresses would be a logistical nightmare.

Instead, it was decided to assign internet addresses in two stages, as Figure A.2 illustrates. In this approach, a central agency first assigns a block of addresses to an organization or to an Internet service provider. The organization or ISP is then responsible for assigning internet addresses to individual hosts. For instance, the University of Hawaii was assigned a block of 65,536 internet addresses for internal distribution.

Note that we were rather vague in the previous paragraph, saying that "a central agency" assigned the block of addresses. This vagueness was deliberate. As discussed later in this module, the Internet is undergoing major reorganizations that will change the makeup of these central agencies. However, this reorganization will retain the process of assigning blocks to individual organizations and ISPs and then making the organization or ISP responsible for internal distribution.

Figure A.2 also shows how blocks are assigned. Each internet address is 32 bits long. This total length is divided into two parts, the **network part** and the **local part.** For the University of Hawaii, the network part is 128.171 or "1000000010101011". All UH internet addresses must begin with 128.171.

This essentially gives the university a block of 65,536 internet addresses. To see why, note that the local part is 16 bits long. The university assigns these to individual hosts. Two to the 16th power is 65,536, and this is how many hosts the university can support. So the size of the local part determines how many hosts an organization has to administer.

HIERARCHICAL ADDRESSES AND ROUTING

As we saw in Chapter 2, routing makes use of this two-part addressing. If a router at the University of Hawaii sees an internet address that begins with 128.171, it knows that this is an internal host. If it sees any internet address beginning with anything else, it sends the packet on to a border router that sends the packet outside the UH, to the Internet backbone.

INTERNET ADDRESS CLASSES

For the University of Hawaii, the network part is 16 bits long, leaving 16 bits for the local part. Do all blocks of addresses assigned to organizations and ISPs have this same 16–16 organization? The answer is "no."

Making all local parts the same size would make no sense. Some organizations and ISPs are enormous and need far more than 65,536 addresses. Others are small businesses that do not need anywhere near that many.

To cope with variations in the sizes of organizations and ISPs, the Internet Protocol defined several *classes* of internet addresses. Each class has a different number of bits in its local part. Each class is assigned a contiguous block within the total range of internet addresses from 0.0.0.1 and 255.255.255.254. Table A.1 summarizes the key differences among the classes.

Class A Networks In a **Class A** network, the network part begins with a 0. This unambiguously designates the network as a Class A network. The next 7 bits designate a specific Class A network.

A Class A network, then, has an 8-bit network part. Its 7 content bits allow only 2^7 or 128 Class A networks.

The good news is that each Class A network has 24 bits in its local part (32 minus the 8 bits of the network part). This gives each Class A network over 16 million internet addresses to assign (2^{24})! Very few organizations and networks need that many internet addresses. This lack of need is fortunate because it is impossible to get a Class A network assigned to your organization today. The few that were possible have been assigned or reserved.

TABLE A.1

Classes of Internet Addresses

CLASS	BEGINNING BITS	BITS IN THE REMAINDER OF THE NETWORK PART	NUMBER OF BITS IN LOCAL PART	APPROXIMATE MAXIMUM NUMBER OF NETWORKS	APPROXIMATE MAXIMUM NUMBER OF HOSTS PER NETWORK
A	0	7	24	128	16 million
B	10	14	16	16,000	65,000
C	110	21	8	2 million	256
D*	1110				

*Used in multicasting.

Problem: For each of the following internet addresses, give the Class, the network bits, and the host bits if applicable.

```
10101010111110000101010100000001
11011010111110000101010100000001
01010101111110000101010100000001
11101110111110000101010100000001
```

Class B Networks Next come **Class B** networks. These are the workhorses of the Internet, thanks to their good balance between the number of networks and the number of hosts per network. Class B networks use 16 bits for the network part.

In Class B networks, the first two bits are 10. This leaves 14 bits to assign to individual network IDs. This is enough for over 16,000 (2^{14}) Class B networks.

The total length of an internet address is 32 bits. So with 16 bits in the network part, there must be 16 bits in the local part. This is enough for more than 65,000 hosts on each Class B network. This is sufficient today even for fairly large and computer-intensive organizations, such as universities. The University of Hawaii (128.171) is a Class B network.

Class C Networks For **Class C** networks, there are 24 bits for the network part. The network part begins with 110, leaving 21 bits to designate individual Class C networks. This allows over 2 million possible Class C networks.

Unfortunately, each of these Class C networks can only have a few hosts. With only 8 of the 32 address bits left for internet addresses, each Class C network can only have 256 possible hosts. This would only be enough for a very small company.

Why were Class C networks made so small? When the Internet Protocol was created, personal computers were barely visible in organizations, and the idea of making a PC a full host computer was almost unthinkable given the power of 1980-vintage PCs. Hosts were large mainframe computers or at least minicomputers. Under these circumstances, the 256 hosts in Class C networks could support thousands of terminal users.

Class D Internet Addresses for Multicasting Although the Internet Protocol created only three types of networks, it created a fourth type of address for special use. **Class D** addresses exist to create multicast groups.

As discussed later in the module, the Internet was created for unicasting—one host sending a packet to another host. Yet sometimes you wish to send the same packet to several hosts. For instance, you might wish to send a video sales presentation to a hundred branch offices. This one-to-several transmission is called multicasting.

Class D networks begin with 1110. This leaves 28 bits to designate individual multicast groups. This is enough to represent over 268 million multicast groups. These addresses, by the way, usually are assigned temporarily, so the only limitation is that there must not be more than 16 million multicast groups on the Internet at any one time.

Classes of Address: Perspective When you see an internet address, the first thing you must do is determine its address class. Only then will you know how to handle it. If the address is given to you in binary, you *look for the first zero in the address*. If it comes in the first bit, you have a Class A address. If it comes in the second or third bit, you have a Class B or Class C address, respectively. If it comes in the fourth bit, you have a Class D multicast address. To test your understanding, identify the network part for the internet addresses shown at the bottom of Table A.1.

Because of the two-step approach that the Internet uses to assign internet addresses, it is impossible to get anywhere near the maximum 4 billion number of possible hosts on the Internet. Most organizations use only a small fraction of their assigned internet addresses. As a result, the Internet is running out of network numbers—especially for the high-demand Class B networks. Later we will see that one goal of the new IP standard, IP Version 6, is to avoid the Internet running out of addresses to assign.

SUBNETS AND SUBNET MASKS

The Need for Subnetting The two-phase assignment of internet addresses shown in Figure A.2 was created for administrative convenience. Although central Internet registrars were willing to keep track of several thousand networks, they were not willing to take on the task of assigning addresses to billions of individual host computers.

Organizations with Class A and Class B networks had a similar problem. They faced the need to assign individual internet addresses to thousands or millions of individual hosts within the organization. Again, this would have been a network nightmare.

As a result, organizations wanted a three-phase process for assigning internet addresses to an individual host. First, a central authority would assign a block of addresses to an individual organization. This would be done in the traditional way by assigning a network part.

Next, however, the organization would give smaller blocks of addresses to suborganizations. It would then make each small organization responsible for assigning the internet addresses within its blocks.

Typically, this suborganization approach would mirror the organization's administrative structure. For instance, at the University of Hawaii, the College of Business Administration is a suborganization.

Typically, each suborganization would have its own LAN to administer. A single network is called a **subnet.** So the goal would be for the organization to assign blocks of addresses to individual subnets.

As Figure A.3 shows, this would require a three-part address. The network part would remain the same. However, the local part would be subdivided into a subnet part and a host part.

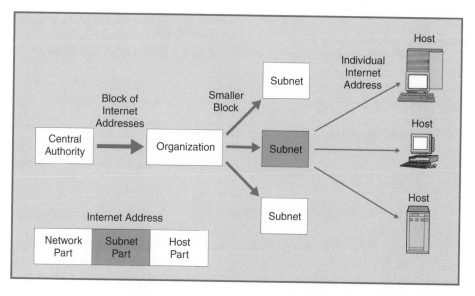

Three-Phase Process for Assigning Internet Addresses

Routers, in turn, would connect the subnets. So when an IP packet arrived at a router, the router would have to look at both its network part and its subnet part to see if the destination host was on one of the subnets connected to the routers.

Subnet Masks Routers, then, would need to be able to tell how the organization divides its local part into a subnet part and a host part.

To recognize the length of the network part, we saw earlier, is very easy. You simply look to see the first zero in the internet address. This tells you the network class. You then know the length of the network and local parts.

When the Internet Protocol was created, the need for subnetting was not foreseen. So no mechanism was provided to distinguish subnet and host components of the local part.

The solution to this problem was to give each network a second number to supplement internet addresses. This is the **subnet mask.** It is also a 32-bit number. It begins with a block of ones and ends with a block of zeros. A typical example would be:

11111111   11111111   11111111   00000000

Here, the subnet mask begins with 24 ones and ends with 8 zeros, for a total of 32 bits. In dotted decimal notation, this is 255.255.255.0. This, by the way, is the most popular subnet mask.

The number of zeros tells you the host bits. If there are 8 zeros, then there are 8 bits in the host part. If there are 10 zeros, then there are 10 bits in the host part. In this example, there are 8 trailing zeros, so the final 8 bits of each internet address in the network represent a particular host on the Internet.

Router Operation To see why subnet masks are useful, consider what routers do when subnetting is used. A router is attached to two or more subnets. When the router receives a packet, it must decide whether the destination internet address is on one of the subnets to which the router is attached. If the destination internet address does belong to a host on one of these subnets, the router can deliver the packet to the destination host. In turn, if the destination internet address is not one of the subnets to which the router is attached, the router must pass the packet on to another router.

To see how this is done, consider a network with a subnet mask consisting of 24 leading ones and 8 trailing zeros, as shown above.

Suppose that the router receives an IP packet for which the internet address of the destination host is the following:

10001000   10101010   00010001   11011011

Then the combined network and subnet parts of this destination address are specified by the 24 initial ones:

10001000   10101010   0001000100

Now suppose that the router is on 3 subnets. We saw in Chapter 2 that without subnetting, a router has different network addresses on different networks. When subnetting is used, a router connects subnets instead of networks and so has different network *and* subnet addresses on each of its subnets. Suppose that its internet addresses on these 3 subnets are:

```
10001000   10101010   10101010   11011011
10001000   10101010   00010001   11011011
10001000   10101010   11101110   11011011
```

From the subnet mask's 24 initial ones, we know that the combined network and subnet parts of these addresses are:

```
10001000   10101010   10101010
10001000   10101010   00010001
10001000   10101010   11101110
```

The second 3 sequences matches the initial 24 bits of the destination address shown above. So the destination host must be on the second subnet. The router delivers the IP packet to the destination host on the second subnet.

Router Operation: A Second Case However, suppose that the internet address in an IP packet that the router receives is:

```
10001000   10101010   11101110   11011011
```

Here, the first 24 bits in the destination internet address specified by the ones in the subnet mask do *not* match the network and subnet parts of any of the router's 3 networks. So the router knows that the destination host is not on one of the router's 3 subnets. The router must pass the IP packet on to another router.

Balancing the Numbers of Subnets and Hosts per Subnet The organization sets its subnet mask to give a good balance between the number of subnets it can have and the number of hosts per subnet.

For instance, suppose that the network is Class B, so that the local part is 16 bits. With the subnet mask 255.255.255.0, there are eight bits in the host part and 8 bits in the subnet part. This allows 256 (2^8) subnets, each with 256 hosts.

Suppose that the subnet mask were changed to 11111111 11111111 11111100 00000000. Here, there are ten bits for hosts on each subnet, so there can be 1,024 (2^{10}) hosts per subnet. However, there are only 6 subnets bits, so there can be only 64 subnets. This is good for an organization with a smaller number of large subnets.

Classless Inter-Domain Routing (CIDR)

The combination of network classes and subnetting leads to administrative convenience in the distribution of internet addresses. However, it has also led to inefficiency in address distribution. Many universities with Class B addresses use only a fraction of their addresses. The same problem exists for Class A networks.

Another problem is that Class D addresses take more internet addresses out of circulation. There is even a reserved set of Class E addresses (beginning with 11110) that have never been assigned and probably never will be.

As a result, although 32-bit Internet addressing should allow for about 4 billion addresses, in fact, the number of supportable addresses is only a fraction of that number.

Class C networks, furthermore, are almost useless. Very few organizations are small enough to have a maximum of 256 hosts, and these probably work with an ISP anyway. The ISP will assign them internet addresses from the ISP's pool.

For all of these reasons, there currently is a crisis in internet address assignment. This is being handled in two ways. One is for a firm to assign internet addresses internally any way it wishes. Its routers at the border between the firm and the Internet then assign outgoing transmissions into the relatively few internet addresses assigned to the firm. Incoming messages to these "fake" addresses are then reassigned to real internal addresses. This is called **network address translation (NAT).**

Another approach is to use **Classless Inter-Domain Routing (CIDR).** As the name suggests, CIDR does not observe the existence of classes. Instead, it uses a full 32-bit mask to designate the number of bits in the network part of the address. This allows network parts of any size, giving much greater flexibility. In practice, CIDR is used to group multiple Class C networks into an equivalent larger network.

Internet number reassignment and CIDR have given us some temporary breathing room in the assignment of internet addresses. However, these are only stopgap measures. As discussed below, the new version of the Internet Protocol, IP Version 6, attacks the address problem head-on by creating 128-bit source and destination addresses. This promises to be enough for everyone in the world to have his or her own internet address. It will even allow us to assign internet addresses to printers, copiers, and a host of other devices, including the proverbial smart toaster.

IP Fragmentation

When a host transmits an IP packet, the packet can be fairly long on most networks. Some networks, however, impose tight limits on the size of IP packets. They set maximum sizes called **maximum transmission units (MTUs).** IP packets have to be smaller than the MTU size. This MTU size can be as small as 512 octets.

THE FRAGMENTATION PROCESS

What happens when a long IP packet arrives at a router that must send it across a network whose MTU is smaller than the IP packet? Figure A.4 shows that the router must fragment the IP packet by breaking its data field up and sending the data field in a number of smaller IP packets.

FIGURE A.4
IP Fragmentation

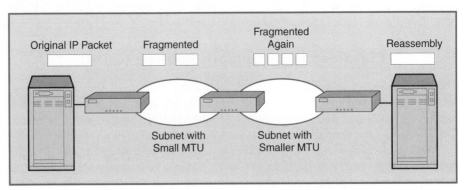

Fragmentation can even happen multiple times, say if a packet gets to a network with a small MTU and then the fragments get to a network with an even smaller MTU, as Figure A.4 shows.

At some point, of course, we must reassemble the original IP packet. As Figure A.4 shows, this happens only once, at the destination host. The internet process on the destination host reassembles the original IP packet from its fragments and passes the reassembled data field up to the next-higher-layer process, the transport layer process.

IDENTIFICATION FIELD

The internet layer process on the destination host, of course, needs to be able to tell which IP packets are fragments and which groups of fragments belong to each original IP packet.

To make this possible, the IP packet header has a 16-bit **identification field.** Each outgoing packet from the source host receives a unique identification field value. Typically, the identification field is initially given a random value. It is then incremented by one for each subsequent transmission.

The receiving internet layer process on the destination host, then, must collect all incoming IP packets with the same identification field value and must then reassemble them.

FLAGS AND FRAGMENT OFFSET FIELDS

The identification field value identifies several fragmented IP packets as belonging to the same original packet. However, the receiving internet layer process must still reassemble the fragments in order.

The IP packet header has a **flags** field, consisting of three 1-bit flags. One of these is the **more fragments** flag. In fragmentation, this bit is set to 1 for all but the last IP packet in a fragment series. It is set to zero for the last fragment to indicate that there are no more fragments to be handled.

In addition, the IP packet has a **fragment offset** field. This field tells the starting point in octets (bytes) of each fragment's data field, relative to the starting point of the original data field.[1] This permits the fragments to be put in order.

DISABLING FRAGMENTATION

It is possible to disable fragmentation. One of the flag field bits is the **Fragmentation Forbidden** bit. If this bit is set (has the value *one*), then a router along the way will not fragment the packet. Instead, it will discard it and send an error message to the source host using the ICMP protocol described later in this module.

ROUTING PROTOCOLS

On the Internet, there are no master control routers. Each router decides, for each packet, whether to send it to another router or to deliver it directly to a destination host. More subtly but more importantly, most routers have multiple "out" ports. When a packet arrives, a router must decide which port to use to send the packet back out. The wrong choice could send the packet on a needlessly long path.

---

[1] If there is no fragmentation, of course, the more fragments field is set to zero, as in the fragment offset field.

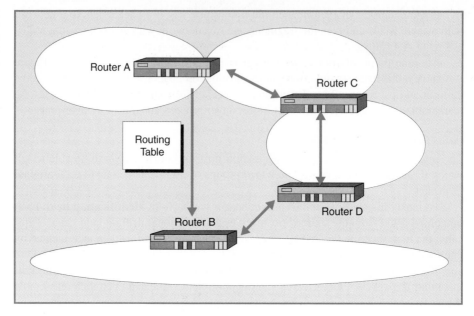

Routing Tables

Every router has a **routing table.** This table is a fairly complete description of the locations, characteristics, and distances of various other routers over some domain. This domain may be a single corporation or the entire Internet.

Good routing tables are essential to good routing. Unless tables are very accurate, packets will go spinning off into the void.

How do routers build their routing tables? The answer is that they talk to one another constantly. Figure A.5 shows one router passing its entire routing table to another router. In other cases, information is only passed on selectively.

Routing Protocols

On the Internet, routers exchange information through **routing protocols.** As Figure A.6 illustrates, there are many routing protocols on the Internet. In general, it is important to distinguish between routing protocols in autonomous systems and external routing protocols.

AUTONOMOUS SYSTEMS

Most large corporations have internal TCP/IP networks that only connect to the Internet through **border routers.** Their internal networks are called **autonomous systems** because companies have total control over what protocols they use internally. In particular, some routing protocols are found mostly in autonomous systems, whereas others connect border routers to one another and to the Internet backbone.

Routing Information Protocol (RIP)

The oldest widely used routing information protocol on the Internet is the **Routing Information Protocol (RIP).** RIP is useful only for relatively small networks, so it is used today only in autonomous systems.

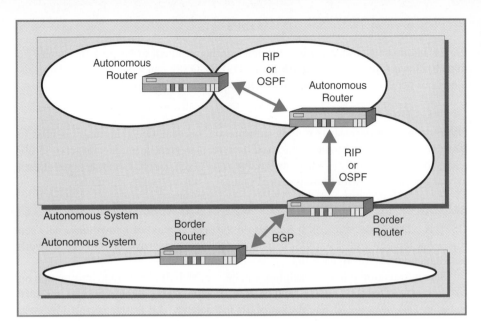

EXCHANGING WHOLE ROUTING TABLES

RIP takes a brute force approach to exchanging routing data. Each router transmits its entire routing table every 60 seconds (see Figure A.5). So routers constantly update one another's routing tables.

BROADCASTING

RIP routers, furthermore, **broadcast** their routing tables to all other routers they can reach. This makes the update likely to get through, but if you have many routers, each broadcasting its routing table every 30 seconds or so, the traffic load on the network will be very large.

DISTANCE VECTOR OPERATION

RIP is a **distance vector** protocol. Basically, it asks how many hops are between itself and other routers. For instance, if a router begins to work in Boston, it will broadcast its existence. A router one hop away, in New York City, will give the New York–Boston pair a vector of one because Boston is one hop away.

Next, the New York router's broadcast will tell a router in Philadelphia that Boston is one hop away from the New York router. Because the router in Philadelphia knows that New York is one hop away from Philadelphia, it adds the Boston router to its routing table. It gives the Boston router a value of two, because Boston is two hops away.

LOCAL KNOWLEDGE

RIP does not record information about routers more than 16 hops away. As a consequence, RIP routers only have limited knowledge of their networks. In a small autonomous system, they may know all routers, but this will not be the case in large networks.

OSPF

Larger autonomous systems use a different routing protocol to keep routing tables up to date. This is **Open Shortest Path First (OSPF).** OSPF can work with very large autonomous networks and can even work between autonomous networks.

LOCAL CONTACTS

OSPF does not broadcast its routing information, because OSPF normally is used in large networks where broadcasting would create too great a burden. Instead, OSPF learns the addresses only of the routers at the ends of the data links out its ports. It then exchanges data only with those routers. Figure A.7 illustrates this situation.

EXCHANGE INFORMATION ONLY WHEN YOU NEED TO DO SO

OSPF is a **link state** protocol. It focuses on the state (status) of known *links* between routers in the network. Each OSPF router has a comprehensive map of the network with data on the status of each link.

The information it has on each link can be very rich. It can include information on cost, security, reliability, latency, and other information. This allows OSPF to optimize traffic in various ways. If one packet needs low latency and another wants low cost, OSPF can optimize their routes through the network differently.

EXCHANGES OF ROUTING INFORMATION

When adjacent routers exchange information, they first exchange information on the time-stamped *version number* of each link between routers in their routing tables. If one router has a newer version number for a link, it sends its newer information about this link to the other. In this way, nearby routers constantly keep one another up to date by simple local communication.

Border Gateway Protocol (BGP)

For your border routers to talk to the outside world, you must use a protocol supported by your ISP. The most widely used is the **Border Gateway Protocol (BGP).** *Gateway* was an early term for *router*, so this is a protocol for border routers. BGP supports a wide array of services, such as Classless Inter-Domain Routing, which was described earlier in this module.

FIGURE A.7

Open Shortest Path First (OSPF) Routing Protocol

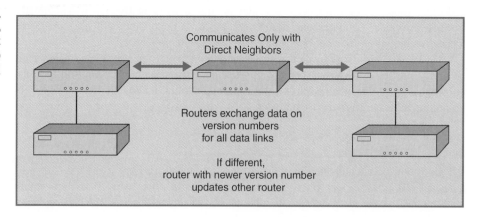

MORE ON INTERNET SUPERVISORY PROTOCOLS

In Chapter 2, we saw that packet delivery is not the only job of the internet layer. We saw that when your host connects to the Internet, it may first have to get an internet address from an autoconfiguration host. When you type a host name, in turn, your application program may have to call on a DNS host to get the corresponding internet address. We also saw, in the previous section, that internet layer standards are needed for routers to perform their routing duties.

In this section, we will look at two additional supervisory protocols. We will look first at ICMP, which is used to deliver several types of supervisory messages. We will then look at ARP, which hosts and routers use when transmitting an IP packet to a host or router on the same subnet.

Internet Control Message Protocol (ICMP)

In some ways, the main *supervisory* protocol in TCP/IP is the **Internet Control Message Protocol (ICMP).** ICMP is a workhorse protocol with several important uses.

ERROR MESSAGES

Figure A.8 shows that hosts (and routers) use ICMP to send error messages. If your application program gives you a "host unreachable" message, it is merely passing on to you what an ICMP error message has told it. Although routers do not ask for the retransmission of IP datagrams with damaged messages, they typically try to send ICMP error messages back to the sending host to indicate this and other problems.

QUERIES

ICMP also allows one host to send queries to another host. The most common of these is handled by a **Ping** program. When a host "pings" another host, it is sending it a message asking the receiver if it is operational. The receiver then sends a reply saying that it is indeed operational. In ICMP terminology, the Ping program sends an ICMP **echo**

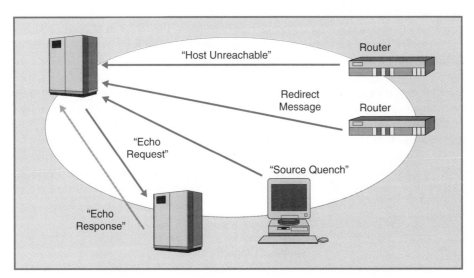

message. It often makes sense to Ping a distant host with an ICMP echo command before attempting a long transmission.

FLOW CONTROL

ICMP also provides flow control. One ICMP message is **source quench.** When a host receives this message from another, it should reduce the rate at which it transmits. It should continue to reduce its transmission rate until it stops receiving source quench messages. When source quench messages finally stop, it should increase its transmission rate slowly. This is a rather weak form of flow control, but it is useful in IP transmission, which does not guarantee packet delivery.

REDIRECTION

ICMP is also useful in routing. When a router receives an IP datagram from a host, it may realize that a different router on the subnet would be better able to handle datagrams to the host. One IP message is a **redirect** message, which advises the sending host to send subsequent messages for this destination address to another router.

PERSPECTIVE

Overall, ICMP offers a rich set of supervisory messages. It supplements the basic IP delivery mechanism. In the introduction to the ICMP RFC, Postel[2] notes that "ICMP is actually an integral part of IP, and it must be implemented by every IP module." The fact that IP is RFC 791 and ICMP is RFC 792 further emphasizes their closeness.

Address Resolution Protocol (ARP)

If the destination host is on the same subnet as the sending host or router, then the host or router delivers the IP packet via the subnet's protocol. For an Ethernet LAN, the internet layer process would pass the IP packet down to the NIC. The NIC's LLC layer process would place the IP packet in the data field of an 802.2 frame and then pass this LLC frame down to the MAC layer. The MAC layer process would place the LLC frame into the data file of an 802.3 MAC layer frame. It would then deliver this 802.3 MAC layer frame to the destination host or router.

To do this, however, the source device must know the 802.3 MAC layer address of the destination device. Otherwise, the source device will not know what to place in the destination address field of the MAC layer frame! This is a problem. The internet layer process only knows the internet address of the destination device. If the internet layer process is to deliver the 802.3 MAC layer frame, the internet layer process must discover the MAC layer address of the destination device. It can then pass this information, along with the IP packet, down to the logical link control layer, which will in turn pass the MAC layer address down to the MAC layer process to allow delivery.

Determining a MAC layer address when you only know an internet address is called address resolution. Figure A.9 shows that the **Address Resolution Protocol (ARP)** allows a source device to broadcast an *ARP request* message to all stations on the LAN.

---

[2] J. Postel, RFC 792, *Internet Control Message Protocol*, September 1981.

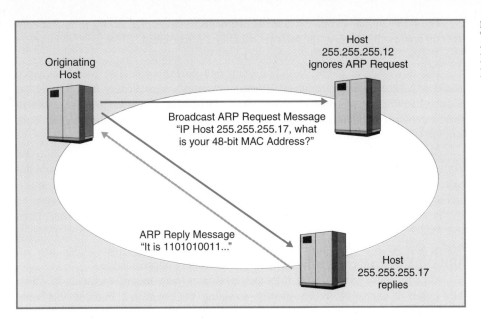

To do this, the source internet layer process creates an ARP packet that essentially says, "Hey, device with internet address X.X.X.X, what is your 48-bit MAC layer address?" The internet layer on the source host passes this packet to the LLC layer program, which passes its LLC frame down to the MAC layer process.

The MAC layer process on the host sends the ARP request message in a MAC layer frame with a destination address of 48 ones. This designates the frame as a broadcast frame. All NICs listen constantly for this broadcast address. If they hear it, they listen to the frame and process it. In this case, all devices on the subnet read the frame and send the internet layer PDU, which is the ARP request message, to the internet layer process.

The internet layer process on every computer examines the ARP request message. If the target internet address is not that computer's, it ignores it. If it is that computer's internet address, however, the internet layer process composes an **ARP response** packet that includes its 48-bit MAC layer address. It sends this packet to the source device, using the MAC layer source address given in the ARP request message.

THE INTERNET OF THE FUTURE

Looking Ahead

THE INTERNET OF THE PAST

The Internet of 20 years from today may look vastly different than the Internet looks today, and not just in terms of technology. Until now, the Internet has been very loosely managed. In fact, many would argue that the term *Internet management* is an oxymoron. The Internet was created by engineers with adventurous spirits, and if the Internet's almost nonexistent management practices sometimes caused problems, this was just the price that had to be paid for creativity to flourish.

The international Public Switched Telephone Network has strong technical controls on quality. In contrast, the Internet backbone sometimes is overloaded to an unacceptable degree because of poor technical control over quality.

The international public switched telephone network also has well-established management mechanisms for the settlement of charges across carriers. The Internet has nothing like this. As transmission costs continue to escalate, national governments will almost certainly demand settlement charges and the other management controls built into the telephone network.

Although the Internet works fairly well today, it is obvious to any user that the Old Net is having some problems. In a 1997 test of ISP availability,[3] many ISPs could not be reached by their customers in over 10% of all calling attempts. Even the best ISP had a failure rate of 3.2%. We would certainly not tolerate this in telephone service.

In addition, Internet end-to-end transmission speed is anything but stellar. Dern and Mace[4] noted in 1998 that end-to-end bandwidth is as low as 40 kbps. In other words, the Internet sometimes is no faster than the speeds offered by the old ARPANET. Throughput speeds, furthermore, are highly unpredictable.

Already, small groupings of ISPs are developing **peering** arrangements in which they agree to exchange traffic directly, avoiding the congested Internet backbone. Some have even speculated that the Internet will survive but only as a lowest-common-denominator service for residential users, for small businesses, and for big companies who must use it when peering and other arrangements to avoid it fail.

THE NEED TO CHANGE

The devil-may-care attitude that characterized the Internet during its first 20 years was sufficient when the Internet was small and was confined primarily to research institutions. Even today, however, the Internet is an important tool for international commerce. In 20 years, it will be indispensable. *Best-effort* packet delivery and the other rough edges of the Internet's protocols will no longer be acceptable. Like it or not, the Internet will go from T-shirts and blue jeans to business suits.

Another big change will be the emergence of a truly international Internet. The Internet was started in the United States. Even today, however, use of the Internet is no longer heavily dominated by U.S. citizens and organizations. In 20 years, Internet use will almost certainly reflect world population and economic distributions.

In the past there was a strong and generally unspoken assumption that the United States controlled the Internet. This was questioned sharply recently when Internet agencies and international standards agencies worked out an agreement for modifying the structure by which domain names would be assigned. (This is discussed below.) The U.S. executive branch ignored this agreement and instead created its own plan for changing domain name assignment—a plan that would keep U.S. control. For a while it looked like the U.S. government would simply force its plan onto the weak Internet community. However, the European Union reacted strongly against the U.S. power grab. This was a watershed event. Never again will the we-made-it-we-own-it assumptions of many people in the United States go unquestioned.

Finally, we need a body of statutes and case law to make Internet electronic commerce work smoothly. We need this at the state, national, and international levels.

---

[3] D. Pappalardo, "Trouble Haunts the Internet," *Network World*, August 4, 1997, 33.

[4] D. P. Dern and S. Mace, "The Internet Revisited," *Byte*, February 1998, 89–96, *passim*.

Managing the Internet Today

Today, the Internet is "managed" by a loose collection of organizations, each jealously protecting itself against interference by others. Figure A.10 illustrates the three most important of these organizations. (Of course, other organizations will disagree with their exclusions.)

INTERNET ENGINEERING TASK FORCE (IETF)

When the Internet was first established, its standards were written under contract to DARPA. The Information Sciences Institute (ISI) at the University of Southern California created TCP, IP, and other initial standards.

Internet TCP/IP standards are now created by the **Internet Engineering Task Force (IETF)**. Initially, academic researchers heavily influenced the IETF. This reduced vendor influence. The IETF had a philosophy of keeping things simple and getting them out fast. In general, it has a focus on "rough consensus and running code." "Rough consensus" meant that votes were rarely held in study groups and unanimity was desirable but unnecessary. "Running code" meant that the IETF members gave greater weight to field demonstrations than to theory.

INTERNET ARCHITECTURE BOARD (IAB)

The **Internet Architecture Board (IAB)** oversees the Internet Engineering Task Force. However, the IETF is very jealous of its independence. Although the two bodies have a complex relationship, the IAB's main power comes in handling disputes that arise within the IETF.

INTERNET SOCIETY (ISOC)

When the U.S. federal government withdrew from most active Internet management activities, it established an open organization to "manage" the Internet. This was the **Internet Society (ISOC)**. The original vision was for ISOC to manage all other groups.

However, the IETF is much older than ISOC and generally refuses to be guided by the society. After many debates, a general compromise has been worked out. ISOC's main job will be to provide the IETF with money. ISOC's influence is felt mostly in the fact that it appoints members of the IAB.

INTERNET MANAGEMENT IN THE FUTURE

It is impossible to predict the future of the Internet. However, it appears that in the long run a much tighter management structure will emerge to handle the growing scope of the Internet.

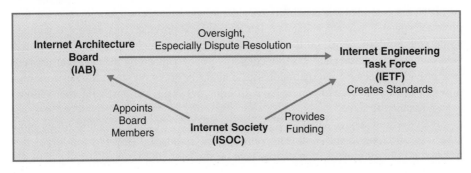

FIGURE A.10

Major Internet Organizations

IPv6

As noted earlier, the most widely used version of IP today is IP Version 4 (IPv4). This is the version that has 32-bit addresses. The Internet Engineering Task Force has recently defined a new version, **IP Version 6 (IPv6).**

128-BIT ADDRESSES

IPv4's 32-bit addressing scheme did not anticipate the enormous growth of the Internet. Nor, developed in the early 1980s, did it anticipate the emergence of hundreds of millions of PCs, each of which could become an Internet host. As a result, as noted earlier, the Internet is literally running out of addresses. The things that have been done to relieve this problem so far have been fairly successful. However, they are only stopgap measures. IPv6, in contrast, takes a long-term view of the address problem.

IPv6 will expand the internet address size to 128 bits. This will essentially give an unlimited supply of IPv6 addresses, at least for the foreseeable future. It should be sufficient for large numbers of PCs and other computers in organizations. It should even be sufficient if many other types of devices, such as copiers, electric utility meters in homes, and televisions become intelligent enough to need internet addresses.

AUTHENTICATION, PRIVACY, AND OTHER OPTIONS

Although IPv4 can have options, they are difficult to use. In contrast, IPv6 has a well-defined way of handling options through **extension headers,** which come after the main header. Extension headers are very easy to add.

One of these extension headers provides **authentication.** As Chapter 6 and Module F discuss, authentication ensures the sender is who he or she claims to be. The authentication header is mandatory.

The authentication extension header also provides **integrity** for the entire packet. This is the assurance that other parts of the packet have not been modified enroute.

Although integrity ensures that changes have not been made, it does not ensure privacy that others have not read the packet enroute. Another option is **encapsulation security.** This option encrypts the packet, ensuring that the message cannot be read enroute. Although the authentication extension header is mandatory, encryption is optional.

AUTOCONFIGURATION

From Chapter 2, recall that if a computer needs an internet address, it can call on an autoconfiguration host. The autoconfiguration host will supply the computer with a temporary internet address.

IPv6 has extended this capability considerably in its autoconfiguration service. For instance, suppose you are using one Internet service provider and switch to another while you are doing work on the Internet. The autoconfiguration service will switch your computer's internet address immediately to one assigned by the new Internet service provider. (Because internet addresses contain information about the network and different Internet service providers have different networks, the host's internet address cannot remain the same.)

Recall from Chapter 2 that, in the past, the process of finding an autoconfiguration host was different in different autoconfiguration standards. However, in IPv6, the process is fully automatic. You simply turn on the host, and it automatically finds an autoconfiguration host and gets an internet address. Although fully automatic autoconfiguration is very useful, it can be restricted for security purposes, so that only authorized hosts are allowed to do automatic autoconfiguration.

QUALITY OF SERVICE

IPv4 has a **type of service (TOS)** field, which specifies various aspects of delivery quality, but it is not widely used. In contrast, IPv6 has the ability to assign a series of packets with the same **quality of service** parameters to **flows** that will be treated the same way by routers along their path. Quality of service parameters for flows might require such things as low latency for voice and video while allowing e-mail traffic and World Wide Web traffic to be preempted temporarily during periods of high congestion. When an IP datagram arrives at a router, the router looks at its flow number and gives it appropriate priority.

PIECEMEAL DEPLOYMENT

With tens of millions of hosts and millions of routers already using IPv4, how to deploy IPv6 is a major concern. The new standard has been defined to allow **piecemeal deployment,** meaning that the new standard is backwardly compatible with IPv4 and can be implemented in various parts of the Internet without affecting other parts or cutting off communication between hosts with different IP versions.

Quality of Service

It was once believed that IPv6 would be adopted rapidly because of the Internet's address crisis. However, slow IPv6 development and temporary fixes have reduced the need for a fast changeover. It now appears that IPv4 and IPv6 will coexist for several years to come.

IPv6, as previously noted, was created with quality of service in mind. It has a large 28-bit flow field for identifying streams of IP packets with similar needs. A related protocol, the **Resource reSerVation Protocol (RSVP)** offers one way to describe flows and to reserve capacity at routers along a particular flow, so that capacity will be there when needed.

A simpler way to give services the throughput they need is to assign a **priority level** to each IP packet. Currently, the IETF **differentiated services** working group is defining one-byte fields for both IPv4 and IPv6 that will be used to specify priority levels. For instance, real-time voice conversations must have high priority at each router, in order to minimize latency. In contrast, e-mail delivery normally can tolerate delays of minutes or even hours and so can be given low priority.

As Module C notes, priority of service is already being added to LANs. This standard has 3 bits, allowing 8 levels of priority. Both IPv4 and IPv6 can use these 3-bit priority measures, so we can have fairly smooth integration between IPv6 parts of the Internet, IPv4 parts of the Internet, and LANs.

Although priority is useful, it raises the issue of **fairness.** Even lower priority traffic should be given a reasonable share of throughput capacity, even when lines are congested. Otherwise, lower-priority traffic might never get through, despite the fact that owners of this traffic are also paying for transmission. Consequently, algorithms that assign priority must consider both the priority of individual packets and also overall fairness.

Multicasting

Normally, the Internet supplies **unicasting.** When you send an IP packet, it goes to one other person. Some applications, however, require you to "narrowcast" the same message to a limited number of people simultaneously. Here are a few examples:

▶ A distance education class sends a television signal to 25 sites simultaneously.
▶ A webpage changes, and this change should be actively pushed to a few hundred thousand sites across the Internet.
▶ A company needs to download a program update to 50 computers.

On the Internet today, these applications require you to send unicast messages to all sites independently. This can be very wasteful, especially if many of the destination host computers are located together physically.

What we would like to do instead is to **multicast** these messages. Figure A.11 illustrates multicasting. Note that when the source host transmits, routers only pass the multicast IP packets out on routers that should receive it. Furthermore, if a multicast message is going to many users along the route, only one multicast IP packet travels over that route. Only where the multicast packet must be divided to reach different destinations is it actually divided. Obviously, this conserves bandwidth. Such bandwidth conservation is especially important for video and for messages that must go out to thousands or even millions of destinations.

Multicasting requires standards. These standards have been developed and tested extensively on the **Mbone,** a subset of the Internet designed to carry multicast traffic.

First, as noted earlier, Class D internet addresses are designed to designate multicast addresses. Each multicast address will be listened to by a group of hosts around the world. So there is no need to design new addresses to handle multicasting.

Second, there must be a standard that allows individual hosts to join a multicast group. For this, there is the **Internet Group Membership Protocol (IGMP).** The

FIGURE **A.11**
Multicasting

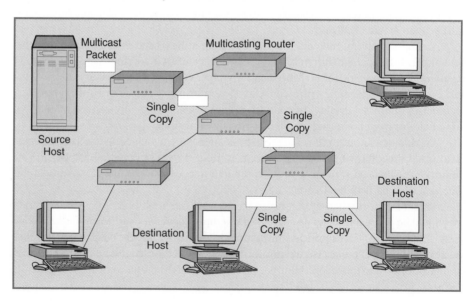

IGMP not only connects the host with the nearest router. It also propagates the membership to other affected routers.

Third, there are **multicast routing protocols** that help routers select paths and that respond to changing topology as routers come and go. There are several multicast routing protocols. The most widely used is the *Distance Vector Multicasting Routing Protocol (DVM-RP)*. Several other newer *multicast routing protocols* also exist.

Overall, there is nothing new about multicasting on the Internet. The *Mbone*, mentioned above, has long carried multicast messages. Most new routers, furthermore, are capable of handling multicasting protocols. However, multicasting works only if all or at least most routers on the Internet activate this capability. Although it is possible to tunnel multicast IP packets in ordinary packets to get through noncompliant parts of the Internet, this is impractical if it has to be used in most parts of the Internet.

One problem comes from ISPs and backbone carriers. Multicasting can reduce their revenues by reducing traffic. For this and other reasons, ISPs have been lagging in the activation of needed protocols on their routers.

Another issue is interactions with LAN multicasting. As Module C discusses, multicasting is being added to Ethernet and other LAN protocols through the mechanism of virtual LANs. Members of a particular LAN multicast group will share a common VLAN. LAN multicasting standards and products have to work together with their Internet multicasting counterparts.

Mobile IP

As Module C discusses, the proliferation of notebooks and other portable computers has brought increasing pressure on companies to support mobile users. Module C discusses wireless LANs as a way to provide such support.

Yet mobile users on the Internet also need support. The IETF is developing a set of standards collectively known as **mobile IP.** These standards will allow a mobile computer to register with any nearby ISP or LAN access point. The standards will establish a connection between a computer's temporary internet address at the site and the computer's "home" internet address. Mobile IP standards will allow mobile computer users to travel without losing access to e-mail, files on file servers, and other resources.

Mobile IP will also offer strong security, based in the IPsec standards discussed in Module F.

IP Telephony

The Internet to date has been used primarily for data. However, corporations also have enormous voice traffic requirements. In the past, the analog and circuit switched Public Switched Telephone Network has handled these voice needs. Now, however, there is growing interest in sending telephone calls over IP networks. The first Internet IP telephony systems were crude hobby applications for placing low-quality but "free" long-distance calls over the Internet. However, such crude systems will be replaced by IP networks that provide the sound quality, reliability, and low latency traditionally enjoyed by telephone users. The Internet Engineering Task Force is currently developing IP telephony standards. Module D discusses IP telephony.

Technology Test Beds

One valuable aspect of the ARPANET and the early Internet was that they allowed relatively small communities to "live in the future." They were test beds for new technology. Of equal importance, they gave us insight into what people really need in such environments.

In the next few years, we will see a number of such *high-technology test beds* that test technology and give us insight into needs. The most exciting project currently is **Internet2.** This is a consortium of universities and corporations that is exploring the impact of tenfold and hundredfold improvements of speed. Users will get at least 10 Mbps unshared at the desktop, and backbone routes will carry data at 500 Mbps or even faster. Universities will connect to the Internet2 backbone at high-speed access points called **GigaPOPs** (gigabit per second points of presence). Among other things, Internet2 will implement the Internet Group Membership Protocol to provide multicasting (discussed in the last section). It will also implement an advanced routing protocol, the Inter-Domain Routing Protocol, which promises high-speed routing without the huge routing tables that Internet routers now carry.

REVIEW QUESTIONS

CORE REVIEW QUESTIONS

1. A TCP-PDU begins with byte 8,658 and ends with byte 12,783. What number does the sending host put in the sequence number field? What number does the receiving host put in the acknowledgment number field of the TCP-PDU that acknowledges this TCP-PDU?

2. How is UDP better than TCP? How is it not as good? When is it the correct choice?

3. At an organization that does not use subnetting, how are internet addresses assigned to hosts? How are they assigned in an organization that does use subnetting?

4. In subnetting, what is a subnet?

5. What class of network is each of the following?

   ```
   10101010101111111110000000010101010
   00110011000000000111111101010101
   11001100111111110000000010101010
   ```

6. What happens when an IP packet reaches a subnet whose MTU is longer than the IP packet? What happens when an IP packet reaches a subnet whose MTU is shorter than the IP packet? Can fragmentation happen more than once as an IP packet travels to its destination host?

7. What program on what computer does reassembly if IP packets are fragmented? How does it know which IP packets are fragments of the same original IP packet? How does it know their correct order?

8. What is a routing table? Why is it important? What do routing protocols do?

9. Compare RIP and OSPF in terms of which routers they transmit information to and what information they transmit.
10. What is an autonomous system? Within an autonomous system, can the organization choose routing protocols? Can it select the routing protocol its border router uses to communicate with the outside world? What does *gateway* mean in the Border Gateway Protocol?
11. What types of ICMP messages were described in this module?
12. A host wishes to send an IP packet to a router on its subnet. It knows the router's internet address. What else must it know? Why must it know it? How will it discover the piece of information it seeks?
13. What nontechnical factors will drive the Internet to change in the next few years?
14. Briefly describe the relationship between ISOC, the IAB, and the IETF.
15. What specific benefits will IPv6 bring?
16. How may IPv4, IPv6, and LANs provide integrated priority treatment for packets and frames?
17. Why do we need multicasting?
18. What is mobile IP?
19. Why is Internet2 an important project? In Internet2, what is a GigaPOP?

DETAILED REVIEW QUESTIONS

1. What does the port number field of a TCP or UDP header tell you?
2. Put the following internet address in dotted decimal notation:

   00000001111111100000000000000011

3. How many Class B networks can there be, and how many hosts can each have?
4. A network has the subnet mask 255.255.255.0. This is 24 ones and eight zeros. How many hosts can it have per subnet? How many subnets can it have if it is a Class A network? How many subnets can it have if it is a Class B network? How many subnets can you have in a Class A network with the subnet mask 255.255.0.0? How many hosts can you have per subnet in a Class B network with the following subnet mask?

   11111111111111111111000000000000

5. How does CIDR help the Internet cope with the shortage of Class A and Class B addresses? How does network address translation help?
6. Explain flow control at the IP layer.
7. Does ICMP provide error correction?
8. What standards are needed to support multicasting?

THOUGHT QUESTION

1. What changes not in the book do you think will take place in the Internet in the next 20 years?

PROJECTS

1. Go to the book's website, http://www.prenhall.com/panko, and read the Updates Page for this module to see any reported errors and for new and expanded information on the material in this module.
2. Go to the book's website, http://www.prenhall.com/panko, and do the Internet Exercises for this module.

More on Propagation

INTRODUCTION

Chapter 3 introduced the central concepts of signal propagation. This module provides more detail on selected topics in transmission:

▶ **Modulation,** including frequency modulation, amplitude modulation, phase modulation, and complex modulation (which combines amplitude and phase modulation). All recent modems use complex modulation.

▶ **Multiplexing,** including time division multiplexing, statistical TDM, frequency division multiplexing, and wave division multiplexing.

▶ **Carrier trunk lines** between switches, including optical fiber links and radio links using microwave and satellite transmission.

This module is not intended to be read front-to-back like a chapter. Rather, it is intended to provide additional information on several distinct (although loosely related) topics.

In courses focusing on telecommunications (which covers telephone technology as well as data networking), the material on carrier trunk lines supplements the discussion of telephone technology and services in Module D.

MODULATION

Here we will look at the main forms of modulation in use today.

Frequency Modulation

Modulation essentially converts 1s and 0s into electromagnetic signals. Electromagnetic signals consist of waves. Figure B.1 illustrates an electromagnetic wave.

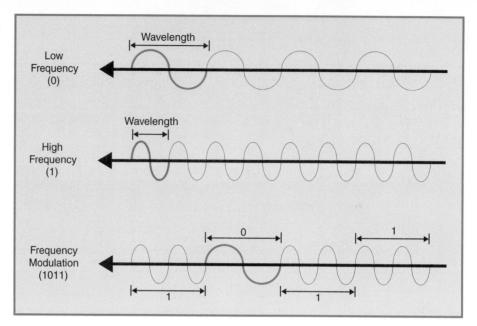

Figure B.1 illustrates that a pure wave oscillates (vibrates) in a regular way. The **frequency** of the wave is the number of times per second it travels through its entire cycle of rising, falling, and rising again. The frequency is measured in **hertz (Hz).** One hertz is one cycle per second. For higher speeds, we use metric notations.

The wave's **wavelength** is the physical distance between comparable parts on adjacent waves. Ocean waves have wavelengths of many meters; a violin's sound vibrations have a very small wavelength. Electromagnetic waves have a wide variety of frequencies and wavelengths, as discussed later in this module.

Frequency and wavelength are related. The wave's wavelength times its frequency equals the speed of the wave in the transmission medium. So if you increase the wavelength, you decrease the frequency, and vice versa. Think about strings vibrating. A shorter string will produce a higher-pitch sound.

We can use frequency differences to represent 1s and 0s, as Figure B.1 illustrates. For instance, we can use a high frequency to represent a 1. We can then use a lower frequency to represent a 0. So to send "1011," we would send a high frequency for the first time period, a low frequency for the second, and a high frequency for the third and fourth. Older modems use frequency modulation.

Amplitude Modulation

Frequency and wavelength are two of the four characteristics of radio waves. The third is **amplitude**—the level of intensity in the wave (see Figure B.2).

In amplitude modulation, Figure B.2 shows that we represent 1s and 0s as different amplitudes. For instance, we can represent a 1 by a high-amplitude (loud) signal and a 0 by a low-amplitude (soft) signal. Then to send "1011," we would send a loud signal for the first time period, a soft signal for the second, and high-amplitude signals for the third and fourth.

Phase Modulation

The last major characteristic of waves is **phase.** As shown in Figure B.3, we call 0 degrees phase the point of the wave at zero amplitude and rising. The wave hits its maximum at 90 degrees, returns to zero on the decline at 180 degrees, and hits its minimum amplitude at 270 degrees. Although the human ear can pick out frequency (pitch) and

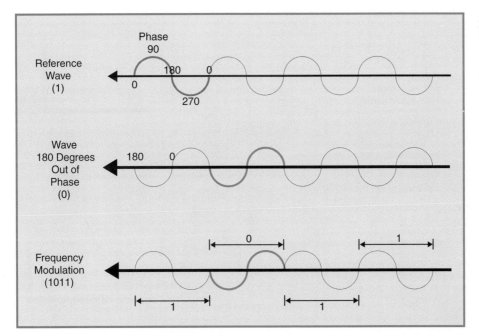

FIGURE **B.3**

Phase Modulation

amplitude (loudness), it is not good at picking out phase differences. Electrical equipment, in contrast, is very sensitive to phase differences.

We will let one wave be our reference wave or carrier wave. Let us use the carrier wave to represent a 1. Then we can use a wave 180 degrees out of phase to represent a 0. The figure shows that to send "1011", we send the reference for the first time period, shift the phase 180 degrees for the second, and return to the reference wave for the third and fourth time periods. Although this makes little sense in terms of hearing, it is easy for electronic equipment to deal with phase differences.

Complex Modulation

We have looked at rather idealized modulation schemes. However, today's high-speed modems really combine multiple forms of modulation, giving **complex modulation.** Figure B.4 shows that they combine amplitude and phase modulation. The sender varies both the amplitude and the phase of the transmitted signal with each transmission.

In the figure, there are two possible amplitude levels and four possible phase angles. (Real modulation standards use more combinations.) This gives eight possible signals to send in each transmission. With eight possibilities, each transmission can represent one of the eight possible sequences of three bits (000 through 111). The standard assigns a specific three-bit sequence to each combination.

Some complex modulation schemes use even more combinations of amplitude and phase, so that they can send more bits per line change. This, however, can increase errors because phase and amplitude detection become more difficult when there are many possible phase–amplitude states. As a consequence, many complex modulation schemes use trellis encoding, in which only some phase–amplitude combinations are used to represent data. If other combinations appear, they are counted as errors. If

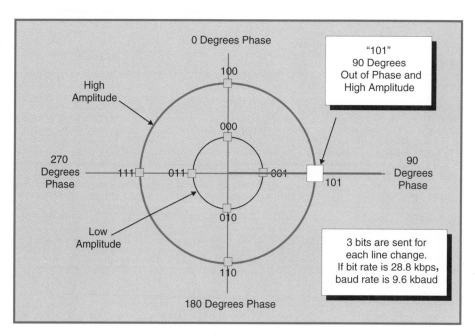

modems begin to detect too many errors, they will slow down and ask their partner at the other end to slow down as well.

Baud Rate and Bit Rate

The transmission's **baud rate** is the number of times the line changes per second. Suppose our modem has a baud rate of 2,400. Then sending 3 bits per line change (baud) gives us a bit rate of 7,200 bits per second. In other words, baud rate is much lower than the bit rate in fast modems. This causes confusion because what modem vendors label as the baud rate is usually the bit rate. If they label the modem using one of the standards discussed in Chapter 3, however, this will tell you the bit rate unambiguously.

MULTIPLEXING

Transmission lines are expensive, especially long-distance transmission lines. As Figure B.5 shows, we would like to be able to reduce costs by **multiplexing**—having several conversations between pairs of end stations that share a single transmission line. Here we are looking at terminal–host communication, but multiplexing is also used in many other situations.[1]

MULTIPLEXERS AND TRANSPARENCY

Figure B.5 shows that multiplexing requires a box at each end of the transmission line. This box is a **multiplexer.** It handles the mixing of multiple signals onto the line at one end and their unmixing at the other end.

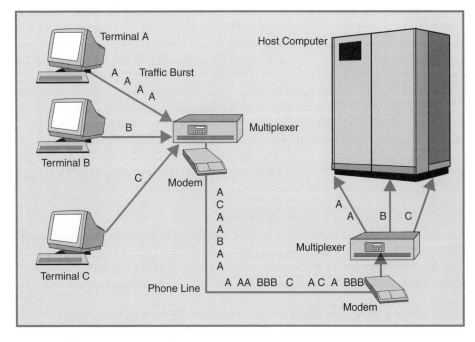

FIGURE B.5
Multiplexing

---

[1] Module H discusses how multiplexing is integral to communication between IBM mainframes and terminals.

Multiplexers work in a way that is **transparent** to the end stations. This means that the end stations do not know that their signals are being multiplexed. They transmit and receive exactly as they do on an unshared line. This means that you can add multiplexing anywhere in a system without changing anything else.

ECONOMIES OF SCALE

One thing that makes multiplexing attractive is **economies of scale** in the purchase or lease of transmission lines. For instance, suppose that each connection between a pair of end stations needs a transmission capacity of 64 kbps. Telephone companies offer 64 kbps lines (sometimes 56 kbps). They also offer T1 lines, which operate at 1.544 Mbps. This high capacity allows T1 lines to multiplex 24 connections operating at 64 kbps. Yet T1 lines cost only about three or four times as much as 64 kbps. Even if you have only a half dozen 64 kbps connections, buying a single T1 line makes economic sense as long as you use it long enough to pay back the cost of the multiplexer.

STATISTICAL MULTIPLEXING

Even further cost savings are possible in data communications because most connections between pairs of stations are **bursty.** This means that they usually consist of short transmissions followed by long silences.

For instance, consider when you work at a PC using the World Wide Web. You may only download webpages every three to five minutes. You will spend most of your online time staring at the screen, printing the webpage, or copying contents to other applications.

The same is true in e-mail. You typically use the transmission line only when you download messages to your PC or upload them to the mail server. Most of your time is spent in the message disposition phase, in which you read your mail, delete messages, copy them to folders by topic, and type replies. These actions only require occasional bursts to and from the mail server. The second most time-consuming phase is the composition of initial messages, which is very long compared to the burst that will be needed to send the message.

As a result of the bursty nature of most types of data communications, most of the capacity of an unshared line goes to waste. In fact, the line will be in use only about 5% of the time. If we can find a way to mix the bursts of many connections onto a single line, we can save a great deal of money. We call this **statistical multiplexing.**

To give an example, suppose you have four 64 kbps connections, each using the line only 10% of the time. Then you can easily support all four connections with a single 64 kbps line instead of four.

ECONOMIES OF SCALE AND BURSTINESS

Economies of scale and burstiness can work together. For instance, suppose that 100 end-station connections need a 64 kbps transmission line and only use it 5% of the time. Without multiplexing, you would need one hundred 64 kbps lines. For simplicity, suppose that each of these lines costs $200 per month. Then the monthly cost would be $20,000.

However, T1 lines can multiplex 24 connections. Without statistical multiplexing, then, you would need 5 T1 lines for the 100 connections. If a T1 line costs $800 per month, simple nonstatistical multiplexing will cost you $4,000 instead of $20,000.

Now add statistical multiplexing. Each connection needs only about 5% of 64 kbps, or 3,200 bps. So 100 connections would require only 320 kbps of capacity. This would require five 64 kbps lines with statistical multiplexing, although six or seven would be better because burstiness is uneven and you do not want to run out of capacity at peak periods. However, a single T1 line at $800 per month would be less expensive because of economies of scale, for a savings of $19,200 per month compared to nonmultiplexed transmission using one hundred 64 kbps lines. This would allow you to recoup the cost of the multiplexer in a few months at the most.

Time Division Multiplexing

There are several ways to do simple multiplexing, that is, multiplexing without accounting for burstiness. The most widely used is **time division multiplexing (TDM).** Figure B.6 illustrates TDM on a T1 line.

64 KBPS PER CONNECTION

As discussed in Chapter 3, the process of coding a single voice connection requires a transmission capacity of 64 kbps. This is why almost all transmission lines are multiples of 64 kbps. (Sometimes the speed is 56 kbps, because 8 kbps is "stolen" from the channel for in-channel supervisory signaling.)

FRAMES AND SLOTS

On a T1 line, each second is divided into 8,000 time **frames,** each of which is 125 microseconds long.

Figure B.6 shows that within each frame, each of the 24 channels is given an 8-bit **slot.** The slot is reserved for that channel in every frame. Over the 8,000 frames that occur each second, then, each channel can transmit 64,000 bits (8,000 slots per second times 8 bits per slot).

SUPERVISORY INFORMATION

A T1 line operates at a 1.544 Mbps. Divided by 8,000 frames per second, this is 193 bits per frame. However, the twenty-four 8-bit slots in the frame collectively have only 192 bits (24 times 8). The extra bit (called the **framing bit**) is used for supervisory signaling such as timing signals to ensure that the T1 multiplexers at each end of the transmission line stay in synchronization.

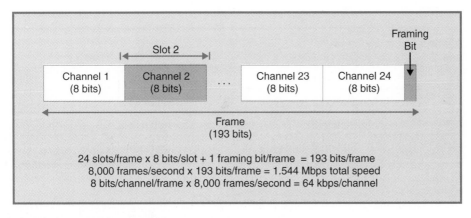

Of course, a single bit provides very little information. So groups of either 12 or 24 frames are treated as **superframes.** Their 12 or 24 supervisory bits are used for simple but effective supervisory signals. For example, in the T1 Extended Superframe standard:[2]

▶ The 6 framing bits in frames 4, 8, 12, 16, 20, and 24 form the pattern 001011. The receiver constantly monitors this pattern. If it sees a different pattern, it knows that framing is off. The sender and receiver are no longer synchronized.

▶ Six other framing bits form a 6-bit cyclical redundancy check. This checks for bit errors within the frame. It allows the devices at the two ends to check for performance degradation over time.

▶ The remaining 12 framing bits are used to send supervisory control codes between the two devices at the ends of the T1 line.

Statistical Time Division Multiplexing

In simple TDM, each channel between stations is assigned one dedicated time slot in each frame. Each slot is reserved for a particular channel, and that channel is guaranteed its capacity. Figure B.7 illustrates a more sophisticated form of time division multiplexing called **statistical time division multiplexing (STDM).**

WASTED CAPACITY IN SIMPLE TDM

Recall that data communication transmissions are bursty. This means that most of the time a channel's dedicated time slot will go unused within the frame if you use simple TDM. This is wasteful of capacity. In Frame B.7, three of the four time slots are going unused.

More importantly, suppose one station has a lot to transmit in its burst. It would like to transmit this burst of data at a much higher speed than 64 kbps. However, even if slots are going unused, the station will still be limited to its single 8-bit slot within each frame.

STATISTICAL TDM

Figure B.7 compares how slots are used in simple and statistical TDM. In simple TDM, most slots go unused, and Station 3, which has much to transmit, gets only a single slot in each frame. In **statistical time division multiplexing,** in contrast, the multi-

FIGURE B.7

Simple and Statistical Time Division Multiplexing

Time Slot	Simple TDM	Statistical TDM
1	Station 1 (unused)	Station 3
2	Station 2 (unused)	Station 3
3	Station 3	Station 3
4	Station 4 (unused)	(unused)

---

[2] In addition, the Extended Superframe standard steals some extra signaling bits from frames 6, 12, 18, and 24.

plexer assigns slots on a demand basis. Stations 1 and 2, which are not transmitting, do not use up slots. In turn, Station 3 gets three slots within the frame.

COST

Years ago, statistical time division multiplexing was prohibitively expensive. Today, however, processing power is cheap, and statistical time division multiplexing is the norm in data multiplexers. Of course, the multiplexers at the two ends must follow the same statistical multiplexing standard.

Frequency Division Multiplexing

In time division multiplexing, each second is divided into a number of frames, and frames are further divided into slots. This is good for digital transmission over wires. However, it is not the most common way to transmit radio signals. For radio transmission, the most common technique is **frequency division multiplexing (FDM).** Figure B.8 illustrates this approach.

RADIO WAVES AND INTERFERENCE

Radio waves consist of electromagnetic signals operating at different frequencies. If two stations transmit at the same frequency, their signals will interfere with one another. As a result, there are regulatory agencies that assign frequencies to prevent or at least minimize interference.

SERVICE BANDS

The entire range of frequencies from zero Hertz to infinity is called the **electromagnetic frequency spectrum.** Figure B.8 shows that a part of the spectrum devoted to a single application is called a **service band.** This is a range of frequencies devoted to a

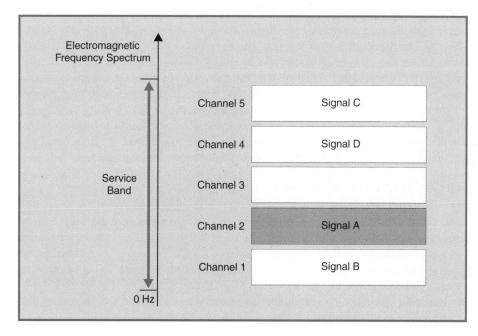

certain service. For instance, in the United States, there are two frequency bands for cordless telephone service and two for cellular communication (see Module D). There are also service bands for television, AM radio, FM radio, and many other purposes.

FREQUENCY CHANNELS

Next, the service band is further divided into **frequency channels.** As Figure B.8 shows, the channels do not overlap in frequency. This means that a transmission in one frequency channel will not interfere with a transmission in another frequency channel.

BANDWIDTH

Each frequency channel has a lowest frequency and a highest frequency. The difference between them is called the channel's **bandwidth.** In the United States, for instance, the bandwidth of a television channel is 6 MHz. As discussed in Chapter 3, faster transmission requires wider bandwidth. Looked at another way, the bandwidth of a channel restricts the maximum speed of transmission, much as the thickness of a garden hose restricts water flow.

SIMPLE FDM

In simple frequency division multiplexing (FDM), each connection is assigned a single channel. The two stations using that frequency channel can communicate anytime, although speed will be limited by the channel's bandwidth.

WAVE DIVISION MULTIPLEXING

Optical fiber traditionally used lasers operating at a single wavelength. Now, however, multiple lasers or other input devices operating at multiple wavelengths may transmit their signals simultaneously into the optical fiber. This allows the fiber to carry several signals simultaneously. This use of multiple wavelengths is called **wavelength division multiplexing** or **wave division multiplexing.**

Wavelength and frequency are related, as discussed earlier in this module. So wavelength division multiplexing is simply another form of frequency division multiplexing. The basic difference is that simple FDM often uses adjacent channels throughout a service band, whereas wavelength division multiplexing on optical fiber uses a series of wavelengths that may be far apart. However, as our ability to control laser frequencies grows, we will be able to send signals at more and more frequencies.

In addition, wavelength division multiplexing normally uses binary (on/off) signaling within each channel. This is sometimes taken as a way of distinguishing wavelength division multiplexing from frequency multiplexing. However, some frequency division multiplexing systems also use binary signaling within channels.

SPREAD SPECTRUM TRANSMISSION

A concept similar to frequency division multiplexing is **spread spectrum transmission,** which Module C discusses. In spread spectrum transmission, multiple stations share channels and can transmit at the same time. We just noted that two signals interfere with one another if they are transmitted at the same frequency. However, spread spectrum transmission uses very wide channels and two different transmission techniques discussed in Module C that reduce interference when two stations transmit at the same time. By reducing interference to tolerable levels, spread spectrum transmission allows channel sharing.

Multiplexing at Other Layers

Multiplexing is used frequently at the subnet layer, that is, the data link and physical layers. In fact, even the PPP protocol discussed in Chapter 1 is capable of multiplexing several connections over a single telephone line.

Multiplexing also is common at higher layers. For instance, consider the transport layer. If two computers are communicating, they will have only one transport connection. If there are several pairs of application programs on these two machines communicating with one another, the application messages can be multiplexed over that single transport connection.

Inverse Multiplexing (Bonding)

Multiplexing sends frames from multiple conversations over a single transmission line. The goal is cost reduction through line sharing.

Inverse multiplexing or **bonding,** in contrast, sends frames from one conversation over two or more transmission lines, as shown in Figure B.9. Here, a single conversation uses two transmission lines. However, inverse multiplexing is not limited to two lines. It can use several lines.

If the goal of multiplexing is to reduce cost, the goal of inverse multiplexing is to increase speed. For instance, suppose you have two telephone lines in your home. If you and your Internet service provider have compatible inverse multiplexing (bonding) modems, you can communicate twice as fast as you can with a single modem. This may be an inexpensive way to increase speed.[3]

We saw in Chapter 3 that some ISDN systems allow you to use both 64 kbps B channels to communicate at 128 kbps with another party. This is another example of bonding. Module C discusses bonding in the context of connections between LAN switches. Finally, if a company using Frame Relay service (see Chapter 5) has a 128 kbps port speed, it might bond two 64 kbps leased lines instead of leasing a single, more expensive T1 line. By the way, most implementations of the PPP standard that we saw in Chapter 1 implement extensions to allow bonding.

Although inverse multiplexing can be useful, keep in mind that both sides must have compatible inverse multiplexing technology. For instance, if you buy a bonding

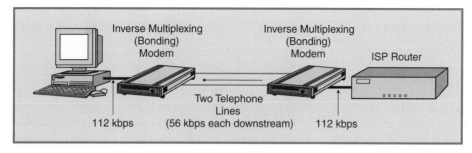

FIGURE B.9

Inverse Multiplexing

---

[3] Of course, if your household got the second phone line precisely because Internet use was tying up your line so much, using bonding modems to tie up both lines might result in serious problems in household relationships.

modem that can inverse multiplex two telephone lines, the ISP at the other end must have a bonding modem that follows the same standard as yours.

CARRIER TRUNK LINES

Trunk Lines

Module D notes that the telephone network consists of many switches connected by transmission lines. The transmission line that connects the customer premises to the first switch is called the local loop. Chapter 3 discussed local loop technology for **small office and home (SOHO)** users.

In turn, transmission lines that connect switches within the telephone system are called **trunk lines.** Trunk lines usually have far higher capacity than SOHO local loop lines. They need this extra capacity to multiplex many voice conversations between switches onto a single line, in order to reduce cost. We looked at multiplexing on T1 lines earlier. T1 lines are the lowest-speed trunk lines.

Sometimes telephone companies provide trunk line technology on the local loop, for instance providing T1 lines to the customer premises. Large companies can use this capacity either to multiplex several voice signals between two sites or as single "fat pipes" to carry large amounts of data to and from switched data networks (see Chapter 5).

For reasonably short distances, such as those found in most local loops, T1 transmission can be run over the same pair of wires that normally carries voice. We saw in Chapter 3 that various types of digital subscriber lines can bring even higher speeds to many SOHO customers over ordinary wire pairs.

It was once believed that if we wanted to provide high-speed connections to the home and small office, we would need to rewire our communities to bring optical fiber to individual homes. However, digital subscriber line technology has extended transmission speed over the existing local loop wiring to several megabits per second. Although optical fiber can bring even higher speeds, the incremental cost of rewiring the local loop with optical fiber is so high that the gains generally are not worth the cost today.

Optical Fiber

Chapter 3 discussed optical fiber briefly. This section looks at fiber in somewhat more detail.

CORE AND CLADDING

As discussed in Chapter 3, optical fiber is a thin glass (or plastic) tube with two components. First, there is a very thin inner **core,** as Figure B.10 illustrates. This core ranges from about 5 microns up to 62.5 microns. Light passes through this inner core.

The core is surrounded by a cylinder of glass or plastic called the **cladding.** The cladding can be up to about 125 microns in diameter. The cladding has a slightly lower index of refraction than the inner core. The difference in index of refraction is set so that when light from the core strikes the core–cladding boundary, there is total internal reflection. In other words, (almost) no light escapes.

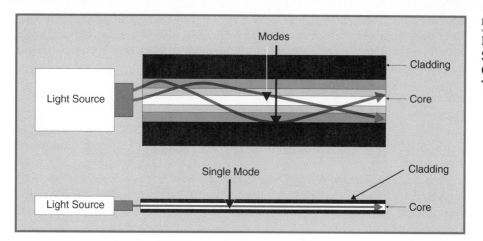

MULTIMODE AND SINGLE MODE FIBER

Chapter 3 noted that rays entering the core at different angles will travel different distances, resulting in rays from successive bits eventually overlapping. This was only an approximation.

More accurately, light waves traveling down the optical fiber's core travel in one of several ways called **modes.** Unfortunately, modes are too complex to characterize without a long technical discussion.

Multiple modes are bad because different modes travel at slightly different speeds. As a result, modes from successive bits will overlap, making the bits unintelligible.

Single Mode Fiber The wider the core of the fiber is, the more modes will be generated. This would suggest that we should make optical fiber extremely thin. In fact, such **single mode** optical fiber exists. As shown in Figure B.10, its core diameter is only about 5 microns in diameter. At typical laser wavelengths, such thin fiber can carry signals several kilometers, as discussed in the next module. Beyond that distance, additional modes begin to appear, even in thin fiber.

Unfortunately, single mode fiber is difficult to use. The light source must be aligned extremely precisely with the axis of the very thin core. Otherwise, there will be high signal injection loss. Splicing two sections of single mode fiber also requires high precision. As a result, single mode fiber is used mostly in long-distance runs, say between buildings in a university campus or as trunk lines between two switches in a telephone network. Single mode telephone trunk fiber is even thinner than the single mode fiber used in building LANs.

Multimode Fiber If the core of the optical fiber is fairly thick, typically 50 to 62.5 microns in diameter, then we will have **multimode** optical fiber. Figure B.10 also illustrates multimode fiber. In multimode fiber, the presence of multiple modes limits distance. Signals travel only 200 to 600 meters. Module C discusses distance limitations for gigabit Ethernet using multimode fiber.

Graded Index and Step Index Multimode Fiber To reduce problems caused by modes propagating at different speeds, most multimode fiber is **graded index** fiber, shown in Figure B.10. The index of refraction in the core decreases from the center to the outer edge. This causes signals at the outer edge of the core to propagate slightly faster than signals in the center, reducing mode time differences. In contrast, single mode fiber uses **step index** fiber, in which the index of refraction is constant in the core and the only change is at the core–cladding boundary.

WAVELENGTH

The number of modes in a tube will depend on the wavelength of the signal. If the wavelength is long, compared to the length of the tube, there will be fewer modes. In optical fiber, too, longer wavelengths mean fewer modes and so longer propagation distances.

For instance, Module C notes that gigabit Ethernet has two variants. The "SX" version uses a "short" wavelength of about 850 nanometers (nm). The "LX" version uses a longer wavelength of about 1350 nm. As a result, LX transmission can travel over longer distances before mode problems appear. Unfortunately, LX is more expensive than SX, first because 1350 nm signaling is somewhat more expensive than 850 nm signaling and second because LX specifies either a higher grade of multimode fiber or single mode fiber.

WORKING WITH OPTICAL FIBER

Because the core is so thin, optical fiber is difficult to splice. This has made optical fiber prohibitively expensive within LANs. However, splicing tools have improved greatly in recent years. In addition, it is now possible to buy premade lengths of optical fiber with simple connectors at their ends. There are two popular forms of connectors, called SC and ST, so connectors on a fiber must be matched with those in hubs, switches, and routers.

SONET AND SDH

The world's telephone companies now use optical fiber for much of their trunking. The dominant technology for telephone optical fiber trunking is **SONET (Synchronous Optical Network)** and its compatible European cousin, **SDH (Synchronous Digital Hierarchy).**

SONET and SDH use a ring topology, as shown in Figure B.11. Like 802.5 and FDDI, SONET and SDH use a dual ring. Multiplexers link devices to the dual ring. As

FIGURE B.11

SONET or SDH Ring

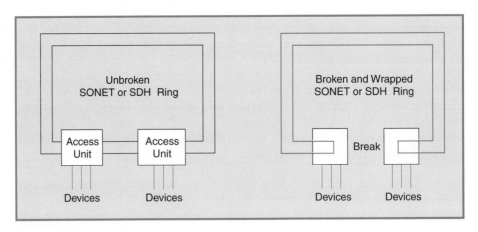

discussed in Module C, if there is a break in the dual ring between two switches, the dual ring can "heal" a single break by being wrapped, even if both optical fiber runs between a pair of switches are broken.

This is an important consideration because one of the most common problems in telephone transmission is for underground lines to be broken by being dug up accidentally by backhoes at construction sites. Another common problem is for aerial lines to fail because of wind damage and other problems. In *SONET* and *SDH*, such breaks cause only momentary disruptions.

Radio Transmission for Trunk Lines

ELECTROMAGNETIC WAVES

A radio signal is caused by getting an electron to oscillate back and forth, like a spring, as shown in Figure B.12. This oscillation generates an **electromagnetic wave** with the oscillation's frequency. This electromagnetic wave propagates as a sphere away from the electron, at the speed of light.

Of course, a single electron does not produce a very strong electromagnetic wave, so many electrons within an antenna must be forced to oscillate at the same frequency. This produces a strong enough electromagnetic wave to detect some distance away.

OMNIDIRECTIONAL ANTENNAS

Figure B.13 shows an **omnidirectional antenna.** From such an antenna, the signal spreads out in all directions (hence, omnidirectional), in an expanding sphere. This spherical propagation is good, because you do not have to know the location of the receiver's antenna. The signal will find it. This is why cellular telephones use omnidirectional antennas.

However, omnidirectional antennas have a serious problem, namely attenuation. As the sphere increases in size, the signal energy is spread over an ever greater area. This reduces the signal strength at the reception site, making the signal harder to receive.

In fact, signal strength is inversely proportional to the area of the sphere. This is a serious problem because the area of a sphere is proportional to the *cube* of the distance from the antenna. Suppose that Point A is 50 meters away from the signal source. Also suppose that Point B is three times as far away. At Point B, the signal strength will be only one twenty-seventh ($\frac{1}{3}^3$) as strong at Point B as it is at Point A. To give another example, if Point B is four times as far away as A, then the signal strength at B will be

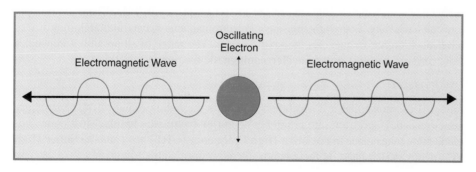

Oscillating Electron

Electromagnetic Wave

Electromagnetic Wave

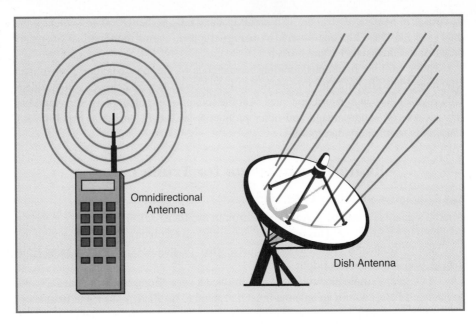

only one sixty-fourth as strong as it is at A. Obviously, omnidirectional antennas are best for short distances.

DISH ANTENNAS

For longer distances, you need a **dish antenna.** As Figure B.13 shows, dish antennas focus part of the radiated energy into a fairly narrow beam. This puts more energy in the direction of the receiver. In addition, beams do not attenuate according to a pure inverse cube law. However, you must know where to point the dish.

RADIO PROPAGATION

As discussed above, in this module's section on modulation, waves have four characteristics: frequency, wavelength, amplitude, and phase. Frequency and wavelength are related by the fact that the frequency times the wavelength equals the speed of the wave in the transmission medium. So if frequency doubles, the wavelength of the signal is only half as long.

FREQUENCY

Frequency varies widely. Of course, the lowest frequency is 0 Hz. There is no upper limit on frequency. Even light consists of electromagnetic waves, although light waves have much higher frequencies than radio waves. The range of all possible frequencies from zero to infinity is called the **electromagnetic frequency spectrum.**

FREQUENCY BANDS: UHF AND SHF

Figure B.14 shows that it is customary to divide the radio portion of the electromagnetic frequency spectrum into a number of **major frequency bands.** Most data communication takes place in the **Ultra High Frequency (UHF)** band and the **Super High Frequency (SHF)** band. In these bands, there is considerable bandwidth (2.7 GHz and

BAND	FULL NAME	USES	LOWEST FREQ.	BAND-WIDTH	UNITS	WAVE-LENGTH OF LOWEST FREQUENCY	UNITS
ELF	Extremely Low Frequency		30	270	Hz	10,000	km
VF	Voice Frequency		300	2,700	Hz	1,000	km
VLF	Very Low Frequency		3	27	kHz	100	km
LF	Low Frequency		30	270	kHz	10	km
MF	Medium Frequency	AM Radio	300	2,700	kHz	1,000	m
HF	High Frequency		3	27	MHz	100	m
VHF	Very High Frequency	VHF TV, FM Radio	30	270	MHz	10	m
UHF	Ultra High Frequency	UHF TV, *Cellular Phones, Radio LANs*	300	2,700	MHz	100	cm
SHF	Super High Frequency	*Satellites, Microwave*	3	27	GHz	10	cm
EHF	Extremely High Frequency	*Future Q/V Band Satellites*	30	270	GHz	10	mm

27 GHz, respectively). In fact, the SHF band is so wide that it is further divided, as discussed in the section on satellite transmission later in this module.

At the same time, signals in the UHF band and lower frequencies of the SHF band travel through walls and around obstacles reasonably well. At higher frequencies in SHF, they do not. In addition, equipment becomes more expensive at higher SHF frequencies. So there is great competition for spectrum space in the UHF band and in lower portions of the SHF band.

SERVICE BANDS

As noted earlier in this module, under the discussion of frequency division multiplexing, major bands are further subdivided into **service bands,** within which users have a common application. For instance, Module C notes that the 2.4 to 2.5 GHz service band is allocated for unlicensed propagation using spread spectrum technology. This makes it ideal for radio LANs.

To create the personal communication service (see Module D) in turn, the U.S. Federal Communications Commission (FCC) assigned frequencies between 1.8 and

2.2 GHz, where waves still pass around obstacles. To do this, the FCC had to move other systems to higher frequencies. Competition for spectrum is always fierce.

Microwave Systems

One of the most important uses of radio in carrier trunk transmission is microwave transmission. Microwave permits the transmission of information over reasonably long distances without the expense of laying ground wires.

Figure B.15 shows a **microwave** system. It shows that microwave systems use dish antennas for point-to-point transmission. They operate in the low gigahertz range, where highly directional transmission is possible with dish antennas only a few meters in diameter.

However, microwave systems only can travel a limited distance before problems occur. Signals may grow too weak because of attenuation. Or, the receiver might be so far away that it falls below the horizon, losing the required line-of-sight connection (the ability of the two dish antennas to see one another). Or, there may be mountains and other obstacles between the dishes. In general, line-of-sight microwave transmission is good for only 30 to 50 kilometers (20 to 30 miles).[4]

To solve such problems, Figure B.15 shows that microwave systems use **repeaters.** These repeaters capture and regenerate the signal, often cleaning it up to remove propagation effects before passing the message on to the next repeater or to the ultimate receiving antenna.

Satellite Systems

After World War II, a young radar engineer named Arthur C. Clarke saw a way to improve on microwave systems. Why not, he asked, put a microwave repeater in space, on a satellite going around the earth? And why not set the satellite's altitude at 36,000 km (22,300 miles), so that it would circle the world every 24 hours and so appear stationary in the sky? (This is called a **geosynchronous orbit.**) Figure B.16 shows his

FIGURE **B.15**

Microwave Transmission

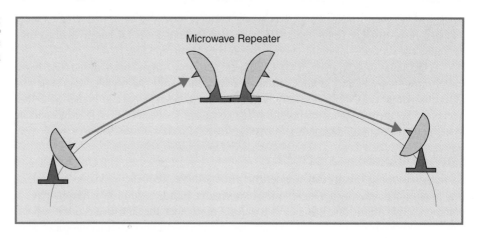

Microwave Repeater

---

[4] G. R. McClain, ed., *Handbook of International Connectivity Standards* (New York: Van Nostrand), 1996, p. 418.

suggestion. Today, a great deal of our long-distance communication travels over **geo-synchronous communication satellites (GEOs).**

Figure B.16 shows that because the satellite appears to be stationary, individual earth stations with dish antennas point directly at the satellite. They use point-to-point transmission for **uplink** transmission.

In contrast, the satellite's **downlink** beam is rather broad, so that it can reach many earth stations. The area a satellite covers is called its **footprint.** This footprint is often the size of a whole country, although it can be larger or smaller.

SATELLITE FREQUENCY BANDS

As noted earlier, the SHF band is so wide that it is normally divided into a number of smaller frequency bands. In general, as frequency increases, dishes can become smaller for the same degree of amplification, but attenuation problems increase, requiring more powerful satellites.

▶ **C Band.** The first satellites operated in the *C Band*, which was originally created for microwave systems. C Band satellites use frequencies of about 6 GHz for the *uplink* (the signal from the earth station to the satellite) and 4 GHz for the *downlink*. (The uplink frequency is always higher than the downlink frequency in satellite transmission.) C Band was a good place for satellite communication to start because C Band equipment was readily available and inexpensive, thanks to widespread terrestrial microwave transmission in this band. Unfortunately, this same widespread terrestrial microwave use tends to create interference between terrestrial microwave systems and C Band satellites.

▶ **Ku Band.** Next, many satellites began to use the Ku Band, with an uplink of about 14 GHz and a downlink of about 12 GHz. In this band, rain produces substantial attenuation, so powerful satellites are needed to burn through the attenuation. Dishes, however, can be smaller than they can be in C Band without losing efficiency. In addition, there are no terrestrial microwave systems to interfere with Ku Band signals.

▶ **Ka Band.** The Ka Band has uplink frequencies of about 30 GHz and downlink frequencies of about 20 GHz. Satellites are just beginning to use these frequencies. Rain attenuation is very high, so satellites must have very high power. New satellite-based telephony systems (see Module D) and satellite data services will use the Ka Band.

▶ **Q/V Bands**. Although the Ka Band is only beginning to be used, some firms are already looking beyond it to the Q/V Bands, where attenuation will be extremely severe.

SATELLITE LIMITATIONS

Although communication satellites are very useful, they have several limitations.

1. There is *limited bandwidth*. Even with dish antennas, directionality is limited, so you cannot place satellites too close together in the geosynchronous orbit. Space on the geosynchronous orbit is a scarce resource.
2. Satellites have long *propagation delays*. Even at the speed of light, it takes a quarter of a second for a signal to go up to a GEO and back down again. This is somewhat distracting for human conversations. For data transmission, it requires special protocols.
3. For high-volume routes between major cities, *optical fiber* has proven to be more economical than communication satellites. Even for overseas transmission, fiber optic cables are rapidly displacing satellites on high-density routes, despite fiber's high deployment expense.

TOWARD SPECIALIZED USES

As a result of these limitations, satellites tend to be used in specialized circumstances.

1. First, they are used in areas with very *low subscriber densities*. These are called **thin route** systems. Indonesia, for example, finds it much cheaper to connect many villages with satellite service than to lay wiring between islands and across many inhospitable types of terrain.
2. Satellites are also good for **multipoint transmission;** that is, transmission from one site to many locations. The television and cable television networks deliver most of their programming to their affiliates via multipoint satellite distribution. **Direct broadcast satellites** even deliver signals directly to homes.
3. Satellites are also ideal for **mobile stations.** You obviously cannot string wire between a fixed station and a moving truck.

VSATs

When communication satellites first appeared, antennas were 10 to 30 meters in diameter. Large dishes allowed weak satellites to be used because a large dish can collect and amplify a very weak satellite signal. They also allowed close satellite spacing because as dishes grow in size, they become more directional. Unfortunately, these giant dishes had to be located far from cities.

SMALL DISHES

In the 1970s, Professor Bruce Lusignan at Stanford began to show that it would make sense to create some satellite systems with very low-cost earth stations. These simple earth stations would use small dishes to reduce their costs. We now call these **very small aperture terminal (VSAT)** systems, where *aperture* means the diameter of the dish (terminal).

Because satellite power was growing, Lusignan reasoned, earth station power could be lower. And at higher frequencies, even relatively small dishes could provide reasonable directionality. Although satellite spacing in orbit would still have to be made wider, if less directional VSAT dishes were used, Lusignan argued that the trade-off would often make a great deal of sense.

HUBS

In VSAT systems, not all stations use VSAT dishes. Figure B.17 shows that VSAT systems have one or more large *hub* stations that are very powerful and have large dishes. This allows the satellite to use most of its limited power to broadcast to weak VSAT stations.

The hub–VSAT approach is especially good for one-way, one-to-many transmission, such as delivering network television program feeds to thousands of television stations or millions of homes. VSATs can also be used for two-way communication, although this requires more complex electronics in *send–receive* VSAT stations, compared to *receive-only* VSAT stations.

BYPASS TECHNOLOGY

We have been discussing VSAT technology within a section on trunking between switches for carriers. Obviously, VSAT technology is not an inter-switch trunking technology. In practice, companies turn to VSAT carriers to avoid traditional carriers.

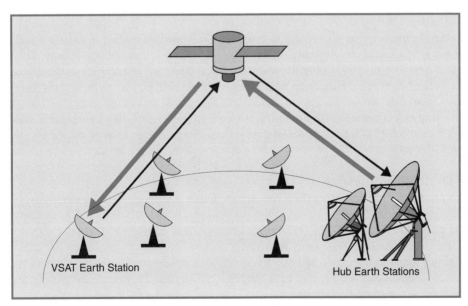

FIGURE B.17

Very Small Aperture Terminal (VSAT) Satellite System

VSAT Earth Station

Hub Earth Stations

VSAT technology is referred to as a **bypass technology** because it bypasses traditional local telephone carriers as well as long-distance carriers. Companies simply place VSAT dishes on roofs at remote sites and deal only with the VSAT carrier. The one exception is that the central VSAT hub often uses a terrestrial carrier's land line to reach the headquarters of the company using the service.

LEOs

LEOs are **low earth orbit** satellites. Instead of circling the earth at 36,000 km, like geosynchronous satellites, LEOs orbit at only 500 to 2,000 km (300 to 500 miles). Like VSATs, LEO satellites give customers the ability to bypass traditional telephone carriers.

ADVANTAGES OF SHORT-DISTANCE TRANSMISSION

As discussed earlier in this module, radio signal strength decreases with the *cube* of distance. So if a LEO satellite is 1,000 km from the user and a geosynchronous satellite is 36,000 km away, the ratio of the two distances is 36. Cubing this, the signal strength of a ground receiver will be 50,000 times stronger at the LEO satellite than at the GEO.

Overall, then, it is much easier for a hand-held *transceiver* (transmitter/receiver) to reach a LEO satellite than a geosynchronous satellite. It is possible to use hand-held transceivers without dish antennas.

PROBLEMS WITH SHORT-DISTANCE TRANSMISSION

On the other hand, whereas a geosynchronous satellite appears to be stationary overhead, a LEO circles the earth once an hour or two. So LEO systems need many satellites, and a receiver on the ground is likely to switch satellites several times during a long session with another user. Overall, LEOs are essentially cellular telephone systems in which the cellsite moves but the receiver remains (relatively) motionless.

LEO CARRIERS

Several companies are now vying to enter the LEO services market in the Ka Band. Some are focusing on telephony, which requires only low transmission speeds. This limits requirements for power both on the ground and on the LEO satellite itself. If you buy a hand-held transceiver from such a company, you will be able to make calls from anywhere in the world.

Other LEO carriers will provide high-speed data services. From remote sites, stations will be able to send and receive data at megabits per second and perhaps even gigabits per second.

MEO (MEDIUM EARTH ORBIT) SATELLITES

Although most trunk-line satellite systems are GEOs and most personal satellite systems are LEOs, technology abhors a distinction. Some newer personal satellite systems are **medium earth orbit (MEO)** satellites orbiting about 5,000 to 15,000 km (3,000 to 9,000 miles). Being farther away than LEOs, MEOs require more power on the satellite, in ground transceivers, or both. In compensation, however, users do not have to switch satellites as often because each satellite stays in view a longer period of time. In addition, fewer satellites are needed.

CORE REVIEW QUESTIONS

1. What characteristics of carrier waves can be modulated in modems? In newer modems, which characteristics actually are modulated?
2. Distinguish between the concepts of baud rate and bit rate. When a modem box says that it has a V.34 modem that transmits at 34.4 kilobaud, why is this inaccurate?
3. In multiplexing, distinguish between economies of scale and the exploitation of burstiness.
4. What common characteristic of data transmission does statistical multiplexing exploit?
5. Distinguish between simple TDM and statistical TDM.
6. Describe FDM.
7. Is multiplexing found only at the physical layer? Explain.
8. Distinguish between single mode and multimode fiber, including both technology and the advantages of using each. Why is wavelength important in fiber optic transmission?
9. Distinguish between omnidirectional antennas and dish antennas, including both technology and the advantages of using each.
10. If one station is 100 miles away from the transmitting antenna and another is 400 miles away, how many times stronger will the signal be at the first station than at the second station?
11. How does bandwidth change with each increase in frequency band? Why do most data communications and voice communications services use the UHF band and lower portions of the SHF band?
12. Distinguish between microwave systems and satellite systems.
13. How are trunk-line satellite systems different than VSAT bypass systems?
14. What is a transceiver?
15. Give the distances for GEOs, LEOs, and MEOs. What is the advantage of each distance range?

DETAILED REVIEW QUESTIONS

1. You have a modem that operates at 2,400 kbaud. Its modulation system uses four amplitude levels and four phases. What is its bit rate?
2. You have a modem that operates at 3,200 kbaud. Its modulation system uses two amplitude levels and eight phases. However, only four of the eight phase combinations are used for signal data. The rest are error states. What is the bit rate?
3. Why is multiplexing especially important on long-distance transmission lines?
4. In what sense is multiplexing transparent? What are the implications of transparency?
5. Distinguish between service bands, channels, and bandwidth. Why is channel bandwidth important?

6. In time division multiplexing, distinguish between frames and slots. In a T1 line, how many frames are there per second? How many slots are there per frame? How many slots are there per second?
7. Distinguish between FDM and wavelength division multiplexing.
8. Distinguish between multiplexing and inverse multiplexing (bonding).
9. Distinguish between step index and graded index optical fiber. Why does graded index fiber dominate the multimode fiber market?
10. What are the main satellite frequency bands? Give the representative frequencies for the uplink and downlink in each band (except Q/V). Which has the higher frequency—the uplink or the downlink?
11. What are the main limitations of satellites? As a result, in what ways do satellites tend to be used mostly for specialized needs?

THOUGHT QUESTIONS

1. You have 40 connections that need 19.2 kbps transmission speeds. A 64 kbps line costs $500 per month. T1 lines cost $1,800 per month. Because of burstiness, lines are in use only 10% of the time. Compare the costs of transmission without using multiplexing, with nonstatistical multiplexing, and with statistical multiplexing. The multiplexer costs $5,000 and has a useful life of 5 years.
2. Voice connections are not statistically multiplexed. Why is this? In your answer, estimate what percentage of transmission line capacity is used in voice connections.

PROJECTS

1. Go to the book's website, http://www.prenhall.com/panko, and read the Updates Page for this module to see any reported errors and for new and expanded information on the material in this module.
2. Go the book's website, http://www.prenhall.com/panko, and do the Internet Exercises for this module.

More on LAN Technology

INTRODUCTION

Module C covers some advanced topics in LAN technology. It is not intended to be read front-to-back like a chapter. It should be read after Chapter 5. This module focuses on these topics:

▶ Older Ethernet physical layer standards, especially the still widely used 10Base5 and 10Base2 standards. It also covers mixing several Ethernet physical layer standards in the same LAN, for instance, to increase the distance span

▶ The newest Ethernet physical layer standards—the 100Base-X and 1000Base-X gigabit Ethernet standards

▶ The sometimes-useful distinction between Ethernet and 802.3 LANs

▶ The distinction between bridges and switches, how to select a switch, and inter-switch trunking

▶ Further information on 802.5 Token-Ring Networks

▶ Information on FDDI (Fiber Distributed Data Interface)

▶ More on 802.11 Wireless LANs

▶ Frame tagging, which supports standards for VLANs and priority levels in 802 frames

ADDITIONAL ETHERNET STANDARDS

In Chapters 4 and 5, we looked at three sets of the Ethernet physical layer standards from the IEEE 802.3 Working Group. We looked at the 10Base-T, 100Base-X and 1000Base-X (gigabit Ethernet) families of physical layer standards.

In this section, we will look more closely at two 802.3 physical layer Ethernet standards that predate 10Base-T, namely *10Base5* and *10Base2*. Both, as you can tell by their names, are 10 Mbps baseband standards. Some organizations that networked early still use these two physical layer standards as their main standards. Others continue to use 10Base5 for longer runs in their 10Base-T networks. As we will see, you can mix 802.3 physical layer standards in a LAN, as long as you separate them by repeaters.

We will also look at newer Ethernet standards: 100Base-X and 1000Base-X (gigabit Ethernet).

Finally, we will look at the difference between 802.3 MAC layer frames and the Ethernet II frames that gave rise to the 802.3 standard.

802.3 10Base5

When the 802 Committee began developing 802.3 variants, it developed a naming system. The **10Base5** standard illustrates this system. The *10* stands for the speed of the standard—10 Mbps. The *Base*, in turn, stands for baseband transmission.

The *5*, finally, means that a **segment** (single unbroken run) of the cable can be up to 500 meters long (1,640 feet). We will see later that several of these segments can be linked to form a larger LAN.

THE TRUNK CABLE

The specific type of coaxial cable used in 10Base5's **trunk** was created especially for the standard. It is 10 millimeters thick (about 0.4 inches). This is much thicker than the coaxial cables used to bring cable television signals to the home or to link VCRs to television sets.

Because of this thickness, the 10Base5 trunk cable is fairly difficult to bend and install. Because 10Base5 cable is traditionally colored yellow (the standard merely specifies a bright color), installers refer to it in frustration as a "frozen yellow garden hose."

MEDIUM ATTACHMENT UNIT (MAU): THE TRANSCEIVER

Figure C.1 illustrates how Ethernet 10Base5 devices are attached to the network.

First, attached to the thick cable is the **medium attachment unit (MAU).** One job of the MAU is to provide a physical attachment to the network. Older MAUs have a

FIGURE C.1

Connecting a Station to 10Base5 Trunking

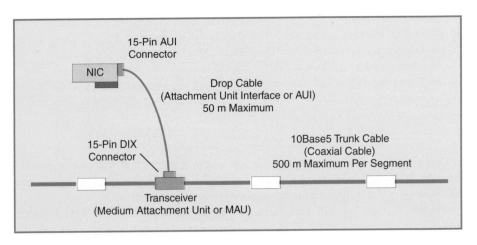

"vampire clamp" whose two "teeth" dig into the cable, making contact with both the inner and outer conductors in the cable. This rather crude attachment method speaks volumes about the antiquity of Ethernet cabling technology. Newer MAUs use screw-on N connectors.

The MAU is also called a **transceiver (transmitter/receiver).** This is the Ethernet Version 2.0 terminology. It is a transceiver because it *transmits* signals over the cable and *receives* signals from the cable. It is an active electronic device, not a mere physical connector.

ATTACHMENT UNIT INTERFACE (AUI): THE DROP CABLE

The station can be some distance away from the cable. To allow this, an **attachment unit interface (AUI)** runs from the MAU to the station itself. Ethernet V2.0 called this wiring bundle a **drop cable.** This seems like a wiser choice of terminology. The AUI attaches to the station via a 15-pin **DIX connector.**

The AUI can be up to 50 meters long. This is another thick, inflexible bundle, but unlike the coaxial trunk cable, the AUI is a bundle of 15 wires. It is slightly more expensive per foot than the trunk cable.

MULTISEGMENT 10BASE5 LANS

As noted earlier, a single unbroken length of 10Base5 trunk cable is called a segment. As in the case of 10Base-T (see Chapter 4), you can connect multiple 10Base5 segments with repeaters. This is like connecting 10Base-T segments, except that 10Base5 segments can have several stations attached to them along their runs.

The rules for connecting segments are the same as they are for 10Base-T segments. First, there must be no loops. Second, there is a 5-4-3 rule. There is a maximum of five segments (four repeaters) between the farthest two stations. This gives a span of 2,500 meters (8,200 feet). The 3 in 5-4-3 means that only three of these 10Base5 segments can be populated, that is, have stations attached to them.

In Ethernet, the term **LAN** means a group of segments connected by repeaters. The 802.3 terminology also calls this a **collision domain** because if two stations on the LAN transmit at the same time, their signals will collide.

802.3 10Base2

Although 10Base5 worked and worked well, it was expensive. The 802.3 Working Group created a standard for a less expensive cabling system. This was **10Base2,** which is also known popularly as *Cheapernet* or *Thinnet.* Like 10Base5, it carries data at 10 Mbps, using baseband signaling. However, its maximum segment length is only 185 meters (607 feet), which is rounded off to "2" in its name. In addition, it can only have 30 stations on a single segment.

THINNER CABLE

10Base2 is attractive because it uses RG-58 A/U and RG-58 C/U cable instead of the traditional Ethernet cable. As the standard's popular names suggest, this cable is thinner than the cable used in 10Base5. The 10Base5 cable is 10 mm in diameter. The 10Base2 cable, in contrast, is only half as thick. This thinner cable is cheaper to buy. It is also cheaper to lay because it is much more flexible.

FIGURE **C.2**

Connections in Ethernet 10Base2

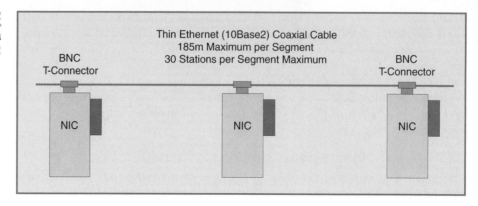

The T·CONNECTOR

Another reason why 10Base2 is less expensive than 10Base5 is that Thinnet does not have a separate trunk cable and AUI drop cables. Figure C.2 shows that 10Base2 uses a simpler arrangement. The cable at each station attaches via a simple T-connector. The stem of the T screws into the NIC, via a **BNC plug** on the NIC. The other connectors on the T-connector are for 10Base2 cable runs to the two adjacent stations. Connections and disconnections can be made in seconds.

In 10Base2, a segment consists of a string (daisy chain) of stations, as shown in Figure C.2. A segment may have up to 30 stations. On the last station, the T-connector not leading to another station must have a terminator installed on the open connector.

CABLING SUBTLETIES

There are only two things that are tricky about 10Base2 cabling. The first is that there must be at least half a meter of cabling between adjacent stations. The second is that the stations at each end of the daisy chain must have a special terminator attached to the T-connections.

DISTANCE IN 10BASE2

As in the case of 10Base5, you can have up to five 10Base2 segments (four repeaters) between the farthest stations. This gives a maximum span of 925 meters (3,035 feet). As in 10Base5, the standard requires that at least two of the segments cannot have stations attached to them if you are using the maximum five segments.

Mixed 802.3 Networks

So far, we have discussed networks that use a single 802.3 physical layer standard. But we would like to mix them together in a network. Figure C.3 shows how to do so.

For longer runs, such a network uses 10Base5 cabling or a 10Base-F interrepeater link (IRL). This provides a high-speed backbone that can run between offices in a building.

For runs to individual stations, networks can mix both 10Base-T and 10Base2. So if a firm still has older 10Base2 cabling in place, it can keep some older cabling while upgrading some of its 10Base2 cabling with 10Base-T cabling.

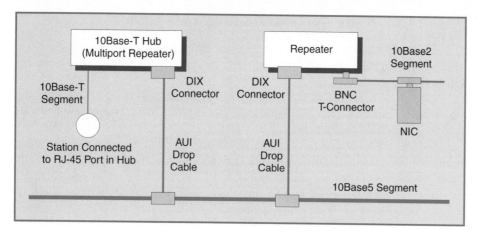

FIGURE **C.3**

Mixing Ethernet Segments with Different Physical Layer Standards

Mixing segments with different physical layer standards requires that you use the proper repeater. Figure C.4 shows a 10Base-T wiring hub, which is properly called a **multiport repeater** in the standard. In addition to its usual 10Base-T RJ-45 connectors, it has a DIX connector, so that it can attach to a 10Base5 segment. Other multiport repeaters come with a BNC connector for connection to 10Base2 segments.

Some repeaters have only two or three ports. These can be any combination of 10Base-T, 10Base5, 10Base2, or 10Base-F. You simply buy the proper multiport repeater for your purpose.

Note that we have talked only about the physical layer. As Chapter 4 noted, all 802.3 standards use the same MAC layer standard. Mixing physical layer standards has absolutely no impact on MAC layer operation.

In mixing 802.3 technologies, it is important to consider the maximum round-trip delay in a network. Each segment adds some latency. So do hubs. Mazzo[1] provides some data on delays and works several examples to show how to compute latencies so they do not exceed the 512 bit times (64 octets) in the 802.3 standard.

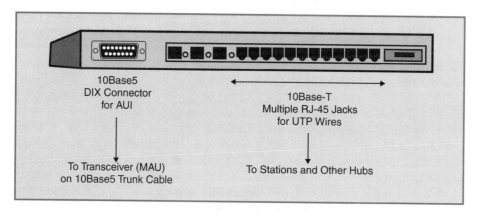

FIGURE **C.4**

Ethernet Hub with 10Base-T and 10Base5 Ports

[1] John Mazzo, *Fast Ethernet* jmazza.shillsdata.com/tech/Fast Ethernet/Design Rules, May 13, 1997.

The Cyclical Redundancy Check

We noted in Chapter 4 that the last field in an 802.3 MAC layer frame is the frame check sequence field. This field provides error detection using a **cyclical redundancy check (CRC).**

The CRC process begins by excluding the preamble, start of frame delimiter, and frame check sequence fields. The remainder of the 802.3 MAC layer frame is treated as a very large binary number, M.

The first 32 bits of M are complemented. In other words, zeros are changed to ones and ones to zeros. This is an obscure step that can be ignored in understanding the basic process.

Next, 32 zeros are added to the complemented M. This creates a frame check sequence field with zeros in all its bit positions. The CRC value will later replace these 32 bits.

Next, this complemented M with 32 zeros added is divided by a generating polynomial, G, which has the value:

100000100110000010001110110110111

This produces a 32-bit remainder, R.

Finally, the remainder is complemented and added to M. This places the complemented remainder in the frame check sequence field.

When the receiver receives the frame, it removes the preamble, the start of frame delimiter, and the frame check sequence fields from the incoming frame. It again performs the operations on the remaining fields and compares the result it calculates to the value in the frame check sequence field.

More on 100Base-X

Chapter 4 looked at the 802.3 100Base-X family, which includes 100Base-TX, 100Base-FX, and 100Base-T4. Since their introduction, products from this family have come screaming down in price for hubs and even for switches. The one exception has been 100Base-T4, which can use category 3 or category 4 wiring. Most organizations did not need a system for Cat 3 and Cat 4 wiring because they had already gone to Cat 5, and firms with older wiring tended either to upgrade wiring or not to upgrade at all. Faced with low market demand and a lack of existing chips, 100Base-T4 has not fared well in either market penetration or price reduction.

We saw in Chapter 4 that 100Base-TX and its cousins faced sharp distance limitations because of collision detection needs and propagation latency. Hubs add to latency. So does translating between 100Base-T4 physical encoding and 100Base-TX/FX encoding. As a result, the 802.3u standard specified two separate types of hubs.

Class I hubs can mix both T4 and TX/FX links. However, this adds so much to latency that there can be only a single hub in a collision domain.

Class II restricts itself to TX/FX links. This eliminates T4-to-TX/FX translation latency. As a result, there can be *two* Class II hubs in a collision domain. However, they must be within five meters of one another. So adding a second hub does not add to distance span. It merely adds a bit to port scalability by letting you add a second hub if your first hub no longer has enough ports.

Each Class II hub has a special "uplink" port. A short length of TX wiring connects this uplink port to any port in the other hub, which becomes the "root" hub.

Remembering the distinction between Class I and Class II hubs is easy because you can have only one Class I hub, but you can have two Class II hubs.

More on Gigabit Ethernet

As companies move increasingly to 100 Mbps to the desktop and in intermediate switches, their largest switches will need gigabit capacity. Chapter 5 mentioned gigabit Ethernet briefly. That chapter merely noted that gigabit Ethernet adds another factor of 10 increase in speed beyond 100Base-TX, 100Base-FX, and 100Base-T4.

STANDARDS FOR DISTANCE

Ethernet 100Base-TX and 100Base-FX "stole" the physical layer technology of FDDI. Gigabit Ethernet did something similar. Most gigabit Ethernet versions are based on the physical layer standard of **fiber channel.** Fiber channel is used in high-end servers as a way to link servers with disk drives. Hardware chips were already built for fibre channel when the gigabit Ethernet standards were developed, and this immediately made the cost of gigabit Ethernet switches attractive.

Two 802.3 groups are developing gigabit Ethernet standards. The 802.3z group focuses on standards to link gigabit Ethernet switches and hubs. The 802.3ab group, in turn, focuses on bringing gigabit service to the desktop using UTP.

1000Base-SX The 802.3z group has focused more specifically on optical fiber standards. It has focused on two basic technologies. In **1000Base-SX,** it focused on relatively inexpensive 770 to 860 nm technology. (The *S* stands for *short wavelength.*) At such lower frequencies, propagation distance is limited but cost is relatively low. So 1000Base-SX is used for relatively short runs, such as for horizontal distribution within a floor in a building. The 1000Base-SX standard was developed for 62.5-micron multimode optical fiber. The February 1998 draft standard allows runs of 220 meters to 275 meters over optical fiber that meets even minimum quality standards.[2]

1000Base-LX The 802.3z group is also developing a long-wavelength standard using 1,270 to 1,355 nm optical fiber transmission. This is **1000Base-LX.** This standard is designed for longer runs, such as those between buildings. For multimode optical fiber, the February 1998 draft standard for 1000Base-LX specifies a maximum distance of 500 meters over optical fiber meeting the high-end quality levels of fiber standards. In addition, for 9-micron single-mode fiber, the maximum draft distance is 5 km.

1000Base-CX In wiring closets, switches are often only a few meters apart. For such short-distance connections, the 802.3z group developed the **1000Base-CX** standard for distances of 25 meters or less. It uses shielded copper wire of a special design.

---

[2] Data in this section are from the Gigabit Ethernet Alliance, "Status of the Gigabit Ethernet Standards Effort FAQ," http://www.gigabit-ethernet.org/technology/overview/status.html, as of March 7, 1998.

1000Base-TX The 802.3ab group developed a UTP version standard to bring gigabit speeds to the desktop. This is **1000Base-TX.** The goal is to bring gigabit speeds to the desktop over CAT 5 UTP.

DATA ENCODING

Recall from Chapter 4 that 100Base-TX uses 4B/5B encoding, in which a package of 5 bits carries 4 bits of data. The 802.3z standards use the **8B/10B** encoding process created for fiber channel. Here, the packages are 10 bits long and carry 8 data bits.

MAC LAYER

Recall from Chapter 4 that 100Base-TX distances are very limited. As speed increased to 100 Mbps, short distances were needed to ensure that collisions would be detected.

In 1000Base-X standards, distance limitations are not as severe because of the almost universal use of full-duplex transmission and switching. In full-duplex transmission, collision detection is turned off, and the switch ensures that this will not cause problems. Although the standard allows complex ways to transmit in half duplex over hubs, the market is not likely to use this option extensively.

Ethernet versus 802.3 LANs

In Chapter 4, we noted that **Ethernet** and **802.3** were not literally the same, although the two terms have become synonyms in common usage. In one area—frame format—it is still useful to understand the distinction between the two, because some systems still use Ethernet II frames. In fact, the frame tagging process discussed at the end of this module is almost a throwback to Ethernet II framing.

ETHERNET

The original Ethernet was a one megabit per second standard created by Bob Metcalfe of Xerox after a trip to the University of Hawaii to see its Aloha packet switched radio system. This was so successful that Xerox, Intel, and Digital Equipment (DIX) cooperated to create a 10 Mbps standard. This was the Ethernet I standard, which appeared in 1980. In 1985, an improved Ethernet II (Version 2.0) standard emerged. Figure C.5 compares the Ethernet II frame to the 802.3 MAC layer frame.

COMMON FIELDS

The first thing to note is the number of identical fields. The Ethernet preamble field is identical to the 802.3 preamble plus start of frame delimiter fields. The destination and source addresses are the same. The frame check sequence fields are also the same.

LENGTH FIELD

Ethernet and 802.3 both use CSMA/CD. Collision detection requires there to be a minimum frame length of 64 octets in both standards. In addition, the receiving NIC must know how long the frame is because frames have variable length.

Ethernet II did not have a length field. All network layer protocols at the time had their own length field. Because the **Ethernet type** field identified the next-higher-layer

ETHERNET II FRAME	802.3 MAC LAYER FRAME
Preamble (8 octets)	Preamble (7 octets)
	Start of Frame Delimiter (1 octet)
Destination Address (6 octets)	Destination Address (6 octets)
Source Address (6 octets)	Source Address (6 octets)
Ethernet Type (2 octets)	Length (2 octets)
Data (variable)	802.2 LLC Frame (variable)
	PAD if Required
Frame Check Sequence (4 octets)	Frame Check Sequence (4 octets)

FIGURE C.5

Ethernet II Frame versus 802.3 MAC Layer Frame

protocol, the NIC could simply read the length field in the packet header to know how long the frame would be.

The 802.3 Working Group decided that it was unwise to gamble on future network/internet layer protocols always having a length field. So the working group put in the explicit length field shown in Figure C.5.

In addition, as noted above, an Ethernet II or 802.3 frame has a minimum length. All network/internet standards when Ethernet II was created had acceptable minimum lengths. Rather than gamble on this continuing, the 802.3 Working Group added a **PAD** field in case the length would be less than the minimum without the PAD.

NEXT-HIGHER-LAYER PROTOCOL

The Ethernet II frame has an Ethernet type (Ethertype) field. This field gives the name of the next-higher-layer protocol, whose packet lies inside the data field. This way, a receiving NIC knows whether to pass an incoming packet to an IP process, an IPX process, or some other process.

Something similar was needed for 802 networks. However, the 802 Standards Committee decided to move the typing function to the 802.2 Link Layer Protocol. As we saw in Chapter 4, the 802.2 LLC standard begins with destination and source SAPs. The SAP codes identify the next-higher-layer protocol.

However, Ethernet II offered a two-byte Ethernet type field, allowing thousands of possible protocols at the next-higher layer. The 8-bit DSAP and SSAP fields only had 6 bits left after 2 bits were dedicated to special purposes. This only allowed 64 possible protocols at the next higher layer. As we saw in Chapter 4, the 802 standards committee then created the rather inelegant SNAP extension to define more options.

RECOGNIZING FRAME TYPE

Fortunately, most NICs are able to distinguish between Ethernet II and 802.3 frames. If the frame is an 802.3 frame, then the two bytes after the source address will give the length. In 802.3 frames, the maximum amount of data is 1,500 octets, so the value in the length field will be less than 1,500. In contrast, for Ethernet II, no common Ethernet type has a value less than 1,500.

So the NIC simply reads the two bytes following the source address. If the value is 1,500 or less, the NIC knows that it is dealing with an 802.3 frame. If the value is larger, the NIC knows that it is dealing with an Ethernet frame.

MORE ON ETHERNET SWITCHING

Bridges and Switches

Many networking textbooks barely mention switches. Instead, they discuss devices called **bridges.** In fact, 802 standards always specify bridges instead of switches. This is not surprising because Ethernet switches in many ways are merely advanced bridges.

Bridges work on MAC layer addresses. When a MAC layer frame comes in one port, the bridge either ignores it (because it is for another station on the LAN connected to that port and does not need to be passed on) or passes the frame out another port. This is exactly how switches work.

Are switches, then, really different from bridges? They do have several characteristics that tend to set them apart from bridges, but some analysts feel that these are minor differences. Basically, when Kalapana introduced a radically advanced bridge, it called it a switch, and the terminology stuck.

NUMBER OF PORTS

One thing that tends to set bridges and switches apart is number of ports. Traditionally, bridges have had two to four ports. Switches, however, often have a dozen or even several dozen ports. Of course, there is nothing to preclude multiport bridges.

VIRTUAL LANS

Another difference is that switches allow virtual LANs. Traditionally, bridges have not done this. However, the 802.1Q standard for virtual LANs described later in this module specifies how to standardize virtual LANs on *bridges*. The same standard, however, will be used on switches, just as switches use the spanning tree standard, 802.1D, which was created for bridges to ensure that there are no loops.

CUT-THROUGH PROCESSING

One of the strongest differences between bridges and switches is how much of an incoming frame they analyze before passing it on. Traditionally, most bridges analyzed the entire frame. This allowed them to detect errors by analyzing the frame check sequence field. Of course, this added latency. In bridges, a typical delay is about 90 to 120 microseconds.[3]

---

[3] Petra Borowka, *Internetworking: The Way to a Structured Network.* (London: International Thompson Press, 1997).

Switches, in contrast, tend to use cut-through processing. They stop analyzing the frame after reaching the source and destination fields. This is all they need to read in the frame to know which port to use to send it out, even if there are virtual LANs. Instead of having to process 1,500 bytes, a cut-through switch only has to analyze the preamble, the start of frame delimiter, and the two addresses. This only requires the switch to process 20 bytes. A typical delay in a cut-through switch is only about 2 to 20 microseconds.[4] Even the new tagged information discussed later in this module will extend processing only another few bytes.

PARALLEL PROCESSING

The biggest advance in the Kalapana switch was **parallel processing.** In previous bridges, there had been only a single processor. While one frame was being handled by that processor, all others had to wait. The Kalapana switch, like all switches after it, instead used parallel frame processing. If a station on Port A is transmitting to Port C at the same time a station on Port B is transmitting to Port D, both transmissions take place simultaneously without being time-shared in a central processor. Even more than cut-through processing, this simultaneous transmission through parallel processing is the key to the extremely low latency of switches.

MARKETING

Although all these differences are debatable, the simple fact is that the term *switch* has replaced *bridge* as the norm in the marketplace. Very few devices being produced today are called bridges, and they tend to be two- to four-port devices without VLAN support. Since the war of names has been lost in the market, it no longer makes sense to keep fighting it in textbooks. However, when reading 802 standards, keep in mind that the term *bridge* has been retained in these standards. Fortunately, 802 bridging standards apply to switches in the marketplace.

Selecting a Switch: Capabilities

Ethernet switches operate at 10 Mbps, 100 Mbps, or 1000 Mbps. However, this is not the only capacity measure to use when examining a switch.

FRAMES PER SECOND

An important measure of a switch's speed is its ability to process frames, which usually is measured in **frames per second.** This number represents the degree of parallel processing in the switch as well as the capacity of the **switching fabric,** which connects any port to any other port.

Ideally, a switch will be **nonblocking,** meaning that even if all ports are receiving incoming packets, there will not be delays. For a 12-port gigabit Ethernet switch, this would require enormous capacity. Although switches do not have to be fully nonblocking, the ratio of the switch's capacity divided by the total speeds of incoming ports is a critical measure. If this ratio is too low, blocking will occur with some regularity.

As switches filter ever more deeply into frames, as discussed at the end of Chapter 6, they will require increasing power to maintain a good ratio of capacity to the speed

---

[4] Borowka, *Internetworking: The Way to a Structured Network*.

of incoming ports. So switches must be purchased not just for their adequacy today but also for their likely adequacy tomorrow.

MAC ADDRESS AND VLAN CAPACITY

If a switch is to implement VLANs, then the switch must be able to handle many MAC addresses and must be able to support many VLANs. Switches have maximum capacities for both MAC addresses and for the number of VLANs they can support. Small switches designed for workgroups might support too few MAC addresses and VLANs to be used in larger networks, even if the switch's processing speed is sufficient.

OTHER CONSIDERATIONS

Mier[5] suggests two other factors to consider when buying a switch. One is what other LAN technologies it can support, such as FDDI or ATM. Pure Ethernet switches are less expensive, but they also limit your flexibility.

Another consideration is what standards the switch supports. For instance, we discuss frame tagging later. Not all switches today support the 802.1Q and 802.1p standards or other emerging standards.

Selecting an Ethernet Switch: Forms

Ethernet switches come in three basic forms, as Figure C.6 illustrates. We will look at these from the least to the most expensive.

STAND-ALONE SWITCHES

As the name suggests, **stand-alone switches** are not designed to link to other switches. This might be good for a small business, but stand-alone switches are not good for corporate networks.

STACKABLE SWITCHES

Next come **stackable switches.** As the name implies, stackable switches can be placed on top of one another. This allows easy growth. If you need 20 ports, you can begin with a 24-port switch. As demand grows, you can add another 24-port stackable switch, doubling your capacity. Stackable switches have high-speed wiring connectors so that they can work together at very high speeds.

FIGURE C.6

Stand-Alone, Stackable, and Chassis Switches

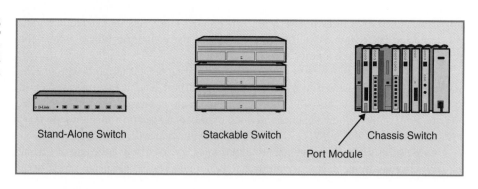

Stand-Alone Switch   Stackable Switch   Chassis Switch

Port Module

---

[5] Edwin Mier, "How to Play for Keeps," *Network World*, January 26, 1998.

CHASSIS SWITCHES

Chassis switches offer the highest growth potential. A chassis contains the switch's basic processing power and switching matrix. The switching matrix, usually called the **backplane,** has extremely high capacity.

The chassis switch also has **expansion slots.** These slots can be filled with **port modules.** Each port module will contain multiple ports—for instance, twelve 10Base-T ports, six 100Base-T ports, two 100Base-F ports, or some other port combination. This allows a firm to add whatever types of ports it needs on an as-needed basis.

Inter-Switch Trunking

Ethernet switching is scalable, growing from 10 Mbps to a gigabit per second. However, its growth comes in large chunks. There is nothing between 10 Mbps and 100 Mbps. Nor is there anything between 100 Mbps and a gigabit per second.

This situation may change in the future. Figure C.7 shows that we may no longer have to link switches together with single 10, 100, or 1000 Mbps trunk lines. We may be able to connect them using a technique called link aggregation or **trunking.** In Figure C.7, we have multiple physical links between the two switches on the left. However, they act as a single logical link. To the two switches, the four 100Base-FX links connecting them act as a single 400 Mbps line. Essentially, a **trunk** is a single logical link made up of several point-to-point physical links.

Overall, then, trunking will allow much finer granularity in inter-switch connections. To connect 100 Mbps switches, companies can use 10 Mbps connections, 20 Mbps connections, and so on, up to 100 Mbps. To connect two gigabit Ethernet switches, in turn, the company can select connections in multiples of 100 Mbps.

Trunking requires new standards. As Chapter 5 discussed, switches must not be connected in a loop. Even a single pair of parallel lines between two switches constitutes a loop. Actually, the **802.1D Spanning Tree** standard will allow switched networks to work even if there are loops. However, it does this by closing some ports to disconnect loops. This would effectively close down all but one line in an aggregated trunking connection. Trunking must override such shutdowns.

The IEEE 802 *LAN MAN* Standards Committee is currently working on inter-switch trunking. This effort is just getting under way at the time of this writing.

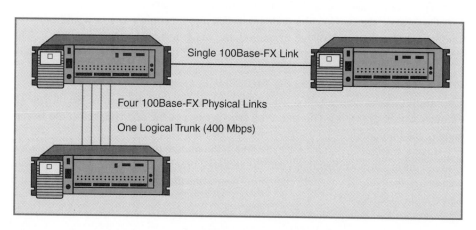

Single 100Base-FX Link

Four 100Base-FX Physical Links

One Logical Trunk (400 Mbps)

FIGURE C.7

Inter-Switch Trunking

THE 802.5 TOKEN-RING STANDARD

Chapter 4 looked at **802.5 token-ring networks (TRNs).** One important point about the TRN standard is that it is strongly driven by IBM. In fact, the actual 802.5 documentation is rather simplified, and most vendors follow IBM TRN standards, which are sometimes incompatible with 802.5 standards for token-ring networks.

Differential Manchester Encoding

In Chapter 4, we saw that to send a signal, you must encode the zeros and ones as combinations of voltage levels. The method that TRN networks use is called *differential Manchester encoding.*

MANCHESTER ENCODING

In Chapter 4, we saw that 802.3 10Base-T uses **Manchester encoding** (as do 10Base5 and 10Base2). In Manchester encoding, there is always a transition in the middle of the bit time. This ensures that the sender will not transmit a long series of bits that all keep the signal high or low. A long voltage transmission without change will not keep the receiver's clock synchronized with that of the sender.

To transmit a 1, Manchester encoding sends a low voltage for half the bit time, followed by a high voltage for the second half of the bit time. A 0, in turn, is a high voltage for the first half of the bit time, followed by a low voltage for the second half. A good way to remember this is that a high ending is a 1 and a low ending is a 0.

There are two possible line changes for each bit transmission. So operating at 10 Mbps, 10Base-T is a 20 Mbaud transmission system.

DIFFERENTIAL MANCHESTER ENCODING FOR A 1

In contrast to simple Manchester encoding, the way that **differential Manchester encoding** represents a bit depends on whether the previous bit time ended high or low. To transmit a 1, there is no transition at the start of the bit time. To prevent a long series of 1s from ruining synchronization, there is a transition in the middle of the bit time.

Suppose the previous bit ended high. Then to transmit a 1, you would keep the signal high for the first half of the bit period. Then you would make it low for the second half. The ending state will be different than the starting state.

Or suppose the previous bit ended low. Then to transmit a 1, you would keep the line low for the first half of the bit period and make it high for the second half. The ending state, then, is always different than the starting state when you send a 1.

DIFFERENTIAL MANCHESTER ENCODING FOR A 0

To transmit a 0, in contrast, you *change* the voltage level at the start of the bit period. In other words, you tell a 1 from a 0 by whether or not the line changes at the beginning of the bit period.

Like a 1, a 0 always makes a transition in the middle of the bit period. In this way, you are ensured transitions that keep the receiver synchronized with the sender. Note that in a 0, there are always two changes. This means that the ending state is always the same as the starting state.

DIFFERENTIAL MANCHESTER ENCODING FOR J AND K

In addition to representing 1s and 0s, differential Manchester encoding defines two special characters, J and K. Actually, they are called code violations, but as we will see, they are used for signaling.

A J is a 1 without the transition in the middle. Whatever the line state was at the end of the last bit time, a J will continue that state for the entire bit.

A K, in turn, is a 0 without the transition in the middle. Whatever the line state was at the end of the last bit time, a K will change the state at the start of the bit and will hold that changed level for the entire bit. The line state at the end will be the opposite of the line state at the beginning.

EXAMPLE

Figure C.8 illustrates how 1, 0, J, and K appear on a line. The situation looks more complicated than Manchester encoding, but most of this complexity comes from viewing representations in terms of line changes instead of line values.

For instance, the initial state of the line (Event 1) is high. Event 2 is the transmission of a 1. As the remark notes in condensed form, a 1 keeps line state constant (high) at the start, then changes it (to low) in the middle. At the end of Event 2, the line is in a low state.

The 802.5 MAC Layer Frame: Token Frame

Chapter 4 discussed the 802.3 MAC layer frame in some detail. We will now do so for the IBM Token-Ring Network MAC layer frame. We will begin with the token frame itself. Figure C.9 shows that a token frame has three fields: start frame delimiter, access control, and end frame delimiter.

START FRAME DELIMITER

The **start frame delimiter** acts like the preamble and start of frame delimiter fields in 802.3 MAC layer frames, although it is much shorter. It is only a single byte long. It has the following pattern of bits:

JK0JK000

This frame, with two J violations and two K violations in specific locations, is highly unlikely to occur in erroneous transmissions. It uniquely marks the start of the frame.

ACCESS CONTROL

The **access control** field is the heart of the token. This is the field that allows stations to know if the token is free and, if so, whether their priority is high enough for them to take it and transmit. Its eight bits are encoded in the following way:

PPPTMRRR

Priority.   The three P bits give the priority of the token. This gives eight levels, from 0 through 7. Unless a station has priority at least as high as these bits indicate, it must let the token pass, even if it has something to send.

FIGURE **C.8**

Differential Manchester Encoding

Event	Bit to be Sent	Initial State of the Line	Change at Start?	Change at End?	Final State of the Line	Remarks
1					High	Starting condition—line high
2	1	High	No	Yes	Low	1 keeps state constant at start, changes in middle. Ends in opposite state
3	1	Low	No	Yes	High	
4	1	High	No	Yes	Low	
5	1	Low	No	Yes	High	
6	0	High	Yes	Yes	High	0 changes state at start and in middle. Ends in same state
7	0	High	Yes	Yes	High	
8	0	High	Yes	Yes	High	
9	1	High	No	Yes	Low	
10	0	Low	Yes	Yes	Low	
11	1	Low	No	Yes	High	
12	0	High	Yes	Yes	High	
13	1	High	No	Yes	Low	
14	J	Low	No	No	Low	J keeps state constant at start and in middle. Ends in same state
15	0	Low	Yes	Yes	Low	
16	J	Low	No	No	Low	
17	1	Low	No	Yes	High	
18	J	High	No	No	High	
19	1	High	No	Yes	Low	
20	K	Low	Yes	No	High	K changes state at start but not in middle. Ends in opposite state
21	0	High	Yes	Yes	High	
22	K	High	Yes	No	Low	
23*	0	Low	Yes	Yes	Low	
24*	K	Low	Yes	No	High	
25	1					Complete this row
26	0					Complete this row
27	J					Complete this row
28	K					Complete this row

*Check these for errors.

Token Bit. The T bit tells whether this frame is a token or a full frame. In this case, it is a token, so its value is set equal to 1. If it were a full frame, it would be 0.

Monitor Bit. The M bit is set to 0 by the transmitting station. A special station called the *active monitor* (discussed later) sets this bit to 1. If it sees a 1 bit in an arriving

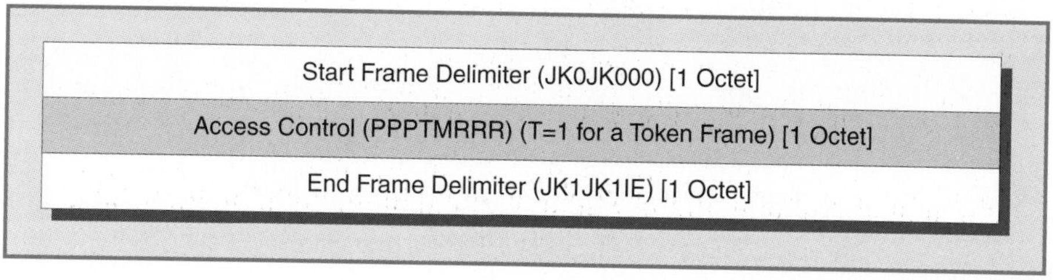

FIGURE **C.9**

**Token Frame
in 802.5**

| Start Frame Delimiter (JK0JK000) [1 Octet] |
| Access Control (PPPTMRRR) (T=1 for a Token Frame) [1 Octet] |
| End Frame Delimiter (JK1JK1IE) [1 Octet] |

frame, the active monitor knows that the frame has not been removed by the transmitting station when the frame completed a full run around the ring. The active monitor then removes the frame.

Token Reservation Bit. The three R bits are the token reservation bits. These come into play when full frames are transmitted, as we will see later.

THE END FRAME DELIMITER

The **end frame delimiter** finishes the token. This one-octet frame has the following pattern:

JK1JK1IE

Here, again, we start with an unusual pattern of bits containing uncommon J and K violations. Although the start frame delimiter begins with "JK0JK0", the end frame delimiter begins with "JK1JK1".

We will discuss the I and E bits next, in the context of full frames.

The 802.5 MAC Layer Frame: Full Frame

If a station has high enough priority, it takes control of the token. It takes its information and wraps it inside the token, forming a full token-ring network frame. Figure C.10 shows a full frame.

ACCESS CONTROL

When the station grabs the token, it changes the T bit in the *access control field* from 1 to 0. This signals receivers that they are looking at a full frame instead of just a token.

In addition, when the transmitting station transmits, it changes the three priority reservation bits (RRR) to 000, the lowest priority. If a station wishes to transmit, it looks at the reservation bits. If its priority is higher, it places its priority level in the reservation bits. In this way, by the time the frame has gotten all the way around to the sender, the RRR bits contain the highest-priority level of stations wishing to transmit. When the sending station releases the token, it places this priority level in the main priority bits (PPP) of the token it releases.

FRAME CONTROL

The **frame control** field tells what kind of frame this is. It has the following pattern in its eight bits:

FFZZZZZZ

FIGURE **C.10**

**Full Frame
in 802.5**

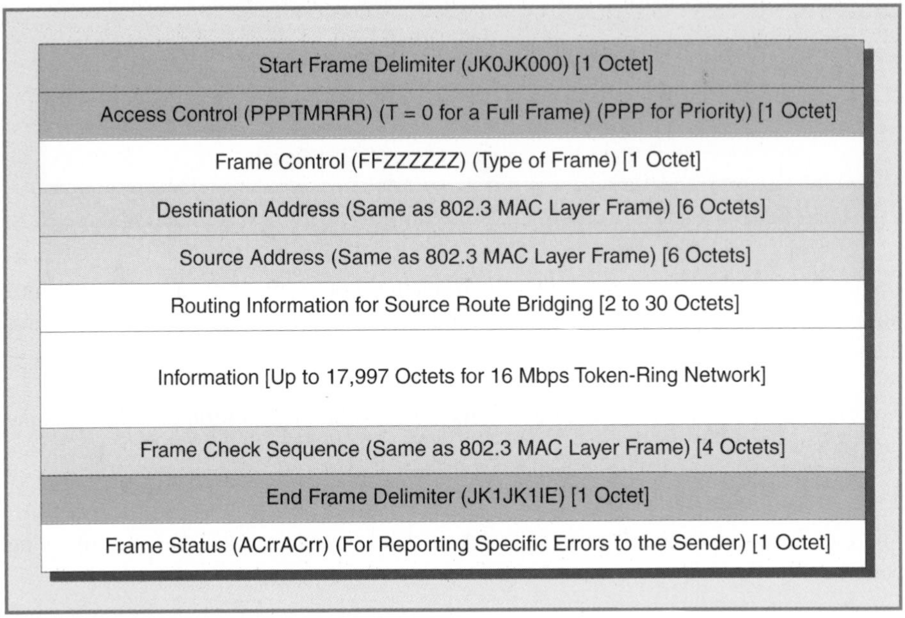

Start Frame Delimiter (JK0JK000) [1 Octet]
Access Control (PPPTMRRR) (T = 0 for a Full Frame) (PPP for Priority) [1 Octet]
Frame Control (FFZZZZZZ) (Type of Frame) [1 Octet]
Destination Address (Same as 802.3 MAC Layer Frame) [6 Octets]
Source Address (Same as 802.3 MAC Layer Frame) [6 Octets]
Routing Information for Source Route Bridging [2 to 30 Octets]
Information [Up to 17,997 Octets for 16 Mbps Token-Ring Network]
Frame Check Sequence (Same as 802.3 MAC Layer Frame) [4 Octets]
End Frame Delimiter (JK1JK1IE) [1 Octet]
Frame Status (ACrrACrr) (For Reporting Specific Errors to the Sender) [1 Octet]

The first two bits tell the stations what type of frame this is. If the F bits are 01, then this frame contains logical link control layer data. In other words, its information field contains an 802.2 frame (discussed in Chapter 4).

In contrast, if the F bits are 00, then this frame is a MAC layer frame only. It is either a token or a supervisory frame.

The six remaining Z bits specify particular types of LLC and MAC layer frames. We will see some MAC layer control frames later, when we discuss errors and error recovery.

DESTINATION AND SOURCE ADDRESSES

Fortunately, the IBM Token-Ring Network frame (and the official 802.5 MAC layer frame) uses the same 48-bit addressing scheme as the 802.3 MAC layer frame, which we discussed in Chapter 4.

ROUTING INFORMATION

The *routing information* field holds information for routing the frame through a series of source routing bridges. Source routing is the bridging standard created by IBM and allowed by the 802 Standards Committee only for 802.5 LANs. This field can be from 2 to 30 octets in length.

INFORMATION

The **information field** holds the data to be delivered. The information field can be very large. In 16 Mbps token-ring networks, frames can be 17,997 octets long. Even in 4 Mbps TRNs, frames can be 4,501 octets.

FRAME CHECK SEQUENCE

The **frame check sequence** field is a 32-bit field for error checking. It is the same as the frame check sequence field in 802.3 MAC layer frames.

END FRAME DELIMITER

In 802.3 MAC layer frames, the frame check sequence field is the last field. In contrast, TRN frames add two final fields. One of these is the **end frame delimiter.** This one-octet field, as we saw earlier, begins with the unusual pattern "JK1JK1." It ends with two other bits, the I bit and the E bit.

The I bit is used to tell the receiver if this is the last frame in a series. It is set to 1 if it is the last frame. If it is not, the I bit is set to 0.

The E bit is for reporting errors. The transmitting station sets this bit to 0. If *any* station along the ring detects a J or K violation or some other transmission error, it sets this bit to 1. When the transmitting station receives the frame back, it looks at the E bit to check for errors.

FRAME STATUS FIELD

The very last field is the **frame status field.** This octet allows the receiving station to tell the sending station whether or not it has received the frame. The form of this field is the following:

A C r r A C r r

Here the r bits are reserved for future use (an unlikely situation at this late date). They are normally set to 0.

The transmitting station sets the A bit to 0. If the receiving station recognizes its address, it resets this address bit to 1. When the frame returns to the sender, the A bits tell if the receiver has seen the frame.

It is possible that a station will recognize its address yet not be able to copy the frame into its NIC's memory. This is the purpose of the C (copy) bit. The sending station sets this bit to 0. The receiver resets it to 1 if it makes a successful copy.

The frame status field comes after the frame check sequence field, so there is no way for the receiver to check for errors in the frame status field. To compensate, the field has two A bits and two C bits. The transmitting station assumes a failure unless it sees 1s on both A bits and on both C bits.

Error Handling

In many ways, a token-ring network is an accident waiting to happen. As we will see, there are two major ways in which a simple failure can disable the network.

Although these dangers are very real, the standard contains several ways of minimizing these risks. As a result, TRNs are not at all the fragile networks that they first seem to be.

BREAKING THE RING

The most obvious problem is that frames have to go all the way around the ring. In addition, the stations do not simply watch the frames go by. They stop each frame, look at it bit by bit, and then regenerate it. As a result, if a single connection breaks, or if a single device fails, no station on the network can transmit.

LOSING THE TOKEN

Another risk in TRNs is losing the token. We know that stations may not transmit until they have the token. What if the token is lost? Then no station may transmit. Again, communication will break down.

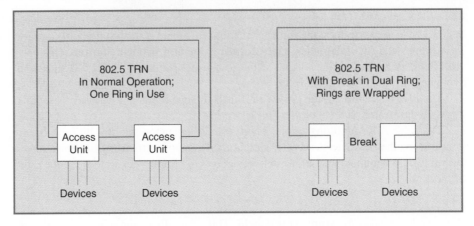

FIGURE **C.11**

Double Ring and Wrapping in 802.5 Token-Ring Networks

WRAPPING THE RING BETWEEN ACCESS UNITS

How can we prevent the loss of transmission if there is a break in the ring between access units? To allow recovery, 802.5 rings are really double rings, as shown in Figure C.11. Normally, all traffic passes through one of the two rings. The other ring goes unused.

If there is a break between access units, the ring is **wrapped.** As you can see from Figure C.11, the result is still a loop. If you trace the wrapped ring going in one direction, you will still come back to the starting point. This is the essence of a ring network.

Wrapping works only once. If there is a second failure, a wrapping will break the ring into two unconnected pieces. So wrapping is a "first aid" practice. The broken link should be reestablished as quickly as possible.

WITHIN AN ACCESS UNIT

Figure C.12 looks more closely at the access unit. Note the way that devices are connected. Essentially, there is still a ring. The ring comes into the access unit. It then goes down to the first station and back up to the access unit in an unbroken connection. If you trace the ring from its entry into the access unit to its exit, you will find a single complete path. The ring is unbroken.

The ring extends to the stations themselves. The two lines between the access unit and the station are part of the overall loop of the network. This is why the link to the station is called a **lobe.**

What if one of the stations turns off its power? Figure C.12 shows that when this happens, the ring remains unbroken. Look at Station C. It has powered off. The access unit automatically bypasses the device.

Of course, there are a few milliseconds between the time when a device powers off and the access unit redirects the ring to pass through the connection. During this time, packets will be lost. However, these errors will be discovered at higher layers, and the packets will be resent.

When you power on a station, there is also a brief interruption as the access unit connects the station to the ring. Again, a few frames will be lost.

The mechanism is remarkably simple. For each port, the access unit has a small

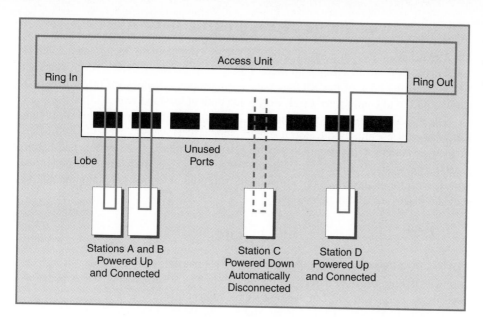

FIGURE C.12

Connections within an 802.5 Access Unit

solenoid. When the station powers up, it sends power to the solenoid. The solenoid closes, connecting the station's lobe to the main ring. When a station powers down, in turn, even accidentally, the solenoid opens, automatically disconnecting the station from the ring.

HANDLING LOST TOKENS AND OTHER PROBLEMS

Handling lost tokens, in contrast, requires a considerable amount of complexity. One station must be designated as the **active monitor.** We saw earlier that the active monitor constantly examines frames that have gone around the ring more than once. It also removes garbled frames with obvious errors.

This station keeps watching for the token. It times the reappearance of the token each time the token passes the station. If that time is too long, it generates a new token. This station also weeds out duplicate tokens.

The active monitor even detects breaks in the ring.[6] When *any* station fails to hear traffic for a long period of time, it issues a beacon control frame with a frame control field of 00000010. By listening to these beacon frames, the active monitor can estimate where the break has occurred. This can allow automatic wrapping of the ring.

What if the active monitor fails? This failure will be addressed automatically.[7] Periodically, the active monitor issues an **active monitor present** control frame. Its frame control field is 00000011. If any station notices an absence of this frame for a long period of time, it may issue a **claim token** control frame, whose frame control field is 0000010. If this token gets all the way around the ring, the claiming station assumes the duties of the active monitor.

---

[6] Andrew S. Tanenbaum, *Computer Networks* (Upper Saddle River, NJ: Prentice Hall, 1988).
[7] Tanenbaum, *Computer Networks.*

The Status of Token-Ring Networks

The 1990s have not been a happy time for Token-Ring Network technology. Even in 1997, only 11% of all NICs sold were Token-Ring Network NICs, while Ethernet NICs comprised 85% of the NIC market.[8] Furthermore, revenues for 802.5 networks were projected to continue to shrink worldwide until at least the year 2000.[9]

The 802.5 Working Group is currently developing a 100 Mbps version of Token-Ring and will eventually develop a gigabit standard. However, even the 100 Mbps standard is coming fairly late, and gigabit Ethernet should be well-entrenched before gigabit Token-Ring emerges. In addition, Token-Ring's ability to enhance quality of service with frame prioritization will soon be available to Ethernet through the 802.1p standard discussed later in this module.

FDDI

FDDI is the **Fiber Distributed Data Interface** standard. Like 802.5 Token-Ring Networks, FDDI uses a ring topology at the physical layer, token passing at the media access control layer, and 802.2 at the logical link control layer.

In fact, FDDI was derived from 802.5 technology, although the modifications were so extensive that 802.5 and FDDI are deeply incompatible. One reason for the differences is that FDDI was designed to run at 100 Mbps, rather than at 4 Mbps or 16 Mbps. This (initially) required the use of optical fiber and a number of other differences. Although a 100 Mbps version of 802.5 is currently being finalized, FDDI achieved megabit speeds in 1987, when few organizations even had 10 Mbps LANs. Thanks to its high speed, FDDI was used primarily in workstation networks when it first appeared.

Another difference between 802.5 and FDDI, however, proved to be more important in the long run. Whereas 802.5 was designed to be a compact LAN technology with distance limits similar to those of Ethernet, FDDI was designed to be a metropolitan area network technology that could span distances typically found in an urban area. An FDDI ring has a maximum circumference of 200 km! Although the metropolitan area network market did not emerge as a major force in networking, the wide distance span of FDDI made it perfect as a backbone network within large site networks to link individual LANs.

A final key difference between FDDI and other LAN technologies is that FDDI did not come from the IEEE. Rather, the FDDI standard is the product of the **American National Standards Institute (ANSI)** X3T9.5 Committee. However, ANSI was careful to develop FDDI within the IEEE framework for LAN standards. It has media access control and logical link control layers, and it uses 802.2 as the LLC standard.

FDDI never fared well in the market for LANs because of its high cost. When its 100 Mbps speed was attractive, its NICs cost $2,000 to $5,000, which was far too expensive to connect the PCs that even then dominated corporate desktops. Although FDDI NIC prices have fallen since then, they have not fallen as far as NICs for other 100 Mbps LAN technologies, such as Ethernet 100Base-TX. In addition, FDDI is not scalable, working only at 100 Mbps. For a while, FDDI was popular as a backbone

---

[8] Jodi Cohen, "The Downfall of Desktop ATM," *Network World*, July 7, 1997, 25.
[9] Paul Korezeniowski, "Is This Token-Ring's Last Gasp?" *PC Week*, February 16, 1988, 104.

network for site networks, but FDDI's single speed now makes it unattractive even for backbones in new installations. Overall, FDDI is a technology whose time never came but has certainly gone.

In one sense, however, FDDI lives on at the physical layer. The 100Base-FX standard is based on FDDI's physical layer standard for optical fiber transmission. The 100Base-TX standard, in turn, was based on FDDI-over-UTP, which adapted FDDI to operation over ordinary Category 5 wiring. This allowed 100Base-TX and 100Base-FX to benefit from the existence of mature chips at the physical layer while avoiding the complexity and cost of token-ring operation.

WIRELESS LANs (802.11)

Most of the LANs we have seen in this book have used wire, optical fiber, or some other physical transmission medium to carry signals. This is fine for many applications, but for some applications, we need wireless transmission.

- ▶ In hospitals, doctors and nurses have to move constantly. They need a wireless LAN so they can carry data entry and lookup devices with them.
- ▶ Some LANs are temporary, such as those set up for conventions or in conference rooms for one-time use. Wireless LANs greatly reduce installation costs for temporary LANs.
- ▶ Most importantly, today's users of notebook computers are second-class LAN citizens. With a wireless LAN, however, they are able to work anywhere yet have constant access to network resources.

The 802.11 Standards Group

Wireless LAN standards are set by the IEEE 802.11 Working Group. In 1997, the working group released its first standards. As Figure C.13 shows, the working group developed a single MAC layer standard for use with multiple physical layer standards. For each physical layer (PHY) transmission standard, in turn, two speeds were specified: 1 Mbps and 2 Mbps.

Modes of Operation

The 802.11 standard specifies two modes of operation, as Figure C.14 illustrates.

DIRECT OPERATION

In **direct operation,** the computers communicate directly with one another in peer-to-peer communication with no control point.

LOGICAL LINK CONTROL LAYER (802.2)					
802.11 Media Access Control Layer Standards					
Infrared PHY		Frequency Hopping Spread Spectrum (FHSS) Radio PHY		Direct Sequence Spread Spectrum (DSSS) Radio PHY	
1 Mbps	2 Mbps	1 Mbps	2 Mbps	1 Mbps	2 Mbps

FIGURE C.13

802.11 Standards

FIGURE **C.14**

Wireless LAN Modes of Operation

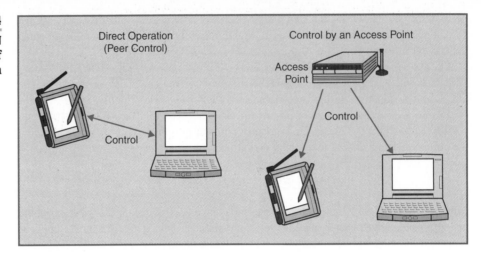

Direct Operation
(Peer Control)

Control by an Access Point

Access
Point

Control

Control

ACCESS POINT CONTROL

Alternatively, computers can be coordinated by an **access point.** This is reminiscent of cellular telephony (see Module D). The access point is like a cell site. It assigns power levels to its stations and exerts other forms of control.

The similarity to cellular telephony extends to roaming. If a computer is being controlled by one access point and passes into an area controlled by another access point, control will switch automatically and smoothly to the new access point.

The access point even stores frames for later delivery. So a station can be powered off at any time. When it next powers on and associates with the access point, the access point will deliver waiting e-mail and other messages.

CONTENTION

The use of an access point allows for two forms of service. One allows **contention,** requiring stations to compete for transmission time as in Ethernet or token-ring networks. We will focus on this form of service.

The other service is for time-bound transmission that cannot tolerate delay, such as voice transmission. This is **contention-free** service, in which the access point controls when stations may transmit and gives priority to services that require time-bound transmission.

The MAC Layer

The MAC layer controls when stations may transmit. Ethernet uses CSMA/CD. In CSMA, stations can transmit only if there is no traffic on the line. In CD, if a station hears another station transmitting while it is sending its own signal, the station will respond to this collision by stopping, backing off a random amount of time, and then transmitting again if the line is free.

CONTENTION SERVICE: CSMA/CA+ACK

In a radio environment, collision detection is very difficult. Two stations whose signals are colliding may be far enough apart that they do not hear each other's transmissions and so cannot detect collisions.

Standards from the 801.11 Working Group use a slightly different media access control method, **CSMA/CA.** This is CSMA with collision avoidance, instead of collision detection. The goal is to reduce collisions instead of dealing with them after they occur.

Collision avoidance is very simple. Suppose that a station is transmitting. As soon as the transmitting station finishes, other stations may try to transmit at once. To avoid such collisions, however, stations do not begin to transmit as soon as they hear no signals. Instead, each backs off for a random amount of time *before transmitting*. This reduces simultaneous transmissions, thus reducing collisions. The backoff period is very short for acknowledgments (discussed next), a bit longer for supervisory communication, and longest for data transmission.

Of course, collisions will still occur sometimes. So whenever a station receives a correct frame, it *immediately* sends back an acknowledgment (ACK) frame. If a station transmits and does not hear an ACK frame immediately, it retransmits the message.

POWER CONTROL

Another aspect of collision avoidance is power control. The access point sends control signals to all stations, in order to limit their transmission power. This reduces the interference between more distant stations while allowing local stations to communicate effectively.

Radio Transmission: ISM Operation

The first 802.11 radio standards operate in the 2.4 GHz **ISM** (industrial, scientific, and medical) band.[10] This band, available throughout the world, is **unlicensed.** When you install an access point or a PC with a wireless NIC, you do not have to apply for a license, which might take several months. Even if you could get a license, it would be for a fixed location only, and this makes little sense for mobile computers.

However, unlicensed operation in the ISM band can create problems. First, if you are in a building shared by multiple tenants, your wireless LAN may interfere with a neighbor's wireless LAN. Because the band is unlicensed, you cannot appeal to some government agency to avoid problems. You must work out such problems locally through negotiation. Second, some terrestrial microwave dishes operate in ISM frequencies, and this too can cause interference.

ISM unlicensed operation means that interference cannot always be avoided. As a result, 802.11 standards are designed to reduce interference problems.

SPREAD SPECTRUM OPERATION

One way to reduce interference problems is to use **spread spectrum** operation. In Chapter 3, we saw that the speed at which you can transmit depends on both bandwidth and signal strength (divided by noise strength). Traditionally, we had to operate in channels of narrow bandwidth. So we had to send the signal very strongly. In spread spectrum transmission, we use very wide bandwidth channels. As a result, we can transmit at reduced power.

---

[10] Specifically, 2,400 MHz to 2,4835 MHz, for a bandwidth of 83.5 MHz.

DIRECT SEQUENCE SPREAD SPECTRUM (DSSS)

Figure C.13 shows that there are two forms of spread spectrum transmission in 802.11. One of these is **Direct Sequence Spread Spectrum (DSSS),** also known as **Code Division Multiple Access (CDMA).** Figure C.15 illustrates 802.11 DSSS transmission at 1 Mbps.

Figure C.15 shows the transmission time for a single bit (in one millionth of a second). During this period, Station A transmits a one. More specifically, it transmits 11 brief radio bursts called **chips.** The chips are sent according to a pre-set time code within the bit period. This time code sequence is specific to the communication between Station A and its partner (not shown in the figure). Station B, also shown in Figure C.15, has a different time code sequence for transmitting its 11 chips within each bit period.

At 1 Mbps, each chip may be either in phase with some reference radio signal or 180 degrees out of phase with the reference signal. (See Chapter B for a discussion of phase.) A one is represented by a specific pre-coded pattern of in-phase (blue) and out-of-phase (white) chips. Figure C.15 shows the pattern for a one. For a zero, all in-phase chips are changed into out-of-phase chips, and all out-of-phase chips are changed into in-phase chips.

What if a second station (Station B) begins to transmit while Station A is transmitting? As Figure C.15 shows, they would probably not begin at exactly the same time. Even during the overlap in their transmissions, however, their different time code sequences for sending chips within each bit period would mean that few chips, if any, would collide. The figure specifically shows a single collision. Although the collision would make that chip unreadable for Station A's partner, the other ten chips would still be received correctly. Given the strong differences between chip sequences for zero and one, the receiver would have no trouble reading the chip sequence correctly as a one.

In Ethernet, only one station can transmit at a time, because interference between transmitted signals will make ones and zeros unreadable. In DSSS, however, two or more signals can transmit at a time. While they will damage one another's transmissions slightly, the damage will rarely be fatal for the bit being transmitted.

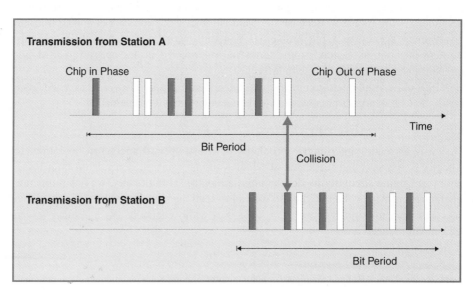

FIGURE **C.15**

Direct Sequence Spread Spectrum (DSSS) Transmission

At 2 Mbps, 802.11 uses DSSS in almost exactly the same way. There are again 11 chips sent in one millionth of a second. However, instead of there being just two possible phases, there are four possible phases (0°, 90°, 180°, and 270°). Consequently, each chip represents two bits (00, 01, 10, or 11), according to its phase. The baud rate, then, is 1 Mbaud, while the bit rate is 2 Mbps.

FREQUENCY HOPPING SPREAD SPECTRUM

Another radio technology is **frequency hopping spread spectrum (FHSS)** transmission, which is illustrated in Figure C.16. Here transmission is done in a very wide channel. This channel is divided into several subchannels.

Before a station transmits, it is given a frequency hopping code. As it transmits, it uses this preset code to hop among the various subchannels. The receiver, which also knows the code, listens on the subchannels at the appropriate times.

Recall that DSSS sends several chips per bit. This makes bit transmission relatively immune to collisions. Although frequency hopping could work the same way, 802.11 uses **slow frequency hopping,** in which the frequency changes only every 20 ms to 50 ms. Several frames can be transmitted during that time.[11] So if two stations transmit in the same frequency at the same time, several frames may be lost. However, frequency hopping reduces the number of frame collisions, and these few lost frames are merely retransmitted. Slow frequency hopping is less expensive to implement than frequency hopping several times per bit.

GRACEFUL DEGRADATION

As noted earlier, 802.11 wireless LANs operate in unregulated radio bands. So you cannot prevent nearby organizations from building systems in the same frequency range. However, as traffic grows due to competition, interference will increase in both DSSS and FHSS, but only very slowly. As more and more stations are added, it will be

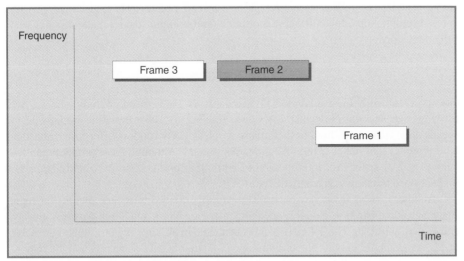

FIGURE C.16

Frequency Hopping Spread Spectrum (FHSS) Transmission

[11] Mahalo to Dean Kawaguchi of Symbol Technologies and to Naftali Chayat of Breezecom for the information on slow frequency hopping in 802.11.

as if there were more and more noise. This **"graceful degradation"** gives time to allow congestion problems to be negotiated among firms before they become serious.

Infrared Transmission

Your television's remote control uses **infrared light,** whose frequencies are just below what the human eye can see. In addition to defining two radio frequency physical layer standards for wireless LANs, the 802.11 standard specified an infrared wireless physical layer. This standard specifies transmission wavelengths from 850 to 950 nm.

The infrared standard has not received as much attention as the two radio frequency standards because infrared technology, while inexpensive, is difficult to implement. If someone walks between the television set and your remote control, that person's body will block your signal. The same is true of infrared LAN signals. To prevent signal blocking, 802.11 can use **diffuse infrared** transmission, which scatters infrared light around a room. However, this still restricts transmission to a single room. In contrast, radio waves pass through normal walls fairly well, allowing much larger cells. Another problem is that while infrared transmission is immune to radio frequency interference, bright sunlight and other light and heat sources do create interference at infrared frequencies.

Security

If you are transmitting signals on open frequencies, you would like to have good security so that eavesdroppers will not be able to read your messages. Although spread spectrum operation inherently offers some security, the spread spectrum technology used in 802.11 is not very secure. It was optimized for collision avoidance rather than for security.

The initial version of the standard did offer techniques for "wired equivalent privacy." Yet this is only a station-to-station form of privacy, not end-to-end privacy across multiple hops. In addition, it is only an option in the standard, and it is not very fully developed.

The Future

One problem with the initial 802.11 standards is their speed of only one or two megabits per second. Now that LANs are moving to 100 Mbps, the initial 802.11 speeds now seem very slow. In fact, many wireless LAN vendors offer faster nonstandard products that run at several megabits per second. Although these products can fall back to 802.11 speeds for interoperability with other products, users would like to see higher-speed transmission standardized.

Another issue is frequency bands. The world is divided into three regions for radio frequency administration. Roughly speaking, these are North and South America, Europe and Africa, and Asia. The 2.4 GHz band is available in all three regions, but other usable bands are available in only one or two regions. Future 802.11 standards may be region-specific. For instance, the United States has allocated 300 MHz of radio spectrum in the 5 GHz region for short-distance transmission at speeds of 10 Mbps to 25 Mbps.

More generally, the ability to serve mobile notebooks and other computers as fully and easily as desktop machines will require much more than the initial version of the standard offers. For instance, roaming between access points was not standardized in the initial version. The 802.11 standard is very much a "work in progress."

FRAME TAGGING FOR VLANS, PRIORITY, AND MORE

The standard Ethernet 802.3 frame introduced in Chapter 4 is relatively simple. This simplicity allows for quick and low-cost implementation. However, this simplicity has some drawbacks. For example, despite the importance of virtual LANs (see Chapter 5), there is no field for the Ethernet frame to indicate the frame's VLAN.

Nor is there a field for priority, which would allow frames for applications that cannot tolerate delay (such as voice conversations) to be delivered ahead of frames that can tolerate some delays (such as e-mail frames).

Frame Tagging

The 802.1 Working Group is beginning to add additional fields to LAN frames. This approach will be used for all types of 802 LANs, not just 802.3 Ethernet LANs.

Frames with additional fields are called **tagged frames.** Although the details are not set, it appears that **tag fields** will follow the source address field in the Ethernet. Token-Ring or other MAC layer frames may place it elsewhere.

The tag fields will contain supervisory information to indicate VLAN membership, transmission priority, and other matters that extend the MAC layer frame beyond its traditional limits.

Explicit and Implicit Tagging

When tags are in the frame to describe VLAN membership and other matters, this is called **explicit tagging.** However, there is also **implicit tagging,** in which the transmitting NIC does not actually insert tags in the frame. Instead, the switch to which the station connects analyzes the frame and treats it as if it were explicitly tagged. This allows NIC hardware and software to remain unchanged. We will focus on explicit tagging in our discussion.

802.1Q and 802.1p

Frame tagging was first introduced in the **802.1Q** standard, which focused on adding a tag for virtual LAN information. Later, **802.1p** extended the standard to include priority information and MAC layer multicasting.[12]

The Tag Format

Specifically, the **802.1 Working Group** has been developing a two-field tag that will initially give VLAN membership, priority level, and one other piece of information. Figure C.17 shows these fields, which are subject to change in the final versions of the

---

[12] In IEEE 802 standards, a capital letter, such as Q, indicates that the standard is a base standard in an area. A lowercase letter, such as p, indicates a revision to a base standard.

FIGURE **C.17**

**VLAN Membership
and Priority in
Frame Tagging**

TAG PROTOCOL IDENTIFIER 2 Octets		TAG CONTROL INFORMATION 2 Octets		
8100 hex (2 octets)		Priority (3 bits)	*	VLAN Identifier (12 bits)

*Canonical Form Indicator (1 bit)

standard. The example in this figure illustrates frame tagging in Ethernet 802.3 networks. Other types of networks, such as Token-Ring Networks, will use the same two fields but will have different internal designs for the fields.

TAG PROTOCOL IDENTIFIER FIELD

The first two octets in the tag form the **tag protocol identifier** field. As the name suggests, this field tells the receiver that the frame is tagged and the type of tag that appears in the frame. For Ethernet 802.3, the tag protocol identifier is 8100 hex.[13] If this looks familiar, it is really the Ethernet II type field reborn. (Ethernet II was discussed earlier in this module.) The 802.1 Tag Protocol Type is an Ethernet II type.

TAG CONTROL INFORMATION (TCI) FIELD

The **tag control information** field follows the tag protocol identification field. This field gives the content of the tagging. Figure C.17 shows that the tag control information field has three subfields.

▶ **User Priority.** This three-bit subfield has the values 000 to 111, representing priority levels from 0 through 7. A higher number means higher priority. The specific meanings of the individual values are still being worked out at the time of this writing.

▶ **VLAN Identifier.** This 12-bit field identifies the frame as belonging to a specific VLAN. With 12 bits, there can be 4,096 VLANs.

▶ **Canonical Format Indicator.** This one-bit flag varies according to the tag protocol identifier field. For our Ethernet 802.3 frame, a one in this field means that a routing information field follows the tag control information field. A zero indicates the absence of such a field.

Virtual LAN Identifier (802.1Q)

As just noted, the virtual LAN identifier's 12 bits allow 4,096 possible VLANs. If a station broadcasts a message to all members of its VLAN, then these stations and only these stations hear the broadcast. As switch vendors implement the 802.1Q standard, the problems caused by proprietary VLAN technology should wane.

---

[13] In binary, this is 1000 0001 0000 0000 (spaces added for ease of reading).

Priority

One important concern in LANs is **quality of service (QoS).** At its broadest level, QoS is a complex matter that may involve guarantees about cost, latency, reliability, security, and other matters. Most commonly, however, network managers are concerned primarily with latency (delays), especially for such latency-intolerant applications as interactive voice.

As we saw in Chapter 5, one way to decrease latency is to increase transmission speed. If there is enough transmission capacity, then *every* frame will get through faster. For LANs, this brute force approach has tended to be the least expensive way to reduce latency in the past.

However, higher speeds can be supplemented with **prioritization.** As Figure C.18 shows, when a frame reaches a switch, it is placed in a queue. Different queues have different priority levels, and high-priority frames will be placed in high-priority queues. Normally, queues will be empty, and frames will be passed on as soon as they arrive. However, if two or more frames destined for the same output port arrive during the time a frame is being transmitted on that output port, they will be placed in queues.

When the outgoing frame is finished being transmitted, the switch will go to the highest-priority queue first and process any frame it finds there destined for that output port. The switch will then work down to successive lower-priority queues. This way, the highest-priority frame will always be the port's "next frame out."

As noted above, the user priority subfield has three bits, giving seven possible priority levels. The exact meanings of these seven levels have not been set, beyond agreement that higher numbers mean higher priority.

In the end, cost is the important issue. Prioritization allows firms to run their networks closer to capacity. This reduces cost. However, implementing 802.1p in switches is also costly. So the brute force method of upgrading to a faster network may actually be less expensive. Of course, this cost trade-off may change over time.

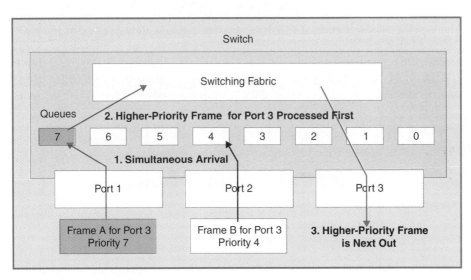

FIGURE C.18

Prioritization in an 802.1p Switch

A final point about prioritization is that if a network is working too close to capacity, prioritization will be futile. Even the highest priority applications will experience delays, whereas lower-priority applications will experience delays so large that latency becomes serious. Prioritization is a tool, but there must always be sufficient capacity in the network.

Multicasting

The 802.1p standard goes beyond prioritization. It also specifies multicasting in IEEE 802 LANs. **Multicasting** allows a frame to be sent to a group of MAC addresses rather than just to a single address. Multicasting allows the transmission of information to all stations in a group. Multicasting is very attractive in videoconferencing, as discussed in Module A, which introduced IP multicasting.

GARP

How does one join a VLAN or multicasting group? There is a general method for registering a station's attributes with the nearest switch. This is the **Generic Attribute Registration Protocol (GARP).** A station registers an attribute with its local switch, and this information is communicated to other switches as necessary.

For VLAN membership, the **GARP VLAN Registration Protocol** uses GARP to register a request by a station to join a particular VLAN.

Similarly, for multicasting, stations can request inclusion in a multicast group through the **GARP Multicast Registration Protocol.**

The Implications of Longer Frames

Frame tagging adds at least four octets to the length of an Ethernet frame. This will make some frames longer than the maximum size of 1,518 octets. This will cause problems for some NICs, hubs, and switches, especially older ones.

Upgrading Issues

Although the standardization of VLANs and prioritization is attractive, it is expensive.[14] Unless all switches in the network comply with the 802.1Q and 802.1p standards, the benefits will be negligible. Many older switches and NICs cannot be software-upgraded to handle these new standards, so companies face buying many new switches or delaying implementation until old switches are gradually replaced over time.

REVIEW QUESTIONS

CORE REVIEW QUESTIONS

1. Name the physical layer options a company has for Ethernet networks running at 10 Mbps. Can you mix these physical layer technologies in a single LAN? If possible, why would you wish to do so?

---

[14] Jim Duffy and Robin Schreier Hohman, "Switch Users in for QoS Cost Surprise," *Network World*, March 23, 1998.

2. In Ethernet 100Base-TX, how many Class I hubs can you have? How many Class II hubs? What is the maximum distance between Class II hubs?

3. The 100Base-TX standard only allows a distance span of about 200 meters because of collision detection problems. How does gigabit Ethernet avoid even smaller distance limitations because of its ten-times-higher speed?

4. Give the two reasons why the 802.3 Working Group decided to change the Ethernet II (Version 2.0) frame.

5. How do switches differ from traditional bridges?

6. In what ways do we measure the capacity of a switch? What are the three forms of switches, and what is the relative advantage of each?

7. Define inter-switch trunking. What is its advantage?

8. Compare and contrast Manchester encoding and differential Manchester encoding.

9. Briefly explain the *main* purpose of the following 802.5 fields: start frame delimiter, access control, frame control, destination address, source address, routing information, information, frame check sequence, end frame delimiter, and frame status. Why is the 802.5 MAC layer frame so much more complex than the 802.3 MAC layer frame?

10. Explain the major risks associated with 802.5 Token-Ring Network and how the standard handles each of them.

11. At what speed does FDDI operate? Where has it been used primarily in the past in site networks? What makes FDDI good for that job, even at large sites? Why does FDDI not have a bright future?

12. What working group creates wireless LAN standards? For what three physical layer transmission techniques and speeds have wireless standards been developed?

13. Explain the difference between CSMA/CD and CSMA/CA+ACK. Why doesn't a wireless LAN use CSMA/CD?

14. Explain the difference between DSSS and FHSS. DSSS transmits 11 chips per bit. How many times does FHSS change frequencies? What is the advantage of slow frequency hopping? What is its disadvantage?

15. Why is spread spectrum transmission used in wireless LANs?

16. Why do we want to add tags to MAC layer frames? What two fields have been defined for frame tagging today? What are their relative purposes? How do we implement virtual LANs, priority, and MAC layer multicasting?

DETAILED REVIEW QUESTIONS

1. Explain the physical connections in 10Base5. What are the distance limits of 10Base5?

2. Explain the physical connections in 10Base2. What are the distance limits of 10Base2?

3. In 10 Mbps Ethernet LANs, what are the limits for the number of segments and repeaters linking the two farthest stations? Explain 5-4-3.

4. Contrast in some detail how Ethernet II and 802.3 handle the minimum frame length problem. Contrast in some detail how Ethernet II and 802 LANs identify the protocol of the next-higher-layer process. How can a receiving device tell whether an incoming frame is an Ethernet II or 802.3 frame?

5. Explain how differential Manchester encoding produces 1, 0, J, and K.
6. Why does the 802.5 start frame delimiter have the pattern JK0JK000?
7. Explain the PPP, T, M, and RRR in the 802.5 access control field.
8. In the 802.5 end frame delimiter, JK1JK1IE, what are the purposes of I and E?
9. In the 802.5 frame control field, what types of frames can a station specify in the FF bits?
10. How do the address fields and the frame control sequence fields differ in 802.3 and 802.5, if they differ at all?
11. What is the purpose of the 802.5 routing information field?
12. Describe the ending fields in 802.5.
13. Explain why a break in the ring between access units is dangerous and how 802.5 reduces the danger. Explain why a station suddenly turning off is dangerous and how 802.5 handles it.
14. What is an active monitor? What happens if it fails? How does 802.5 handle this danger?
15. What are the two modes of operation in 802.11 wireless LANs? What are the two ways of controlling when a station may transmit in 802.11? For what type of data would each control approach be used?
16. In 802.1Q and 802.1p, how does a station join a VLAN? How does it indicate that a particular frame is destined for a particular VLAN? How does a firm join an IP multicast group? How does a firm indicate a frame's priority?

THOUGHT QUESTIONS

1. Now that you know more about 802.5, why do you think its market penetration has been lower than 802.3? Why do you think that many companies feel that 802.5 is a much better choice anyway?
2. Complete Figure C.8 by filling in the last four lines.
3. Why must power be controlled in radio LANs?
4. In ISM bands, why is it possible for two firms to build wireless LANs that interfere with one another? In spread spectrum transmission, explain graceful degradation and explain how it gives firms time to negotiate if their wireless networks do interfere.
5. How can VLANs and multicasting avoid the need for explicit frame tagging? What problems does this avoid?
6. Unless stations can send and receive at high speeds, there is no sense in placing them on a very fast network. Older PCs have ISA busses, which only move eight bits in each clock cycle and have a clock cycle of 10 MHz. Newer PCs have PCI busses. Often they can move 32 bits at a time and have a clock speed of 33 MHz. Faster PCI busses are coming and some computers have them, but the PCI speed just given is illustrative. New external ports can connect to networks without adding a NIC. For example, a universal serial bus can send and receive at 12 Mbps. Ignoring problems of computer software being able to use the full bandwidth of a bus, would you be limited to 10 Base-T or 100Base-TX, or could you benefit from gigabit Ethernet if you have an ISA NIC, a PCI NIC, or a universal serial bus port?

PROJECTS

1. Go the book's website, http://www.prenhall.com/panko, and read the Updates Page for this module to see any reported errors and for new and expanded information on the material in this module.
2. Go the book's website, http://www.prenhall.com/panko, and do the Internet Exercises for this module.

MODULE D

Telephone Service

POTS

Its official name is **PSTN—Public Switched Telephone Network**—but even telephone professionals call it **POTS (plain old telephone service).** Telephony gets little respect and causes even less excitement. It is simply there, always available, like a comfortable old pair of jeans.

However, corporations must take the telephone seriously. Telephony is extremely important in corporate life, and it is also important to data communications professionals.

▶ Although data communications is flashy and new, companies spend far more today on telephony and will for years to come. People talk a lot on the telephone. Managers, for instance, spend 5% to 10% of the day on the phone.[1]

▶ In addition, voice transmission generates a great deal of bandwidth. Although data tend to come in short bursts, people fill up a telephone channel constantly when they talk.

▶ Furthermore, the job of managing telephony is exploding in complexity. Technology is creating many new products and a bewildering array of options in each product category. In particular, "IP telephony" technology may revolutionize long-distance calling.

▶ Finally, *deregulation*—the relaxation of protectionist regulation—has brought the competition needed to get new products to users.

In one critical respect, even basic voice service has changed profoundly in recent years. In real dollars, interstate long-distance prices have fallen dramatically over the last 20 years. International calling charges have fallen even more dramatically.

[1] R. R. Panko, "Managerial Communication Patterns," *Journal of Organizational Computing* 2, no. 1 (1992): 95–122.

Because of falling prices, use is growing several times faster than the GNP. We now make even international calls without giving much thought to cost. Compared to even 10 years ago, telephony today has a much wider role in organizations, and this role will grow in the future.

THE TRADITIONAL TELEPHONE SYSTEM

A Telephone Call

Figure D.1 shows what happens when you place a telephone call. The call begins in your **customer premises**—your home or office.

Next the signal travels over a transmission line to the first switch of the telephone company. This transmission line is called the **local loop.** It usually consists of one or

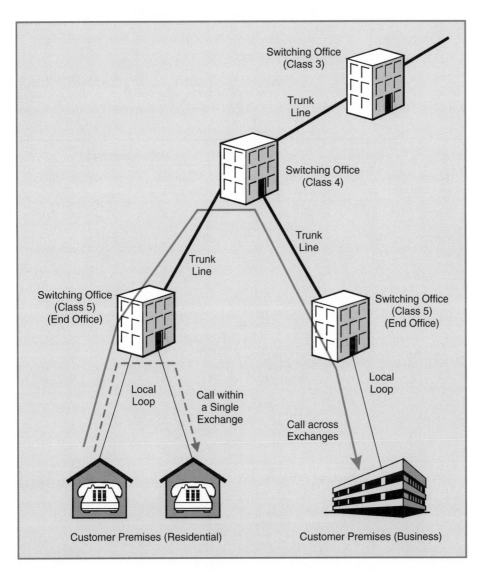

FIGURE **D.1**

Public Switched Telephone Network (PSTN)

Switching Office (Class 3)

Trunk Line

Switching Office (Class 4)

Trunk Line

Trunk Line

Switching Office (Class 5) (End Office)

Switching Office (Class 5) (End Office)

Local Loop

Local Loop

Call within a Single Exchange

Call across Exchanges

Customer Premises (Residential)

Customer Premises (Business)

two pairs of copper wire. In the future, the local loop is likely to switch (at least in part) to optical fiber. Fiber will allow much higher speeds.

The call may travel through several more **switching offices,** also called **central offices.** The lines between switching offices are called **trunk lines.** Each trunk line usually carries 24 or more voice calls. Some carry hundreds or thousands of simultaneous calls. Module B contains more information on trunk-line technology, including optical fiber trunking and satellite trunk lines.

At the other end, the final switching office connects you with the party you are calling. Your connection goes over the local loop to the customer premises of the party you are calling.

Carriers

As we saw in Chapter 5, carriers are regulated organizations that carry your signals outside your customer premises.

CARRIERS IN THE UNITED STATES

Figure D.2 shows that when we deal with carriers, there are four geographical tiers of service. The customer premises is your corporate site, your building, or, in the case of residential service, your home. Carriers no longer control transmission on the customer

FIGURE **D.2**

Tiers of Carriers

UNITED STATES		MOST COUNTRIES	
Geographical Tier	Carriers Regulators	Carriers Regulators	Geographical Tier
International	International Common Carriers (ICCs) Bilateral Negotiation		International
Domestic Inter-LATA	Interexchange Carriers (IXCs) Federal Communications Commission (FCC)	Public Telephone and Telegraph Authority (PTT) Competitive Carriers Ministry of Telecommunications	Domestic
Domestic Intra-LATA	Local Access and Transport Area (LATA) is the region Local Exchange Carriers (LECs) Competitive Access Providers (CAPs) Competitive Local Exchange Provider (CLEP) State Public Utilities Commission (PUC)		
Customer Premises	Completely Deregulated	Completely or Heavily Deregulated	Customer Premises

premises in most countries (they once did). We show the customer premises primarily to illustrate the fact that customer premises telephony cannot be divorced from carrier services. The term *customer premises*, by the way, is always written in the plural.

Next, there is **domestic** service, that is, service within a country. In the United States, there are two tiers of domestic service. Note that this is peculiar to the United States. Most countries do not divide domestic service.

First, the United States is divided into 161 regions called **local access and transport areas (LATAs).** Traditionally, there was a single monopoly telephone carrier in each LATA. This monopoly carrier, usually called just "The Telephone Company," is officially known as the **local exchange carrier (LEC).** The LEC once had a monopoly on providing the line to your home and transmission services within the LATA. It also connected you with inter-LATA carriers and provided integrated intra-LATA and inter-LATA billing.

In the future, regulation will allow increasing competition for local connection and transmission services. The companies challenging the LEC are known collectively as **competitive access providers (CAPs)** or **competitive local exchange providers (CLEPs).** Both terms are commonly used. Cellular companies are already acting as CAPs, but we also should see more traditional "wireline" competition in the future.

Second, companies that provide services *between* LATAs are known as **interexchange carriers.** For consistency, we would expect them to be called IECs. Instead, they are called **IXCs.** Note also that the *I* does not stand for *international* (a mistake commonly made on exams). Once, there was only a single monopoly IXC in the United States. This was AT&T. Today, there are many IXCs, although AT&T is still by far the largest IXC and MCI and Sprint have most of the other customers.

How can you call someone if you use different carriers? The answer is that each LEC must provide a **point of presence (POP)** where different vendors can interconnect (see Figure D.3).

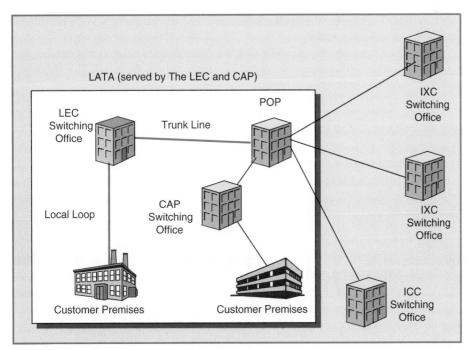

FIGURE D.3

Transmission Service in the United States

For example, if an LEC customer needs to communicate with a CAP customer in the same LATA, the POP will provide the connection point. The calling customer merely keys the number of the other party.

If you are calling someone in a different city, the POP in your LATA connects you to your preferred IXC. Your IXC connects you to the POP in the other party's LATA. The POP in that LATA connects you to the other party's LEC or CAP. That carrier connects you to the party you are calling.

CARRIERS IN OTHER PARTS OF THE WORLD

Most other countries do not have a two-tier structure for carriers. Historically, there was a monopoly telephone company that provided all domestic services. This was the **Public Telephone and Telegraph (PTT) authority.** Sometimes there was a second company for international service. For instance, in Japan, the NTT was the domestic PTT. KDD handled international calls.

The **deregulation** (relaxation of competition rules) that brought competition in the form of CAPs and many IXCs in the United States is also strong in many other countries. Most countries now allow competing carriers, although most limit what competitors can offer to a greater extent than does the United States.

Regulation

Regulation is relatively complex in telephony, especially in international calling and especially in the United States.

REGULATION IN THE UNITED STATES

In the United States, there are two tiers of regulation, reflecting the country's political system. At the national level, there is the **Federal Communications Commission (FCC).** The FCC regulates interstate transmission. It also regulates the entire telephone system, for instance, by setting technical standards and basic service conditions that must be met within states.

At the state level, there are **public utilities commissions (PUCs)** that monitor the day-to-day work of telephone companies operating within the state. The PUCs set many rates and set limitations on services.

Historically, the FCC has been more aggressive in deregulating telephone companies than the PUCs. Today, however, PUC resistance to deregulation is crumbling in many states, and competition is increasing at the local level.

Breaking Up Ma Bell In the United States, there never was a national telephone monopoly. However, **AT&T,** sometimes known as *Ma Bell,* came very close to having a monopoly. It controlled most local telephone companies, and it had a de facto monopoly on long-distance transmission.

In 1984, an antitrust suit by the Justice Department broke up AT&T. One resulting company, which maintained the name AT&T, kept long-distance service and most equipment manufacturing capacity. Local telephone companies, in turn, were divided among seven **Regional Bell Operating Companies (RBOCs).** The seven RBOCs are often called the "Baby Bells." The agreement signed with the Justice Department kept AT&T out of the local markets (intra-LATA service). It also kept the Baby Bells out of long-distance telephony beyond their borders (inter-LATA service).

The Second Breakup of AT&T In 1996, for competitive reasons, AT&T voluntarily decided to split itself further into three companies: a carrier that retained the name AT&T, an equipment manufacturing company called Lucent, and a computer equipment and software company, NCR.

The Telecommunications Act of 1996 That same year, Congress passed the **Telecommunications Act of 1996,** which vastly increased competition in both intra-LATA and inter-LATA service. AT&T can now compete in local telephony, and the RBOCs can compete in long-distance service.

Although the Telecommunications Act of 1996 may eventually create extensive local competition in the United States, local telephone companies are engaging in a number of stalling tactics to keep competitors out of their markets. However, local telephone companies have taken advantage of another provision of the Telecommunications Act of 1996—the deregulation of prices. The intent of regulators was to allow telephone companies to drop their prices to meet the lower prices of new competitors. Of course, in the absence of real competition, telephone companies used price deregulation to raise prices instead.

REGULATION IN OTHER COUNTRIES

In most other countries, there was a national PTT to provide service. There was also a government **Ministry of Telecommunications** to oversee the operation of the PTT. Most ministries are now implementing deregulation to varying degrees. This is bringing in new competitors to the PTT.

Two recent developments should increase competition within countries in the future. First, the **European Community** has mandated that most of its member nations must drop many of the preferences they have given to their PTTs. Although this was to have been implemented in January 1998, implementation is (as usual) taking longer than anticipated. However, the removal of preferences for PTTs does seem to be moving forward.

At a broader level, the **World Trade Organization (WTO)** created a worldwide telecommunications services agreement that would gradually open competition in national markets around the world. However, this agreement did not have strong deadlines, and not even all WTO member nations signed the agreement. Although the WTO agreement is welcome, its effects will be felt only in the long term.

International Telephony The ITU-T (see Chapter 1) sets standards for telephone equipment and transmission lines. It also standardizes many services. However, in most cases, international calling conditions between each pair of countries are largely unregulated. The governments of the two countries engage in **bilateral (two-country) negotiations.** As a result, long-distance calling rates reflect politics much more than they do cost and distance.

Trends in Regulation Although countries vary in the degree to which they have deregulated telecommunications, most follow the same rank ordering in what aspects of telecommunications they have deregulated.

First, the most deregulated aspect of telecommunications is usually the *customer premises.* In many countries, firms can do anything they want on their own premises, as long as they obey the technical and legal rules for connecting to public networks.

Next usually comes *long-distance domestic service*. Most countries deregulate long-distance transmission several years before they deregulate local service.

Then usually comes *international calling*. Deregulation here requires bilateral co-operation between the two countries in allowing each country's international common carriers (ICCs) into the other country's market.

Finally, the least deregulated aspect of telecommunications is almost always *local service*. Regulators often fear that if they allow open competition here, poorer people may be left without telephone service.

CUSTOMER PREMISES EQUIPMENT

Up to this point, we have looked at facilities owned by telephone carriers. Now we will return to the **customer premises;** that is, the building and grounds owned by the customer.

In the past, telephone companies owned all telephone equipment on the customer premises, including all copper wires and even telephone handsets. In most countries, regulators have turned this around completely. The customer now owns everything on the premises, unless the customer specifically chooses to lease equipment from a telephone company. In effect, companies operate their own internal telephone companies.

PBXs

Many large companies have internal switches called **private branch exchanges (PBX).** A PBX is somewhat like having your own end office switch. In fact, this is the origin of the term *branch exchange*. (*Exchange* is another word for *switch*.) Figure D.4 illustrates customer premises wiring using a PBX.

In large buildings, a key consideration is where to leave space for the PBX, wiring, and other equipment. PBXs are about two-thirds of a meter deep, allowing them to fit into standard equipment racks. A small PBX that serves "only" a few hundred lines is about 2 meters tall and 1 meter wide. A large PBX that serves 10,000 to 70,000 lines typically is the same height but may be twice as wide. Companies also need room for the mandatory **termination equipment** that telephone carriers require you to place between the PBX and outgoing lines to protect the telephone system.

In addition, most companies have internal telephone operators. These operators need room for an office. It is common to put operators near the central equipment, but it is not necessary. The telephone manager and his or her office staff and technicians need room as well.

WIRING

If a PBX serves many users, the company needs to run hundreds or thousands of telephone wires from the PBX to individual telephones. As shown in Figure D.4, the wires leave the PBX in thick **cable bundles** that contain hundreds of wire pairs.

The cable bundles move vertically through a building inside **riser** spaces that are 6 inches to 2 feet thick. For new buildings, it is important to leave ample room for riser spaces.

At each floor, the riser terminates in a **wiring closet.** This wiring closet is about the size of a hall closet in a home or apartment. Inside the wiring closet, the thick vertical bundle splits into smaller bundles. Some continue to travel upward to the next floor. Others run out horizontally on that floor of the building. Typically, they run through false ceilings. In other cases, they run inside walls. In improperly built buildings, there are neither false ceilings nor wall space. In that case, the horizontal distribution has to take place through relatively unsightly conduits that look like water pipes.

Finally, the last cable splits into a bundle destined for an individual telephone. As we saw in Chapter 3, this bundle usually contains four pairs (eight wires). It terminates in an RJ-45 connector.

IMPORTANCE OF CUSTOMER PREMISES WIRING

There are two reasons we have spent a considerable amount of time talking about customer premises wiring. The first is that the company must manage its own wiring system, so telephone professionals need to be familiar with customer premises wiring.

In addition, several LAN technologies use high-quality telephone wiring, including repeaters that fit into wiring closets. To understand building wiring is to understand many forms of LAN wiring.

PBX Networks

Many large companies have multiple sites. Figure D.5 shows that each site is likely to have a PBX.

The figure shows that the company can link its sites together with leased lines. For instance, a single T1 leased line can handle 24 conversations between two sites. Especially busy connections require T3 lines or even faster leased lines.

If a firm buys all of its PBXs from a single vendor, they will be able to function together like the central offices of the telephone company. A single system of extension numbers will be able to serve everyone in the firm, regardless of their sites. A PBX at some master site should even be able to do remote maintenance on the PBXs at other sites.

For communication outside the firm, the PBXs will have access lines to the local telephone company. The PBXs will also have links to various other transmission carriers than the local telephone company. This allows the PBXs to select the least-cost line whenever someone makes an outgoing call.

Although the leased lines are likely to be put into place for voice service, they are also good for data transmission. Even if a firm does not completely integrate its voice and data transmission within sites, it usually sends both along the same leased lines between sites.

In effect, the company sets up its own private telephone system. Technically, this is known as a **private telephone network.** By creating private networks, companies can reduce their costs while providing a high level of services.

FIGURE D.5

Private Network via PBXs

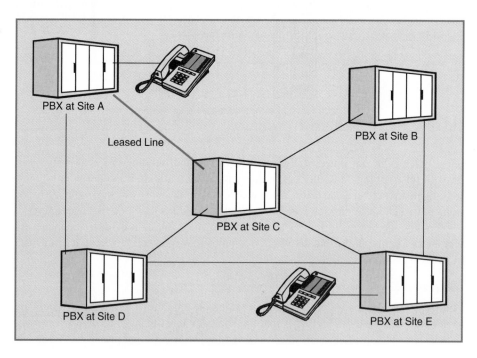

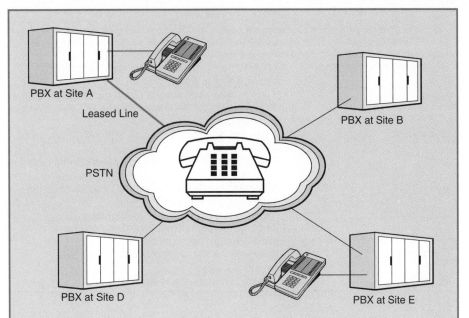

PBX at Site A

Leased Line

PBX at Site B

PSTN

PBX at Site D

PBX at Site E

Many telephone carriers are trying to get back the business they have lost because of private networks. They now offer **virtual private network** service. In this service, the firm appears to have an exclusive private telephone network. Calls between sites are inexpensive, and so are outside calls. However, the telephone company provides this service using its ordinary switches and trunk lines. Virtual private network service is a matter of pricing, not of technology. Figure D.6 shows a virtual private network in telephony.

The term *virtual private network* is a little confusing. It began in telephony as described in the previous paragraph. Later, as Chapter 5 discusses, the term *virtual private network* became popular as a way to describe the use of the Internet instead of a commercial carrier for data transmission. This is why Figure D.6 is titled "Virtual Private Network *in Telephony*.

User Services

Figure D.7 shows that, because digital PBXs are essentially computers, they allow vendors to differentiate their products by adding application software to provide a wide range of services.

CARRIER SERVICES AND PRICING

Having discussed both technology and regulation, we can finally turn to the kinds of transmission services that telecommunications staffs can offer their companies. Figure D.8 shows that users face a variety of transmission services and pricing options.

FOR USERS	
Speed dialing	Dial a number with a one- or two-digit code
Last number redial	Redials the last number dialed
Display of called number	LCD display for number the caller has dialed. Allows caller to see a mistake
Camp on	If line is busy, hit "camp on" and hang up. When other party is off the line, he or she will be called automatically
Call waiting	If you are talking to someone, you will be beeped if someone else calls
Hold	Put someone on hold until he or she can be talked to
ANI	Automatic number identification. You can see the number of the party calling you
Conferencing	Allows three people to speak together
Call transfer	If you will be away from your desk, calls will be transferred to this number
Call forwarding	Someone calls you. You connect them to someone else
Voice mail	Callers can leave messages

FOR ATTENDANTS	
Operator assistance	In-house telephone operators can handle problems
Automatic call distribution	When someone dials in, the call goes to a specific telephone without operator assistance
Message center	Allows caller to leave a message with a live operator
Paging	Operator can page someone anywhere in the building
Nighttime call handling	Special functions for handling nighttime calls, such as forwarding control to a guard station.
Change requests	Can change extensions and other information from a console

VOICE RESPONSE	
	In interaction, user hits keys for input. System gives prerecorded voice responses. Allows menu operations to allow callers to get access to telephone numbers and other information. Reduces operator time

FOR MANAGEMENT	
Automatic route selection	Automatically selects the cheapest way of placing long-distance calls
Call restriction	Prevents certain stations from placing outgoing or long-distance calls
Call detail reporting	Provides detailed reports on charges by telephone and by department.

Tariffs

In looking at services in regulated areas, it is important to look at the carrier's tariffs. A **tariff** is a contract with a regulatory agency that specifies what the carrier will offer. There is a separate tariff for each service the carrier offers.

Local Calling
    Flat rate
    Message units
Toll Calls
    Intra-LATA
    Inter-LATA
Toll Call Pricing
    Direct distance dialing
        Anytime, anywhere
        Highest rate
    800/888 numbers
        Free to calling party
        Reduced rate per minute
    WATS
        Wide area telephone service
        For calling out from a site
        Reduced rate per minute
    900 numbers
        Calling party pays
        Called party charges the calling party a price above
        transmission costs
Personal Telephone Number
    Number for a person, not an instrument
    Can reach the person anywhere

SERVICES

Tariffs specify *two* things. First, they specify the details of the *service* to be provided. It is important to read tariffs carefully because they sometimes leave out things that you assume would be included. They may not make these service features available at all or may do so only for an additional charge.

PRICES

Second, tariffs specify how the service will be *priced.* This can be extremely complex. For instance, pricing may depend on usage volume, with larger customers getting price discounts. In addition, there are likely to be initial charges for activation and installation, flat monthly charges, and volume-dependent charges.

Tariffs from competing carriers may have very different pricing structures, making them difficult to compare. You almost always must be able to estimate traffic volume to make comparisons.

NONTARIFFED SERVICES

Under deregulation, a growing number of services are becoming nontariffed. This allows carriers to compete with one another by negotiating services and pricing with individual customers.

Basic Voice Services

The most important telephone service, of course, is its primary one: allowing two people to talk together. Although you get roughly the same service whether you call the next-door office or another country, billing varies widely between local and long-distance calling. Even within these categories, furthermore, there are important pricing variations.

LOCAL CALLING

Most telephone calls stay within a LATA. There are several billing schemes for local calling. Some telephone companies offer **flat-rate local service** in which there is a fixed monthly service charge but no separate fee for individual local calls.

In some areas, however, carriers charge **message units** for some or all local calls. The number of message units they charge for a call depends on both the distance and duration of the call. Economists like message units, arguing that message units are more efficient in allocating resources than flat-rate plans. Subscribers, in contrast, dislike message units even if their flat-rate bill would have come out the same.

TOLL CALLS

Although the local situation varies, all long-distance calls are **toll calls.** The cost of the call depends on distance and duration for both intrastate and interstate calls. Because of PUC rate control, some intrastate toll rates are more expensive than interstate calls over longer distances.

800/888 NUMBERS

Companies that are large enough can receive favorable rates from transmission companies for long-distance calls. In the familiar **800/888 number** service, anyone can call *into* a company, usually without being charged. To provide free inward dialing, companies pay a carrier a per-minute rate lower than the rate for directly dialed calls. Initially, only numbers with the 800 area code provided such services. Now that 800 numbers have been exhausted, the 888 area code is offering the same service to new customers.

Unfortunately, some unscrupulous companies have you call an 800 or 888 number and then switch you to one of the 900 numbers discussed later. This requires you to pay for the call, despite having dialed an 800 or 888 number. There usually is no indication that you have been switched.

In the past, AT&T dominated 800 calling. Now, however, **800/888 number portability** is allowing AT&T customers to move to competitors without losing their numbers. As expected, this competition is driving down prices. Now even people who operate companies out of their homes or apartments may have 800/888 numbers.

WATS

In contrast to inward 800/888 service, **wide area telephone service (WATS)** allows a company to place *outgoing* long-distance calls at per-minute prices lower than those of directly dialed calls. WATS prices depend on the size of the service area. WATS is often available for both intrastate and interstate calling. WATS can also be purchased for a region of the country instead of the entire country.

900 NUMBERS

Related to 800/888 numbers, **900 numbers** allow customers to call into a company. Although 800/888 calls are usually free, callers to 900 numbers pay a fee that is much *higher* than that of a toll call. Some of these charges go to the IXC, but most of them go to the company being called.

This allows companies to charge for information, technical support, and other services. For example, customer calls for technical service might cost $20 to $50 per hour. Charges for 900 numbers usually appear on the customer's regular monthly bill from the local exchange carrier. Although the use of 900 numbers for sexually oriented services has given 900 numbers something of a bad name, they are valuable for legitimate business use.

UNIVERSAL AVAILABILITY

A potential new service is the **personal telephone number.** In this service, a number would be linked to an individual rather than to a telephone. A call would be able to reach the person anywhere in the country and eventually anywhere in the world. People might even be assigned a personal telephone number at birth.

Advanced Services

Although telephony's basic function as a "voice pipe" is important, telephone carriers offer other services to attract customers and to get more revenues from existing customers.

ELECTRONIC SWITCHING SERVICES

Earlier we saw that most digital switches are really computers. We also saw the types of applications that vendors now program into their PBXs. Many carriers now offer the same services to home and residential customers.

Unfortunately, different carriers throughout the country tend to offer very different digital switching services. We will see later that one reason for creating the Integrated Services Digital Network is to standardize services. This will allow them to be offered even for calls that span multiple carriers.

Perhaps the most controversial electronic switching service is **automatic number identification (ANI)** in which the caller's number is displayed in an LCD display on the receiver's telephone.

On the positive side, ANI can allow **service customization.** The caller can automatically be routed to his or her personal service agent or to an agent serving the caller's state or geographical location within a city. ANI could also allow a computer to pull up information on the caller, so that the agent would have full background information for servicing the call.

On the negative side, ANI has serious privacy implications. The telephone has always been an anonymous calling device, and many people are loath to give up their privacy. This is a special problem if the person wants to call up a crisis hot line or some other service for which anonymity is desirable. On the other hand, call receivers rightly complain about prank calls and feel that they should be able to know who is calling their own homes or businesses.

One potential problem with call screening is geographical *red lining*. In red lining, companies refuse service to people living in certain parts of a city. Although explicit red lining may be illegal, ANI would provide geographical information that could allow companies to subtly discourage service to red-lined areas.

Because of these problems, many nations are limiting ANI usage. Some permit ANI **call blocking,** in which the caller can block the ANI feature. The receiver, however, can still know that ANI has been blocked in most cases. The receiver can then decide whether to accept an ANI-blocked call.

CELLULAR TELEPHONY

Cellular telephony is probably the most dynamic service in telephony today. Cellular telephony use is growing explosively, and new technologies are likely to fuel this growth for some years to come.

Cellular Concepts

Until the 1980s, mobile telephones were rare. There were only 44 channels in the United States, and other countries had similar limits. Not everyone is on the telephone all the time, so a system can have more subscribers than channels, but in general, only about 20 subscribers can share a radio channel. So early mobile radio could serve only 800 to 900 subscribers, even in the largest cities. This kept prices astronomically high.

During the 1960s, AT&T invented a technology that would bring prices down, making it possible to serve thousands of users rather than a few hundred. It would do this by allowing available channels to be used multiple times in each city, not just once. Figure D.9 shows AT&T's **cellular telephone** concept. The figure shows that cellular service divides a city into a number of geographical regions called **cells.**

FREQUENCY REUSE

Cells are the key to **frequency reuse**, that is, using a channel several times in each city. Cellular uses low power, so signals do not travel far. You can use the same channel in nonadjacent cells. If someone talks on Channel 1 in Cell E, someone can be talking on Channel 1 in Cell A.

In practice, you can reuse a channel roughly every 7 cells. So with 21 cells, you can reuse channels about three times. Following the 20-to-1 rule, you can support about 60 subscribers with each cellular channel, not just 20.

LOW-POWER OPERATION

Because **cellular telephones (cellphones)** only have to transmit over short distances, they can have very low power. A typical hand-held cellphone only uses 0.6 watts of power. This brings small size, relatively long battery life, and most important of all, relatively low cost.

Hand-held cellphones are common sights. In addition, there are *mobile cellphones* designed to stay in cars. They have a bit more power, so they operate in some areas where hand-held units will not. They also cost less because they use the car's electricity. However, they cannot leave the car when the subscriber does.

SPECTRUM CAPACITY

The third advantage of cellular service, besides channel reuse and low-cost phones, is not intrinsic to cellular operation. This is the fact that national regulators give cellular service much more spectrum capacity than early mobile services. Most cellular systems have about 800 channels. We will see later that this will soon quadruple.

More spectrum is possible because regulators are putting cellular services in high-frequency bands—450 MHz, 800 MHz, 900 MHz, and 1.8 GHz to 2.2 GHz. These higher-frequency bands are less crowded than traditional mobile bands.

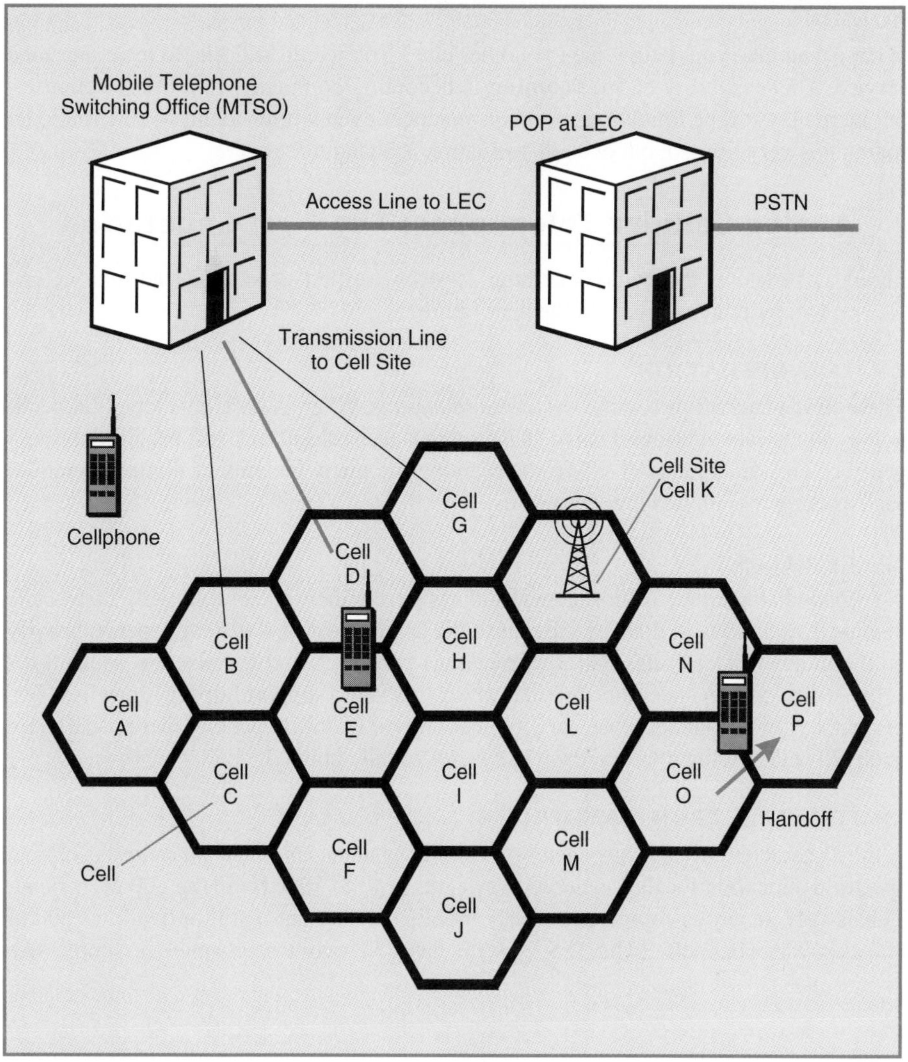

Mobile Telephone
Switching Office (MTSO)
POP at LEC
Access Line to LEC
PSTN
Transmission Line
to Cell Site
Cellphone
Cell Site
Cell K
Cell
G
Cell
D
Cell
B
Cell
H
Cell
N
Cell
A
Cell
E
Cell
L
Cell
P
Cell
C
Cell
I
Cell
O
Handoff
Cell
Cell
F
Cell
M
Cell
J

FIGURE D.9

Cellular Telephone System

HANDOFFS

What if a subscriber moves from one cell to another? When that happens, the system will automatically execute a **handoff,** passing responsibility for service to the subscriber's new cell site. This happens so rapidly that few people are aware when a handoff occurs.

Handoffs are possible because all of the system's cell sites (antennas plus other equipment) are coordinated from a central point. This is the **mobile telephone switching office (MTSO).**

All cell sites pass their signals to the MTSO. If the other party is also a cellular customer, the MTSO sends the signal back out to the other party's cell site.

If the other party is on a regular (**wireline**) telephone, the MTSO passes the signal to the local exchange carrier. The LEC handles the rest of the connection to local customers. For long-distance calls, the MTSO connects to an IXC or even an ICC.

ROAMING

What if you take your cellphone to another city? You would still like to have the same service. This capability called **roaming** is becoming common within most countries, but there may still be limitations or inconveniences even within countries. International roaming is very limited, but even this situation is changing.

Analog Cellular Telephones: The First Generation

Figure D.10 shows that today's cellular services are first generation and that we can foresee two more generations in the near future.

ANALOG OPERATION

These **first-generation** cellular systems are *analog*. When AT&T developed the technology in the late 1960s and early 1970s, digital technology was still prohibitively expensive. This prevented AT&T from receiving the many benefits of digital operation, such as compression and low error rates.

LARGE CELLS

A second characteristic of first-generation systems is their use of relatively *large cells* that are 1 to 5 miles in diameter. Because the capital cost of a system depends heavily on the number of cell sites that a carrier must construct, and because the demand for cellular service was uncertain, cellular power was set to support fairly large cells. This, of course, limits channel reuse. In a typical city of 1 million people, there usually are about 20 cells, giving a frequency reuse factor of only about 3.

LIMITED SPECTRUM BANDWIDTH

A third characteristic of first-generation cellular systems is *limited spectrum*. A typical spectrum allocation for first-generation systems is 40 to 50 MHz in the 800 MHz band. This is very generous compared to early mobile service, but it still only allows 600 to 800 two-way channels. (The U.S. system has 832 two-way channels.) Simple fre-

FIGURE D.10

Three Generations of Cellular Service

	1ST GENERATION		2ND GENERATION		THIRD GENERATION	
Service	Analog		Digital		Digital	
Cell size	Large		Large		Small*	
Total bandwidth	Large		Large		Very Large*	
Compression	Usually Not		Usually Not		Yes*	
Standards	U.S. Good AMPS	Elsewhere Poor Many	U.S. Poor	Elsewhere Good GSM	U.S. Poor No standards	Elsewhere Good DCS-1800

*Allows greater spectrum efficiency (more subscribers per Hz of bandwidth)

quency reuse only boosts this to 1,800 to 2,400 channels. So with the 20-to-1 rule, cellular could only serve 36,000 to 48,000 subscribers in a typical million-person city. Even with the reuse tricks described earlier, this can only double or quadruple. This is not enough for larger cities, even today.

COMPRESSION

A fourth characteristic of first-generation cellular systems is that voice is not compressed. Channels are fairly wide, about 30 kHz. This lack of compression also limits subscriber capacity.

LACK OF STANDARDS

A final characteristic of first-generation cellular systems is a *lack of standards*. The U.S. AMPS technology is different from technologies in Europe. In Europe, furthermore, there are several competing standards. Not even the frequency range of cellphones is standardized around the world. There is not even standardization in frequency bands. Most countries use the 800 MHz band, but some use the lower 450 MHz band.

Digital Cellular: The Second Generation

The **second-generation** systems now being introduced are similar to first-generation systems in some ways. Cell sizes and spectrum allocations tend to be the same or similar, for instance. However, there are two important differences.

DIGITAL OPERATION

The big change in second-generation systems is the use of *digital technology* instead of analog technology. This is better for data. It also produces cleaner systems. With multiplexing, it is even possible to have more subscribers for the same amount of bandwidth, although this is not always implemented.

STANDARDS

Although second-generation systems are not perfectly standardized around the world, there have been improvements. There seem to be two competing standards around the world. In the United States and some other countries, there is **cellular digital packet data (CDPD).** Generally, existing analog systems have some of their channels refitted for CDPD service. So CDPD is an incremental addition to existing cellular systems.

In Europe and most other parts of the world, in contrast, there is an entirely new system operating in the 900 MHz band. This is **GSM, the Global System for Mobile telephony.** As countries around the world move from their chaotic mix of first-generation systems to GSM, they will be able to have true worldwide roaming. Unfortunately, the United States will be left out of this worldwide roaming possibility, because the Federal Communications Commission failed to adopt GSM.

COMPRESSION

As in first-generation systems, there typically is no compression of the voice signal.

Personal Communication Services:
The Third Generation

Although GSM and CDPD will offer many improvements, they still use large cells and have fairly limited bandwidth. Unless forecasts for cellular demand are extremely optimistic, first- and second-generation cellular systems will not be able to meet subscriber requirements in the near future.

MICROCELLS

The most important gains in third-generation digital systems are due to their use of much smaller cells called **microcells.** Instead of being a mile or more in diameter, a PCS microcell may be only a quarter of a mile in diameter or even smaller.

The number of cells increases as the inverse square of the cell size. For instance, decreasing cell size by a factor of 5 increases the potential number of cells by a factor of 25. Although the gains in capacity are not completely proportional, microcells can support about 10 times as many subscribers as large cells. Having many microcells and, therefore, massive amounts of reuse is the real key to capacity increases in PCS.

In addition, power requirements fall by the *cube* of the cell size. Reduced power requirements will make PCS cellphones very small, light, and inexpensive. It should also reduce concerns about radiation. At the time of this writing, power levels and, therefore, cell sizes have not been set for PCS. So the ratios we have just given are only for purposes of illustration.

GREATER BANDWIDTH

A second key to improved service is increased bandwidth. By assigning third-generation service to the 1.5 GHz to 3 GHz range, countries can typically allow about 150 MHz of capacity—three times the amount of earlier systems.

COMPRESSION

A third key to improved capacity is signal compression. The voice signal usually is compressed to about 12 kbps to 20 kbps, instead of 64 kbps. This further increases the capacity of third-generation systems. It roughly triples the possible number of subscribers per channel per cellsite.

PCS

In the United States, the third-generation service is called **personal communication service (PCS),** with a generous allocation of 160 MHz of capacity in the 1.8 GHz to 2.2 GHz band.

To create competition, the FCC has authorized several PCS carriers to compete in each market. (In first-generation systems and second-generation systems, there were only two carriers per market.)

MORE SUBSCRIBERS

So smaller cells increase subscriber capacity by a factor of perhaps 10. Greater bandwidth again roughly triples capacity. Compression roughly triples it again. Overall, then, third-generation cellular systems can serve roughly 100 times as many subscribers as first-generation systems.

Unfortunately, in the spirit of "not invented here," the FCC did not adopt the world's DCS-1800 technology discussed below. In fact, in the spirit of "let's cause chaos," it did not standardize any PCS technology at all! It allowed PCS carriers to use whatever technology they wanted!

In fact, no single standard has emerged. Three technologies, however, have emerged as leaders. One is the DCS-1800 standard adopted by the rest of the world. The others are a specific time division multiple access (TDMA) technology and a specific spread spectrum technology. Module B discusses time division multiplexing, whereas Module C discusses direct sequence spread spectrum technology.

The problem with having multiple technologies is that it limits roaming, both within the United States and internationally. However, having learned nothing from the PCS disaster, the FCC has decreed a no-standards approach to digital television.

DCS

Europe, in contrast, is taking a more conservative approach. The third-generation cellular system will be the **distributed communication service (DCS).** DCS will operate at 1710 to 1785 MHz and 1805 to 1880 MHz, so it is called DCS-1800. It is a modification of GSM technology, so it is easy to develop DCS equipment. Just as the world outside the United States has standardized on GSM for second-generation cellular service, it is standardizing on DCS-1800 for third-generation cellular telephony. Often, to emphasize continuity, marketers are calling third-generation systems GSM systems.

DIGITAL SERVICES

Because third-generation cellular systems are digital, each cellphone contains a microprocessor. As a result, many vendors have added software to the cellphone to handle such nontelephone applications as paging and even e-mail.

Many third-generation cellular systems are keeping their prices high by offering additional services, instead of taking advantage of the inherent cost advantages of third-generation cellular technology. This has reduced the hope that PCS will attract a much larger percentage of the population to cellular telephony. However, as more competitors enter markets, prices for PCS should drop substantially. We may even see high-service/high-price PCS carriers and low-service/low-price PCS carriers focusing on different market segments in the same community.

PERSONAL SERVICE

The *personal* in PCS signifies that the telephone number eventually will not be linked to a piece of equipment. Rather, it will be linked to an individual person. You may have a credit-card-sized *access card* that you can plug into whatever cellphone you are near. This credit card will recognize you as the number's owner. You could plug it into your home telephone, your car phone on the way to work, your desk phone at work, and a cordless telephone tied to your organization's wireless PBX.

Even if you use a single phone, it will be able to serve multiple uses. At home, it will act as a cordless telephone working with a low-power unlicensed base unit. The cell in this case will be about the size of your house. On the way to work, the phone would act as a traditional cellphone, using a cellular carrier. At work, it would link to a wireless PBX using unlicensed operation.

Whether you use one phone or several, people will be able to get you anywhere, simply by calling your PCS number. DCS is also likely to see extensive use as a personal communication service.

Although the idea of personal service is exciting, you should not expect it to be fully implemented for some years to come. However, phones that double as home wireless telephones and PCS telephones already exist. For the long term, the ITU-T is working toward person-based systems under the **IMT-2000** (International Mobile Telecommunications 2000) initiative.

LEO Services

All of the services we have discussed so far use ground-based transmission facilities. However, several companies are now attempting to produce satellite-based systems that will work with low-cost radio transceivers.

All of these systems use **low earth orbit (LEO) satellites,** which circle the earth at orbits of only 500 to 2,000 km (300 to 500 miles), as shown in Figure D.11. This allows inexpensive hand-held cellphones to reach them. In contrast, traditional communication satellites circle the earth at an orbit of 36,000 km (22,300 miles). This provides a geosynchronous orbit, making the satellite appear to hover over one position. This allows you to aim a dish at the satellite. LEOs, in contrast, race across the sky. This makes dishes impossible to use, but the distance to the user is so much less that this inability to use a dish is unimportant. See Module B for more information on LEOs and other satellites.

IP TELEPHONY

Looking to the future, one of the biggest threats to traditional telephone service is **IP telephony,** in which the human voice is packetized and sent over an IP network. IP telephony began as a toy service for making inexpensive long-distance and international telephone calls over the Internet. However, the crude service that these early offerings provided should not be taken as an indicator of where IP telephony may go in the future.

FIGURE D.11

Low Earth Orbit (LEO) Telephony

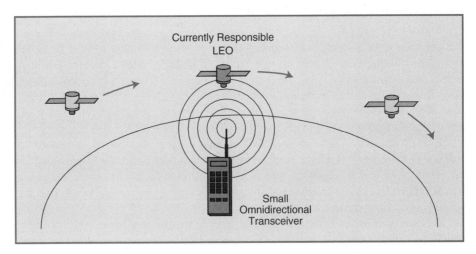

Why IP Telephony?

THE WASTEFULNESS OF CIRCUIT SWITCHING

The Public Switched Telephone Network has always been *circuit switched*. Even the ISDN, which was designed as an all-digital replacement for the PSTN, is almost always implemented through circuit switching. As Chapter 5 discussed, circuit switching allocates dedicated capacity for each call. Other customers cannot cut into your dedicated bandwidth. On the downside, if you do not use your bandwidth, you still pay for it by the minute.

Even in lively telephone conversations, people roughly take turns talking. Each person, then, only talks about half the time on average. So transmission in each direction only uses about half the allocated bandwidth. In other words, simply compressing silences out of the transmission could cut the required bandwidth in half.

In IP telephony, the outgoing signal would first be encoded with a *codec*, as Chapter 3 discussed. It would then be placed into IP packets. The packet-transmission circuitry could simply not send packets without noticeable sound content.

Furthermore, as Chapter 5 discussed, packet switching multiplexes the packets from many different sources over the trunk lines between packet switches. This further reduces costs.

THE WASTEFULNESS OF 64 KBPS VOICE ENCODING

In addition, as Chapter 3 discussed, it has been traditional to encode human voice as a 64 kbps data stream. This uses a simple technique in which the voice is sampled 8,000 times per second and in which 8 bits are recorded for each sample. The 8 bits represent the absolute loudness of the voice signal.

Newer forms of encoding can reduce the number of bits per sample. For example, **adaptive encoding** does not measure the *absolute loudness* of a sample but rather the *change in loudness* from the previous sample. Given the fact that human voice amplitude changes fairly slowly, you can store fewer bits per sample. With adaptive encoding, voice can be sent at 16 kbps or 32 kbps with only a slight loss in sound quality. Voice can even be encoded at 8 kbps at significant loss in signal quality.

Overall, compressing the human voice, packetizing it, and sending it over an IP network offers the promise of very significant cost reductions.

IP'S CORPORATE DOMINANCE

Another reason for interest in IP telephony is that many organizations have already implemented corporate-wide IP networks and see IP as their strategic direction for all corporate data networking. If voice could also be sent over IP networks, corporations could eventually move toward their long-term goal of integrating voice and data communications.

Why Not IP Telephony?

Although the potential economic benefits of IP telephony are persuasive, networking professionals pale at the prospect of sending voice over IP.

THE SENSITIVITY OF VOICE TO DELAY

When you speak to someone face to face, it only takes a few milliseconds (thousands of a second) for your voice to reach him or her. This lets you talk back and forth with little delay. The telephone system introduces a slightly longer delay, but even this delay is negligible. It is no impediment to the give and take of normal conversations.

As delay increases, it becomes more difficult to carry on a normal conversation. At a **latency** (delay) of about a fifth of a second (200 ms), people begin having a difficult time carrying on a normal conversation. The other person does not seem to respond promptly, and both sides often start talking at the same time in response to a "silence" that is really a delay in transmission. At about a 300 ms delay, conversation becomes unbearable. At about 500 ms, it becomes impossible.

THE SENSITIVITY OF VOICE TO JITTER

Circuit switching delivers voice in a steady stream, just as the air does in a face-to-face conversation. But packet switching creates the possibility of **jitter**—variability in latency. Sometimes, adjacent packets are delivered immediately after one another. At other times, there can be significant delays between packets. This is called jitter because that is precisely what it sounds like. It is as if the other party is sitting on a vibrating machine.

IP, LATENCY, AND JITTER

As discussed in Chapter 2, IP is a **best-effort** service. It can offer no guarantee of either short latency or constant latency. It was designed for applications in which even significant latency causes few problems. Latency of 300 ms from end to end across the Internet is extremely common, and even 500 ms delays are not unusual.

However, one must not confuse IP telephony with the Internet. The Internet's latency and variable latency problems stem in large part because so many different carriers are involved and because the Internet is often congested. IP can also be done on a private network or a commercial network offering **service-level agreements** of low congestion. In such cases, latency and jitter may be imperceptible.

Internet IP Telephony: The First Generation

When IP telephony first appeared, it came in the context of the Internet, and its main purpose was to save money, even at the expense of very poor voice quality.

Most users pay a flat monthly fee to use the Internet. This usually buys them unlimited use. So if you could talk over the Internet, you could do so at zero incremental price.

TECHNICAL PROBLEMS

Of course, there are some technical problems with this approach. We have already seen that IP is only a best-effort service and that the Internet often has very high congestion.

In addition, **Internet IP telephony** is often done from home computers, using modem transmission for Internet access. As we saw in Chapter 3, modems are quite slow, and this limits voice quality. To accommodate modem speeds and congestion, the voice bandwidth is often limited to 8 kbps in Internet telephony systems.

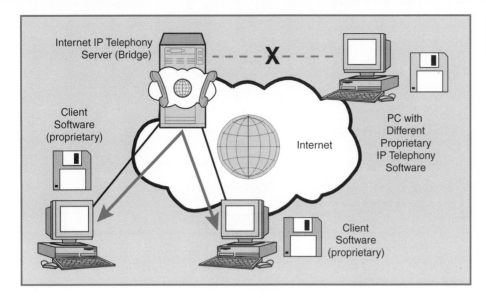

THE SERVICE

Figure D.12 shows how Internet IP telephony works. Each user must have client software designed for IP telephony. This software contains a codec program that translates between analog voice and the Internet's digital transmission.

Figure D.12 shows that client PCs do not communicate directly. Rather, they both connect to an IP telephony server called a **bridge.** The bridge links them together.

PRACTICAL DIFFICULTIES

This approach creates several practical difficulties. First, different vendors offer different bridge services. They differ in call connection and disconnection protocols. They also differ in the encoding and decoding methods they use in their software codecs. As a result, an Internet IP telephony user who has client software from a different bridge service provider cannot call users of the bridge shown in the figure. Figure D.12 illustrates this difficulty.

In the future, different bridges are likely to be able to interoperate. IP telephone bridge vendors have already agreed to interoperate using the **G.723.1** codec standard for voice compression. However, many supervisory signaling protocols still need to be agreed upon, and developing these agreements is likely to take some time.

The other practical difficulty is that bridge service is not free. First, you often have to buy the client software. Second, you have to pay the bridge service provider, often on the basis of a flat monthly fee. Although with moderate use this arrangement is far cheaper than long-distance domestic and international calling, it means that Internet IP telephony is not really free.

Corporate IP Telephony

Internet IP telephony is fine for "hobby users." However, it does not offer the quality of service necessary in corporate environments. **Corporate IP telephony** also uses client software and may use bridges as well. However, it replaces the Internet with more reliable transmission technologies.

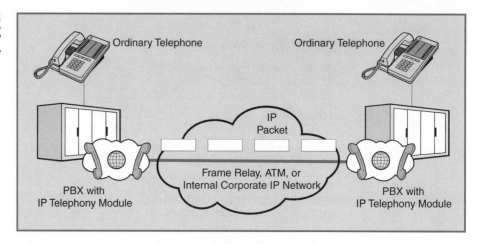

CARRIER SERVICES

Recall that although IP was not designed for voice service, the biggest problem with Internet IP telephony is that the Internet is highly congested. In addition, a packet may take 30 hops between routers to go from one user to another user.

Figure D.13 shows that corporations instead use corporate IP networks or send their IP traffic over public Frame Relay or ATM carriers. This greatly reduces the number of hops. In addition, most carriers offer service-level agreements that limit congestion to a degree where latency and jitter are not problems.

INTERNAL IP TELEPHONY NETWORKS: A PBX-ONLY SOLUTION

Figure D.13 shows that corporations also have to modify their internal networks. The figure shows the simplest approach, in which the internal corporate telephone network is linked to the carrier or internal IP network through a PBX. The PBX will need a voice-to-IP module.

With this approach, there is no need to involve user PCs at all. Employees can use their ordinary telephones. In fact, they probably will not even know that their call is being routed over an IP link. This is attractive because it means that there is no need to change the internal telephone network, beyond adding a module to the PBX.

INTERNAL IP TELEPHONY NETWORK: COMPUTER–TELEPHONY INTEGRATION (CTI)

Although PBX-only solutions are the simplest to implement, there are reasons to have **computer–telephony integration (CTI),** in which voice and data are integrated using the employee's desktop computer.

With CTI, for example, you could handle your incoming e-mail, voice mail, and facsimile messages through a single integrated in-box. To give another example, if you wanted to call someone, you could just select the person's name from a list on the computer screen, and the IP telephony network would connect you.

Unfortunately, CTI requires an internal system that goes far deeper than the PBX. For such systems, there are many unanswered questions. For instance, should all conversations travel over the building's telephone wiring, over LANs, or using some combination of the two? The same question needs to be asked about supervisory signals.

Also, telephone systems are extremely reliable compared to data networks, and IP telephony users will expect similar reliability. However, even with circuit switched traffic, the reliability of telephony systems is very difficult to achieve. When IP transmission is added to the picture, traditional levels of reliability may be extremely difficult to obtain.

Finally, there is the whole issue of billing. One of the main benefits of PBXs is their ability to generate monthly bills for individual telephones. Corporations will not be willing to give this up.

Overall, the PBX-only solution is possible today. Full internal systems that bring CTI to every desktop raise many issues today.

The Carriers Weigh In

Although IP telephony is still a new idea, several major carriers in the United States have already presented their initial plans for integrating data and voice services. Although these plans will change over time, perhaps radically, it is clear that all long-distance carriers see packetized voice as a way to drop voice calling rates to under five cents per minute in response to competitive pressures.

AT&T

In the purest IP play, AT&T has been working within the Internet Engineering Task Force to design standards for IP telephony. For instance, the **Diffserv** (differential services) group is creating standards to allow different types of service for different types of traffic. In addition, several IETF groups are working on specific aspects of IP telephony.

One way to get high performance using IP within the telephone network is to put packets directly on high-speed physical layer SONET lines (see Module B) instead of placing them in data link layer frames. SONET is already widely used within telephone networks, so the big cost would be the creation of routers that can work with SONET.

SPRINT

Sprint is taking a more traditional telephone company approach. It is basing its integrated voice-data network on ATM (see Chapter 5). ATM was originally created for the multiplexing of digitized voice over high-speed lines, such as SONET, so Sprint is essentially bringing ATM back to its roots. Sprint notes that ATM already has the quality of service tools needed to make packetized voice as reliable as circuit switched voice.

DATA AND VOICE TRAFFIC RATIOS

One crucial consideration is the ratio of data to voice traffic. Some estimates indicate that data and voice are already roughly equal in size and that data will soon be far larger. Other estimates indicate that voice is still far larger than data and will be for some years to come. This is an important debate, because it drives the choice of technology. A mostly-data network would benefit from very different technology than a mostly-voice network.

Estimates that favor data tend to talk in terms of *call minutes*—connect time between two stations. However, voice traffic is fairly constant, filling the line during a call. Data traffic, in contrast, tends to be bursty, so that there is a great deal of *dead time*, during which no bits are sent. Estimates that look at bits transmitted tend to see voice as being far larger than data.

PRICING

One potential issue in IP telephony is that demand is being skewed by regulatory considerations in the United States. For large customers, carriers are already willing to offer long-distance prices under five cents per minute. However, the customer also must pay about five cents per minute in **access fees,** which go to the local telephone company. This makes the total cost per minute about ten cents. Internet service so far has been exempt from the access fee. However, if IP telephony grows rapidly, the Federal Communications Commission may extend access fees to such calls. If that happens, IP telephony may no longer be a bargain.

GLOBAL TELECOMMUNICATIONS ALLIANCES

Today, many large organizations do business throughout the world. As things stand now, they have to establish service agreements with telecommunications carriers in each country—sometimes several in each country. This makes central administration of the firm's telephone system very difficult.

Another problem for central administration is billing. Bills come in from different carriers in different countries in different formats. Yet sometimes calls billed in one country have to be charged back to departments in other countries.

What corporations doing business globally would like, of course, is to be able to do what they do in the United States and other individual countries—work with a single carrier to provide service among all sites as well as integrated billing.

Although this is impossible today, it may be possible in the next decade. A number of large carriers or small groups of large carriers are establishing **global telecommunications alliances.** In these alliances, they work with carriers in other countries to establish service agreements and, to the extent possible, integrated billing.

To give some examples of global telecommunications alliances, *World Partners* involves AT&T, KDD (the Japanese national international common carrier), Singapore Telecom, and PTTs in several other countries. *Phoenix*, in turn, is a partnership of Sprint, Deutsche Telekom, and France Telecom.

Although alliances hope to become completely global, most instead are largely regional with stronger coverage in some parts of the world than others. They only address some of a firm's needs. Even with their stable of countries, integrated billing is far from complete.

In addition, some large firms have found that even in countries served by global telecommunications alliances, firms can negotiate better financial conditions and service-level agreements by themselves.

CORE REVIEW QUESTIONS

1. Define the following terms for the Public Switched Telephone Network: *customer premises*, *local loop*, *switching office*, *trunk line*. Trace the route a call takes from one customer premises to another in a local call.

2. Explain each of the following in the United States: LATA, LEC, CAP, CLEP, IXC, ICC, RBOC, Baby Bell, and POP. Trace what happens in a local call involving a LEC customer and a CAP customer. Trace what happens in a long-distance call between states. Trace what happens in a call from a U.S. customer premises to a party in another country.

3. What is a PTT? Explain the relationship between the PTT and the Ministry of Telecommunications.

4. Explain the two levels of regulation within the United States. Describe the two phases of AT&T's splitting up into smaller firms. What is the significance of the Telecommunications Act of 1996 in the United States? For other countries, discuss the importance of European Community and WTO mandates.

5. Rank order the following in terms of degree of deregulation: customer premises operation, local service, and long-distance service. Use the terms *most*, *middle*, and *least*.

6. What is a PBX? Why are PBXs attractive to businesses? What are private telephone networks? Virtual private networks? How does the term *virtual private network* differ in telephony and data communications?

7. Describe the main elements in the vertical and horizontal distribution of telephone wiring. (Be sure to explain the function of the wiring closet.)

8. What is a tariff? What two things does it specify? Are all carrier services tariffed?

9. Compare and contrast 800/888 numbers, 900 numbers, and WATS, in terms of whether the caller or the called party pays and the cost compared to the cost of a directly dialed long-distance call.

10. Explain why cellular telephone systems can serve thousands of simultaneous callers in a large city.

11. Explain the differences between first-generation cellular systems and third-generation (PCS) cellular systems in terms of number of subscribers served. Explain reasons for the difference. Explain why third-generation cellular phones should be less expensive and smaller than first-generation cellphones. How will LEO-based systems differ from traditional cellular telephony systems?

12. Why is IP telephony attractive? Why is it not attractive? Distinguish between Internet IP telephony and corporate IP telephony. Why does using an internal network or a public carrier reduce the problems found in Internet IP telephony? Why is a PBX-only approach desirable? What do you lose with this approach? What issues are raised by CTI-based IP telephony?

13. Why is the ideal of global alliances attractive? To what extent do global alliances exist today?

DETAILED REVIEW QUESTIONS

1. Explain the requirements of a telephone system for building space.
2. What is a PBX network? Why do organizations create such networks? Distinguish between private telephone networks and virtual private networks.
3. In PBXs, what is the difference among user services, attendant services, and management functions? List at least three services in each category. Be able to explain all of the PBX services in the module if given their names.
4. Distinguish between voice recognition and voice response systems. What are the relative advantages of each?
5. How do countries decide which ICCs will serve their customers? How are ICC rates set?
6. Describe pricing for local calls and toll calls. What is the advantage of 800/888 numbers for customers? For companies that subscribe to 800/888 number service? What is 800/888 number portability, and why is it important to competition?
7. For what do the initials ANI stand? What does this service do? Why is it good for business? Why is it good for individual people? Why may it be bad for individual people? What is ANI call blocking?
8. Explain the benefits of dividing a service area into cells in cellular telephony.
9. How do cellular systems serve many people? (Some overlap with the preceding question.)
10. Distinguish between handoffs and roaming.
11. What are the characteristics of first-generation cellular systems? Why are these characteristics limiting? Describe standardization for first-generation services.
12. Distinguish between first-generation and second-generation cellular. Which limitations of first-generation cellular does second-generation cellular relieve? Which does it not relieve?
13. Distinguish between first-generation and third-generation cellular. Which limitations of first-generation cellular does third-generation cellular relieve?
14. LEO transceivers will not use directional antennas. Why will this be possible? What benefits will this bring? What costs will it create?

THOUGHT QUESTIONS

1. Compare building wiring with LAN and local internet wiring in Chapters 4 and 5. Do you think the similarities are accidental? If not, why do you think LAN wiring so closely follows traditional telephone building wiring?
2. How do you feel about 900 numbers, ANI, and cellular radiation's effects on the body? Do you think we should have new regulations?
3. Do you think that people should be allowed to use cellular telephones while driving?

PROJECTS

1. Go to the book's website, http://www.prenhall.com/panko, and read the Updates Page for this module to see any reported errors and for new and expanded information on the material in this module.

2. Go to the book's website, http://www.prenhall.com/panko, and do the Internet Exercises for this module.

3. From your local cellular company, find out how many cells serve your city. If possible, locate the cell sites on a map. Note: it is important for not everyone in the class to do this. Also, some cellular firms will be unwilling to give out this information.

4. Determine the cost of cellular telephony in your area. Determine activation (initial) charges and monthly charges. Most cellular systems provide several alternatives based on monthly calling volume. Compare them.

5. Go to a store that sells cellphones. Compare prices with features, size, and power. Determine if low-price cellphones require you to get an account with a particular cellular provider. If so, determine the activation fee and monthly service charge. See if it is possible to get a contract with a lower activation fee and/or a lower monthly service charge. See if this raises the price of the cellphone.

More on Large-Scale Networks

INTRODUCTION

This module is designed to be read after Chapter 5. The two exceptions are the sections on server technology and quality of service, which should be read after Chapter 6. This module is not intended to be read front-to-back, like a chapter. Rather, it supplements the material in Chapters 5 and 6 by offering additional readings in the following areas:

- ▶ **Server Technology.** Chapter 6 discussed server technology. This section discusses three additional topics in server technology: using RAM for disk caching, power supplies, and disk technology.
- ▶ **Quality of Service (QoS).** Carriers make claims about the quality of service they maintain in their transmission offerings. Service-level agreements (SLAs) make those claims enforceable. An important QoS consideration is the handling of high-priority traffic, which may be given preference either through priority or by reserving capacity.
- ▶ **Leased Lines.** The section on leased lines discusses trends and covers leased line offerings from analog voice-grade leased lines to ultra-high-speed SONET and SDH leased lines. The section focuses most heavily on the area of main user demand: 64 kbps to 1 or 2 Mbps.
- ▶ **Frame Relay.** Frame Relay is the most popular packet switched data network. The section on Frame Relay describes this service in some detail.
- ▶ **ATM.** As corporate transmission demand grows beyond Frame Relay speeds, most switched data networks offer a smooth growth path to ATM. The section on ATM covers this technology in some detail.
- ▶ **Switched Data Network Pricing.** This section discusses what organizations will have to pay for Frame Relay or ATM service. There are several components to the pricing equation, and it is important for users to understand each of them.

ADDITIONAL TOPICS IN SERVER TECHNOLOGY

Chapter 6 discussed server technology for enterprise servers, which have to serve large numbers of users. This section presents some additional topics in server technology.

RAM

All servers have a great deal of RAM. This allows them to keep many commonly used files in RAM, a process called **disk caching.** It is much faster for the microprocessor to retrieve a file from a disk cache in electronic RAM than from a relatively slow mechanical disk drive.

RETRIEVAL OF FILES

For instance, as shown in Figure E.1, system files, which users and other programs call frequently, are stored in a section of RAM called the **disk cache.** When a user calls for a system program or data file (labeled as "File A"), the file is retrieved from the disk cache instead of from disk.

What if the file is not in RAM? In this case, it *is* retrieved from disk. However, after being sent to the user, it is also copied into the disk cache section of RAM. Later, if the user calls for the file again, the operating system retrieves it from the disk cache instead of going all the way back to disk. If the disk cache becomes full, the user files used the longest time ago are deleted first.

SAVING FILES

Figure E.2 shows that disk caching also makes saves to disk faster—or at least makes them seem faster to users. Here, the operating system needs to save two files. One is a system file, S. The other is a user file, U.

Contrary to what you might expect, the user file is given higher priority and is saved first. System files are saved only when there are no user disk reads or writes

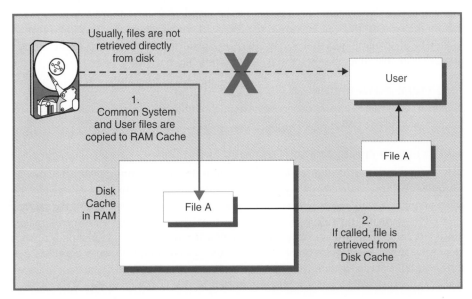

FIGURE **E.1**

Retrieval from Disk Cache

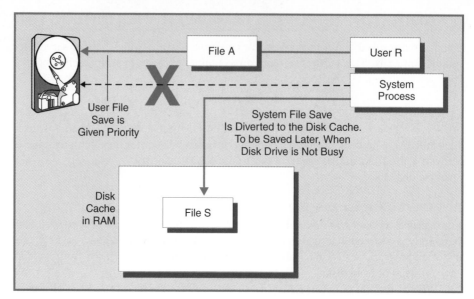

waiting to be done. User files are given higher priority because users experience delays during their file saves. They typically will not be able to do other work until after the save. Giving priority to user file saves reduces this waiting time.

Power Supply

Power supplies translate high-voltage wall power into the low-voltage power that computer components need. Power supplies are not glamorous, but if the power supply fails, the server fails.

Power supplies are especially important on servers. Priority-based saves in disk caching means that system files that need to be saved often have to wait. If power fails before the system files can be saved, the disk will contain the wrong system information. The systems administrator may have to spend hours or days restoring system files. During that time, the server may not be available to users.

MULTIPLE POWER SUPPLIES

Superservers typically have two power supplies within their systems unit. This gives redundancy. If one power supply fails, the system can keep running.

UNINTERRUPTIBLE POWER SUPPLIES

Power supplies sit inside the server's systems unit. In contrast, **uninterruptible power supplies (UPSs)** sit outside the systems unit, between the systems unit and the electrical wall plug. If wall power fails, the UPS continues to supply electricity to the server.

UPSs normally provide only enough electrical power to keep the server running for a few minutes. However, this is long enough for the systems administrator to shut down the server properly, so that all system files are written to disk. Many UPSs, in fact, can tell a server to shut itself down if wall power is lost for more than a few seconds. The server will shut down properly even if no one is around to shut it down.

Disk Technology

Obviously, servers require enormous amounts of hard disk storage. Webservers are likely to store thousands of webpages and associated image, sound, and video files. Database application servers, in turn, may store enormous databases.

SCSI DISK DRIVES

Most client PCs use **EIDE** disk drive technology, which is relatively inexpensive. In contrast, most high-end PC servers use **SCSI** (pronounced "skuzzy") drives, which are somewhat faster and considerably more expensive.

FIBRE CHANNEL

For extremely high-speed disk access, high-end servers are beginning to move beyond SCSI drive access to **Fibre Channel** disk access. Whereas SCSI hosts must be within about 12 meters of their disk drives, fibre channel allows disk drives to be hundreds of meters or even kilometers away from their hosts. In addition, fibre channel is significantly faster than SCSI. Fibre channel is leading to the creation of a new type of network, the server area network, which connects one or more servers to a hard disk "farm" containing many drives.

RAID DISK DRIVES

Disk drive speed is often the limiting factor in server performance. One way to get around this limitation is to use a disk technology called **RAID (redundant array of Inexpensive[1] drives).** As shown in Figure E.3, RAID does not use a single disk drive. Instead, it uses multiple disk drives controlled by a single controller board.

Note that the controller board has a separate line to each RAID drive. (In the example, there are six drives.) This means that the controller can transmit or receive several bits at a time in each clock cycle. In contrast, if you have only a single drive, the

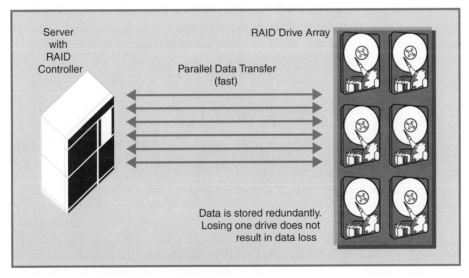

FIGURE E.3

Redundant Array of Inexpensive Drives (RAID)

Server with RAID Controller

RAID Drive Array

Parallel Data Transfer (fast)

Data is stored redundantly. Losing one drive does not result in data loss

---

[1] The standard uses the term *independent* instead of *inexpensive*, but *inexpensive* is more widely used.

controller can only send or receive a single bit in each clock cycle. As a result of this *parallel data transfer*, RAID can transfer data to and from the RAID drive extremely rapidly. No single drive, no matter how expensive, can match the speed of a good RAID array.

In addition, the most widely used versions of RAID store information *redundantly*. For instance, if the controller is saving eight bits, it will actually store more than these eight to represent the information. It will also distribute the bits across the drives. If one disk drive fails, the controller can still recover the original eight bits. In fact, most RAID arrays use hot-swappable drives, which can be switched while the RAID system is still running.

QUALITY OF SERVICE (QoS)

Quality of Service Parameters

When carriers market their services, they make certain claims about speed, latency, reliability, security, and other matters. Collectively, these service claims are called **quality of service (QoS)** guarantees.

Service-Level Agreements (SLAs)

Increasingly, users are demanding that carriers go beyond marketing claims and provide warranties, that is, legally enforceable guarantees. These warranties are called **service-level agreements (SLAs).** Service-level agreements specify such things as maximum latency times, percentage of time that the service will be available, and other quantitative QoS parameters.

Typically, there are penalties if the carrier fails to meet its SLA targets. This creates strong incentives for the carrier to avoid adding more subscribers than its network can handle.

Some companies now use service-level agreements internally. In such cases, the information systems (IS) department offers SLA guarantees to internal users. Although there are no monetary penalties if service-level agreements are not met, failing to meet SLAs will harm personnel performance reviews and, therefore, salaries, bonuses, and promotions.

High-Priority Traffic

A major concern in quality of service is the treatment of high-priority traffic that cannot endure latency (delay) or variable latency. Two obvious examples are telephony and video transmission. Another is real-time interactive terminal–host communication. Such applications must get through with very little delay and with very little variability in delay.

INSTALLING A HIGH-CAPACITY CAPACITY NETWORK

The simplest way to achieve low latency for high-priority traffic is to *ensure low latency for all traffic* by installing extremely high transmission capacity in the network. When any frame or packet reaches a switch, it will (probably) not have to wait to be processed.

Installing high transmission capacity is a brute force approach. It does not give special treatment to high-priority messages, and it certainly makes no guarantees. However, installing high capacity often is far less expensive than the two other techniques we discuss below for handling high-priority traffic. It also tends to be simpler technologically and organizationally. Often, the simplest approach is the most effective.

Of course, companies are not always good at estimating their capacity needs. If demand grows more than expected, the network will begin to approach its capacity. High-priority applications will begin to experience unacceptable degradation long before the network is saturated.

It is always important to consider network capacity, however. If a network does not have sufficient capacity, then problems are guaranteed. To ensure that high-priority traffic gets through on a network with insufficient capacity, you will have to create such excessive delays in lower-priority traffic that the situation will be unacceptable to users.

PRIORITIZATION

There are two general ways to handle high-priority data. One is to define **priority** levels for traffic. If frames or packets of different priority levels enter a switch at the same time, the switch will send high-priority transmission out first.

For instance, as discussed in Module C, the IEEE 802 LAN MAN Standards Committee is now defining a way to introduce priority levels in LANs. The effort will create eight levels of priority from zero to seven. Frames with higher-priority levels will always be sent out first.

As Module C discusses, there are two ways to implement priority levels. One is to add a priority field to each frame or packet. This is **explicit tagging.** When a frame or packet arrives at a switch, the switch places it in a queue consistent with its priority level. Frames in higher-priority queues will be sent out before frames in lower-priority queues.

In **implicit tagging,** in contrast, nothing is added to frames or packets. Instead, the frame examines each incoming message. Based on the source address, the contents of the application PDU header, or some other criterion, the switch affords priority to a frame or packet and places it into the appropriate priority queue.

In networking, it is important to distinguish between quality of service (QoS) on the one hand and **class of service (COS)** on the other. QoS is a very broad concept. It guarantees certain transmission service parameters. COS is one of several techniques used to implement QoS. Other QoS techniques do not divide traffic into categories in order to achieve guarantees.

RESERVATION

Priority levels give preference to higher-priority frames and packets. Yet if the network is congested, all frames will suffer latency, even frames of the highest priority. Priority levels *do not guarantee* a target level of latency.

A more robust approach to handling high-priority data is to guarantee throughput by reserving capacity for a stream of messages on each switch along the path between the two end stations. This **reservation** system ensures that when a frame or packet in such a stream arrives at a switch, the switch will have the capacity available to handle it immediately.

The problem with reservations approaches is that when the reserved capacity is not used, it is wasted. Unless reservations are very carefully managed, there will not be enough capacity for other applications that may have lower performance but that are still very important to an organization.

Policy Enforcement

With both prioritization and reservation systems, companies have to create reasonable **policies** and enforce them carefully. Otherwise, many users may give their applications higher priority or reserved bandwidth when it is not justified.

One method of policy enforcement is to give switches enforcement powers. For instance, when a switch sees a high-priority frame or packet arrive, it can check to see if the source address is authorized to set high priority. In the case of reservation systems, the switch can see if the source address is authorized to make high-priority reservations.

Or, the switch can examine the header of the application PDU. Usually, priority depends on the application. If a frame containing e-mail or a World Wide Web download arrives with a high-priority tag, the switch can override the tag and give the message lower priority. It can do the same if the frame arrives in a reserved channel.

Another approach is to use free market principles and charge more for priority service or reservations. Instead of creating arbitrary rules, this approach allows users to decide when low latency is worth the cost of providing it. For instance, in web-enabled transaction processing (see Chapter 8), World Wide Web download speed is critically important to productivity. In other cases, World Wide Web downloads can be highly tolerant of delays. Rather than creating business rules that deal with such subtleties, companies can rely on the business judgments of their managers.

LEASED LINES

As Chapter 5 discussed, **leased lines** provide point-to-point service. On the negative side, this makes them very limiting. You can communicate only between two points.

On the positive side, you reduce the cost of communication between those two points. For telephone calls, you will pay much less per minute than you would if you use direct distance dialing. This is particularly true because leased lines allow you to multiplex many voice calls.

Leased Lines and Switched Data Networks

For data transmission, however, if you have even three or four sites, a switched data network almost always will be cheaper than a mesh of leased lines connecting all the sites (see Chapter 5). Overall, a mesh of leased lines makes little sense for data communications.

At the same time, if you use a public switched data network (PSDN), you need an access line from each site to the PSDN's point of presence, as discussed in Chapter 5 and later in this module. This access line is almost always a leased line. So while switched data networks may eliminate the need for large meshes of leased lines for data transmission, access line requirements will continue to keep leased lines important in corporate planning.

To connect a site to a switched data network, you need a router or some other access device. As Chapter 5 discussed, the access device probably will have multiple ports.

Each port going to the PSDN really connects to a leased line. This leased line connects you to the PSDN's point of presence (POP). So even if you are connecting to a switched data network, at the physical layer, you are using a leased line connection from your access device.

Leased Line Categories

As Table 5.1 in Chapter 5 showed, leased lines come in a variety of speeds. We will look briefly at each of the categories of leased lines.

ANALOG VOICE-GRADE LEASED LINES

The slowest leased lines use the analog voice-grade technology that you use every day when you call people on the telephone. Analog voice-grade leased lines are slow and have high error rates. Faster lines are always digital. This reduces errors dramatically. Once, analog voice-grade lines were the most widely used leased lines. Today, they are only a memory in most firms.

DIGITAL 64 KBPS LEASED LINES

The slowest digital leased lines run at 64 kbps (often 56 kbps). Chapter 3 explained that if you digitize a voice signal, this generates a 64 kbps data stream. So the slowest digital lines were designed to transmit voice in digital form.

T1 AND E1 LEASED LINES

Higher-speed digital leased lines range from small multiples of 64 kbps to more than one gigahertz. For telephony, these higher-speed lines allow the carrier to multiplex several 64 kbps voice conversations on a single leased line. Originally, the slowest multiplexed line ran at 1.544 Mbps in North America and some other parts of the world (**T1** line) or 2.048 Mbps in Europe and some other areas (**E1** line). T1 and E1 leased lines multiplex 24 and 30 voice calls, respectively. Module B discusses how multiplexing is done on T1 lines. Of course, the firm can also use the entire capacity of the T1 or E1 line to send high-speed data or video, instead of using the leased line to multiplex voice calls.

FRACTIONAL T1 LEASED LINES

Most corporate demand for long-distance transmission falls into the range from 64 kbps to 1 or 2 Mbps. Because 64 kbps lines and T1/E1 lines bracket the extremes of this range, we would like lines with intermediate capacity, in order to give customers more choices.

For companies with intermediate needs, many carriers offer **fractional T1** leased lines. As the name suggests, these lines have a fraction of a T1 line's capacity. Typical speeds are 128 kbps, 256 kbps, 384 kbps, and 768 kbps. Most carriers offer only one or two of these speeds.

T3 AND E3 LEASED LINES

For companies with very heavy transmission needs, **T3** and **E3** leased lines are attractive. (Carriers normally do not offer T2 and E2 service.) Until recently, only the largest companies needed such lines, and they needed them only on their most dense routes.

These lines can multiplex large numbers of telephone calls or can be used as high-capacity data pipes.

SONET/SDH LEASED LINES

For even higher speeds, there is a new series of high-speed digital leased lines. In the United States, these are called **SONET (Synchronous Optical Network)** lines. In Europe, they are called **SDH (Synchronous Digital Hierarchy)** lines. However, although there are naming differences, SONET and SDH leased lines are compatible.

SONET/SDH service normally begins at 156 Mbps and offers the next speed of 622 Mbps. Very few end user organizations require such speeds, but they are available if needed. Some very large websites connect to the Internet at such speeds.

FRAME RELAY

As Chapter 5 noted, Frame Relay dominates packet switched data networking today.

Origins

The first commercial packet switched data network was **X.25,** which borrowed heavily from ARPANET technology. However, given the concerns of commercial customers for reliability, X.25 focused much more on error reduction. In fact, it did error detection and correction at each hop between X.25 switches! This made X.25 very slow. Its maximum speed was only 64 kbps, and most links ran at only 9,600 bps or even less. This was sufficient for terminal–host communication but is not sufficient for modern transmission needs. X.25 is still available in many parts of the world. In less-developed countries, it may be the only choice.

X.25 was notable for introducing permanent virtual circuits (see Chapter 5). Instead of the ARPANET's switch-by-switch routing (similar to router operation on the Internet), X.25 created what were in effect layer 2 connections between end points.

Despite some important differences, Frame Relay is fairly similar to X.25. In fact, some X.25 switches can be upgraded with software to handle Frame Relay transmission. However, although X.25 was designed to be bulletproof, Frame Relay lives dangerously. Frame Relay does not do error detection and correction on each hop between pairs of switches. Nor does Frame Relay have very good flow control.

As a result, however, Frame Relay places much lower processing burdens on switches than does X.25. This allows much higher speeds, much lower costs, or some combination of the two. It also reduces the latency (delay) at each switch.

The Frame Relay Frame

Figure E.4 shows the basic Frame Relay frame for carrying user information. Note that it is very simple, consisting of only two header fields and two trailer fields. (We will later see that the address field has internal structure.)

OUT-OF-BAND SIGNALING

Note also that there is no control field. There is no way to send commands within Frame Relay frames. Switches have to communicate with one another through other types of frames if they are to send control information. This is called **out-of-band signaling.**

FLAG 01111110	ADDRESS (2–4 octets)	INFORMATION (variable)	FCS (2 octets)	FLAG 01111110

Note: FCS = Frame Control Sequence

FIGURE **E.4**
The Frame Relay Frame

FLAGS

The frame begins and ends with one-octet **flag** fields that have the value 01111110.[2] The **start flag** at the beginning of the frame is like the Ethernet preamble and start of frame delimiter fields we saw in Chapter 4. However, start flags are only one octet long, compared to the eight octets that begin the Ethernet MAC layer frame. The start flag signals the beginning of the frame and allows synchronization.

The **stop flag,** in turn, ensures that the receiver knows that the frame has ended. With the stop flag, no length field is needed.

FRAME CHECK SEQUENCE

The **frame check sequence (FCS)** field allows each switch to check for errors in the Frame Relay header. If it finds such an error, the switch discards the frame. Note that only the brief header is checked—not the full frame.

ADDRESS FIELDS

The **address** field is fairly complex. Figure E.5 shows the two-octet version of the address field. We will see later that there are also three- and four-octet versions.

ADDRESSING

Data Link Control Identifier (DLCI) The **data link control identifier (DLCI)** field identifies a specific virtual circuit. In the 2-octet address option, it has 10 bits. This allows 1,024 (2^{10}) virtual circuits to be identified.

Note that the DLCI does not give the address of the destination computer. Instead, it identifies a route for getting there. To give an analogy, when you fly commercially, your aircraft has a flight number instead of being called by the name of the destination city.

1	2	3	4	5	6	7	8
Data Link Control Indicator (High Order)						C/R 0/1	AE 0
Data Link Control Indicator (Low Order)				FECN	BECN	DE	AE 1

FIGURE **E.5**
Address Field in Frame Relay Frame

Notes:
C/R = Command/Response
AE = Address Extension
FECN = Forward Explicit Congestion Notification
BECN = Backward Explicit Congestion Notification
DE = Discard Eligible

---

[2] What if the pattern 01111110 appears somewhere in the data being delivered? There is a process called "bit stuffing" that adds another "1" in the octet where the reserved 01111110 pattern appears.

Address Extension (AE) The **address extension (AE)** bit is set to one if the octet it ends is the last octet in the address field. Otherwise, it is set to zero. In Figure E.5, there are two octets. So the AE bit in the first octet is zero, and the AE bit in the second octet is one.

Using the address extension bit, it is possible to add either one or two more octets to the address field. If more octets are added, each will contain 7 more DLCI bits plus an AE bit. In other words, adding a third octet raises the size of the DLCI field from 10 to 17 bits. Adding a fourth octet raises the DLCI to 24 bits.

Local Significance The DLCI in the address field has only local significance, that is, significance within the customer's internal network. This means that the access device must map internal DLCIs into the Frame Relay carrier's DLCIs established for the firm's virtual circuits on the network.

CONGESTION CONTROL

Three fields are used for a crude form of congestion control in Frame Relay.

Discard Eligible As discussed later in this section, most Frame Relay networks offer two speeds to customers. The lower rate—the **committed information rate (CIR)**—is guaranteed, although not completely. The higher rate—the **available bit rate (ABR)**—is for bursts at speeds above the CIR. For transmissions within the CIR, the **discard eligible (DE)** bit is set to zero. For frames going faster than the CIR, the discard eligible bit is set to one. If there is congestion, the Frame Relay vendor will begin by discarding only frames with the discard eligible set to one. In high congestion, however, even frames with the discard eligible bit set to zero may be discarded.

Explicit Congestion Notification Fields If a Frame Relay switch begins to experience congestion, it will tell stations to reduce their transmission rate. It does this by setting one of the two explicit congestion notification fields. The receiving station will see the explicit congestion notification field and act appropriately.

The **Backward Explicit Congestion Notification (BECN)** field is set to tell the station that receives the frame to slow down. This is easy to implement.

The **Forward Explicit Congestion Notification (FECN)** field is more complex. If a station receives this notification in an incoming frame, it should tell its communication partner *at the other end* of the Frame Relay network to slow down.

COMMAND/RESPONSE

The **command/response (C/R)** field allows the two communicating parties to indicate that a message is either a command or response message. If the command/response distinction is not meaningful for the communication, the two parties ignore this field.

ATM

The Status of ATM

We saw **ATM** in Chapter 5. At one time, many analysts felt that ATM would become the "everything network." It would carry both voice and data. It would be our main networking technology for both LANs and WANs. In the words of a famous *Saturday Night Live* skit, it would be both a dessert topping *and* a floor wax.

Yet ATM faltered when it first appeared. First, standards for this complex technology took a long time to emerge. Then, Frame Relay speeds proved adequate for most corporate WAN needs. Finally, in site networks and LANs, Ethernet switches offered products in roughly the same speed range as ATM with far lower technology and training costs. Although ATM had its niches, such as LANs for scientific computing, it did not penetrate broader markets. In addition, although technically superior to its alternatives, it was also complex to install and manage. In the final analysis, it initially had clear advantages—when it had them at all—only at speeds much higher than most corporations needed. As one pessimist said, "It's the wave of the future. And always will be."

Despite its initial disappointments, ATM is now moving into the mainstream, at least for wide area networking. Frame Relay dominates public switched data network demand today because it offers the speed range corporations need most at reasonable cost. However, as discussed in Chapter 5, many companies need ATM speeds for at least some of their site-to-site links.

Most switched data network vendors now offer Frame Relay and ATM as a paired team, with seamless pricing from 64 kbps to over a gigabit per second. Over time, as demand grows, ATM should eventually dominate the PSDN market.

On the Internet, furthermore, many of the BFRs (big routers) in the fastest parts of the Internet's core backbone are really ATM switches. Given ATM's likely eventual dominance in PSDNs, ATM has the potential to be used for a good portion of all long-distance transmission in the next few years.

For site networking, the picture is less clear. As Chapter 5 discussed, Ethernet has proven to be amazingly scalable. Certainly, 100Base-TX and 100Base-FX switches give most corporations the speed they need today, and gigabit Ethernet promises to extend Ethernet speed into the heartland of ATM service speeds.

Even with doubtful conditions at the site level, however, ATM's slow march into wide area networking should make it a critical technology for new IT specialists to learn.

Layering: ATM versus AAL

ATM follows OSI layering for subnets. Its standards are limited to the physical and data link layer.

We saw in Chapter 4 that the IEEE subdivided the data link layer into the media access control and logical link control layers. Figure E.6 shows that the ITU-T also subdivided the data link layer into two layers in ATM. These are the **ATM layer** and the **ATM adaption layer (AAL).**

▶ The (lower) ATM layer is application-*independent*. It provides the same frame transmission process regardless of the application (voice, videoconferencing, timing-insensitive data, and so forth.) Think of ATM as a train carrying boxcars whose contents are irrelevant to the railroad.

▶ The (upper) ATM adaption layer (AAL), in turn, handles different requirements in different applications. For instance, voice needs constant frame delivery rates, whereas for data it is more important to get more capacity when sending a large burst. The job of the ATM Adaption Layer is to build on ATM layer services to provide the specific transmission characteristics each application needs.

OSI	ATM	
Data Link	ATM Adaption Layer (AAL) (Application-Dependent)	Convergence Services (CS)
		Segment Assembly/Reassembly (SAR)
	ATM (Application-Independent)	
Physical	Physical	

The ATM Layer: Built for Speed

Most people who have heard about ATM have heard about the characteristics of the ATM layer. They have heard, correctly, that ATM transmission consists of fixed-length frames called **cells.** These cells, furthermore, are extremely short, consisting of only 53 bytes—5 bytes of ATM header and 48 bytes of payload (data).

LOW LATENCY AT EACH SWITCH

This short and constant cell length was selected to minimize the latency (delay) at each switch. ATM was created to carry telephone calls as well as data, and human conversation is extremely intolerant of delay. So the latency at each switch must be kept to an absolute minimum, even over intercontinental distances, when transmissions must travel through several switches.

PREDICTABILITY

One reason why it is possible to have low latency at each switch is processing efficiency. When a cell arrives at a switch, the switch does not have to waste time examining a length field before allocating temporary storage space to the frame. It knows exactly how long the frame will be.

SHORT DELAYS AT EACH SWITCH

Another way that cells minimize delays follows from the fact that the frame may have to be read entirely before being sent out again. For a 53-octet cell, this delay will be only 424 bit periods. In contrast, for an Ethernet frame of 1,500 octets, the delay would be 12,000 bit periods! So when a cell arrives at a switch, it will not have to wait long before being sent out again.

VIRTUAL CIRCUITS

Another way in which ATM reduces latency at each switch is by using virtual circuits, that is, connection-oriented service. Recall from Chapter 5 that virtual circuits allow simple table lookups to be used when a frame arrives in order to decide which port on the switch should be used to send the cell out again. The software merely notes the virtual circuit number (DLCI), looks up the output port for that virtual circuit number, and sends the frame back out again.

Bit 1	Bit 2	Bit 3	Bit 4	Bit 5	Bit 6	Bit 7	Bit 8
Generic Flow Control				Virtual Path Identifier			
Virtual Path Identifier				Virtual Channel Identifier			
Virtual Channel Identifier							
Virtual Channel Identifier				Payload Type		reserved	Cell Loss Priority
Header Error Control							
Payload (48 Octets)							

The ATM Cell

Figure E.7 shows the ATM cell. As noted above, the header is 5 octets long. The data field, called the **payload,** is 48 octets long.

GENERIC FLOW CONTROL

These four bits can be set for flow control. However, their use is still under development. Furthermore, these bits are used only for flow control within a site network. When the router sends the cell to the network, it creates a new header in which these four bits are not used.

VIRTUAL CIRCUIT

Note that the ATM header does not contain a destination address per se. Rather, it contains two fields, the virtual path identifier (VPI) and the virtual channel identifier (VCI). Collectively, they label the cell's virtual circuit in a way we discuss a bit later.

To give you an analogy, if you want to go someplace by bus, you do not look for that place name on the front of the bus when the bus arrives. Instead, you look for the bus's route number. Virtual circuit labels are like route numbers on a bus. They specify the path, rather than the end destination.

The two parts of the ATM virtual circuit reflect the realities of corporate communication. First, from any particular site, your frames may have to flow to another site. Second, once there, your cells must go to a particular computer at that site.

Similarly, in ATM, the **virtual path identifier (VPI)** can point to a particular site. Within this flow from site to site, **virtual channel identifiers (VCIs)** can point to particular computers at that site.

Figure E.7 shows that the VPI field is 8 bits long. This is enough to represent 256 VPIs. So a user can specify 256 sites. The 16 bits of the VCI field, in turn, are enough to represent 65,536 VCIs within each VPI. Collectively, these 3 octets provide a very rich address space.

Figure E.7 shows the header for cells transmitted by a computer within an organization. As noted above, the access device that connects the site to the ATM network access line creates a new header when submitting the cell to the ATM carrier. This new header uses the first 12 bits to form a longer virtual path identifier meaningful to the ATM carrier. It also may create a new 16-bit virtual channel identifier meaningful to the ATM carrier. So the VPI and VCI in the header sent by the user have only local significance. The access device must translate the user's VPI and VCI into the VPI and VCI meaningful to the ATM carrier's network.

PAYLOAD TYPE

The **payload type** field is set to 00 for information cells—cells containing information to be delivered end to end.

RESERVED BIT

Another bit is reserved for future use.

CELL LOSS PRIORITY

The **cell loss priority (CLP)** bit is set to one if discarding is allowed or to zero if discarding is not allowed. If a station is sending a burst of data above its guaranteed committed information rate, it must set the cell loss priority bit to one.

HEADER ERROR CONTROL

The fifth octet of the ATM cell header is the **header error control** field. As its name implies, this field is used to detect errors *in the header*, not in the entire cell. This is needed because a header error can lead to serious network problems, such as misdirecting a cell to the wrong virtual path or virtual channel. If errors are found, the ATM switch discards the cell.

PERSPECTIVE ON THE ATM LAYER

Overall, the ATM layer is designed for speed. There is minimal processing at each node. This sacrifices flow control, end-to-end correction, and other desirable propagation characteristics. However, these sacrifices are needed to achieve very low latency at each switch.

At the same time, ATM cells have high overhead. The five header octets that are sent for each 48 octets of data represent an overhead of 10%. As we will see next, there is also considerable overhead in the ATM Adaption Layer (AAL).

The ATM Adaption Layer (AAL)

The ATM layer is application-*independent*. All cells are transmitted in exactly the same way whether they are snippets of voice in a conversation or parts of a data file transfer.

However, the ATM standard needs a way to serve the specific needs of different types of services. For instance, telephone conversations need very steady delivery with almost zero latency. File transfers, in turn, are more sensitive to the support of large traffic bursts.

The ATM Adaption Layer (AAL) adds whatever functionality is needed for specific applications to work effectively and efficiently over the ATM cell delivery express in the ATM layer.

AAL CLASS OF SERVICE SAR TYPE OF OPERATION	CLASS A TYPE 1	CLASS B TYPE 2	CLASS C TYPE 3	CLASS D TYPE 4
Exact timing (no jitter)	Yes	Yes	No	No
Bit rate	Constant	Variable	Variable	Variable
Connection oriented (CONS) or connectionless (CNLS)	CONS	CONS	CONS	CNLS
Example	Telephony	Video-conferencing with varying motion	Connection-oriented data transmission	CNLS data transmission

CONVERGENCE SERVICES LAYER

Figure E.6 shows that the ATM Adaption Layer is further subdivided into a convergence services layer and a segmentation and reassembly layer.

The **convergence services (CS)** layer examines the application and decides what class of service is needed. Figure E.8 shows that the convergence services layer specifies four **classes of service,** labeled A, B, C, and D. For each class of service at the convergence services layer, there is a corresponding **type of service** at the segmentation and reassembly layer.

▶ **Class A** service has exact timing, a constant bit rate, and connection-oriented service. It is good for telephony.

▶ **Class B** service is like Class A service but allows a variable bit rate. This is useful in videoconferencing, where sudden motion may benefit from a larger bandwidth for a second or two.

▶ Class C and Class D are good for data. Both provide a variable bit rate for high-speed data bursts. **Class C** service supports connection-oriented data transmission, which allows error correction and flow control. **Class D** service is good for connectionless service with its simple operation and high-speed delivery.

THE SEGMENTATION AND REASSEMBLY SUBLAYER

The bottom layer of the ATM adaption layer (see Figure E.6) is the **segmentation and reassembly (SAR)** sublayer. As the name suggests, this layer accepts whatever the convergence services sublayer above it sends down. The SAR sublayer then fragments the convergence services sublayer PDU and places the segments in one or more SAR-PDUs. The SAR layer then passes the SAR-PDUs down to the ATM layer for transmission. At the other end, the receiving computer reverses the process. Its ATM layer passes the SAR-PDU up to the SAR sublayer.

SAR Protocol Data Units (SAR-PDUs) Just as the ATM layer has a protocol data unit structure, the segmentation and reassembly sublayer has a 48-bit SAR-PDU, which is carried in the payload field of an ATM cell.

Type 1 SAR-PDUs Each type of operation has a different SAR-PDU organization. For example, in Type 1 operation, where voice must be sent with minimum delay, the SAR-PDU contains only a single octet of header containing only a 4-bit sequence number for the SAR frame and another 4-bit number designed for sequence number error detection.

Type 4 SAR-PDUs For other types of operation, the situation is more complex. For example, Figure E.9 shows the SAR-PDU for Type 4 operation.

The **ST (segment type)** field tells whether the cell is the beginning of a multi-SAR-PDU convergence services layer PDU, the continuation of a multi-SAR-PDU convergence services layer PDU, the end of a multicell message, or a single-cell message.

The **SN (sequence number)** allows missing cells to be detected.

Like the segment type field, the MID field is used for the convergence services sublayer PDU segmentation. The **MID (Multiplexing Identification)** value is the same for all SAR-PDUs carrying a single convergence services sublayer PDU. So the receiver collects all SAR-PDUs with the same MID value and then orders them by sequence number.

The **(LI) length indicator** field, in turn, indicates the number of bytes of convergence services layer PDU contained in the payload field. This 6-bit field is needed because there are a fixed number of bits (48) in the payload field, and the convergence services sublayer PDU may not fill them all.

Finally, there is a 10-bit **CRC (Cyclic Redundancy Check)** field, which is used for error detection. The CRC field covers the entire SAR-PDU.

More Overhead SAR-PDUs add still more overhead to ATM transmission. In Type 4 operation, for instance, only 44 octets of convergence services layer data are sent in the SAR data field. Another 9 octets of SAR and ATM fields are overhead. So the combined ATM–SAR overhead adds 20% to convergence services layer data delivery!

THE CONVERGENCE SERVICES SUBLAYER

The **convergence services** sublayer uses the capabilities of Type 1 through Type 4 SAR operation. It builds upon them to offer whatever is needed for Class A through Class D service at the overall ATM Adaption Layer. It provides the selected class of service to the next-higher layer.

The convergence services sublayer also adds to overhead. Most obviously, there is a **convergence services layer PDU,** which also has a header and a trailer. Fortunately,

FIGURE E.9

Type 4 Segmentation and Reassembly PDU

ST (4 bits)	SN (4 bits)	MID (10 bits)	SAR-PDU PAYLOAD (44 octets, 352 bits)	LI (6 bits)	CRC (10 bits)

Notes:
   ST = Segment Type
   SN = Sequence Number
   MID = Multiplexing Identification
   SAR = Segmentation and Reassembly
   LI = Length Indicator
   CRC = Cyclic Redundancy Check

a convergence services layer PDU does not have to fit into a single cell, so this header and trailer overhead will be spread across several cells.

More subtly but of considerable importance, the convergence services layer offers a **streaming mode** option for applications that need very low latency. In this case, the layer above the convergence services layer provides data in very short blocks. Each block is sent in a separate SAR-PDU, so that there will be no waiting while SAR-PDU data fields are filled to capacity. As soon as a block arrives, it can be sent in an outgoing cell. Of course, this also saves time at the other end because there is no complex reassembly.[3]

Although the streaming mode option reduces latency, it can add strongly to overhead. Suppose that the block supplied by the next-higher layer is only 2 octets long. In this case, only 2 octets in each ATM cell will contain data. The other fields—ATM header and trailer, SAR header and trailer, and unused octets—constitute 51 octets of overhead. This represents an overhead of over 2,000%! Although this example may be extreme, streaming mode convergence services sublayer operation has the potential to raise overhead to an alarming degree.

The ATM Physical Layer

To move data at 156 Mbps, 622 Mbps, or even higher speeds, ATM needs a very good physical layer. We will look first at framing and then at sublayering within the physical layer.

CELL-BASED PHYSICAL LAYER

The ITU-T has designed two approaches to framing at the physical layer. The first is the simplest. This is just to send cells back to back, with no gaps between successive frames. This is like placing data on successive stairs on an escalator. Although this approach has very low overhead, it does not offer a good way of handling supervisory signaling.

SONET/SDH–BASED PHYSICAL LAYER

A more elegant approach is used in most ATM installations. This approach uses the SONET/SDH technology now used by telephone companies for a growing fraction of their long-distance communication. **SONET (Synchronous Optical Network)** is the name of this approach in the United States. Other countries use a slightly different but fully compatible technology called **SDH (Synchronous Digital Hierarchy).**

For speeds of 155.52 Mbps, the SONET/SDH ATM frame has 2,490 octets. A frame is sent every 125 microseconds, giving the 155.2 Mbps aggregate transmission rate.

For supervisory purposes, each frame has 324 octets of control information. This represents an overhead of 15%.

PHYSICAL SUBLAYERS

Just as ATM subdivides the data link layer, it subdivides the physical layer into four layers.

---

[3] Actually, there is one small complication. A convergence layer PDU will contain a header, a trailer, and multiple blocks. The first block must share its cell with the convergence layer header, while the last block must share its cell with the convergence layer trailer. However, this changes the picture only slightly.

- ▶ **Path Layer.** The highest layer is the *path layer*, which is responsible for end-to-end data transmission across multiple switches between two computers.
- ▶ **Line Layer.** Between the two end computers, there are likely to be multiple *multiplexers* that add data streams to the overall frame and remove them from the frame. Multiplexers are like highway on-ramps and off-ramps, which allow new cars to come onto the freeway and to leave it. The *line layer* handles transmission between multiplexers.
- ▶ **Section Layer.** The *section-layer* controls information between *repeaters*, which periodically regenerate the signal to keep it from being damaged during transmission. There are likely to be multiple repeaters between multiplexers.
- ▶ **Photonic Layer.** The *photonic layer* is the bottom-most physical layer. It is concerned with light transmission through the optical fiber carrying the signal. (ATM was designed for optical fiber transmission but has been extended to use unshielded twisted pair wire for desktop runs.) As Module B discusses, the ATM photonic layer uses a ring topology to connect the multiplexers that allow frames to enter and leave the network.

Other ATM Complexities

If ATM transmission seems complex, that is because it really is complex. In fact, there are many complexities we have not discussed. We will mention only two of them.

LANE

ATM has a **LAN emulation (LANE)** standard that allows a local ATM network to act like a (very expensive) traditional Ethernet network. This allows ATM to fit into existing corporate networks. It also allows the emulation of virtual LANs (VLANs) for security purposes and to reduce broadcast transmission. Chapter 5 and Module C discuss VLANs.

MPOA

Multiprotocol over ATM (MPOA) describes how IP, IPX, and other internet layer packets can be transmitted over ATM networks. It allows ATM networks to act much like routed networks.

ATM in Perspective

In many ways, ATM is like a racing car. It is extremely fast and sophisticated. It is also very complex and expensive. Much of its cost stems not so much from equipment costs (although these are high too), but from training and management time. Racing cars need large pit crews. So do ATM networks.

Another concern with ATM is overhead. As we have just seen, every layer adds overhead to cell transmission. In the case of the streaming transmission option that is good for voice transmission, the added overhead is especially problematic. Although this overhead adds to the capabilities of ATM, it makes ATM less attractive compared to switched Ethernet for local transmission.

For wide area networking, ATM has much higher overhead than Frame Relay. As a result, when organizations move from Frame Relay transmission to ATM transmission, they must be careful to calculate the actual improvement in throughput they can expect. Moving from 1 Mbps Frame Relay to 156 Mbps ATM does not bring a 156-fold increase in throughput.

SWITCHED DATA NETWORK PRICING

If you wish to buy Frame Relay or ATM service, Figure E.10 and Figure E.11 show that there are several costs involved.

Access Equipment

Most obviously, you need an **access device** to connect you to the carrier's network. At the data link layer, each port must handle the type of communication activities that the switched data network requires.

At the physical layer, each access device port must have a CSU/DSU matched to the type of leased line being used. The **data service unit (DSU)** translates between the site network and leased line digital formats, as discussed in Chapter 3. The **channel service unit (CSU)** limits voltages and other transmission characteristics that might cause harm to the carrier network.

Leased Line to the POP

You also need a **leased line** from your site to the PSDN's **point of presence (POP).** This leased line can be quite expensive, especially if the SDN does not have a POP in your site's city. In that case, you must get a leased access line to the PSDN carrier's POP in another city.

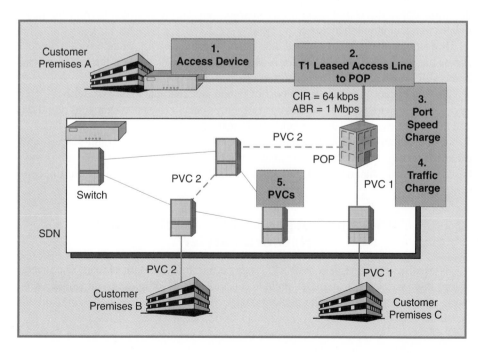

FIGURE E.10

Switched Data Network Pricing

ELEMENT	VENDOR	DETAIL
Access Device	Hardware vendor	Hardware to connect your site network to the first switch through the leased access line
Leased Access Line	Telephone company	To connect your site to the switched data network
		Setup charge and monthly charge; sometimes per-megabyte charge
Port Charge	PSDN carrier	Single port speed charge
		Based on both committed information rate and available bit rate
Traffic Charge	PSDN carrier	Charge per megabyte transmitted
PVC Charge	PSDN carrier	Charge per permanent virtual circuit; may include speed and traffic charges
SVC Charge	PSDN carrier	Charge per SVC is systems that offer switched virtual circuits

Note a subtle but important fact. The public switched data network carrier usually does not supply the leased access line. Instead, you get the leased line from the telephone company or another carrier.

Sometimes the public switched data network provider will arrange for the leased access line and may even bill you for it. However, even in such cases, the leased access line is still provided by a different carrier.

So you cannot just look at the cost of public switched data network service. You also need to consider the substantial costs of leased access lines between your premises and the public switched data network's POP nearest each site.

Usually, there is a hookup charge for installing the leased line (and perhaps another for taking it down). There is also a monthly charge to the telephone company based on speed, distance, and perhaps the amount of traffic on the leased access line.

Hookup Charges by the Switched Data Network Carrier

Normally, switched data networks assess a one-time **hookup charge** to connect you to their service. This handles the administrative work of adding you to their network. This is separate from the hookup charge you pay to the telephone company to install the leased access line.

Port Charges

You connect to a port on one of the PSDN's switches. You will be charged a monthly fee for using this port. This port fee usually is the most expensive aspect of Frame Relay or ATM Service.

SIMPLE PORT SPEED CHARGES

The simplest **port speed** charges are based on the speed of the port. Usually, port speeds start at 64 kbps.

CIR AND ABR PORT SPEED CHARGES

As noted earlier in this module, many Frame Relay and ATM vendors offer a more complex port charge based on two speeds—a **committed information rate (CIR)** and an **available bit rate (ABR).**

As noted above, the committed information rate is pretty much guaranteed, although in times of very high congestion, the vendor may not be able to support the CIR. To give an example, suppose that the CIR is 64 kbps.

You can transmit bursts above the CIR rate. You can transmit as fast as the available bit rate. To continue the example, suppose the ABR is one megabit per second. However, bits sent faster than the CIR will be the first bits to be discarded if there is congestion.

PORT SPEED AND ACCESS LINE SPEED

The speed of the leased access line must be able to support the port speed. There is not much point having a one megabit per second port speed if you have only a 64 kbps leased access line. You cannot transmit faster than your access line. For a port speed of one megabit per second, for example, you need a T1 (1.544 Mbps) or E1 access line (2.048 Mbps). The access line must be as fast as the port speed or faster.

What about access lines if you have a CIR and an ABR? If you have an access line at the CIR speed, in this case, 64 kbps, you will not be able to transmit any faster. So having an ABR of 1 Mbps will do little good. You need an access line as fast as the ABR.

Traffic Charges

Some vendors charge only by the port speed. Others have a lower port speed charge but add a **traffic charge** for each bit sent. This gives use-sensitive pricing.

Permanent Virtual Circuits (PVCs)

Over the one leased access line from your site to the public switched data network cloud, you may multiplex several **permanent virtual circuits,** each connecting you to a different site.

There will be a separate charge for each PVC the PSDN must support. Usually, the charge per PVC is small compared to the charge for the port. Some carriers have a flat monthly fee per PVC while others have usage-sensitive pricing.

The PVC charge may also depend on the speed of the PVC. If there are set speeds for PVCs, both your access line speed and your port speed must be great enough to support the total of all PVC speeds.

Switched Virtual Circuit Pricing

Some Frame Relay and ATM vendors also offer **switched virtual circuits (SVCs).** Chapter 5 discussed SVCs. Basically, they are like lease lines, limiting you to two points. However, SVCs are set up only when one party wishes to call another, not weeks or months ahead of time, as in PVCs. Establishing an SVC is more complex than placing a telephone call, but they are similar in operation.

At the time of this writing, SVC pricing is still in its infancy. However, we do know that SVC setup and breakdown places fairly heavy burdens on the PSDN carrier's switches. In addition, per-setup billing will be much more complex than charging a flat monthly fee for dedicated connections.

REVIEW QUESTIONS

CORE REVIEW QUESTIONS

1. Why does a server need a great deal of RAM? In what two ways does disk caching speed service to the user?
2. Why does a server need an uninterruptible power supply (UPS)?
3. Why do most servers use SCSI drives? What is RAID? What are the two benefits of RAID?
4. What are some benefits sought in quality of service (QoS)? What is a service-level agreement (SLA)? Why is it important?
5. What are the three main ways of reducing latency for high-priority applications?
6. Why are leased lines important even if you use a public switched data network?
7. What is the slowest speed digital leased line? What is the speed of a T1 line? What is the speed of an E1 line?
8. Why do organizations want fractional T1 lines?
9. In Frame Relay and ATM, why does the frame header NOT give the address of the destination station?
10. What are the layers in ATM? Describe the function of each.
11. Why does ATM have high overhead?
12. What are the main costs in Frame Relay and ATM?

DETAILED REVIEW QUESTIONS

1. What is the advantage of fiber channel? What new way of organizing disks does it allow?
2. Explain why sufficient capacity is needed in all three ways to reduce latency for high-priority applications.
3. Explain why policy enforcement is important in techniques for reducing latency in the delivery of high-priority frames.

4. In the T-series of leased lines, which line follows the T1 in speed? How many times faster is it?
5. What are common speeds of SONET/SDH?
6. How long is the address in Frame Relay?
7. Explain flow control in Frame Relay.
8. How long is the address in ATM? Describe the four service types in ATM.

THOUGHT QUESTIONS

1. Distinguish between quality of service and class of service. Why is QoS the broader category?
2. What two types of leased lines do you think are in broadest use today? Justify your answer.

PROJECTS

1. Go to the book's website, http://www.prenhall.com/panko, and read the Updates Page for this module to see any reported errors and for new and expanded information on the material in this module.
2. Go to the book's website, http://www.prenhall.com/panko, and do the Internet Exercises for this module.

More on Security

INTRODUCTION

This module is designed to be read after Chapter 6. It is not designed to be read front-to-back like a chapter, although later topics tend to build upon earlier topics. The sections on the Secure Sockets Layer (SSL) and Secure Electronic Transactions (SET) are designed to be read after Chapter 8, which deals with electronic commerce over the Internet.

ENCRYPTION

To read this module, you should understand security basics, especially the concept of **encryption.** In encryption, plaintext is converted into unreadable ciphertext, transmitted over a network, and converted back to plaintext at the other end.

PUBLIC KEY ENCRYPTION

You should know that **public key encryption** is the easiest and safest kind of encryption to use because there is no need to keep your public key secret and because you only need one private key no matter how many business partners you have.

It is important to remember that in a transaction, there are two public and two private keys—one of each for the two parties that are communicating. In each direction, the sender encrypts with the *public key of the receiver*. Only the receiver can decrypt the message after it has been encrypted with the receiver's public key.

SINGLE KEY ENCRYPTION

On the other hand, public key encryption and decryption are about a hundred times more computer processing–intensive than **single key encryption,**[1] in which there is a single secret key that both sides use to encrypt and decrypt. As a result, it is com-

---

[1] W. Ford and M. S. Baum, *Secure Electronic Commerce* (Upper Saddle River, NJ: Prentice Hall, 1997), p. 122.

mon to have the two parties begin with public key encryption. Then, one party will generate a single key and send it to the other party encrypted with the other party's public key. This way, only the sender and the receiver will know the secret single key.

AUTHENTICATION

Before you begin communicating with someone, you should **authenticate** the other party, that is, determine that the other party is who it says it is. Public key encryption can do this. A sender can encrypt appropriate information with its *private* key. The receiver, who knows the sender's public key, can decrypt the message with the sender's *public* key. If the decryption works, then the sender holds the sender's secret private key. Only the sender should know this.

PASSWORD POLICIES

Many security techniques at some point rely on passwords. For instance, a user might keep his or her public key on his or her hard disk drive. To prevent someone else from using his or her computer, the user might set a password on the computer. In many other cases, elaborate security systems are vulnerable if a user password is stolen or guessed.

Obtaining Passwords

WRITING IT DOWN

The easiest way to get someone's password is to steal it. Many people write their password on a sheet of paper and then place it in a nearby drawer or even stick it on their computer!

LONG PASSWORDS

One principle of good password policy is to require fairly long passwords, say six to eight characters. This makes it more difficult for an intruder to guess the password by doing an exhaustive search, in which he or she tries all possible passwords. Even with six characters, there are 26^6 possible passwords. This is a very large number. Doing an exhaustive search would be prohibitively expensive.

COMMON WORDS

However, exhaustive searches are rarely necessary. Users often pick a password that is easy to remember, such as their name or the name of one of their family members. Often, it takes only a dozen or fewer tries to guess the correct password.

If people do not choose something personal, they often choose a common English word (or a common word in their own language). There are relatively few common English words. Only a thousand or two thousand tries may be necessary to crack the password based on a common word, instead of a billion or more through exhaustive search.

RANDOM PASSWORDS

As a result, some firms assign random combinations of letters and numbers, but these tend to be so difficult to remember that people write them down next to the computer.

USING CASE AND DIGITS

A better approach is to require that the person select a password with at least one character capitalized and with at least one digit in the password. In this case, a person thinking about using "dreamcoat" might choose "dream5Coat" This is a little more difficult to remember but not unreasonably more difficult. Yet this still beats simple guessing strategies.

Network Administrators

What if users forget their passwords? Usually, a network administrator cannot determine a lost password. However, the administrator usually can change any password. So if a person loses his or her password, the administrator might give the person the new password "changeme," plus instructions to change the password immediately.

If this is done, it means that the network administrator can always get into a file by changing the password, logging in as the person, and then changing it again. The administrator cannot change this to the original password, but the victim might think that he or she had simply forgotten the password.

If it is not possible for the network administrator to change a password, this enhances security. At the same time, it means that if a user loses his or her password, the user will not be able to read the encrypted message. This could be far riskier than security breaches.

COMPUTER SECURITY

Securing the network will not be effective unless you can also secure client PCs and servers. Unfortunately, even server operating systems were not designed for high security. Client PC operating systems, in turn, were designed with almost no thought given to security.

SERVER SECURITY

For servers, most network attacks exploit **known weaknesses** in the operating system. Operating system vendors frequently post **security patches**—software to be added to the operating system to remove newly discovered weaknesses. Unfortunately, busy systems administrators often fail to install the patches, leaving the server vulnerable to these known weaknesses.

CLIENT PC SECURITY

As noted in the Introduction, the biggest weakness of client PCs is their reliance on passwords to create any form of security at all. Few employees use passwords, and as noted earlier in this module, many create passwords that are easy to guess or write difficult passwords somewhere near the computer.

APPLICATION SECURITY

Application software can also cause security problems. One person was using online banking software supplied by his local bank. He discovered that the software stored his password on the computer in unencrypted form.[2] Anyone could read it if he or she got onto his system.

---

[2] Brian McWilliams, "Hacker Finds Online Banking Security Hole," *PC World News Radio*, March 11, 1988.

JAVA SECURITY

Java applets are a particular problem. When you download a Java program, you accept the danger that the program may do something improper. Although the **Java virtual machine** that runs Java programs constantly checks them for improper activities and tries to block such activities, problems have been found in all versions of Java virtual machines to date. In addition, although every Java applet is registered, authenticating its developer, a registered gun can kill as easily as an unregistered gun.

PROCEDURES AND THE HUMAN FACTOR

The biggest weakness in any security system is people. Often, procedures must be followed exactly or the system will become vulnerable. More fundamentally, employee attacks have long dominated computer security threats. The system must not only require that employees follow proper procedures. It must also ensure that individuals cannot violate procedures in ways that allow them to exploit the system.

Overall, although this book understandably focuses on network security, you need to understand that network security means nothing unless there is security in all hardware, software, and people.

DIGITAL SIGNATURES AND DIGITAL CERTIFICATES

Authentication is the requirement that the sender prove its identity. To do this on a message-by-message basis, the sender must add one of two things to each message. One is a digital signature. The other is a digital certificate. Chapter 6 discussed these concepts briefly. We will look at both in more detail in this module. We will focus especially on digital certificates, which are more powerful but are also more complex and more prone to be misunderstood by users and network professionals.

Digital Signatures

A sender wishes to send a series of messages to a receiver. The receiver needs to know that each message really came from the sender, rather than from a third party pretending to be the sender.

The receiver already knows the sender's public key. So the sender must prove that he or she has the private key associated with that public key. The way to do this is to encrypt something with the sender's public key and attach it to the message. Then, the receiver will decrypt the "something" with the sender's public key. If the decryption works, then the sender's authenticity is proven.

The problem is what to encrypt. As Chapter 6 noted, the sender encrypts a **message digest,** also called a **message authentication code (MAC).** The message digest is constructed from the message but is much smaller. The receiver, who has the entire message, can also compute the message digest. The message digest that the receiver computes and the contents of the message digest field after decryption with the sender's public key must match.

Normally, the message digest is computed by hashing the message. **Hashing** is a way of doing calculations so that even if the message to be hashed is very long, the computed hash string will be of a certain length or smaller. This guarantees that message digests will always be no longer than a certain size. A simple case would be to treat the message bit stream as a large binary number and divide it by a standard binary number. The remainder will always be less than the size of the standard binary number. So the remainder would be the hash value.

Hashing algorithms must be selected carefully. If they are not almost perfectly random (as our example was not), it will be easy for intruders to defeat the hashing algorithm. There are two popular hashing algorithms for creating message digests. One is **MD5 (Message Digest 5),** which was created by RSA Data Security, Incorporated. This company owns the rights to the popular RSA public key encryption algorithm. RSA Data Security, Inc., placed MD5 in the public domain, so now any company can use it. The other common hashing algorithm is the **Secure Hash Algorithm (SHA),** which was created by the U.S. Department of Defense and is also freely usable.

One good thing about hashing is that it creates **message integrity**—proof that the message has not been captured, changed, and then retransmitted by an intruder. If the message is altered, the computed hash string will not match the decoded message digest string.

Digital Certificates

CERTIFICATION
If you visit a doctor's office, you see diplomas and other certificates on the wall. This gives you reasonable assurance that the doctor has passed various types of formal training and testing.

DIGITAL CERTIFICATE USE
In a similar way, instead of adding a message digest to each outgoing message for authentication purposes, a sender can also add to each message a **digital certificate** created by a third party, a **certificate authority.**

You must apply to the certificate authority for a digital certificate. Most certificate authorities offer varying grades of assurance with several classes of certificate. For instance, the lowest **grade of certificate** may only require you to have a valid e-mail address. For the highest grade, the certificate authority may visit your firm, inspect its operations, and examine its business licenses.

SOURCES OF CONFUSION
Having multiple grades of certificate allows a merchant to compare the higher costs of higher certificate grades against the need for greater authentication. Unfortunately, having multiple grades of certificates is also confusing to business partners, especially residential consumers. Consumers or business partners may believe that the certificate authority really has checked the business operation, and this may not be the case.

Another source of confusion is the fact that few certificate authorities check into the legitimacy or practices of the business. They merely certify that it exists. Some certificate authorities do offer some assurance by guaranteeing protection against fraud committed by a certified company, but this guarantee normally varies by certificate grade and is normally quite limited.

Finally, there is no way to ensure that the certificate authority itself is legitimate. Any company can set itself up as a certificate authority, and it can even certify its own subsidiaries!

Overall, there is a general feeling that governments will have to regulate the digital certification industry to avoid shady business practices and also to standardize terminology so that business partners will know what certificates do and do not mean.

CHECKING THE CERTIFICATE

How do digital certificates provide assurance? First, the digital certificate itself has a digital signature encrypted by the *private key of the certificate authority*. So when a receiver gets a message containing a digital certificate, the receiver will decrypt the certificate's digital signature with the public key of the claimed certificate authority. If the decryption works, the receiver will know that the certificate authority really created the certificate.

How can the receiver get the certificate authority's public key? The receiver can get it from the certificate authority's website. The receiver can also use other information there. For instance, the receiver should check the certificate number against the certificate authority's list of operational digital certificates. The receiver should check that the digital certificate has not been revoked. In addition, most browsers know the public keys of many widely used certificate authorities.

IS THE SENDER LEGITIMATE?

The certificate may be legitimate, but is the sender really the company named in the certificate? After all, anyone can copy the certificate and attach it to their messages.

To prevent this from happening, the digital certificate contains the public key of the certified sender. The sender should add a digital signature to the message. If the public key named in the digital certificate can decrypt the digital signature, the sender is authenticated.

THE X.509 DIGITAL CERTIFICATE STANDARD

OSI offers a standard for the syntax of digital certificates. This is the **X.509** standard. In this standard, the digital certificate begins with a number of required fields. These include:

- ▶ **Version Number.** Three versions of X.509 have been released to date, and more are likely. New versions have added fields, so it is important for the receiver's software to know the version number.
- ▶ **Serial Number.** Each digital certificate issued by a certificate authority must be given a unique serial number.
- ▶ **Signature Algorithm Identifier.** There are several algorithms for digital signatures (not certificates). This field tells which algorithm the certificate authority will use to sign the digital certificate.
- ▶ **Issuer.** This is the name of the certificate authority in X.500 name syntax.
- ▶ **Valid Period.** Certificates are valid for limited periods of time. At the end of the valid period, the company wishing certification must update its certificate information and apply for a new certificate.
- ▶ **Subject.** This is the name of the certified company in X.500 format.
- ▶ **Public Key Information.** This field has two pieces of information. The first is the public key algorithm used by the subject company. The second is the subject company's public key. As noted above, this allows the receiver of a certificate to test whether the sender really is the subject company.

These required fields are followed by a number of optional fields that provide more detailed but less essential information.

The last field in the X.509 digital certificate is the certification authority's own digital signature, which is based upon all the other fields in the digital certificate. This digital signature uses the algorithm in the **Signature Algorithm Identifier** field.

DISTRIBUTING THE DIGITAL CERTIFICATE

We have said that the digital certificate will be sent with every message. However, there are other options.

One option is for one party to send its digital certificate to its partner only at the beginning of a series of interactions. This reduces processing time for each message. On the other hand, it also allows a third party to send a fake message during subsequent transmissions in a transaction.

Another option that will soon be emerging is to place the digital certificate in a company's directory server. When the other party checks the directory server to find out about the sender, the other party can also see the sender's digital certificate.

CERTIFICATE REVOCATION LISTS

The X.509 standard even standardizes the creation and distribution of **certificate revocation lists (CRLs).** These CRLs identify certificates that have been revoked by the certificate authority before the end of their original period of validity.

HIDING OPERATIONAL DETAILS

Current browsers handle the details of digital certificate processing appropriately without user intervention. This makes the user's life easier. However, browsers often do not provide nuances of the digital certification to users, such as the level of certification and the implications of the level of certification.

DATA ENCRYPTION STANDARD (DES)

Created in 1977, the **Data Encryption Standard (DES)** is one of the oldest encryption methods still in operation. The U.S. federal government sponsored DES's development. It was due to be replaced in the early 1990s, but no agreement on a replacement emerged. It is still widely used despite growing concerns about its safety.

DES Characteristics

DES is a **block cipher** method. This means that it encrypts messages in blocks. For DES, each block is 64 bits long. DES uses a key that is 56 bits long,[3] and this is the source of concern over the algorithm's safety. This is a fairly short key, and it is breakable with enough effort.

In DES encryption, the 64-bit plaintext block goes through a series of transformations. IBM developed this method but never explained why it chose the algorithms in DES. This lack of candor probably is justified on the grounds that if the entire rationale were published, this information might lead someone to find a way to break DES. At the same time, there is concern that IBM left a "trap door"—an easy way to break encryption—for law enforcement officials to use.

---

[3] Actually, the key is 64 bits long, but 8 of the bits are parity bits.

Triple DES (3DES)

Because of concerns over key length, many organizations now use a variant called **Triple DES** or **3DES.** In this approach, two keys are used.

First, each 64-bit block is encrypted with the first key. This is the equivalent of simple DES. It creates a new 64-bit block that is DES-encrypted.

Second, the block from the first step is *decrypted* with the second key. This seems odd at first, but the DES algorithm can be applied in two directions. If you apply the algorithm in the reverse of the normal direction, this is called decryption. This "decryption" is still capable of scrambling a block in a way that can be undone only by the encryption process using the same key.

Third, the block from the second step is encrypted again with the first key. Although this seems like it might somehow undo the work of the first steps, it really does not, thanks to the scrambling in the second step.

At the other end, the receiver undoes the process. It first decrypts with the first key, encrypts with the second, and decrypts with the third. This convoluted process restores the original 64 bits of plaintext.

Triple DES obviously requires a good deal more processing time than simple DES. However, given the vulnerabilities of simple DES, many organizations have adopted 3DES for their most sensitive information transfers and business transactions.

SECURE SOCKETS LAYER (SSL)

Netscape was the first company to deal with security on the Internet. Its creation was the **Secure Sockets Layer (SSL)** protocol. As Chapter 8 indicated, SSL is less secure than the SET protocol discussed in the next section. Nevertheless, it offers a good deal of security and has become a de facto standard for Internet electronic commerce security. Both Netscape and Microsoft browsers support it. Netscape has even submitted its latest version, 3.0, to the IETF for ratification as a standard. In the future, the IETF may manage the SSL standard. It has already renamed it Transport Layer Security (TLS).

Socket Layer Protection

In TCP/IP, there are two common transport layer protocols, TCP and UDP. Both have a "port" field that indicates which application layer process should receive the application PDU within the TCP or UDP protocol data unit.

WELL-KNOWN PORTS

The IETF has defined a number of **well-known port numbers.** For instance, "80" is the well-known port number for the HTTP protocol used in the World Wide Web. In turn, FTP and Telnet have the well-known port numbers "21" and "23," respectively.

SOCKETS

To reach a particular application program on a particular server host, we need to know two things. First, we need to know the internet address of the server, so that our IP packets can reach it. Second, we need to know the port number that the destination host uses for the particular application program we seek.

Application Layer	HTTP	FTP	E-Mail	etc.
Transport Layer	Secure Sockets Layer			
	TCP or UDP			

Reflecting these two necessary elements, a **socket** is the combination of an internet address and a port number. When we specify a socket, we do so by writing out the internet address, then a colon, and then the port number. So if we are trying to reach the webserver application (port 80) on host 128.171.17.13, we write the socket as 128.171.17.13:80.

SOCKET LAYER

The Secure Sockets Layer (SSL) protocol in effect creates a sublayer, the **socket layer,** at the top of the transport layer, as Figure F.1 illustrates.

In operation, the socket layer grabs all communication from TCP or UDP to application layer protocols and processes the communication before the application layer protocol receives the data. So if the application protocol data unit is encrypted by the SSL protocol on the sending host, the socket layer will decrypt the APDU and then pass the plaintext APDU up to the application layer program indicated by the port number.

In the other direction, when the application layer protocol sends data, the socket layer intercepts the APDU before TCP or UDP sees it. This allows SSL to encrypt the APDU and take other actions necessary for security.

SSL Operation

SSL provides two basic services. First, it authenticates the server to the client and, if possible, the client to the server. Second, it encrypts messages to frustrate anyone who intercepts them.

INITIAL HANDSHAKING INTERACTIONS

Client Application Program Initiation In World Wide Web service, when a browser user wishes to communicate with a webserver application on a webserver host, he or she types a URL, as Figure F.2 indicates. For SSL communication, the URL begins with *https://* instead of http://. Here, https:// indicates that the client will be dealing with a secure host using SSL.

Note that the browser program initiates the interaction. More broadly, any client application program can initiate the interaction because SSL's socket layer placement allows it to work with any application.

Establishing Socket Layer Parameters Before passing on any HTTP-Request-PDUs, the socket layer program on the client browser first establishes a secure connection with the webserver's socket layer program. It uses the SSL standard to establish this connection.

First, the client and server socket layer programs negotiate to determine which al-

```
┌──────────┐
│ Browser  │
└──────────┘
     │ 1. Browser Sends
     │    https:// call
     ▼
┌──────────┐        2.                              ┌──────────┐
│   SSL    │◄─── SSL Programs Negotiate Security ──►│   SSL    │
│ Software │        Parameters                      │ Software │
│   on     │        3.                              │   on     │
│ Customer │◄─── Server Authenticates Itself ──────│ Merchant │
│   PC     │        to Browser                      │   Host   │
│          │        4.                              │          │
│          │──── Browser Authenticates Itself ─────►│          │
│          │    to Server (Optional)                │          │
│          │        5.                              │          │
│          │──── Exchange of Single Key ───────────►│          │
│          │    (Usually, Browser Creates Key)      │          │
│          │        6.                              │          │
│          │◄─── Secure Exchanges Using ───────────►│          │
│          │    Single Key                          │          │
└──────────┘                                        └──────────┘
```

gorithms will be used in their interactions. SSL offers a small but useful and widely implemented set of algorithms for authentication, key exchange, and single key encryption.

Server Authentication The server's socket layer program uses the chosen authentication algorithm to authenticate itself to the client. Digital certificates, as noted above, offer a powerful way to do authentication.

Client Authentication (Optional) Next, if the client has a digital certificate, its socket layer will authenticate the client to the webserver's socket layer.

Key Exchange for Single Key Encryption Following authentication, the two socket layer programs select a single key to be used for subsequent transactions. This key exchange normally uses public key transport via RSA. It is also possible to use the Diffie-Hellman key agreement protocol described later in this module under IPsec, or the U.S. secret government KEA algorithm, which is based on Diffie-Hellman.

If RSA key exchange is used, the *client* generates the secret key and sends it to the server encrypted with the server's public key. The two socket layer programs on the client and server are now ready to communicate.

Transaction Exchanges

Passing the HTTP-Request-PDU Recall that the interaction began when the client application issued a call to the transport layer to deliver an HTTP-request-PDU. Instead of delivering this APDU immediately, the client socket layer program first authenticated the webserver and negotiated communication parameters with the webserver. Now that this has been accomplished, the browser's socket layer program turns its attention back to the HTTP-request-protocol.

Encryption The client socket layer program encrypts the APDU so that if it is intercepted enroute, the interceptor will not be able to read it.

Digital Signature for Message Authentication and Integrity The socket layer program also adds a digital signature. This ensures integrity. If the APDU is intercepted and changed, the digital signature will no longer be correct. It also authenticates the APDU.

Sequence Number The sockets layer also adds a sequence number to each APDU, so that an attacker cannot send false messages to the client application or to the web-server application.

Advantages and Disadvantages of SSL

The Secure Sockets Layer (SSL) protocol has several advantages. First, because it creates a new layer (sockets) below the application layer, it can work with any application layer program. Although we have seen how SSL is used in HTTP exchanges, SSL is not limited to HTTP World Wide Web exchanges.

Second, because SSL works just below the application layer, the transaction is still secure even if there are security breaches at lower layers. Interceptors will still not be able to read application PDUs, insert false application PDUs, or compromise the communication in other ways.

On the negative side, SSL trusts the merchant operating the application program on the server host. Most importantly, when the browser sends a credit card number, the merchant application program can read it. This means that although SSL protects customer–merchant communication, it does nothing to protect the customer against a merchant who will misuse the customer's credit card number. This is an omission that the SET protocol discussed in the next section tries to repair.

At the same time, SSL is not standing still. More precisely, both Netscape and Microsoft are building on it to compete with SET. Microsoft is developing extensions that it currently calls Private Communication Technology (PCT). Netscape, in turn, is developing a very SET-like Electronic Payment Protocol (EPP). It remains to be seen how these extensions will do against SET in the future.

SECURE ELECTRONIC TRANSACTIONS (SET)

To reduce risks in credit card purchasing over the Internet, Visa, MasterCard, and other companies have cooperated to produce a rather comprehensive standard for customer–merchant interactions. This is **Secure Electronic Transactions (SET).**

Parties

As noted at the end of the section on the Secure Sockets Layer (SSL) protocol, if SSL is used, the merchant can see the customer's credit card number. This allows the merchant to misuse the customer's credit card number. Figure F.3 shows that SET avoids this by bringing two additional players into the picture. One is the **card issuer** company that issued the customer's credit card. This usually is a bank. The other is the **gateway,** which links merchants and card issuers.

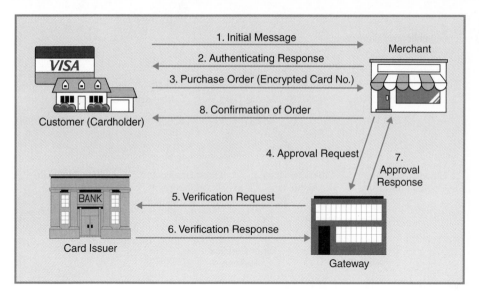

FIGURE F.3

Secure Electronic Transactions (SET) Organizations

We saw in Chapter 8 that SET encrypts the credit card number so that the merchant cannot read it. Instead, the merchant passes the encrypted credit card number and the purchase price to the gateway organization, which passes this information to the card issuer. The card issuer approves the purchase amount and sends an authorization back to the merchant. The merchant then confirms the order. The merchant is protected but cannot misuse the customer's credit card number.

Layer Organization

Figure F.4 shows how SET fits into the TCP/IP–OSI hybrid layering scheme we have been using since Chapter 1. The figure notes that SET is a flexible top-level protocol. It can work directly with the transport layer. It can also work using SSL for additional security. It can also work via HTTP, whether or not using SSL below HTTP.

The figure also illustrates that other standards can be working at other layers to enhance security. At the internet layer, the IPsec standards discussed later in the module may be in place. At the data link layer, the Layer 2 Tunneling Protocol (discussed later in this module) may be in place. Overall, security is safest when it operates at all layers.

Application	HTTP	SET	
Transport	SSL/TLS		
Internet	IPsec		
Data Link	L2TP, PPTP		
Physical	Locks, etc.		

FIGURE F.4

Secure Electronic Transactions (SET) and Layering

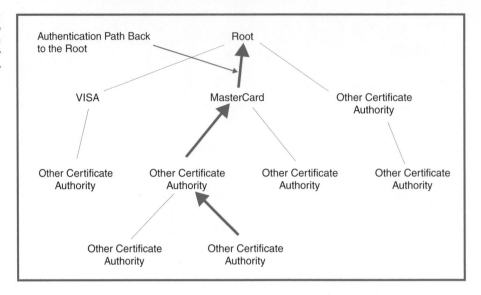

Getting a Client Certificate

To use SET, the customer needs a digital certificate for each credit card. For this, the customer will have to go to a SET-authorized certificate authority. The consumer will apply for the digital certificate and receive it electronically. Afterward, the digital certificate will stay in the consumer's electronic wallet on his or her PC.

The consumer may also need special client software until browsers become SET-compatible. This software is expected to be widely available and may be free.

Who will certify the certificate authority? As Figure F.5 shows, SET has a hierarchical scheme in which there is a master root and a few top-level certificate authorities, such as VISA and MasterCard. Each of these top-level certificate authorities can certify next-lower-layer authorities. These authorities can then certify next-lower-layer authorities. This process can continue to lower layers. This way, any certificate authority's certification can be traced back to the master root.

Making a Purchase

Now we will trace a single purchase using SET. This is a fairly complex process, but it can all happen very automatically and quickly. Software will hide most details from users. We will not present the full details, such as signing every message with a digital signature, adding digital certificates (except in some cases), and other normal matters. This will allow us to focus on the aspects of SET that make it unique.

SELECTING ITEMS TO PURCHASE

The user working at the browser will search a website for items to purchase. He or she may add several items to an electronic shopping cart. At some point, the customer will be finished shopping. He or she will hit a *purchase* button or take some other similar action.

THE INITIAL MESSAGE

First, the browser will send an initial message to the webserver. This will be a SET-PDU. It will begin the purchasing process.

RESPONSE TO THE INITIAL MESSAGE

The server will respond to the initial purchase message. The response will contain the merchant's digital certificate. This will assure the customer that the merchant is certified.

The message will also contain the digital certificate of the gateway the merchant will use. This will assure the customer that a legitimate gateway is being used.

CREATING THE PURCHASE ORDER

The customer's software can check the message digest, the merchant certificate, and the acquirer certificate. Checking certificates will require tracing certificate authorities back to the root.

The customer will then create a purchase order. This will contain ordering information and purchasing information. The purchasing information contains the customer's credit card number and other sensitive credit card information.

The cardholder will then encrypt the purchasing information so that the gateway can read it but the merchant cannot. The cardholder does this by encrypting the purchasing information with a new single key that it generates itself. The cardholder program then encrypts the single key with the gateway's public key. Now only the gateway can read the single key and therefore decrypt the purchasing information.

The customer then sends the purchase order, including the customer's own digital certificate. It sends the purchase order encrypted with the merchant's public key.

MERCHANT RECEIVES THE PURCHASE ORDER

When the merchant receives the purchase order, the merchant decrypts it and authenticates the customer. The merchant then checks to be sure that the order entry information is proper.

The merchant now needs an authorization from the company that issued the credit card. To do this, it creates an authorization request message, to be sent to the acquirer gateway.

This authorization message passes on the ordering information and the encrypted purchasing information to the gateway.

AT THE GATEWAY

The gateway decrypts the authorization request message and authenticates the merchant. The gateway then decrypts the purchasing information. Finally, it authenticates the customer.

COMMUNICATING WITH THE CARD ISSUING COMPANY

The gateway now checks with the company that issued the customer's credit card. This check ensures that the card is still valid and that the purchase amount will not put the card over its credit limit.

The gateway communicates with the card issuer the same way it would if the purchase order had been called in over the telephone. This process has been in place for many years and is very mature.

AUTHORIZATION RESPONSE TO THE MERCHANT

Once the gateway has heard from the card issuer, the gateway sends an authorization response message to the merchant.

CONFIRMATION ORDER RESPONSE TO THE CLIENT

Finally, the merchant sends a confirmation of the customer's order to the customer. The process is finished.

Perspectives on SET

Although SET is sophisticated technologically, it remains to be seen whether practical problems will slow its growth or even kill it entirely.

Currently, the credit card companies have the most to gain. By reducing fraud, they will reduce costs substantially.

Will credit card companies pass their lower costs on to merchants, and to what degree will they do so? This is by no means certain today. Even if they do, furthermore, the benefit will be small.[4] Merchants now pay a fee of 2.5% for today's Internet purchases without SET. This is the same rate they now pay for mail-order transactions. In contrast, when a customer presents a card to a merchant in a retail store, the fee is only 1.2%. It is doubtful that the SET fee could be lower than the card-presented fee.

What is certain, on the other hand, is that SET will cost money to implement. If merchants will not get enough benefits to overcome their costs, they will not join the program.

Another issue is the security of credit card information. From the customer's point of view, the real benefit of SET is that the merchant will not know the customer's credit card number. However, the current rules of SET allow the merchant to ask for this information from the gateway! So the main customer benefit is illusory.

Finally, to really work, SET needs each customer to have a digital certificate. The discussion assumed the presence of such a certificate, but SET 1.0 does not require it. If digital certificates are not mandatory in later versions, the system will not work well. If digital certificates are not free and painless to obtain, customers are not likely to obtain them.

IPSEC

The Internet Engineering Task Force has been working on a set of standards generically called **IPsec,** which is short for the **IP Security Protocol.** As the name suggests, IPsec is concerned only with security at the internet layer. However, if the internet layer is secure, interceptors will not be able to read higher-layer protocol data units.

This does not preclude security from being used at other layers as well. For instance, a user might use SSL or SET to secure a transaction at the application layer (see Figure F.4). IPsec then provides additional security at the internet layer. IPsec can also be used by itself as the only security method.

Our discussion of IPsec is necessarily conditional because IPsec is still in the process of development. Check the book's website for updates on IPsec.

---

[4] Ellen Messmer, "Visa and CompuServe get SET for Net Sales," *Network World*, September 29, 1997, 10.

Basic Mechanisms

IPv4 AND IPv6

The most widely used version of the Internet Protocol today is Version 4. IPv4 has 32-bit internet addresses. Except in Module A, "IP" is largely synonymous with IPv4 in this book.

IPv6 is the new version of the Internet Protocol. Described in Module A, IPv6 has 128-bit internet addresses.

IPsec has defined two headers that can be added to either IPv4 or IPv6. This means that, in terms of security at least, the two versions will work in the same way.

ENCAPSULATING SECURITY PROTOCOL (ESP)

The most complete alternative is the use of an **encapsulating security protocol (ESP)** header. Added after the main IP header, this header provides for authentication, integrity (being able to detect if the IP packet has changed), and privacy (the inability of others to read the message because it has been encrypted).

Instead of requiring specific algorithms to achieve these goals (beyond specifying that digital signatures should be used and giving some other general direction), the ESP header can use any of several acceptable protocols. Of course, this means that when two systems begin to communicate, they must negotiate which algorithms they will use for different purposes. We will describe this negotiation process below.

AUTHENTICATION HEADER (AH)

Like the encapsulating security protocol header, the **authentication header (AH)** provides for authentication and integrity. Unlike ESP, however, AH does not provide privacy. It does not provide encryption.

At first, this seems odd. Why give up encryption? Privacy, also called confidentiality, is extremely important. Ford and Baum[5] argue that the AH avoids problems with U.S. restrictions on strong encryption for messages going into and out of the United States and on hardware and software sold for use in other countries.

Modes of Operation

TUNNELING

Both the encapsulating security protocol header and the authentication header can be used in two ways. One of these is tunneling. In **tunneling,** the entire IP packet is encrypted and then placed within another IP packet. Looked at another way, the entire IP packet is encrypted and a new IP header is added.

As Figure F.6 illustrates, the destination internet address in the added IP header may be a host, but it is also likely to be a **security gateway,** such as a firewall or IPsec-enabled router. This way, even if a packet is captured, the interceptor will not learn much by examining the destination address. The interceptor will not be able to tell which host beyond the security gateway will receive the IP packet.

---

[5] Ford and Baum, *Secure Electronic Commerce*, p. 128.

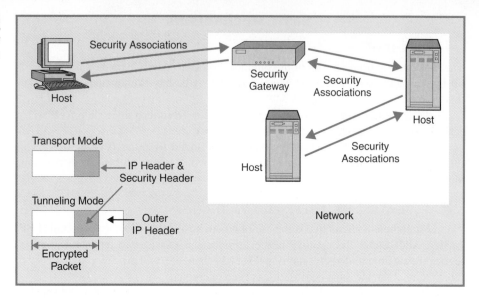

TRANSPORT MODE

In transport mode, the IP packet is sent directly to a destination without being encapsulated. The main IP header is followed by the ESP or AH header and then by the remainder of the IP packet (encrypted in the case of ESP).

Negotiation (ISAKMP/OAKLEY)

SECURITY ASSOCIATION

When two hosts begin to communicate, or if a host connects to a security gateway such as a router or firewall, the two devices must establish a security association. A **security association** is a relationship that describes how two parties will use security services. This includes such things as whether authentication services will be used and, if so, which authentication algorithm will be used.

Security association is a one-way concept. If there are two devices, A and B, two security associations must be established. One will govern how A transmits to B. The other will govern how B transmits to A. These usually are the same, but they can be different.

For security association management, IPsec uses **ISAKMP**, the **Internet Security Association Key Management Protocol.** As the name suggests, this standard governs how security associations will be managed.

NEGOTIATION

Given the past history of algorithms that have failed to be as secure as originally promised, ISAKMP avoids specific standards and is a general way for two devices to negotiate security association parameters. ISAKMP provides a general mechanism for establishing security associations, modifying them, and deleting them.

ISAKMP describes how one device can tell the other device what security alternatives it can support and prefers. By exchanging such information, the two sides can quickly agree upon what services they will use and what algorithm they will use for each service.

KEY EXCHANGE (OAKLEY)

Although ISAKMP manages most aspects of the initial exchanges between the two devices, it does not manage **key exchange**—the establishment of specific keys for security algorithms that the communicating partners have selected. The IETF selected the **OAKLEY** key exchange standard for that purpose. Because ISAKMP and OAKLEY are so closely related, they are usually referred to collectively as ISAKMP/OAKLEY.

Although OAKLEY can support multiple key exchange approaches, most firms are likely to use OAKLEY's modified Diffie-Hellman key agreement protocol.

The innovative feature of **Diffie-Hellman key agreement** is that even if an interceptor breaks the exchange communication between the two communication partners, it will do them no good. The key exchange data are not enough to reconstruct the common key.

To see how Diffie-Hellman works, suppose that there are two parties that wish to communicate. We will call them Party 1 and Party 2.

First, using the Diffie-Hellman algorithm, each party generates a string that has two parts—a secret part and a public part. Party 1 generates secret part a and public part A. Party 2 then generates secret part b and public part B.

Next, the two parties exchange their public parts. Party 1 transmits A to Party 2, and Party 2 transmits B to Party 1.

As the name implies, A and B are public, like public keys. There is no need to encrypt them. Intercepting them will do no good because knowledge of A and B is not enough to generate the secret single key, x, which will be used to encrypt subsequent transactions.

However, thanks to an ingenious algorithm, it is possible to generate the secret key x from a and B. Party 1 generated the secret part a, and Party 2 sent it public part B, so Party 1 can determine x.

It is also possible to generate the secret key x from b and A. Party 2 has this information and so can generate x.

Overall, by exchanging public information, the two sides can agree upon a secret session key, x. This is why the technique is called **key agreement.**

Perspective on IPsec

Given the growing importance of security on the Internet, especially in virtual private networks and extranets, IPsec's development has been followed with keen anticipation. Even before the standard was fully specified, in fact, there was a major demonstration of IPsec product interoperability in the Automotive Network Exchange (ANX) demonstration project designed to show how the automotive industry's 8,000 suppliers can communicate with car makers and other purchasers.

In general, where IPsec offers options, it presents what is generally considered to be an acceptable list of standards from which to select. Although more standards will be offered in the future, the ones available initially are attractive.

One weakness of IPsec is that it only focuses on internet layer security. It is only part of a broad package of multilayer security standards, such as those shown in Figure F.4.

One bright spot is that the ISAKMP standard is not limited to the internet layer. It establishes a method for managing security association and keys that can be used at any layer.

Another known weakness of IPsec is that it requires digital certificates. However, except in SET, we lack a good digital certificate architecture that would control certificate authorities and their mutual relationships.

A final major known weakness is that IPsec is designed for TCP/IP networks. Other internet protocols, such as IPX, can be encapsulated within IP datagrams, but this is an underdeveloped area.

All new protocols will evidence some weaknesses over time, and the IPsec family of protocols—ESP, AH, ISAKMP, OAKLEY, and various allowed algorithms—will almost certainly do the same. However, IPsec offers a fairly comprehensive and very standardized way of managing security in private virtual networks over the Internet in other TCP/IP network environments.

OTHER SECURITY TOPICS

The Layer 2 Tunneling Protocol (L2TP)

In **tunneling,** a PDU is encrypted and placed within another PDU for transmission. This is also called **encapsulation.** Often, the destination address of the outer header is a security gateway such as a firewall (see Figure F.6). The receiving device will remove the outer header and either decrypt the PDU or encapsulate it inside another PDU for a second tunneling transfer.

Microsoft and Cisco Systems (the leading router vendor) both developed tunneling protocols. Working together, they later created a new standard, the **Layer 2 Tunneling Protocol (L2TP).** This protocol ensures that frames at the data link layer can be transmitted with high security. However, in Windows 98, Microsoft only implemented the earlier **Point-to-Point Tunneling Protocol (PPTP).**

Radius

A major problem for corporations is dial-in access from traveling users and users working from home. Because users can dial into the firm through many access points, it is very difficult to provide consistent security across many access points.

Many firms are attempting to increase their dial-in security by adopting **RADIUS,** the *Remote Access Dial-In User Service* standard.

In RADIUS, there is a central RADIUS authentication server. This server maintains access information about employees and anyone else who is authorized to dial in.

When a user dials into an access server, he or she gives the login name and password to the access server. Rather than relying on a local database, the access server asks the RADIUS authentication server to authenticate the user.

The RADIUS authentication server sends authentication information back to the access server. This may tell the access server to deny the dial-in, accept the user, or place certain restrictions on what the user may do.

RADIUS is popular because of its centralized policy and data control. A user on the road can dial into the system from anywhere with the assurance that he or she will be able to get into the network. Network administrators, in turn, know that hackers cannot simply try many different access servers to find one with weak security.

Smart Cards

Nearly everyone now carries credit cards. As discussed earlier in this module, when people present a credit card, the risk of fraud is far lower than when they place an order by phone.

Smart cards look like credit cards but contain a microprocessor, some RAM, and programs in ROM. This allows them to respond intelligently when passed through a scanner. It is virtually impossible to crack the encryption of a smart card, although people must remember their password or code number.

Smart cards are especially safe if they are used as debit cards. A bank can transfer a certain amount of "money" to the card. A retailer later runs the card through a scanner and deducts the amount of the purchase. Because the retailer already has its money, the risk of fraud is almost negligible. There is no need to pay the credit card company a fee based on risk.

Smart cards are much more popular in Europe, where they were developed, than they are in the United States. Eventually, we may have smart card readers built into our PCs for truly low-cost online purchasing.

Biometric Authentication

Despite the common saying "I forgot my head," our body is always available when we shop. In authentication, the goal is to prove that you have something that nobody else has. In **biometric** authentication, this "something" can be your finger print, the irises of your eyes, your hand print, your voice, or some other measurable body component. (*Metric* means measurement.)

There are several types of biometric readers. The least expensive units read your fingerprint. An almost infallible way to use a smart card is to use it with a finger print reader that can be compared to data on the smart card. The most accurate biometric readers measure the patterns of one of your irises, but these are very expensive.

Kerberos

Many systems use the **Kerberos** authentication system named after a three-headed dog in Greek mythology. As Figure F.7 illustrates, the Kerberos system has three elements—the two communicating devices and the Kerberos server.

Figure F.7 shows that the computer that wants to initiate communication is called the **principal.** The other computer is called the **verifier** because it needs to verify the authenticity of the principal.

GETTING A SESSION KEY AND TICKET

Each computer in the network has a secret single key it can use to communicate with the Kerberos server. Different computers have different keys, so each can have a private conversation with the Kerberos server. Kerberos communication uses the DES single key standard discussed earlier in this module.

When a principal wishes to communicate with a verifier, the principal first sends an authentication-request message to the Kerberos server, using the key that the principal shares with the Kerberos server. The message says that the principal wishes to communicate with the verifier.

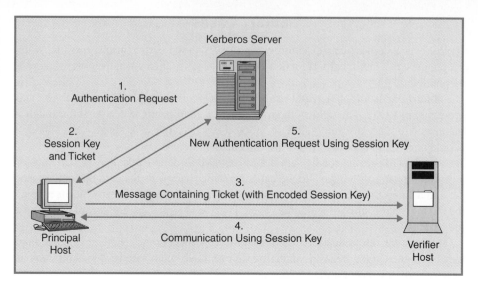

The Kerberos server responds by sending the principal a temporary DES **session key** that the principal and the verifier will use to communicate with one another during the communication session.

SENDING THE TICKET TO THE VERIFIER

The Kerberos server also sends a **"ticket"** to the principal. The principal sends this ticket to the verifier without encryption. The ticket is encrypted by the server with the secret single key that the *verifier* shares with the Kerberos server. This allows the verifier to read the ticket. The ticket contains the same session key that the Kerberos server sent to the principal. Both the principal and the server now have the session key and may communicate.

AUTHENTICATION

The verifier is willing to communicate because it knows that the principal is authentic. Only the Kerberos server knows the DES key that the verifier shares with the Kerberos server. So the ticket must have come from the Kerberos server. In addition, if subsequent communication can occur using the temporary session key, then the principal must have gotten the ticket from the Kerberos server for communication with the verifier.

SUBSEQUENT TICKET SERVICES

The ticket is only good for a short time period. If the principal needs to renew it, it communicates with the Kerberos server again, this time using the session key instead of its permanent single key that it shares with the Kerberos server. This minimizes the number of times the permanent single key will be exposed.

The Kerberos server then sends the principal an extended ticket to communicate with the same verifier or a new ticket to communicate with a new verifier, depending on what the principal specifies.

Key Recovery

To maximize security, only the two parties that are communicating should know the keys they use to communicate. Otherwise, someone could eavesdrop on their conversations or take other malicious actions.

However, there are two situations in which it might be desirable to have **key recovery** possible, that is, to allow a third party to gain access to a secret key. One is that people sometimes forget passwords and other secrets. If a user forgets his or her private key in public key encryption, for instance, the results can be disastrous.

The other is that governments have traditionally had the right to monitor communication to and from criminals or suspected criminals. Many criminal convictions have been made possible by wiretaps on telephones, and quite a few terrorist attacks have been thwarted in this way. The United States, in order to make keys breakable so that terrorists can be monitored, limits key length to 40 bits in exported products. In January 1998, such a key was broken in only 40 seconds. Assured key recovery would eliminate the need for very short keys.

One possibility for key recovery is **key escrow,** in which the secret key is stored in a secure place managed by trusted administrators and secured against attack. It is even possible for the secret key to be broken into parts, each of which is stored in a different place and is under the control of a different authority. Only strong collusion could cause a key to be reassembled without proper authorization.

Pretty Good Privacy (PGP)

Philip Zimmermann is a hero to many people. When the U.S. federal government was fighting against strong encryption, Zimmermann created a strong public key technology and made it available for free around the world. This was **Pretty Good Privacy (PGP),** which actually offers *very* good privacy.

Once the battle was lost, the U.S. government stopped prosecuting Zimmermann. PGP even went commercial, through PGP, Incorporated.

PGP is available for encryption in many systems, including e-mail systems. However, its use is being surpassed by other technologies in the marketplace.

Secure E-Mail

Although e-mail security is important, the IETF has not been successful to date in creating a secure e-mail standard. However, check the book's website because such a standard will be coming.

REVIEW QUESTIONS

1. Why are passwords important in terms of threats to overall security? Why are passwords usually easy to guess? What is the danger of giving people long random passwords? What does the book suggest as a minimum length for passwords? What guidelines does the book give to make passwords difficult to guess?

2. Why are network administrators a source of danger?

3. Why is network security not enough? Describe one problem with security on each of the following: servers, client PCs, and application programs. Why must you make sure that security procedures protect you against your own employees?

4. Distinguish between digital signatures and digital certificates.

5. For what is "message authentication code" another name? What is hashing? What is hashing used to create?

6. What protection do you have against someone copying your digital certificate and claiming to be you?

7. How can a receiver check to see if a digital certificate is from the certificate authority it claims created it?

8. Why is it problematic to have several grades of digital certificates? Are certificate authorities regulated today? What is a certificate revocation list, and why is it important?

9. Is DES a single key or public key system? What are the weaknesses of DES? Why is it popular anyway? How does 3DES strengthen it? Explain how 3DES works. How long is the DES key?

10. In IETF terminology, what is a port? What is a well-known port number? What is a socket? In SSL, what is a socket layer? How does its placement allow it to protect multiple applications? Who created SSL? Does it support authentication? Does it support privacy? What browsers support it? What is its biggest limitation?

11. What limitation of SSL does SET address? Does it really provide protection against that threat?

12. How does SET protect a merchant from knowing your credit card number? How can merchants get around this protection? (This question overlaps the previous question.)

13. In terms of TCP/IP–OSI layering, where is SET?

14. What parties are involved in a SET transaction? What is the role of each?

15. In SET, who is likely to benefit the most? Who is likely to pay the costs? Does this sound like a recipe for success?

16. What organization is standardizing IPsec? Name the main standards in the IPsec family. Briefly describe what each standard does.

17. Does IPsec work with both IPv4 and IPv6?

18. Distinguish between what the ESP and AH approaches provide. Why do we have AH, given its limitations?

19. What is tunneling? What is a security gateway?

20. What does ISAKMP do? Describe the negotiation process briefly.

21. What does OAKLEY do? Describe the Diffie-Hellman key exchange protocol briefly.

22. What does L2TP do? PPTP?

23. How does RADIUS work? What are its benefits?

24. Why will smart cards lower transaction costs?

25. What is measured in biometrics? What is the cheapest form of biometrics? What is the most expensive form? How can biometrics work with smart cards?

26. In Kerberos, describe the process a principal goes through to establish authenticated and secure communication with a verifier. What two keys will a principal use? How do they differ?

27. What is Pretty Good Privacy (PGP)?
28. What is the security standards situation in e-mail?

PROJECTS

1. Go to the book's website, http://www.prenhall.com/panko, and read the Updates Page for this module to see any reported errors and for new and expanded information on the material in this module.
2. Go to the book's website, http://www.prenhall.com/panko, and do the Internet Exercises for this module.

Internet Applications

Internet applications have appeared throughout this book, beginning in Chapter 1. This module looks somewhat more closely at the World Wide Web and at some smaller applications, including FTP, LISTSERVs, USENET newsgroups, and Telnet. Chapter 7 examines e-mail.

THE WORLD WIDE WEB

Hypertext

Nearly everyone is familiar with the World Wide Web. The Web is based on the concept of hypertext. As Figure G.1 illustrates, **hypertext** *consists of a collection of pages scattered across multiple host computers; pages may contain links that point to other hypertext documents on the same host or on different hosts.*

Early Developments

BUSH AND MEMEX

In a 1945 magazine article, Dr. Vannevar Bush[1] described a hypothetical machine called **Memex.** This machine would allow individuals to collect sources of information and index them in ways that would show *associations* between items of information. This would allow the user to return later and jump from one article to another based on associations among them.

---

[1] Reprinted in Irene Greif, ed., *Computer-Supported Cooperative Work: A Book of Readings* (San Mateo, CA: Morgan-Kaufman, 1988).

ENGELBART AND NLS/AUGMENT

In the early 1960s, Dr. Doug Engelbart actually built a Memex-like system at Stanford Research Institute. He called this system **NLS**, short for oN-Line System. As the name suggests, NLS was not only the first hypertext system, it was one of the first time-sharing systems of any type that allowed users to work at interactive terminals. Later, this name was changed to **Augment.**

In NLS/Augment documents, writers could insert links to other documents. As a result, when NLS was used to document software development projects, the documentation formed a web of associated papers and memos. Unfortunately, NLS/Augment used a proprietary linking technique and document format. This limited its use. However, NLS/Augment demonstrated the feasibility and power of hypertext systems. (Engelbart's project also gave us the mouse, integrated text and graphics, and numerous other seminal inventions.[2])

NELSON, HYPERTEXT, AND XANADU

While Engelbart was developing NLS/Augment, Ted Nelson was also being captivated by Bush's article. It was Nelson[3] who coined the term **hypertext.** He envisioned a universal hypertext document base called **Xanadu.**

---

[2] Several of Engelbart's papers have been reprinted in Greif, ed., *Computer-Supported Cooperative Work: A Book of Readings.*

[3] T. H. Nelson, "Replacing the Printed Word: A Complete Literary System," *IFIP Proceedings*, October 1980, 1013–1023.

The World Wide Web

BERNERS-LEE, HTTP, AND HTML

The real breakthrough in hypertext came when Timothy Berners-Lee created **World Wide Web** hypertext standards for the Internet in the early 1990s. As discussed in Chapter 2, the Internet already offered standards below the application layer. So Berners-Lee only had to create application layer standards.

This use of existing standards meant that the system that Berners-Lee developed, the World Wide Web, allowed new information servers to be added easily. Existing computers with Internet capability only had to add application software and data. They would then be immediately available to users.

Users, in turn, needed only an Internet connection and application software. An undergraduate student, Marc Andreesen, developed a program called **MOSAIC.** This was the first browser. Andreesen went on to form Netscape Corporation to commercialize his browser under the name **Navigator.** MOSAIC was also the basis for the first versions of Microsoft's browser, Internet Explorer. In a triple play, MOSAIC itself was commercialized under its own name.

HTTP

In order to allow any browser to talk to any webserver application program, Berners-Lee had to develop *two* standards, as shown in Figure G.2. First, he had to create a standard that would allow the client host to send a request to the webserver application program and for the webserver application program to send back a response. In Chapter 2, we saw that this standard was the **HyperText Transfer Protocol (HTTP).** To keep things simple, Berners-Lee based HTTP on the simple SMTP Internet standard for exchanging messages between e-mail systems (see Chapter 7). By adapting an existing simple standard, Berners-Lee made transfers easy to implement.

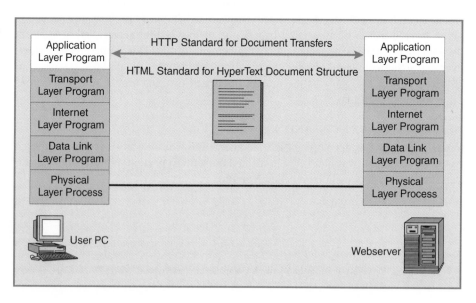

FIGURE G.2
World Wide Web Standards

HTML

Second, Berners-Lee had to create a standard for the structure of webpages themselves. As an editorial note, at the application layer, it *usually* is necessary to create two standards—one for application exchanges and another for document structure. HTTP can only transmit printable ASCII characters (basically, the characters on your keyboard). So links and other aspects of document structure had to be represented as tags within the text.

In proofreading, inserting notes about how to format a document is called marking up the document. Accordingly, Berners-Lee called his standard for specifying such tags the **HyperText Markup Language (HTML).**

Again, Berners-Lee borrowed from an existing standard, specifically the **Standard Generalized Markup Language (SGML)** standard. Although HTML is sometimes called a subset of SGML, it is not. SGML is not a markup language itself but rather a standard for creating specific markup languages, such as HTML. Each specific markup language is characterized by a **document type definition (DTD).** HTML is properly called an SGML DTD.

XML

In order to keep things simple, Berners-Lee used only a little of the functionality allowed by SGML. This was a good choice at first, and in fact HTML has shown how much functionality can be created with a simple markup language.

However, even with continual updates, HTML began to demonstrate serious limitations. As a result, another SGML DTD markup language has emerged with more functionality. This is the **Extensible Markup Language (XML).** XML gives document creators almost unlimited ability to create categories for new entities, such as attribute fields in databases. To give an example, if one tag is 〈Product Name〉 and another is 〈Price〉, a user can type a product name and ask for its price. HTML brought us open **text publishing;** XML will bring open **database publishing** and many things beyond that.

Increasingly, browsers are able to read XML documents as well as HTML documents, so the user typically is unaware of what markup language is being used in a document.

STREAMING AUDIO AND VIDEO

Typically, a browser downloads a file completely and only then displays it. This causes a delay in the file's appearance on screen. This delay is not bad for text, and it usually is only somewhat annoying for graphics of reasonable size. For large audio and video files, however, the delay is prohibitive.

As a result, many websites now offer **streaming** audio and video, in which audio and video files begin to be played (almost) as soon as the first bytes begin to arrive. This dramatically reduces the initial wait between the download command and the time when audio and video start playing. It also means that you do not have to store large temporary audio and video files on your hard disk, as you do when files are downloaded entirely before beginning to be played.

However, streaming technology does have one major downside. There are competing streaming technologies in both audio and video, and if you wish to hear or see a streaming presentation, you may have to download a special **player program.**

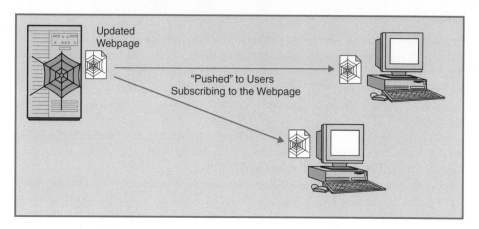

Updated Webpage

"Pushed" to Users
Subscribing to the Webpage

PUSH TECHNOLOGY

One of the most radical changes in the Web since its initiation has been the creation of **push** technology, shown in Figure G.3. Traditionally, if there were several webpages important to you, you had no way of knowing when they changed. You had to download each webpage periodically to check for changes. Often, there would be no changes, so the downloading would be a waste of time.

In push technology, the effect is as if the webservers periodically downloaded updated versions of subscribed webpages to you without your conscious effort. Whenever you read one of these webpages, it would be a very recent version. The webservers would *push* the webpages to you, instead of your having to *pull* them.

Actually, the webservers do not really take the initiative. Your push-enabled browser periodically sends requests to the webservers to push any updated webpages to your computer. However, to the user, the webservers really do appear to be taking the initiative.

File Standards

When the Web first appeared, most browsers could handle only HTML and one or two other file standards, such as GIF and JPEG for images. Over time, browsers have become much broader in the file standards they will support natively. However, developers still face a difficult choice when building webpages. If they use advanced file formats, many browsers will not be able to read them unless potential readers download special add-ins. So website vividness must be considered in the context of lost viewership.

Improving the World Wide Web

Although the World Wide Web has already brought dramatic benefits, we are beginning to see some problems caused by its basic simplicity. We have already mentioned some of these.

DOWNLOAD SPEEDS

As Chapter 2 discussed, downloading a single webpage may require multiple HTTP request–response cycles. The first will download the HTML document. Successive

HTTP request–response cycles will download images, sound clips, Java applets, and other files referenced in the base HTML document.

Chapter 2 noted that each HTTP/1.0 request–response cycle requires the creation of a new TCP connection, the transfer of the request and response messages, and the breakdown of the TCP connection. Setting up and breaking down TCP connections for each download is very time consuming.

In addition, when TCP first begins to transmit, it usually does so fairly slowly, to avoid overloading the other host. Later, if no problems appear, TCP begins to transmit faster. In brief HTTP request–response cycles, however, TCP never gets up to speed.

Newer versions of HTTP, beginning with HTTP/1.1, create a single TCP connection that will be used to download not only the initial HTML page but also all referenced pages as well. This avoids multiple TCP connection setups and breakdowns. It may also give TCP a chance to get up to speed in its transfers. Overall, requiring only one TCP connection per HTTP request–response cycle could cut some download times in half.

STATES AND COOKIES

When HTTP was created, it was envisioned that each request–response cycle would be separate. A webserver host would not remember you from request to request. It would simply get the file you requested and send it to you.

Not having to remember users has advantages. Most obviously, it reduces work on the webserver host, which does not have to consult its files to see what the user has asked for in the past.

More complex actions, however, such as financial transactions, consist of a sequence of HTTP request–response cycles that build upon one another. Each action in the sequence creates a **state** (condition). The next action builds upon that state to create a new state.

For example, to place an order, you must first give your name, then add a number of items to your electronic in-basket, and then agree to pay the total. Giving initial information creates a state. The host must remember this information in later phases of the transaction. Each item you add changes the state. Finally, agreeing to pay for the total may require several messages, each changing the state.

To help webservers keep track of what users have done in the past, browsers allow webservers to store brief text files on the user's PC hard disk drive. These short text messages are called **cookies.** When the user sends a message to the webserver, the webserver can also get the cookie to see what has been done in the past.

One common use of cookies is to store passwords. Some websites require you to log in. Many of these sites will store your login information in a cookie on your hard disk. Later, if you connect to the site, the webserver will use your password stored in your cookie, instead of requiring you to remember the password.

Cookies are somewhat controversial because they allow a webserver to store files on your hard disk drive. However, because they are text files, they are not programs. They cannot act like viruses.

FTP

The World Wide Web is a very nice way to **download** information from a server host to a client host. The process is very simple, and webpages can be rich with graphics, animation, and other elements that are attractive to users. However, the Internet also

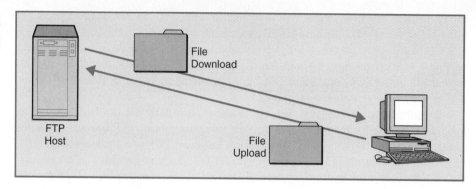

offers a much older way to download files from server to client. This is the **File Transfer Protocol (FTP),** which was one of the earliest application standards on the Internet.

Both Downloading and Uploading

Although the Web is glamorous, FTP offers one important thing that HTTP does not. As Figure G.4 shows, this is the ability to **upload** files in the other direction, from the client host to the FTP server host. So if you work with someone, FTP allows you to send files to that person for his or her use.

Logging In

If someone can download files from a host computer, this is potentially dangerous. Uploading files is also potentially dangerous. So before you can work with a host computer, FTP requires you to log into that computer.

For this, you need a **username** and a **password**—things you do not need on the World Wide Web with its limited but highly controlled transfer process. In some directories, you will only be allowed to upload files. In other directories, you will only be allowed to download them. In some directories, you will be able to do both. In *most* directories on the computer, you will not be able either to upload or to download files.

The need for the user to obtain a username and password ahead of time and the requirement for the server authority to make certain directories read-only make FTP more cumbersome to use than the World Wide Web.

Anonymous FTP

Some host servers offer **anonymous FTP.** Actually, this is normal FTP with two exceptions. First, you log in with a standard user name, **"anonymous."** For the password, in turn, you give your e-mail address.

You then have access to certain directories set aside for public files. You do not have access to all files on the computer.

In addition, you usually can *only download* files from these directories. File uploading usually is forbidden. Before webservers, anonymous FTP was the most popular way of offering information to the public.

By the way, anonymous FTP is not really anonymous. The host knows your internet address because all IP packets that you send to the server host contain your internet address.

No File Structure Standards in FTP

We have said that application standards usually consist of two types of standards—transfer standards and file structure standards. FTP, however, is a pure **transfer standard.**

The benefit of not defining a file content standard is that there is no limit to the type of file that FTP can transfer. You can transfer word processing files, spreadsheet files, or any other type of file you need.

On the negative side, the receiver of the file must know how to recognize and handle the transferred file type. This often requires prior communication between the two parties involved in the transfer, often via e-mail. If the type of file is new to the person trying to read it, problems are likely to occur.

Archiving

In addition, files on the FTP server often are archived. As Figure G.5 illustrates, **archiving** combines several files into a single file. Next, that single file is compressed so that it takes up less room. At the other end, of course, the file must be dearchived. This decompresses the file and turns it back into multiple files. By the way, you can archive a single file in order to take advantage of compression.

Unfortunately, there are many archiving standards. Although the **zip** archiving standard is the most common, it is far from universal. As a result, the user has to know what archiving process (if any) was used on a file before storage, as well as how to deal with the dearchived file format. FTP is not for the faint of heart.

One help in dearchiving is that many archived files are now **self-dearchiving.** These files end with the *.exe* extension. Running the file as a program causes the embedded dearchiving program to decompress the archive and break it into separate files. You do not need separate dearchiving software. You do not even need to know how the archiving was done.

One danger of .exe files of any type is that they may contain viruses. So your "self-extracting game program" may actually be a self-extracting malicious virus. You must be careful with self-extracting files.

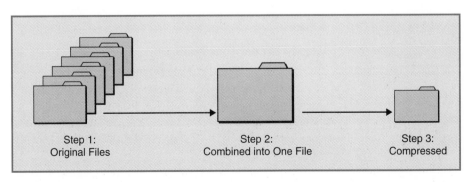

Step 1:
Original Files

Step 2:
Combined into One File

Step 3:
Compressed

LISTSERVs

Suppose you have a project team or wish to participate in a discussion group. You would like to have a shared mailing list that has everyone's name instead of having to type the names individually. In addition, you would like a single person to maintain the mailing list so everyone will be using the same list. (Otherwise, not everyone would get every message.) Maintaining such a list would be difficult because in many project teams, people join and leave the team during the course of the project.

LISTSERV software provides exactly that functionality. A program called a LISTSERV manager resides on a server. Team members can post messages to the LISTSERV manager when they have something to say to the group. The LISTSERV manager will then send the posting to other members of the group via ordinary Internet e-mail.

Users can also send **supervisory messages** to the LISTSERV manager. Most importantly, they can send *subscribe* and *unsubscribe* messages. These add them to the group mailing list and drop them from the group mailing list, respectively.

Another common supervisory message allows a user to see a list of his or her group's members.

Supervisory messages are also provided for each LISTSERV group's moderator, such as the ability to drop members from a mailing list if these people cannot send unsubscribe messages themselves.

Subscribing to a LISTSERV Group

Figure G.6 shows the process of subscribing to a newsgroup. Here the LISTSERV management program is called *LISTSERV*. It manages two LISTSERV groups, *GLOBAL-L* and *CRIME-L*. The host is *puka.org*.

FIGURE G.6

Subscribing to a LISTSERV Group

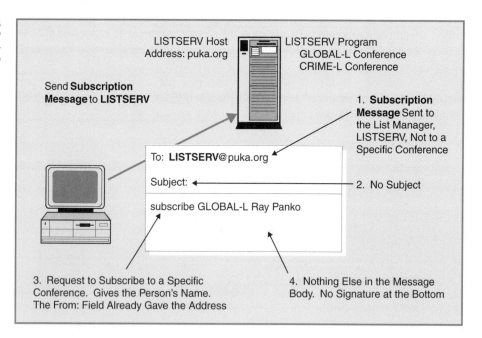

LISTSERV Host
Address: puka.org

LISTSERV Program
GLOBAL-L Conference
CRIME-L Conference

Send **Subscription Message** to **LISTSERV**

To: **LISTSERV**@puka.org

Subject:

subscribe GLOBAL-L Ray Panko

1. **Subscription Message** Sent to the List Manager, LISTSERV, Not to a Specific Conference

2. No Subject

3. Request to Subscribe to a Specific Conference. Gives the Person's Name. The From: Field Already Gave the Address

4. Nothing Else in the Message Body. No Signature at the Bottom

TO:

To subscribe, you must first know the name of the LISTSERV manager, which in this case is called *LISTSERV*. The names of two other popular LISTSERV program managers are Majordomo and Maiser (Mail Server).

You must then know the name of the LISTSERV host computer, which in this case is *puka.org*.

In the To: field, you type *LISTSERV@puka.org*. Note that the **subscription message** goes to the LISTSERV management program, not to the name of the conference.

SUBJECT:

The subject field will be ignored, so you can leave it blank or put in anything you wish.

BODY:

The body's contents must be entered very precisely.

A Single Line   As Figure G.6 shows, the body must have only a single line, and it must have this form exactly:

subscribe conferencename yourname

Note that the line begins with the word *subscribe*, not *subscribe to*.

Note also that there is no period at the end of the line.

Subscribe is the keyword.

GLOBAL-L is the conference to which you wish to subscribe. Many LISTSERV group names end with "-L" to indicate that they are lists. However, this is far from universal.

Finally, *yourname* is your name. You can also give a **handle,** such as "Spidey" or "Ra3y." Using a handle preserves your anonymity to some extent. However, your e-mail address may appear in postings sent on to group members, so you usually do not have real anonymity.

Nothing Else in the Body, Including Signatures   Note also that there is nothing else in the body. If you have a signature file that is added automatically at the end of the body in messages you send, you must suspend its use for this message.

RESPONSE MESSAGE

If your subscription message is accepted, the LISTSERV manager sends a **response message** to your e-mail address. This message welcomes you to the conference. It also lays out any conference rules.

Always keep this message in a folder. It is considered rude to send a message to everyone in the conference saying, "Hi, there. I've forgotten how to unsubscribe. Can someone unsubscribe me?"

Posting Messages

Now that you are a member of the group, you can post messages to everyone in the group. Figure G.7 shows how this is done.

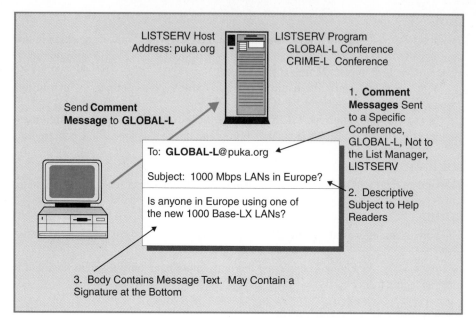

LISTSERV Host
Address: puka.org

LISTSERV Program
GLOBAL-L Conference
CRIME-L Conference

Send **Comment
Message** to **GLOBAL-L**

1. **Comment
Messages** Sent
to a Specific
Conference,
GLOBAL-L, Not to
the List Manager,
LISTSERV

To: **GLOBAL-L**@puka.org

Subject: 1000 Mbps LANs in Europe?

Is anyone in Europe using one of
the new 1000 Base-LX LANs?

2. Descriptive
Subject to Help
Readers

3. Body Contains Message Text. May Contain a
Signature at the Bottom

TO:

Supervisory messages are sent to the **LISTSERV manager.** In the previous example, for instance, we sent the supervisory subscribe message to LISTSERV@puka.org.

When you wish to **post** a message to your group, however, you put the *name of the group* in your message's To: field, rather than the name of the LISTSERV manager. In this example, you put GLOBAL-L@puka.org in the To: field.

This is quite confusing. You must keep in mind that when you send a supervisory message, you are communicating with the conference supervisory, the LISTSERV management program. When you send a posting, however, you are communicating within the group.

OTHER FIELDS

There are no restrictions on other fields in the message, although you should follow the conference rules. For instance, there usually are rules against sending long messages or posting messages with attachments.

Receiving Postings

When other members of your LISTSERV group post messages, the LISTSERV manager forwards the messages to everyone in the group, using ordinary Internet e-mail.

The nice thing about this approach is that postings appear in your e-mail in-box, along with your regular e-mail messages. There is no need to load a special program to read your LISTSERV postings, just as there is no need for a special program to subscribe, to submit postings, or, as we will see next, to unsubscribe.

The bad thing about this approach is that postings appear in your e-mail in-box, along with your regular e-mail postings. If you are in one or more active conferences, you may get a dozen or more postings each day. In the swarm of messages arriving in your mailbox each morning, you may find it difficult to find important regular e-mail messages addressed specifically to you.

Users who receive a large number of LISTSERV postings often set up a filtering rule in their e-mail program. The rule specifies that if the name of a LISTSERV group appears in the From: field of the arriving message, then the message should be moved automatically from the in-box to a folder for that conference. This way, when you first read your mail, you will see only messages sent specifically to you. You can go to the folder where you store your incoming LISTSERV messages when you have time.

LEAVING A LISTSERV GROUP

To join the group, you send a *subscribe* message. To leave the group, you send an **unsubscribe** message.

TO:

Again, you send the message to LISTSERV@puka.org. This is a supervisory message, so you send it to the LISTSERV manager, not to your entire group. As noted earlier, it is considered rude to send an unsubscribe message to the entire group.

SUBJECT:

The LISTSERV manager ignores the subject field, so you can put anything here that you want, as was the case in your subscribe message.

BODY:

Again, the body must have a single line. It must be typed exactly, and there must not be a signature file attached to your message. The single line is:

unsubscribe listname yourname

USENET NEWSGROUPS

Although LISTSERV works, it is something of a brute force approach. There is a more elegant conferencing system on the Internet. This is **USENET.**[4]

USENET Hosts and Replication

Figure G.8 shows that there are many **USENET hosts** on the Internet. These hosts run the **USENET host program.**

To read or post messages, you need a **newsreader program** on your PC. You can get a special newsreader program designed specifically to read USENET newsgroups. In addition, most browser suites now come with a newsreader module.

To read postings, you can connect to *any* USENET host in the world that will accept your connection. The ability to connect to any USENET host is possible because USENET hosts **replicate** (send) their postings to all other USENET hosts, as shown in Figure G.8. When you post a message to one USENET host, your message will go to all other USENET hosts, often within a single day.

---

[4] USENET actually began outside the Internet as a collection of UNIX host computers. However, USENET hosts now usually employ the Internet to communicate with one another and with users.

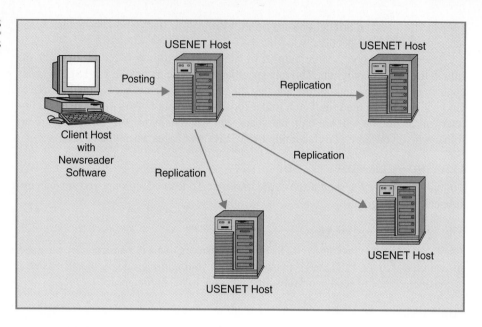

Similarly, a posting anywhere in the world will arrive at your selected USENET host within hours or days.

Newsgroups

Each USENET host supports thousands of **newsgroups,** which are discussion groups on particular topics. Figure G.9 shows that newsgroup names are arranged hierarchically. Not all USENET hosts carry all newsgroups, especially those in the "Alt" category, in which, generally speaking, "anything goes." The "Comp" family—especially the Comp.dcom subfamily—is very popular with networking professionals.

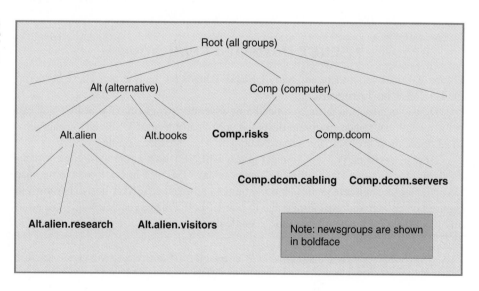

Subscribing to Newsgroups

Originally, newsgroups were seen as being like newspapers and magazines. It was envisioned that you would **subscribe** to a few, just as you do newspapers and magazines. You would see only these subscribed newsgroups when you connected to your USENET host, making your life easier.

As a result, dealing with newsgroups is still a two-step process in most USENET hosts and newsreader programs. You first look through a list of available newsgroups to select ones that interest you. You then subscribe to them. Afterward, you see only subscribed newsgroups unless you specifically ask to see the whole list again.

Reading Postings

When you have finished subscribing, your USENET newsreader program will show your subscribed newsgroups in a window in the upper left part of the screen. You then select a particular newsgroup you wish to read.

Another window in the upper right portion of the screen shows one-line summaries of recent postings in the selected newsgroup. If you click on a posting, you will see its contents in another window at the bottom of the screen.

Submitting Postings

It is also easy to submit a posting. Your newsgroup reader will have a "post" command or button. If you hit it while in a newsgroup, a window will open up that will look very much like the window you use to send e-mail. You will type your posting, and your newsreader will post it to your USENET host.

Threads

Another way to send a posting is to give a REPLY command while reading a particular message. As Figure G.10 shows, replies are not listed in chronological order. Instead, a reply is listed as a subposting under the original posting. This grouping of a message

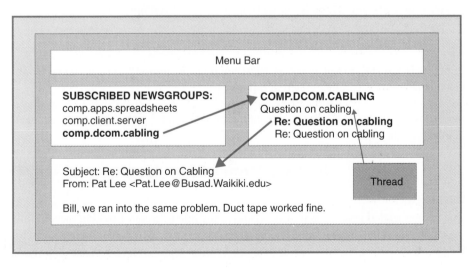

FIGURE G.10

Reading a Newsgroup's Recent Postings in USENET

and subsequent replies to it is called a **thread.** Threads are important because we often want to see not only a posting but also subsequent comments on the posting as well.

LISTSERVs VERSUS USENET NEWSGROUPS

LISTSERVs and USENET newsgroups are both "computer conferencing" systems that support communication within groups. However, they operate differently, and this creates relative advantages.

Delivery: Ordinary E-Mail versus Newsreader Programs

The most obvious difference between the two is message delivery. In LISTSERV, you use your ordinary e-mail program to subscribe, send and read postings, unsubscribe, and send other supervisory messages.

As we saw earlier, this is both a blessing and a curse. It is a blessing because you do not have to learn how to use a newsreader program and because you do not have to take any special action to receive postings. The postings arrive in your ordinary e-mail in-box.

The curse is that active LISTSERV groups can glut your in-box with messages, making it difficult to find messages sent specifically to you.

USENET is the opposite. You will not get any postings unless you specifically start your newsreader program, connect to the USENET host, and go to a subscribed group.

Finding the Host

One problem with LISTSERV conferences is that you need to know the name of the LISTSERV host. Note in Figure G.6 and Figure G.7 that the name of the host appears in the To: field of all messages. There is no central list of LISTSERV hosts on the Internet, much less a list of individual LISTSERV groups.

In contrast, most USENET hosts carry most newsgroups. So to look for interesting newsgroups, all you have to do is connect to *any* USENET host and read through the list of available newsgroups. The newsgroups are even listed hierarchically, to make your searching easy. You can then subscribe to a particular newsgroup and watch the postings for a few days to see if it is a group you wish to continue following.

PROPER BEHAVIOR IN CONFERENCES

In both LISTSERV groups and USENET newsgroups, proper behavior is important. Good behavior is sometimes called **netiquette.**

Good behavior is important because many LISTSERV and USENET groups have thousands of readers. If you send an inappropriate message, you will waste a great deal of other people's time.

Adopting Proper Behavior

LURKING

One recommended practice is to lurk when joining a new group. **Lurking** means simply reading postings, without making contributions of your own. Lurking allows you to see the style of the conference. Some conferences are positively rude in the directness of exchanges, whereas others adopt a more professional style. Learn a group's style before jumping in with postings of your own.

READ THE FAQs!

Most conferences have **frequently asked questions (FAQs)** that are posted periodically. You should not send postings unless you have read the FAQs.

One reason for FAQs is to provide answers for frequently asked questions, so that you will not post one of these questions. Long-time members of the group are tired of seeing these questions asked. One good way to see how many members there are in a group is to post a frequently asked question and count the number of angry responses you receive.

Another reason for FAQs is to post the rules for the group. These rules lay out what is considered to be legitimate and illegitimate in message postings.

Flaming

As noted in Chapter 7, **flaming** is the posting of angry messages. Flaming is bad in one-to-few e-mail, but it is disastrous in LISTSERV and USENET conferences. When you send flames to a conference, you are flaming many people.

Spamming

We saw in Chapter 7 that **spamming** is the sending of commercial messages. In LISTSERV and USENET conferences, it is easy to spam all members of a newsgroup. You simply post your message. It is much easier than spamming in e-mail, where you need to develop large distribution lists. Spamming began in USENET and has since spilled over to e-mail.

LONG MESSAGES AND ATTACHMENTS

It is almost always inappropriate to send long messages in LISTSERV and USENET. In LISTSERV conferences, furthermore, adding attachments to an e-mail posting is also considered rude. Long messages waste a great deal of reader time. In LISTSERV, long messages can even run the receiver's in-box over its maximum capacity.

Moderated Conferences

Some LISTSERV and USENET conferences are moderated. In a **moderated** conference, postings do not go automatically to all members. Instead, they first go to a human moderator. The moderator checks the message for appropriateness. He or she then deletes inappropriate messages. Unfortunately, moderating a conference can be a great deal of work. As a result, moderated conferences are fairly rare.

TELNET

We saw in Chapter 7 that if you have a POP or IMAP client program, you can download your e-mail from anywhere on the Internet. All you need is a POP or IMAP mail client program on your PC.

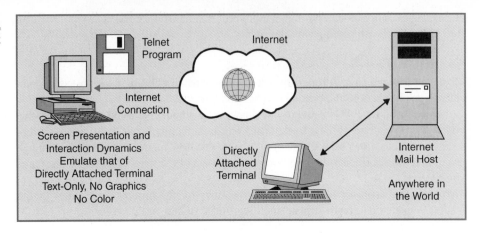

Access from Anywhere

Telnet offers another way to read your mail from anywhere, if your mail host supports terminal access. Figure G.11 shows that you first connect to the Internet. You then connect to your mail host using a **Telnet** program. To the host, you look exactly like a terminal user attached directly to the host. To you, your client PC looks like a terminal.

Terminal User Interface

Once connected, you can run any program on the host computer that a directly connected VT100 terminal user can run.[5] Obviously, this includes a mail program. However, Telnet is not limited to e-mail. You can run statistical analysis programs, database programs, or any other programs that are on the host and that will work with Telnet terminals.

Unfortunately, Telnet only offers a very limited terminal. It is limited to simple text, without boldface or other emphasis, without multiple fonts, and without graphics. There is a single color against a contrasting background.

Why Not POP or IMAP?

Chapter 7 noted that there is a more attractive way to read your mail remotely. This is to have a mail client program on your PC. Such mail clients have attractive graphical user interfaces. Like Telnet programs, mail clients can attach to any mail host anywhere in the world. When they download mail, however, they show it to you with an attractive user interface.

However, not all mail hosts support POP and IMAP. In addition, basic POP, which is more common than IMAP, does not give you the ability to manage your messages on the host computer. Telnet does this, as does IMAP.

Also, while POP and IMAP deal only with e-mail, as noted above, Telnet can run any terminal-based program. It is a broader product.

---

[5] Module H discusses VT100 terminals.

In general, however, Telnet is yesterday's way of dealing with Internet hosts, especially Internet mail hosts. As IMAP becomes more popular, Telnet should fade even further in importance.

Of historical note, the original ARPANET, which gave rise to the Internet, was created specifically for Telnet. The idea was to let researchers at different sites use one another's host computers. This way, DARPA money spent to develop software would not be wasted because the software could run only on a single machine, as was common in those days.

This Telnet focus was so strong that when the first e-mail systems appeared, they were bootleg efforts developed without permission by individual ARPANET users, such as Ray Tomlinson. It actually took some time for e-mail traffic to be accepted as legitimate by ARPA. The big breakthrough came when Larry Roberts, who headed the ARPANET effort at DARPA, wrote the first complex program for reading ARPANET mail.

REVIEW QUESTIONS

CORE REVIEW QUESTIONS

1. What did Berners-Lee have to invent to create the World Wide Web? How did he simplify his work?
2. Distinguish between HTML and XML.
3. Why do users like streaming audio and video? What limitations does streaming technology have?
4. Explain "states" in the context of a financial transaction. Can native HTML keep track of a transaction's state? How can the webserver keep track of state?
5. What is FTP? What can FTP do that HTML cannot?
6. Distinguish between FTP and anonymous FTP in terms of the need for an account and password and in terms of what you can do on the host.
7. In LISTSERVs, to what address do you send supervisory messages? To what address do you send postings to a particular group?
8. In LISTSERV *subscribe* and *unsubscribe* messages, what must be in the body? What must NOT be in the body? Are signatures allowed?
9. Distinguish between USENET and newsgroups.
10. Explain replication in the context of USENET hosts.
11. Explain how you would search for an interesting newsgroup.
12. In USENET newsgroups, what is a *thread*?
13. Distinguish between LISTSERV and USENET in terms of how postings are received. What are the relative merits of these approaches?
14. Discuss the relative difficulty of finding interesting LISTSERV groups versus interesting USENET newsgroups.
15. What are FAQs, and why is it important to read them?
16. What are moderated conferences? Why are they good? Why are they fairly rare?
17. Compare Telnet and IMAP in terms of ease of use and what they can do.

DETAILED REVIEW QUESTIONS

1. Define hypertext. Trace its origins before the World Wide Web.
2. Explain why HTML and XML are not subsets of SGML. What is a document type definition?
3. In what two ways can we improve TCP to enjoy faster World Wide Web downloads?
4. Explain the problems of file formats in FTP compared to the problem of file formats in World Wide Web.
5. What two things does archiving do? What are self-dearchiving files? Why are they good? Why are they dangerous?
6. Give the names of some popular LISTSERV management programs.
7. In LISTSERV conferences, what is a *response message*, and why should you keep the response message when you join a conference?
8. Explain the following: netiquette, lurking, flaming, and spamming.
9. Why should you lurk when first joining a group?
10. Why should you not send long messages or messages with attachments to a conference?

THOUGHT QUESTIONS

1. Do you think cookies are bad for you?
2. How does the LISTSERV program know your e-mail address? What must you do if you wish to have LISTSERV messages delivered to two or more e-mail addresses?
3. How do you think unmoderated LISTSERV conferences and USENET newsgroups reduce improper behavior among their members? When do you think this is effective? When do you think it is ineffective?

PROJECTS

1. Go to the book's website, http://www.prenhall.com/panko, and read the Updates Page for this module to see any reported errors and for new and expanded information on the material in this module.
2. Go to the book's website, http://www.prenhall.com/panko, and do the Internet Exercises for this module.

More on Terminal–Host Communication

INTRODUCTION

Although client/server computing dominates organizational computing today, terminal–host communication is still very widespread and will continue to be important for many years to come. Even if a corporation wanted to get rid of its legacy terminal–host systems, the cost of rewriting host software would require a transition of several years.

MATCHING TERMINALS WITH HOSTS

Terminal–host systems were designed long before the days of open standards. So you cannot use any terminal you wish with any host. Rather, each host will work only with a few types of terminals. So if you want to use a host computer, you will need a terminal acceptable to that host.

This insistence on working with only a single terminal or a few terminals is not just a whim on the part of host designers. As the name terminal–host system suggests, terminals, hosts, and communication capabilities are designed as an overall system to give optimum performance and costs under certain conditions of use. Changing just one part of a system, such as a terminal, can undermine the performance of the entire system.

Although this lack of freedom in mixing terminals and hosts can be frustrating to users, it has a key advantage. It allows terminal–host systems, including terminals, hosts, and communication links, to be optimized for specific uses.

VT100 SYSTEMS

For instance, the first terminal–host system we will see in this module, the VT100 system, is designed for people who will use the terminal only a few minutes per day. For these users, having an inexpensive terminal is crucial, because a high-cost terminal could not be justified for such light use. The VT100 terminals used in such systems cost only about two hundred dollars to buy. In fact, we will see that software allows your existing PC to emulate a VT100 terminal.

Although every host system has a preferred terminal, many host systems make an exception and allow access through VT100 terminals. In effect, the VT100 terminal has become a lowest common denominator terminal that is accepted, at least grudgingly, by many host systems.

IBM MAINFRAME SYSTEMS

The second terminal–host system we will see, in contrast, is designed for environments where users will be online most of the day, such as order entry departments. This is the IBM mainframe terminal–host system. Although this system uses a much more expensive terminal, it dramatically reduces transmission costs and the load on the host computer. In high-volume applications, it can even be less expensive overall than a VT100 system.

In addition, IBM mainframe systems are designed for high reliability in transmission, because the operations that depend on them cannot suffer outages or poor service without having a serious impact on the firm. So instead of using the TCP/IP architecture with its best-effort protocols, IBM mainframe systems use IBM's own Systems Network Architecture (SNA), which is designed to link terminals to hosts in real time. This requires almost zero latency.

AS/400 TERMINAL–HOST SYSTEMS

VT100 and IBM mainframe systems are undoubtedly the most important terminal–host systems in use today. However, there are two other terminal–host systems that we should at least mention in passing.

Large companies buy IBM mainframes when they need terminal–host systems. However, for smaller firms, it would be prohibitively expensive to buy or lease a mainframe and pay for the systems programming staff needed to keep the mainframe running.

As a result, many smaller and midsize firms use an IBM small-business computer called the **AS/400** (Application System/400). AS/400s are relatively inexpensive to buy, and they do not require a large systems programmer staff to keep running. In addition, they offer high-level languages to increase programmer productivity. Finally, many small-business software packages have been designed to run on the AS/400. IBM has even developed webserver software to run on this popular system that is the computer equivalent of a light pickup truck.

NETWORK COMPUTERS AND WINDOWS TERMINALS

As discussed in Chapter 1, many organizations are concerned about the high cost of buying and maintaining their large fleets of desktop personal computers. As a result, several alternatives to general-purpose desktop PCs have been put forth as ways to reduce the total lifetime cost of ownership of desktop machines.

One alternative discussed in Chapter 1 was the **network computer (NC).** NCs, in principle, have no hard disk drives. When they need a program, they download it from a program server on the network. To reduce costs further, NCs are limited to programs written in a single language, Java. Even when the total cost of NCs, program servers, and network transmission is considered, NC vendors claim that the cost of network computer systems would be much lower than the cost of personal computers.

One of the ways in which Microsoft has tried to counter the NC movement was to develop **Windows terminals.** Obviously, the Achilles heel of NCs is their inability to run programs created for Windows PCs. Windows terminals attack that weakness directly. Their program server runs regular Windows applications, drawing the results on the screens of relatively dumb Windows terminal devices. This allows inexpensive desktop devices to run all Windows software. Again, the burning issue is the total cost of the entire system, including Windows terminals, program servers, and higher loads on the transmission network.

Although the NC–Windows terminal war has produced more heat than light, it does have the potential to revolutionize the role of terminals. As we will see below, dumb VT100 terminals have poor user interfaces. IBM mainframe terminals also tend to have clumsy user interfaces. Both NCs and Windows terminals, in contrast, have the potential to bring extremely good user interfaces to places where terminals are being used and will continue to be used—for example, in hotel registration desks and ticket booths at theaters.

Such applications use only one or two application programs, so even the NC's inability to run the full spectrum of Windows applications is not an issue. Also, such applications have enough outlets to justify the cost of writing new Java software. Both NCs and Windows terminals can serve such niche markets with excellent user interfaces.

VT100 TERMINAL–HOST SYSTEMS

As noted earlier, systems using VT100 terminals are designed for casual users who can live with low performance in order to achieve low terminal cost and in order to connect to many different types of hosts, including Internet hosts.

Terminals and Hosts

Figure H.1 illustrates a basic **VT100-based terminal–host system.** It is very simple. It consists of a VT100 terminal on the user's desk, a host computer (minicomputer or mainframe), and a transmission line connecting the two devices. We will see later that IBM mainframe systems are far more complex.

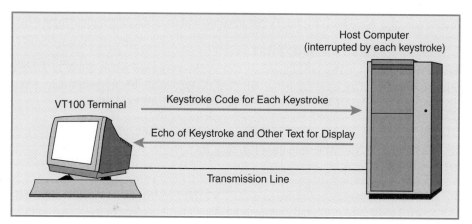

FIGURE H.1

VT100-Based Terminal–Host System

Host Computer
(interrupted by each keystroke)

VT100 Terminal

Keystroke Code for Each Keystroke

Echo of Keystroke and Other Text for Display

Transmission Line

This simplicity creates a problem, however. When the VT100 terminal was designed, there were no microprocessors. So there was no way to give it intelligence. The VT100 terminal could only be a remote keyboard and display. It could only be a **dumb terminal.**

Consequently, all processing in a VT100 system is done on the host. In normal operation, when you type a key, you send a frame to the host computer containing that key's designation. The host echoes the key back to you, along with the results of any processing it has done.

This approach has two obvious disadvantages. First, if the host computer is heavily loaded, it may take a second or two for what you type to be echoed back to your screen. This is very disconcerting.

Second, sending every keystroke separately places a very heavy load on the host computer. Every time a keystroke arrives, the host has to stop the job it is processing and handle that keystroke. Each of these interruptions takes a long time to process (as far as the host is concerned). The host must transfer what it is working on to storage, then load a special interrupt-handling program to process the keystroke. Afterward, it must reload the original job. In other words, if you type a sentence with only 10 words, you will cause this interrupt handling cycle to occur about 60 times in the space of only a few seconds.

VT100 Terminals

WIDESPREAD USE

We have said that VT100-based terminal–host systems are lowest-common-denominator systems that are widely supported. There are three reasons for this widespread support.

1. Digital Equipment Corporation created the VT100 terminal in the 1960s for use with Digital's minicomputers. Because of Digital's high market share, other minicomputer vendors designed their systems to work with VT100 terminals. Mainframe vendors eventually followed suit as a way to reach light users.
2. Later, when the American National Standards Institute (ANSI) wanted a standard for low-end terminals, it settled upon the VT100 design.
3. In addition, the ARPANET was created originally to allow a terminal user in one location to log into a host computer in another location. The VT100 design was selected as the basis for the Telnet standard that supports such remote logins.

A DESIGN FROZEN IN THE PAST

Today, even users of Digital Equipment Corporation computers see the VT100 as a relic of the past. They have far better terminal designs available to them today. Standardization froze the VT100 terminal in time, like a fly in amber.

NO GRAPHICAL USER INTERFACE

One problem with VT100 terminals is that they do not offer the user a modern graphical user interface.

▶ The user interface is limited to text. A VT100 terminal has no graphics capability. Users must give up the attractive graphical user interfaces they have on PCs.

▶ There is only a single font for the screen. The font's characters have fixed widths, in contrast to proportional fonts, in which narrow letters such as "i" are given less space than letters such as "M." This paragraph is shown in a nonproportional font.

▶ Finally, text is monochrome, consisting of a single color against a contrasting background color.

SLOW SPEED

Another limit of VT100 terminals is low-speed operation. These terminals communicate with the outside world using the EIA/TIA-232-F serial plug we saw in Chapter 3. The standard limits such plugs to 20 kbps. Although PCs today can drive their serial plugs at higher speeds, VT100 terminals respect the limit. In fact, 9600 bps is high for VT100 terminals.

ASCII

Another limit of VT100 terminals is that they use a character code called **ASCII,** the American Standard Code for Information Interchange. It is also known as International Alphabet 5. When we write in English, we have to spell our words using the 26 letters of the alphabet. In digital transmission, we have to "spell out" everything in ones and zeros.

ASCII encodes each character as a string of 7 bits (ones or zeros). Figure H.2 shows the ASCII code for "Happy Birthday." Note that each letter is represented by a

FIGURE **H.2**

ASCII Codes for "Happy Birthday"

LETTER	ASCII CODE
H	1001000
a	1100001
p	1110000
p	1110000
y	1111001
	0100000
B	1000010
i	1101001
r	1110010
t	1110100
h	1101000
d	1100100
a	1100001
y	1111001
.	0101110

Notes: Every character to be printed needs a 7-bit ASCII code. Capital *H* and lowercase *h* have different codes so they will print differently. The space between "Happy" and "Birthday" needs a code so it will print. The period needs a code so it will print.

7-bit code. We also have to represent the period and even the space by ASCII codes. (Otherwise, they would not print or appear on our monitor.) Note also that upper case *H* and lower case *h* have different codes, so that monitors and printers will be able to display them differently.

Strict ASCII, using only 7 bits per character, is limited to printing characters—the characters you see on your keyboard—plus a few control codes to let the terminal and host send rudimentary supervisory commands.

In contrast, personal computers use **extended ASCII,** which has 8 bits per character. This eighth bit doubles the number of possible symbols. These additional symbols are often used by applications for such things as formatting codes. These formatting codes are hidden from the user, but they allow boldface and other formatting information to be embedded in word processing files. Extended ASCII is also used on PCs to represent graphics. Overall, not using extended ASCII is why VT100 terminals are limited to monofont monochrome text.

Asynchronous ASCII Transmission

In Chapter 2, we looked at protocol data units (PDUs). We saw that PDUs are highly structured internally, with a header, a data field, and sometimes a trailer. The data field can contain hundreds or thousands of bytes of data.

Transmission using this type of organization is called **synchronous** transmission. At the data link layer, when a frame arrives, the receiver's clock must be synchronized to the sender's clock. This synchronization happens at the beginning of the frame. Chapter 4 showed how this initial synchronization is done in Ethernet 10Base-T. Once synchronization occurs, the receiver can read long frames.

In contrast, VT100 terminals use **asynchronous transmission,** in which each character is sent in its own 10-bit frame. Figure H.3 illustrates this character-by-character transmission.

START AND STOP BITS

When nothing is being transmitted, the sender keeps the line in the 1 state. Each character begins with a **start bit** to indicate the beginning of a new character frame. The start bit is always a 0. By changing the line state from 1 to 0, the start bit signals the receiver that a new character is beginning.

FIGURE **H.3**

Asynchronous Character Frames

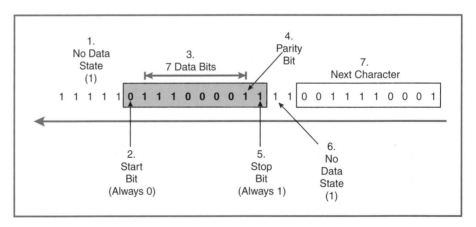

In turn, each character ends with a single **stop bit,** which is always a 1. This returns the line to the no-data condition for at least a single bit time. This ensures that the next start bit will change the line state from 1 to 0, signaling the start of a new bit.

DATA BITS

After the start bit come the frame's **data bits.** As noted earlier, the ASCII standard uses only seven data bits.

PARITY BIT

If you are using seven data bits, there is still an eighth bit sent. This is the **parity bit,** which offers a crude form of error detection. Figure H.4 shows that in **even parity,** the parity bit is set so that there is always an even number of ones in the seven data bits and the parity bit. For example, if the seven data bits are 1111111 (odd), the parity bit must be set to 1 to give an even number of ones for the data bits and parity bit combined. In **odd parity,** the parity bit is set to give an odd number of ones. In **no parity,** the parity bit is ignored. Note that the start and stop bits are *not* included in the calculation.

The receiver can use parity to detect errors. In even parity, a character with an odd number of ones in the data bits plus the parity bit must be incorrect.

Unfortunately, asynchronous transmission does not have a way of asking for the retransmission of the damaged character. The receiver either marks the character as incorrect, painting an error character on the terminal screen, or throws the character away. So parity offers **error detection** but not *error correction.*

In fact, parity is not even good at error *detection.* If two bits are changed instead of one, the changed character will still have the correct parity. The receiver will think that the character is correct. Parity was created when transmission speeds were a few bits per second, so multibit errors due to noise fluctuations (see Chapter 3) were rare. As noted in Chapters 2 and 4, we now use error detection *fields* in synchronous transmission. These fields are two to four bytes long, allowing even multibit errors to be detected.

8-BIT ASCII

Given the universal use of 8-bit ASCII in personal computers and the poor error detection ability of parity, many asynchronous transmissions use 8 data bits and no parity. This still gives a 10-bit frame.

EVEN PARITY			
Character	Number of 1s	Odd or Even	Parity Bit
1110001	4	Even	0
1110000	3	Odd	1

ODD PARITY			
Character	Number of 1s	Odd or Even	Parity Bit
1110001	4	Even	1
1110000	3	Odd	0

FIGURE **H.4**

Parity

HALF- AND FULL-DUPLEX OPERATION

Chapter 3 covered the difference between full-duplex and half-duplex transmission. In full-duplex transmission, both sides can transmit at the same time. In half-duplex transmission, they must take turns. When you set up a VT100 terminal, you have to specify whether the transmission is full-duplex or half-duplex. If you are not sure, the full-duplex option is a safe bet, because almost all terminal–host systems today use full-duplex transmission.

LACK OF STANDARDS

There are no standards for speed, number of data bits, parity, or duplex. Some systems even use more than one stop bit. So users have to set up their terminal or communications software for each host separately. Users may even get information about hosts in cryptic ways, such as "9600E1" (9,600 bps, even parity, and one stop bit). In general, for novice users, VT100 terminal and terminal emulation setup are a little daunting. Although VT100 terminals are technically simple, their setup is not.

Terminal Emulation and Telnet

It often seems that "desktop PCs" got their name because they take up your entire desktop. Certainly you do not want to add a terminal to your desk, just so that you can use host computers occasionally. Fortunately, you can use your PC to reach a host computer.

TERMINAL EMULATION

Figure H.5 shows that you can use your PC through a process called **terminal emulation,** in which your PC emulates (mimics) a terminal. In effect, your PC lies to the host computer. It says, "Hi, I'm a terminal." It lies so effectively that the host cannot tell that it is dealing with something other than a terminal.

FIGURE **H.5**

Terminal Emulation and Telnet

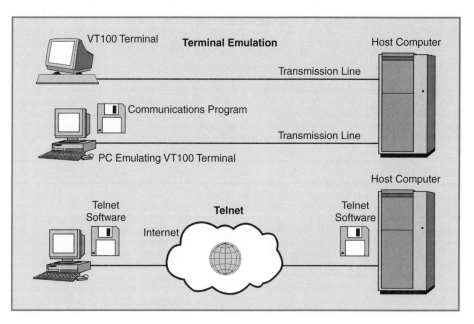

VT100 terminal emulation is simple and inexpensive. You only need to add a **communications program** to your personal computer. Communications programs are widely available for free or as shareware. Even commercial communications programs are inexpensive.

Your PC already has the serial port used by VT100 terminals. Your PC serial port automatically handles asynchronous transmission, and ASCII is a PC's native code. (The 7-bit versus 8-bit difference is not a problem.) So you do not even need special hardware to connect your emulated VT100 terminal to the outside world.

In fact, your PC is better than a real terminal in several ways. First, you can create scripts—prewritten series of commands—to automate common actions such as logging into a host computer and going to your mail program. This is especially important for dial-in access, which may take too many steps to remember easily.

In addition, you can transfer files between your PC and the host, as Figure H.6 illustrates. You can *upload* files from your "lowly" PC to the "exalted" host. You can also *download* files from the host to your PC. File transfer tends to be fairly simple once you begin the transfer. Before you begin, however, you have to select a file transfer protocol supported by both your communications program and the host computer. Some common protocols for PC file transfers are XMODEM, YMODEM, ZMODEM, and Kermit.

TELNET

Figure H.5 also shows **Telnet.** The ARPANET was originally created to link terminal users to distant host computers. This application was called Telnet. Telnet is still widely used on the Internet, especially to read e-mail from remote locations.

The big difference between Telnet and terminal emulation comes in transmission. Terminal emulation merely gives you a terminal and does not help you with transmission. You still need to arrange a telephone line and a modem or some other transmission system to link you to the host.

Telnet assumes that you are already connected to the Internet. It uses this connection, and it does so automatically. It also dispenses with such complexities as setting

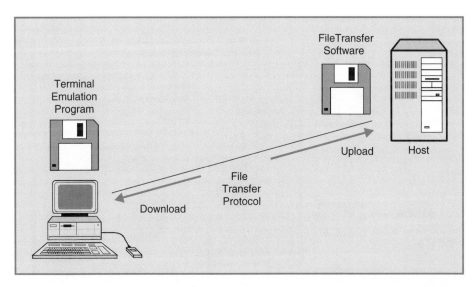

Terminal Emulation Program

FileTransfer Software

Host

Upload

Download

File Transfer Protocol

up the number of stop bits, the number of data bits, odd versus even versus no parity, and half- versus full-duplex. All of this is standardized in Telnet.

Telnet is attractive to mobile users because they can reach any host computer from anywhere. For example, if you are traveling and want to read your e-mail, you simply connect to the Internet, start the Telnet program on your PC, and type the name of your host. The next thing you will see is your host's login screen. You can use Telnet to read your mail host from home, from your desktop PC at work, or from a PC in a computer lab at school.

VT100 Terminals in Perspective

Using a VT100 terminal is like taking a trip back in time. You will not see color or graphics, your speed will be low, and setup can be daunting for novice users. Although Telnet removes the setup problems, it still offers only a slow character-based interface.

For light users, however, the VT100 or its software equivalents are appropriate choices when they have to deal with terminal–host systems only an hour or so a day.

IBM MAINFRAME COMMUNICATION

Introduction

We have just seen the relatively simple terminal–host technology that is present when users have VT100 terminals or software equivalents. This section introduces the more complex technology of IBM mainframe communication.

COMPLEXITY

In VT100 communication, the terminal talks directly to the host computer. Figure H.7 shows that **IBM mainframe communication** uses two intermediate devices. One is a **cluster controller** at the terminal site. The other is a **communications controller** at the host site. We will look at these devices in detail later.

FIGURE **H.7**

IBM Mainframe Communication

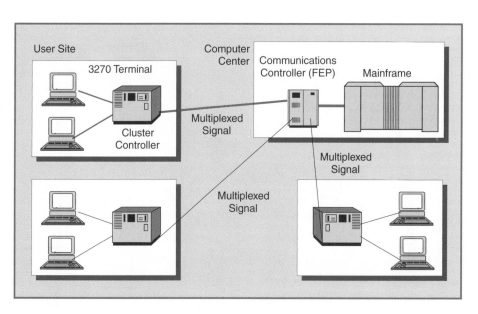

SYNCHRONOUS PACKAGING

Another big difference is that VT100 communication uses asynchronous transmission, whereas IBM mainframe communication uses more sophisticated **synchronous** transmission. Synchronous transmission uses the long PDUs we saw in Chapters 2 and 4.

RAPID RESPONSE

Several considerations drove the design of IBM's complex mainframe communication architecture, which is actually older than VT100 communication. The first and most important is that IBM designed its mainframe systems for **clerical transaction processing,** such as entering new orders into the computer. Clerical workers need a rapid response time when they hit a key.

Transaction processing involves high volumes of interactions. Mainframe performance, in addition to being rated on the basis of **MIPS (millions of instructions per second),** is measured on the basis of **transactions per second (TPS).** With a good database management system (DBMS), a mainframe can execute several hundred transactions per second. Very large applications, such as airline reservation systems, constantly press mainframe vendors and database vendors to increase throughput.

EFFICIENT LONG-DISTANCE TRANSMISSION

The second design consideration was that many terminal sites would be very distant from the central computer—often hundreds or even thousands of miles away. (In contrast, VT100 technology was designed for terminals located near the host computer.) Long-distance communication was extremely expensive when IBM created its mainframe architecture. The reduction of long-distance transmission costs was a critical design goal.

VERY LARGE NETWORKS

Third, IBM designed its mainframe communication for large networks. Designers expected mainframes to serve hundreds or even thousands of terminal users. They have not been disappointed.

RELIABILITY

Fourth, and finally, IBM mainframe communication had to be reliable. Transaction processing is mission-critical. Companies literally fail within a few days if their transaction processing is cut off, and even brief outages can be extremely costly.

Having looked at these four crucial design considerations, we will now look at how the components shown in Figure H.7 achieve IBM's design requirements.

The User Site

As just noted, IBM expected users to be hundreds or thousands of miles away from the mainframe computer. In addition, IBM expected users to cluster in offices having a number of terminals and one or more high-speed printers. Some examples of terminal cluster sites are bank branches, travel agencies, sales offices, and individual departments in headquarters buildings.

THE CLUSTER CONTROLLER

As shown in Figure H.7, the terminals and printers in the user site are connected to a device called a **cluster controller.**

This cluster controller has two functions. First, as shown in Figure H.7, the cluster controller **multiplexes** (combines) the traffic to and from the mainframe onto a single transmission line. Multiplexing, which we saw in earlier chapters and modules (especially Module B), dramatically reduces long-distance costs.

Second, the cluster controller supports limited **text editing** by the terminal user. Recall that IBM designed its mainframes for transaction processing. In transaction processing, the user basically fills out **forms.** As shown in Figure H.8, an IBM terminal screen shows a form to be filled in. Cluster controllers support text entry and very limited text editing, but not full word processing.

If IBM were designing its mainframe communication system today, it would put the editing intelligence into the terminal itself. In fact, it would probably use a PC instead of a terminal to take advantage of the PC's extensive processing power. However, when IBM designed its mainframe communication in the 1960s, this was not possible. Microprocessors had not even been invented yet. Intelligence had to be "hard-wired" into the cluster controller.

Many people call IBM terminals **smart terminals** because they can do basic editing—in contrast to VT100 terminals, which many people call *dumb terminals*. The name **smart terminal,** however, is misleading. The intelligence is really in the cluster controller, not in the terminal itself. Yet the name does remind us that there is local intelligence at the user site.

Doing editing at the user site is strategically important to the design. With VT100s, the host itself does all processing work, including simple editing. Every time the user presses a key, the terminal sends the character to the host for processing. This interrupts the host. After processing the character, the host sends the character back to the terminal.

Doing editing locally cuts down on this enormous communication traffic. Only completed forms need to be sent (in practice, partially completed forms are often sent if the user action demands a functionality the controller cannot support). Overall, traf-

FIGURE **H.8**

IBM Terminal Screen

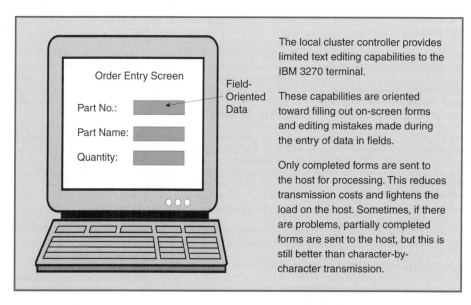

Order Entry Screen

Part No.:

Part Name:

Quantity:

Field-Oriented Data

The local cluster controller provides limited text editing capabilities to the IBM 3270 terminal.

These capabilities are oriented toward filling out on-screen forms and editing mistakes made during the entry of data in fields.

Only completed forms are sent to the host for processing. This reduces transmission costs and lightens the load on the host. Sometimes, if there are problems, partially completed forms are sent to the host, but this is still better than character-by-character transmission.

fic is an order of magnitude less than it is with host-based editing. This is critical for long-distance networking

Local editing also reduces the workload on the host computer. Even with local editing, each of the hundreds of transactions per second sent to the host interrupts the host and creates extensive work. With host-based text editing, the mainframe would have to service thousands of interruptions per second. This would be physically impossible.

A third benefit of local editing is that it improves response time. If the user types a character, the cluster controller instantly paints the character on the screen. Cursor movements are also instantaneous. In contrast, as every VT100 terminal user knows, editing with host-based processing is sometimes fast, sometimes very slow. Constant slow response is destructive of productivity, and variable response time is frustrating to users.

3270 TERMINALS

Most people refer to IBM mainframe terminals generically as **3270 terminals.** This is because IBM's earliest mainframe terminals had model numbers beginning with the digits "327." Current terminals have very different model numbers and offer more functionality, but they share the same core design as the first 3270 terminals.

IBM designed 3270 terminals for high performance. IBM eschewed the EIA/TIA-232-F electrical interface used by VT100 terminals because of the slow 20 kbps speed limit. IBM designed its own electrical interface, and 3270 terminals can run as fast as 2 Mbps. A more common speed, given the cost of long-distance lines, is about 64 kbps.

A computer screen has 25 rows, each with 80 columns. This gives 2,000 characters on a screen. At 64 kbps, even a full screen can change in a thirtieth of a second. This is as fast as video images change.

Modern 3270 terminals, furthermore, have both color and graphics, allowing attractive user interfaces. In contrast, we saw earlier that VT100s are monochrome, character-only terminals. Although later Digital Equipment Corporation VT terminals have both color and graphics, most hosts that support VT100s do not support more advanced VT terminals.

So IBM 3270 terminals offer faster speeds and higher functionality. Given the costs of long-distance transmission lines, the local editing and multiplexing built into IBM mainframe communication can even produce lower overall costs.

3270 TERMINAL EMULATION

VT100 terminal emulation is very simple. All you need to add to a standard PC is a communications program. This simplicity was possible because PC hardware has a lot in common with VT100 terminals. Like them, a PC uses the ASCII character code. Also like them, the PC has built-in electronics for EIA/TIA-232-F serial communication.

However, the PC is very different physically from 3270 terminals. As discussed below, a 3270 terminal uses a different character code, EBCDIC. In addition, a 3270 terminal sends data using a complex *synchronous* communication process. Finally, a 3270 terminal has to move data much faster than VT100 speeds; this even requires a different physical interface than the EIA/TIA-232-F serial plug.

To emulate a 3270 terminal, a PC user must buy a **3270 terminal emulation kit** consisting of both an expansion board of considerable processing power and a communication program tailored to this particular controller board. This kit costs several hundred dollars.

With this kit, a PC emulating a 3270 terminal can plug directly into a cluster controller. Consequently, a site office can mix and match PCs and 3270 terminals.

Sometimes, a remote site only has a single PC. In this case, the PC needs to emulate both a 3270 terminal and a cluster controller. The needed kit consists of a single expansion board that does both tasks, plus a single communication program. These kits are understandably more expensive than terminal emulation kits.

SYNCHRONOUS GATEWAY SERVERS

If your PC is on a LAN, another alternative is to use a **synchronous gateway server.** As Figure H.9 shows, this gateway downloads terminal emulation software to the PC. The PC communicates with the gateway server. The gateway server translates between LAN PC communication protocols and IBM's SNA protocols. It also acts as a cluster controller.

In general, gateways translate between communication architectures. In the figure, your PC is using standards from the IPX/SPX architecture to communicate with the synchronous gateway server. (It could as easily have used TCP/IP.) The mainframe communicates with the gateway server through SNA protocols. The gateway translates between IPX/SPX and SNA at all layers.

Calling these servers synchronous servers is misleading, because the name suggests that they can implement any synchronous protocol in communicating with outside devices. In fact, they are limited to SNA synchronous protocols.

The Computer Center

The mainframe and its attendant hardware, peripherals, software, and operations staff are located in a **computer center.** IS people often call the center the **glass house,** because companies used to show off their mainframes by putting them on the ground floor of a building, in an area surrounded by floor-to-ceiling glass windows, in order to show off their new technology. Today, the computer center is more likely to be in an industrial area of the city, where rents are cheaper, or in the countryside. Falling data

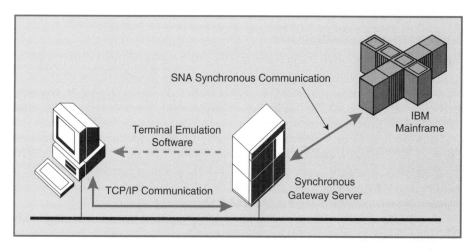

FIGURE H.9

Synchronous Communication Gateway Server

SNA Synchronous Communication

IBM Mainframe

Terminal Emulation Software

Synchronous Gateway Server

TCP/IP Communication

communication costs have allowed this freedom in placing data centers where costs are lower.

Large corporations—especially multinationals—usually have multiple data centers. Each serves a geographical region, a country, or a cluster of countries. Placing data centers near the users they serve was once required by high communication costs. However, falling data communication costs are making it economical for many firms to consolidate their data center functions. Some large multinationals that formerly had two or three dozen computer centers now have only a handful. This gives economies of scale in the use of specialized staff members, and it reduces management overhead.

Consolidation is also being driven by the desire to bring more standardization to such core applications as accounting. In the past, each data center might develop its own accounting system, giving the organization dozens of different accounting systems.

MAINFRAMES

The most important elements in any data center are its **mainframe computers.** Most centers have several mainframes to maintain.

Scientists and engineers sometimes work with **supercomputers.** The architectures of these ultra-fast "number crunchers" are superoptimized for arithmetic calculations, especially floating point (decimal) calculations.

In contrast, mainframes are **business computers.** This means that they are optimized for database processing. Database applications, most notably management information systems (MISs), depend primarily on very rapid disk access. (Their mathematical operations are comparatively simple.) So mainframes are optimized for ultra-rapid disk access. Whereas supercomputers push the state of the art in arithmetic-logic units, mainframes push the state of the art in disk access and transfer speeds. Mainframes have multiple disk controllers that can access disk drives in parallel. In addition, the disk drive controllers themselves are dedicated computers of considerable processing power. For database applications, I/O loads would swamp most supercomputers.

In evaluating mainframes, it is important to look at database indices of merit, such as transactions per second, rather than simple processing scores, such as MIPS (millions of instructions per second).

IBM OPERATING SYSTEMS

IBM has developed a number of operating systems for its mainframe computers. Some lived and died in the era of batch processing. IBM created others for unusual circumstances, such as airline reservation systems.

In the commercial world today, two operating systems dominate on IBM mainframes. These are MVS and VM. **MVS** is used most widely and is especially good for transaction processing. **VM** is used more for end user applications.

MVS was created before interactive terminals. To handle interactive terminals, IBM later added another layer of software. This was a **teleprocessing layer.** IBM offers several products for this layer. The most popular are **CICS** and **IMS.** CICS is the **Customer Information Control System.** IMS is the **Information Management System.** An IBM mainframe offering MVS with CICS is said to be offering MVS/CICS.

VM also requires a teleprocessing layer to manage the user interface. In VM, the most popular teleprocessing layer is **CMS,** short for **Conversational Monitoring System.** VM systems that use CMS are called VM/CMS systems.

Because IBM offers so many operating systems, and because these operating systems can be customized for each machine's needs, it is critical to plan the entire environment of systems software in mainframe environments. Two IBM mainframes with the same hardware model number may have very different capabilities and limitations for running programs, depending on their software environments.

Although customization can bring benefits, it is expensive. IBM mainframe sites need large **systems programming staffs** to maintain the system. These large systems programming staffs are expensive. Many smaller organizations cannot afford them.

COMMUNICATIONS CONTROLLER

Every time a cluster controller sends information to the mainframe, several back-and-forth messages may have to be sent to be sure that the message has arrived. (See Chapter 2.) In addition, the mainframe has to check on its cluster controllers and its transmission network constantly to be sure that everything is functioning properly.

Although this work is critical and necessary, it takes time away from the mainframe's main job and architectural strength—database file processing. If the mainframe has to do this work, it will not be able to support as many terminals or perform as many transactions per second. Instead, its expensive hardware will be used to support rather simple communication control.

As shown in Figure H.7, IBM mainframes handle this dilemma by "delegating" communication-related tasks to a separate computer. IBM calls this computer a **communications controller.** Others call it a **front end processor (FEP).**

As shown in Figure H.7, the communications controller manages the cluster controllers attached to the mainframe. In addition, communications controllers can cooperate, as shown in Figure H.10, so that they can transmit traffic from a cluster controller attached to one communications controller to the mainframe attached to another.

FIGURE H.10

Complex IBM Mainframe Network

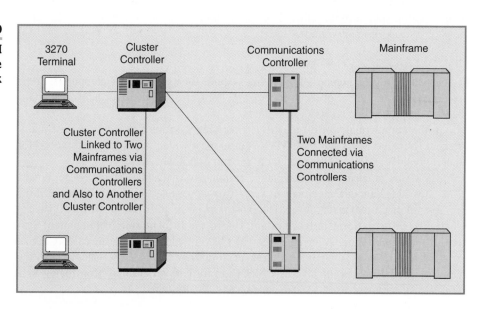

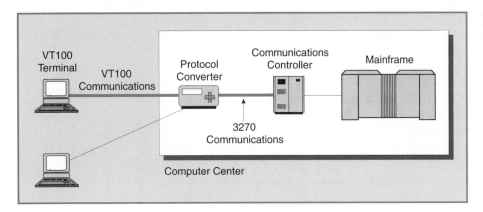

VT100
Terminal
VT100
Communications

Protocol
Converter

Communications
Controller

Mainframe

3270
Communications

Computer Center

PROTOCOL CONVERTERS

What if the user only has a VT100 terminal? We have seen that these terminals use entirely different technologies.

When two humans speak different languages, they need an interpreter to translate between them. These interpreters exist for IBM mainframe communication as well. They are called **protocol converters.** Figure H.11 shows that they translate between IBM protocols and other protocols, typically VT100 protocols.

Translation is never perfect, and protocol conversion is not magical. VT100 terminals are still slow and cannot support applications that use color and graphics. In addition, the protocol converter must handle the functions of the cluster controller, including on-screen editing. These chores, added to its translation tasks, can sometimes result in sluggish screen editing.

Overall, protocol converters make sense for casual terminal users who use their VT100 terminal (or a PC emulating such a terminal) only an hour or so a day. In addition, protocol converter users do not need high speeds and should be able to reach the mainframe via local calls or via low-cost data networks, not expensive dial-up lines. Managers working from home in the evening or on a weekend are typical protocol converter users.

Systems Network Architecture (SNA)

IBM SYNCHRONOUS COMMUNICATION

IBM mainframe communication uses two different synchronous protocols at the data link layer. The older is **Bisynch.** This was a half-duplex protocol that assumed 8-bit character data fields. It still sees some use.

Most mainframes use IBM's newer, more sophisticated, and more widely used **SDLC (Synchronous Data Link Control) protocol.** SDLC is full-duplex and has a transparent data field, meaning that it can carry any type of data. SDLC actually is part of **IBM's Systems Network Architecture (SNA).**

SOFTWARE

To implement SNA, users must have software running on their host computer, their communications controllers, and their cluster controllers.

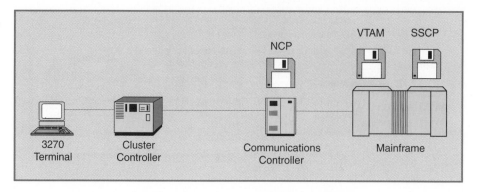

Network Control Program (NCP) The software on the communications controller is the **network control program, NCP.** As shown in Figure H.12, NCP manages communication between the communications controller and the cluster controllers connected to it.

Virtual Telecommunications Access Method (VTAM) The key communication software on the mainframe is the **Virtual Telecommunications Access Method, VTAM.** This software governs communication between the mainframe and its communications controller.

System Services Control Point (SSCP) A network must set up and maintain hundreds of connections each second. A program called the **Systems Services Control Point (SSCP)** initiates and maintains these connections. This is a highly centralized approach consistent with SNA's general hierarchical structure.

A single SSCP can control several mainframes, their communications controllers, associated cluster controllers, and terminals. It is not necessary for each mainframe to have its own SSCP.

Some extremely large SNA networks are divided into a number of **domains.** Each domain has its own SSCP.

APPN IBM has extended SNA to deal with peer-to-peer networking via its **Advanced Peer to Peer Networking (APPN)** extensions to SNA. APPN does not require an SSCP, because in APPN, peer entities can link without asking permission from a central authority. APPN does require additional software on the mainframe, communications controller, and cluster controllers, and in some cases the hardware of these devices must be upgraded to process the software.

NETWORK ADDRESSABLE UNITS

Another key concept is the **network addressable unit (NAU).** As Figure H.13 shows, SNA considers three types of entities: end users, network addressable units, and a transmission network (Path Control Network). The purpose of SNA standards is to *define communication between NAUs.*

SNA has three types of NAUs. The System Services Control Point (SSCP) software is its own distinct type.

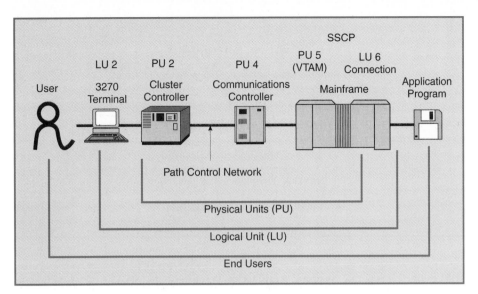

FIGURE **H.13**

End Users, Network Addressable Units, and the Path Control Network in SNA

Then there are **logical units (LUs).** This type of NAU *deals directly with an end user*—either a person or an application program. For instance, LU 2 is a terminal. In turn, LU 6.2 deals with application programs in APPN. Notice that *logical* does not mean software. It includes terminals. It is merely the name for NAUs that deal with end users.

Third, **physical units (PUs)** *do not deal directly with end users*. PU 2 is software residing in a cluster controller. PU 4 is in the communications controller. PU 5 is in the VTAM software on the host itself.

LAYERS

Figure H.14 shows layering in SNA when two NAUs communicate. SNA layering is extremely complex, and for details, the reader should refer to Kapoor[1] or another advanced source. For our purposes, we wish to note that there are two clusters of layers.

To deal with transmission over the Path Control Network, that is, the transmission network, SNA has the **Physical Control, Data Link Control,** and **Path Control Network** layers. These are roughly similar to the three lowest OSI layers: physical, data link, and network. In fact, this similarity is no accident. SNA's layering heavily influenced OSI at the bottom three layers.

The next three layers are more difficult to describe. In terms of the OSI framework, they act more like OSI session layer protocols. The **Transmission Control**, **Data Flow Control,** and **NAU Services** layers basically create a session between NAUs and manage flow control, duplex, and other matters when the NAUs communicate.

There is nothing really like an OSI transport layer in SNA, perhaps because this layer was created to deal with design differences between platforms, and there are no such differences in IBM mainframe systems because all devices were created by IBM.

Although most writers draw an **End User** layer in SNA and show it as being similar to the application layer in TCP/IP, application standards really lie outside SNA.

---

[1] Atul Kapoor, *SNA: Architecture, Protocols, and Implementation* (New York: McGraw-Hill, 1992).

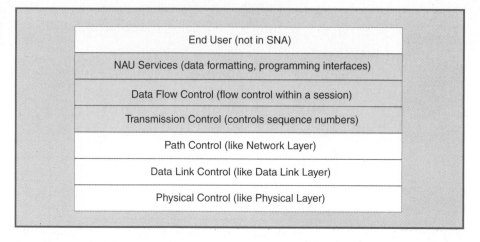

End User (not in SNA)
NAU Services (data formatting, programming interfaces)
Data Flow Control (flow control within a session)
Transmission Control (controls sequence numbers)
Path Control (like Network Layer)
Data Link Control (like Data Link Layer)
Physical Control (like Physical Layer)

IBM defined a separate **Systems Application Architecture (SAA)** to deal with standards linking applications.

EBCDIC

Although the data field of the SDLC frame can contain any information, IBM mainframes normally encode character data in an 8-bit code called **EBCDIC (Extended Binary Coded Decimal Interchange Code).** This is a direct competitor of ASCII.

The extra bit gives EBCDIC 256 possible codes—twice as many as 7-bit ASCII. As a result, there is not a perfect one-to-one correspondence between ASCII and EBCDIC codes. However, for printing characters, translation is possible.

Routing SNA

Today, many corporations have created router-based transmission networks. Most of these networks use multiprotocol routers, which can route both IP and IPX efficiently. Unfortunately, SNA was not designed for routing. As a result, sending SNA through a routed network is difficult. When SNA must be routed, organizations often use a standard **called data link switching (DLsw).**

Another problem is that SNA was designed for real-time communication between a terminal and a host. If communication between the terminal and host is broken, even briefly, the host assumes that the terminal has been disconnected and breaks the session. Even delays caused by network congestion often cause such breaks to occur. **TN3270E** servers fool devices into believing that they are in constant communication, even when they are not.

Perspective

Recall that IBM mainframe communication was designed with the assumptions that workload on the host would need to be minimized, that terminals would be very far away, that there would be many terminals, and that reliability would be critical.

REDUCING THE LOAD ON THE HOST

To optimize the mainframe's ability to do database transaction processing for hundreds of terminals, as much work was removed from the host as possible.

First, almost all editing of forms is done at the user site, in the cluster controller. The mainframe does not have to worry about such low-level but processing-intensive chores.

Second, the communications controller by the host off-loads almost all communication work. It deals with the complex mechanics of creating synchronous frames, dealing with the competing demands of many cluster controllers, and breaking synchronous frames into simple data streams for the mainframe.

REDUCING LONG-DISTANCE COSTS

The IBM mainframe communications system reduces long-distance costs in several ways. First, it uses synchronous transmission, which has lower overhead than asynchronous transmission.

Second, IBM mainframe communication uses the inherent ability of synchronous transmission to multiplex transmissions. The cluster controller is a very efficient multiplexer that combines all of its terminals' and printers' traffic onto a single transmission line to the communications controller.

Third, because most simple editing is done at the user site, by the cluster controller, there is no need to transmit large numbers of characters for editing.

LARGE NETWORKS

Individual mainframes can handle several hundred terminal users simultaneously. As we saw in Figure H.10, furthermore, it is possible to create networks that contain multiple mainframes and their associated terminals. IBM mainframe networks can be enormous.

RELIABILITY

Everything about IBM communications is designed for reliability because the loss of mainframe communication for even a few days can be crippling in heavy-use environments. Its SNA protocols, for instance, are highly reliable. This concern with reliability colors everything that IBM does in communications. For instance, IBM initially rejected Ethernet (802.3) LAN transmission, in favor of more reliable Token-Ring Network (802.5) technology that it introduced in the 802 Standards Committee.

RAPID RESPONSE TIME

Clerical workers and other employees who use a terminal constantly cannot tolerate delays. Frequent delays would seriously reduce their productivity. The use of cluster controllers makes this possible. For simple tasks, such as text editing, the processing power is in the on-site cluster controller. Text entry and editing, at least, are almost instantaneous.

For heavier tasks, work is done on the host. Rapid response time depends critically on having adequate host processing power and adequate transmission throughput.

COMPLEXITY AND COST

Unfortunately, all of the characteristics of IBM mainframe communication tend to make it costly to implement. The hardware and software are very expensive. In addition, the mainframe needs a staff of systems programmers to keep it working, and

SNA requires a staff of SNA programmers to manage the complex transmission network.

SUMMARY

Although terminal–host systems are less important than they once were, they are still used widely in organizations. Especially in long-distance communication, terminal–host communication still makes up a substantial portion of all data traffic in many organizations.

As the name *system* implies, terminal–host systems carefully design their hosts, terminals, and communication subsystems to work together to achieve certain goals. VT100 systems, for instance, are designed to give low-cost host access to casual users. IBM mainframe systems, in contrast, are designed to serve many simultaneous users in geographically distributed, heavy-use environments. In such environments, response time, transmission cost, reliability, and the ability to support many simultaneous users are crucial.

As a result of optimization to particular circumstances, terminal–host system designs are not "open" in the sense that you can use any terminal with any host. Most hosts support only a few types of terminals.

However, many hosts that prefer their own terminals will give at least grudging support to VT100 terminals, which are lowest-common-denominator devices that have low speeds, poor user interfaces, and no error correction. In addition, VT100 terminals use obsolete asynchronous ASCII transmission. On the positive side, if you have a PC, communication software will allow you to emulate a VT100 terminal when linking to a host. In addition, on the Internet, the VT100 terminal is the basis for Telnet, which allows you to log into a remote Internet host.

IBM mainframe systems have four major devices in addition to transmission lines. These are terminals, hosts, communications controllers, and cluster controllers. IBM "3270" terminals are relatively expensive, but for this higher cost, they offer reasonable graphics and high-speed interfaces. The cluster controller and communications controllers, in turn, handle multiplexing, reduce the load on the mainframe, and provide 3270 terminals with limited local editing power.

To optimize processing on the host, firms have to maintain systems programming staffs. IBM supports two different operating systems on its mainframes, and both offer many optimization parameters. This systems programming staff, unfortunately, is very expensive.

IBM mainframe communication is governed by the Systems Network Architecture (SNA), which predated both OSI and TCP/IP. SNA is a master–slave standards architecture, in which devices are under the command of the System Services Control Point (SSCP) program on a mainframe. Although SNA now has a peer–peer option, APPN, it is still largely used in master–slave mode. SNA requires certain programs to run on the mainframe and on the communications controller.

SNA was not designed for routing. As a result, sending SNA through a routed network is difficult. When SNA is routed, it often uses a standard called data link switching (DLsw). Another problem is that SNA was designed for real-time communication between a terminal and a host. Delays caused by network congestion can cause broken terminal–host sessions.

The module also looked briefly at AS/400 terminal–host systems for smaller businesses. It also looked at two types of devices that are likely to be used heavily as replacement for dumb terminals: network computers (NCs) and Windows terminals.

REVIEW QUESTIONS

CORE REVIEW QUESTIONS

1. In general, can you use any terminal with any host? Explain. What terminal do many hosts support? Is it a full-featured terminal? In what sense are terminal–host systems "systems"?
2. What are the design goals for VT100 systems? What are the design goals for IBM mainframe systems? Why would companies use AS/400 systems instead of IBM mainframe systems? What are the relative advantages of network computers (NCs) and Windows terminals?
3. In what sense is the VT100 a dumb terminal? Why does it place a heavy load on the host computer? Why does it place a heavy load on transmission lines? What are the limitations of its user interface? What are the limitations on its speed?
4. Describe the bits of the asynchronous frame with 7-bit ASCII. Describe them with 8-bit ASCII.
5. Is parity good for error detection? Describe a situation in which parity would fail to detect an error. Does parity offer error correction?
6. Why is terminal or terminal emulation setup difficult for novice users? What must they know to set the parameters for VT100 terminal emulation?
7. What is terminal emulation? Why is VT100 terminal emulation easy? What do you need for terminal emulation? What can you do with terminal emulation that you cannot do with a terminal? How does terminal emulation differ from Telnet?
8. What were the design goals for IBM mainframe systems? Name the four hardware boxes in IBM mainframe communication. What does each do? What is the difference between asynchronous and synchronous communication?
9. How do IBM mainframe terminals (3270 terminals) differ from VT100 terminals? Why is 3270 terminal emulation expensive?
10. When you are filling out a form on a 3270 terminal, where is the processing power for doing the editing located? How does this improve response time? How does this lighten the load on the host? How does this reduce transmission costs?
11. How does the cluster controller in an IBM mainframe system reduce transmission costs? How does it reduce the load on the mainframe?
12. To implement SNA, what software is added to various devices in the network?
13. Standards architectures govern communication between two entities. What are the entities called in SNA? What are the three types of these entities? How do logical units and physical units differ?
14. Name the layers in SNA. Which layers correspond approximately to the physical, data link, and network layers in OSI?

DETAILED REVIEW QUESTIONS

1. Explain the purpose of having the start bit be a zero. Explain the purpose of having the stop bit be a one.
2. What does a synchronous communication gateway server do on LANs? Why is it called a *gateway*?
3. What are IBM's two major mainframe operating systems? Why do they need teleprocessing layers?
4. What is the function of a protocol converter on IBM mainframe systems?
5. Distinguish regular SNA from APPN.
6. What standard is used in SNA routing? What problem can occur if there is network congestion?

THOUGHT QUESTIONS

1. Multiple stop bits in ASCII transmission were used in the past, when even low transmission speeds could outpace the ability of terminals to handle incoming ASCII frames. Why would multiple stop bits reduce the load on the terminal?
2. You are sending the ASCII character *H*. (See Figure H.2 for its ASCII representation.) You wish to have even parity. What are the 10 bits of the asynchronous ASCII frame? Before you begin, note that the 7 ASCII bits are sent backward. So if you are sending the ASCII character "1111000," you would send 3 zeros and then 4 ones.
3. You are setting up a VT100 terminal to communicate with a particular host. What must you know to be able to set up VT100 terminal emulation on a PC and log into a host?
4. Under what circumstances can an IBM mainframe system be less expensive than a VT100 terminal–host system?

PROJECTS

1. Go to the book's website, http://www.prenhall.com/panko, and read the Updates Page for this chapter to see any reported errors and for new and expanded information on the material in this chapter.
2. Go to the book's website, http://www.prenhall.com/panko, and do the Internet Exercises for this module.
3. Windows has a built-in communications program. This is Terminal in Windows 3.1 and Hyperterminal in Windows 95. Use it to set up the parameters for connection to a particular host. Use the parameters 9600E1. What would you assume about parity?

Index

Boldface entries indicate boldfaced terms in text.

Convergence services layer PDU, 378–379
Conversational Monitoring System (CMS), 443
Conversion, 21, 212, 445
Cookies, 415
Cooperative processing, 16–17
CORBA. *See* Common Object Request Broker Architecture
Core in optical fiber, 284–285, 286
Core business functions, 232–233
Corporate IP telephony, 355–357
Cost, 4, 22
  advertising, 238
  alternative routing and, 144
  ATM switches and, 142
  dedicated services and, 153
  Ethernet switches and, 138
  of Ethernet vs. ATM, 155
  filtering and, 187
  of Frame Relay vs. ATM, 155
  IBM mainframes and, 449–450
  intelligent devices and, 24
  IP telephony and, 358
  link state, 260
  multiplexing and, 281, 283
  packets and, 151
  prioritization and, 327
  of PSDN, 362, 381–384
  switches vs. routers and, 145
  of videoconferencing, 211
  virtual circuits and, 152
  See also Accounting management; Economics
Cost per thousand impressions (CPM), 238
CPM. *See* Cost per thousand impressions (CPM)
CRC. *See* Cyclic redundancy check (CRC)
Credit card fraud, 236–237, 240
CRLs. *See* Certificate revocation lists (CRLs)
Cross-talk, 70
CS. *See* Computer science (CS); Convergence services (CS)
CSLIP. *See* Compressed serial line internet protocol (CSLIP)
CSMA/CD. *See* **Carrier sense multiple access with collision detection (CSMA/CD)**
CSU. *See* Channel service unit (CSU)
CTI. *See* Computer-telephony integration (CTI)
Customer Information Control System (CICS), 443
Customer premises, 333–334
Cut-through processing, 306–307
Cyclic redundancy check (CRC), 302, 378

DARPA. *See* Defense Research Projects Agency (DARPA)
Data bits, asynchronous transmission, 435
Data caching, 165–166, 363–364
Data circuit termination equipment (DCE), 76–78
Data compression, 76. *See also* Compression
Data encoding, 304. *See also* Encoding
Data Encryption Standard (DES), 392–393, 406
Data fields, 33–40, 44, 110
  filtering and, 185–186
  length field and, 109
Data Flow Control in SNA, 447
Data link control, 447
Data link control identifier (DLCI in Frame Relay), 371–372, 374
Data link layer (DLL), 10, 11–12, 13, 14
  filtering and, 187
  and home use of Internet, 32–63
  LLC vs. MAC layer, 96–97, 101
  multiplexing at, 283
  OSI and, 26, 28

PDUs and, 32
security at, 397
site/enterprise networks and, 129–157
standards for, 106–113
tunneling and, 404
Data link switching (DLsw) in SNA, 448
Data marts, 230
Data mining, 229
Data safety, 223
Data service unit (DSU), 86–87, 381
Data terminal equipment (DTE), 76–78
Data warehouses, 228–229, 230
Database management system (DBMS), 439
Database middleware, 226
Database publishing, 413
Database servers, 15, 16–17, 21, 222
Databases, 222, 443. *See also* Internal databases
DBMS. *See* Database management system (DBMS)
DCE. *See* Data circuit termination equipment (DCE)
DCOM. *See* Distributed Component Object Model (DCOM)
DCS. *See* Distributed communication service (DCS)
DE. *See* Discard eligible (DE)
Decryption, 180, 181, 182, 393
Dedicated capacity, 151, 152–153
Dedicated connections, 152–153, 155
Defense Research Projects Agency (DARPA), 9, 265, 427
Denial-of-service attack, 176, 177
Depth of filtering, 185–186
Deregulation, 332, 336, 337
DES. *See* Data Encryption Standard (DES)
Design rationale, 207
Desktop conferencing, 213–215
Desktop groupware, 205–210
Destination addresses, 54, 57–59, 109, 249, 314
  firewalls and, 184
  switches and, 134–139
Destination hosts, 34, 38–39, 44, 55–56, 257
  headers and, 54
Development utilities, 242
Device hierarchies, 138, 142
DHCP. *See* Dynamic Host Configuration Protocol (DHCP)
Dial-up service, 152–153
Differential Manchester encoding in 802.5, 310, 311
Differentiated services, 267
Diffie-Hellman key agreement, 395, 403
Diffserv in IP, 357
Diffuse infrared, 324
Digital cellular telephones, 349, 351
Digital certificates, 183, 236–237, 390–392, 395
  IPsec and, 404
  SET and, 398, 404
Digital signatures, 182–183, 389–392
Digital subscriber line (DSL), 88–89, 90
Digital television, 351
Digital transmission, 66–68, 80–81, 85–87
  conferencing and, 212
Direct broadcast satellites, 292
Direct operation, 319–320
Direct sequence spread spectrum (DSSS), 322, 323, 351
Directory access protocols, 169–170
Directory servers, 166–170
Discard eligible (DE) in Frame Relay, 372
Dish antennas, 288, 290, 291, 292
  small, 293

Disk cache, 363
Disk caching, 363–364. *See also* Caching
Disk technology, 365–366
Distance vector routing protocol, 259
Distance Vector Multicasting Routing Protocol (DVM-RP), 269
Distortion, 69, 72
Distributed communication service (DCS), 351
Distributed Component Object Model (DCOM), 228
Distributed operation, 58, 173
Distributed processing, 23
Distributed programming, 2
Distribution list, 195, 196
DIX connector, 299
DLCI. *See* Data link control identifier (DLCI)
DLL. *See* Data link layer (DLL)
DLsw. *See* Data link switching (DLsw)
DNS. *See* Domain name system (DNS)
Docubases, 217
Document conferencing, 214
Document type definition (DTD), 413
Documents
  EDM and, 207, 217
  Web-based systems for, 217
Domain name registrars, 59
Domain name system (DNS), 32, 57–59, 261
Domain names, 264
Domains, 58–59, 446
Domestic service, 335
Dotted decimal notation, 54
Downlink, 291
Downloading, 415–416, 437
Downsizing, 21
Drop cable in 10Base5, 299
DSAP field, 111–112
DSL. *See* Digital subscriber line (DSL)
DSSS. *See* Direct sequence spread spectrum (DSSS)
DSU. *See* Data service unit (DSU)
DTD. *See* Document type definition (DTD)
DTE. *See* Data terminal equipment (DTE)
Dumb terminals, 20, 22, 440
DVM-RP. *See* Distance Vector Multicasting Routing Protocol (DVM-RP)
Dynamic Host Configuration Protocol (DHCP), 59

E-mail. *See* Electronic mail (e-mail)
E-mail hosts, 197, 198–199
E1 line, 369
E3 line, 369
EBCDIC. *See* Extended Binary Coded Decimal Interchange Code (EBCDIC)
Echo, 261–262
Economies of scale, 278–279
Edge switches, 145
EDI gateways, 239
EDI. *See* Electronic data interchange (EDI)
EDM. *See* Electronic document management (EDM)
EE. *See* Electrical engineering (EE)
EIDE, 365
8B/10B in 100Base-X, 304
800/888 number portability, 344
800/888 number, 344
802 LAN MAN Standards Committee, 99–100, 115, 309, 367
802.1 Working Group, 325–326
802.1D Spanning Tree, 309
802.1p standard, 325, 328
802.1Q standard, 325, 326, 328
802.2 standards, 110, 113, 115, 116
802.3 10Base-F, 300–301